NASF20 R104.95

INITIATION INTO
THEOLOGY

THE RICH VARIETY OF THEOLOGY AND HERMENEUTICS

SIMON MAIMELA • ADRIO KÖNIG
(editors)

JL van Schaik
RELIGIOUS BOOKS

Published by J L van Schaik Publishers
1064 Arcadia Street, Hatfield, Pretoria
All rights reserved
Copyright © 1998 The authors

No part of this book may be reproduced or transmitted
in any form or by any electronic or mechanical means,
including photocopying and recording, or by any
information storage and retrieval system, without written
permission from the publisher.

First edition 1998
ISBN 0 627 02146 8

Cover design by Deirdré Bartie
Typesetting in 10 $\frac{1}{2}$ on 12$\frac{1}{2}$ pt Palatino by
  Sonja Reinecke, Studio S
Printed and bound by Creda Press, Eliot Avenue, Eppindust II, Cape Town

Contents

1. Introduction	The editors	1

Section A: Theology

Contents		7
2. Biblical Theology	Adrio König, Unisa	11
3. Theology: the first 19 centuries	Brian Gaybba, Rhodes	27
4. Theology: the 20th century	Daniël Veldsman, Pretoria	49
5. Evangelical Theology	Adrio König, Unisa	81
6. Black Theology	Simon Maimela, Unisa	111
7. Feminist and Womanist Theology	Marie-Henry Keane, Oxford	121
8. African Women's Theology	Christina Landman, Unisa	137
9. African Theology	John S. Mbiti, Uganda	141
10. African Initiated Church Theology	Stephen Hayes, Unisa	159
11. Pentecostal Theology	Francois Möller, Johannesburg	179
12. Charismatic Theology	Jacques Theron, Unisa	191
13. Ecological Theology	Martien E. Brinkman, Utrecht	203
14. Postmodern Theology	Marius D. Herholdt, Top Teach	215
15. The theological challenge of other religious traditions	J.N.J. Kritzinger, Unisa	231

Section B: Hermeneutics

Contents		257
16. Biblical Hermeneutics	W.J. Wessels, Unisa	261
17. Biblical Hermeneutics: the first 19 centuries	Dirkie J. Smit, Western Cape	275
18. Biblical Hermeneutics: the 20th century	Dirkie J. Smit, Western Cape	297
19. Evangelical Hermeneutics	William Klein, Denver	319
20. Black Hermeneutics	Timothy G. Kiogora, Nairobi	337
21. Feminist and Womanist Hermeneutics	Denise M. Ackermann, UWC	349
22. African Women's Hermeneutics	Mercy Amba Oduyoye, Nigeria	359
23. African Hermeneutics	Cornel du Toit, Unisa	373
24. African Initiated Church Hermeneutics	Allan H. Anderson, Tshwane	399
25. Pentecostal and Charismatic Hermeneutics	Marius D. Herholdt, Top Teach	417
26. Ecological Hermeneutics	Luco van den Brom, Groningen	433
27. Postmodern Hermeneutics	Marius D. Herholdt, Top Teach	451
28. The hermeneutical challenge of other religious traditions	Farid Esack, UWC	471

Introduction

The Editors

1.1 THE VARIETY OF THEOLOGICAL AND HERMENEUTICAL FORMS

During the 1960s we entered the era of the "theologies" – such as the theology of hope, of revolution, of liberation, of history, of the world. One single type of theology, the Theology of Liberation, has even branched out into a number of subdivisions: Latin-American Liberation Theology, Black Liberation Theology, Feminist Theology, Womanist Theology, African Woman's Theology and Ecological Theology. And still the process is not complete.

Prior to the Sixties, theology was subdivided according to ecclesiastical traditions such as Catholic Theology, Lutheran Theology, Reformed Theology. And even when it was not clearly indicated, it was pretty easy to "place" a book as Catholic or Lutheran or Reformed.

These lines have become dotted as time goes by and in some cases they have simply disappeared – obviously not to everyone's satisfaction. But it is true that today it has become difficult, and in some cases impossible, to identify a commentary on Galatians or a monograph on salvation as Catholic or Lutheran or belonging to any other theology. What is obvious today is rather whether it presents Liberation Theology or Postmodern Theology or African Theology and so on.

However, with the decline of the major ecclesiastical theologies, some new ones have developed, like Pentecostal Theology, Charismatic Theology and, to a lesser extent, African Initiated Church Theology, which is still very much in its infancy. Some of the older ones are still alive and well, such as Evangelical Theology.

The result is that we have to cope with a virtually incalculable number of theologies. A mere introduction to the most important of these theologies would create somewhat of a library on one's table.

Still this is only half the story. For the other theological "explosion" that occurred during the same period is in the area of communication theory, understanding, reading and interpreting; which is known as hermeneutics.

There has been a dramatic development in our understanding of the processes of communication. One of the first insights during the middle of the twentieth century was that meaning is not conveyed as much by single words as by groups of words, such as phrases or sentences. The implication is that so-called literal translations (word for word translations) are in fact bad ones, which has resulted in numerous new translations of the Bible along different lines. We have been flooded by problems and new insights in the process of understanding, some of which are difficult to understand and formulate, but for all that are no less important.

One could, of course, decide not to enter these vast fields of theology and hermeneutics, and simply to stick to one's own tradition. However, the one great disadvantage would be that one is not exposed to the most original and challenging theology done during the past few decades. Inbreeding never results in excellence. Which does not mean we have to accept at face value whatever is offered on this diversified market, but rather that we enter into serious discussion with other theologies so that we are able to strengthen or enrich or adapt or let go of our own – whatever our preference might be.

As virtually every form of theology has developed its own hermeneutic, we have introduced two sections in this volume: Section A deals with the different types of theologies, and Section B with the corresponding types of hermeneutics. It is often true that one can only thoroughly understand a specific type of theology if one comes to grips with its hermeneutic, and vice versa.

Therefore, the aim of this volume is to enable the reader to enter into a thorough discussion with most of the important current theologies and hermeneutics in one volume.

1.2 THE CONTRIBUTORS

This volume does not attempt to choose between good or bad types of theology or hermeneutics. There is no hidden apologetic motive.

Each contributor is an authoritative representative of the appropriate type of theology or hermeneutics. Contributors themselves therefore accept explicitly or implicitly the meaningfulness of the view they present. For this reason, readers will surely feel invited to consider for themselves seriously the meaningfulness of every contribution. Also, no contribution reflects negatively on any other. Each is presented and evaluated in its own right. This ensures the reader of the most trustworthy orientation in the variety of theological and hermeneutical approaches offered.

The racial and sexual composition of the contributors should not pass by unnoticed. Out of the 23 contributors, 16 are white men, 3 black men, 3 white women and only 1 is a black woman.

First, it should be mentioned that originally 6 more black men and 3 more black women were invited to contribute, and indeed accepted, but for various reasons they were unable to do so in the end. However, it should be noted that none of them withdrew because of differences with the editors or dissatisfaction with the volume.

Second, it should be stated that the overwhelming percentage of white male contributors is part of the legacy of colonialism, racism and sexism. It is a basic fact that there are not scores of highly skilled women and black people knocking at the academic doors of the world. They have not only been excluded in South Africa, although we are possibly the worst of examples.

1.3 AFRICA

The volume was born and bred in Africa. Most of the contributors also live and work in Africa. Africa is one of the major growth points of Christianity. There is therefore a great need for theological training here. On the other hand, there are some important theological developments in Africa which need be brought to the attention of the rest of the theological world. The time has passed when Africa merely sat at the feet of the west in order to learn theology. Africa has something unique to offer – like chapters 6, 8–10, 20, 22–24. Some of the theologies that have developed in Africa should make the western world aware of the fact that what they have offered to the third world as "pure gospel" was often drenched in old and new forms of western philosophy. For example, the formulation of the doctrine of the trinity (three persons and one being) cannot even be translated meaningfully into some African languages.

Because this volume is from Africa, the language is simple and straightforward, since for most people in Africa, English is a second or even a third language. We believe that this does not necessarily detract from the academic value of the contributions. The gospel is a simple message which originated from, and was intended for, simple people, and we see no reason why it necessarily needs to be researched and presented in complicated and highly learned language.

In conclusion, this volume originated in South Africa during and immediately after the dramatic change to a democratic government. We rejoice in this and offer this contribution to the rest of the world as a symbol that South Africa will play a new role in the world in the years to come.

1.4 THE TOPICS

The list of contents does not present topics simply chosen at random, although virtually every interested person will note with regret the absence of a few types of theology and hermeneutics he or she would have included. It was simply not possible to include everything. So we decided to include four groups of topics. First, we wanted to investigate where we come from as Christian theologians (chapters 2–5 and 16–19). We come from the Jewish-Christian tradition of the Bible (2, 16), via the first nineteen centuries of Christianity (3, 17) to the twentieth century (4, 18) which, in a very special sense, has paved the way for what we have here. Added to this is the Evangelical tradition which has formed part of the development in the western world over the past few centuries (5, 19) and the great missionary enterprises which are of special importance for the church in Africa.

Second, we wanted to reflect the contribution of Africa to Christian thought (6–10 and 20–24). That is why we refrained from a separate discussion of Latin-American Liberation Theology and Hermeneutics and concentrated instead on Black Liberation Theology and Hermeneutics (6, 20) which has developed particularly in North America and Southern Africa. Feminist Theology has diversified to such an extent that we have included three forms: Feminist Theology and Hermeneutics (7, 21) which is a world-wide phenomenon, Womanist Theology and Hermeneutics (7, 21) which has mainly developed in North America, and African Woman's Theology and Hermeneutics (8, 22). Added to these is African Theology and Hermeneutics (9, 23), which is an older phenomenon and has developed in the historic churches. We conclude this African section with African Initiated Church Theology and Hermeneutics (10, 24) which, together with African Woman's Theology and Hermeneutics, is of very recent origin. In both cases, very little scholarly literature is available as yet.

Third, we offer the theologies and hermeneutics of the Pentecostal and Charismatic Movements (11–12, 25) which are in many ways related, but not identical. Together with the African Initiated Churches, these are the fastest growing Christian movements in the world, but they also show the least theological and hermeneutical development.

Fourth, we reflect on the major and most important recent developments in the world of theology (13–15) and hermeneutics (26–28). Ecological Theology and Hermeneutics deals with the gravest problem that confronts humankind: continued human existence on this small planet; Post-modern Theology and Hermeneutics reflects a new way of doing theology in which some of the basic presuppositions of theology over the past centuries are dismissed. The final aspect of this section is the challenge of other religious traditions, which concerns the new consciousness among Christians and the important question of how we should relate to them.

The contributors were asked to use inclusive language which they did to differing extent. Some still used masculine forms for God, and one requested that the concept of *kingdom* of God be retained in his contribution.

SECTION A

Theology

Contents

2 Biblical Theology — 11

- 2.1 Four different views of Biblical Theology — 11
- 2.2 The Bible as source and norm for theology — 14
- 2.3 Some biblical landmarks for theology — 17
- Reading List — 25
- Bibliography — 25

3 Theology: the first 19 centuries — 27

- 3.1 Introduction — 27
- 3.2 The first two and a half centuries — 28
- 3.3 The first major disputes and dogmatic developments (300–500) — 32
- 3.4 Developments from the 4th century to the end of the Patristic Period (8th century) — 33
- 3.5 Stirrings of revival and reopening the debate about reason: 9th to 11th centuries — 36
- 3.6 The 12th century — 37
- 3.7 From the 13th to the end of the 15th centuries — 40
- 3.8 The 16th century — 42
- 3.9 Seventeenth to nineteenth centuries — 43
- Reading List and Bibliography — 48

4 Theology: the 20th century — 49

- 4.1 Introduction — 49
- 4.2 Germany — 51
- 4.3 The Netherlands — 64
- 4.4 The United States of America — 70
- 4.5 Trends of the trendsetters in retrospect — 78
- Reading List and Bibliography — 79

5 Evangelical Theology — 81

- 5.1 The Evangelical Movement — 81
- 5.2 Evangelical spirituality — 83

5.3	The history of the Evangelical Movement	84
5.4	Some basic aspects of Evangelical Theology	93
5.5	Fundamentalism	103
Reading List		109
Bibliography		109

6 Black Theology — 111

6.1	Introduction	111
6.2	The social context of Black Theology	111
6.3	The origins of Black Theology	112
6.4	The term "Black Theology"	113
6.5	Theological trends in Black Theology	114
6.6	Some emphases in Black Theology	116
Reading List and Bibliography		119

7 Feminist and Womanist Theology — 121

7.1	Introduction	121
7.2	Defining Feminism	122
7.3	Feminist Theology	122
7.4	Different streams of Feminist Theology	123
7.5	What has already been achieved – a brief overview	125
7.6	Womanist Theology	131
7.7	Gender studies: the point of meeting	133
Reading List		135
Bibliography		135

8 African Women's Theology — 137

8.1	Introduction	137
8.2	Theologies of mind and body	137
8.3	A diversity of theologies	138
8.4	Women as theological and religion educators	138
8.5	In summary	140
Reading List and Bibliography		140

9 African Theology — 141

- 9.1 African Theologians and their context — 141
- 9.2 African Theology and its history — 144
- 9.3 Theological streams — 146
- 9.4 Sources and tools for doing theology in Africa — 149
- 9.5 The main issues of African Theology today — 150
- 9.6 Conclusion — 155
- Reading List and Bibliography — 157

10 African Initiated Church Theology — 159

- 10.1 What are the "African Initiated Churches"? — 159
- 10.2 Historical background — 160
- 10.3 The theological approach of the African Initiated Churches — 164
- 10.4 Some theological themes — 167
- 10.5 Summary and conclusion — 176
- Reading List and Bibliography — 177

11 Pentecostal Theology — 179

- 11.1 Introduction — 179
- 11.2 Historical background of the Pentecostal Movement — 179
- 11.3 Historical background of the Charismatic Movement — 180
- 11.4 A comparison between the Pentecostal and Charismatic Movements — 181
- 11.5 A Pentecostal paradigm — 184
- 11.6 The implications of the Pentecostal paradigm — 186
- 11.7 Conclusion — 188
- Reading List — 188
- Bibliography — 188

12 Charismatic Theology — 191

- 12.1 Introduction — 191
- 12.2 The roots of Charismatic Theology — 191
- 12.3 From Oral Theology to formal systematic theology — 193
- 12.4 A variety of theologies — 194
- 12.5 Spirit-baptism seen from different angles — 194

12.6	Systematic theologies from different traditions	196
12.7	Conclusion	200
Reading List		201
Bibliography		201

13 Ecological Theology — 203

13.1	Introduction	203
13.2	God in nature and history	204
13.3	Justice, peace and integrity of creation	205
13.4	Main issues in the ecumenical ecological reflection	206
13.5	Open questions	208
Reading List and Bibliography		212

14 Postmodern Theology — 215

14.1	Introduction	215
14.2	Postmodernism and Modernism	215
14.3	Self-organization	217
14.4	The agenda of Postmodern Theology	218
14.5	Comparing world-views	220
14.6	An alternative epistemology	222
14.7	The consequences for theology	223
14.8	Participation	224
14.9	Metaphors	225
14.10	Cosmology	227
14.11	Interdisciplinary dialogue	228
Reading List and Bibliography		229

15 The theological challenge of other religious traditions — 231

15.1	The contect out of which this theology emerges	231
15.2	Major trends in the Christian Theology of Religions	235
15.3	Central biblical notions	242
15.4	The forms of praxis for a theology of religion	246
Reading List		252
Bibliography		253

Biblical Theology

Adrio König

2.1 FOUR DIFFERENT VIEWS OF BIBLICAL THEOLOGY

2.1.1 Introduction

In section A of this volume theology is viewed form fourteen different perspectives, most of which are taken from the last half century. But a few from previous centuries are also included (chapters 2–4), amongst them this first chapter on Biblical Theology.

The reasons for the existence of most of the types of theology are obvious. Hardly anyone would question the right to existence of, for example, Black Liberation Theology or Post-modern Theology – even though they may not necessarily evaluate them positively.

However this is not the case with Biblical Theology. Even the possibility of its existence is often doubted. At least four different positions can be distinguished, two for and two against.

There are two positive views on Biblical Theology. One defines Biblical Theology as theology according to or in agreement with the Bible. The other sees Biblical Theology as theology that inquires into the interrelatedness of different themes in the Bible. Let us deal with the first of these views.

2.1.2 Theology according to the Bible

This view on Biblical Theology originates from one of the premises of the Reformation of the 16th century: *sola scriptura* (only the Bible). This means that the Bible is the only norm for Christian doctrine and life. In terms of this theological approach, theologians simply have to systematically formulate the doctrines that are already contained in the Bible. Despite different emphases and historic developments, there is a doctrine on every major subject available in the Bible. Theology is in fact

SECTION A

THEOLOGY

"saying after" the Bible. Some very conservative Evangelical groups still adhere in principle to this view on Biblical Theology and dogmatics.

The doctrine of creation can serve as an example. It is supposed that in its briefest form this doctrine in the Bible reads that in six days God created everything out of nothing. One of the main problems with this approach is that it does not take the variety of biblical materials seriously or that these are all too easily harmonized. In terms of the material on creation, the amazing variety of concepts of creation simply cannot be accommodated in such an inarticulate formulation (König 1988:70ff.). Just think of the differences between concepts such as creation through an act, creation through separation, creation and conflict, creation through origination (like the earth producing plants, Gen 1:12).

2.1.3 Theology interrelates different themes

This type of Biblical Theology more readily accepts the variety of concepts and traditions in the Bible and enquires into the possibility of meaningfully interrelating these. We find this type of Biblical Theology particularly in the German-speaking world. The father of this approach is J.P. Gabler (late 18th century).

Actually, one has to distinguish between two approaches. The one is to interrelate specific themes in the Bible, while the other is to attempt to understand the Bible as a whole – or either the Old Testament or the New Testament as separate units – in terms of one central concept or theme.

Let us first look at the more inclusive approach. It is particularly systematic theologians that favour this approach. The question is whether it is possible and meaningful to interrelate the major biblical themes through one basic concept such as the covenant, the reign of God, or law and gospel, or sin and grace. During the past few decades, different forms of Liberation Theology have developed: Latin American Liberation Theology, Black Liberation Theology, Feminist Theology, Womanist Theology, Ecological Theology – to mention only the most important ones. All of these theologies see liberation as a key concept in the Bible, and take it that one can formulate the entire gospel, or at least important aspects of it, in terms of the concept of liberation. Depending on what type of Liberation Theology is involved, the liberation of suppressed classes or races or sexes or natures is at stake. Some Old and New Testament theologians have tried to develop either an Old Testament Theology or a New Testament Theology by identifying a concept to interrelate the main themes of either of the Testaments. The division of Biblical Theology into Old Testament Theology and New Testament Theology is virtually as old as Biblical Theology itself (end of the 18th century). Especially during the 20th century, the question has continually been asked as to a centre or central concept of either Testament.

For the Old Testament, Eichrodt suggested the covenant, Sellin the holiness of God, Köhler God as the Lord, Vriezen community, Schmidt the first commandment – to mention some of the most important ones. However, each one of these central concepts met with serious criticism.

Today many theologians are convinced than one cannot speak of a centre of either Testament. Concerning the Old Testament, we are reminded of the long history involved during which time new situations and issues developed so that one could at its best speak of God as a central theme – or rather the central Person (Kraus 1970:384; Haacker 1977:117ff.; Hasel 1972:99ff.).

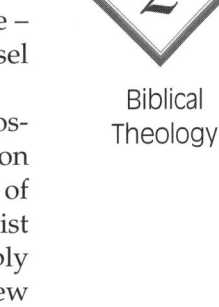

The same debate has been conducted on the New Testament. As possible centre has been proposed: the human person (Bultmann), salvation history (Cullmann), the covenant (Loretz, Fensham), the justification of the godless (some Lutheran theologians), the reign of God (Klein), Christ (Reicke) and the resurrection of Christ (Künneth). One could presumably say with perfect justice that Jesus Christ stands at the heart of the New Testament, at least in the sense that none of the books of the New Testament would have been written had he not lived and especially not risen (Hasel 1978:chapter III). And this means that one can at least say that a Person stands at the heart of both Testaments. One should however realize that the mere names Yahweh and Jesus Christ can not function as a key concept without being filled with content. And the moment this process starts, the debate is on again.

There is also a second form of this type of Biblical Theology. In this case theologians work less inclusively and rather try to relate specific themes in the Bible. A good example is the way Gese deals with the Prologue of John, where Jesus is referred to as the Word (1977:152ff.). While many New Testament scholars in the past looked for the background of the concept Word (Logos) in sources outside the Bible, Gese turns to the Old Testament and identifies a very interesting background in the Wisdom literature, especially in Proverbs 8 and Job 28. He then tries to show meaningful dependence of the Logos concept on the Wisdom figure.

This is but one example of how this type of Biblical Theology looks for interdependence and interrelatedness of concepts and images in the Bible. Important work has been done by i.a. Kraus (1970, 1972, 1983), Gese (1974, 1977), Haacker (1977) and Weber (1989).

While we have been referring to the doctrine of creation in dealing with the first form of Biblical Theology, it may be interesting to use the same example now. In this approach the effort will be made to interrelate the variety of material on creation in the Bible. From the fact that both God, Jesus and the Spirit are referred to in connection with creation in different parts of the Bible, it will be concluded that the work of creation is a Trinitarian act. The variety of creation concepts will also be dealt with much more seriously. Some may try to harmonize them, while others may find it impossible and therefore simply accept the diversity and try to make sense of it. Reference may be made to the fact that biblical writers are using much the same concepts as other religions in the Ancient Near East (König 1988:74ff.), which may imply that the actual message of the Bible does not consist in exactly how God created but rather in **which** God is the Creator, namely the God of Israel. Others may go further and conclude that as the writers of the Bible freely made use of creation con-

Biblical Theology

cepts of other religions, we could follow them and use some of the concepts of traditional African religion and of the theory of evolution. Obviously disagreement will exist on issues such as these amongst biblical theologians.

After this fairly long treatment of positions that are positive about the possibility of Biblical Theology, we can now consider two negative ones.

2.1.4 The Bible by definition has no theology

Again there are two views rejecting the possibility of a Biblical Theology. The first is a very conservative approach which holds that there is no theology in the Bible simply because the Bible is something totally different from theology. The Bible contains proclamation, and it is our duty to try to understand and formulate this message. Theology is to reflect theoretically on the message of the Bible and this, by definition, the Bible writers did not do. In this vein one should not speak of the theology of Paul or whatever other Bible writer. Older forms of Reformed Theology still reflect this view.

2.1.5 There is no meaningful interrelatedness in the Bible

The second negative view on the possibility of Biblical Theology maintains that what we do have in the Bible is rather a variety of materials, as different writers made their contributions in different times and situations. What we can and should do is to research what the individual writers in the Bible produced and in this way put forward the theology of specific books or writers. But they will never concede the existence of more inclusive theologies like an Old or New Testament Theology or even a theology of the Sinoptic Gospels, as to their mind the books differ too much. Like Käsemann (1970:124ff.) they would rather accept that the New Testament contains a variety of views on e.g. the church in fact such a variety that no one authoritative view on the church can be deduced from it. Both Roman Catholics and Protestants can call with equal right on the Bible for their ecclesiologies. In the same way there is no possibility of reconciling Paul and James on justification.

We have now dealt with four different views on Biblical Theology. Obviously each of them makes some sense. The truth does not always lie clearly with one position against all others. Often one sides more strongly with one view, but can simultaneously accept some aspects of others. It is more enriching to foster such a critical-elective approach rather than a more exclusive and strict dogmatic one.

2.2 THE BIBLE AS SOURCE AND NORM FOR THEOLOGY

2.2.1 Source

The fact that the Bible is fairly generally accepted as source and norm for theology offers the most important reason why people make a scholarly study of the Bible.

Though there is some connection between source and norm, it has some advantages to discuss them separately.

The Bible is an important source of theology, but it is not the only one (Grenz 1993). Not all theological disciplines make equally intensive use of it.

First a brief remark on the last-mentioned fact. Old and New Testament disciplines and some forms of Systematic and Ethical Theology make much more use of the Bible than, for instance, Practical Theology or Church History, simply because of their fields of study.

Now something more on the fact that theologians do not work with the Bible as the only source of theology. Besides the Bible there are also the Apocryphal books which are indeed included in the Bible used in the Catholic Church. Furthermore there is the environment, both of time and of place, in which the events of the Bible occurred. These three sources may be grouped together as the Bible-and-its-environment, which many see as by far the most important source for theology.

The second source is the Christian tradition, including the history of dogma and of theology, which is one of the main objects of Church History. Those of us who today try to understand the Bible and live faithful to the Lord, can only benefit from taking serious what previous generations understood and did. But more is at stake than only the history of the Christian Church. The history of certain other religions is also important, especially that of Judaism and Islam – often wrongly called Mohammedanism – because there are certain historic ties between these religions. As second source of theology we could therefore speak of the Christian tradition and the traditions of other religions.

As third source we can mention the situation or the context in which we live. There is much truth in the saying that one should read the Bible and the newspaper together daily. Contextual Theology is not only a modern phenomenon. Since the origin of the Theology of Revolution and Political Theology in the early Sixties, and the development of the range of fully-fledged Liberation theologies, it has become convention to call these "contextual" theologies. But what else has the theology of the reformers been than contextual? Just think of Martin Luther, who, in a situation of the utmost uncertainty on how to be saved, called out: Where do I find a gracious God?

Present day contextual theology differs from earlier forms in that oppression, poverty and inhumane living conditions now play a decisive role. Why? Haven't there been such conditions in earlier times? There have! But theologians and the church in general did not experience these as part of their context, i.e. the context they question and address, at least partly because they were not poor themselves. We have to distinguish between a total context and a constituted or conscientized context. Every person or group of persons lives in a much bigger context than the one they consciously engage and question. Poverty and oppression were simply not part of Luther's constituted context, part of the problems he wrestled with. Even slavery and in South Africa apartheid, has for very long not been "noted" by very many Christians. It was of course a different matter when people defended these phenomena. In that case they

2

Biblical Theology

SECTION

A

THEOLOGY

indeed conscientized them – which makes their moral blame all the graver. But for many people it simply was outside of their conscientized context.

Under 2.3.5 it will be argued that the Bible itself is very much a contextual book, that the different authors were very sensitive to the situations in which they wrote. This fact should encourage Christians all the more consciously and questioningly to engage with their situation and to try to relate their faith meaningfully to it. There is no doubt that context is an important source of theology that leads to new questions being put to the Bible and the faith in general. Black Liberation Theology, Feminist Theology and Ecological Theology are clear present day examples of this. But one can also think of the way in which the division between the Protestant churches and Missionary societies encouraged the churches early in the 20th century to rethink the unity of the church in light of the Bible and to act accordingly.

We have now considered three sources of theology but again (see 2.1.5) it is advisable to refrain from choosing one of them to the exclusion of the others. There will always be particular emphases by certain theologians, some working more with biblical materials and others with one of the other sources, like the history of doctrine or the context in which they live. We should leave theologians the liberty to choose as, on the whole, these different emphases lead to the enrichment of theology.

2.2.2 Norm

The question of the Bible as norm is more complicated. During the Reformation, Luther and Calvin took a strong stand on "only the Bible" but this is often misinterpreted as though they meant that the Bible is the only source of theology. In fact, Luther himself stood strongly on the tradition of the church, especially on the ecumenical creeds. One of his strong arguments against Roman Catholic Theology was that while he honoured the true tradition, the Catholic Church had deviated from it on decisive points and thus had become a "new" church – with the implication of an illegitimate one (Küng 1964:96ff.).

It is very interesting to note Luther's justification for this argument. According to him, his teaching agrees with that of the apostles and the tradition of the early church, while it is the Catholic Church that has decisively deviated from them.

The aim of this reference is not to take a position vis à vis the polemic between Luther and Rome, but to indicate what meaning the Reformers attached to "only the Bible". They did not mean that the Bible was the only source for their theology. The ecumenical councils of the early church and also the Fathers were simply too important to them. What they meant was that the Bible was the only (or at least the final) **norm** for doctrine and life.

Even though there are still Christians who maintain that the Bible is in fact the only source of their convictions, it has become all too obvious how difficult it is to determine exactly what is in agreement with the

Bible and what not. There is virtually no group of Christians that does not present its convictions as "biblical". But the Bible is a collection of books written over a thousand or more years in different situations. Furthermore, the biblical writers are generally very sensitive to there context, which means that they take the problems of their day very seriously. For all these reasons it is often extremely difficult, if not impossible, to determine in new situations what is in accordance with the Bible and what not.

There is no easy answer to this problem. It is simply not enough to say, no matter with how much force, that "we are only true to the infallible Word of God". The least that one should be willing to do is seriously to listen to other Christians – and also to non-Christians – especially to those who differ substantially from oneself. Our biggest opponents are in fact our biggest friends! From them one will receive the clearest views on positions that differ from one's own, and the sharpest criticism on one's convictions. If I want people to take me seriously, I have to do the same. Virtually all of us all too often simply try to justify our own position and use the Bible for that purpose rather than to listen, "together with all Gods people" (Eph 3:18), to what the Bible is really saying.

And reflecting back on the position of the Reformers, it may be necessary to say that the Bible is the main norm rather than the only norm for doctrine and life. The history of the church and the situation also have some normative value, even if subordinate to the Bible. Especially some liberation theologians and those from the Pentecostal and Charismatic movements assess the value of the present speaking of God in their concrete situation very highly. We should also allow some authority to Christian convictions of the past and not all too easily claim that our insights are biblical in cases where they speak against the tradition or are in no way reflected in it.

We have again reached the conclusion that Christians should not only be critical of one another, but should also try to be enriched by other traditions.

2.3 SOME BIBLICAL LANDMARKS FOR THEOLOGY

2.3.1 Introduction

There is not only one "pure" Biblical Theology or one pure doctrine on every issue in the Bible. The Bible is not a book of doctrine with ready answers to our problems if we only know where to look. The Bible is rather a book of history – at least to a large extent. It tells the story of people who witness that they met a God who revealed himself to them and what further experiences they had with this God. This means that there is a wide world in which theology can be done. One theologian may emphasize one aspect like the covenant, while another a different like sin and grace. The one need not be right while the other one is necessarily wrong. Each one may develop important insights that enrich our faith.

For this reason it is preferable to accept that there are a number of landmarks that can direct our thought, rather than strict prescriptions on exactly what shape our theology should take. All these landmarks need not function in the same way and have equal importance, but no theology should move outside these or develop views contrary to them.

For the sake of convenience these indicators are grouped together in five groups. The way they are organized is not a case of principle, nor is it suggested that all the important indicators are included. It is rather an attempt to help us critically to enrich our own theology by looking at some important perspectives in the Bible.

2.3.2 Christ, God the Father, the Holy Spirit, covenant, reign of God, sin and grace, law and gospel

Christ It is not for nothing that we speak of the **Christian** faith and call ourselves Christians. Christ is central in the New Testament. If the references to Christ, to what he said and did, to what happened with him and to how he was understood, were to be excluded from the New Testament, only a few discontinuous pages would have been left. The gospels are in their entirety a witness about him, the Acts are his acts through his Spirit in the world, and the Letters have an unimaginable concentration on his significance for the early church – to say nothing of the book of Revelation which again is **his** revelation to John. Ephesians 1:3–14 is an interesting example. There is virtually no phrase in it which does not refer to Christ. In fact, one should take the time to make a list of all that is said about him in this one long sentence.

The implication of all this is that thinking about Jesus Christ should occupy a central place in any theology. A good example of such a theological approach was that of Karl Barth during the first half of the 20th century. Christ is central in every aspect of Barth's theology. In terms of the doctrine of revelation he is the revelation of God (1956); in terms of the doctrine of God he himself is God, and God is this Jesus of Nazareth (1957); according to the doctrine of creation he is the Creator(1958); and as far as reconciliation is concerned he reconciled us to God, being himself the reconciling God and the reconciled human being (1961). And although Barth could not write an eschatology, there is no doubt that also in this doctrine Christ would have been the central person.

But this is not only true of Barth's theology. Even in Pietistic Theology Jesus is in the centre as the Saviour of souls, and in Liberation Theology as the great Liberator. In the "Four Square Gospel" Jesus Christ is the Saviour, Healer, Baptizer with the Spirit, and coming King.

This central position of Christ in the New Testament is, however, never at the expense of the Father or the Spirit. The long sentence in Ephesians 1 that has already been referred to, is a good example. Without any tension, the Father and the Spirit act alongside of Christ. In fact, the Father is the subject of that long sentence. There need be no tension, as Christ is the Son of the Father, and the Spirit is Christ's Spirit. The Father has sent the Son and the Son now works through the Spirit.

This means that a Christocentric theology need not neglect the Father or the Spirit even though this has been done in the past. In fact, if we have a clear understanding of Christ, we will necessarily include his Father and his Spirit with him in the centre.

Covenant The covenant is one of the central features in the Bible. It occurs in many places and in many forms. In fact, the one sentence that occurs most in the Bible is the sentence that gives the content of the covenant in a nutshell: "I shall be your God and you shall be my people." Covenant implies relatedness, mutuality, community. The covenant consists in the relationship between God and Israel, in the mutual relationship of human beings, and can even be interpreted to include our relationship with nature. Israel as the people of God has to live in communion with God and with one another, and has to care for the land which is part of God's covenantal blessings to them. The church is the household of God, but also the body of Christ in which interrelatedness and mutual service express the essence of the community. The Spirit binds all believers together by his gifts through which they have to serve one another. The fruit of the Spirit (like love, kindness, faithfulness, patience) also binds people together, while the "works of the flesh" tears people apart. And by his death on the cross, Christ created one new humanity out of the estranged groups (Eph 2).

This means that in whatever type of theology, the idea of covenant should never be neglected – even though it need not be the key concept and even though different concepts for the idea of covenant are used, like community (Grenz). God and humans, humans amongst themselves, and humans and nature are interrelated in love. In opposition to this, any divisive factors should rather be treated with misgiving.

Traditional Africa knows something of this interrelatedness of human beings amongst themselves, and of humans and nature – as opposed to western individualism.

The reign of God This is likewise a central biblical concept. It is deemed the essential feature in the words and deeds of Jesus. He both announces and realizes the reign (kingdom) of God because He acts on behalf of God. For this reason also the reign of God should play a part in any type of theology.

Of course much is at stake in the way a concept features in a specific theology. In some theologies the reign of God features one-sidedly in terms of authority and obedience. God is seen as King, Lord, sovereign who speaks with authority and should be obeyed – which is good enough as far as it goes. But it is one-sided and less than the full picture, because with the prophets God is pre-eminently the one who **cares** for the poor and the oppressed (i.a. Ps 72!). God's justice means that God gives justice to the exploited. These perspectives add tenderness to the reign of God making it more than merely authority and obedience. Because of God's care, God's people obey God in gratefulness and love.

Sin and grace, law and gospel These are equally central issues in the Bible which may not be neglected in any theology. The very fact that God is the faithful and caring God of the covenant gives us the courage to approach God with confidence and confess our sins with the assurance that God will forgive. It is meaningful that some theologians prefer the sequence grace and sin and also gospel and law, to emphasize that we must first have the confidence that God will forgive before we can ever dare to approach God with our sin. If God were only the holy God who hates sin, and only the sovereign to be obeyed, we would have had no choice but to flee from God, as we are unholy and disobedient.

Black Liberation Theology rightly emphasizes God as the true covenant God who cares and delivers, but it does not emphasize as much the God who forgives the contrite sinner. Various forms of Liberation Theology tend to emphasize the law and the judgement of God one-sidedly, but so did Amos as long as there was no clear repentance and confession by the oppressors! Obviously under special circumstances some aspects of the gospel have to be emphasized stronger than others.

2.3.3 Human beings, individuals and groups

Up to now we have concentrated on aspects of the gospel where God is in the centre. However, it should be noted that we had again and again also referred to humans. This may be an indication that we cannot speak in the right way about God if we do not also speak of humans – which may be an indication of the fundamental significance of the covenant. God is the God of Abraham, Isaac and Jacob, the Father of Jesus of Nazareth – thus the God of humans.

For this reason it will come as no surprise that humans are also central in the Bible. Even though there is one book that does not refer to God (Esther), there is no book that does not refer to human beings, in which humans are not in the centre.

The Old Testament starts off with humanity as a whole (Gen 1–11), and from there concentrates on Israel, though not at the exclusion of the nations. In fact, one of the important future perspectives of some prophets is the flocking of all nations to Jerusalem to unite with Israel – a prophecy to whose fulfilment the New Testament authors witness more than once. Just think of Jesus (re-)creating one new humanity on the cross (Eph 2), of the Spirit being poured out exactly when the entire (then known) world is represented in Jerusalem (Acts 2), and the prophecy that all nations of the saved will flock into the New Jerusalem (Rev 21–22).

In a certain sense everything in the Bible is viewed in terms of human beings (Berkhof 1979:178). It is human beings that are created, God lives in a covenant with humans, humans are saved, God's law is given to humans, and so we could carry on. As is the case in Africa (Mbiti 1971), so in the Bible human beings are most important, though not only some exclusive groups but rather humanity as such, as is clear from these references. This means that humanity should be in the focus of theology. The gospel is not only for a selected few. God loves the (sinful!) *world*.

On the other hand, humanity does not function as an unstructured mass in the Bible. There are important distinctions. The emphasis is often on individuals and also on specific groups, but our attention is also drawn to a few remarkable structures in humanity.

Individuals are important in certain parts of the Bible. Even in the Old Testament, where Israel as a group is in the centre, we have the prophet Ezekiel emphasizing the individual's responsibility (Ezek 18 and 33), and also the many individuals prominent in the Psalms. In the New Testament, individuals and the personal experience of the grace of God becomes even more important. Heathens are called to a personal decision of faith in Christ as Lord, and individuals receive gifts of the Spirit for the benefit of all. The justice of God, which in the Old Testament is pre-eminently a societal feature, is applied by Paul to individual justification. This legitimizes the Evangelical emphasis on individual conversion and a personal relationship with Jesus Christ. Theology and proclamation that remain general and have no individual application are therefore unacceptable.

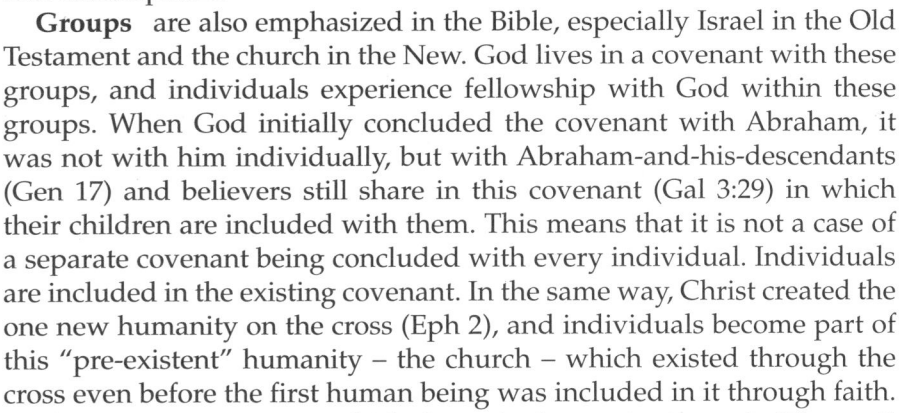

Groups are also emphasized in the Bible, especially Israel in the Old Testament and the church in the New. God lives in a covenant with these groups, and individuals experience fellowship with God within these groups. When God initially concluded the covenant with Abraham, it was not with him individually, but with Abraham-and-his-descendants (Gen 17) and believers still share in this covenant (Gal 3:29) in which their children are included with them. This means that it is not a case of a separate covenant being concluded with every individual. Individuals are included in the existing covenant. In the same way, Christ created the one new humanity on the cross (Eph 2), and individuals become part of this "pre-existent" humanity – the church – which existed through the cross even before the first human being was included in it through faith.

There is even a sense in which the entire humanity is a unit. We are all represented by, and somehow incorporated in Adam, just as Christ represented all and included all in his death and resurrection (Rom 5:12–21; Rom 6). It is this basic unity of the entire humanity that is presupposed by the doctrine of original sin and the substitutive death of Christ, and is often suggested as a basis for infant baptism.

A few very important issues in the Bible which should at least not be negated by any theology have in this way been dealt with in some detail. There are more such issues. We mention some of them.

2.3.4 The earth, the body and nature

The earth, the human body and nature in general are important features in some biblical traditions (Zimmerli 1971). The earth is not only the dwelling-place of humans, but also the place where God wants to have fellowship with us. The earth is so important to God that God has even promised to renew it and to come and live with us on it in the new Jerusalem (Rev 21–22). This does not form an alternative to a longing for heaven, since heaven is where God is. On the new earth it will be "heaven on earth".

One implication that this has, is the emphasis on the land in the Old Testament (Wright 1990). Israel receives a land from God, not merely as a place to live and to earn a living, but first and foremost as a place to live in fellowship with God and in which to praise God. The meek shall inherit the earth (Matt 5:5). Some prophecies in the Bible reflect an interesting view on the new earth as free from violence and suffering (Isa 11:6ff.; 65:17ff.), and supplying an abundance of food for its inhabitants. There is at least some comparison with the importance of land in Africa, and more specifically the position in South Africa.

Even though the pollution of the environment, the depletion of resources and overpopulation were not on the agenda in biblical times, perspectives on the future of the earth, such as those mentioned above, should function as a powerful inspiration to preserve and care for nature. It is here on the earth that God has placed us and wishes to live in the harmony of the covenant with us. Therefore an ecological theology should encourage the church to respond to the ecological challenges around us. Some very meaningful innovative initiatives have been taken in this regard by Innus Daneel in Zimbabwe, who has convinced a number of the African Initiated Churches to include tree planting as part of their regular communion service (Daneel 1995:87ff.).

Emphasis on the importance of the earth includes the human body. Our salvation will only be completed at our resurrection. God has created us as *bodily* beings to live on the *earth*. This means that our prayer for daily bread is as important as our prayer for the forgiveness of our sin. Also, it is as much the task of the church to care for people's needs as to provide them with "spiritual" food. The ministry of healing is essentially part of the gospel – just think of the life of Jesus! – and not only a bait to draw people to the "real" gospel (Jas 2:14–17). On the new earth there will be no more sin, but also no more sickness. All this should be part and parcel of any inclusive theology.

2.3.5 The context

The Bible is not a book with timeless, eternal values, but much rather a contextual book. One repeatedly feels the warmth of the life of specific people, their sufferings and their joys, their oppression or deliverance. The Gospels tell the story of what Jesus did and suffered in Palestine. The Letters deal with the problems of the early churches. The gospel comes to us in the robe of the life- and world-view of the time: the earth is flat, heaven is above the earth and hell below, the sun moves around the earth, a dome retains the water in the sky, and God supplies rain by opening up some of the windows in the dome (Mal 3:10). Nothing of this is scientifically true.

In the same way, women are spoken of in a most humiliating manner and they were treated no better than the women from amongst the neighbours of Israel (Gen 19:6–8)! A man's wife is simply one of his possessions – not even the first on the list (Exod 20:17).

This contextuality of the Bible is very important because it reminds us that our theology should also be contextual. The gospel wants to address our concrete situation. It cannot be understood and proclaimed in the same way in Europe as it is in Africa. Amos is not identical to Paul! The gospel is like a diamond with many facets. The position of the sun determines which facet will shine. In a situation with bad pollution, one should rather emphasise other aspects of the gospel than those where women are discriminated against. A situation of consuming diseases and poverty asks for other facets of the gospel to be discussed than when rich atheists are addressed.

On the other hand, this contextuality of the gospel also creates problems. It is not easy to distinguish between the gospel and the culture or world-view in which it comes to us. For centuries, Christians were convinced that it is part of the truth of the Bible that the earth is flat. Even in modern times, Christians still defended slavery as the will of God. Even today, there are Christians who are convinced that no woman may ever act in a position of power and authority over men.

There is no easy solution to such problems. Often it takes a long time and much discussion before Christians reach any sort of consensus.

Again we face the important issue of contact and dialogue with Christians of different convictions and people of other faiths or no faith.

2.3.6 Goal and future

There are Christians who believe that in the Bible we have a detailed plan of whatever God is doing on earth, even that God has predetermined everything that is happening. Just think of the popular belief that the time of death of every person is fixed by God.

The motives behind these views are often to be praised, as they intend to give the honour to God and to praise God's greatness and sovereignty. However, these views encounter serious problems with regard to human responsibility and in dealing with the injustices and suffering on earth.

If it says too much that God has a detailed plan which He executes, at least there is enough reason to accept that God has a goal for creation which will be realized in future.

It is possible that Israel came to know Yahweh from the earliest times as the One who gives promises and thereby directs the people to the future (Moltmann 1967; Preuss 1968). Israel never stagnated. They were repeatedly drawn into the future by this God.

In some sense, Jesus fulfilled the promises of God. According to some of the Evangelists, a multitude of prophecies are fulfilled in him. But at the same time they see him as still moving into the future, giving new promises that again direct his disciples to the future, but this time an imminent one.

This emphasis on the future is so prominent in many parts of the Bible that one could build an entire theology around the contrast old/new. We have an Old Testament and a New Testament, an old covenant and a new covenant, a first and a new exodus, Jerusalem, heaven and earth, old and new (born again) human beings who have received a new life and a new commandment from Jesus. And Jesus himself is the new human being and the new Adam, in contrast to the old Adam.

This prominent directedness to the future makes a restoration theology unacceptable. The Bible does not continually look back to Adam as if redemption would mean that we are restored to what he was. The Bible rather looks into the future, and we are recreated in terms of the new Adam. The Bible starts out with a garden (which is threatened and should be protected [Gen 2:15, Gen 1:4, 6, 18 etc.]), but ends with a city (Rev 21–22) which is no longer to be protected and which is the symbol of safety, in contrast to the unprotected countryside. Also, the Bible starts with the sun and moon, but ends with God and the Lam as the light (Rev 21:23). As Christians, our calling is therefore not to look back to the "good old days" and to restore, but rather to work for the future when God's justice will shine through and God's reign will come, when the covenant will be fully realized in the lives of human beings who will love God and live in love and peace with their fellows and with nature.

Here we have tried to summarize the goal of God for creation. Justice, reign, covenant and peace are some of the key concepts.

2.3.7 A closing remark

These landmarks need not all be fully developed in every theology. More clarity is reached by distinguishing between different types of theology.

There are inclusive theologies and theologies with limited scope. In an inclusive theology, the intent is to deal with the entire body of the faith, all the relevant loci – in many cases in terms of one specific key concept. In a limited theology, the focus is on one main issue of the faith, such as a Theology of Hope, or an Ecological Theology or Womanist Theology. In such an approach, a few aspects may be included. The Theology of Hope develops a very specific view of God (as the One who opens up the future) and of history (as open so that new things can happen). Feminist Theology isolates the oppression of women and employs a very specific view on the biblical concept of liberation. So all these limited theologies deal with a restricted area of the faith.

Obviously, not all the landmarks discussed above can be included in these theologies. But at least they should not be countered. No theology should try to argue against the centrality of Christ, or minimize the importance of the earth or the body, or disclaim the value of the gospel for all humans.

In the case of inclusive theologies, more of the landmarks can be included, but even then some concentration occurs, not so much in terms of aspects of the faith, but rather in terms of key concepts. Often more than one is involved, but it is possible that too many will diffuse the impact. The point of an inclusive theology is to show how one or two concepts meaningfully interrelate the different aspects of the faith. A covenant theology may make some use of concepts such as the reign of God or sin and grace, but will not develop them extensively. Again, no theology which works mainly with one concept should discredit the others. It should rather try both to benefit from other key concepts and theologies and to develop its own in a way that will enrich the others rather than oppose them.

The overall aim of this chapter is therefore not to be prescriptive and to motivate people to always try to show that their theology is the best, the soundest and the only truly biblical one, but rather to encourage them to look at other theologies in a more informed way and to be able to "place" them and to enrich their own approach through them. In fact, throughout this treatment of the relationship between Bible and theology there is a thread of openness towards others. The gospel is so rich and diversified, the situations in which Christians work so different, and we are all so inclined to justify only our own convictions against all others and to use the Bible as an arsenal against other Christians and their theologies, that we can only benefit from a more open approach – something of an "ecumenical" approach if by "ecumenical" we mean trying to understand the faith in communion with all God's people (Eph 3:18).

READING LIST

Berkhof, H. 1979. *Christian Faith*. Grand Rapids: Eerdmans.
Haacker, K. et al. 1977. *Biblische Theologie Heute*. Neukirchen: Neukirchen Verlag.
Hasel, G. 1972. *Old Testament Theology*. Grand Rapids: Eerdmans
– 1978. *New Testament Theology*. Grand Rapids: Eerdmans.
Kraus, H-J. 1970. *Die Biblische Theologie*. Neukirchen: Neukirchen Verlag.
Weber, H-R. 1989. *Power. Focus for a Biblical Theology*. Geneva: WWC.

BIBLIOGRAPHY

Barth, K. 1956. *Kirchliche Dogmatik* I/2. Edinburgh: T and T Clark.
– 1957. *Kirchliche Dogmatik* II/1. Edinburgh: T and T Clark.
– 1958. *Kirchliche Dogmatik* III/1. Edinburgh: T and T Clark.
– 1960. *Kirchliche Dogmatik* III/2. Edinburgh: T and T Clark.
– 1961. *Kirchliche Dogmatik* IV/1. Edinburgh: T and T Clark.
– 1962. *Kirchliche Dogmatik* IV/3, 2. Edinburgh: T and T Clark.
Berkhof, H. 1979. *Christian Faith*. Grand Rapids: Eerdmans.
Daneel, I. 1995. In: *Religion and Theology* 2/1. Pretoria: Unisa
Gese, H. 1974. *Von Sinai bis Zion*. München: Chr. Kaiser.
– 1977. *Zur Biblische Theologie*. München: Chr. Kaiser.
Grenz, S. 1993. *Revisioning Evangelical Theology*. Downers Grove, Illinois: Intervarsity Press.
Gutierrez, G. 1973. *Theology of Liberation*. Maryknoll: Orbis.
Haacker, K. et al. 1977. *Biblische Theologie heute*. Neukirchen: Neukirchener Verlag.
Hasel, G. 1972. *Old Testament Theology*. Grand Rapids: Eerdmans.
– 1978. *New Testament Theology*. Grand Rapids: Eerdmans.
Käsemann, E. (ed.). 1970. *Das Neue Testament als Kanon*. Göttingen: Vandenhoeck und Ruprecht.
König, A. 1983. *Menslike Mense. Gelowig Nagedink Deel 5*. Halfway House: Orion.
– 1988. *New and Greater Things. Re-evaluating the Biblical Message on Creation*. Pretoria: Unisa.
Kraus, H-J. 1970. *Die Biblische Theologie*. Neukirchen: Neukirchener Verlag.
– 1972. *Biblisch-theologische Aufsätze*. Neukirchen: Neukirchener Verlag.
– 1983. *Systematische Theologie im Kontext biblischer Geschichte und Eschatologie*. Neukirchen: Neukirchener Verlag.

Küng, H. 1964. *Structures of the Church*. London: Burns and Oates.
Mbiti, J.S. 1971. *African Religion and Philosophy*. London: Heineman.
Migliore, D.L. 1991. *Faith seeking Understanding*. Grand Rapids: Eerdmans.
Miguez-Bonino, J. 1975. *Doing Theology in a Revolutionary Situation*. Philadelphia: Fortress.
Moltmann, J. 1967. *Theology of Hope*. New York: Harper and Row.
Nürnberger, K.G. 1975. *Sistematiese Teologie*. Durban: Lutheran Publishing House.
Piper, J. and Grudem, W. 1991. *Recovering Biblical Manhood and Womanhood*. Wheaton: Crossway Books.
Preuss, H.D. 1968. *Jahweglaube und Zukunfterwartung*. Stuttgart: Kohlhammer.
Spykman, G. 1992. *Reformational Theology. A new paradigm for doing Theology*. Grand Rapids: Eerdmans.
Weber, H-R. 1989. *Power. Focus for a Biblical Theology*. Geneva: WCC.
Zimmerli, W. 1971. *Die Weltlichkeit des Alten Testaments*. Göttingen: Vandenhoeck und Ruprecht.

Theology: the first 19 centuries

Brian Gaybba

3.1 INTRODUCTION

All theology is ultimately a reflection by Christians on their faith. This reflection can take many forms, and that is what distinguishes one type of theology from another. It can take the very basic form of a personal attempt to apply one's faith to one's own life. Or it can take the form of a very abstract, detailed and highly sophisticated analysis of a particular aspect of the faith, utilising the latest philosophical insights or whatever other insights contemporary knowledge can give us.

It would be impossible to list all the different types of theology that can exist and trace their development here. However, it will be useful to list four ingredients that are found mixed up in all forms of theology. These four are: the Scriptures, tradition, experience and reason. Theologies have a different flavour according to the way in which they stress one ingredient more than the other. These ingredients operate mostly as "sources", that is to say theologians go to them to get their basic working material. Sometimes these sources are used consciously, as when a theologian examines a particular text of the Bible. Sometimes they are used subconsciously, as when one's own experience colours the way one views or understands something without being aware of the extent of that influence. The fourth ingredient mentioned above – reason – operates not only as a source but also as a tool in theology. It operates as a source when theologians use the products of human reasoning and discovery – for example, philosophical ideas. It operates as a tool when theologians use the techniques of reason to analyze their faith or the sources of their faith – for example, logic, grammar, hermeneutical theory.

In the story that follows, it will be worth remembering these ingredients, for the history of theology is very much the history of the way in which those ingredients shaped theology at particular periods in its history.

Finally, it is only a decadent theology that continues to repeat past ideas without consideration for present needs or concerns. All good theology responds to particular needs, whether those needs be the addressing of a specific problem – for example, how can God be three in one? – or providing a detailed, integrated account of all aspects of the Christian faith. In the story that follows, be on the lookout then for the needs that led to particular emphases or ideas developing. In the brief space available to this section, such needs can only be mentioned in passing. The details will have to be filled in from works devoted specifically to the history either of theology or the broader history of the church.

3.2 THE FIRST TWO AND A HALF CENTURIES

The earliest theological writings of this period reflect two needs that will recur again and again in the church's history: (a) the need to defend Christianity's faith against attacks from the outside; (b) the need to think through a pastoral crisis.

3.2.1 The defense of the faith

The defense of the Christian faith against outside opponents is the province of the theological discipline known as "apologetics". The earliest such defenses were directed against two opponents: the Jews and pagan intellectuals. The former accused Christians of distorting the Jewish Scriptures (what came to be called the "Old Testament"). The latter accused them, amongst other things, of having ludicrous beliefs that were an affront to reason.

The earliest post-apostolic defense of the faith against Jewish attacks is to be found in the *Letter of Barnabas*, which may even have been written in the first century. It is itself an attack on Jewish practices, claiming that the Jews failed to take note of the deeper meaning of the Scriptures (by which they meant the Old Testament).

In this polemical work, we see the ingredient of Scripture holding the centre of the stage, in the sense that the theological reflection is a constant interaction with the biblical text. This will remain characteristic of theology up to the 13th century. However, we see something else here that is worth noting, and that is the idea of a "deeper meaning" to the Scriptures.

This idea of a "deeper meaning" to the Scriptures was something common to Christianity and Judaism. Later Old Testament works used it in interpreting earlier ones and the New Testament writers made use of it in interpreting Old Testament texts. On the surface, the idea of a "deeper meaning" is a very dubious one, since it opens the way for making

Scripture mean almost anything you want it to mean. On the other hand, it is one way of expressing a conviction that all Scripture is an expression of a living faith, a faith that has its origin in God's revelatory action, and that it is that faith that guides the theologian when interpreting the Scriptures.

The idea of a "deeper meaning" to the text will play an important role in theology, especially for the first thousand years of the church's existence. As we will see, Origen will give it a theoretical structure in the third century.

As regards attacks from pagan intellectuals, these were responded to by a group of well-educated converts to Christianity who have come to be known as the "Apologists". The most famous of them is Justin Martyr. With them, we see another ingredient that will play a major role in theology's development moving into clear focus: reason, in the form of philosophical ideas.

The Apologists took up the Stoic idea of a "logos" or rational principle inherent in everything to argue that all rationality everywhere comes from Christ, whom John's gospel describes as the Word or "Logos", and that therefore Christian beliefs represent the highest and greatest truth known to humanity.

Such use of philosophy and philosophical arguments did not go unchallenged. One famous challenge came from the pen of a third century western theologian, Tertullian, who questioned whether Jerusalem (representing the Christian faith) and Athens (representing Greek philosophy) had anything in common. However, the use of philosophy rapidly established itself as a legitimate tool in theology and it was explicitly defended as such by an eastern contemporary of Tertullian, Clement of Alexandria. He listed the objections against the use of philosophy and refuted them one by one.

Barely two generations after the end of the apostolic age, therefore, the use of philosophy in theology had already become an issue in the church. However, its use would become accepted as normal. This is not surprising, since as theological works became more sophisticated so too they needed to draw increasingly on the secular knowledge that the educated believer had to interact with.

3.2.2 Thinking through a pastoral crisis

Pastoral crises were with the church from the beginning. They form the occasion for several of the letters which make up the New Testament. They provide superb opportunities for probing and therefore deepening one's understanding of the faith.

One such crisis that hit the early church was whether or not Christians who sinned after baptism could be forgiven, since it was felt by many that they could not. The *Shepherd of Hermas* was written in the first half of the second century to argue that such forgiveness was indeed possible. It is written in the style of an apocalypse, viz., as a series of heavenly visions. The issue of forgiveness of sins after baptism would continue

SECTION A

THEOLOGY

to be an issue for quite some time to come – especially when dealing with those who denied their faith under the pressure of persecution and who wished to be readmitted to the church.

Crises such as these led to the development of ideas about baptism and the role of penance in the church. It even raised issues about where the Spirit was active: for example, were baptisms performed by sinners, heretics or apostates valid? Did the Spirit work through them? Some, such as the third century bishop of Carthage, Cyprian, denied that the Spirit did. Others, such as the bishop of Rome at the time, believed that such sacraments were valid and that by implication the Spirit was indeed active even through sinners and unbelievers, at least as regards the conferring of baptism. Rome's view prevailed. But the issue clarified the church's insight into the fact that it was not the goodness or faith of the minister that gave the sacraments any value, but the action of Christ through his Spirit.

3.2.3 The first theological schools

It is remarkable that within a very short time after the end of the apostolic age, schools of theology made their appearance. These were not academic institutions in the modern sense of the word, with a clear curriculum leading to a diploma or a degree. That would come much later. But they were institutions devoted explicitly to providing a deeper understanding of the Christian faith. Their existence was due to the influence of intellectuals who also brought to their Christianity a familiarity with pagan schools of philosophy.

By the end of the second century, we find them in Cappadocia, Edessa, Jerusalem, Caesarea, Alexandria, Antioch and Rome. However, only two of them were to play a major role in the intellectual formation of Christian ideas: the schools of Alexandria and Antioch. The one at Rome was founded by Justin Martyr and would have played some role in spreading the ideas of the Apologists, which was to have its own influence on western views on Christ and the Trinity. But the major schools of Christendom were the two eastern ones of Alexandria and Antioch.

Each school had its own emphasis.

Alexandria, founded about 150 AD, was renowned for the theological use it made of current Platonic philosophy (known as "middle Platonism") and for its allegorical approach to the Scriptures. The philosophy and biblical approach went together. Platonism saw the world around us as but shadows of the real spiritual world behind it and the search for a "deeper meaning" saw the literal meaning as but a shadow of the more spiritual one. Its most renowned scholars were Clement and Origen.

Antioch, founded about the year 200 AD, was critical of what it saw as Alexandria's excessive dependence on Platonic mysticism and therefore of its use of allegory in biblical interpretation. Antiochene theologians preferred to stay within the literal meaning of the text. Debates about the techniques for interpreting the Bible had already started!

Sad to say, the great names of the school that had its feet more firmly on the ground, Antioch, established a reputation for themselves as heretics rather than as orthodox theologians – Paul of Samosata, Theodore of Mopsuestia and the great Nestorius.

The schools were not destined to develop into permanent institutions, as the medieval universities did. But for a few centuries they played an important role in shaping Christian thought, especially about the nature of Christ.

3.2.4 The first theological giants: Tertullian and Origen

It was during this early period that we also see emerging the first truly great theologians. There were of course quite a few good theologians of the period. But two of them stand head and shoulders above the others because of their subsequent influence on theology. One was a western theologian – Tertullian. The other was an eastern thinker – Origen.

Tertullian (160–230 AD)

Tertullian was the first outstanding Christian thinker to write in Latin. He had a legally trained mind, one that enabled him to bring a precision to his writing that was missing from much earlier work. For example, it was he who provided the west with two distinct terms for thinking through the Trinity: person and substance. There were three persons, he noted, but only one substance. In its slightly changed form of "three persons, one essence", it was to become the classic formulation of the doctrine of the Trinity. These, and other terms coined by him, were to become part and parcel of western theological language.

He also expressed himself very strongly about the relationship between the Scriptures and the faith of the church. The two belong together, so much so that he refused to heretics the very ability to understand the Scriptures properly. It is only in the church, to whom the book belongs, that the faith can be found that will give us the true key to the Scriptures.

Ironically, Tertullian ended his days outside the church whose faith he said could alone give the key to the Scriptures. For he became a Montanist, a member of a charismatic-apocalyptic group that eventually found itself rejected by mainstream Christianity.

It was his Montanism that led him to take an especial interest in the doctrine of the Holy Spirit and so was the first to describe the Spirit as a distinct "person". He stressed the authority of the Spirit's guidance – which underpinned the claims of the Montanists – and so triggered off possibly the earliest debate in the church on the relationship between the institutional and charismatic elements in the church.

For him experience – of the Spirit and of the world around us – was of paramount importance in theology (see Danielou 1977:344). He had an aversion to the sort of high-flown speculation that he saw in much eastern-influenced theology. And it was in this context that he made his famous remark: "What do Jerusalem and Athens, the church and the academy have in common?" *(On Prescription 7.)*

Theology: the first 19 centuries

SECTION A

THEOLOGY

Finally, we also see in him an attempt to systematise the data of faith, to put things together in a way that shows their relationship with each other (see Danielou 1977:344). This is the first sign of the maturing of a truly systematic theology. It is something that will be even more characteristic of Origen.

Origen (died 254 AD)

Origen's contribution to theology can be summed up in three points (see Congar 1968:42ff.).

First of all, he can be called the founder of a scientific approach to biblical exegesis. He rejected the Gnostic idea that there was a secret source of Christian knowledge that existed outside the Scriptures (something his mentor, Clement of Alexandria, accepted in principle). Instead he stressed the sufficiency of Scripture and devoted his energies to commenting on and clarifying the techniques for interpreting it. Accepting the idea of a "deeper meaning" to Scripture, he distinguished between the literal, the allegorical and the spiritual levels of meaning. As we saw above, this meshed in well with the Platonic cultural framework within which he worked.

Secondly, he developed a theory to explain the difference between faith and the knowledge built on it. We have here the beginnings of theological epistemology – of an investigation into how the knowledge of faith differs from other forms of knowledge, including those built on faith.

Thirdly, he composed the first great work of Systematic Theology called *Principles*. Its four volumes cover, in turn, God and heavenly creatures, the material world and human beings, free will and its consequences and, finally, Scripture.

3.3 THE FIRST MAJOR DISPUTES AND DOGMATIC DEVELOPMENTS (300–500)

As the church moved into the 4th century, doctrinal crises became more severe. One reason, no doubt, was that as persecution waned and Christianity became the official religion, so too in-fighting increased dramatically. The doctrinal in-fighting revolved around the natures of Christ and the Spirit and therefore also around the Trinity.

Theological literature of this period is composed mainly of polemical works. That is to say, they are works directed against theological positions that the writer disagrees with. The themes dealt with therefore reflect the theological battlegrounds of the time: Christology, Pneumatology and the doctrine of the Trinity.

The period is instructive for a student of the history of theology because it demonstrates the unavoidable role of philosophy in shaping not only a culture, but theologies developed within that culture. In trying to think through how Christ could be both divine and human, how there could be but one God and yet distinguish between the Father, the Son and the Spirit – in trying to think through these issues, the problems that arose, as well as the tools used for their solution, were philosophical ones. For example, if you believe, as Platonist philosophy did, that God is totally unchangeable, how can you say that God became a human being, suffered and died? If you saw it as illogical, as Platonism did, that the infinite and all perfect divinity should have any division or multiplication within it, how can you talk of three persons sharing a single substance?

Philosophical ideas, embedded in the intellectual culture of the day, contributed to the sharpness of the intellectual problems believers found themselves faced with. The theologians who made the greatest contribution to the solution of such problems were those who took up the challenge by using philosophy's own ideas and arguments to show how Christian beliefs could withstand the most rigorous philosophical assault.

The result was the development of a series of terms that have entered into the mainstream of Christian theology: for example, "substance", "person", "nature", "relationship" and "procession", to name but a few. Indeed, the use of such terms became so important in trying to clarify orthodox and heterodox views on Christ's divinity that the Council of Nicea (325) broke with tradition by inserting a non-biblical, philosophical word into the church's solemn creed. The word was the Greek word for "of one substance" and to this day Christians reciting the Nicean creed profess Christ to be "of one substance" with the Father.

The disputes also bequeathed to posterity a way of thinking about God, Christ and the Spirit that has become part and parcel of Christian theology ever since. The idea of God as being "three persons in one substance" was eventually accepted into Greek thought in the form of "three *hypostaseis* in one *ousia*". At the Council of Chalcedon (451), Christ was said to be a single person possessing two natures, divine and human, which must not be confused with each other. Christians have thought of Christ like that ever since. The Spirit is seen as not only fully God, but also a distinct person and the relationships between Father, Son and Spirit have been clarified (though east and west would develop a bitter dispute about the relationship between the Spirit and the Son).

3.4 DEVELOPMENTS FROM THE 4TH CENTURY TO THE END OF THE PATRISTIC PERIOD (8TH CENTURY)

To begin with the west, by the time Augustine of Hippo (354–430) appeared on the scene, the west was already becoming increasingly isolated from the east and developing its own, distinctive theological approach. Moreover, Augustine was able to work in an environment that was spared the major Christological disputes that tore the east apart. Arianism had been settled – Christ had been officially proclaimed to be "of one substance with the Father". Disputes about whether or not Jesus of Nazareth and the Word of God were one and the same person (Nestorianism) and whether his humanity was a true humanity distinct from the divinity (Monophysitism) were still to come. The issues that August-

SECTION A
THEOLOGY

ine was faced with were issues that related very closely to his own personal experience of helplessness in the face of the attractions of sin: issues concerning grace, predestination and the relationship of both to free will. The East would develop the reputation of putting divinised humanity at the centre of its thinking. The west, thanks to Augustine, developed the characteristic of putting sinful humanity at the centre of its thinking. The two approaches were not incompatible, but did represent quite different emphases.

Augustine's influence on western theology is so great that whatever can be said here will be woefully inadequate. However, we can summarise it under the following headings.

First of all, he created what were to become the west's classic theologies of the Trinity, grace, predestination, the sacraments and original sin. He was to have a massive influence on the west's views on sexuality and marriage. And in his book, *The City of God*, he created a theology of history that was also a theology of the relationship between church and state.

Secondly, he gave the full weight of his authority to relating faith and reason to each other in a positive way. He saw them as interacting – reason giving one an initial understanding of what the faith teaches, faith opening one's eyes to the fullness of truth present there. He expressed this in a couplet that became famous and from which Anselm of Canterbury would later derive his equally famous description of theology: "Understand in order to believe; believe in order to understand" (Sermons 43,7). He also stressed, in his *On Christian Doctrine* (bk 2), the usefulness of all the human sciences and arts in order to understand the Scriptures better (see Congar 1968:49).

Thirdly, he stressed the role of love in enabling us to understand the faith (see Gaybba 1985), thereby providing a valuable corrective to those who would see logical and conceptual analyses as being sufficient. This illuminating role of love was to become central to a type of theology that reached its zenith in the 12th century and was to become known as "monastic theology".

Fourthly, he cast Christian ideas within a neo-Platonic mould that was to remain their framework for centuries, until Aquinas re-cast them within an Aristotelian one. However, unlike Aquinas, Augustine did not deliberately set out to utilise neo-Platonic ideas. Those ideas were rather the philosophical and cultural air that he breathed.

Augustine lived to see an event that was the greatest imaginable crisis for the west: the fall of Rome in 410 to the invading barbarian armies. As a result, the west witnessed the breakdown not only of traditional political and social structures but also of educational ones. Schools for the education of lay citizens of the empire ceased to exist. The only education available was that which the church provided for its clergy, since the latter had to be able to read the Scriptures and the liturgical texts. The effect of this on the educational level of Christians can be seen from the fact that Boethius, who died round about 524, was the last well-educated layperson in the church for centuries. He wrote extensively on philosophical themes, but also produced a short treatise on the Trinity that was influential in medieval times.

The breakdown of educational structures in the west, not surprisingly, resulted in the fact that there were no truly creative theological works there for the next four centuries. The few works that did make their mark had as their aim the conserving of the insights of the past rather than developing new insights for the future. Thus Prosper of Aquitaine, a pupil of Augustines, put together a collection of texts culled from his master's works. And Isidore of Seville (560–636) put together a collection culled from a wider range of authors. These collections were known as *Books of Sentences* and such collections became widespread after the 9th century. They represent the moving to centre stage of tradition in western theology. Theology came to be seen as the faithful exposition not simply of the Scriptures, but of the understanding of the Scriptures to be found in the writings of the Fathers.

Turning briefly to the east, two names stand out above all others in terms of the history of theology as a discipline.

The first is Pseudo-Denys or Denys the Areopagite, as the author used to be called. His name derives from the belief that he was the person referred to in Acts 17:34 and it was that belief that gave his writings enormous authority in medieval times. However, what interests us about him is the stress he laid on mystical experience and on theology's radical inability to describe God accurately. As such he is regarded as the father of what is called "apophatic" (i.e., "negative") theology. His idea that we cannot really say what God is like, but only what God is not like, entered into the mainstream of Christian thinking. This had implications for the way in which theological language has to be understood, and in medieval times the principle enunciated by Pseudo-Denys led to widespread and detailed discussions on the way in which theological language is able to represent the realities it talks about. In short, the principle enunciated in Apophatic Theology raises the issue about the meaningfulness of theological language in all its sharpness.

The second person who needs to be mentioned is the one who closes the patristic period in the east: John Damascene (675–749).

We have already seen how, in the west, this period saw a shift to preserving the past, a veneration of the tradition of wisdom built up by the Fathers. The breakdown of learning contributed to this. However, Platonic Philosophy provided a framework that supported it too. For such philosophy saw change as a sign of imperfection and therefore as undesirable. The truth, once attained and clarified, should simply be passed on. To try to change it would be to distort it.

Where could one find this unchanging truth? It was felt, in both west and east, that the place to look for it was in the writings of the Scriptures and of the revered thinkers of the past who expounded those Scriptures – the Fathers. We see this in Maximus the Confessor (580–662). But its best expression in a major work is to be found in John Damascene's *Fount*

Theology:
the first
19 centuries

SECTION A
THEOLOGY

of Wisdom. The work has three parts: philosophical; an account of heresies; an exposition of the true faith. This last section is no more than a systematic account of all that the Fathers taught, and in it John deliberately avoids trying to give his own ideas. It was to have an immense influence in both east and west (see Pelikan 1974:136).

By the end of the patristic period, therefore, the biblical ingredient is still at the centre of the stage. Theology is still seen as a matter of interpreting the Scriptures. However, that interpretation is itself seen as largely done by the Fathers of the past. So tradition also moves onto the centre of the stage as an ingredient of theology. Henceforth, the theologian would interpret not simply the Scriptures, but the interpretations of the Scriptures done by the Fathers. These latter interpretations were given such veneration that in practice they were accepted without question.

3.5 STIRRINGS OF REVIVAL AND REOPENING THE DEBATE ABOUT REASON: 9TH TO 11TH CENTURIES

Towards the end of the 8th century, the newly established emperor of the west, Charlemagne, decided to establish schools of learning in every diocese (a diocese was the geographical area ruled over by a bishop). As a result, despite set-backs, the systematic pursuit of learning, including theological study, began to revive.

The idea that the theologian's primary job was to conserve the past remained. Creativity and novelty were frowned upon.

Moreover, philosophy did not play much of a role except insofar as it provided theologians with analytical tools, such as dialectics (the art of clear and logical thinking), thus enabling one to prove or disprove something. And even this tool was not all that widely used, the best example of its use being found in John Scotus Erigena's work in the 9th century.

Theology was still seen as being no more than the interpretation of the biblical texts. In interpreting the text, the writings of the Fathers provided an essential guideline and many relied on the collections of patristic sayings (the *Sentences* referred to above) for their knowledge about the Fathers' ideas.

Since theology was still mostly a matter of explaining the meaning of the Scriptures, grammar (the science of how to communicate meaning in language) was the only area of secular knowledge that was widely used by theologians. However, even this mild intrusion of reason into the realm of theology was frowned upon by some.

The intrusion of reason into theology was to become a major source of dispute in the 11th century (and an even greater one in the 12th). The dispute was, in fact, over whether or not the science of dialectics had any role to play in theology. Could one impose the logical demands made by dialectics on the Word of God? The debate between dialecticians and anti-dialecticians was, in effect, a debate concerning whether or not human reason had any contribution to make to the understanding of the faith.

The dialecticians felt it had not merely a useful, but an essential contribution to make. Berengarius was the one who made this point most forcefully in the 11th century. He argued that since it is by virtue of our reason that we are made in God's image, we must use that same reason in order to become more like the image of God we are meant to be. He caused a storm of protest when his use of dialectics led him to reject the, by then, traditional belief that the eucharistic bread and wine literally became the body and blood of Christ. His conclusions only served to confirm the view of those who held that dialectics had no contribution to make to our understanding of the faith. Indeed, it was dangerous.

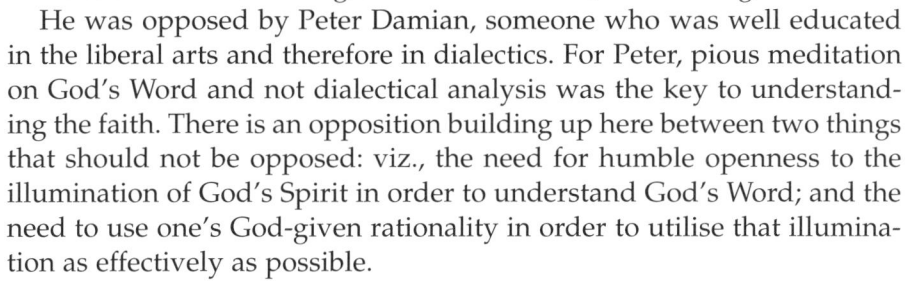

He was opposed by Peter Damian, someone who was well educated in the liberal arts and therefore in dialectics. For Peter, pious meditation on God's Word and not dialectical analysis was the key to understanding the faith. There is an opposition building up here between two things that should not be opposed: viz., the need for humble openness to the illumination of God's Spirit in order to understand God's Word; and the need to use one's God-given rationality in order to utilise that illumination as effectively as possible.

That the two need not be opposed was demonstrated in the work of the undisputed giant of 11th century theology: Anselm of Canterbury. His theological starting point was always his faith. But he then proceeded to attempt to understand it, using the resources of reason. His motto – taken from Augustine – was *fides quaerens intellectum* (faith seeking understanding). This has become one of the most frequently given definitions of theology. Anselm's aim was to lay bare, as far as is possible, the inner reasonableness, the inner rationality of the Christian faith. He displays this technique in his two most famous works. The first is his *Cur Deus Homo?* (Why did God become a human being?), in which he gave a reasoned argument for the necessity of the incarnation that has captured the imagination of Christian thought ever since. The second is his *Proslogion*, in which he gives his famous "ontological proof" of God's existence. Anselm has been accused of taking reason too far. However, he was aware of its limitations.

3.6 THE 12TH CENTURY

By the close of the 11th century, the revival of learning had resulted in the emergence of three types of schools. The first was the cathedral school, situated in the big cities and attracting masters and students interested not only in theology, but also in secular studies. The second type was the monastic school. This was attached to a monastery and the tuition was aimed mainly at teaching monks what they needed to know to be good monks, not to provide all-round tuition. The third type was the personal school. This lacked any institutional structure and was composed of nothing more than a famous teacher and whatever pupils gathered around him.

Of the three, the monastic school was the commonest. However, it was

SECTION A

THEOLOGY

in the cathedral schools that major developments were about to occur. This was not surprising, seeing that they offered a more broadly based education and attracted an increasing number of outstanding masters. It was from these schools that universities were to develop towards the end of the century.

The shift from a cathedral school to a university occurred when the teachers decided to form a single institution, one that would have its teaching organised into different faculties and that would grant degrees, testifying to the level of proficiency achieved. The first such university was formed at Bologna, in Italy. However, the most famous and influential of them all (in medieval times) was to be the second university to be formed – the one at Paris.

With the creation of universities, a structured programme of studies came into existence, one that all students had to go through and on which all students would be examined. As regards theology, it meant that it now became an academic subject, one in which an individual could achieve a clearly measured degree of proficiency. This in turn meant that a certain standardisation of theological learning rapidly occurred, which in turn raised the general level of theological learning in Europe. It also created a common pool of theological knowledge that could be regarded as given and on which others could build by focusing on specific points of debate or problematic areas.

Once it began to be taught as one subject amongst several, theology needed to define its identity in relation to them.

The first result of such an attempt at self-definition was to use the term "theology" to mean a field of study covering all that can be known about God through revelation. Up to the 11th century, the term usually referred to what we would to-day call the doctrine of God. The broader area of theological knowledge was usually referred to by other terms such as *doctrina christiana* (Christian doctrine), *sacra scriptura* (sacred Scripture; recall that theology was seen as being but the exposition of the Scriptures), *sacra eruditio* (sacred learning); *sacra pagina* (sacred page), *sacra doctrina* (sacred doctrine).

The second result was to try and clarify the basic rules of procedure of the new discipline and its specific terminology. All the other disciplines had in common the fact that they began with a consideration of their basic axioms or presuppositions and with an attempt at clarifying the definition of key terms. Hence we now come across theologians, such as Alan of Lille and Nicholas of Amiens, who attempted to clarify what theology's basic axioms are and the meaning of its key terms (see on all this Evans 1980).

The movement towards becoming an academic discipline raised, yet again, the issue of the relationship between philosophy and theology. More deeply, it raised serious questions about the very nature of the theological enterprise. This was particularly so as more and more of Aristotle's works were rediscovered by the west, thanks to the new trade routes that had been opened up. In particular, Aristotle's works on logic and his rules for debating and probing an issue were to have an immense effect on the development of theology and would sharpen the debate between what now became the progressives (who were all for the use of Aristotelian logic in theology) and the conservatives (who felt that its use was going too far and was breeding pride and presumptuousness rather than a true respect for the Word of God).

The leader of the progressive wing was Peter Abailard. He argued forcefully that Christ, the Logos incarnate, was the ultimate source of logic and therefore logic too can and should be used in his service. His influence was enormous and it is he who introduced into theology a method that would change the face of theology for centuries.

What he did was to make the heart of future Systematic Theology a question or issue, rather than a particular text to be explained (see Congar 1968:73). He did this by writing a book called *Sic et Non*, which means "yes and no". The book gathered together in one place 158 contradictory viewpoints of the Fathers and urged his students to resolve the contradictions by taking each one as a specific issue that needed to be debated and argued out.

The background to the book was the fact that the collections of *Sentences* that we referred to earlier had shown that the holy Fathers contradicted themselves now and then. This was something of a scandal for people who believed that the views of the Fathers were beyond questioning. Earlier attempts had been made at reconciling their views. What Peter Abailard did, was to use those contradictions as a way of forcing students to think and debate and argue a point for themselves.

As noted, he thereby introduced – alongside traditional biblical commentary – a new way of doing theology: viz., by regarding each topic as an issue that needed to be debated and argued out.

His method was taken up by Peter Lombard and used in a work that was to make him one of the most famous names in the history of theology: *The four books of Sentences*.

This was a massive survey of the entire field of Systematic Theology. In the 13th century, Alexander of Hales introduced it as a text book alongside the Bible at his lectures in Paris. It was destined to become the longest used text-book in the history of theology.

But let us return to the central point: the introduction of the *quaestio* or question as the typical way of dealing with a theological topic.

This method had its origins, as we saw, in the contradictions that are to be found in the writings of the Fathers. However, it drew its philosophical inspiration and its structure from Aristotle's logical works. For the method demanded following a clear pattern and logical argumentation that followed clear rules. The broad pattern was as follows: a thesis would be stated, briefly explained, and a brief argument given in its defense (the "yes" bit). Then arguments for rejecting the thesis would be presented (the "no" bit). The problematic character of the issue was now made clear and the master or student would have to decide which of the two options it was to be – yes or no. This would be made clear in the course of the solution that would now be offered, which would in turn be followed by a refutation of the arguments advanced for opposing

Theology: the first 19 centuries

viewpoints. Anyone who would like to see this pattern being used can open any page of Thomas Aquinas' famous *Summa Theologiae* and see how he structures his discussion of each issue.

The method itself held enormous benefits for the rapid development of theological expertise. First of all, it demanded a highly trained mind. Every student had to learn to debate and hence philosophy became part and parcel of every theological student's programme of studies. Secondly, it focused attention on issues which could be arranged in a systematic and logical way. This meant that from now on treatises that would deal with the Christian faith would systematically multiply. Thirdly, this in turn meant that we begin to see the development of Systematic Theology and biblical studies as two distinct types of theology. For alongside the continuing practice of commenting on the Scriptures, there is now the practice of studying Christian beliefs in a logically ordered, systematic way.

The leader of the opposition was Bernard of Clairvaux, a monk. He and other "monastic theologians" (for example, William of St Thierry and Rupert of Deutz) believed that the Abailards of this world had turned theology into an intellectual exercise, one that fed rather than corrected their pride through their incessant arguing and debating about points. Theology should rather proceed in a meditative manner. The brightest illumination of God's Word can only come from God and so the would-be theologian must open him or herself up to God's grace through humble and prayerful reading and reflection on the Scriptures and the writings of the holy Fathers. Above all, the theologian must be a person who loves, since it is love – of God and neighbour – that makes us more like the God who is love and which therefore opens our eyes and enables us to understand that God's revelation. Love, rather than logic, should be the theologian's greatest tool (see Gaybba 1985).

However, the impetus of the movement created by theology becoming an academic discipline was unstoppable. While all the great "scholastic" theologians (as they will be called) believed that to be a good theologian you had to live a good life and be in humble dependence on God's illuminating grace, the way they actually did theology – viz., through the cut and thrust of academic debate – pushed such ideas into the realm of piety rather than to the centre of theories about the skills needed to do theology. Such ideas instead found a home in mysticism and the writings of mystical theologians, where they became quite divorced from mainstream theology.

3.7 FROM THE 13TH TO THE END OF THE 15TH CENTURIES

The developments described in the previous section gave rise to a type of theology known as "Scholastic" Theology, that is to say, the theology to be found in the "schools". It was to be a form of theology that would endure for centuries. It reached a peak towards the end of the 13th century, was still very much alive for most of the 14th, but then began to decline. However, it experienced a revival within Catholicism in the 16th and again in the 19th and 20th centuries. It was to be so influential that it would develop even a Protestant form in the late 16th and 17th centuries.

In the 13th century, it found its most famous exponent in Thomas Aquinas (1224–1274). By the time Aquinas appeared, all of Aristotle's philosophical works had been discovered and not only his works on logic. The entire corpus of Aristotelian writings posed a major challenge to Christian thought, since it not only provided a well-reasoned survey of the entire field of human knowledge, but did so in a way that stressed the human mind's inherent ability to discover truth in the world around it. The rationalist threat that this posed to Christianity cannot be imagined any longer. But it was an immense threat and it was Aquinas who took up the challenge by mastering Aristotle's thought and forcing it to serve Christianity. He recast the entire Christian faith in Aristotelian categories of thought, thus ending the centuries-old domination of Platonic categories. So successful was he, that Scholastic Theology and Aristotelian Philosophy came to be seen as inextricably intertwined, to the point where Luther had to protest against the idea that one could not be a good theologian without using Aristotelian Philosophy!

Aquinas not only became scholasticism's most famous exponent, but he created a particular form of scholasticism known as "Thomism". A somewhat different form of scholasticism was created in the early 14th century by John Duns Scotus, whose system came to be known as "Scotism". A third form was developed some years later by one of Scotus' followers, William Ockham, who gave rise to a system known as "Ockhamism", also known as "nominalism". The differences between each of these is too technical for us to go into. The most basic differences concern ideas about the way the mind knows things, especially things about God.

Towards the end of the 14th and for the whole of the 15th century, Scholastic Theology lost its earlier creativity and degenerated into a mindless repetition of previous viewpoints. One may be tempted to think that this was simply theological conservativism raising its head once again, as it did towards the end of the patristic period. However, this time the conservativism was different because it was due to the development of group loyalties. Scholasticism became split into three groups: the followers of Aquinas, the followers of Scotus and the followers of Ockham. The ideas of their great masters were simply repeated, usually verbatim. Moreover, there does not appear to have been much of an attempt to enter into dialogue with the other viewpoints, but simply to condemn them. Early in the 15th century this led to complaints about the degenerate character of theology. But the complaints were not listened to. Matters were not helped by the fact that creativity had become a dangerous activity at this time. This was because the church and the university increasingly attempted to control or censure any ideas that appeared to them to be dangerous. It is significant that the only work of the 15th century which dealt with theology as a discipline that showed any real creativity was written by someone who was condemned as a heretic: John Hus.

SECTION A

THEOLOGY

Worse still was the fact that whatever debates did develop were so abstract and so concerned with technicalities that theology became a lifeless discipline. It had become cut adrift from a living contact with the Scriptures and the biblically based writings of the Fathers and had got lost in its own intellectual analyses.

We saw how, in the patristic period, the ingredient of tradition had moved to a central position alongside the biblical one, leading eventually to a situation where theologians saw their task as simply conserving the wisdom of the past's understanding of the Bible. The period we have just looked at shows how the ingredient of reason can not only revitalise theology (as it did in the 13th century) but, when cut adrift from the other ingredients, contribute rapidly to its degeneration.

3.8 THE 16TH CENTURY

The 16th century saw a massive rejection by the Reformers of the style of theologising that had characterised the west up to that period. It was now referred to not simply as "theology" but as "Scholastic Theology".

All the reformers agreed on rejecting the scholastic way of doing theology, where abstract speculations and Aristotelian Philosophy had a dominant role. Luther himself castigated Scholastic Theology in his *Disputatio contra scholasticam theologiam*. The reformed theologian, Danaeus, mounted a major onslaught on the work that, he argued, had given rise to Scholastic Theology and was the foundation on which it rested – Peter Lombard's *Sentences*. Nevertheless, as will be noted below, Protestantism was soon to develop its own form of Scholastic Theology.

All reformers also agreed on placing Scripture once more at the very centre of theologising. The subjection by the reformers of the authority of tradition to that of Scripture meant that Scripture became the main authoritative source. Debates would occur within Protestantism as to the precise way in which the authority of Scripture was to be understood and how that authority operated entirely on its own (for details see Evans, McGrath & Galloway 1986:145ff.). But that Scripture was the main authority in theology was unquestioned. This stress on Scripture also led to a revival of interest in the biblical languages as well as in the interpretative tools being developed by the Humanist movement.

The usefulness of tradition was in no way ruled out by reformers such as Luther, who made a strong move back to the Fathers, to the patristic period that preceded the scholastic one. Interestingly enough, the Fathers were valued on the grounds that they were reliable guides to the true meaning of the Scriptures – which was the way in which their contribution was viewed in former times. Hence, the authority of the Fathers was not seen as one that existed alongside the Scriptures, but as one that derived from the Scriptures. The old unity between the church and its Scriptures that had been unquestioned up to the 13th century, now became a unity between the Fathers and the Scriptures.

Reason was regarded with suspicion – at least initially. None of the reformers had any time for the rampant abstract speculations that had become typical of the decadent scholasticism of the 15th century. However, Luther's own reaction to any use of reason in theology was one of outright rejection. It is God's revelation that illumines our sin laden minds, not our minds that illumine God's revelation. One finds echoes here of the old monastic tradition. This is not surprising, since Luther was an Augustinian monk. However, just how difficult it is to exclude reason can be seen from the fact that Luther's own disciple, Philip Melancthon, had a much more positive attitude to it. So too did John Calvin. Of course, a culture conducive to affirming a limited, though valuable, role for reason (and one that rejected the scholasticism of the past) was created by the Humanist movement. But even apart from Humanism, any attempt to exclude a role for reason on a massive scale would have met with great difficulty.

As regards developments within the Catholic camp, it is not surprising that a fair amount of attention was given to refuting the attacks by the Protestants on Scholasticism. That, combined with the Humanist stress on the importance of sources (see Congar 1968:163), occasioned the writing of one of the most influential Catholic works of the period: Melchior Cano's *De locis theologicis*. It was a work devoted to a detailed examination of theology's sources, defending the use of reason and tradition. The century was also to see the Thomist form of scholasticism becoming the dominant one and the Ockhamist one virtually disappearing from it. The only creative works of the period were works derived from within the Thomist stream. The centre of Catholic theological work had also shifted – from Paris to Salamanca in Spain, where Thomism was the major force.

3.9 SEVENTEENTH TO NINETEENTH CENTURIES

Protestantism never became a homogeneous, united reform movement. Instead, it was to experience its own divisions. These took on a permanent shape in the formation of different Protestant churches which owed allegiance to different doctrinal confessions of faith, though most of the churches fell into one of two broad groups: Lutheran (or, as it was called in Germany: *evangelisch*, which simply means "Protestant," and not Evangelical as in the Anglo-Saxon world) and Calvinist (or, as it is more widely known, "reformed". In Germany, the few Reformed churches were included under "evangelisch").

With the formation of confessions of faith, the importance of doctrinal orthodoxy came to be stressed, leading to the movement known as "Protestant Orthodoxy" (see Evans, McGrath & Galloway 1986:151ff.). At the same time, a period of consolidating the insights of the reformation set in. This expressed itself in detailed theological treatises in which the stress was placed on the defense, systematisation and elucidation of doctrines. In the organisation and analysis of the material, Aristotelian logic as well as quite a few Aristotelian philosophical concepts were used. Hence, Protestant Orthodoxy became Protestant scholasticism. The positive attitude to reason displayed by reformers such as Melancthon and

SECTION A

THEOLOGY

Calvin was able to provide a platform undergirding this extraordinary development barely fifty years after the reformation. It is curious to see a Protestant author such as Musaeus, who wrote in the 17th century, quite happily regarding himself as one of a long line of scholastic theologians stretching back to Aquinas.

We saw how the old scholasticism came to be condemned for its aridity. Something similar occurred with regard to its Protestant version. For this evoked a strong reaction in the 17th century and led to the ingredient of experience coming to the fore once more.

As we saw above, experiencing God was at the heart of the monastic form of theology which achieved its zenith in the 12th century. The triumph of scholasticism meant that spiritual experience came to be sidelined as a source of theologising. Its importance was, of course, recognized when dealing with the topic of spiritual growth. But that was seen as something different from theologising.

Experience was important for reformers such as Luther. However, its role as a source in theologising only came to the fore in the rejection by 17th century Pietists of the aridity of Protestant scholasticism.

For the Pietists, it was essential to the work of the theologian that he or she be able to experience the realities of salvation to which the Scriptures witnessed. Indeed, the implication was that unless a person had such an experience he or she could not really practice theology at all (see Evans, McGrath & Galloway 1986:172). It is only such experience that will fill theology's concepts with real content.

The Pietist stress on experience bore fruit in a variety of ways, two of which can be mentioned here. One stream of influence flows through John Wesley to the Holiness Movement in the United States, from which sprang contemporary Pentecostalism. A second stream of influence flows through the 19th century theologian, Schleiermacher and on to all those forms of contemporary theologising that appeal to a core religious experience, accessible to all human beings, as a source illuminating or validating the Christian message.

We will return to Schleiermacher in a moment. But before doing so we need to take a brief look at two other developments in 18th century theology. Both concern the role of reason.

The first was the interest that developed in theological method, due especially to Wolf's philosophy. The mathematical method was especially admired and many attempts were made to absorb this into theology. This was not something completely new, since some attempts at doing that had been made in the 12th century (e.g., Alan of Lille's *Regula de sacra theologia* and Nicholas of Amien's *De arte catholicae fidei*; see Evans 1980:113ff.). But such attempts became quite fashionable now. Closely connected to this was the desire to organise the whole of theological knowledge into a single system. This, too, is not completely new of course. We see a drive for systematisation as early as Tertullian and Origen (see 3.2.4). And we see an even more notable version of it in Aquinas' *Summa Theologiae*. But at this stage, theology had developed into several separate disciplines and the "Encyclopedists", as they were called, attempted to reunite the various branches of theology by integrating them and their contents into an overarching system, with each part being allocated its proper place.

The second point concerning the role of reason was the challenge reason began to pose to theology's very foundations.

The 18th century gave rise to what is known as the "Enlightenment". This was an intellectual movement that had little time for the supernatural. In some places (e.g., in France) the Enlightenment was positively anti-religious. In other places (e.g., in Germany) it supported religion, but only that form of religion that could be founded on purely rational arguments. All claims to a supernatural revelation were rejected. Here we see reason becoming the chief ingredient in theology. Indeed, it has booted out the traditional faith basis, expressed in Scripture and tradition. The event that symbolised this supremacy of reason most dramatically was the setting up, in 1793, of an altar dedicated to the "goddess of reason" in Paris' most famous church – Notre Dame.

The mentality that rejected all ideas of the supernatural was also one that was willing to be very critical of the historical claims made by Christianity. The Humanist movement had bequeathed to the Enlightenment a concern for historical accuracy. In the 18th century, this resulted in the emergence of historical-critical studies of the Bible and of the way in which Christian beliefs had developed down the ages. As regards the Bible, an attempt was made to discover the "real" Jesus behind what were now believed to be the distortions arising out of later developments in the faith of his disciples, distortions that mar the picture of Christ presented in the Gospels. This "real" Jesus was now pictured as a person of immense moral stature whose main message was about how to live a good moral life. The idea that he was a divine being who became human in order to save the world through his death was rejected as a distortion of the original facts.

The Enlightenment therefore bequeathed to Christian Theology the idea of studying its own history critically. This has been immensely beneficial, despite the rationalist presuppositions that gave birth to it.

Towards the end of the 18th century, a general reaction set in against the rationalist, analytical approach of the Enlightenment. The reaction was typified by a stress on the living unity that was believed to exist between all things and on the importance of experience and feeling in developing one's knowledge and understanding of reality. The movement embodying this reaction is known as the "Romantic" movement.

For the Romantics, life was much larger than logic. All things were interconnected, especially all living things. A favourite idea, and one we see embodied in Hegel's philosophy, is that the whole universe is shot through with a life-giving, energising Spirit. As regards religion, the world's religions were expressions of the different ways in which this spiritual heart of the universe was experienced. The period was also one in which the Christian west had become very much aware of the varieties of religious traditions that existed in the world and had begun to study them in depth, giving rise to the discipline known as "Comparative Re-

SECTION A
THEOLOGY

ligion". The fashionable theory developed that at the heart of all religions there was a common spiritual experience.

It was against such a background that the 19th century Protestant theologian, Friedrich Schleiermacher, utilised his Pietist tradition to develop his own response to the challenge posed to Christianity by the Enlightenment. From his Pietism, he got the conviction that Christian beliefs can only be understood in relation to the religious experiences that underlie them. Christianity – and indeed all religion – is primarily not a matter of doctrinal beliefs or even of moral directives, but rather of experiencing God. From the Romantic movement and the developing interest in world religions, he got the conviction that there was a core religious experience that all people have and which is at the heart of all religions, including Christianity.

This core religious experience he described as a "feeling of absolute dependence". By this he meant an experience of being dependent on a reality that completely transcends oneself, an infinite reality. His defense of Christianity was that the Christian faith, and it alone, made complete sense of this core experience.

The details of his argument need not concern us here. What is important, however, is his theological method: he starts with an experience common to all human beings and shows how Christianity makes sense of it. This way of showing the reasonableness and convincing character of Christianity and of explaining the relevance of its key doctrines has been adopted by many theologians since then, both Protestant (e.g. Paul Tillich) and Catholic (e.g. Karl Rahner). An Anglican example can be found in John Macquarrie.

As we saw, Schleiermacher's method also accepted the idea that Christianity is but a particular example of the universal phenomenon of religion. This was to lead, in the 20th century, to a burgeoning literature on the relationship between Christianity and other faiths, with a wide spectrum of opinions developing on the topic amongst Christian theologians. Indeed, the experience of other religions has become, for not a few theologians, a fifth ingredient in Christian Theology (cf. 3.1).

As can be imagined, the 19th century was a traumatic time for Christian Theology. This was especially the case for Protestant Theology, since it entered into a far greater dialogue and contact with the Enlightenment than Catholic Theology did. Not only did it have to cope with the rationalism of the Enlightenment, but it had to adjust to the critical-historical spirit of the age as well as to new ways of understanding the world, humanity's place in it and the nature of religion. Towards the end of the century there was, in addition, a tremendous optimism about humanity's ability to progress and build a new world – an optimism that fed on the sort of evolutionary ideas found in Darwin, but also on Hegel's ideas about the way the Divinity develops all its inner potentialities.

This optimism and the challenge to Christianity to come to terms with a world in which a critical spirit had become widespread, led to the movement known as "liberal Protestantism". Its full story belongs to the 20th century, but its roots are to be found in the 19th. Its chief characteristic was an attempt to reinterpret Christianity in such a way as to make it more acceptable and meaningful to the critical, scientific spirit of the late 19th century. At its heart was perhaps the programme we saw initiated by Schleiermacher – start with humanity and show how Christianity explains humanity's deepest concerns and experiences, discarding or reinterpreting whatever may not be able to perform that explanatory function. In the early 20th century, after the disillusionment of the First World War, Karl Barth mounted an enormous opposition to such a theological method by insisting that theology can be built on God's Word alone and that no human experience other than the hearing of that Word can be used to interpret or analyze it.

So far I have concentrated on the development of Protestant Theology. Let me close this section by taking a brief look at Catholicism.

There is little in Catholic developments of this time that were to be as influential as those that occurred within Protestantism. Scholasticism continued to be a feature of Catholic Theology, but towards the end of the 17th century it began to slide into a new decadence. Congar (1968: 185) attributes this to the fact that the scholastic form and structure were retained, but the unifying Christian philosophy that underpinned it had been abandoned. It was significant, then, that the revival of scholasticism in Catholic circles that began in the late 19th century did so through a papal decree (known as *Aeterni Patris*) that forcefully recommended the scholastic philosophy of Thomas Aquinas for institutions teaching Catholic Theology. This led to a flowering of Thomist scholasticism, known as neo-scholasticism, that dominated Catholic Theology for the first half of the 20th century.

The resurgence of scholasticism also had the negative effect of stifling, for a time anyway, the beneficial effects of the spirit of the Romantic movement on 19th century Catholic Theology. In Germany it had led to a form of theologising at Tübingen that stressed the living unity that bound the members of the church together, from which would develop the revitalising of the old biblical idea of the church as Christ's body. In England its influence can be seen on John Henry Newman's famous theory about how doctrines developed – he compared the development of doctrine to a very fertile idea that develops almost as a living organism does.

The rationalist challenge of the Enlightenment did cause some problems within Catholic Theology, but Catholicism's main response to it was the simple and outright condemnation of its major presuppositions. This condemnation occurred in the First Vatican Council, which met between 1869 and 1870. It was only towards the end of the 19th and the opening years of the 20th century that a major movement within Catholicism developed which attempted to come to terms with the historical-critical mentality that had been fostered by the Enlightenment and which was rampant throughout the main intellectual centres of Europe. The movement came to be known as "Modernism". At its heart was the conviction that doctrines are the product of historical developments and therefore cannot be absolutised, but need reinterpretation as the church moves

SECTION A
THEOLOGY

from one historical setting to another. The movement – which certainly threatened the sort of commitment to truth that was traditional in Christianity – was condemned in the early 20th century by Pope Pius X. The condemnation was given teeth by imposing strict sanctions on any Catholic theologians who embraced its ideas. The net result was to kill any real creativity within Catholic Theology for quite some time to come. But that story belongs to the 20th century.

The Catholic response to the Enlightenment's rationalism, to Modernism as well as to the imposition of scholastic philosophy, especially as expounded by Aquinas, demonstrates the powerful role of authority in Catholic Theology. Moreover, because authority saw itself as the guardian of tradition, the late 19th century saw tradition become *the* major ingredient in Catholic Theology. But, once again, it is not the broad tradition that moved to the fore, with all its complexities and riches, but rather a narrow one, one that was formed in the high Middle Ages and one that was reverted to simply because it appeared to offer the only safe haven against the onslaughts of the age. Already in the 19th century, Pope Pius IX made the extraordinary comment that *he* was tradition ("tradition – that is me!"). In the 20th century, tradition was for a long time narrowed down pretty much to papal decrees and conciliar decisions (see Mackey 1962:1–52, esp. 23).

From the above sketch – and it must be emphasised that it is barely more than a rapid sketch – one can see the importance of maintaining a balance between the "ingredients" that go into any pot of theology. The history of theology as a discipline is very much the history of the varying fortunes of those ingredients (3.1).

READING LIST AND BIBLIOGRAPHY

Congar, Y.-M. 1968. *A History of Theology*. New York: Doubleday.
Danielou, J. 1977. *A History of Early Christian Doctrine, vol 3: The Origins of Latin Christianity*. London: Darton, Longman & Todd.
Evans, G.R. 1980. *Old Arts and New Theology*. Oxford: Clarendon.
Evans, G.R., McGrath, A.E., Galloway, A.D. 1986. *The History of Christian Theology. Vol 1: The Science of Theology*. Basingstoke/Grand Rapids: Marshall Pickering/Eerdmans.
Gaybba, B. 1985. "Love and know what you will. The Epistemological role of love in Augustine." In Landman, C. and Whitelaw, D.P. (eds.), *Windows on Origins*. Pretoria: Unisa.
Mackey, J.P. 1962. *The Modern Theology of Tradition*. London: Darton, Longman and Todd.
Pelikan, J. 1974. *The Christian Tradition, vol 2: The Spirit of Eastern Christendom*. Chicago: University Press.

Theology: the 20th century

Daniël Veldsman

4.1 INTRODUCTION

In reading this overview of 20th century western theological thought, the serious student of theology need not feel confused when exposed to and confronted with a wide spectrum of trends. Theology is, after all, not a heavenly enterprise, but a form of the human scholarly quest (Hendrikus Berkhof). This quest, like any quest in any other discipline (albeit very different), is subject to the laws of trial and error, to methodological preferences, to historical contexts and to sociological predicaments (Thomas Kuhn). Theological thought, therefore, does not only display a wide variety of approaches, but also a wide spectrum of focal points. Like a moth towards a burning flame, Christian theological reflection has, throughout history, been driven towards the candle of truth. And this truth has as its inexhaustible "object" the life-giving and sustaining God in Jesus Christ through his Spirit.

The circling quest for theological truth finds expression in systematic-theological concepts such as Trinity, Christology, pneumatology and eschatology. Every Christian community gives an account of the gospel as its source and norm by forming concepts. Conceptualisation is the act of (re-)interpreting the significance of the gospel from a specific historical, geographical, linguistic and sociological situation or context. The danger of (re-)interpreting the gospel for one's own selfish protection and profit is a very real problem – to which the theologian is very vulnerable and of which he/she must be very aware.

SECTION A

THEOLOGY

The aim of this overview is to introduce the thought of leading 20th century western theologians. Since it is impossible to cover all lines of thought in the space of this chapter, two criteria were used for selection, namely:

- The theologian should have had written constructively on a broad range of theological issues, and
- his/her theological contribution should be widely studied at present in universities, seminaries or colleges.

The choice that follows will hopefully give the student some grasp of this vast field. It is important to have an historical overview of a wide spectrum of theological trends because it gives us a responsible and enriching insight into our own theological position (where we come from theologically) and also stimulates further reflection within one's own context (where we stand now).

Before we discuss the work of each theologian separately, let us note the main issues which they all address:

- The questions raised by the inherited agenda of doctrines; that is, the traditional topics of Systematic Theology: how are we to understand God and revelation, creation and providence, election, the human being, sin and evil, Jesus Christ, atonement, the Holy Spirit, Christian living, the church, ministry and sacraments, and eschatology;
- The problem of how to integrate a theology; that is, how to relate these various topics to each other;
- The recovery and criticism of the past; that is, the question of the relationship of faith and history, and the related question of hermeneutics (that is, the art and theory of interpretation as well as the act of interpretation itself);
- The special significance of the 19th century; that is, the period in which the issues of modernity were comprehensively tackled for the first time. The 19th century is the main dialogue partner for many 20th century theologians (although other important periods are also addressed such as the patristic period, Medieval Theology and the Reformation);
- The conditioning of theologies by their contexts and interests; that is, historical and sociological insights which urged theologians to take fuller account of the situation in which theology is done (context and theological framework) and for whom (society) and by whom (male/female, academic or grassroots level etc.) it is done.

In one way or another, these issues are addressed by 20th century theologians from their specific backgrounds and in relation to their own contexts. These contexts, however, are directly or indirectly influenced by certain conditions, events and forces. Some of these can be mentioned here: the two World Wars with their unprecedented scale of mass killings, the Holocaust and concentration camps, various revolutions all over the world and the emergence of new post-colonial societies, struggles against racism and sexism, the spread of mass communication, business corporations and technological advances and innovations and the ecological crisis. More specific to religion have been the rise of the Pentecostal movement, Christian and interreligious ecumenism, the formation of the World Council of Churches, the influence of the Second Vatican Council of the Roman Catholic Church, the spread of Islam and Christianity (especially in Africa), new religious movements outside the main world religions, the multiplication of "base communities", liturgical reforms and new translations of the Bible.

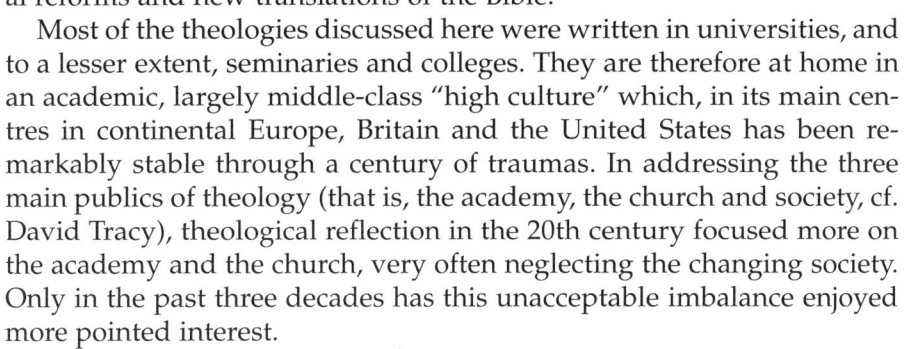

Theology: the 20th century

Most of the theologies discussed here were written in universities, and to a lesser extent, seminaries and colleges. They are therefore at home in an academic, largely middle-class "high culture" which, in its main centres in continental Europe, Britain and the United States has been remarkably stable through a century of traumas. In addressing the three main publics of theology (that is, the academy, the church and society, cf. David Tracy), theological reflection in the 20th century focused more on the academy and the church, very often neglecting the changing society. Only in the past three decades has this unacceptable imbalance enjoyed more pointed interest.

The brevity of an overview of this nature makes it impossible to stress all the subtle nuances or to explain all complexities of every theologian. At most, it can be an invitation to self-reflection and engagement within one's own theological context and, through this context, with the broader spectrum of theological trends.

The chosen trendsetters of 20th century western theological thought in Continental Europe (Germany and the Netherlands) and the United States of America come from the Protestant tradition. We start with the theological tradition in Germany, as it is the most sustained and intensive example of engagement in the enterprise of Modern Theology.

4.2 GERMANY

The Germany of the late 19th century had to come to terms with a rapidly changing world. Traditionally more at home in a world of images and ideas, the fast-growing influence of empiricism changed the face of the European world. Its effects were embodied in steam power and mechanics, rail roads and ocean-going vessels, in opposition between capital and labour and in imperialism and militarism. At the same time, Germany enjoyed a period of political superiority. Progress, human power and freedom were the fashionable values to ponder on and attain.

This was the world of the Lutheran scholar Albrecht Ritschl (1822–1889), a professor in dogmatics in Bonn and later in Göttingen, who historically laid the theological table for his student Johann Wilhelm Herrmann (1846–1922). Herrmann, the "firstborn" son of the Ritschlian school and professor for thirty-seven years in Marburg, was the inspiring teacher of Rudolf Karl Bultmann (1884–1976) and Karl Barth (1886–1968), two of the most influential scholars of the 20th century. Barth and Bultmann, and to a much lesser extent Dietrich Bonhoeffer (1906–1945) have become, together with great historic figures like Luther, Schleier-

SECTION A

THEOLOGY

macher and Kierkegaard, and the philosophers Kant, Hegel and Heidegger, the constant dialogue partners of almost all modern theologians in Germany. Apart from Ritschl, Herrmann, Barth, Bultmann and Bonhoeffer, the other influential contemporary theologians that will be discussed are Jüngel, Moltmann and Pannenberg. We start with the pivotal figure from the 19th century, Albrecht Ritschl.

4.2.1 Albrecht Ritschl: The gospel as moral power

The systematic theologian of Göttingen, Albrecht Ritschl, represents a most significant anticipation and inspiration for more than one type of German Systematic Theology in the 20th century, albeit that few scholars of name (including Barth!) will acknowledge their Ritschlian heritage.

Confident of the rule of the Spirit in the world and particularly in the historical process, Ritschl was convinced that this rule could only be established by a long journey through historical studies. This was the vantage point of his journey. On this journey he shifted from historical studies to dogmatic theology. In his philosophical orientation, he shifted from Hegel to Kant. For Ritschl, disinterested knowledge of God was unacceptable. All metaphysical speculation was unacceptable. Natural Theology and mysticism were unacceptable, as well as the form of piety which was no more than a flight from the world.

Being a Lutheran, Ritschl's aim was to fashion a comprehensive interpretation of the Christian religion based on the doctrine of justification and reconciliation as set forth by the New Testament (particularly Paul) and by the Protestant reformers (particularly Luther). According to Ritschl, the reformers had failed to order their religious insights in a theological system. This left the impression that Christianity was primarily a religion of personal redemption from sin, and not equally one of corporate ethical activity directed at the moral reconstruction of society. For Ritschl, the Protestant Reformation was, in this sense, unfinished. Ritschl therefore took it as his own vocational task to effect a true reformation of Protestant Theology by recovering the reformers' religious root ideas through critical historical scholarship and by integrating them, under the influence of the theology of Schleiermacher and the philosophy of Kant, in a theological system. Thereby the unfinished reformation could be brought to theological completion.

In his three volumes, *The Christian Doctrine of Justification and Reconciliation* (1870–1874), Ritschl set the German scene for a specific understanding of the relationship between God, humanity and world. For a Christian to say something of God was, for Ritschl, to say something of the value that faith in God has for him or her (that is, faith as a value judgement). The strong accent which Ritschl placed on the value of faith was to oppose a purely intellectual affirmation of doctrinal propositions. In the face of the experience of the saving encounter with the victorious life and suffering of the Christ of revelation, a person finds him/herself forced to make this value judgement. Faith – as trust in Christ's saving activity and in God's fatherly providence – could only indirectly express such a value judgement ("Christ is God") because Christ manifests himself only in his works and can only be read from his works (cf. the words of the 16th century reformer Melanchton: "For to know Christ is to know his benefits"). In Jesus, God revealed his own final goal, which must also become our own goal in life: practical proof of our sonship of God in spiritual freedom and dominion over the world (not only a technical dominion, but in the first place a moral lordship!) and labour for the kingdom of God. Animated by faith in progress and moral self confidence, the kingdom of God was seen by Ritschl as a moral entity in which morality and salvation merged. The moral goal of justification was reconciliation. The form in which spiritual lordship over the world was exercised was faith in God's providence, that is, faith in the fatherly providence of God was for Ritschl the Christian world-view in an abbreviated form. Providence thus stood in the service of human world rule.

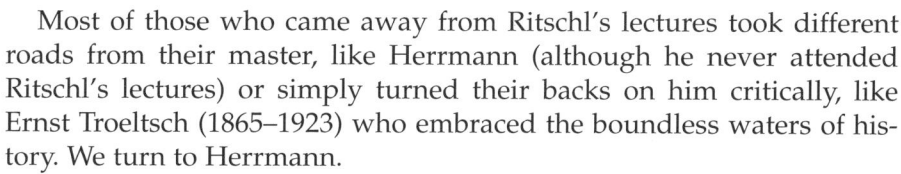

Most of those who came away from Ritschl's lectures took different roads from their master, like Herrmann (although he never attended Ritschl's lectures) or simply turned their backs on him critically, like Ernst Troeltsch (1865–1923) who embraced the boundless waters of history. We turn to Herrmann.

4.2.2 Wilhelm Herrmann: The inner life of Jesus

Although the systematic theologian Wilhelm Herrmann (1846–1922) of Marburg was almost 25 years younger than Ritschl, and much more lively and personal in his theological reflection, one of Ritschl's basic convictions attracted Herrmann to him: the calling of people to relate and conduct themselves as free personalities within a deterministic world (that is, a world determined by the laws of nature). However, in Herrmann's mind, Ritschl was still too objectivistic in his theological reflection. For Herrmann, the essence of faith was a liberating encounter with God as a Person-to-person encounter. The foundation of our life is the experience of meeting the person of God in the person of Jesus. Jesus makes us into personalities who are able, for our part, to evoke personhood in others, by handing down the tradition, education and personal encounter. Ethics was to be the guide and religion the power. In his understanding of ethics as guide and religion as power, Herrmann philosophically diverted from Ritschl, following Kant more closely, as well as Hermann Cohen (1842–1918) and Paul Natorp (1854–1924), two philosophers from Marburg.

At the centre of increasing attacks and criticism on religion at the dawn of the 20th century, Herrmann retreated in his *The Communion of the Christian with God* (1886) to the one place he thought that was safe: to individual introspection. No research could ever lead to or be the basis of the certainty of faith as there is no link between knowledge and faith. Although Herrmann did not deny that faith took on historical shape, it is based on something above history and beyond the reach of research, namely the "inner life of Jesus". Through the stories in the Bible, our personhood achieves contact with Jesus' as the one presently at work in us.

SECTION A
THEOLOGY

The inner life of Jesus was the foundation as well as the content of our encounter with faith.

In his *Ethics* (1901), in which Herrmann seek to build a bridge between the gospel and the modern world, he clearly stated his vantage point: Divine revelation was the answer to the misery of our moral condition. The unity of religion and morality was to be founded in the figure of Jesus. Jesus was, however, more than just an ethical ideal. In and through him, the faithful received the forgiving and redeeming grace of God which alone enables them to live a new life of moral rebirth. Only faith in Christ could bring about a saving personal encounter. It was not to be confused with faith in the authority of Scripture, dogma, or creed. Such a faith was not a redemptive faith! Faith and knowledge had to be sharply separated.

This very conviction in the separation between faith and knowledge, and the personal character of the encounter of faith, laid the foundation for two of his most influential students, namely Barth and Bultmann. Although they built their theologies on the foundation laid by Herrmann, each went his own way: Barth focused on God's sovereign and merciful revelation in his Word, namely Jesus Christ; Bultmann focused on humanity's existential response to the message *(kerygma)* of the community of faith about Jesus Christ. We turn to their respective theologies.

4.2.3 Bultmann: Faith as a new self-understanding

Although he was a New Testament scholar by profession, Rudolf Bultmann's (1884–1976) Theology is many-sided and displays many interests. Like Barth, Tillich, Brunner and others, he belonged to the circle of dialectical theologians during the second decade of the 20th century. He was an exegete of distinction. He was co-founder of the form criticism of the synoptic Gospels. He was a theological existentialist who flirted with Heidegger in terms of his terminology. In content however, his theological ear was sympathetic to a wide and diverse spectrum of scholars: from poets to philosophers, from historians to theologians (especially his teacher Herrmann). Bultmann's influence, which ranged from New Testament history, theology and the general problem of hermeneutics to gnosticism, caused more than just a stir in theological circles throughout the world. Bultmann was ultimately a Christian theologian who did all his historical work in service of the church and its witness. He engaged in historical research for the sake of theological understanding.

Our interest here is the systematic side of his multifaceted theological thought. Two features of his thought contribute largely to his significance. First, his quest for making the gospel understandable and credible in terms that men and women are able to understand today. He took the chasm of almost two thousand years between the world of the New Testament and the world in which he lived very seriously. The relationship of faith and history was the central focus in all his work. Second, this chasm (according to Bultmann) could only be bridged through the interpretation of the Christian faith in existentialistic terms – that is, its significance for "existing". The term "existentialistic" should not be confused with "existential", which refers to the structures of existence. The programme which Bultmann proposed for such an interpretation was demythologization, that is, the intelligible interpretation of biblical myths. In his opinion, faith itself demanded demythologization.

Bultmann felt that the liberal theologians (such as Troeltsch and Von Harnack) were only securing a knowledge of the human past. This was a knowledge attained by the application of critical historical methods. The question was: Did it contribute to knowledge of God? Of this Bultmann was suspicious. Karl Barth's *Epistle to the Romans* (especially the 1922 edition) offered Bultmann a workable solution for this problem, namely speaking of God in a modern world. In it, he found a way to bridge the gap between the world of the texts and the world of the interpreter. In his interpretation of Paul, Barth spoke of God's judgement and grace, thus speaking with Paul, but in a new cultural situation. For Bultmann, this was the answer to a new way of doing theology, namely as self-understanding within a specific historic context through the interpretation of texts. Put differently: an "hermeneutical" style of doing theology. Bultmann thus developed a Kerygmatic Theology. This Kerygmatic Theology could, in his opinion, do better justice to the subject matter of the New Testament than the historical exegesis of his liberal teachers could do. Theological exegesis inescapably included theological criticism. In practice, this meant that the biblical formulation had to be challenged in the light of one's understanding of what the writers were getting at. Whereas Barth attempted to speak of God *with* the biblical author, and therefore had to be utterly loyal to the text, Bultmann refused to identify the word of God with the words of Scripture. This explains the infamous introductory paragraph of his *Theology of the New Testament* (1948), in which he stated that "Jesus Christ is the presupposition of the message of the gospel and not a part thereof". Bultmann thus sought to express the theological content of the New Testament in a way relevant for modern times. His was the existentialist way, that is, he took humanity's being-in-the-world, self-understanding, freedom, choice, relationships and death very seriously.

Bultmann's theological existentialism entertained a number of presuppositions which can briefly be formulated as follows: Theology is "talking about God", yet God cannot be made the object of the "talking about God", that is to say, God is non-objectifiable. To speak of God is only possible if we speak of humanity before God, that is, if out of faith we speak about the relationship between humanity and God. In this sense, faith discloses a new self-understanding of humanity in the world as it exists before God. This new self-understanding paves the way for authentic existence, that is, a new life in Christ before God.

The new self-understanding finds its impetus in the biblical voices from the past. These voices mediate an encounter with reality by asking questions which concern humanity's significance and fate in the world in a way which is structurally similar to the effects of Christian proclama-

4

Theology: the 20th century

tion (challenging readers to give an answer to these questions). These voices thus challenge modern hearers and may transform their present understanding of themselves by presenting them with an understanding in which their inauthentic existence before God is laid clear.

Two important points with regard to the Christian proclamation should be stressed. First, the heart of the proclamation is the message that God, the wholly transcendent, has acted decisively for the salvation of humanity in the death and resurrection of Jesus Christ. The proclamation of God's act is called the kerygma. It is only properly heard (understood) as a call to the radical decision of faith, that is, a total surrender of the self to God. For a person to believe the kerygma is, at the same time, for God to act in that person's death to her/his old self and resurrection to the life of freedom in love. Theology for Bultmann is, therefore, the methodical exposition of the self-understanding that comes into being with faith, a self-understanding which at the same time includes an understanding of God and the world.

In the wake of his controversial influence, the questions posed by his theology were either taken seriously or were solemnly rejected as heretical.

4.2.4 Barth: God's sovereign "yes" for humankind in Jesus Christ, God's "no" for sin

The Swiss Reformed dogmatic theologian, Karl Barth (1886–1968), is unquestionably one of the most influential theologians of the 20th century. As a prophetic voice in turbulent times, Barth called the Christian church back to the Bible and to its foundation in Jesus Christ. He challenged the influential legacy of the Enlightenment (see 3.9 and 17.5). He challenged the liberal theologies of his teachers (especially the so-called Jesus of history of the liberal quest). In short, he challenged the West's established religion through the very message of the gospel itself. Whereas Bultmann's theological criticism focused much more strongly on the non-objectifiability of God and the chasm between his world and the world of the text, Barth's focus was on the sovereignty of God and a Trinitarian Theology as source (and not as an intellectual problem!) of our faith, determined by the qualitative difference between heaven and earth, God and humanity. In addressing the theological significance of this difference, Barth exposed the influence which many other great thinkers such as Kierkegaard, Schleiermacher and Herrmann had on his own theology.

As young pastor in an industrial community in Safenwil (Switzerland), he found that he could not read the Bible in the same way as he had learnt in the classroom of his liberal teachers. The issues of social justice, poor wages and trade union affairs which affected the people in his parish did not allow such a "comfortable" intellectual reading. Although he became a member of the Social Democratic Party, he refused to identify socialism with the kingdom of God.

Theologically speaking, Barth's second edition of his commentary, *The Epistle to the Romans* (1922), heralded the start of the 20th century. It became the banner for a generation of the German-speaking church's young pastors and teachers. Barth himself compared the effect of this edition to when, as a child, he accidentally yanked the bell-rope in a dark church – which brought the whole village running!

Having taught in Göttingen, Münster and Bonn, Barth became the theological leader of the "confessing" opposition to the National Socialism's attempt to rule the German Church. He was also the chief drafter of the opposition's *Barmen Declaration* (1934). Forbidden to teach in Germany, he returned to Basel and remained there for the rest of his life. During his years in Basel, he wrote extensively on his magisterial and massive *Church Dogmatics* (1932–68), which appeared in thirteen volumes.

Barth was to interpret Christian dogmatics as the function of the Christian church, scrutinizing the content of the Christian faith with the revelation of God in Jesus Christ as attested to in Holy Scripture. It, and it alone, was the criterion of truth. The church had to listen to the divine word of judgement on their political and intellectual towers of Babel. Barth discovered in the Bible a strange new world, namely the world of God which is the kingdom of God, established by God and not by humanity. Like Luther, he was gripped by the Pauline message of the righteousness of God which calls into question all human righteousness.

The voice of God could only be heard in Scripture, in encounter with Christ. That which God is to us in Jesus Christ, He is eternally in himself. All that we know and say about God and humankind is controlled by our knowledge of Jesus as the true God and the true human being. By looking at Jesus Christ through the Holy Spirit, we know the heart of the eternal Father. In Jesus Christ we see the inner meaning of creation, as well as of redemption. In terms of creation, Christ is the One by whom and for whom all things were created. In terms of redemption, Christ is God's fulfilment of his purpose with the human race.

God meets us in moments of crisis and decision, creating his own point of contact in us ("senkrecht von oben", that is, directly from above) and summons us to radical obedience. Put differently: God's revelation is made possible by God alone and comes "from above" without any human intervention. The chasm between God and humanity can therefore only be bridged by God, not by (wo)man. The possibility of knowledge of God is grounded in the actuality of the revelation in Jesus as He makes himself known to faith by the Holy Spirit. For Barth, the doctrine of the Trinity was the starting point and "grammar" (that is, the structure of theological reflection) for all knowledge of God. Within this self-revelation of the triune God, we can distinguish three forms of the one Word of God: the eternal Word incarnate in Jesus Christ, the written Word in the witness of the Bible to that primary Word, and the Word of God as proclaimed in the church.

For Barth, the Word of the cross means that God says "No" to our human sin and pride. At the same time however, God, in grace, says "Yes" to his own creatures in a word of forgiveness (Barth stressed God's "Yes", as the triumph of grace through Jesus Christ, more powerfully than the "No"). The task of Christian dogmatics was to be faithful to this Word, and therefore to examine the content of the church's preaching by tracing it back to its source in God, by the standard of Holy Scripture, and under the guidance of its creeds and confessions. In short: Barth's Theology challenged all theologies of his day to enquire not into Jesus' place in our life story, but into our place in the history that He made on our behalf.

4.2.5 Dietrich Bonhoeffer: Messianic suffering with Christ in a non-religious world

In responding to the challenges of his times, the Lutheran theologian Bonhoeffer (1906–1945) was much more than just an academic theologian. His response represents a deep personal wrestling with the fundamental question: What does it mean to be a Christian here (in Germany) and now (in the period of the nazification of the churches by Hitler)? In his response to these challenges, he blended spirituality and discipleship. His life and works, especially his *The Cost of Discipleship* (1963), *Ethics* (1964) and his posthumously published *Letters and Papers from Prison* (1971) testify to this.

Although he travelled to America, England, Spain and Italy for the purpose of study and work, he kept returning to his home town, Berlin, in commitment to the task that he had passionately chosen, a task that consisted of a radical criticism of the contemporary church and theology, actively fighting Hitler and Nazism, and a task for which he paid with his life at the age of only thirty nine. The way in which he answered these challenges with his own life, constitute his most enduring legacy.

Bonhoeffer's own theology, which is greatly influenced by Barth, is characterised by his commitment to the concrete as opposed to the abstract. Jesus Christ as God-man, as the Word made flesh, as the person for others was the focus of this commitment. In Christ, God graciously acted to reconcile the world with himself. In Christ, God's being is revealed as a "being for others", that is, as vicarious suffering love. The incarnation declares God's love for the world. The crucifixion is God's judgement on sin and evil. The resurrection reveals God's will to renew the world. For Bonhoeffer, Christ therefore defined the true and the real and the good – once and for all.

Because Christ's being is a being for others, neither Christ nor humans can be conceived in isolation, but only in relationship to others. Relationships can be broken by sin, which, in essence, is the desire to be for oneself. For Bonhoeffer, formal religion – as opposed to a life of faith in Christ – was also the product of sin, that is, religion as a self-centred interpretation of God as either individualistically "within us" or metaphysically "beyond us". Christ brings the restoration of relationships by showing in himself what it means to exist in the image of God. That is, He lived, suffered and died *for others*. By doing so, He became the new Adam, the new being, the new humanity. For Bonhoeffer, Christ is – until his visible return – hidden in the church, that is, the community of persons called and formed by the Word through the work of the Holy Spirit. The church, therefore, is church only in as far as it exists *for others*. To live in Christ is to overcome the world by loving it, that is, to join God's suffering in the midst of the world. Bonhoeffer's plea for a "non-religious" faith must be understood in this sense. Religion, according to Bonhoeffer, includes both a false piety, which ignores this world, and a false worldliness, which ignores God. Both are therefore useless. The Christian life, which has neither idolized the world nor written it off, is one of proclamation, praise, prayer, of doing right, of opening the mouth for those who cannot speak and of risking acts of liberation on behalf of the oppressed. Only a life lived in this way avoids "cheap grace" (which Bonhoeffer called the deadly enemy of the church) and witnesses the love of God for the world.

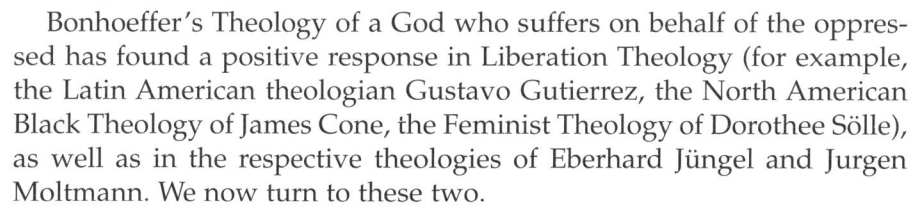

Bonhoeffer's Theology of a God who suffers on behalf of the oppressed has found a positive response in Liberation Theology (for example, the Latin American theologian Gustavo Gutierrez, the North American Black Theology of James Cone, the Feminist Theology of Dorothee Sölle), as well as in the respective theologies of Eberhard Jüngel and Jurgen Moltmann. We now turn to these two.

4.2.6 Eberhard Jüngel: God as open secret of the world

The Tübingen theologian and philosopher of religion, Eberhard Jüngel (1934–), is one of the most serious-minded and perceptive theologians on the contemporary scene. He chose to address two tasks, namely that of exegesis (in the broadest sense) and hermeneutics. The intellectual rigor and passionate engagement with which he assumes his task can find few equals in German Protestant Theology. A reading of Jüngel, from his *Paul and Jesus* (1962) through his *God's Being is in Becoming* (1965) to his *God as the mystery of the world* (1977) is an extremely difficult task, a task which is made even more difficult by the argumentative style of close dialogue with many great thinkers, philosophers (such as Aristotle, Hegel, Descartes, Feuerbach, Nietzsche) and theologians (especially Luther, Barth and Fuchs, but also Bultmann, Bonhoeffer, Ebeling and Pannenberg). It is therefore not easy to characterise his writing in a straightforward manner.

Jüngel's work mounts a serious challenge to the easy dismissal of some of the central problems concerning Trinity, incarnation and God's action in the world. In addressing these problems, language and time determine his focus.

For Jüngel, God has made himself "utterable" in human speech. By becoming "speakable", God has also become "thinkable". And so theology has the task of thinking about the faith in order to keep it "tellable" in each new human situation. According to Jüngel, Trinitarian doctrine is needed for the responsible telling and retelling of the tale which finds definitive linguistic expression in the writings of the New Testament. The cross reflects the sharpest distinction between the Father and Jesus, but at the very same time, the closest identification. The resurrection re-

SECTION A

THEOLOGY

veals that their unity was maintained throughout by the Holy Spirit, that is, by the bond of love. The distinction between Father and Son, as well as their unity in the Spirit, is eternal. The living unity of love is what came and still comes to expression in God's having come and continued coming to the world. On the basis of this, the being of God may and must be said to lie in becoming. The incarnation, death and resurrection of the Son show that God never willed to "come to himself" without humanity. God's humanity thus belongs to his eternal being and nature. As justification, humanity is given a share in God's selflessness, a selflessness to bring "another" into being. This selflessness works itself out in love that entails the reception of the true self from the "other".

The heart of the Christian proclamation and confession is therefore the death and resurrection of the Word of God incarnate in Jesus. In a human person, Jesus the divine Word came to worldly expression, and the resurrection reveals God's self-identification with the Crucified One whose death for others integrated his whole life of selflessness. In the life, death and resurrection of Jesus, the being of God was realized historically as a unity of life and death in favour of life. This is an act of love by God – who is love – into which men and women may let themselves be drawn by the Spirit. Towards their justification, sinners can and must do nothing except allow themselves – in pure passivity – to be drawn into this act and in this way be "made righteous" by God's own effective righteousness. Only then, and for that reason, are they set free to love in a more active participation in the secret by which God has bound and binds himself to the world, that is, his humanity. Only in this way can the human God remain human. Humans may become more human only as they remain redeemed by a God who by a word created what did not exist, and brings the dead to life.

Human beings thus find themselves "having been addressed". The Christian church has to proclaim that God has spoken and also what God has spoken. Theology is to reflect in a responsible way on how God becomes "speakable", that is, how God has become part of our words (language), and how God continues to be part of our words. After all, human words are the only language that human beings understand. Furthermore, God's coming to the world does not take away the reality of this world, but grants this world further possibilities, such as exploring being human in this world. It is in this sense that God must be understood as the open secret (mystery) of the world of which theology has to speak: God is the mystery of the world because his self-communication is that which brings about the renewal of that world by disclosing its possibilities. Stated more simply: having made his hidden reality (secret) manifest in Jesus Christ, God is the one who makes us and our world interesting in new ways.

4.2.7 Jürgen Moltmann: The crucified God as our hope in this world as we live in the power of the Spirit

As a young prisoner of war (1945–1948), the Protestant systematic theologian, Jürgen Moltmann (1926–) of Tübingen, was confronted with two themes which were to form the two complementary sides of his theology: God as the power of hope and God's presence in suffering. This has greatly shaped his sense of involvement, not only in Academic Theology, but also in public and political issues. Through his first three works, *Theology of Hope* (1964), *The Crucified God* (1972) and *The Church in the Power of the Spirit* (1975), he has become one of the most influential contemporary theologians in the world.

The influence of many and diverse scholars can be found in his work. Initially, Barth and Bonhoeffer were the major influences, but, apart from the influence of his teachers at Göttingen (Otto Weber, Ernst Wolf, Gerhard von Rad, Hans Iwand and Ernst Käsemann), he was also influenced by the Dutch theologians Van Ruler and Hoekendijk and later on, by the Jewish theologians Rosenzweig and Heschel. However, the greatest influence on his thinking came from the Jewish Marxist philosopher Ernst Bloch's philosophy of hope.

In Moltmann's Theology, the cross and resurrection are the two key concepts which he relates dialectically (that is, the one presumes the other) to one another within a Trinitarian framework. God experiences a history with the world in which He both affects, and is affected by, the world. The cross and the resurrection are the decisive moments within the Trinitarian history (the history of God's own Trinitarian relationships as a community of divine persons who include the world in their love). The cross is an event between the Father and the Son in which the Father suffers the death of his Son in order to redeem sinful humanity. The cross and the resurrection of Jesus represents complete opposites: death and life, the absence and presence of God. Yet the crucified and risen Jesus is the same Jesus who paradoxically brings new life through his death. By raising the crucified Jesus to new life, God created continuity in the radical discontinuity: As God has spoken (acted) in the past, He has now spoken (acted) again, but spoken (acted) anew and differently in Jesus Christ and the Holy Spirit. The contradiction of cross (death) and resurrection (life) corresponds with the contradiction that exists between what reality is now and what God promises to make it. By his death on the cross, Jesus identified himself with the present reality of the world in all its negativity. This included subjection to sin, suffering and death. However, since the same Jesus was raised, his resurrection constitutes God's promise of a new creation for the whole of reality which the crucified Jesus represents. The cross therefore represents the themes of dialectical love, suffering and solidarity; the resurrection represents the themes of dialectical promise, hope and mission. For its part the Spirit, whose mission derives from the event of the cross and resurrection, moves reality towards the resolution of the dialectic, filling the godforsaken world with God's presence and preparing it for the coming kingdom in which the whole world will be transformed to reflect the resurrection of Jesus.

Moltmann's Theology in its dialectic of cross and resurrection displays a strongly christological centre in the particular history of Jesus. At the same time, it has a universal direction. The resurrection as eschatological

Theology: the 20th century

SECTION A THEOLOGY

promise opens theology and the church to the whole world and its future. Their function is to transform the world in anticipation of its promised eschatological transformation of God. The cross as God's identification, in love, with the godless and the godforsaken, requires that theology and the church show solidarity with them. This implies that theology's task is not merely to interpret the world as God's world, but to change it. However, theology is not only significant for changing the world. It also means the enjoyment of God and participation in the pleasure of his creation. It also means an openness towards one another, that is, to critical dialogue on all fronts and levels. The reason for this openness is that theology does not already know all the answers and can learn from others and from other approaches.

4.2.8 Wolfhart Pannenberg: re-learning to "think God" in universal history

The Protestant (Lutheran) systematic theologian, Wolfhart Pannenberg (1928–) of Munich, was to challenge both Barth and Bultmann on the issue of their understanding of the relationship of faith and history. For Pannenberg, the integrity of Christian Theology requires that faith be grounded in knowledge which can be rationally established outside faith. It requires an understanding of the entire reality which can match atheist and other world-views. It also requires an awareness of the necessity for interdisciplinary co-operation with the human sciences and, to a certain extent, with natural sciences – in which Christian Theology interacts with the intellectual efforts of its time. The intellectual thoroughness, style and impact with which Pannenberg addresses these challenges makes him one of the leading contemporary theologians, not only in Germany but also in America. His ideas stimulated a theological debate far beyond the borders of Protestant Theology.

A varied spectrum of formative influences can be noted in Pannenberg's theological reflection: from the earlier influences of the philosopher Hegel, the Old Testament scholar Von Rad, the New Testament scholar Bornkamm, the church historian Von Campenhausen to the later influence of the American process theologians. All these formative influences are blended together by Pannenberg in his new emphasis on the theological significance of history to Christian faith. Of this new emphasis, God's indirect self-revelation ("Revelation as History") is the basic idea, while history is the most comprehensive horizon of Christian Theology. For Pannenberg, the experience of reality as history constitutes the historicity of human existence. Historical research can thus help to establish the foundations of faith. And faith has to be based on knowledge. This does not imply a special kind of knowledge which is accessible only to believers, but "natural" knowledge which is the object and objective of all scientific inquiry. Faith and reason can thus be comfortable "bedfellows". This meant that, for Pannenberg, the new theological battleground was anthropology!

In Pannenberg's view, God does not reveal himself directly, but indirectly through his acts in history. God's self-revelation is therefore not complete in specific historical events or series of events. It can only be complete at the end of history. It will be in the light of the end of history that every preceding event and the whole of reality will be illuminated. For Pannenberg, this eschatological perspective constitutes the universality of revelation. The distinctive claim of Christian faith is that God's eschatological self-demonstration is actualized in anticipation through the destiny of Jesus of Nazareth, more precisely, in his resurrection. The preceding history of Israel has to be understood as a gradual universalization of the understanding of God's action in history. This action reaches its final stage in Jewish apocalypticism in which the end of history is expected as the complete revelation of God. In the light of the end, the course of history will become clear as God's indirect self-revelation. The universality of God's self-revelation, as it is anticipated in the resurrection of Jesus, has the important implication that it is accessible not only to a specifically privileged group of people, but to everyone. Since it happened for everyone, it is, in principle, open for all who have eyes to see.

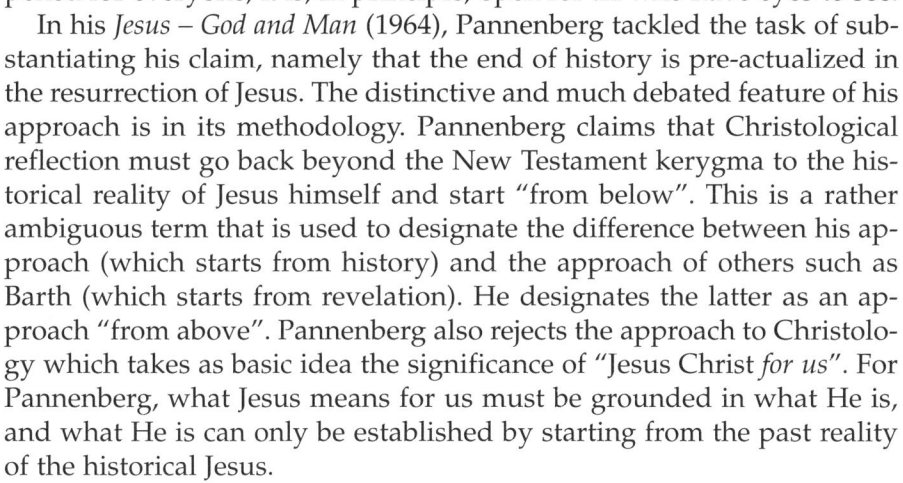

In his *Jesus – God and Man* (1964), Pannenberg tackled the task of substantiating his claim, namely that the end of history is pre-actualized in the resurrection of Jesus. The distinctive and much debated feature of his approach is in its methodology. Pannenberg claims that Christological reflection must go back beyond the New Testament kerygma to the historical reality of Jesus himself and start "from below". This is a rather ambiguous term that is used to designate the difference between his approach (which starts from history) and the approach of others such as Barth (which starts from revelation). He designates the latter as an approach "from above". Pannenberg also rejects the approach to Christology which takes as basic idea the significance of "Jesus Christ *for us*". For Pannenberg, what Jesus means for us must be grounded in what He is, and what He is can only be established by starting from the past reality of the historical Jesus.

However, starting "from below" does not mean that Christology remains "below". Knowledge of the divinity of Jesus is grounded in the resurrection. His unity with God is established in such a way that his claim to be the son of God, implied by his pre-Easter appearance, is proven. The resurrection is the crucial point for the validation of the claim of Jesus' divinity. It is also the foundation for understanding the true humanity of Jesus as the fulfilment of human destiny. For Pannenberg, the identity of Jesus as the Son of God is established indirectly through his relationship of absolute obedience to God the Father. The appeal to the resurrection as the foundation for christological statements about the unity of Jesus and God, and the fulfilment of the human destiny in Him, presupposes that the apocalyptic expectation of the end of history as the disclosure of the totality of meaning can be justified on general anthropological grounds. Furthermore, the fact that the identity of Jesus and the eternal Son is established indirectly through his humanity, presupposes that the openness for God, which is the hallmark of Jesus' obedi-

SECTION A THEOLOGY

ence to the Father, is the determining feature of the human condition. To put this mouthful in a nutshell: Anthropology becomes the battleground on which the validity of theology's claim to universality has to be demonstrated. Pannenberg undertook this task in an admirable way in his *What is Man?* (1962), *Theology and the Philosophy of Science* (1973) and *Systematic Theology*, vol I–III (1988–1993).

In *Theology and the Philosophy of Science*, Pannenberg's understanding of the methodology and the status of theology as a science is spelt out. Starting from the traditional definition of theology as the science of God, Pannenberg immediately qualifies this definition by asserting that God as the subject matter of theology must be understood as an hypothesis. This is necessary if one is to avoid the twofold pitfall of religious subjectivism and dogmatic positivism. If the word "God" can meaningfully refer only to the reality that determines everything, God cannot be directly experienced as an object in the world. God can only become indirectly accessible in the subjective anticipation of the totality of meaning which is presupposed in all particular experiences. Put differently: The question of the meaning of human existence is a question which receives its answer only in God. But God, as the answer, remains ahead of every attempt to fully express his being and nature.

Since the experience of reality as a whole finds symbolic expression in the historic religions, a theory of the history of religions is the place where the indirect "co-givenness" of God has to be substantiated against the background of this general reflection, which Pannenberg now calls Fundamental Theology.

On the basis of this understanding of the nature of theology, Pannenberg characterizes theological statements as hypotheses. While their complete verification can only be expected from the eschaton (that is, from the end of history), there are nevertheless specific criteria for their proleptic substantiation. These criteria are that theological hypotheses are to be considered unsubstantiated if

- they cannot be shown to present implications of the biblical tradition;
- they are not related to the whole of reality in a way that can be validated by present experience and substantiated against the background of contemporary philosophical reflection;
- they are not capable of being integrated with the relevant experience;
- they are deemed to be inadequate in relation to the present stage of theological debate.

Pannenberg's continuing influential contribution to contemporary theology, particularly after the publication of his *Systematic Theology*, vol I–III (1988–1993), is still hotly debated in approval and criticism.

4.3 THE NETHERLANDS

The Dutch theological heritage of the 19th century can be characterised as modernistic theology. This heritage was influenced not only by the Leyden professor, Jacob Arminius (1560–1609), but also greatly by the philosopher Descartes (who lived in Holland for twenty years from 1629 onwards). In concrete terms, this meant that the rational autonomy of the human mind, rather than the response of the believer, set the theological agenda with regard to the relationship of theology to science and culture. In short: the modern spirit was elevated to the level of ultimate truth and norm. This modernistic theology appeared to capitulate the truth of divine revelation to the critical and rational human mind.

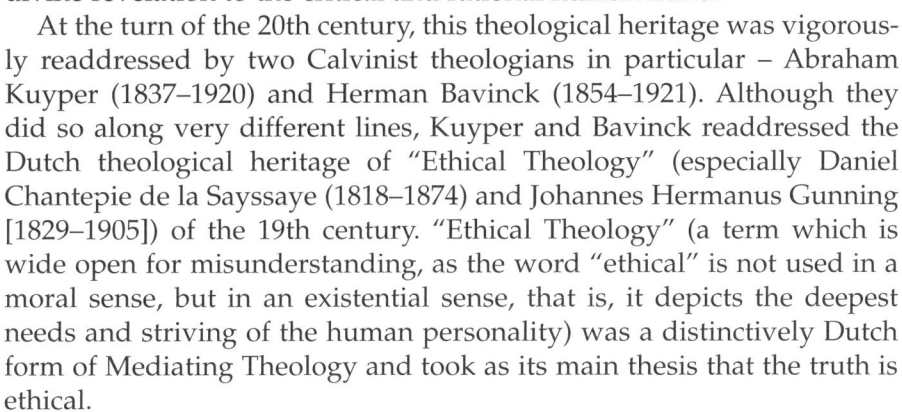

At the turn of the 20th century, this theological heritage was vigorously readdressed by two Calvinist theologians in particular – Abraham Kuyper (1837–1920) and Herman Bavinck (1854–1921). Although they did so along very different lines, Kuyper and Bavinck readdressed the Dutch theological heritage of "Ethical Theology" (especially Daniel Chantepie de la Sayssaye (1818–1874) and Johannes Hermanus Gunning [1829–1905]) of the 19th century. "Ethical Theology" (a term which is wide open for misunderstanding, as the word "ethical" is not used in a moral sense, but in an existential sense, that is, it depicts the deepest needs and striving of the human personality) was a distinctively Dutch form of Mediating Theology and took as its main thesis that the truth is ethical.

In this short overview, however, the emphasis will fall on the two 20th century scholars, Gerrit Cornelis Berkouwer (1903–1996) and Hendrikus Berkhof (1914–1996) whose theological orientation – albeit with sharp differences – continues in the tradition established by Kuyper and Bavinck. It is therefore necessary to make a few introductory remarks on Kuyper and Bavinck.

Kuyper was the founder of the Free University in Amsterdam (1880) and its first professor of theology. After having first thought along the lines of Ethical Theology, Kuyper turned his back on this theology because the ecclesiological and political thinking of this theology was, to his mind, not clear and vigorous enough. He then turned to Calvin and started afresh. Closely following Calvin and seeking the renewal of Reformational Theology, Kuyper's main emphasis is the common grace of God which made possible the organic connection between knowledge of the empirical world and knowledge of God. For Kuyper, true knowledge of God is only possible through the Holy Spirit and regeneration. It is knowledge of God which leads to a knowledge of the world and society as an integrated whole. Kuyper therefore vigorously seeks the renewal of the church and the society, convinced that no stone (read "inch"!) should be left unturned. His theological approach was labelled Neo-Calvinism. In the same year that he founded the Free University, Kuyper discovered a highly gifted young systematician, Herman Bavinck.

Herman Bavinck, seventeen years Kuyper's junior, was professor at a small seminary of the Christelijke Gereformeerde Kerk in Kampen. He refused Kuyper's numerous invitations to join the faculty in Amsterdam. However, in 1902, he become Kuyper's successor. In his search for the right response to modernism, Bavinck was fascinated by Ethical Theology. In contrast to Kuyper, who turned his back on Ethical Theology, this

Theology: the 20th century

SECTION A
THEOLOGY

influence stuck with Bavinck even though a shift in his theological focus is noticeable. In the theological orientation of his Dutch heritage, Bavinck found a lack of distance between God and humanity, a deficiency in the sense of the transcendence of God. For Bavinck, there was too little authority and sovereignty and not enough recognition of the transethical elements in revelation and faith. There was too great an immanence placed on the heritage of theological reflection, an excess of "humanizing the divine", of the normativity of the experience of the Christian church, of self-fulfilment at the expense of self-denial. It was this very road of self-denial which Bavinck was to explore and undertake in his four volumes of *Gereformeerde Dogmatiek* (1895–1901). He rejects both idealism and empiricism. There is no road from human needs to the truth as God reveals it to us. Bavinck distinguishes two principles of knowledge: the subjective and the objective. The objective principle is primary, that is, the Holy Scriptures, the fruit of the final act of the Spirit in the objective revelation of God. Faith's final ground in the testimony of the Holy Scriptures which spontaneously communicates to us the certainty of being children of God, is the subjective principle. Bavinck holds that there is a correspondence between an object and its representation in the experiencing subject. God's creative wisdom, the *Logos*, has been implanted in the human mind as the divine image. All knowledge is ultimately revealed knowledge and not ascertainable through direct empirical observation nor through independent mental activity. Thus all knowledge rests on faith.

4.3.1 Gerrit Cornelius Berkouwer: God's Word, as heard in Holy Scripture, as the true correlation between faith and knowledge, or: true faith honouring the sovereignty of grace

The same issues which preoccupied Kuyper and Bavinck prompted the attention of Berkouwer (1903–1996) when he began his theological studies at the Free University. After serving as a pastor for 18 years in the Gereformeerde Kerken, he was appointed as Bavinck's successor to the chair of dogmatics at the Free University. Berkouwer's fourteen volume series, *Studies in Dogmatics* (1952–1976), offers one of the most comprehensive and systematic expositions of theology from an evangelical perspective available in the English language.

Berkouwer began his theological career with the same concern which was to remain with him throughout his life: the relationship between faith and revelation. In his theological orientation, he continues in the tradition established by Kuyper and Bavinck, but differs from them in two ways. First, for Berkouwer, both Kuyper's and Bavinck's understanding of the relationship between faith and knowledge points towards the fact that God must himself provide the necessary connection between the human mind and natural knowledge, as well as the human mind and religious knowledge. Berkouwer does not employ this analogy and reacts strongly to the parallel between natural faith and Christian faith. Second, Berkouwer does not pick up the emphasis which both Kuyper and Bavinck placed on the corporate aspect of the witness of the Holy Spirit. Berkouwer stresses the relation of the Spirit to the words of Scripture, but not the witness of the Spirit to the corporate church body. With regard to the saving purpose of Scripture, however, Berkouwer does not deviate from them. The authority of Scripture is affirmed by the inward testimony of the Holy Spirit, rather than by the principle of external evidence. Berkouwer is open to the full humanity of Scripture and accommodating to its historical context. Textual problems do not present a contradiction to the truth of the Word of God as received through the witness of the Spirit in the text itself.

Berkouwer directs his theology in opposition to two fronts: the liberal as well as the orthodox. The former has moved toward the subjective side of the relationship between faith and revelation, with the experiencing human subject as the criterion for divine revelation. The latter has moved toward the objectivity of revelation as an abstract construct of doctrinal formulations. Berkouwer argues that it is the very nature of divine revelation as Word of God spoken and heard in Holy Scripture that provides true correlation between faith and knowledge, between faith-subject and revelation-object.

For Berkouwer, faith has no value in and of itself. The value of faith comes entirely from its object: salvation in Jesus Christ – and it is only in correlation with this object that faith has reality. Faith is therefore not only the response to the word of God which is revealed to us through Holy Scripture, but also has epistemological significance in that it is only through faith that true knowledge of God and revelation comes to us. In short: for Berkouwer it is true faith as a human act which honours the sovereignty of God's grace. But as a human act, it is always a gift of God, a result of the working of the Holy Spirit.

Berkouwer is committed to the absolute authority of Scripture as the source of divine revelation which faith grasps in a knowing way. The Bible serves as the "boundary" which qualifies both existential faith and rational knowledge. The message of salvation contained in the Scripture summons one to faith and personal involvement. Without this correlation between faith and revelation, revelation would either have a purely external authority subject to critical reason, or a purely inward authority subject to human experience alone. The Word of God is thus decisive as a criterion by which all of humanity is to be seen as being under condemnation due to sin and through which the gospel of salvation is offered to all. Salvation through Christ is not for the sake of the church, but for the sake of the world.

Theology must therefore serve revelation and faith, not theology itself as an independent discipline of study. Berkouwer's concern is to create a theology which speaks directly to the need of faith as a personal experience which has practical results in human lives.

4.3.2 Hendrikus Berkhof: Addressing modernity and affirming the gracious and irreducible character of Christian proclamation (or: Christian faith comes of age in the contemporary world)

Speaking as part of a theological generation that was shaped between the two World Wars, Hendrikus Berkhof (1914–1996) has in recent decades forged a mediating theology that combines elements of Apologetic and Revelational Theology. The influence of Schleiermacher, Ernst Troeltsch, Oepke Noordmans, Herman Kohlbrugge and, in particular, of his teacher Karl Barth, is the most notable in his works. Berkhof's excellent *Two Hundred Years of Theology: Report of a Personal Journey* (1989) is acclaimed as a book which reflects the harvest of a fruitful theological career. Berkhof's own career has, however, regularly shifted positions. This makes a straightforward characterisation of these influences and the development in his theological thought very difficult. These shifts in his career were brought about – in his own words – by his personal quest and ongoing struggle to find a theological answer for a generation "gluttonous for reality". New theological answers have to be sought since (in Berkhof's opinion) classic dogmatics was giving deep-argumented answers to questions which no-one was asking any more. In this sense, Berkhof's Theology moved over the years toward a theology that can be called "public".

Having studied in Amsterdam and Leiden (Netherlands), as well as in Berlin (Germany), he became a minister of the *Nederlandse Hervormde Kerk* in Lemele, and six years later in Zeist. During this period, he was imprisoned by the Germans for six months on the grounds of a "German hostile sermon"! His career as an academic stretches from 1950 to 1981, when he eventually retired after twenty one years as professor of Dogmatic and Biblical Theology at the Rijksuniversiteit, Leiden.

Berkhof's theological vantage point, from which he claims that God is the object of a science of experience, is directed by the question: How can the relevance and authority of the metaphysical Christian faith be discussed in the context of a contemporary technological and atheistic world that has come of age? In addressing this question of the co-existence of the gospel and modern thought, Berkhof attempts to resolve the dilemma of the relationship between revelation and experience. Berkhof wants to avoid two theological mistakes. In his view, one can err by subsuming "God" into "experience", or by clinging to conceptions of "God" that inadequately account for "experience". Assertations about God should therefore neither be devoid of experiential warrants nor should they be reducible to claims about human experience. The theologian must affirm revelation without losing contact with experience. Language about God may therefore not be reduced to an expression of experience, but at the same time it is unacceptable to speak about God in ways that do not resonate with contemporary experience.

Berkhof's increased emphasis on the need for experiential warrants for theological claims shows his responsiveness to a shift towards empiricism in academic circles both in the Netherlands and in Europe generally. As a correlational theologian, Berkhof seeks to mediate between the gospel and the contemporary situation which is alien to the gospel. New experiences lead to new questions which face the gospel, and in response to these questions, surprising new answers are found. Berkhof is, therefore, concerned with how this revelation, and therefore its relationship to experience, is to be understood.

Berkhof addresses this relationship from two angles. From the first, he states: Revelation is an event in which God makes himself known to humans. God meets us from beyond the limits of what we call experience. In this event, humans learn something that transcends their own possibilities of knowledge and the centre of their existence is addressed. Revelation is therefore a special kind of experience. In Christ, these experiences find their unity. Systematic reflection (dogmatics) on these experiences mirrors a faith that enters the revelational circle not by logical argument, but by an act of surrender. However, the leap in the circle of revelation appears absurd to the outsider.

For Berkhof, experience can mean many things and is, admittedly, a confusing word. Nevertheless, he understands experience to be that which, as an event, penetrates our consciousness from the outside. It is the Spirit who is the "binding force" between revelation and experience and who makes the encounter between God and humanity possible. The Spirit is the name of God in action and therefore the whole creation can be the field of his operation. A Christian can discern the presence of the Holy Spirit in historical events, even in such developments as secularization in the west. Berkhof then addresses this very problem from another angle, thus affirming the value of Apologetic Theology. The claims of the Christian faith are accessible to those outside the faith by means of experience which confirms these very claims. Four experiences are, according to Berkhof, common in the contemporary situation and support the plausibility of God: wonder, bewilderment, a sense of obligation and expectation. These experiences correspond to the notion of creation, sin, expectation of renewal, and hope for redemption.

Although the claims of the Christian faith are accessible to those outside the faith by means of experience, the truth of the Christian faith can ultimately only be communicated by means of an explication of the content of that faith. The challenge to communicate the Christian faith in this way is determined by the very nature of such reflection. For Berkhof, all theological reflection is provisional, fragmentary and incomplete since what we have now is only a "wayfarers" theology. Theology should therefore be a co-operative effort. The question of relations between Christianity and the modern world constitutes a burden that should be shouldered collectively by theologians. Consequently, in situations of conflict, possibilities for inclusive, complementary conceptions should be explored. It is this openness that suggests possibilities for resolving theological disagreements. In this sense, all theology is ultimately ecumenical.

SECTION A — THEOLOGY

4.4 THE UNITED STATES OF AMERICA

Moving across the Atlantic Ocean from Europe to the United States is not only a shift from one continent to another, but also a shift from one theological world to another, despite the European heritage and (apparent) similarities that the American theological tradition shares with Europe. The reason is simple: The United States is a melting pot of nations and cultures. Consequently, almost everything that the American theological tradition inherited has, in due course, been turned into something else! The underlying implication is that the American mind has little or no time nor inclination for theoretical problems and reflections. The theoretical question of truth, which is so important in Europe, has to take a back seat to a concern for efficiency. In America, whatever works is true. Ethics is more valid than dogmatics, and pragmatics counts for more than metaphysics. The typical focus is not on tradition, nor is it directed, speculatively or meditatively, towards what is "above", but towards plans for the future. Its concern is with progress and renewal. There continues to be a feeling of respect, if not of inferiority, towards the intellectual traditions of Europe, although this is mixed with opposing feelings. Be this as it may, the United States now shares continental Europe's leading role in Modern Theology.

A straightforward characterisation of theology in the United States is impossible. Within the five mainline church traditions (Episcopalian, Presbyterian, Congregational, Baptist and Methodist), a broad field of trends in theological reflection and types of theologies are discernable today: Evangelical, Fundamentalist and Revisionist theologies, Liberal and Post-liberal theologies, Liberation and Process theologies – to name only the most important trends and types. These trends and types are, historically, greatly influenced by the religious mindset of Americans. Three successive intellectual-spiritual foundations are responsible for the composition of this mindset: A Puritan form of Calvinism which dates from the 17th century; a revivalism largely stamped by Methodism; and the Enlightenment. These three layers are interwoven with each other within subsequent theological reflection. The story of American Theology begins with the thinking of Jonathan Edwards (1703–1758). It is in his mind that the three layers mentioned above flow together. The focus here, however, is the 20th century and so a basic historical introduction must suffice. After that, the emphasis will shift to three of the most influential figures of 20th century theology in the United States, namely the Niebuhr-brothers, Reinhold and Richard, and Paul Tillich.

The prelude to 20th century American theological thought is sung by the Social Gospel movement (in particular its founder, Washington Gladden [1836–1919], a Congregational pastor, and Walter Rauschenbusch [1861–1918], a Baptist professor in Church History and the leading theologian of the movement) which came about in the 1870s and reached a climax between the turn of the century and the start of the First World War. The challenge of building a new society, the westward push of the pioneers and, in particular, the Civil War between North and South

(1861–1865) continually demanded far-reaching ethical decisions. In the second half of the 19th century, a great new ethical challenge had to be faced: advanced capitalism. In the eastern states, industrialisation took giant strides forward and brought with it many side effects, including urbanization, the development of poor quarters, exploitation of women and children, unemployment, alcoholism, disease, illiteracy and premature deaths. At this point, the ethical ideals of the past proved powerless.

The Social Gospel movement pointed in a new direction. It discovered the social dimensions of the gospel and from there arrived at a radically new interpretation of concepts that were originally religious. However, World War I ended the heyday of the Social Gospel and a period of searching and confusion followed. People looked for new directions and to that end often had to position themselves against the Social Gospel and its advocates. It is this challenge that was addressed by the Niebuhr brothers and Paul Tillich. The Niebuhr brothers were from the United Church of Christ. The United Church was an union of the Evangelical and Reformed Churches on the one hand, and the Congregational Christian Churches on the other hand. The Niebuhrs remained in close contact with European Theology, despite the fact that their thinking belonged totally to the young American tradition. With Paul Tillich, who emigrated from Germany to America at the age of 47, the situation is quite different. He does not quite fit into the framework of American Theology as he remained a European (read German) thinker. However, he fascinated American intellectuals and found an influential hearing both in America and in Europe. Especially after World War II, his thinking came as a welcome answer to deep-seated existential questions. Against this brief background, we now turn to a discussion of our subjects.

4.4.1 Helmut Richard Niebuhr: The sovereignty of God and culture

Although Richard Niebuhr (1894–1962) was the younger of the two brothers, he was regarded by his brother, Reinhold, as the greater man. After completing his studies at the Eden Theological Seminary, Washington University and Yale, Richard Niebuhr served as a pastor for two years in St. Louis. His academic career began in 1919 at Eden Theological Seminary and at the time of his death in 1962, he was professor in Theology and Christian Ethics at Yale. In his theological thinking, one can identify the influence of Ernst Troeltsch, Karl Barth, Max Weber and the emerging discipline of the sociology of religion. These influences underpin his theological reflections, as can be seen in his better known writings such as *The Kingdom of God in America* (1937), *The Meaning of Revelation* (1941), *Christ and Culture* (1951) and the posthumously published *The Responsible Self* (1963). Richard Niebuhr is, arguably, the most influential American theologian of the 20th century.

Niebuhr was a sociologist of religion, an historian as well as a theologian and ethicist. In each of these areas he made fundamental contribu-

SECTION A

THEOLOGY

tions. Several creative tensions mark his writings. His thinking grasps polarities in thought and experience and seeks to hold them together: subjectivity and objectivity, relativity and absoluteness, power and powerlessness, form and spontaneity, revelation and reason.

Rather than reflect on particular social issues, Niebuhr tends toward broader reflections on faith and culture. He argues that the differences in the beliefs and practice of various Christian denominations and groups have more to do with ethnic, social class, racial and economic factors than with dogmatic convictions. He prophetically exposes the scandal and moral impotence of a divided church and aims, through his reflection, at helping the church gain faithful freedom from its divided loyalty to temporal values. Although initially unable to formulate a helpful theological alternative to the church, Niebuhr gradually develops a directive for the church through the central conviction of the reality and sovereignty of God. Niebuhr, in formulating his directive for the church, spells out his epistemological vantage point at the same time. The foundation of his epistemology is that the being and character of the ground of all being (God) is not directly or comprehensively accessible to finite knowledge. All our insight into God is partial, limited and inevitably relative to our particular times and places in history and the traditions of revelation and interpretation in which we stand. Niebuhr maintains that this does not imply the acceptance of relativism (that is to say that in the plurality of theological interpretations, no position has any foundation for claiming more adequate truthfulness than another). He prefers to think in terms of "relationism" (God-in-relation-to-humanity and humanity-in relation-to-God) because theological interpretations are necessarily relativised by the transcendence of the reality they try to apprehend. However, this realisation neither negates the possibility of criteria for determining the greater or lesser adequacy of these interpretations, nor renders theological work the subjective projection of personal or group consciousness. Niebuhr refuses to opt for either a theology that begins with human experience and consciousness or a theology which starts with the absolutising of particular moments of revelation. Instead, Niebuhr formulates the meaning of the conviction of God's sovereignty in three central metaphors which clarify his "relationism", namely God as Creator, God the Judge and Ruler, and God the Redeemer and Liberator.

First: God as Creator. From the theocentric perspective of his theological ethics, Niebuhr states: Whatever is (has being), is good. If God as Creator is the source of all being, then all being has value because of the Creator's investment in and care for it. All other centres of value are therefore relativised and dethroned from their claim to ultimacy in the light of the fact that God is the source and centre of value.

Second: God the Judge and Ruler. Through this metaphor, Niebuhr stresses God's capacity and commitment to incorporate human sinfulness and self-assertion into the realisation of his divine purpose. We are called to respond to God's action in history and to enter into partnership with his divine purpose. For Niebuhr, the most crucial aspect of human life is our utter dependence upon and responsibility to the Author of all life is our utter dependence upon and responsibility to the Author of all being.

Third: God the Redeemer and Liberator. By submitting to death on the cross, Jesus as the Christ could show both the impoverished destructiveness of human sinfulness and the loving, faithful heart of a God seeking reconciliation with alienated humanity. But Jesus is past. In this sense we may not interpret the revelation of God solely from within the person of Jesus, even though we do not know God apart from Jesus. Nor dare we locate the presence of God in the church. Revelation is present only where God discloses himself to us in personal encounter. The God who reveals himself in Jesus Christ is now trusted and known as the contemporary God who reveals himself in everyday events. Human response in faith to this self-giving God is what brings about the transformation in our value system and response that aligns our will and action with God-ruling.

From his starting point in the conviction that God as Creator, Ruler and Redeemer is the fundamental reality with which we have to deal, Niebuhr provides powerfully illuminative descriptions of the relative, variegated patterns of the human struggle of faith. Niebuhr's greatest contribution to theological reflection and the church is perhaps, above all, the intellectual honesty with which his work is rooted in his own struggle of faith.

4.4.2 Karl Raul Reinhold Niebuhr: social reform in the tradition of Christian realism (or: the quest for right Christian action)

Reinhold Niebuhr (1892–1971) was a pastor in Detroit for thirteen years (1915–1928) before his distinguished academic career took off. During his career as an academic, he profoundly influenced the theology and culture of the United States in general. He was professor of Philosophy of Religion and eventually professor of Ethics and Theology (for four decades) at the Union Theological Seminary in New York. Niebuhr's influential and lasting contribution was in the area of Christian social thought and international relations. Reinhold Niebuhr was essentially an ethicist, as can clearly be seen in the titles of his best known works, which include *Does Civilization Need Religion?* (1927), *Moral Man and Immoral Society* (1932), *An Interpretation of Christian Ethics* (1935), *The Nature and Destiny of Man* (1941–43), (1944), *Christian Realism and Political Problems* (1953) and *Pious and Secular America* (1958).

His Christian realism came to dominate the World Council of Churches, the American National Council of Churches and American denominational thinking in social concerns up to this day, despite the critical challenges from liberation theologies. Whereas people found an answer to the question concerning life's meaning in the thinking of Niebuhr's American contemporary, Paul Tillich, people found in Niebuhr's thinking an answer to the question concerning right action.

Niebuhr's thinking was less influenced by World War I than by the labour situation in Detroit. Detroit, the large and rapidly growing city of

Theology: the 20th century

SECTION A

THEOLOGY

the world-renowned automobile manufacturer, Henry Ford, was Niebuhr the pastor's harsh everyday reality which he had to come to terms with theologically. Detroit was a theatre of murderous conflict between capital and labour – as one writer called it – the exploitation of workers by the acquirers of capital. The seriousness of the situation was masked by Henry Ford's social policies. Despite the perception that Ford, through his generous wages, was an exception to the exploitive rule of the acquirers of capital, Niebuhr soon saw through the fine veneer. Ford, too, hardly saw labourers as human beings. The unfit and exhausted workers were thrown away as people without rights. The sudden great influx of black labourers to Detroit brought something new to the scene. Niebuhr unexpectedly linked the social question with the issue of race. He himself became a revisionist socialist and came close to Marxism in addressing the question of the exploitation of workers.

For Niebuhr, the two pillars on which the Social Gospel movement, and liberalism in general, rested were rotten. These pillars were: faith in social and cultural progress and the confidence that the gospel proclaims the kingdom of God as an optimistic and moral entity which can and ought to be realised by human beings. These two convictions had reinforced each other for decades. This harmonious synthesis had now collapsed.

In his own approach to the situation, Niebuhr replaced the rotten pillars with two new pillars which supported each other. The first pillar is the insight into the world's powerlessness to redeem itself, since every liberation leads, sooner or later, to new idolatry and oppression. The revolutionaries are as dangerous as the oppressors! The second pillar is the discovery that it is the gospel that tells the exact truth about the world, and by the offer of a higher reality, namely that of grace, enables us to uphold ourselves and always again to find a way.

As a theologian, Niebuhr saw himself as an apologist. It was his purpose to show the secularised intelligentsia of the eastern seaboard of the North American continent that the gospel alone is the answer to the contradictory experiences under which they laboured. The relevance of the gospel for us lies not, as liberalism believed, in its conformity with us, but in its non-conformity. What is needed therefore, is not a new ideology, but a perspective on human aspirations and limitations that accepts the inevitable clash of divergent interests without destroying the hope for greater justice.

Niebuhr finds this perspective uniquely expressed in the biblical narratives that present the human being as both a finite, limited creature and as the image of God. As a result, each person and group is bound to a definite point in history and troubled by anxiety over the fragility of life and achievements. But each person and group is also capable of an "indefinite transcendence" of these limitations. This capability lies in humanity's unique capacity to raise itself above the two components of its being, namely nature and reason. That is humanity's freedom and at the same time its responsibility. However, human beings inevitably choose to rebel against God, their source of freedom, and against human freedom itself. In pride, humanity forgets its dependence on God and strives for an absoluteness that humanity cannot possess. Pride corrupts social life through the pride of possessing power and through the struggle for power. It also corrupts the life of the spirit in its expression in religion as spiritual pride, in morality as moral pride, and in education as the pride of knowledge. All human institutions are therefore influenced by corrupting influences that are rooted in the very meaning of human existence.

The root of human disorder lies in the anxiety caused by human freedom. The anxious conditions of human life produce great works, but also the distortion of those works. As long as human history continues, it will be this mixture of great works of freedom and great corruption of freedom. For Niebuhr, there is only a divine remedy. The revelation of God in Christ meant that the source of all life took human failure into the divine nature and suffered. God's victory was in forgiving love. People can live by the acceptance of divine love and respond with responsible love to both the revelation and their human companions. As a theologian in the tradition of the reformation, Niebuhr was convinced that grace, and not works, will provide the support for human life. The consequence of this view is intended as a realistic contribution to the Christian's pursuit of social justice.

In conclusion, it is important to note how Niebuhr sees the relationship between social justice and truth. His own implicit understanding of truth and meaning remains squarely within the traditions of American pragmatism. He does not see himself as a theological craftsman of precise and timeless formulations. To him, what verifies Christianity is the power of Christian faith to motivate further action. Not only does he provide a strong motivation for political action, but offers a substantive account of what responsible action is. His stress on human finitude yields a political realism that gives an important place to interests, conflict and balances of power. It is in this sense that the famous words of a prayer by Niebuhr must be understood: "O God, give us serenity to accept what cannot be changed, courage to change what should be changed, and wisdom to distinguish the one from the other".

4.4.3 Paul Johannes Oskar Tillich: The quest for the meaning of life in the shattered existence of the post-war world

Born in Prussia and raised in a conservative Lutheran pastor's home, Paul Tillich (1886–1965) studied at the universities of Berlin, Tübingen and Halle. However, the outbreak of World War I utterly transformed the sheltered and conservative existence of the young Army chaplain. His whole life and lifestyle changed, and he became a religious socialist and cultural pessimist. His academic career began after the war when he taught philosophy and religious studies at different German universities. In 1933 he was expelled from Germany by the Nazis because he attacked Nazi ideology in one of his books. On the invitation of his friend Rein-

SECTION A
THEOLOGY

hold Niebuhr, he emigrated to the United States where he become professor of Theology and Science at the Union Theological Seminary in New York. In his new homeland, and particularly after World War II, Tillich encountered another kind of quest, namely the quest for the meaning of life and for a place to stand in the shattered existence of the post-war world.

For more than fifteen years he taught at Union in relative obscurity, although he was widely respected in small circles of academic theologians. Two publications, however, changed this and the name Tillich suddenly became a household name in America. The first was the publication of a small volume of sermons *(The Shaking of the Foundations,* 1948) which he had preached in the chapel at Union and which became a bestseller. The second publication was Tillich's *Systematic Theology* (1951–1963), which was given considerable press coverage and elevated him to the status of an intellectual superstar in America. After his retirement, he continued teaching at Harvard University and at the University of Chicago. With his death in 1965, the once obscured, but respected, theologian became perhaps the most widely known academic theologian in American history.

Paul Tillich was not only an imposing person, but also a penetrating thinker. In his reflections, the influence of Kant, Schleiermacher, Kierkegaard, Nietzsche and Heidegger, but especially that of Schelling comes to the fore. However, Tillich's appropriation of such influences is original and direct lines can not be drawn easily. In his writing and teaching, Tillich's principle goal was to make Christianity understandable and persuasive to religiously sceptical people, modern in culture and secular in sensibility. He wanted to mediate between contemporary culture and historical Christianity to show that faith need not be unacceptable to contemporary culture and that contemporary culture need not be unacceptable to faith.

As a theologian, Tillich is best known for his Philosophical Theology which not only introduced aspects of Existential Theology into the United States, but also stands as one of the major systematic Protestant statements on Christian Theology. His works are regarded as an adaptation and expansion of the Lutheran principle of the justification by grace through faith alone, and the specific method which he employs in his own exposition of this principle is that of correlation.

Tillich was convinced that the mediatory task between theology and culture had to be undertaken by means of exhibiting the correlation between the two. The relation between the two is like the correlation between "questioning" and "answering" in a conversation, like "form" and "content" in a work of art. It is possible to relate them to one another because in concrete reality, religion and culture are always a single whole of which the form of religion is culture and the substance of culture is religion. The human condition always raises fundamental questions which human cultures express in various ways in the dominant styles of their works of art and to which religious traditions offer answers expressed in religious symbols. Tillich consequently structured his *Systematic Theology* according to the principle of correlation, namely "question" (major human questions) and "answer" (major religious symbols).

In this short overview, the focus will fall on this structure (correlation), as it provides a very useful key to the interpretation of Tillich's theological thinking, which is otherwise not that easily accessible. However, two concepts which are fundamental to Tillich's mediatory theological approach must be taken into account if we are to understand his specific utilisation of the method of correlation. The two fundamental concepts are his theory of symbols and his concept of human existence.

Firstly, objects, persons, images and the like, are symbols when these are spontaneously connected with meanings. Symbols thus have an intermediate status between ideas and things, that is, they participate in the reality to which they refer. Furthermore, symbols thus differ, on the one hand, from conventional signs (in which we arbitrarily assign a meaning to a figure) and, on the other hand, from mere objects (with which we do not associate any meaning at all).

Secondly, human existence is understood by Tillich as a question, that is, as an existence which, by its openness and by its predicaments, points away from itself to something else which gives it meaning. Question must therefore be understood in the sense of a quest, that is, as an existential search. An existential question of this sort is like an empty symbol, because it points to a meaning, yet does not convey that meaning. The emptiness is filled when it is brought into correlation with the religious symbol that conveys the meaning sought.

In practice, Tillich formulates five major questions (Q) and answers (A) in his Systematic Theology which clarify his understanding of correlation:

1. Q: How can we know with certainty any humanly important truth? (This is a question about revelation.)
   A: The religious symbol "Jesus as Logos" correlates as answer with this sceptical question expressed by modern culture.
2. Q: How can we withstand the destructive forces that threaten to disintegrate our lives? (This is a question concerning humanity's finitude.)
   A: The symbol of "God as Creator" correlates as answer with the modern culture's expressions of the question of finitude.
3. Q: How can we heal the alienation that we experience from ourselves and from our neighbours? (This is a question concerning the threats of destruction and chaos.)
   A: The symbol "Jesus as the Christ", that is, "new being" as salvation, correlates with the modern secular expressions of the questions of humanity's estrangement.
4. Q: How can our lives be authentic when our morality, religious practices and cultural self-expressions are so thoroughly ambiguous? (This is a question concerning "spiritual life".)
   A: The symbol "Spirit" correlates as answer with modern culture's expressions of the question of ambiguity.

5) Q: Has history any meaning? (This is a question concerning "everyday living".)
A: The symbol "kingdom of God" correlates as answer to the modern question of meaning.

Through this approach of correlation, Tillich seeks to mediate between contemporary culture and historical Christianity. His task as theologian is not to defend the tradition nor the exegesis of Scripture, but rather to answer humanity's basic contemporary questions in terms of all that can be known, guided by the conviction that ultimate reality is decisively manifest to us in Jesus Christ. His theological approach can thus be characterised as a theology of culture in which the "ultimate concern" of being human, that is, the threats of non-being, of destruction and chaos are taken seriously. To the question of the ultimate concern of humanity, "god" is the answer. For Tillich as Christian theologian, the answer (that is, the content of "god") is provided by the Christian symbols referring to God. The Christian God, however, is not an object which we may know or fail to know. God is the symbol of the Other, the most universal concept. God is the power of being or the foundation of being. Foundation of being is "being itself", that is, utterly unconditioned by anything else while at the same time being present to everything. We participate in being by the very fact that we exist in God's Being-itself. Revelation, as the manifestation of our ultimate concern, is a very subjective, inner experience as one ecstatically experiences the power and ground of being. Anyone who completely involves her/himself in the ultimate concern of her/his existence will be grasped by God and will enter a transforming union with true Being-itself.

Tillich's "answering theology" exerted a great influence in America, as the principle of correlation proved fruitful not only for theological reflection, but also for preaching and church education. It was a simple and convincing alternative for its time, which showed what theology should be: humans ask questions, God answers.

4.5 TRENDS OF THE TRENDSETTERS IN RETROSPECT

Since this overview focused only on theologians from Germany, the Netherlands and the United States, it must be immediately stated that much more could have been said, and much more is still to be said. The theological enterprise is an ongoing quest that is displayed and unfolded in a wide variety of approaches and focus points within different (geographical and theological) contexts.

In retrospect, the following trends or foci, formulated in the broadest terms, can be identified which characterise the foregoing trendsetters of 20th century western theological thought:

- The relationship between faith and history, and the related question of hermeneutics (Germany);
- The significance of and relationship between: Revelation (Scriptures) faith and/or contemporary experience (Netherlands);

- The pragmatic-societal implications of being followers of Jesus, not only here and now, but also in the future (United States).

READING LIST AND BIBLIOGRAPHY

Berkhof, H. 1989. *Two Hundred Years of Theology.* Grand Rapids: Eerdmans.
Cobb, J.B. (Jr). 1986. *Living Options in Protestant Theology.* New York: University Press of America.
Hughes, P.E. 1969. *Creative Minds in Contemporary Theology.* Grand Rapids: Eerdmans.
Maimela, S.S. 1990. *Modern Trends in Theology.* Braamfontein: Skotaville.
Smith, D.L. 1992. *A Handbook on Contemporary Theology.* Wheaton: Victor Books.

Evangelical Theology

Adrio König

5.1 THE EVANGELICAL MOVEMENT

In this chapter, Evangelical Theology is understood to be the theology of the Evangelical Movement (which drew and still draws supporters from most Protestant Churches), especially as it developed in England and North America, and from there moved into Africa.

"The theology of the Evangelical Movement" needs some qualification because both the specific concept "Evangelical Theology" and the concepts "Evangel" and "Evangelical" in general, have been used in different contexts and meanings (Humphreys 1983:13ff.; Wells and Woodbridge 1977:22ff.; Bloesch 1983:14ff.).

The rather unfamiliar word "Evangel" is related to the Greek word *evangelion*, which is used for the gospel of Jesus Christ in general and also for each one of the four Gospels included in the New Testament. In this sense, all Christians may be said to be Evangelicals, and all Christian Theology Evangelical Theology, simply because it is concerned with the gospel of Jesus Christ.

After the Reformation in the 16th century, Protestant Theology was – and still is – referred to in Europe as Evangelical Theology, as opposed to Roman Catholic Theology and Orthodox Theology. The latter is the theology of the Eastern Orthodox Churches in Eastern Europe and elsewhere. There are also instances where Lutheran Theology is called Evangelical Theology, as opposed to Reformed (Calvinistic) Theology.

During the Reformation, the Church of England constituted itself as an independent Church, as some sort of midway between the Roman Catholic Church and Protestantism. It soon became clear that there were two main emphases in the Church of England: the High Church which

SECTION A
THEOLOGY

tended more towards the Catholic Church and which held a very high view of church offices and the sacraments; and the Low Church, which held a low view of the church, church offices and sacraments, and developed a superficiality and "enlightened" worldliness. Other than is often thought, the beginning of the "Evangelical Movement" was not associated with this Low Church, but was thoroughly High Church, with Wesley himself honouring the Church of England and the sacraments dearly till his death. The Methodist Movement within the Church of England rather protested against the superficiality and worldliness of the Low Church approach that overrode the High Church approach early in the 18th century. It was only during the 19th century that the term "Low Church" became practically identical with "Evangelical", which had originally been in sharp contrast to the Low Church approach (Voll 1963: 13ff.). It is the theology of this movement that is addressed in this chapter.

The Evangelical Movement has a very definite forerunner in the Puritan Movement that developed in the Church of England during the late 16th century. It was intended to reform the Anglican Church from within, as the Puritans believed that it still was too much like the Roman Catholic Church (Hindson 1976:17ff.). As part and parcel of the 16th century Calvinist branch of the Reformation, they rediscovered the sovereignty of God and the all-sufficiency of Christ, and were disgusted at what they saw as the Catholic emphasis on human ability to merit our own salvation. In 1662, hundreds of Puritan preachers were ejected from the Church of England, making Puritanism a nonconformist movement. Puritanism thus became the basis for modern day Evangelicalism (Hindson 1976:18). Well-known names of Puritan theologians are Thomas Cranmer, William Tyndale and Edwin Sandys.

The Evangelical Movement has been, and still is, a major force in Great Britain, North America and Africa – to mention only what are perhaps the three major areas of their influence. In the United States, it consists of a great percentage of Euro-American ("White") Christians, but is also well represented amongst other groups, like the Afro-American ("Black") Christians.

During the 19th and 20th centuries, a great number of Missionary Societies from the Evangelical Movement, like the London Missionary Society from England and the American Board of Commissioners for Foreign Missions from the USA, sent missionaries to the old "Mission Fields" in, inter alia, Africa and Asia.

Implicit in this description is the fact that the Evangelical Movement is a very broad and diversified movement and also that Evangelical Theology has never been monolithic. The movement includes representatives of an amazing variety of churches (denominations). In his volume on 19th century Evangelical Theology, Humphreys has, for example, included the following number of contributors from the different churches: Anglicans 8, Scottish Presbyterian 7, Baptists 6, Congregationalists 4, Presbyterians 3, Lutherans 2, Reformed 1, Roman Catholic 1 (1983:15). The variety in the Evangelical Movement is, in fact, much bigger, as it also includes members of denominations from Holiness, Pentecostal and Charismatic backgrounds.

This means that the theology of the Evangelical Movement will also reflect a variety that is in fact so big that some scholars doubt whether it is still meaningful to use the concept "Evangelical" at all (Dayton in Dayton and Johnson 1991:245ff.).

However, others differ and continue to speak of the Evangelical Movement and Evangelical Theology. Johnston, the co-editor with Dayton, characterizes American Evangelicalism as "an extended family" (Dayton and Johnson 1991:252ff.). This is true, especially in the sense that Evangelicalism provides an important identity to many Christians. Especially in North America, the fact that one is "Evangelical" is often more important than denominational affiliation. Christians will change denomination without much ado and for secondary reasons (convenience, the person of the minister, youth programme), but only within the Evangelical Movement. In a sense, the Evangelical Movement provides them the sort of unity and identity that the denomination does in Europe or in southern Africa. And this identity includes a fairly clearly identifiable theological conviction – even though it is true that this theology is characterised by a wide variety of emphases, some even strongly militating against others, like the revivalist tradition (often related to Armenianism) which opposes the scholastic Reformed Theology of the Old Princeton Presbyterians.

It is also true that Evangelicals are often better known for a specific spirituality. Therefore we first turn to Evangelical spirituality.

5.2 EVANGELICAL SPIRITUALITY

In general, one may characterize Evangelical Christians in three ways (cf. Grenz 1993:30ff.):

First, they are Christians who have had a personal experience of Jesus Christ. They claim that they are born again or converted and that they have assurance of salvation.

Second, they have a very high view of the Bible. They are a Bible centred people who refer to themselves as "people of the Book". They especially emphasize the authority and the inspiration of the Bible. Evangelicals love the Bible, encourage regular personal Bible reading and Bible study. They learn Bible verses by heart and love to quote the Bible in conversation. They try to relate the Bible to their personal life situations. They have a conservative view of the Bible and a fairly direct and literal understanding of it. They tend to personalize the Bible ("The Bible says ...") or to identify the Bible with the speaking of God ("This morning the Lord said to me ...")

Third, Evangelicals want to share their faith with others. They emphasize evangelism. Most of the great American Evangelists, like Billy Graham, are Evangelicals. It is probably fair to say that, proportionately, no other group of Christians has supported more missionaries and gained more converts abroad than the Evangelicals.

SECTION A
THEOLOGY

There is no clear-cut division possible between their spirituality and their theology, so that these characteristics will again be touched on under their theology. But at least the first point has to be elaborated on here: their personal experience of Jesus Christ. Evangelicals feel themselves in many respects very close to the Reformation. They share the emphasis on sin and grace, on salvation only through Christ, only through grace and only through faith *(solus christus, sola gratia, sola fide)*.

The modern western world, dominated as it is by individualism, has strongly influenced Evangelical Christians. They see true Christianity as a matter of personal commitment. In the decision for Christ, each individual stands alone. During evangelistic services, the evangelical preacher will appeal to the audience as individuals: "Make a personal decision for Christ." In addition, to become like Christ is one's personal responsibility. No one can act on anyone else's behalf. You cannot claim to be a Christian because of the faith of your parents or because you are baptized or because you belong to a specific Church. "God has no grandchildren" is a well-known adage in Evangelical circles.

This emphasis on a personal relationship with Christ includes a personal faith that is alive and vibrant and that clearly distinguishes Christians from non-Christians or nominal Christians. As part of their Christian lifestyle, they emphasize prayer. They have specific ways of referring to prayer. They do not "say a prayer", they "join in prayer" and individually they have a daily – or preferably a twice daily – "quiet time" or personal devotions of Bible reading and "speaking with the Lord".

Their worship services have some characteristic emphases. They do not see the official church as a dispenser of grace, but as a fellowship of believers, and their worship services are seen as particular occasions for experiencing fellowship. Hymns play an important role in their meetings. They do not restrict hymn singing to one hymn at a time at specific points in the liturgy; instead, they sing a number of hymns in praise of God with great enthusiasm and dedication. In this way, they create an atmosphere that is quite unique to services in which the Evangelical spirit dominates. In big churches that reflect Evangelical spirituality, there may even be a specific ministry of music.

Grenz summarized Evangelical identity as "a specific vision of what it means to be Christian – a specific way of being Christian. This vision includes a fervent desire to make the Bible alive in personal and community life, a sense that faith is to be vibrant and central to life, a way of praying, an understanding of the church as a fellowship of believers, and a desire to express our joy and praise through vehicles of worship and testimony". He adds: "As evangelicals we share a common religious experience. We have met God in Christ, we declare" (1993:33–34).

5.3 THE HISTORY OF THE EVANGELICAL MOVEMENT

5.3.1 Great Britain

Just like its spirituality, the history of the Evangelical Movement is very important to an understanding of the movement and its theology. We will deal with the history of the Evangelical Movement in Great Britain, North America and Africa: Great Britain, because it all started there; North America because there we have by far the greatest breach of this movement and because there it has influenced a major society more than in any other place in the world; Africa, because most of the contributors to this volume are from Africa, and in few other places in the world (if any) has this movement gained more converts in missionary situations.

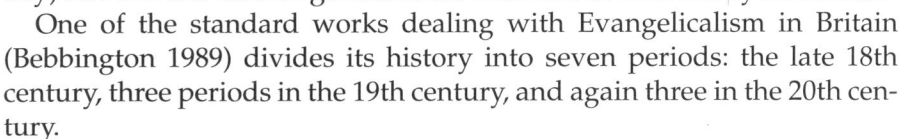

One of the standard works dealing with Evangelicalism in Britain (Bebbington 1989) divides its history into seven periods: the late 18th century, three periods in the 19th century, and again three in the 20th century.

The decade 1734–1743 is seen as the birth of the movement which started with a number of people in Great Britain who experienced Christ and his saving power in extraordinary ways. The names of George Whitefield (an Oxford student who was converted in 1735) and Charles Wesley (Whitefield's mentor in his religious quest, who himself only attained assurance in 1738) were closely related to this movement right from its start. Both were members of the Church of England (often referred to as the Anglican Church, though in the United States it is called the Episcopal Church). Both began open-air preaching and soon a revival broke out near Glasgow. At the same time, Jonathan Edwards was involved in a revival in Massachusetts – later to become part of the USA. Edwards published an analysis of the revival that impressed Wesley prior to the start of his travelling ministry. In the meantime, Whitefield visited America and the already existing movement was fauned into what is usually called the "First Great Awakening" – part of "The Eighteen Century Revival" in Britain and beyond. This revival signified the birth of Evangelicalism, and revivalism has remained an essential element in Evangelicalism ever since. It changed the spiritual life of the churches in Britain. Throughout the 18th century, membership increased rapidly in most denominations: Baptists, Independents, Methodists, Presbyterians (in Scotland).

Evangelicalism initially had less influence on the Church of England and the Church of Scotland. In fact, in these churches developed forms of persecution against the movement. Students were expelled from Oxford for "Methodist practices", young men were denied ordination (Church of England), and ministers who did not favour Evangelicalism were imposed on Evangelically-minded parishes in the Presbyterian Church (Scotland).

The early emphasis of Evangelicals was on justification by faith alone. Lost sinners must trust in Christ for salvation. Christ had done all that was needed to achieve salvation. It remained only for men and women to accept forgiveness at his hands. The insistence on faith alone implied a rejection of at least three alternatives: salvation by works, or by faith and works, or by sincerity, Henry Venn wrote in the classic compendium of Evangelical faith, *The complete duty of Man* (1763) (Beddington 1989: 21ff.). The objection that such a faith would lead to licentiousness as

SECTION A
THEOLOGY

morality and good works would become of no avail, was countered by the conviction – already shared by John Calvin – that while faith alone is necessary for salvation, such faith does not remain alone, but necessarily produces good works. So Paul (justification by faith alone) and James (true faith does not remain without good works) could be meaningfully related.

Added to justification by faith alone was the emphasis on assurance of salvation. Not that this was something new in Protestant Theology. Moravians (Germany) and Puritans (England) had well-established doctrines in this regard, being part and parcel of Protestant Theology. But Evangelicalism transformed it. Puritans held that assurance was rare and achieved only late in the believer's life as the fruit of a long struggle. In fact, Catholic Theology also held to the doctrine of assurance, but only in exceptional cases. But Evangelicals believed it to be general, given at conversion when it should simply be accepted as a gift from God. Jonathan Edwards claimed that Christians could no more doubt assurance than the existence of a blazing sun in a clear sky (Bebbington 1989:46).

At least two other characteristics of early Evangelicalism resulted from this special emphasis on assurance: optimism and mission (Bebbington 1989:ch 2). Christian optimism may be related to the Enlightenment's optimism about humanity's great potential for improvement. It was the Armenianism of the Methodists, in particular, that paved the way for an equivalent "optimism of grace," as opposed to a more strictly Calvinist approach that holds that we can never attain a position of fulfilling the law of God. Methodists accepted the perfectibility of human beings – not humans in general, as later English liberalism believed – but the regenate. According to Wesley, experience told him that believers may reach a state in which they are free from all known sin, though he also emphasized that this state can readily be lost.

Also related to assurance was the missionary endeavour of Evangelicals that lasts till this day. In the 16th and 17th centuries it was rare to find a Protestant minister or theologian who propagated a Christian missionary outreach into the unchristianized world – contrary to Roman Catholic endeavours. Some founding members of Evangelicalism still clung to ideas such as that God bestowed the means of grace only on particular nations and not on all (Jonathan Edwards), views that often were related to the Calvinistic doctrine of election and rejection. But even these ideas did not prevent Edwards from participating in the growing Evangelical missionary outreach. In this time (towards the end of the 18th century), William Carey argued strongly that the Great Commission was still binding. He established the Baptist Missionary Society, the first foreign missionary society that resulted from the revival, and in 1793 he himself took the lead in the work in India. Evangelicals came to acknowledge that missionary work was obligatory to Christianity. One of the Methodist preachers explicitly related this conviction to his conversion: "Now the same Spirit that witnessed my adoption, cried in me, night and day: 'Spend and be spent for God'" (Bebbington 1898:41).

At first the Methodists took the lead, but soon they were followed by Independents and Baptists. In 1795, the well-known London Missionary Society was set up to concentrate on the South Seas. In 1796, interdenominational societies were formed in Edinburgh and Glasgow, and in 1799 the Church Missionary Society was established on lines acceptable to the Church of England.

An important development in early Evangelicalism, that fell into disfavour in the 20th century, was their social involvement. Philanthropy was actively promoted by Evangelicals from the early days on (Voll 1963: 21). In many ways Wesley set the tone himself. Evangelicals saw this as part and parcel of the gospel itself. Good works were fundamental to Christian faith. Didn't Wesley himself teach that though we are saved by faith alone, faith does not remain alone but produces good works? The establishment of orphanages was a most striking example of this philanthropy. Whitefield spared no pains in caring for his orphanage. Other than the general optimism of the early Evangelical Movement, its charitable work could scarcely be related – even indirectly – to the Enlightenment (Bebbington 1989:71). It was a spontaneous expression of Christian principles.

But it is somewhat different with the major contribution made by Evangelicals to the anti-slavery campaign. This was undoubtedly related to the humanism of the Enlightenment. Benevolence, happiness and liberty were three leading principles amongst Enlightenment philosophers. Only Evangelicals that shared these principles took initiative in this campaign. This means that what Evangelicals (like Wilberforce, Clarkson, Stephens and the Clapham Sect of which Wilberforce was a member, Voll 1963:21) brought into the campaign, was not a new theoretical perspective, but their Christian motivation. Though other groups co-operated, Evangelicalism must be accorded a large share of the credit for the final abolition of slavery by an act against slave trade (1807) and an act to extinguish slavery itself in British dominions (1833).

So much for an overview of the first, decisive period in the history of the Evangelical Movement in Britain. Though many new emphases would develop in the coming centuries, and especially tensions and even divisions, some of these early characteristics have remained central to the movement up to the present time. That is the reason why a comparatively large portion of this chapter was devoted to this early period.

5.3.2 North America

The history of North American Evangelism must be added to that of Britain for at least two reasons. First, some features of Evangelism developed in a very distinctive way in America, like Fundamentalism and anti-evolutionism, and second, many more missionaries from more missionary societies were sent to Africa from North America than from England.

North America was colonized by England towards the end of the 16th century. The first "Pilgrim" fathers and mothers to arrive there were

SECTION A

THEOLOGY

"Puritans" and they founded Massachusetts in 1620. "Puritans" is written in inverted commas because these people differed from the main body of Puritans in England in at least one sense. While the British Puritans tried to purify (the word from which Puritan is derived) the Church of England from *within*, these Pilgrims broke away from the official Church and formed a separate, independent structure – a style which the English Puritans had bitterly opposed. In later years, this style became characteristic of many American evangelicals: when under pressure, break away from the established Church. Theologically, these pilgrims to the new world shared the same faith and theology as those in Britain. But, in addition, they had very distinct convictions about themselves and about the future. To a large extent they identified themselves with Israel, the people of God in Old Testament times. They saw themselves as the people of God, the new Israel. They regarded their emigration from England as a new Exodus. They were to build a new Jerusalem, the biblical "city upon a hill" (Grenz 1993:24).

But there was more. Through them, God would bring human history to an end. At least some of them believed that before 1700 God would introduce the Millennium, the thousand years of peace on earth, through them. The following two notions are deeply ingrained in American Evangelicalism: The Americans are a special people, and God has a special purpose for America in realizing God's reign on earth.

Though in these early days there were also some Roman Catholic immigrants – Maryland was founded by some of them – the majority were Protestant. Right up to the end of the 19th century, the majority of Americans would have thought of themselves as Evangelicals, and of America as an evangelical Christian nation. These convictions were strengthened by the First Great Awakening (1740s) and the Second Great Awakening (1790s).

The influence of John Wesley, the 18th century English revivalist, on the Second Great Awakening is very important to an understanding of some of the later developments in Evangelicalism. Wesley had a decisive influence on Charles Finney, particularly with regard to two things: sanctification and social reform. Wesley not only preached conversion, but also sanctification. Converts should go on to perfection through the power of the Holy Spirit. Ordinary Christians should seek to exemplify absolute moral standards in their everyday lives, and introduce these into society. In this way social reform became part and parcel of English and American Evangelical revivals. Social reform included more than charity. Just laws had to be made to change malpractices. It is not surprising that Wilberforce and Clarkson, the great champions of the abolition of slavery in England, were devoted Methodists and stood firmly in the English Evangelical tradition.

While they belonged to a variety of Protestant denominations, the Evangelicals were a determining force in the early history of North America and were very much united in their understanding of the gospel till late in the 19th century. McLaughlin writes: "The story of American

Evangelicalism is the story of America itself in the years 1800 to 1900" (1968:1), and Wells and Woodbridge: "... evangelicals were effectively shaping American culture" (1977:10). In fact, at times it must have been very difficult to distinguish between Evangelical faith and American civil religion.

The Civil War (1861–1863) and the introduction of Liberal Theology into North America in the late 19th century resulted in the Fundamentalist Movement early in the 20th century. This movement shattered the unity amongst Evangelicals and terminated their prominence in American society.

The Civil War was waged between the more liberal, industrialized northern States and the rich, conservative agricultural southern States over the issue of slavery. In the South, a more literal use of Scripture prevailed, so that slavery could be defended because no direct condemnation or repudiation of slavery was found in the Bible nor any clear admonition to abolish it. The furthest these Evangelical leaders were willing to go was to appeal for the more humane treatment of slaves. In the North, a more free and innovative interpretation led to the condemnation of slavery. They held that the biblical teaching on the equality and freedom of all human beings implied that slavery was against the will of God, even if this implication had not as yet been drawn in biblical times. Although the North won the Civil War and slavery was finally abolished, it became clear that the mentality behind slavery offered strong resistance, so strong that it eventually led to the dissolution of the reform impulse and broader social concern of the revivalistic tradition that Charles Finney developed in faithfulness to the heritage of John Wesley (Dayton 1976:124ff.). What remained was the propagation of personal morality ("no smoking, no drinking, no dancing, no gambling" – the elements which came to characterize the revivalistic ethic of later days). Moberg's book (1972) is revealing and enlightening in this regard. Eventually, social involvement came to be identified with Liberal Theology (e.g. Rauschenbush and the Social Gospel early in the 20th century, Moberg:23ff.).

The issues of evolution and a critical approach to Scripture led to the clearer demarcation of Liberal Theology which had started as a small movement, but eventually won the day after the disastrous Scopes Trial in 1925.

When we speak of the critical approach to the Bible, we mean the historical-critical exposition of the Bible that originated mainly in Germany and entered North America towards the end of the 19th century. On scholarly and historical grounds, age-old traditions were challenged, such as that Moses was the author of the first five books in the Bible. Some scholars went much further and challenged doctrines such as the virginal birth of Christ, and even fundamental ones like the substitutional value of his death, and his resurrection – though the historical-critical method does not necessarily lead to these conclusions.

This introduction of Liberal Theology into North America created a

SECTION A

THEOLOGY

vehement response from Evangelical theologians, in this case especially from the Princeton Theological Seminary, a seminary of the Presbyterian Church. The main contributors were Charles Hodge, his son A.A. Hodge and B.B. Warfield, who defended a very conservative view of Scripture in the Protestant Scholastic tradition of Francis Turretin. Their views reflected little sensitivity for obvious differences between some of the books in the Bible (such as the Synoptic Gospels) and the problems created by these differences, or for the importance which the historical situations in which Bible books originated has for interpreting them. In his *Systematic Theology*, first published in 1871, Charles Hodge compared the method of theology to that of the natural sciences (which in his day was supposed to work according to fixed laws from which one deduced indisputable conclusions from the clear facts available). He writes: "The Bible is to the theologian what nature is to the man of science. It is his store-house of facts; and his method of ascertaining what the Bible teaches, is the same as that which the natural philosopher (read: scientist, A. K.) adopts to ascertain what nature teaches" (1952:10). His son, A. A. Hodge, and B. B. Warfield continued this tradition by asserting that "all the affirmations of Scripture of all kinds, whether of spiritual doctrine or duty, or of physical or historical fact, or of psychological or philosophical principle, are without any error ..." (Rogers and McKin 1979:350).

Such views laid the foundation for a doctrine of biblical inerrancy that was fully developed early in the 20th century under the impact of the theory of evolution.

Charles Darwin published his book *The Origin of Species* in 1859 (Darwin 1979). He claimed that by observations from nature he could substantiate the theory that organisms developed gradually over immense periods of time through small random changes, and that only the fittest of these survived. The full title of Darwin's book in fact reads *The Origin of Species by Means of Natural Selection or the Preservation of Favoured Races in the Struggle for Life*.

Just as was the case with the historical-critical approach to Scripture, conservative theologians experienced this theory as a violation of biblical authority and inspiration. They maintained that it was clear biblical teaching that the earth and everything on and around it was created from nothing in only six days *(creatio ex nihilo)* only by the word (command) of God. This position was maintained despite a number of efforts from liberal theologians to reconcile Darwin's theory of evolution with biblical perspectives on creation.

By the beginning of the 20th century, the historical-critical approach to Scripture, combined with the support Darwin's theory received in some theological circles, challenged a number of evangelical theologians to publish a series of booklets under the title *The Fundamentals: A Testimony to the Truth* (1909–1915). These books were edited by A.C. Dixon, and "became the rallying point of the Fundamentalist Movement" (Moberg 1972:31). A deeply divisive controversy regarding biblical interpretation developed in the mainline churches. In opposition to the liberal approach, fundamentalism stood as the old Evangelicalism which, under pressure, had turned defensive and dogmatic, rigid and reactionary (Carnell 1959:113).

The disaster of the Scopes Trial of 1925 finally turned the scale against the Evangelical Movement. The defender was a teacher, John Scopes, who was accused of teaching the theory of evolution against the State law in Tennessee. He was accused by the silver-tongued, but aging, William Jennings Bryan, ex-presidential candidate for the Democratic Party, who was clearly outwitted by Scopes' brilliant defender, Clarence Darrow. Conservative Christianity was not only repulsed, but seemingly crushed. Conservative Evangelicals were disheartened (Wells and Woodbridge 1977:12). They no longer formed the dominant group in the mainline churches. They were replaced by Fundamentalism, a reactionary movement which led people to oppose and separate from the traditional denominations. Evangelicals were widely admired prior to 1870. By 1925 fundamentalists were the object of ridicule in the public press (Marsden 1980:6ff.).

Only by the middle of the 20th century did a new phase in the history of the Evangelical Movement, called Neo-Evangelicalism, set in (Wells and Woodbridge 1977:306). Most of the leaders in this new phase still had their roots in separatist Fundamentalism, but they opposed the narrow focus and isolationism of the Fundamentalists, and desired to bring the gospel they preached into creative contact with American society. Whereas they remained committed to "the fundamentals" of the 1920s, they took a new position in terms of the role of the church in society.

In 1942, H. J. Ockenga took the initiative in forming the National Association of Evangelicals (NAE). The return of the NAE to the term evangelical rather than fundamentalist, is significant. The need for an intellectual and training centre was provided in the formation of the Fuller Theological Seminary (after Charles E. Fuller, a radio evangelist). The first resident president, E. J. Carrell (1954), involved the Seminary in a truly open scholarship and a commitment to academic freedom.

Closely related to this new development was the rise of Billy (William Franklin) Graham to public prominence (1949). He also fostered openness and challenged American society at large. He made racial integration a policy of his crusades and co-operated with all churches who were willing to sponsor him.

In 1955 Graham, Ockenga and others joined forces to launch Christianity Today, a national magazine that presented the Neo-Evangelical approach. In 1966, *Christianity Today* sponsored the important *World Congress on Evangelism* in Berlin.

Although the isolationism and separatism of Fundamentalism was replaced by a new involvement in society at large, the Neo-Evangelical Movement still reflected strong social and theological conservatism through the 1960s and into the 1970s. They initially opposed the Civil Rights Movement, supported the war in Vietnam, defended Nixon, and opposed the equality of men and women in home and church (Dayton 1976:3).

Evangelical Theology

SECTION A

THEOLOGY

5.3.3 Africa

The Evangelical Movement and compatible missionary societies played an important role in bringing the gospel to sub-Saharan Africa in the 19th century. Britain and Germany were the major dispatching countries. Societies like the Church Missionary Society, London Missionary Society, British Baptist Missionary Society and the German Moravians (Basel Mission, Berlin Mission, etc.) led the way in opening up the interior of Africa for the gospel (Hastings 1979:39; Falk 1979; Beetham 1967:13ff.).

Prior to the second half of the 20th century, little was done to interrelate and organize co-operation between these societies and the denominations resulting from their work. The founding of the Association of Evangelicals of Africa and Madagascar (AEAM) in 1966 changed the situation. According to Adeyemo, the organisation includes almost two hundred denominations and mission agencies, representing over fifty million evangelical believers (1991:92). In 1973, the AEAM founded a Theological Commission with Byang Kato as Executive Secretary. The Commission strove to develop graduate theological education and to raise theological standards by establishing ACTEA (Accrediting Council for Theological Education in Africa – Tienou 1985). Important African Evangelical theologians outside of South Africa are Byang Kato (died 1975), Tite Tienou and Tokunboh Adeyemo.

The main issues Evangelical theologians in Africa have to deal with are the authority of the Bible, the relationship between the Christian faith and the traditional religion of Africa, the proper contextualization of theology in Africa, cultural identity, the issue of race and colour and the problem of poverty (Tienou 1985:86; 1987:156). An interesting example of Evangelical activity is the *Evangelical Witness* in South Africa, which addresses the fact that "most Evangelical churches and groups supported the apartheid regime" – a fact that was also highlighted by Walker (1989). The *Evangelical Witness* was published by a group of "Concerned Evangelicals" in 1986. A variety of denominations are represented amongst the 130 signatories, especially Baptists and Pentecostal denominations like the Apostolic Faith Mission and the Assemblies of God.

It is, however, rather difficult to identify Evangelical theologians and denominations in South Africa (Jackson 1978:20), which is the country with the strongest theological output in Africa. Other than in North America and in Britain, the Evangelical movement in South Africa is not an overarching movement which includes supporters from major denominations. The large Afrikaans Reformed tradition does not deem itself part of the Evangelical movement, nor does the large Methodist and Anglican Churches, though much of the theology and spirituality in these churches would be deemed Evangelical in North America and Britain. Only relatively small groups like the Baptists and the Church of the Nazarene deem themselves Evangelical. On the other hand, there were and still are, quite a number of individuals and local churches from both the English speaking mainline churches and the Pentecostal churches who form part of the Evangelical Movement, so that de Gruchy can even say: "South African history has been largely shaped by Evangelical Christianity" (1978:53). The Evangelical Fellowship of South Africa takes most of the initiative in the Evangelical Movement, but there are a few other important organizations associated with the Evangelical Movement, like Africa Enterprise (AE) headed by Michael Cassidy. It played a major role in organizing both the Pan African Christian Leadership Assembly (PACLA) in Nairobi (1976) and the South African Christian Leadership Assembly (SACLA) in Pretoria (1978), two major conferences that brought together Evangelicals and like-minded Christians, but also Christians from different backgrounds ("from Roman Catholic to Pentecostal" – Jackson 1978:20). AE also played a major role in organizing the National Initiative for Reconciliation (NIR) in Pietermaritzburg (1985), which spoke out strongly against apartheid and the malpractices of government. The "Concerned Evangelicals" link up with these major events in forming what Jackson calls the New Evangelicals who have strongly opposed apartheid in South Africa.

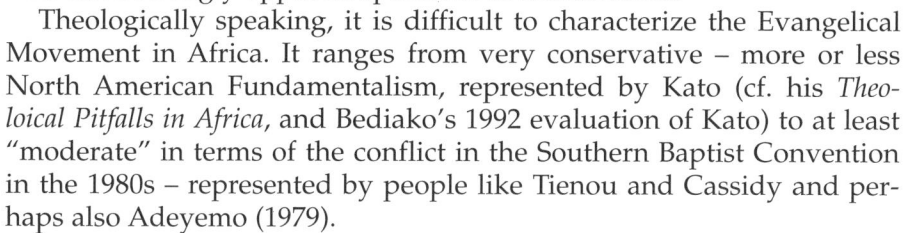

Theologically speaking, it is difficult to characterize the Evangelical Movement in Africa. It ranges from very conservative – more or less North American Fundamentalism, represented by Kato (cf. his *Theoloical Pitfalls in Africa*, and Bediako's 1992 evaluation of Kato) to at least "moderate" in terms of the conflict in the Southern Baptist Convention in the 1980s – represented by people like Tienou and Cassidy and perhaps also Adeyemo (1979).

5.4 SOME BASIC ASPECTS OF EVANGELICAL THEOLOGY

5.4.1 The core of the evangelical faith

It is not an easy task for Evangelical Theology to identify an essence or core of the evangelical faith. It might have been easier earlier in the 20th century, but over the last few decades, Evangelical writers have become more aware of the variety and diversity of groups amongst Evangelicals (Dayton in Dayton and Johnston 1991:245, 262). Dayton indicates that at least some of the characteristics that were accepted as common to the movement at large in the past are in fact no longer treasured by all subgroups. He refers, inter alia, to the inerrancy of Scripture, to which most Pentecostal and holiness churches are in fact not committed. He also questions the characterization of Evangelicals as *conservative* against the *liberal* theology of the mainline churches. If this were true, one would have expected Evangelical churches to resist the ordination of women and mainline churches to practise it. But the opposite is true. Many Evangelical churches have a long history of ordained women as opposed to mainline churches like the Anglican Church in North America, Britain and elsewhere. In fact, Dayton submits that it can hardly be true to view Pentecostal churches (and one may add: independent Charismatic Churches) as conservative and traditional. Rather, they can be seen as modern and on the newer and innovative edge of Christianity, breaking the patterns of classical Protestant thought and forcing new questions to be asked.

SECTION A
THEOLOGY

These insights have resulted in characterizations of the evangelical faith that are more tentative and allow for exceptions to the rule. It is with this firmly in mind that the following effort is presented.

Traditionally the evangelical faith, especially in its earlier form, has generally been characterized in terms of a few clear and strong distinctives.

In its shortest form, it is described simply as salvation by grace (Bloesch 1979:276). The same author describes it more fully in the following way:

> The hallmark of evangelical faith is not the inerrancy of Scripture, nor even its divine authority, nor is it the person of Christ or the Trinity. Instead, it is the cross of Christ, the doctrine of salvation through the righteousness of Christ procured for us by his sacrificial life, death and resurrection. It is the cross that gives authority to Scripture, and it is the cross that reveals and confirms the Messianic identity of Jesus as the Son of God. (1979:238)

Bloesch also offers a much longer list: the absolute sovereignty and transcendence of God; the divine authority and inspiration of Scripture; the radical sinfulness of human beings; the deity of Jesus Christ; his vicarious substitutionary atonement; the eschatological and super historical character of the kingdom of God; a final judgement at the end of history; the realities of heaven and hell; and evangelization as the primary dimension of the Christian mission (1978:14).

Again, Bloesch (1983:17) devotes an entire chapter to defining evangelical identity, and it may make good sense to see how he adds flesh to the bones of the briefer formulations:

> An evangelical is one who affirms the centrality and cruciality of Christ's work of reconciliation and redemption as declared in the Scriptures; the necessity to appropriate the fruits of this work in one's own life and experience; and the urgency to bring the good news of this act of unmerited grace to a lost and dying world. It is not enough to believe in the cross and resurrection of Christ. We must personally be crucified and buried with Christ and rise with Christ to new life in the Spirit. Yet even this is not all that is required of us. We must also be fired by a burning zeal to share this salvation with others. To be evangelical therefore means to be evangelistic. We are not to hide our light under a bushel but manifest this light, so that God might be glorified in the world (Matt 5:15–16).

Following on this, he lists the following key elements: biblical fidelity, apostolic doctrine, the experience of salvation, the imperative of discipleship, and the urgency of mission. Commenting on these, he emphasizes that evangelicals stress the need for a personal experience of the reality of Christ's salvation, as well as the need to carry out the great commission to teach all people to be his disciples and to call all nations to repentance. A number of further elements then follow.

First, Evangelicals have an eschatological hope, a hope for the second coming of Christ. The kingdom that is already present is still to be consummated and fulfilled, not merely by a gradual evolution of humanity, but by a cataclysmic intervention of the Son of God.

Second, Evangelicals maintain a high view of Scripture. They affirm its divine authority and its full inspiration by the Holy Spirit. They speak of the inspiration of words as well as authors, though they do not commit themselves to any theory of mechanical inspiration or dictation. They acknowledge Scripture as the medium through which those who earnestly seek, will hear the voice of the living God.

Third, Evangelicals have a high view of God. They affirm his sovereignty over the world, and their absolute dependence on Him, although they are reluctant to speak of God's absolute power, since this connotes arbitrariness and lawlessness. They prefer to speak of God's sovereign will and to understand this as a will to love. Instead of focusing on God's eternal decree, they dwell on the power of his suffering, yet conquering love. By contrast, theologies that concentrate on the unrestricted, absolute power of God, as well as those that posit a secret will of God at variance with his revealed will, are in philosophical rather than biblical territory. The heart of the gospel is that God loves the whole world, and that He justifies the ungodly.

Fourth, Evangelicals have a high view of human beings. We were given dominion over the animals and made only a little lower than the angels. We were created in the image of God. Evangelicals are pessimistic about what human beings can do on their own, but optimistic about what God can accomplish in and through them. Grace does not reduce humans to nothingness, but instead raises them to fellowship with their Creator. On the other hand, Evangelicals are agonizingly aware of humanity's despair and sense of being lost. Therefore, they accept the responsibility to call all human beings to trust in Christ for their salvation. Thus far Bloesch's definition of Evangelical Theology.

Let us consider attempts by different authors to identify a few central aspects of the evangelical faith.

Bebbington, writing about modern Britain, offers what he calls a quadrilateral ("four corners") of priorities as the basis of Evangelicalism: *conversion*, evangelism, *the Bible* and the cross of Christ (1989:3 – he uses a different terminology). Askew numbers four characteristics most Evangelicals affirm (note Askew's use of a qualifying term: "most"): the Bible as the sole authority for belief and practice; conversion as a personal experience; the *nurture* of spirituality and holiness; and *mission*, including both evangelism and social reform (Dayton and Johnston 1991: 261). In one of his brief descriptions, Bloesch goes more or less in the same direction:

> The key to evangelical unity lies in a common commitment to Jesus Christ as the divine Saviour from sin, a common purpose to fulfil the great commission and a common acknowledgement of the absolute normativeness of Holy Scripture (1983:5).

In more or less the same manner, Smith describes what Evangelicals have in common:

SECTION A
THEOLOGY

a thoroughgoing commitment to the authority of the Bible; a personal experience of salvation from sin, received in a moment of living faith; and finally an outreach in missionary evangelism (Dayton and Johnston 1991:262).

A further point he makes is that Evangelicals have these in common notwithstanding the fact that they include at least four different (in fact, widely divergent) branches in America: Methodist Armenianism, Puritan Calvinism, Pietism and the so-called "Peace Churches". Yet another voice can be added with the same effect. Packer characterizes Evangelical Theology as the doctrine of God's free and sovereign grace to sinners that is again and again expressed in opposition to what is false, as Paul spoke against the Judaizers, Augustine against Pelagius, Luther against Erasmus, Calvin against the Scholastics. He then lists four key features of Evangelical Theology.

First, a *biblical perspective*. The Bible is God's instruction: true, trustworthy. The Holy Spirit inspired and interprets it.

Second, a *Trinitarian shape*. God is Yahweh, the Father, Son and Holy Spirit. Grace is the work of this triune God, whereby the Son redeems and the Spirit renews sinners whom the Father chooses.

Third, *a radical view of sin and grace*. Human nature fails through badness, not just weakness. Our fallen state is one of total depravity and therefore total inability to respond to God in the correct way. Thus salvation is by grace only, through Christ only, received by faith only, and presupposes nothing in us other than total need. No theology takes a lower view of the natural human being, but no theology takes a higher view of saving grace or of the glorious hope God has provided for us in Christ.

Fourth, *a spiritual view of the Church*. This is what the Reformers called the *invisible* church, which does not mean that the church is altogether invisible, but rather that the deepest truth and reality of the church is invisible and is an object of faith. The church is believing people, and as such it is visible. But its faith is not visible, nor is Christ in whom it believes nor the Spirit through whom it believes, nor the fact that it is the body of Christ or the temple of the Spirit. Nor is the fact visible that some of the participants may not be believers. All this means that it is improper to identify the church with what we see. The church is always more a mystery of faith than an object of sight. Thus far Packer (King 1973:20ff.).

From the fairly extensive treatments of Bloesch and Packer, it is obvious that the more detailed a description becomes, the more the specific background and peculiar emphasis of the author will shine through. Packer is Reformed and strictly Calvinistic in his theology. Bloesch is Neo-Orthodox. Evangelical theologians from Holiness or Armenian backgrounds will have different emphases. However, on the whole it is clear that a high view of the Bible, a definite experience of conversion as a personal relationship with Christ and active involvement in witnessing to Christ will be included in all or at least most of the descriptions of the core of Evangelical Theology.

5.4.2 Diversity and disunity in Evangelical Theology

The Evangelical Movement draws on an amazing variety of churches which are directly or indirectly related to it. A list of these churches – even restricted to North America – would be unmanageable. What is offered here, is only the traditions from which these churches come: the Reformed tradition, Mainline Pietist traditions, Holiness churches, Pentecostal Churches, Independent Charismatic Churches, Restorationist Churches, Dispensationalist Churches, churches of the Radical Reformation, the Free Church tradition, Lutherans and other mainline churches such as the Southern Baptist Convention, which is the largest of the United States Protestant churches and includes some prominent members of the Evangelical Movement like Billy Graham and Harold Lindsell (Ellingsen 1988:136ff.).

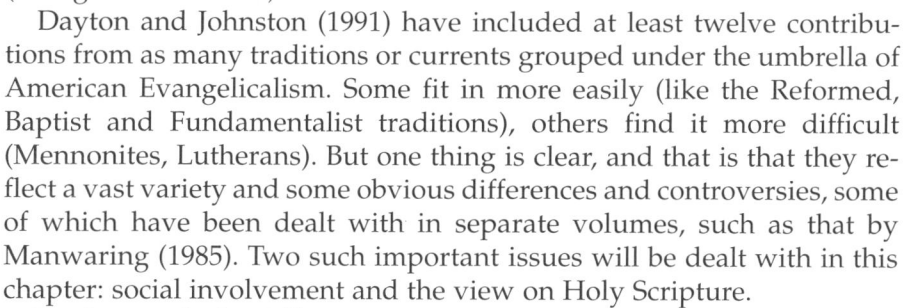

Dayton and Johnston (1991) have included at least twelve contributions from as many traditions or currents grouped under the umbrella of American Evangelicalism. Some fit in more easily (like the Reformed, Baptist and Fundamentalist traditions), others find it more difficult (Mennonites, Lutherans). But one thing is clear, and that is that they reflect a vast variety and some obvious differences and controversies, some of which have been dealt with in separate volumes, such as that by Manwaring (1985). Two such important issues will be dealt with in this chapter: social involvement and the view on Holy Scripture.

Dealing with the differences in the Evangelical Movement regarding social involvement will include a number of related problem areas like eschatology, slavery, the feminist issue and the so-called Social Gospel. Let us start with one major difference on eschatology.

Eschatology and social involvement

Pre-millenialism stands sharply contrasted to post-millenialism, claiming to be not so much a theology as a view on history, and a very negative and pessimistic view for that matter (Dayton and Johnston 1991:6), whereas post-millenialism has an optimistic view and opts for active involvement of Christians in society at large (Marsden 1980:48ff.).

Pre-millennialists expect the second coming of Christ *before* (pre-) the millennium (that is, a thousand years of peace on earth) and they expect it **soon**, while post-millennialists expect Christ's return *after* (post-) the millennium. Evangelical eschatology in North America was dominated by post-millenialism up to the Civil War (1861–3), but largely turned pre-millennial after the war. This resulted in opposing views on involvement in society. Christians who expect a time of peace before Christ's return tend to see social involvement and reform as part of a process in preparation for this millennium. The pre-war revival tradition (Finney, Blanchard, Wesleyan Methodists) took this position as part of the Old American dream of a Christian America (Ellingsen 1988:64), and has therefore fostered a strong social involvement. The recent surge of Dominion Theology is part of this mindset.

Pre-millennialism has a strongly negative view of history, particularly

SECTION A
THEOLOGY

because they expect an *imminent* end. Things will go from bad to worse until Christ comes to judge. Pre-millenialists reject popular notions of human progress and believe that history is a game that the righteous cannot win. People may be redeemed in history, but history itself is doomed. History's only "hope" lies in its own destruction (Weber in Dayton and Johnston 1991:6). Some even argue that efforts to ameliorate social conditions would merely postpone the "blessed hope" of Christ's return by delaying the process of degeneration that is to be completed before his second coming (Dayton 1976:126). Obviously, this attitude resulted in radical withdrawal from social reform and stands virtually diametrically opposed to the earlier involvement in social issues, such as the anti-slavery campaign (Wilberforce et al) that we dealt with earlier on. Moberg entitles his book on the Evangelical withdrawal from societal issues *The Great Reversal* (1972). Dayton calls it the tendency to abandon long-range social amelioration for a massive effort to preach the gospel to as many as possible before the return of Christ. The vision is now one of rescue from a fallen world (1976:127). According to Dayton, this shift in eschatology is difficult to overestimate. One of the most striking contrasts between pre-Civil War revivalists and those who come after the war is that the former founded liberal arts colleges (introducing students into cultural values) while the latter established Bible schools which provided a minimal knowledge of the Bible before the students were rushed into mission situations to gather as many souls as possible before the imminent return of Christ.

The rise to prominence of the Reformed Theology of the so-called "Old Princeton School" during the 19th century strengthened this aloofness towards social involvement (Dayton 1976:128ff.). This Reformed aloofness continued well into the 20th century (Dayton and Johnston 1991:217ff.). The theology of the Old Princeton school is represented in the 19th century by theologians like Charles Hodge, A.A. Hodge and B.B. Warfield. This theology sided with the aristocracy and higher social classes, and incarnated extremely conservative social views, explicitly affirming that the church should be a conservative force in society. Towards the end of the 19th and the beginning of the 20th century, they strongly opposed the Social Gospel (to which we shall return shortly) but earlier on they opposed various social reforms, including the abolitionist (anti-slavery) campaign, insisting only that slave-holders follow certain biblical norms that would moderate the extremes of slavery. They also opposed the women's movement that emerged from abolitionism and which spoke up against the subjection of women in society, church and family. Charles Hodge defended a very specific role model for women. He lauded "a delicate woman adorned with the inward graces and devoted to the peculiar duties of her sex," but he deplored "a woman forgetful of her nature and clamorous for the vocations and rights of men". Princeton theologians opposed suffrage for women, arguing that the idea of two autonomous votes in a single household was irreconcilable with the biblical doctrine of the headship of the husband.

In contrast to this reaction against social involvement (represented by post-millennialism, Old Princeton Theology and Fundamentalism – which will be dealt with later on), we find not only the pre-millennialist views, but also the Social Gospel as part of Evangelicalism.

Although it is often questioned, it seems that the Social Gospel of the end of the 19th and beginning of the 20th centuries can indeed be related to a specific Evangelical background, *inter alia* to the revivalist tradition of Charles Finney (1792–1875). The Princeton theologians reacted negatively against Finney. He identified strongly with the poor, the slaves and the masses, and advocated very definite social involvement with their plight.

The differences between Old Princeton Theology and Finney have specific theological backgrounds. The Princeton theologians emphasized the graveness of sin and total depravity. They strongly resisted any notion that the grace of God can overcome sin in this life. Finney, on the other hand, placed great weight on the power of God to transform sinful persons and society. The discussion of women's issues is a good example of the different implication these views have for societal matters. The Princeton theologians focus on the curse in Genesis 3, arguing that the subordination of women as part of the curse provides a universal principle to be adhered to. By contrast, Finney sees the curse as a result of sin that can be overcome by redemption. This implies that women should be elevated to a position of equality, especially in the church (Dayton 1976: 131ff.).

The woman issue is at present again a highly divisive factor in Evangelical Theology. Conservative theologians tend no longer to emphasize the subordination of women and the inequality of men and women, but rather the different roles divinely allotted to both, so that women have a divine calling to serve and especially to raise the next generation, whereas men have the role of leadership in the family, the church and society at large. The issue of the ordination of women has brought this controversy to a head, and a fierce battle is currently being fought in the Evangelical Movement. The Social Gospel can rightly claim a place in the background of the Evangelical Movement:

> Evangelical Christians in other eras previous to the 20th century had been extremely active in the social realm. One of the most damaging myths perpetrated by those evangelicals ... committed to the status quo is that orthodox Christianity has always been the ally of the establishment. (Wells and Woodbridge 1975:218)

The fact that social involvement need not counter the basics of the Evangelical Faith is clear from the writings of the foremost representative of the Social Gospel, Walter Rauschenbusch, who emphasizes the indispensability of "spiritual regeneration" and states: "If, therefore, our personal religious life is likely to be sapped by our devotion to social work, it would be a calamity second to none" (in: Scott 1971:301). However, he goes on to warn against egotism and self-seeking religious individualism (referring to Thomas à Kempis and John Bunyan) which teach us "to see

5

Evangelical Theology

SECTION A
THEOLOGY

the highest good of the soul by turning away from the world of man" (304), and advocates a Christianity that offers a full salvation. Because sin is a social force, so is salvation. "A full salvation demands a Christian social order which will serve as the spiritual environment of the individual."

After the Fundamentalist "take over" in the 1920s and its gradual decline after the Scopes trial, there has in fact been a general resurgence of Evangelical social conscience in the middle of the 20th century, depicted by Wells and Woodbridge as "The slumbering Giant finally reawakes" (1975:220).

Ellingsen distinguishes between three Evangelical positions of social concern at present: conservative, moderate, and radical social concern (1988:273ff.). The following presentation relies largely on his division.

The conservative social concern accommodates quite a variety of approaches, from Arch-fundamentalists (Bob Jones University), through Jerry Falwell's Moral Majority to the views of *Christianity Today* and the Billy Graham group. Some Arch-fundamentalists even strongly criticized Jerry Falwell for entering the political scene at all – however conservative he is, because that would mean co-operating with people who are not born again.

This conservative approach, though taken from a variety of sources, generally has a lot in common. It supports legislation against abortion, pornography, homosexuality, and against the propagation of secular humanism in the schools. Advocates of this approach are either strongly opposed to, or at least suspicious of the feminist movement and the peace movement, and traditionally opposed communism and government welfare. They uncritically accept democracy and the "American way of life". On the other hand, most of these people are not reactionary. Both Jerry Falwell and *Christianity Today* are on record in support of racial justice and equal rights, and Billy Graham, though emphasizing the individual and conversion, clearly teaches that, through the individual, the gospel has social implications and that these implications are part of the gospel itself, because there is but one gospel (Moberg 1972:165ff.).

The moderate social concern is represented by Carl Henry, *The Reformed Journal* (of the Christian Reformed Church in the USA), John Montgomery and like-minded theologians. Again, this is not a monolithic group, and can be distinguished in a moderate conservative (like Carl Henry) and a moderate liberal group (like *The Reformed Journal*). In general, however, one could say that they do not accept western capitalism uncritically, they support the limited use of abortion in certain special circumstances, and they insist on the necessity of reforming social institutions, not just individuals. On the other hand, they are to be distinguished from the radical Evangelicals in that they still have confidence in the possibility of reform *within the structures of the American system.*

The radical social concern is represented by people like John Alexander *(The Other Side)*, the Evangelical liberation theologian Orlando E.

Costas, radical Evangelicals like John H. Yoder, Lucille S. Dayton, Clark Pinnock and Ron Sider. Some of them come from the new left of the 1960s like the "Jesus Movement". Again, this is not a well-defined group, but in general they tend to argue for international resource distribution, the simple lifestyle, disarmament, feminism, and they strongly identify with the poor. They are Evangelical in that they are committed to the authority of the Bible (though they would not support the inerrancy views of Fundamentalism), the importance of a regenerated lifestyle and evangelism.

Most of the radical Evangelicals add another dimension to the commitment to a regenerate lifestyle: an overwhelming focus on Christian community. According to them, the only context in which human beings can become truly human, is in a community based on the biblical model, a type of alternative community or extended family in which all goods are shared.

John Yoder (a Mennonite theologian) has developed an Anabaptist model according to which the faithful withdraw in such communities, renunciating all political power and opting for absolute pacifism. Reference can be made to the Peace Churches and the Mennonite and Brethren Churches, which are still part of the Evangelical Movement.

Needless to say, the more conservative Evangelical constituency severely criticizes some of these positions, but the radicals are still somehow part of the broader Evangelical Movement. This illustrates the point already made more than once about the profound diversity the Evangelical Movement accommodates. (Ellingsen 1988:282)

The Bible

Turning to the second major issue of diversity and even disunity amongst Evangelicals, their view of the Bible, the differences are as grave as those on the social involvement of the Church.

A high view of Scripture has always been part and parcel of Evangelical thought. The summaries of the main points of the evangelical faith testify to this. But the development of Fundamentalism in the early 1920s radicalized the view on Scripture. This was the peak of a reaction against the liberal views of German theology in particular (called "higher criticism" in those days by conservatives).

Although the appeal of the Fundamentalist Movement on the power structures and public life at large in North America died down after 1925 because of the Scopes trial, the movement intensified its efforts to book growth in countryside areas and even grew strongly in the period after World War II. Its very conservative views on Scripture continue to make a great impact even today. This can be illustrated by the conflict in the Southern Baptist Convention, where conservatives have tried to oust Neo-Orthodox faculty members from the Seminaries during the past fifteen years (Hefley 1986, 1987, 1988, 1989).

It is not easy to clearly distinguish certain positions. There are extremes, and also a number of positions in between. In Britain, the strug-

SECTION A
THEOLOGY

gle has not been so grave, and the more moderate views on the Bible have remained dominant. In a very general statement, Bebbington writes: "It was rare for spokesmen, let alone scholars, in the Evangelical community (in Britain, A.K.) to claim that the Bible is free from error" (1989:189). He gives a number of reasons and circumstances for this.

In North America, however, it was a different situation ever since the 1920s. From the Fundamentalist side, theologians were not satisfied with the confession of the inspiration, authority and even inerrancy of the Bible, but opted for much more strict formulations such as *verbal* inspiration, *absolute* authority and the *total* inerrancy and infallibility of *everything* the Bible affirms. These views were accompanied by very strong emotions. Those who did not hold them were seen as a danger to the faith and the church.

The group(s) on the other side can also not all fit neatly into one specific view. They were (and are) called liberals and modernists, but many of them see themselves as Neo-Orthodox and have been influenced by Karl Barth and German Biblical Theology in general. They tend to give much more thought to the history of theology and to some important distinctions concerning the Bible. They claim adherence to specific Lutheran and Calvinistic views. Bloesch states that

> Calvin, too, upheld biblical infallibility and inerrancy without falling into the delusion that this means that everything that the Bible says must be taken at face value. He felt remarkably free to exercise critical judgement when dealing with textual problems. He tells us ... that Jeremia's name somehow crept into Matthew 27:9 "by mistake" ... Again he was prone to doubt the Petrine authorship of 2 Peter ... (1978:66)

Bloesch continues by pointing out that the Reformers tended to make meaningful distinctions in their view of the Bible, like the inward content and the outward form of the Bible, or the Bible as the certain and unerring rule – but then rule of *faith* and not of science. Views like those of Calvin speak against the sweeping statement by Lightner (1986:6) that for two thousand years the Christian Church has agreed that the Bible is "... infallible and inerrant" simply because Lightner reads his views on inerrancy back into Church history, instead of taking seriously what the Fathers meant by such concepts.

During the 1970s an intensive discussion was waged, especially in Western Europe, on the meaning and intentions of the Bible. Some agreement was reached on the general view that there are specific things Bible writers want to say, and in these they are trustworthy or infallible, but not in general, nor in the cultural idiom they use to express their message.

This more relaxed view is, however, strongly and emotionally rejected by the Fundamentalists and their soulmates. Francis Schaeffer claims that what he calls "the limited inerrantists" have shattered Evangelicalism (Ellingsen 1988:296), the argument mostly being that if there would be only one mistake in anything a Bible writer affirms, we can no longer be sure about anything the Bible affirms. This again is rejected by Neo-Orthodoxy as a modern, neutral definition of inerrancy which is not applicable to the specific intentions of the Bible. It demands total inerrancy, that is "literal, exact, mathematical precision, something the Bible cannot provide" (Bloesch 1978:66).

This controversy in the Evangelical Movement is so important and devastating to the identity of the movement, that in his discussion Ellingson suggests that "all distinctiveness of the Evangelical movement seems forfeit" – and adds what may come as a shock to people tendering the Evangelical Movement: "To be sure, this could be a real cause for ecumenical celebration." However, he limits this observation to the "left" of the Evangelical Movement, and suggests that for the right the well-known Evangelical characteristics still hold good, especially the inerrancy doctrine of the Bible (1988:296ff.).

5.5 FUNDAMENTALISM

The phenomenon of Fundamentalism needs a separate discussion. It is often simply used as a synonym for Evangelicalism, but this is not acceptable. In fact, one should distinguish three possible meanings of the concept "Fundamentalism." If used in a restricting theological sense, Fundamentalism refers to a specific view on the inspiration of the Bible, the belief that since the Bible is the Word of God and God cannot err, the Bible must be inerrant. Fundamentalism taken in a sociological sense describes "a group so fanatically committed to its religion that it lashes out against opponents in mindless denunciation." Fundamentalism used in a more general theological sense refers to the defense of fundamental Christian beliefs. Only in this sense can the term be applied to the Evangelical Movement with any degree of plausibility (Bebbington 1989: 275ff.).

In fact, it is exactly this third meaning that the term had at the inception of the Fundamentalist Movement early in the 20th century: a defense of the fundamental Christian beliefs against the rise of Liberal Theology, and more specifically, against the historical-critical approach of the Bible, and the theory of evolution. Reference has already been made to the introduction of the historical-critical method and to the reaction of the Old Princeton School against it.

Opposition grew towards the end of the 19th century, and the organized form of this opposition came to be known as Fundamentalism in the early 20th century. According to Bloesch, "Fundamentalism has for the most part been a defensive movement designed to safeguard the supernatural elements of faith" (1983:24), but Marsden calls it "militantly antimodernist Protestant evangelicalism" (1980:4). A series of twelve booklets were published from 1910 to 1915 entitled *The Fundamentals: A Testimony to the Truth*, defending the fundamental doctrines of traditional Evangelical faith. Some 300 000 copies were distributed free of charge to ministers and theological students throughout the English-speaking world. The general tone of the contributions was irenic and well-balan-

SECTION A

THEOLOGY

ced. Distinguished conservative Calvinist and Armenian scholars from America and England contributed, but the series originally had only minimal effect (Ellingsen 1988:50).

During the same time, the *Scofield Reference Bible* (1909) was published. It took a strong pre-millennialist-dispensationalist position and was widely accepted and employed by Fundamentalists. Also in this time (1910), the Presbyterian Church in the USA accepted the Five Point Deliverance, which included

- the inspiration and infallibility of the Bible;
- the virgin birth of Christ;
- the substitutionary atonement of Christ's death;
- his literal resurrection; and
- his second coming (Ellingsen 1988:49,89).

The deity of Christ was later added to the virgin birth, but it should be noted that the inerrancy of the Bible was not part of the earlier movement. Gradually, other important issues came to the fore, so that Wells and Woodbridge put the following list together, which represents a later stage of development:

- The eternal pre-existence of the Son as the second person of the one God;
- the incarnation of God the Son in man as the divine-human person – two natures in one person;
- the virgin birth, the means by which God the Son entered into the human race and, without ceasing to be fully God, also became fully man;
- the sinless life of Christ while sharing the life and experiences of alien men apart from sin;
- the supernatural miracles of Christ as acts of his compassion and signs of his divine nature;
- Christ's authoritative teaching as Lord of the church;
- the substitutionary atonement in which God did all that was needed to redeem man from sin and its consequences;
- the bodily resurrection of Christ as the consummation of his redemptive work and the sign and seal of its validity;
- the ascension and heavenly mission of the living Lord;
- the bodily second coming of Christ at the end of the age;
- the final righteous judgement of all mankind and the eternal kingdom of God;
- the eternal punishment of the impenitent and disbelieving wicked of the world.

From the two preceding lists one can form a fairly clear picture of the main emphases of the earlier part of the programme of the Fundamentalist Movement. Generally speaking, however, it should be characterized a little further. Marsden does it in the following way:

> Fundamentalism was a mosaic of divergent and sometimes contradictory traditions and tendencies that could never totally be inte-

grated. Sometimes its advocates were backward looking and reactionary, at other times they were imaginative innovators. On some occasions they appeared militant and divisive; on others they were warm and irenic ... (1980:43)

The emphasis should, however, be on the first half of every pair of opposites. He also includes a diversity of traditions in this movement, like the Holiness tradition, the Millennial tradition, and denominational traditionists – the latter including both Calvinists and Arminians. B.B. Warfield (to mention but one specific person) was a Presbyterian who represented the Old Princeton (scholastic) Theology, and he despised the newer holiness teachings and disdained dispensationalism, yet he co-operated with them in the larger Fundamentalist Movement and, in fact, made an important contribution to Fundamentalism, as did the Old Princeton theologians in general (Marsden 1980:102ff.).

Bloesch identifies four hallmarks of the Fundamentalist Movement: its eschatology, separatism, rationalism, and emphasis on personal salvation (as opposed to social involvement). These will briefly be discussed, as well as the Fundamentalist view of the Bible and its opposition to Darwinism.

The first hallmark of the Fundamentalist Movement is its eschatology. The eschatology most generally taught in these circles includes a visible, imminent return of Christ prior to his millennial reign on earth, which, in turn, will be prior to the final consummation of all things – a view rejected by supporters from both Reformed Theology (which is amillennial) and Puritan and Pietist Theology (which are post-millennial). One strand of Fundamentalism has adopted the dispensational scheme in which the total course of history from creation till consummation is divided into seven dispensations. The one prior to the New Testament times is the dispensation of the law; the New Testament one (in which we still live) is the dispensation of grace, and the coming millennial reign of Christ on earth will be the final dispensation. Dispensationalism has been given strong support and prominence by the Schofield Reference Bible.

The second hallmark is Fundamentalism's separatism. In the early 1920s, when they were very influential in some of the bigger churches, they tried to take control and purify these churches, but after the Scopes trial they fell into disfavour and started separating themselves from these churches (whom they called apostate churches). In some cases they even enacted a so-called "double separation" in which they also separated themselves from those Evangelical churches who were not willing to separate from the apostate mainline churches. Many Fundamentalist groups were even annoyed with Billy Graham, who co-operated with non-fundamentalist Christians in his crusades.

The third hallmark is Fundamentalism's rational approach. As a defensive movement, it tends to be strongly apologetic in its approach to justify the Christian faith in terms of human reason. C. van Til calls Christianity "an absolute rationalism". Other fundamentalist groups,

SECTION A

THEOLOGY

however, maintained an anti-intellectual attitude, becoming anti-Rome, anti-ritual, anti-biblical criticism, anti-Darwin and anti-worldliness (Manwaring 1985:121).

The fourth hallmark of Fundamentalism is its very specific emphasis on personal salvation (like the rest of the Evangelical Movement) and on the *spiritual* task of the church. Fundamentalists do have some social involvement, but tend to associate with capitalism, neglecting the plight of the poor and the oppressed. They foster a very close relationship between Christian values and "the American way of life" and regard prosperity as a blessing from God on his obedient children.

Fundamentalism's high view of the Bible can come as no surprise, since it originated as an opposition group to the growing influence of the historical-critical method of exegesis. In general, the reaction was less strict in Britain than in North America (Henry 1976:48ff.). In Britain, strong views on verbal inspiration and total inerrancy were seldom held by spokespersons and scholars of the Evangelical Movement, and were rather restricted to popular Evangelical circles. Even very conservative scholars tended to be more articulate, like Henry Wace, Principal of Kings College, who represented a strong conservative position, but nevertheless held only to the "substantial truth" of the Bible – which fell short of absolute inerrancy. Like Luther, he had an eagerness to grasp the leading truths of the Bible "without becoming a slave to verbal inerrancy" (Bebbington 1989:188ff.).

In North America, the situation was different, at least partly due to the strong and strict views of the Old Princeton School. B.B. Warfield developed an extensive view on the Bible. On inerrancy, his position was that the Bible is "through and through trustworthy in all its assertions, authoritative in all its declarations, and down to its last particular, the very World of God ..." (Rogers and McKin 1979:345). For Warfield this meant "the complete trustworthiness of Scripture in all its elements and in every, even circumstantial statement."

These views held by Warfield and other Princeton theologians became institutionalized in the "Five Point Deliverance" of the Presbyterians in the early 1920s and in this way became a "fundamental confession of faith" for the Fundamentalist Movement (Ellingsen 1988:74). This fact is easily recognised in some of the well-known statements by Fundamentalist theologians, such as "the Bible is inerrant in everything it asserts" (or declares).

A number of arguments have been used to support this view, like:
- The Bible is the Word of God and because God cannot lie, there can be no errors in the Bible (cf. Lightner 1986:28).
- If we concede even only one error in the Bible, everything may be false and our faith in total jeopardy.

The influence of this view of Fundamentalism never died away and has recently been defended in North America during the controversy that erupted between the Conservatives and the Moderates in the Southern Baptist Convention in the 1980s (Hefley 1986, 1987, 1988, 1989, especially 1986:27ff.).

In conclusion, Fundamentalism's opposition to Darwin's theory of evolution will be discussed in some detail because it ended in a public fiasco for the movement.

The anti-evolution campaign developed quite differently in North America and in Britain. This is yet another example which shows that there often were significant differences between these two countries. Like the inerrancy issue, this one was handled with a lot more venom by the Fundamentalists in America, and the outcome was much more disastrous for Fundamentalism.

In America, evolution did not become a divisive issue within Fundamentalism, but rather a common cause to unite fundamentalist groups and make them more aggressive than before. In fact, the issue of evolution was one of the main causes which led to what is often called a dramatic transformation of conservative evangelicals between 1917 and 1920 (Marsden 1980:141ff.).

Partly as a result of more radical forms of theological liberalism after World War I, the World's Christian Fundamentals Association (WCFA) was formed in 1919, and the cultural and the school issue was tackled aggressively by the fundamentalists. Pleas like "Make the country safe for children" captured the imagination. A.C. Dixon, former editor of *The Fundamentals*, articulated the connections between the school issue, civilization and theological decline, emphasizing the danger of the theory of evolution that was in those days fairly widely taught at public schools (Marsden 1980:161ff.). He portrayed evolution in the darkest possible colours. It was part of the "conflict of the ages, darkness versus light, Cain versus Abel ...". He related Darwin to Greek philosophers before 300 B C who "descended from Cain". Darwin, he said, had added the idea of the survival of the fittest, which Dixon described as giving "the strong and fit the scientific right to destroy the weak and the unfit." This again could be linked with Germany, with Nietzsche's doctrine of the super-man (*Übermensch*), and with the historical-critical approach to the Bible that developed primarily in German theology. According to him, if taken together, these things inevitably led to the atrocities of the Germans in World War I. Against this dark onslaught on Christian values and civilization, he glorified American civilization as one founded on the Bible, and on democracy and freedom. America had always defended the weak and the oppressed against the oppressors, as in World War I when she defended Britain and her allies against German aggression. In this way Dixon, as one amongst a number of fundamentalist leaders, set the agenda for a massive public onslaught on what they saw as the anti-democratic, "might is right", Bible-denying theory of evolution.

Soon after the 1920 conference of the Northern Baptists, where Dixon launched his major attack on evolution, Williams Jennings Bryan emerged as a prominent spokesperson for the movement (Marsden 1980: 161ff.). He was not a theologian but a politician, in fact a three-time candidate for the presidency of the United States (Ellingsen 1988:84ff.). Bryan described evolution not only as merely an hypothesis, "guesses

Evangelical Theology

SECTION A
THEOLOGY

strung together", but also as brutal atheistic materialism which should be removed from schools and colleges. Bryan's cause resulted in an immense surge in the popularity of the Fundamentalist Movement, and the campaign to keep Darwinism out of American schools swept through the South, especially in rural areas. After 1923, several Southern States had adopted some type of anti-evolution legislation. The law passed in Tennessee (1925) was the strongest. It banned the teaching of Darwinism in any public school (Marsden 1980:185ff.; Ellingsen 1988:90ff.). A biology high school teacher, John Scopes, was soon accused of teaching evolution, and a test case was financed by the American Civil Liberties Union. Bryan came to the fore to assist the prosecution. The most famous American criminal lawyer, Clarence Darrow, volunteered his services to help the defence.

Though Scopes was found guilty (but later acquitted on a technicality) the result of the "Monkey Trial" was disastrous for the cause of Fundamentalism. Brian, who testified as an expert witness (but who was a politician and not a theologian) and insisted on a literal interpretation of the Bible, could not handle the questions posed by Darrow. He again and again had to admit that he could not reconcile apparent conflicts and that he did not have answers to many relevant questions. For example, he acknowledged that he never thought about what would happen if the earth stopped in its rotation so that the sun could "stand still". Towards the end of the cross-examination, Darrow objected to Bryan's aggressive innuendoes by saying: "I am examining you on your fool ideas that no intelligent Christian on earth believes." The press sided with Darrow and Scopes against Bryan and the majority of the population of Dayton, ridiculing the Fundamentalist position as that of mindless bigots (fanatics) opposed to all that was intellectually respectable. This spelled the end of Fundamentalism's popular support, at least in the centres of American power (Ellingsen 1988:90ff.).

But that was not the end of Fundamentalism. It entered a period of withdrawal and separation, creating its own subculture that enabled it to survive America's great economic depression in the 1930s. In fact, the years prior to World War II proved to be a time of numerical growth similar to that encountered at the beginning. The movement made use of media shows like Charles Fuller's "The Old Fashioned Revival Hour". In the 1950s, its social involvement regained some strength, inter alia in the strident anti-communism of Billy Hagis and the American Council of Christian Churches of Carl McIntire (later changed to the International Council of Christian Churches – the ICCC).

The emergence of the Neo-Evangelical Movement (Bloesch 1983:29ff.) in the middle of the 20th century won over many Fundamentalists, but the Fundamentalist Movement nevertheless continued to flourish in the 1950s and 1960s. In the 1970s and 1980s their influence was even more profound, as can be seen in the growth of the Moral Majority of Jerry Falwell that has already been referred to.

During the 1980s, Fundamentalism clearly developed into two major segments. The "militant" Fundamentalism carries the commitment to separation to the extreme, and insists on "double separation" (already referred to). The second segment is the more "open" Fundamentalism (represented by Jerry Falwell and the Baptist Bible Fellowship) which does not demand double separation (Ellingsen 1988:93ff.).

The problem of evolution remained on the agenda of the Evangelical Movement, but different views developed and, on the whole, American Evangelicals do not seem as traumatized by this issue as their predecessors in the 1920s were (Wells and Woodbridge 1977:269ff.).

In Britain it was a different story. Evangelicals learned to live with the theory of evolution. A.C. Dixon, with his vehement attack on Darwinism, was seen by British Evangelicals as flogging a dead a horse. When the anti-evolution campaign reached its climax in North America in 1925, there was virtually no interest in Europe in the relations between science and religion (Bebbington 1989:207).

READING LIST

Bloesch, D.G. 1978. *Essentials of Evangelical Theology. Volume One.* New York: Harper and Row.
– 1979. *Essentials of Evangelical Theology. Volume Two.* New York: Harper and Row.
Dayton, D.W. and Johnston, R.K. 1991. *The Variety of American Evangelicalism.* Downers Grove: Intervarsity Press.
Ellingsen, M. 1988. *The Evangelical Movement.* Minneapolis: Augsburg.
Grenz, S.J. 1993. *Revisioning Evangelical Theology.* Downers Grove, Illinois: Intervarsity Press.
Henry, C.F.H. 1976. *Evangelicals in Search of Identity.* Waco: Word Books.
Manwaring, R. 1985. *From Controversy to Co-existence. Evangelicals in the Church of England 1914–1980.* London: Cambridge University Press.
Marsden, G.M. 1980. *Fundamentalism and American Culture.* New York: Oxford Press.
Moberg, D.O. 1972. *The Great Reversal. Evangelism versus Social Concern.* London: Scripture Union.
Rogers, J.B. and Mckin D.K. 1979. *The Authority and Interpretation of the Bible.* New York: Harper and Row.

BIBLIOGRAPHY

Adeyemo, T. 1979. *Salvation In African Tradition.* Nairobi: Evangelical Publishing House.
– 1991. In: *Scriptura* 39.
Bebbington, D.W. 1989. *Evangelicalism in Modern Britain – A History from the 1730s to the 1980s.* London: Unwin Hyman.
Bediako, K. 1992. *Theology and Identity.* Oxford: Regnum Books.
Beetham, T.A. 1967. *Christianity in the New Africa.* London: Pall Mall Press.
Bloesch, D.G. 1978. *Essentials of Evangelical Theology. Volume One.* New York: Harper and Row.
– 1979. *Essentials of Evangelical Theology. Volume Two.* New York: Harper and Row.
– 1983. *The Future of Evangelical Christianity.* Garden City: Double Day.
Carnell, E.J. 1959. *The Case of Orthodox Theology.* Philadelphia: Westmister Press.
Darwin, C. 1979. *The Illustrated Origin of Species.* London: Faber and Faber.

SECTION A

THEOLOGY

Dayton, D.W. 1976. *Discovering an Evangelical Heritage*. New York: Harper and Row.
Dayton, D.W. and Johnston, R.K. 1991. *The Variety of American Evangelicalism*. Downers Grove: Intervarsity Press.
De Gruchy, J. 1978. In: *Journal of Theology for Southern Africa*. No. 24.
Ellingsen, M. 1988. *The Evangelical Movement*. Minneapolis: Augsburg.
Evangelical Witness in South Africa. Dobsonville: P O Box 200.
Falk, P. 1979. *The Growth of the Church in Africa*. Grand Rapids: Zondervan.
Grenz, S.J. 1993. *Revisioning Evangelical Theology*. Downers Grove, Illinois: Intervarsity Press.
Hastings, A. 1979. *A History of African Christianity*. London: Cambridge University Press.
Hefley, J.C. *The Truth in Cirsis*. Vol 1: 1986; Vol 2: 1987; Vol 3: 1988; Vol 4: 1989. Hannibal: Hannibal Books.
Henry, C.F.H. 1976. *Evangelicals in Search of Identity*. Waco: Word Books.
Hindson, E. (ed.). 1976. *Introduction to Puritan Theology – A Reader*. Grand Rapids: Baker Book House.
Hodge, C. 1952. *Systematic Theology*. Volume One. Grand Rapids: Eerdmans.
Humphreys, F. (ed.). 1983. *Nineteenth Century Evangelical Theology*. Nashville: Broadman.
Jackson, G. 1978. In: *To the Point*. June 2.
Kato, B.H. 1975. *Theological Pitfalls in Africa*. Kisumu: Evangel Publishing House.
King, J.C. 1969. *The Evangelicals*. London: Hodder and Stoughton.
– 1973. *Evangelicals Today*. London: Lutterworth.
Lightner, R. P. 1986. *Evangelical Theology*. Grand Rapids: Baker Book House.
Manwaring, R. 1985. *From Controversy to Co-existence. Evangelicals in the Church of England 1914–1980*. London: Cambridge University Press.
Marsden, G.M. 1980. *Fundamentalism and American Culture*. New York: Oxford Press.
Mclaughlin, W.G. 1968. *The American Evangelicals, 1800–1900*. New York: Harper.
Moberg, D.O. 1972. *The Great Reversal. Evangelism versus Social Concern*. London: Scripture Union.
Rogers, J.B. and Mckin D.K. 1979. *The Authority and Interpretation of the Bible*. New York: Harper and Row.
Scott, W.A. (ed.). 1971. *Sources of Protestant Theology*. New York: Bruce Publ. Co.
Tienou, T. 1985. In: *Evangelical Review of Theology*. 9.1
– 1987 In: *Evangelical Review of Theology*. 11,1.
Voll, D. 1963. *Catholic Evangelicalism*. London: The Faith Press.
Walker, D. 1989. In: *Journal of Theology for Southern Africa*. No 67.
Wells, D. F. and Woodbridge J.D. 1977. *The Evangelicals*. Grand Rapids: Baker Book House.

6

Black Theology

Simon Maimela

6.1 INTRODUCTION

Black Theology refers to an aspect of the rather recent theological genre known as Liberation Theology. This world-wide theological phenomenon encompasses a variety of related, but nuanced and distinctive features, *inter alia*: the Latin-American Theology of Liberation which wrestles with class domination and oppression; Black Theology which deals with problems of racial domination and oppression in North America and South Africa; the Feminist Theology which calls the attention of the church to the perennial problem of male domination and exploitation of women in all societies. What characterizes this type of Liberation Theology is that it arises from the experience of one or other form of human oppression, thus focusing attention on the concrete and particular broken relationships in society. These relationships manifest themselves in various forms of alienation and these theologies try to find ways of resolving the conflicts in the light of the gospel, so that people can at least break out of oppression and bondage and come to liberation and freedom.

6.2 THE SOCIAL CONTEXT OF BLACK THEOLOGY

Black Theology owes its origin to the unique experience of the people of colour (especially of African descent) in North America and South Africa, where people's blackness was enough justification to subject them to a life of pain, humiliation, degradation, exploitation and oppression. That is, Black Theology is a particular theological response and is correlative to a unique situation of racial domination and oppression. By racial dom-

SECTION A

THEOLOGY

ination we refer to that conscious or unconscious belief in the inherent superiority of all people of European ancestry, a superiority which entitles Whites to a position of power, dominance and privilege, and which justifies their systemic subordination and exploitation of people of colour, who are regarded as inferior and consequently doomed to servitude.

In North America, racial domination revolved around the history of slavery which was brutal, degrading and had a shattering effect on the Black personhood. For after being captured, millions of Africans were driven like animals, treated as beasts of toil, shipped across the seas and stripped of their language and culture. Not only did racism determine the most basic institutions of American society, but also ensured that Blacks were to remain on the fringe of society, deprived, dependent, humiliated, depersonalized and without justice, freedom or a share in the political, economic and cultural spheres. In South Africa, Blacks were victims of racial oppression not because of slavery per se, but because of European settler colonialism, which used its cultural, scientific, economic and military power to subjugate the people of colour, to rob them of their dignity by subjecting them to a systematic destruction of their personhood through physical and spiritual torture, intimidation, degradation as well as denial of basic human rights.

Put somewhat differently, Black Theology owes its origin to a painful racial situation in which the colour of one's skin had enormous socio-political value. In this context, your colour determines your fate and the quality of life that is open to you, because your entire life is determined by the fact that you are black or white. Where a person may live, where a person may work, what bus or train to use, which schools or churches to attend, which restaurant or toilet s/he may use, whom s/he may love and become a neighbour to – all these things were determined by whether s/he is black or white.

6.3 THE ORIGINS OF BLACK THEOLOGY

It is out of this painful context of oppression, dehumanization and destruction of black personhood that Black Theology was born as a theological protest against racial domination and human beings' inhumanity to other human beings. Black Theology can thus be defined as a conscious, systematic, theological reflection on black experience, characterized by oppression, humiliation and suffering in white racist societies in North America and South Africa. But the history of black struggle against the forces of white racism, domination and oppression stretches further back in history, when black church leaders broke away from white churches for racial, political and theological reasons, thereby laying the foundations for later explicit Black Theology. Indeed, in racial societies where the Christian faith was co-opted and used to justify the enslavement and colonial domination of one racial group by another, it was only natural that the oppressed Blacks, reflecting on their situation in the light of the Gospel, would reject current Christianity and affirm their humanity, thus turning the Gospel into an instrument for resisting the extreme demands of racial oppression. In doing so, the oppressed Blacks gave birth to Black Theology, which seeks to interpret these oppressive conditions in the light of the biblical God whose justice demands that the oppressed and downtrodden be set free. Black Theology, as a response to White Theology which sanctifies racist social institutions, is thus a passionate call to freedom; it invites all the people of colour to authentic human existence and freedom in God's name.

6.4 THE TERM "BLACK THEOLOGY"

Black Theology derives its name from the unique black experience in racist societies upon which it reflects, where one's human identity is determined by one's whiteness or blackness. In order to appreciate what is at stake here, it is important to note that the concept "black" in western cultural and religious societies has always had a negative connotation, apart from the fact that Whites tend to be dominant and oppressive towards Blacks. In these societies, the concept "white" has always been understood as positive and good while "black" was negative and bad. Scriptures tended to reinforce that outlook by teaching that Jesus would wash our hearts whiter than snow while sin blackens us. Black clothes thus became the symbol of mourning while white clothes were the symbol of joy. People speak of "a black day" or "a black mood". Now in situations in which skin colour play a decisive role and people are divided into white and black, the very blackness of some people is often spontaneously understood to refer to something that is dirty, bad, inferior and shameful, and therefore something which is to be rejected. Indeed, because racism has racially undermined and called into question the human-beingness of the people of colour, it has caused Blacks to despise themselves and feel ashamed of their God-given black humanity, because it is difficult for them to understand why their blackness should call forth such contempt, hatred and wanton violence from white people.

Against this background it was to be expected that, if it was to have any positive message to proclaim to black people – so that Blacks could once again affirm and seek to realize their God-given true humanity – Black Theology could not identify itself with White Theology that tends to reinforce the myth of making whiteness the norm of what is authentically human. Rather, Black Theology had to speak positively about blackness as a legitimate form of human existence, authorized by God the Creator. It had to declare unequivocally that humanity includes black humanity and that, if God became truly human in Jesus to liberate humanity, Jesus Christ was a black liberator from white racist oppression. In other words, to talk about blackness is to make both theological and philosophical statements: it is to declare, on one hand, that blackness is one's gift from God about which Blacks need not feel ashamed or apologize for, and on the other, it is to say that because to be black is *not* to be a *non person*, a nothing, a person without a past worth knowing about, **Black is beautiful and is something to be valued and feel good about**.

SECTION A

THEOLOGY

Now, this affirmation of black humanity by Blacks themselves, in racist societies where black personhood was questioned and denied, is nothing short of the miraculous. For it involves a qualitative leap of the sort that can only be comparable to a radical transformation of the heart and mind of the black person; it amounts to a rebirth and total conversion that enables Blacks to participate in the creation of their new humanity in Christ, the black liberator.

In order to avoid misunderstanding about the name Black Theology, it needs to be borne in mind that (apart from the fact that in a situation where one's identity is determined by one's whiteness or blackness, it is a logical consequence of the incarnation that Christ or theology be represented as white or black) the concept blackness has a twofold meaning in the black theological rhetoric: First, blackness is a physiological trait, referring to particular people who happen to have a black skin colour and are historically the victims of white racism. Second, blackness is an *ontological* symbol which refers to a situation of oppression as well as to an attitude, a state of mind that is determined to work with and alongside God, who always sides with the oppressed and underdogs to liberate humans for the freedom for which they were created. The latter aspect of blackness is the universal note of Black Theology, pointing to human solidarity in suffering and struggle on behalf of and together with all the oppressed peoples. When Jesus is called the black liberator, it concerns this latter meanings of blackness.

6.5 THEOLOGICAL TRENDS IN BLACK THEOLOGY

Given the fact that Black Theology has undergone two phases of evolution in its development, it was to be expected that there would be different emphases within it. In other words, Black Theology is not monolithic and does not say the same things all the time. This is simply because its production involved many theologians of different persuasions and temperaments – all they shared was their common black humanity which was under attack from white power structures. Without trying to be exhaustive, a few of these trends will be highlighted here.

6.5.1 The Black Solidarity trend

This type of Black Theology, which covers the period 1970–1980, emerged in South Africa during the first phase of Black Theology and is represented by Black Solidarity theologians such as Sabelo Ntwasa, Mokgethi Mothlabi, Ernest Bartman, Manas Buthelezi, Bonganjalo Goba, Allan Boesak and Desmond Tutu. Sabelo Ntwasa, who was director of the Black Theology Project under the auspices of the University Christian Movement, played a major role in the early stages of this theological trend. After he was banned, Mokgethi Motlhabi carried forward the major thrust of the Black Solidarity trend as director of the Black Theology Project and helped to edit the first book on Black Theology, entitled *Essays on Black Theology* (Johannesburg: UCM, 1972). Manas Buthelezi, as a young professionally trained theologian, made a greater contribution to Black Theology, leaving an indelible stamp on it. Not surprisingly, Motlhabi refers to him as "the leading black theologian at the time of the inception of Black Theology" (Mosala & Tlhagale 1986:47).

The formative contributions of Desmond Tutu and Ernest Bartman, through sermons and writings, were also of significance. It was during the middle of 1970 that Boesak also played a part in this first trend through his published doctoral thesis entitled *Farewell to Innocence* (1976). Bonganjalo Goba, who was also among the early proponents of Black Theology, has become the standard-bearer for the solidarity type of Black Theology. Even though he appreciates the new insights that emerged in other trends of Black Theology, Goba has not been persuaded to move away significantly from the Black Solidarity type of Black Theology.

6.5.2 The Black Solidarity-Materialist trend

This theological trend began to emerge towards the end of the 1970s, especially after the banning of black consciousness organisations in 1977. However, it gained prominence after the revival of the Black Theology Project under the auspices of the Institute for Contextual Theology (ICT) in 1981. It was particularly during the theological conferences sponsored by the ICT in 1983 and 1984 under the respective themes of *Black Theology revisited* and *Black Theology* and *Black Struggle*, that one could sense the tensions that existed within the Black Theology Movement.

Proponents of the Black Solidary-Materialist trend also argue that Black Theology and black consciousness should be closely correlated because the latter is the ideological framework of the former. To put it somewhat differently, Black Theology builds on, and is parasitic on, black consciousness. Hence, Mofokeng correctly points out that Black Theology and the philosophy of black consciousness are not only "inseparably united" but are also "twin sisters", that is, two sides of the same coin. Indeed, the one cannot exist without the other; for it is in their mutual complementarity that they constitute useful instruments for effective liberation for the oppressed Blacks. Therefore, the Black Solidarity-Materialist trend agrees with the first trend on one fundamental point, namely that the philosophy of black consciousness is the basis in forging Black Solidarity in the struggle for the liberation of oppressed Blacks. Both would further agree that such a liberation cannot be effected by Whites, however sympathetic they might be to the cause of the black struggle. This is because Whites lack the fundamental existential experience of what it means to suffer humiliation and oppression as Blacks under white power structures.

However, the Black Solidarity and the Black Solidarity-Materialist trends differ in some important respects. The former puts a greater emphasis on white racism as the root cause of all evils in their social analysis of the black oppression, while the latter argues that the former South African society should be viewed as basically a class society in which class divisions were determined by racial divisions (Kritzinger 1988:140). In other words, it is the systematic concentration of material wealth and political power in the hands of the white race which has enabled it to propagate and perpetuate a rigid racially-based class structure in South Africa (1988:140)

The major representatives of the Black Solidarity-Materialist trend are Simon Maimela, Takatso Mofokeng, Itumeleng Mosala, David Mosoma, Lebamang Sebidi and Buti Tlhagale. One distinguishing feature of the exponents of this trend is that they put emphasis on both theory and praxis, arguing that theoretical analysis is as important as fighting in the streets. Hence they have been very prolific in their writings.

6.5.3 The non-racist trend

Some of the proponents of this trend originally belonged to the Black Solidarity trend, especially during the formative stage of Black Theology in the 1970s. However, in the 1980s they moved from the Black Consciousness Movement in order to identify themselves particularly with the non-racial United Democratic Front (UDF) which was largely based on the Freedom Charter. The distinguishing feature of this trend is that it has openly softened the traditional black consciousness stand on no alliances with the white "democrats" or "progressives". Instead of emphasising the racial character of oppression, they have now embraced categories of class and gender – thus showing a strong influence of the Latin American Theology of Liberation. Since they emphasise the need for solidarity with the poor and oppressed, regardless of existing racial divisions, the non-racialist trend has given rise to a Black Theology which rejects the tenets of an exclusive black consciousness perspective on the black struggle for liberation, which is characteristic of the other two theological trends. Whether theologians who belong to this camp will, in the future, still continue to call themselves black theologians remains to be seen, especially after the election of a non-racial and non-sexist democratic government during April 1994.

The main representatives of the non-racialist trend are Manas Buthelezi, Allan Boesak, Frank Chikane, Shun Govender, Smangaliso Mkhatshwa and Desmond Tutu.

The above discussion should give a fairly good idea that Black Theology, as it has been developed in South Africa over the past 25 years, does not speak with one voice. Its proponents advocate divergent approaches to the analysis of oppression. Hence, some give priority to the racial character of oppression, while others also add the categories of class and gender.

6.6 SOME EMPHASES IN BLACK THEOLOGY

6.6.1 The world is in conflict between the oppressor and the oppressed

As already indicated, Black Theology is born out of the historical experience of suffering and pain because of white oppression and domination of people of colour. In consequence, Blacks could not help but become aware that they are poor, powerless and dominated not by accident or by divine design. Rather, they are made poor and impotent by another class of people, the white dominant group that denies Blacks the right to shape their lives. It is this awareness of being *made* poor and *rendered* powerless that leads Blacks to opt for a radical change which often involves them in a confrontation with white racists who want to maintain the present unequal material relationships. Thus, reflecting theologically on the inhumanity to which white racism has subjected them, Blacks find themselves thrown into a situation in which they cannot avoid seeing the world as a battleground between the white oppressors and oppressed Blacks. Indeed, the fact that white racism tries to encourage Blacks to accept the already established social order, despite the fact that it is unjust, oppressive and dehumanizing to Blacks, is taken as a conclusive evidence that far from being serene and normal, the world is in a state of conflict. It is polarized between two groups, the powerful and dominant Whites who benefit from the oppressive socio-political conditions and the exploited and dominated Blacks who are victims of racism.

In view of this conflict between the dominant Whites and oppressed Blacks, Black Theology insists that *the reality of our conflictory world should become a subject, a datum for theological reflection*. This constitutes a major departure from traditional theology which, as a theology practised from the point of view of the privileged, well-fed and rich Whites, tries to close the eyes of many Christians to the reality of conflict between White oppressors and oppressed Blacks, who are unable to live and work together in harmony. By focusing on the conflictory nature of the racist societies, Black Theology is able to confront more realistically and concretely the reality of the sinful alienation between Whites and Blacks. It thus highlights the fact that the conflictory nature of our world is symptomatic of human fallenness into sin, namely, one of a fundamental breach of fellowship between God and humans, and between human beings themselves. Racism is understood as the sinful refusal to love, to have fellowship and to be available for the well-being of one's neighbour, who happens to have a different skin colour. This fundamental sin of alienation is the cause of injustice, oppression and the will to dominate others, resulting in conflict and polarization between white oppressors and oppressed Blacks. In order to confront this sin of racism, Black Theology calls for the radical transformation of individual and social structures, because the gospel message proclaims that, in Christ, the alienation between God and humans, and between human beings themselves has been overcome. Indeed, the gospel as the free gift of God holds the promise that reconciliation and fellowship between the oppressor and the oppressed could become experienced realities in this conflictory world, for the gospel has the power to bring a total conversion from, and a break with, past oppressive tendencies, thus creating a profound solidarity between white oppressors and oppressed Blacks. Black Theology contends that it is as people candidly face the racial factors that breed alienation and conflict that they will be open to the transformative power of the gospel, which will lead Whites and Blacks to acquire qualitatively new ways of becoming human in their relationships to one another.

SECTION A

THEOLOGY

6.6.2 The divine preferential option for the poor and oppressed

Given the fact that the racist world is characterized by a conflict between the oppressors and oppressed Blacks, it follows that any theology which acknowledges this conflict can no longer afford to remain socially and politically neutral. The struggle between the oppressor and the oppressed is ultimately one of life and death, in the midst of which the church and its theology must take sides out of the conviction that the demands of the gospel are incompatible with unjust, alienating, and polarizing social arrangements in racist societies. In consequence, Black Theology, as an incarnational theology, places a high premium on the fact that in becoming human in Jesus, God, the King of kings was not born in the sumptuous palaces of kings. Rather, the Almighty and transcendent God chose to empty the Godhood of divine power and glory in order to take on the nature of a slave. God came down from his throne and chose to be born of poor parents, to live and die as a poor and oppressed human being so as to give the oppressed Blacks new life and hope. In doing so, our Creator, in Jesus, chose to identify the divine Being with human suffering and pain and to let Him share in it so that God might win freedom and life in its fullness for the downtrodden. This, as Black Theology points out with insight, is what lies at the core of the lowly birth of Jesus in a stable manger, because there was no room in the inn for the God-incarnate. In his ministry, too, Jesus is numbered among those who are despised and rejected by society, thus demonstrating that God is no neutral God, but a thoroughly biased God who was forever taking the side of the oppressed, of the weak, of the exploited, of the hungry, homeless and of the scum of society.

Black theologians are persuaded that the motif of God's preferential option for the poor and oppressed runs through the Bible like a red thread. It is discernable in the Exodus, in which God took the side of the oppressed Israelites against the oppressive Pharaoh and his underlings. God did not side with the Israelites because they deserved to be delivered. No, the issue was not that a particular people were sinless, loveable and therefore savable. Rather, the issue was the concrete evil of oppression, injustice and suffering to which the enslaved and exploited Israelites were subjected. It is in an encounter with those manifestations of evil that God cannot help it but feel constrained to come out on the side of the poor, the oppressed and downtrodden. Similarly, this divine partiality in defense of the interests of the poor and underdogs is made known also by the fact that Jesus identified himself with the marginalized in the manner of his birth, his life and his death. As a consequence, Jesus was numbered among those who were rejected by society. For he deliberately chose as friends, not the Priests, Sadducees, Pharisees and Scribes, but the sinners, the prostitutes, the traitors, the scum of society. In short, his companions were the *sick ones who desperately needed a physician and knew it*. The others thought they were whole. And in opting to side with the oppressed and downtrodden, God declared that He is not prepared to put up with social situations in which the poor and the powerless are oppressed and humiliated on the grounds of colour, religion or class. Consequently, black theologians argue that, just as God liberated Israel not only from spiritual sin and guilt, but also from oppressive socio-political and economic deprivation, God will liberate the oppressed Blacks both from their personal sins and guilt and from historical structures of evil, exploitation and oppression, embodied in racist social structures.

Black theologians are fully aware that advocating God as the One who takes sides with the powerless in situations of injustice and oppression may sound ruthless and harsh to those who are well placed and privileged in the society. For it now appears that God is no longer neutral, that God has his favourites, and does not love everyone in the same way, be they masters or slaves. However, it is important to remember that we are not dealing here with a question of favouritism or sentimentalism for the sinless poor and oppressed group. In their arguments for the preferential option for the poor, black theologians are proposing a sophisticated hermeneutic approach to the Bible; it is this hermeneutic approach which is important because it provides theology with a critical principle whose sole aim is to provide critical insights for the building up of a more humane society by directing theological reflection to those who are powerless, who are defenceless and disadvantaged, who remain oppressed and marginalized. This critical principle is rooted in the divine principle and God's special concern for the disadvantaged who cannot enforce their rights and defend their personal dignity in a racially dominated society. It aims to provide guidance for Christians working for justice for everyone before, during and after social revolution so that new rulers are prevented from becoming oppressors themselves in the newly created social order by reminding us all that God is offended by human oppressors.

READING LIST AND BIBLIOGRAPGHY

Boesak, A.A. 1977. *Farewell to Innocence*. Maryknoll: Orbis Books.
Goba, B.C. 1988. *An Agenda for Black Theology*. Johannesburg: Skotaville Publishers.
Kritzinger, J.N.J. 1988. *Black Theology: A Challenge to Mission*. (Unpublished doctoral thesis submitted at the University of South Africa, Pretoria, South Africa).
Maimela, S.S. 1987. *Proclaim Freedom to my People*. Johannesburg: Skotaville Publishers.
– 1990. *Modern Trends in Theology*. Johannesburg: Skotaville Publishers.
Mofokeng, T.A. 1983. *The Crucified among the Crossbearers*. Kampen: J H Kok.
Motlhabi, M. 1984. *The Theory and Practice of Black Resistance to Apartheid*. Johannesburg: Skotaville Publishers.
Mosala, J.I. 1989. *Biblical Hermeneutics and Black Theology in South Africa*. Grand Rapids: Eerdmans.
Mosala, J.I. & Thagale, B. (eds.). 1986. *The Unquestionable Right to be Free*. Johannesburg: Skotaville Publishers.
– 1986. *Hammering swords into ploughshares*. Johannesburg: Skotaville Publishers.
Nthintile, P.V. 1992. *Contending Notions of Liberation in Black Biblical Theology in South Africa* . (Unpublished doctoral dissertation at Drew University, Madison, New Jersey, United States of America).

7
Feminist and Womanist Theology
Marie-Henry Keane

7.1 INTRODUCTION

Christian Theology is manifestly pluralistic both in its approach and content. Different theologians have different sets of priorities; they find themselves in different situations; they come from different cultures; and are formed by different religious traditions. Some take Scripture as their starting point and interpret faith and all of reality by reflecting on the holy writ and its message. Others look at the church's beliefs and examine the developments which have occurred over the centuries and attempt to add their own insights to those of scholars who preceded them. Still others look at the contemporary world and try to interpret what God is saying in the circumstances of peoples' lives. Following the example of Christ, they offer a message of hope and salvation in a world in need of both. There are painful questions concerning the elderly, handicapped people, people of colour, women, the poor, and many others, which they would like to see addressed. Has theology, others ask, anything to say to the victims of ageism (the practice of discriminating against people on the basis of their age)? Can it combat the evils of ableism (the lack of consideration and justice towards those with physical or mental disabilities); or racism (antagonism against people on the basis of their race); or sexism (the system of discriminating against women on the basis of gender)? Does it take seriously the lot of the poor in a world where wealth abounds? The answer must be yes and this "yes" must, if need be, result in the emergence of new and creative theologies. Theology should, there-

SECTION A
THEOLOGY

fore, be dynamic and not static, since life itself is dynamic and not static. We have seen, for example, the emergence of Black Theology and Feminist Theology, which focus almost exclusively on the struggles of Blacks and of women. But having said that, we have also to admit that Black Theology did not have its origins in the church or in the academy. It arose out of the Black Consciousness Movement of the 1950s and 1960s. So, too, did Feminist Theology; it developed from the secular Women's Movement of the 1960s. Both movements did, however, awaken theologians to problems related to race and gender and obliged them to reflect on these dilemmas from a perspective of faith.

In this chapter I would like to give an overview of the phenomenon which we call Feminist Theology and say something about Womanist Theology (which emerged a little later at the instigation of black women). I shall also take a brief look at the attempts made by women and men to go beyond feminism to gender studies, that is, to the point where women and men can approach each other as equal partners.

7.2 DEFINING FEMINISM

The term "feminism" originally meant "having the qualities of females" (Tuttle 1976:108). In time, however, it became identified with a movement for the liberation of women. The starting point was woman's experience of being treated as a second class citizen. Not simply the male view, but the white western male opinion had become the yardstick for measuring excellence. That myth had to be debunked, not only for the sake of women but also for the sake of men themselves. Patriarchy (literally, "rule by the father") perpetrates a system of male domination at the expense of women. One of the chief aims of feminism, therefore, is to correct that imbalance by promoting an alternative way of looking at life which takes seriously woman's giftedness and woman's experience. However, one of the major aims is not to "feminize" the world, but to make it more human and hence more just. In its more moderate forms, it should not be seen as an anti-men as much as a pro-people movement. Moreover, it should demonstrate the extent to which life can be enriched when women are allowed to exercise their gifts without hindrance, for the sake of the common good, for the sake of the reign of God.

7.3 FEMINIST THEOLOGY

Christian Feminist Theology, which is a branch of feminism, drew its inspiration from the secular Feminist Movement. Women of faith are aware of their disposition in church and society and are asking critical questions in this regard. Special attention is given to their situation in the church, because far from condemning injustices perpetrated against them in social, political and economic life, the church practised and still practises its own forms of discrimination against them. An examination of the church's two thousand year history shows the extent to which it reflects societal injustices. The task of feminist theologians today, therefore, is to criticize abuses in the church which seriously affect them. They react against being excluded from church offices, and will not submit to their ministries being perceived as "marginal". They are not willing to conform to the feminine stereotypes of patriarchal culture. They feel, in fact, that the sexism of Christian tradition requires the critiquing of virtually all areas of church life; its structures, many doctrinal presuppositions, its use of sexist language, particularly in liturgy and official church documents, and the systematic way in which woman's identity as the image of God has either been denied or distorted (Chopp 1986:140). Many Christian feminists (and these include a sizable number of men who are empathetic towards the cause) are involved in serving the church in a number of ways.

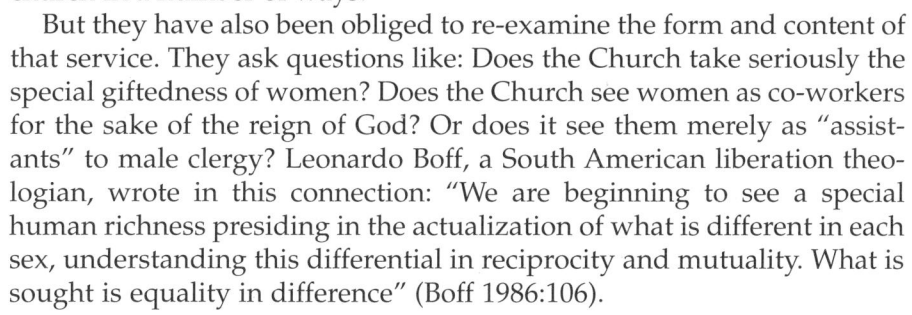

But they have also been obliged to re-examine the form and content of that service. They ask questions like: Does the Church take seriously the special giftedness of women? Does the Church see women as co-workers for the sake of the reign of God? Or does it see them merely as "assistants" to male clergy? Leonardo Boff, a South American liberation theologian, wrote in this connection: "We are beginning to see a special human richness presiding in the actualization of what is different in each sex, understanding this differential in reciprocity and mutuality. What is sought is equality in difference" (Boff 1986:106).

7.4 DIFFERENT STREAMS OF FEMINIST THEOLOGY

Feminist Theology takes context, culture, and religious traditions seriously. The woman's own experience is of primary importance but, since women come from different cultures and have been exposed to different religious traditions, not one but many streams of Feminist Theology have gradually emerged. It is important to bear this in mind, since those who are critical of Feminist Theology tend to paint them all with the same tar brush. Feminist Theology is not a monolithic system. But, in general, we could say that Feminist Theology is either revolutionary or reformist.

Revolutionary feminists believe that the Judaeo-Christian tradition is so intrinsically biased in favour of the male, and so fundamentally patriarchal, that it has to be rejected outright. Radical revolutionary feminist theologians like Mary Daly, for example, advocate a separatist approach. They strive to create an alternative female-centred community and a social life "purged" of male control. Rosemary Radford Ruether on the other hand cautions against seeing men as the enemy, as "defective" members of the human species, for to dehumanise the other ultimately means dehumanising oneself. Moreover, to promote separatism would be counter-productive since it would make it impossible for "moderate" and reformist feminist theologians to realise their dream of building a world where women and men alike can work together, respecting their individual and collective giftedness (Radford-Ruether 1973:13).

Reformist feminist theologians advocate mutuality between the sexes and recognise the importance of examining "her-story" as well as "his

SECTION A

THEOLOGY

story". Women and men alike, they point out, are made in the image and likeness of God (a notion denied by certain of the Early Church fathers)[1]. They suspect the notion of a "male" God. The church fathers argue that everything found in man (sin excepted) is derived from God and had its origin in God. By the same token, feminists would say, everything found in woman (sin excepted) is derived from God and had its origin in God. It is not surprising, therefore, that the notion of the masculine as well as the feminine in God should appear on the feminist agenda and, furthermore, that the notion of the feminine in God can be well supported by referring to very many metaphors found in the Scriptures, as I shall try to show presently.

Reformist feminist theologians recognise, in particular, that patriarchy is not an occasional or localised evil. On the contrary, it is clearly a "universal political structure which privileges men at the expense of women" (Radford-Ruether 1983:108, 230–231). On that account, patriarchy can never be condoned. The reformists opt, therefore, for a steady programme of consciousness raising, in order to make women and men more aware of the effects which systematic tyranny and injustice towards women have on women and men alike. Let me add at once that sexism, like racism, can never be "reformed". It is intrinsically evil. It denies the fundamental truth that in Christ neither gender, nor race nor culture determines the value of a person.

Reformist feminist theologians are aware that they have to persist in their efforts to bring about gradual change and reform. They acknowledge that it will take time to correct the ills resulting from centuries of male domination. Some feminist theologians are more patient than others. Letty Russell, for example, tries to facilitate reconciliation between the sexes since, she holds, human unity is preferable to divisions and whatever damages the integrity or the unity of humanity is wrong because it is wrongly grounded (Russell 1974:62). That is not to suggest that the reformist option is a soft option. It acknowledges that amends have to be made to women who have been sinned against. Indeed, feminist theologians of this kind acknowledge that the physical, mental, psychological and spiritual health of humankind is threatened when artificial restraints are put on the capabilities of people not only because of their gender, but also because of their age, their race, their place on the social ladder or their physical or mental limitations. In other words, far from being an egotistical journey which women embark on for their own ends, the movement has made women conscious that they are not the only ones who have been the victims of circumstance and history. Nor does that blind them to the sad fact that some of their sisters have been bound three times over, not only by being women, but also by being poor and being black. From their perspective, black women found that their agen-

---

1 Augustine expressly denied that woman was made in God's image: "She is not the image of God but as far as man is concerned, he is by himself the image of God" (*De. Trinitate* 12:17). Augustine did subsequently revise his teaching.

da was not fully provided for by Feminist Theology, and as a result they developed Womanist Theology. More will be said about that later.

7.5 WHAT HAS ALREADY BEEN ACHIEVED – A BRIEF OVERVIEW

Feminist theologians today realize that little account has been taken of women's story. They had either been written out of history or neglected or misinterpreted. What has been written was very much "his"-story and very little "her"-story. They feel that a serious re-interpretation of certain areas of Scripture and of tradition needs to be done, and that they themselves are going to do it, using all the skills and tools of serious researchers. They are going back to primary sources, to the Hebrew and Greek Bibles and to historic documents. Let us look very briefly at some of the things that have emerged as a consequence of these studies.

7.5.1 The Scriptures revisited

Bearing in mind that the Scriptures are regarded by Christians as the most important written source of divine revelation, it is unfortunate that they should have been used for centuries to keep women in thrall. Feminist theologians believe that the Bible has to be re-examined. They ask whether their life-experience with its hopes, needs and fears can find "an echo" in the Scriptures. Does the Bible speak meaningfully to their condition? Does it have to be read with "male spectacles", or can it be read through the eyes of women without doing an injustice to the text or compromising women?

It is well to remember that a century ago some work had already been done by Elizabeth Cady Stanton (1815–1902). Stanton was an American philosopher and abolitionist, a woman with many causes, not least of them women's rights and organised religion (which she saw as a way of justifying women's oppression). With the help of several women scholars, she wrote a feminist analysis and critique of the Bible. It was published in two parts in 1895 and 1898 respectively. Today her *Woman's Bible* may not be held in high esteem, for it has not stood up to the rigorous examination of serious biblical scholarship. Nevertheless, she pioneered and gave impetus to further studies by women.

Phyllis Trible has taken up the gauntlet. By focusing on texts in the Hebrew Bible, and at the same time using Feminist hermeneutics, Trible attempts to bring out what she considers to be the neglected themes and lost tokens of faith in the Old Testament Scriptures. In her book, *Texts of Terror: Literary Feminist Readings of Biblical Narratives* (1984), she reinterprets, amongst others, the stories of Hagar, Tamar and Amnon, Jephthah's daughter, and the concubine of Judges 19. She puts on "women's spectacles", as it were, and "digs up" some of our foremothers in the faith and gives them the attention she believes they deserve. In her book, *God and the Rhetoric of Sexuality* (1978), she uses the same approach, but this time she takes a serious look at Genesis 2 and 3. Her interpretation

SECTION A THEOLOGY

of these chapters and of the Song of Songs draws attention to "female" metaphors about God. She looks, for example, at the notions "womb" and "compassion", at "pangs of labour" and at "birth" as found in the texts and does not hesitate to highlight the "feminine" in God. To do this kind of exegesis in the 1970s was regarded as revolutionary, to say the least, but now the "shock" dimension of that way of interpreting Scripture is fast disappearing. Which only confirms feminist belief that commitment to the cause will bear fruit.

When one mentions New Testament feminist scholarship, the name Elizabeth Schussler Fiorenza comes to mind. Her book, *In Memory of Her: A Feminist Theological Reconstruction of Christian Origins* (1987), has already become a classic and is studied by many who investigate the New Testament from a feminist perspective. Fiorenza, like Trible, sets out in search of women's heritage. She attempts to "write women back into early Christian history". She sees this not only as a service to women, but also as a way of giving a richer and more accurate account of our early Christian beginnings. The title of her book comes from Mark 14:9: "Wherever the gospel is preached in the whole world, what she has done will be told in memory of her." The name of the betrayer, says Fiorenza, is remembered, but the name of the faithful woman disciple who anointed Jesus for his burial is forgotten. Fiorenza, too, is a pioneer in her field. She admits that there are hermeneutical, textual and historical problems to be overcome. She succeeds, however, in producing what critics call ground-breaking Feminist Theology, while remaining in communion with the Christian tradition.

On the other hand, certain revolutionary feminist theologians have come to the conclusion that it is impossible to live within the Christian Church, accept the Christian Scriptures and Church discipline and remain a Christian. But Fiorenza, and others like her, have chosen to remain in the church and try to bring about reform from within. They realise, furthermore, that new and creative feminist theological and ethical theories have to be developed to assist the "sisterhood" collectively, since the texts of the Christian tradition are products of an androcentric patriarchal culture and history.

7.5.2 Continuing to reclaim our past

Feminist historians, philosophers and anthropologists alike acknowledge that historiography offers only a selective view of the past. But it is also true that, in general, history has been written by a male hand, a white hand and, furthermore, by a hand of one who belonged to the dominating social class (Chopp 1986). So to reclaim their own story, women researchers have to "dig up the bones" of their valiant foremothers and, using primary sources wherever they can, to reconstruct their own past. We can now take pride in many feminist church historians, but because of the constraints of space, I shall refer briefly only to one of them, namely Elizabeth Clark.

Just as Phylis Trible's work on the Old Testament and Elizabeth

7

Feminist and Womanist Theology

Schussler Fiorenza's work on the New Testament will survive, so too, I believe, will Elizabeth Clark's research on the Early Church period, for she, too, fills in the gaps, weaving her contribution into the "woman tapestry" (as it has often been called) with authority.

Elizabeth A. Clark earned a doctorate in patristic studies and subsequently received many awards and scholarships and was highly respected internationally for her books on the fathers of the early church. These include *Clement's Use of Aristotle* and *The Aristotelian Contribution to Clement of Alexandria's Refutation of Gnosticism*. These are impressive works but, in feminist theological circles, she will probably be best remembered for her role in unearthing the significant women who contributed to the life of the early church.

According to Clark, the fathers' attitude towards women was ambivalent. On the one hand, woman was considered to be God's creation and God's good gift to man. On the other hand, she was regarded as a curse to the world, and weak in mind and character. Furthermore, it seems that early in the church's life, the fathers were convinced, and indeed found "biblical justification", for attributing subordinate status to women. They blamed Eve for original sin and exonerated Adam of all blame. It was through Eve, they said, that sin entered into the world. Tertullian called woman the Devil's doorway. It was her fault, he said, that the Son of God had to die. Using many of the Fathers' letters and treatises, Clark showed how woman has been made a scapegoat from the beginning. She was regarded as morally weak and a trouble-maker. She had to bear on her shoulders the guilt for all humankind. Jerome went a step further: he attributed to women responsibility for all heresy. He even offered an extensive list of the women who were behind every heresy. In the light of the evidence produced by Elizabeth Clark, we cannot take Jerome seriously. The worst that can be said is that certain women were either accomplices or associates of male heretics.

Feminist theologians have tried to account for the anti-women feelings frequently demonstrated by the fathers. Certainly moderate feminist theologians believe that the fathers did not take their cue from Jesus, for New Testament sources do not attribute a single negative statement about women to Him. More than that, He made it clear that relationships within the Christian community were free from dominance (Matt 23: 7–12). Jesus did not subscribe to the social norms of the Graeco-Roman world which distinguished between people on the grounds of race, class, religion or gender (Keane 1988:7–12). He made it possible not only for the "ethne" (gentiles) and slaves, but also for women to participate in the missionary leadership of the church. Yet Origen reduced the ministry of Phoebe to "Paul's assistant", and ever since women in the church have been regarded, more often than not, as assistants or appendages of male ministers and not as protagonists in their own right. (This issue has been taken up again in our own time by women lobbying for the ordination of women).

There was enough evidence to show, says Elizabeth Clark, that there

SECTION A

THEOLOGY

were women of dauntless courage in the early church. Among them were counted the martyrs Perpetua and Felicitas, and women who undertook "prodigious feats of scholarship" (Clark 1983:212) such as Melania the Younger and Melania the Elder. Moreover, Clark draws attention to at least five women who were acknowledged by the fathers as "models" and even became their mentors. Let me just mention one such a woman in passing: Paula, Jerome's friend who laboured with him in promoting monastic life. Together they established a monastery at Bethlehem and when she died in 404, Jerome lamented her passing and wrote an epitaph in her honour. It read: "Farewell, Paula, and with your prayers assist the ripe old age of your friend. Your faith and works unite you with Christ in whose presence you will more easily receive what you ask. I have raised a monument more lasting than bronze which no longer passage of time can destroy. I cut an epitaph on your sepulchre, which I append to this work, so that wherever my letter may go, the reader may know that you were buried in Bethlehem and lauded there" (Clark 1983:212). Collaboration between women and men, it seems, was possible even in an age and culture where the sexes were not generally thought to be equal partners in society at large or within the church.

At the end of the day, it must be admitted that serious injustice has been done to our foremothers. Perhaps one of the reasons why women have not been taken seriously in the past is that women tend to function rather differently from their male counterparts. Feminist theologians today acknowledge those differences and work with them. For one thing, women theologians are more inclined to work in an interdisciplinary way than male theologians do (although this tendency among men is changing too). This could be because, in general, women wish to see the whole picture by viewing it from a number of perspectives simultaneously. Feminist systematic theologians, ethicists, church historians, biblical scholars, sociologists, and other scholarly women have been known to collaborate regularly for the sake of their common objective. This has led to the development of "the sisterhood". In other words, women generally see themselves contributing corporately to the work of reconstruction within the church, the academy and society. They are less inclined to see their contribution as an independent or "private" one. That tendency is, of course, very much in the spirit of the early church with its notion of "corporate personality".

7.5.3 Women who beat the system

Given that able and devout women like Paula, Thecla, Perpetua, Melania and others lived their lives in the shadow of the fathers; that their names are not household words in the way that the fathers are; that they had access to learning only by studying the fathers and under the tutelage of the fathers; that religious women who entered monasteries in relatively large numbers had to submit to rules compiled by men, and not by a rule of life composed by one of their own sex; given that women were regarded not only as morally but also intellectually weak (feeble minded), the time is now long overdue for our foremothers in the faith to be reinstated and given the reverence that is their due. Attempts by feminist theologians and feminist historians to resurrect women's history piecemeal or in part, will undoubtedly have a significant effect on future Christian anthropologies. We have come to realise, and not a moment too soon, that women and men alike share a common history and, having learned from the mistakes of the past, can approach the future with a better sense of what is due to both.

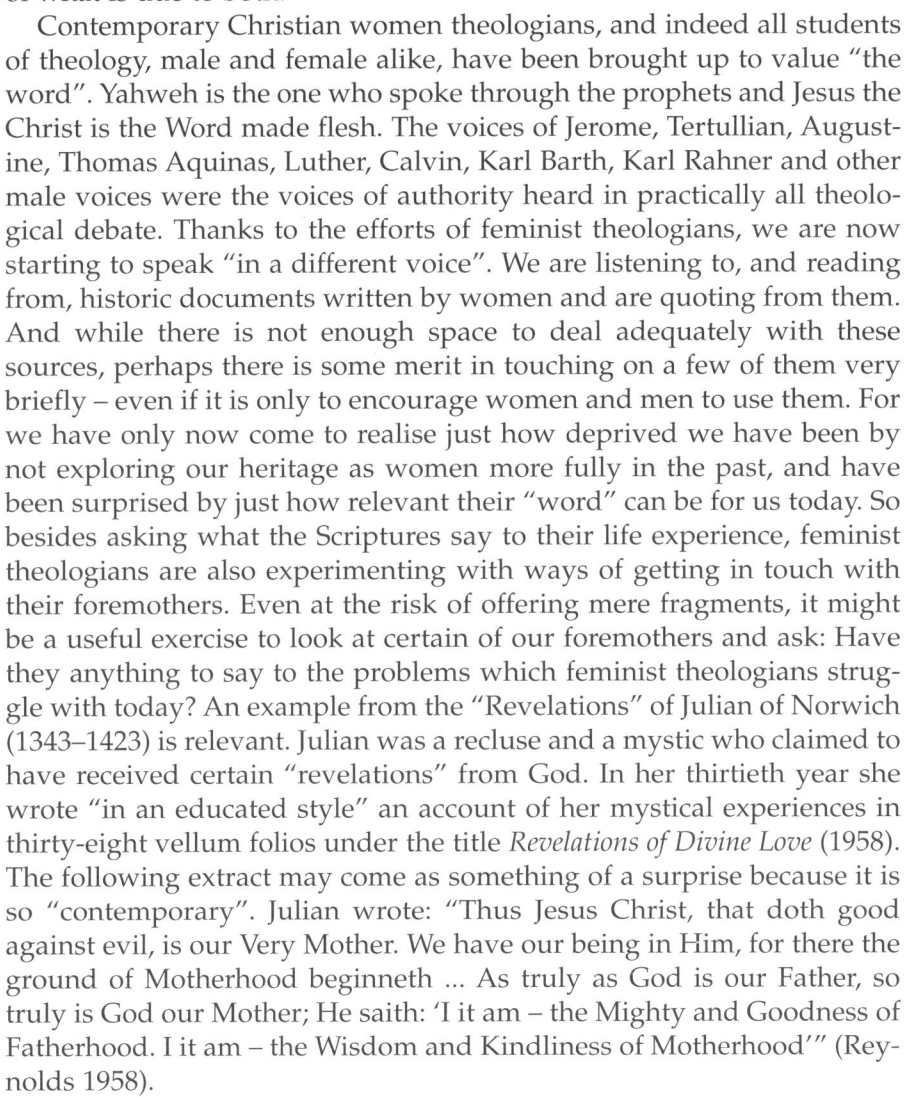

Contemporary Christian women theologians, and indeed all students of theology, male and female alike, have been brought up to value "the word". Yahweh is the one who spoke through the prophets and Jesus the Christ is the Word made flesh. The voices of Jerome, Tertullian, Augustine, Thomas Aquinas, Luther, Calvin, Karl Barth, Karl Rahner and other male voices were the voices of authority heard in practically all theological debate. Thanks to the efforts of feminist theologians, we are now starting to speak "in a different voice". We are listening to, and reading from, historic documents written by women and are quoting from them. And while there is not enough space to deal adequately with these sources, perhaps there is some merit in touching on a few of them very briefly – even if it is only to encourage women and men to use them. For we have only now come to realise just how deprived we have been by not exploring our heritage as women more fully in the past, and have been surprised by just how relevant their "word" can be for us today. So besides asking what the Scriptures say to their life experience, feminist theologians are also experimenting with ways of getting in touch with their foremothers. Even at the risk of offering mere fragments, it might be a useful exercise to look at certain of our foremothers and ask: Have they anything to say to the problems which feminist theologians struggle with today? An example from the "Revelations" of Julian of Norwich (1343–1423) is relevant. Julian was a recluse and a mystic who claimed to have received certain "revelations" from God. In her thirtieth year she wrote "in an educated style" an account of her mystical experiences in thirty-eight vellum folios under the title *Revelations of Divine Love* (1958). The following extract may come as something of a surprise because it is so "contemporary". Julian wrote: "Thus Jesus Christ, that doth good against evil, is our Very Mother. We have our being in Him, for there the ground of Motherhood beginneth ... As truly as God is our Father, so truly is God our Mother; He saith: 'I it am – the Mighty and Goodness of Fatherhood. I it am – the Wisdom and Kindliness of Motherhood'" (Reynolds 1958).

The notion of the motherhood of God and, even more surprisingly, the notion of the motherhood of Christ, ranks high on the feminist theological agenda. It has been the subject of some controversy but, clearly, it is well-grounded in a tradition which has often been overlooked and ignored.

Investigation into women's past has disclosed the presence of a significant number of women mystics, but not all of them were recluses like

7
Feminist and Womanist Theology

SECTION A

THEOLOGY

Julian. Some were seriously involved in public life: Birgitta of Sweden (1303–1373) was one such. Again we see "contemporary" themes running through her writings. She used her power and rank to have the Bible translated into Swedish; she was known to assemble archbishops, political leaders and doctors of theology and quoted to them from her "revelations". She refers, for example, to the "evils of slavery and abortion" which appalled her. She rightly believed that all life was sacred and had to be preserved at all costs. She defended with passion the life of unborn children. She wrote: "Some women behave like harlots; when they feel the life of the child in their wombs they induce herbs or other means to cause miscarriage, only to perpetuate their amusement and unchastity" (quoted in Chevin 1991:27).

One of the most controversial and emotive issues associated with the women's movement is the notion that "biology is destiny", or biological determinism, as it is sometimes called. This notion works from the premise that human nature and society, and the way they function, are dictated by human biology. This notion acknowledges that there are essential and unchanging differences to be found between women and men which are dictated by their physiology. Women are declared "natural home makers" and their bodies are seen primarily as vessels for childbearing. Feminists react strongly against this kind of biological determinism and declare that they are mistresses of their own bodies and their own destiny. This has led certain feminists to adopt a pro-abortion stance. It is also a subject on which feminists are divided for personal, ethical and political reasons. The notion that it is "a woman's right to choose" includes, in the opinion of many, her right to decide whether or not to terminate her pregnancy. This issue is perhaps the most divisive among feminists. Many believe the issue of biological determinism has surfaced in our own day for the first time, but "women sources" in the past confirm that the woman's body, men's attitude towards it, women's sexuality, and especially thinking surrounding her womb and her breasts, have often determined her destiny and kept her in thrall. So the "biology is destiny" experiences of the past need to be heard and abuses addressed even now.

There are a number of recurring themes which appear in the literature of feminist theologians. I have already mentioned some of them above. But "feminine" themes are legion. Let me mention a few and suggest names of foremothers one can associate with them. Women's role in the church: Catherine of Siena (1347–1380) and Teresa of Avila (1515–1582). Women who suffered opposition from church authority: Joan of Arc (d. 1190), Elizabeth Seton (1774–1821), Margaret Hallahan (1803–1868). Women who suffered physical abuse at the hands of men: Rita of Cascia (1381–1457); Maria Goretti (1890–1902). Women who had husbands who were unfaithful to them: Elizabeth of Portugal (1271–1336), Marguerite d'Youville (1701–1771). Women who were the victims of incest: Winifred of Wales (c. 650), Laura Vicuna (1891–1904). Women who were discriminated against because they were disabled: Angela Merici (1474–1540), Germaine de Picrac (c. 1579–1601). Women who suffered extreme poverty: Margaret of Castello (d. 1312).

7.6 WOMANIST THEOLOGY

Clearly, one does not have to be a woman to suffer poverty, be disabled, find oneself at odds with the official church, or be the object of physical or verbal attacks, but feminist theologians and ethicists all over the world are now examining such phenomena from a feminist viewpoint. They recall the experiences of many women who found themselves powerless with no form of redress. Furthermore, research has shown that the women who have suffered most are black and poor. They have endured a triple dose of discrimination on the basis of gender, race and social status. The majority are nameless: black mothers trying to raise families on a pittance; women of colour struggling to educate themselves and their children against all odds; female domestic workers fighting against discrimination and sexual harassment; black women working in industry for long hours in conditions which are injurious to health. Those kinds of abuses could not go on indefinitely.

In North America, black women took up the gauntlet, especially since their problems, their hopes and their fears did not feature prominently in the white middle class feminist agenda, or, for that matter, in the Black Liberation Movement under male leadership. Rosemary Radford-Ruether wrote: "The Black and the Feminist Movements have betrayed the Black Woman" (Radford-Ruether 1975:25).

In 1988, Angela Davies, a black North American activist turned professor of philosophy, wrote authoritatively about the plight of the black women's triple bondage in her book *Women, Race and Class* (1981). She pointed out that black women were not newcomers on the scene. Their long history as slave women still affected their selfperception. Furthermore, emancipation did not substantially reduce their struggles for autonomy or grant them automatic entry to a good education or a comfortable lifestyle. Current struggles had to be seen in the light of that history. She appealed to historians to make the fact of women's pain known so that justice could be done to the memory of our foremothers and that contemporary black women would be able to reflect on their own story. Once again, we come back to woman's root experience and to what it has to say to Womanist Theology today.

Toinette Eugene, an American womanist theologian, is convinced that there is ample material which focuses on the distinctive experience and consciousness of black women during slavery. She quotes from some of her valiant foremothers, who, even today, can be seen as role models. She cites Mary Steward, whose biblical exegetical abilities, coupled with her "modernist thinking", gave black women in the first half of the 19th century a freer rein to express and act upon ideas that liberated them from the oppression of both sexism and racism. Steward wrote in 1832: "God at this eventful period should raise up your females to strive ... both in public and private, to assist those who are endeavouring to stop the

Feminist and Womanist Theology

SECTION A
THEOLOGY

strong current of prejudice which flows so profusely against us at present". And when she and her followers faced ridicule, she retorted; "No longer ridicule our efforts. It will be counted as sin" (Eugene 1984–1985: 23).

In 1851, a Women's Rights Convention took place in Akron, Ohio. On that occasion Sojourner Truth, mystic and abolitionist, delivered her legionary "Ain't I a woman?" speech. She spoke of woman's moral strength and of the power of women's collective efforts to establish justice for black women. She believed that "Moral values, asserted by black women who give credence to the black Judaeo-Christian tradition, honour reconciliation as highly as liberation" (Foner 1972:103). Black women had been hurt physically, emotionally, psychologically and spiritually, but until they had forgiven their oppressors, and had been reconciled to them, they would never be truly free, she said. The rich legacy they had to pass on to their daughters and sons, was their own high moral system which persisted in spite of toil, lash, rape and verbal abuse. In the face of multiple wrongs directed at them, they continued to believe in the salvific power of God.

The emancipation of slaves in North America was dearly paid for, and while it brought great joy and hope to black men, it seemed at times to compound women's problems. Well into the 20th century, lack of education kept black women poor and, at best, semi-literate. But it was their practical biblical faith that was their guiding force, supporting them in their struggles for better educational opportunities, better working conditions and better housing for their families. Black women like Mary McLeod Bethune and Nannie Helen Burroughs ran church schools for Blacks and were impelled by a prophetic sense of purpose. Their agenda was geared towards consciousness raising. Their humble efforts were taken further in due course. Martin Luther King and the Civil Rights Movement drew the attention of the world to racism in North America, but still inherent inequalities persisted on the basis of gender and class.

In 1979, the black feminist writer, Alice Walker, coined the word womanist. It had its roots, she said, in black folk culture, for "womanish" was an expression used by mothers to describe daughters who were courageous, outrageous and wilful (Tuttle 1986:325, n. 24). She did not regard the term womanist as "better" than feminism, but she preferred "the sound, the feel and the fit of it".

A few points need to be made here. First, Feminist, and hence Womanist Theology starts from women's experience (and that includes their cultural reality) which is then reflected upon theologically; second, "abstract ideas" are generally not the focus of interest; third, there is not, as is the case in certain "classical" forms of theology, a sharp line drawn between the sacred and the secular – everything lies within the provident care of God; fourth, womanist theologians remain true to the spirit of the women's movement in using the self-descriptive term "womanist". New and creative forms of theology need new terminology, new symbols and a new inclusive language to express adequately the needs of women of all races. They have heard themselves called "the sons of God" or worse still, the "sons of Abraham, Isaac and Jacob". They have been obliged to praise God in hymns that took no account of the fact that they were women and not men. They heard that "Christ died for all men", and they were taught western forms of theology which ignored their world-view or their reality. Their role within the church was determined by their gender. At the end of the day, feminists/womanists do not intend to eliminate traditional or much loved expressions from the Scriptures or elsewhere, but rather to enrich and expand theological language and imagery by including words that are acceptable from a gender and racial perspective. Third World theologians like Mercy Amba Oduyoye, a Ghanaian, avail of and contribute to this more inclusive approach to language and ideas. They look at the damage done, not only by sexism, but also by racist attitudes and by the injustices of class distinction.

But having said that, womanist theologians are now moving away from seeing themselves as victims; they have self-consciously and in faith begun to take control of their own lives in solidarity with the crucified Christ and with third world women. Oduyoye writes "... Jesus bears in his person the conditions of the weak and hence those of women. However, African women warn that it is vicarious suffering, freely undertaken, which is salvific, and not involuntary victimization" (1988: xvi). Dolores Williams reminds us that Womanist Theology is biased in favour of community and consequently is less concerned with self-interest or self-aggrandizement. The common cause or "sisterhood" is seen as primary. Furthermore, the movement is cyclic and democratic – as opposed to the pyramidal structures of male hierarchical models. Womanist Theology is also mission-minded. It can now go beyond inordinate preoccupation with First World woman issues, conscious that it possesses a truth which neither the church nor the world has yet clearly heard and consequently are the poorer for that. They wish to share their truth with their Third World sisters (and indeed with anyone who has ears to hear) and to learn from the Third World. Katie Cannon writes: "Third World women theologians are long suffering custodians of truth. As outstanding pioneers in the struggle for a globally inclusive church, they are protesting against an uncompleted Christianity"(Oduyoye 1988:vii). The church can try to ignore Womanist and Feminist Theology, but women will not permit it. Cannon believes that Christians are obliged to co-operate with the forces of good and are bound to avoid collaboration with evils such as patriarchy.

7.7 GENDER STUDIES: THE POINT OF MEETING

"When Adam cried 'bone of my bone', 'flesh of my flesh,'" wrote Elaine Storkey, "he was not claiming ownership of the woman, but marvelling at their unity, their oneness." Storkey continues: "In creation terms, humanity was not divided into two autonomous units, each with individual 'essences', but made as an interdependent bi-unity. Each sex needs the other. Each sex complements the other" (Storkey 1985:154).

SECTION A

THEOLOGY

That, in a nutshell, is the basic philosophy of gender studies – mutuality between the sexes.

There are some people who suggest that the war between the sexes is over, that patriarchy has been overcome, that mutuality between women and men has been acknowledged and that men are now willing to rethink who they are, and what their role is in the post-feminist era. It would be too much to think that this is a general tendency, but a start has been made at least. In some quarters, it has been claimed that men are now becoming the victims of oppression, that feminism has taken men apart and not bothered to put them back together again. On the positive side, many men are taking gender studies seriously, for they are beginning to see that it has value, not only for women, but also for men. Women's attempts to re-examine their identity, their role, their interpersonal relationships, their position in church and society, and so forth, had inspired certain men to do the same. Roy Mc Cloughry writes: "It is ironic that men have pontificated about life, the universe and everything ... except themselves. Men seem to be silent about their feelings, their fears, and their hopes ... Men are silent above all about why they have done what women allege they have done" (Mc Cloughry 1989:115). There is an emerging "New Man" who is seriously trying to present himself as the "converted" male. To be acceptable, he is expected to be sensitive, nurturing, friendly, loving as well as dynamic. He is expected to be a good listener, to share the household chores and to like his new image! Theologians, too, are attempting to "reconstruct" man.

The Imago Dei (Image of God) concept is one that comes up in this discussion. It is as women and men together that we express most fully the image of God, as I mentioned earlier. Theologians are also suggesting that Christ is the role model par excellence for man for he is indeed the "New Man", that is the man for others. Men have been perceived as self-centred, competitive, aggressive, as self-assertive, and self-determined. They, too, have suffered from being stereotyped. Not only the Feminist Movement, however, but economic realities, unemployment and new technologies force women and men alike into the market place as equal partners. The move to ordain women has caused ministry, sacramental life, liturgy, ecclesiology and the doctrine of the Trinity, among other fundamental aspects of our Christian life, to be re-examined. Far from fostering unorthodox thinking, feminist theologians claim that such re-thinking will play a significant role in the renewal of the church. It should enrich our notion of what it means to be the body of Christ, the temple of the Holy Spirit and the people of God.

Contrary to what has sometimes been suggested, Feminist/Womanist Theology is not a self-indulgent form of theology. It is about doing justice to more than half of the human race in the first instance, and in the longer term, to all of humanity. Furthermore, it has a significant part to play in the on-going development of a more complete theology and it offers to church and society the richness of woman's history and woman's giftedness.

READING LIST

Paterson Corrington, G. 1992. *Her Image of Salvation: Female Saviours and Formative Christianity*, John Knox Press.
Bethke Elshain, J. 1984. *Public Man, Private Woman*. Princeton Press.
Fiorenza, E.S. 1984. *Bread Not Stone*. Beacon Press: Boston.
Thomas, D. 1993. *In Defence of Modern Man*. Weidenfeld and Nicholson: London.
Tamez, E. 1986. *Against Machismo*. Meyer Stone Books.

BIBLIOGRAPHY

Augustine *De Trinitate* 12:17.
Boff, L. 1986. *Ecclesiogenesis*. Orbis Press: Maryknoll, N.Y.
Chevin, R. de Sola. 1991. *Treasury of Women Saints*. Mercier Press: Cork.
Chopp, R. 1986. *The Praxis of Suffering: An Interpretation of Liberation and Political Theologies*. Orbis Press: Maryknoll, N.Y.
Clark, E. 1983. *Women in the Early Church*. Glazier: Delaware.
Davies, A. 1981. *Women, Race and Class*. The Womens' Press.
Deist, F.E. 1984. *A Concise Dictionary of Theological Terms*. Pretoria: J.L. van Schaik.
Eugene, T.M. 1984–1985. "Moral Values and Black Womanists." *The Journal of Religious Thought*, 41(2).
Fiorenza, E.S. 1987. *In Memory of Her: A Feminist Theological Reconstruction of Christian Origins* Crossroad: New York.
Foner, P.S. (ed.). 1972. *The Voice of Black America*. New York: Simon and Shuster.
Gilligan, Carol. 1992. *In a Different Voice*. Harvard University Press: Mass.
Keane, M.H. 1988. "Women in the Theological Anthropology of the Early Fathers." *Journal of Theology for Southern Africa*, 62
Mc Claughry, R. 1989. *The New Man*. Bath: Ashgrove.
Oduyoye, M.A. 1988. *With Passion and Compassion: Third World Women doing Theology*. Maryknoll, N.Y.: Orbis Press.
Radford-Ruether, R. 1973. *Liberation Theology*. Paulist Press, p.13.
– 1975. *New Woman, New Earth*. Seabury Press:
– 1983. *Sexism and God - Talk: Towards Feminist Theology*. Boston: Beacon Press.
Reynolds, A.M. (ed.). 1958. *A Shewing of God's Love* (The shorter version of *Revelations of Divine Love*). London: Sheed and Ward.
Russell, L. 1974. *Human Liberation in Feminist Perspective*. Westminster Press: Philadelphia.
Storkey, E. 1985. *What's Right with Feminism?* London: SPCK.
Trible, P. 1978. *God and the Rhetoric of Sexuality*. Fortess Press: Philadelphia.
– 1984. *Texts of Terror: Literary Feminist Readings of Biblical Narratives*. Philadelphia: Fortess Press.
Tuttle, Lisa. 1986. *Encyclopedia of Feminism*. Longman.

7

Feminist and Womanist Theology

African Women's Theology

Christina Landman

8.1 INTRODUCTION

African Women's Theology is to be distinguished from Womanist Theology which is practised mostly in North America where black women have a different situation and agenda from black women in Africa. African Women's Theology addresses the specific situation of black women in Africa.

The main issues in African Women's Theology centre around redefining the nature of theology in terms of African women's experiences and re-analysing the relation between traditional theology and culture with reference to patriarchy as an unhealthy contact point between the two. In order to execute these tasks, the training of women in lay and ordained ministries is emphasised. Apart from theological training, religion training is advocated for people of both genders who are religiously minded, but not involved in church-related ministries. The aim of religion training is to create opinion makers in society who will change the patriarchal nature of cultures based on religious stereotypes from within.

8.2 THEOLOGIES OF MIND AND BODY

For a long time, the main difference between men's and women's theologies was this: male theologians took as their point of departure dogmatic principles, while women concentrated on real life stories as the substance of their theologies. Consequently, women theologians were criticised for basing their theologies on "stories from the countryside" and thus for a lack of a philosophically based methodology.

African women's theologians have, in the meanwhile, made an important contribution in the field of methodology by insisting on drawing the "intuitive, the poetic, the lyrical" into theology (Ortega 1995:viii). African Women's Theology acknowledges an integration of mind and body, of philosophical thinking and experience, of academia and activism. Their theology is not dependent on the philosophical meta-language of traditional theologies, but on the language of storytelling, stories which testify to hope as well as to anger, to laughter and sorrow alike, to liberation and to oppression.

8.3 A DIVERSITY OF THEOLOGIES

Theology based on experience leads, of course, to a diversity of theologies, so that it seems more appropriate to speak of African Women's Theologies in the plural. Amongst African Women's Theologies, there are theologies which serve different cultures, theologies which cater for different sexual preferences (including homosexuality) and theologies for church women as well as for men and women who prefer uninstitutionalised forms of inner religion.

However, the diversity itself creates an urgency amongst African women theologians for dialogue and solidarity. A "dialogue of cultures" (Ortega 1995:x), for instance, would offer a critique of African cultures but would also explore the potentially liberative aspects of cultures for the women participating in them. And although not all African Women's Theologies are church theologies, the role of churches in establishing solidarity for women is explored in most of the theologies published.

8.4 WOMEN AS THEOLOGICAL AND RELIGION EDUCATORS

It is only recently that African women were able to take co-responsibility for theological and religion training. Mercy Amba Oduyoye (Ghana/WCC) and Denise Ackermann (South Africa) are an older generation of African women theologians who established a culture of theological literacy amongst women in Africa. This tradition has been cultivated further by a new generation of professional academic theologians and religion scientists such as Isabella Phiri (Malawi), Elizabeth Amoah (Ghana), Nyambura Njoroge (Kenya/WARC), Musimbi Kanyoro (Kenya/LWF), Theresia Hinga (Kenya) and Christina Landman (South Africa). However, many of these women teach and work outside of Africa and influence theological training here only through their publications. At present, many African women theologians train themselves and listen to one another through organisations such as EATWOT and the Circles of African women theologians established all over Africa.

Religion training in Africa, whether it is for ministerial formation or for societal conscientisation in general, aims at establishing the following theologies, ministries and religious insights.

8.4.1 Theologies

Theologies of the mind and the womb not only demystify the superiority of the mind in analysing religious experience, but also deconstruct myths surrounding the physical bodies of religious females – myths based on the high value placed on virginity, and beliefs in the fragility and natural inclination of women to stay away from participation in public life.

Theologies of sexuality create new possibilities for relationships amongst friends, amongst members of families and amongst people in the workplace.

Theologies of relationships replace hierarchal relationships based on dependence with relationships of mutuality (see De Oliviera in Ortega 1995:72).

Theologies of interrelatedness address solidarity between women of different denominations as well as women from different faiths. Theological interrelatedness does not, however, only refer to relationships between God and people, between people themselves and between a person's body and his/her mind. It also includes the relationship between people and nature, a field in which rural women and their experiences can make a special contribution.

African women theologians direct their theologies almost exclusively towards the official scriptures of their traditions. Christian African Women's Theologies are, for instance, primarily Bible-orientated. The stories of people, especially women, in the Bible, bind women from a variety of cultures in Africa together and provide a common source for their healing.

8.4.2 Ministries

One of the special contributions of African Women's Theologies is their emphasis on story-telling ministries as healing ministries. In these ministries, not only the healing of the voiceless, the poor, the powerless and those at the bottom of the hierarchical ladder is at stake, but also the healing of the breach between soul and body, spirit and body, mind and body and other traditional dualities. Healing comes through telling one's story and listening to the previously muted voices of women who are harassed by unfriendly systems and customs.

8.4.3 Religious insights

According to African Women's Theologies, the future for religious women does not lie solely in training women for the ordained ministry. It is the conscientization of religious women from all walks of life that will change patriarchal systems. In this regard it is important to teach women a new type of God-talk that will change societal concepts of a male God who abuses people who challenge the stereotypes of society prescribed to women. Also relevant is the development of a new type of spirituality, a cosmic spirituality which will put women in touch with themselves, with one another and with nature.

8.5 IN SUMMARY

African Women's Theologies aim, in the first place, to incultrate their religious beliefs, that is, to confront culture with belief, but also to accommodate the one within the other. They do this, on the one hand, by critically re-reading their official scriptures and by developing new forms of God-talk and spirituality. On the other hand, they reclaim from their scriptures and religious insights liberative models which they apply to their traditional cultures, thereby acknowledging their African heritage.

In the second place, African Women's Theologies seek the empowerment of women against women-unfriendly social, economic and political systems. Again, they do this by reclaiming models from the source of their theologies, which are the official scriptures.

In the third place, African Women's Theologies wish to provide a climate for interreligious dialogue. The search for solidarity, for healing themselves and nature, binds women together over the traditional boundaries of religions.

The way forward for African Women's Theologies is twofold. On the one hand, the experiences of religious women need to be exposed to the written tradition and retrieved from muteness. A certain level of literacy and academic training is needed for this in order to convey African women's experience to women in other parts of the world. On the other hand, liberative religious insights should be made available to women who do not have access to academic training, and may not even have access to the written word.

READING LIST AND BIBLIOGRAPHY

Ackermann, D. et al. (eds.). 1991. *Women hold up half the sky. Women in the church in South Africa.* Pietermaritzburg: Cluster.
EATWOT women theologians on violence against women. 1995. *Voices from the Third World* 18.1.
Emerging concerns of Third World Theology. 1993. *Voices from the Third World* 16.1.
Fabella, V. & Oduyoye, M.A. (eds.). 1989. *With passion and compassion. Third World women doing theology.* Maryknoll, New York: Orbis.
Maimela, S.S. (ed.). 1994. *Culture, religion and liberation.* Pretoria.
Mosala, I.J. & Tlhagale, B. (eds.). 1986. *The unquestionable right to be free. Essays in black theology.* Johannesburg: Skotaville.
Oduyoye, M.A. 1986. *Hearing and knowing. Theological reflections on Christianity in Africa.* Maryknoll, New York: Orbis.
Ortega, O. (ed.). 1995. *Women's visions. Theological reflection, celebration, action.* Geneva: WCC.
Shope, G. et al. 1994. *Women in Africa.* Potchefstroom: Institute for Reformational Studies.
Spirituality for life: women struggling against violence. 1994. *Voices from the Third World* 17.1.
Vorster, W.S. (ed.). 1984. *Sexism and feminism in theological perspective.* Pretoria: University of South Africa.

African Theology

John S. Mbiti

9.1 AFRICAN THEOLOGIANS AND THEIR CONTEXT

African theologians are people who belong to a particular ethnic group out of 2000 tribes. They live at a particular time and place in history. They are also Christians, members of one of the hundreds of imported church groups, or of one of the thousands of African Initiated (Independent) Churches that have arisen in Africa since the beginning of the 19th century; or they are members of the ancient churches of Egypt and Ethiopia. In this chapter, we will speak of theologians in the latest phase of Christian presence in Africa since the 19th century. They are members of the divided body of Christ which is severely marred by divisions which have arisen in Europe and America or produced locally in Africa.

As African Christians, these theologians are either converts from African religion which evolved without a founder and predates Christianity and Islam; or they belong to the first, second or third generation of Christians. For their local church, the gospel is still very fresh, apart from Christians in Egypt and Ethiopia. They do not have a long history of Christian life behind them, except that which has been imported from overseas through missionaries or other contacts with older Christendom. And because they come from the first to third generation of Christians, the traditional world in all its fullness or richness of culture, history and world-view is still very close to them and their fellow Christians.

Conversion to Christ (and therefore joining the church) does not mean that the individual or the community comes empty-handed into the church. It takes many generations for the gospel to germinate and permeate individuals and the community at all levels of language, culture,

SECTION A

THEOLOGY

world-view, social institution and values. Theologians are part and parcel of this traditional African world – it influences them directly or indirectly, and their theologising cannot ignore this fact.

Furthermore, this traditional African world is very close to the world of the Bible, with many parallels in the social, political, cultural and religious aspects of life. Indeed, the African Christian feels much at home in the world of the Bible. For traditional Africa, the world of the Bible is not a past world of two to three thousand years ago, but a real world of yesterday, today and tomorrow. Theologians are at home in the mythological stories of creation in Genesis, in the social institutions of Jewish people at the time of the kings and judges, at home in the sentiments of the Psalms, in the wisdom of the Proverbs; indeed, they are at home in the parables of Jesus, in the encounters of Jesus with the sick and those possessed by unwanted spirits. The Bible is very much an African book, in which African Christians and theologians see themselves and their people reflected and in which they find a personal place of dignity and acceptance before God.

At the same time, African theologians live in a rapidly changing world, with many social, political and economic challenges. Some of the contemporary events are devastating, such as the ethnic war which took place in Rwanda during 1994 and cost the lives of an estimated one million people. Most of these people were killed in brutal ways, including thousands who had taken refuge in churches. Since political independence from colonial rule started from 1955, many military coups, civil wars and dictatorial regimes have shaken our continent (including Madagascar and other islands) and have resulted in the deaths of thousands of children, women and men, as well as producing millions of refugees. In many places, human rights are broken daily and in the Sudan, Africans are enslaved by the Arab immigrants (Serrill 1996:30). Natural catastrophes like drought, famine and epidemics still rage with costly devastation on human life.

One of the practical problems facing the theologian is the question of language. Africa is richly blessed with some 2000 languages, not counting the dialects. Besides, there are colonial languages imposed on us which, out of necessity, we have adopted: English, French, Spanish, Portuguese and Afrikaans, as well as the language of the slave traders, Arabic. In order to communicate across our ethnic groups, we are forced to use foreign languages that we have not necessarily mastered fully. The art of theologizing in a foreign language is a burden which limits us considerably.

We are, naturally, free to use our own languages. However, writing theology in one's mother tongue means that, in most cases, there are not enough readers to make theological publications economically viable. The number of speakers of the various languages varies from a few thousand to over twenty million, as is the case with Zulu and Xhosa in South Africa, Yoruba in Nigeria, Hausa in western Africa and Swahili in eastern-central Africa. At a deeper level, the question arises as to how far an indigenous language, which has been exposed to Christianity for only fifty or a hundred years, can fully assimilate, sustain and articulate Christian concepts that may be foreign in that language milieu. Even simple terms like salvation, sin, end of the world, Holy Spirit and church require considerable time to be integrated into the deeper conceptual level of local languages.

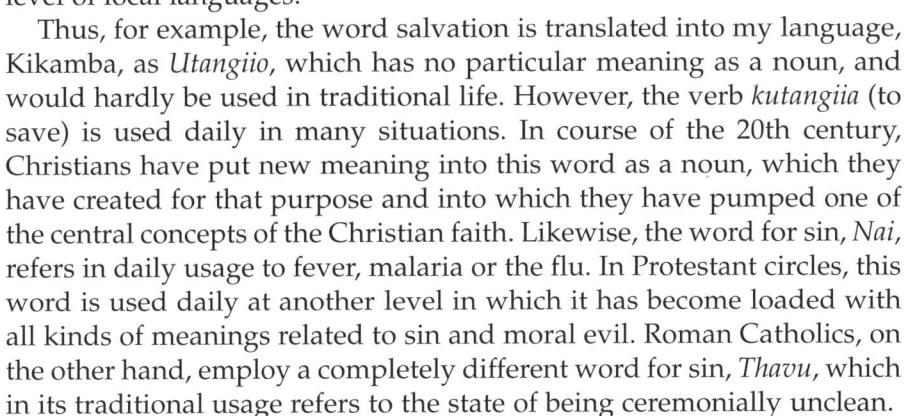

Thus, for example, the word salvation is translated into my language, Kikamba, as *Utangiio*, which has no particular meaning as a noun, and would hardly be used in traditional life. However, the verb *kutangiia* (to save) is used daily in many situations. In course of the 20th century, Christians have put new meaning into this word as a noun, which they have created for that purpose and into which they have pumped one of the central concepts of the Christian faith. Likewise, the word for sin, *Nai*, refers in daily usage to fever, malaria or the flu. In Protestant circles, this word is used daily at another level in which it has become loaded with all kinds of meanings related to sin and moral evil. Roman Catholics, on the other hand, employ a completely different word for sin, *Thavu*, which in its traditional usage refers to the state of being ceremonially unclean.

But now, how do you convince someone who has stolen a sheep, that s/he is in a state of *Thavu* (ceremonial uncleanness)? Or what do you say to a mother who brings her baby to the doctor and explains that the child has *Nai* (fever, not sin)? Will the doctor say that the child has sin and needs only forgiveness? How do you talk about the Trinity, the incarnation, transsubstantiation, or to use the jargon compiled by the World Council of Churches a few years ago: "Towards a Just, Participatory and Sustainable Society"?

All this means that for the African theologian, nearly every Christian concept is open for re-examination, re-interpretation, re-consideration. This makes the theological task both difficult and exciting. Some issues of Christian faith and biblical passages take on a new and meaningful form in the process of theologising. For example, the circumcision of Jesus in Luke 2:21 is hardly given attention by theologians in the West or East, apart from liturgical observation of the day in the church calendar. But as an African theologian, when I read about the circumcision of Jesus, this passage explodes with meaning and becomes a key that opens the way for understanding dimensions of Christology which have not been explored in the history of Christian Theology. From my conceptual and cultural situation, the circumcision presents Jesus as a full and complete person, in a way that would not be the case if He were not circumcised. I can immediately associate with Him, respect and pay attention to Him. Why? According to the world-view and social life of my people, the Akamba of Kenya, as well as many other peoples, an uncircumcised person is socially underdeveloped and immature, s/he is considered to be still a child, a minor who is not yet of age even if s/he may be twenty or forty years old. Traditional society does (did?) not allow such a person to marry and raise a family, girls avoid talking with him or boys laugh at her, s/he is not allowed to take an active role in ceremonies, and cannot

African Theology

SECTION A

THEOLOGY

exercise authority over anybody. Indeed, there are no such people among the Akamba.

To know that Jesus was circumcised means that, socially, He became a full person who can shoulder responsibility and exercise authority and guidance over other people. He is thereby qualified and authorised to be followed as such; He has sound wisdom and experience. He can speak to us about life and guide us into full life. Indeed, some theologians such as Engelbert Mveng of Cameroon and Anselme Titianma Salon from Burkina Faso talk of Jesus as the Master of Initiation (Aklé 1989:87ff.). This means that Jesus has been properly initiated into life through circumcision and has travelled the full way up to death and beyond. He knows the right way of life better than others because He has also risen from death. Through initiation and experience, He is in the position of authority, wisdom and understanding, from which He can lead us and show us the way of life and command our respect and love. We can entrust ourselves to Him without fear of being misled.

9.2 AFRICAN THEOLOGY AND ITS HISTORY

African Theology is the articulation of the Christian faith by African Christians, both theologians and lay people. There is nothing mystical about the use of this term. Christians ask themselves what their faith means and try to explain or simply live it within the context of their history, culture and contemporary issues. They look at it through their reading, hearing and understanding of the Bible. They try to bring into it their rich cultural heritage which has evolved over many generations. They sing their Faith through liturgies or express it through literature, art, drama, song and dance. Christian Theology in Africa is not a new phenomenon. Its beginning and history go back to the very early church in Egypt, Northern Africa, the Nile Valley and Ethiopia. Indeed, the first translation of the Jewish Bible into Greek, the Septuagint, was done in Africa (Alexandria). Africans were already reading it before Christianity spread widely. There is the story of the Ethiopian government minister of finance described in Acts 8:26–40, who had been reading the Hebrew Bible before he heard the gospel and was eventually baptised by Philip. Tradition says that Christianity was introduced to Egypt by the evangelist Mark in the year 43 AD. It spread quite rapidly westwards and over north Africa, as well as to the south in Sudan and Ethiopia. Some names of early African theologians are well-known, such as Origen, Clement, Athanasius, Tertullian, Justin, Cyprian and Augustine. That was in the first phase of Christianity in Africa.

We are now in another phase of Christian presence in Africa, which was initially brought by missionaries from Europe and later America, and has, since the 19th century, spread to the extent that today the southern two thirds of Africa is predominantly Christian. Our immediate concern in this chapter is to look at the theological development and activities of this new phase of African Christianity, which started slowly with Portuguese colonial expansion in the 15th century, but spread more rapidly in the latter part of the 19th century and in the 20th century.

Wherever the gospel comes, theological activity begins to take place. People respond to the Gospel, they reflect on it, some accept it and others reject it. Theology begins to take shape, to be formulated. And that is exactly what has happened in Africa. African Theology started to germinate when the gospel arrived through missionary preaching and the work of African converts, evangelists, pastors, teachers and lay persons. Theology is done orally before it is written down. Historical factors have played their role in this. For example, through missionary work, schools were established in many parts of Africa. More and more African Christians were able to read and write where previously there had been no alphabet. Some began to write down their theological reflections.

At the same time as missionary expansion into Africa, colonial rule was established or strengthened its grip on Africa. In course of the 20th century, Africans began to agitate and fight for political freedom, though resistance to colonial domination had always been there, but was often silenced or driven underground by the brutal power of guns. Similarly, in church circles the feeling increasingly grew that the church and its theology needed to be liberated from missionary domination and be made more relevant to the African setting. Christians began to articulate their theological reflections, some of which critiqued missionary theological and ecclesiastical traditions, others of which attempted to express the gospel in terms that are more relevant and meaningful in the African cultural and contemporary context. At the same time, the Bible, in full or in part, was translated into more and more African languages. The Bible became the mirror and authority of Christian thought and life, especially for members of the Anglican and Protestant Churches who could read it without prohibition from church authorities. Using the Bible to reflect on the Christian Faith, some of the Africans even broke off from Mission Churches and founded their own Independent (Indigenous, Autonomous) Churches of which there were about 9 000 in 1996. Among other things, these churches try to formulate and evolve forms of Christianity that are more directly related to the African background and religious needs than is generally the case where Christianity is still loaded with western culture and traditions.

A major factor in the development of African Theology is the feeling and reflection that our cultural context is rich in values which do not conflict with the gospel. On the contrary, such values enhance people's understanding and application of the gospel. Therefore they need to be seen positively, to be retained and integrated into the life of the church. Indeed, they have prepared the ground for the reception of the gospel in Africa. Some of these values include a deep religiosity in which God is central, in which the spiritual world is very close to the physical world and in which life is seen as a religious phenomenon. There are values associated with life in community, human harmony with nature and the departed members of the family. The basic philosophy here is: "I am because we are, and since I am therefore we are."

9

African Theology

SECTION

A

THEOLOGY

Theological reflection and articulation in Africa has risen out of people's joy in receiving the gospel. At the same time, the injustices wrought by colonial presence, or produced by Africans themselves, and the resultant cultural injuries, created a spirit of "fighting", not only for political, but also ecclesiastical independence and justice. Connected with this was the spirit of wanting to be Christians in our own continent, using our own values and re-interpreting the gospel in the light of our own context. Yet it was, and still is, necessary to remain open to the ecumenical dimensions of the world-wide church and fellowship with it, which means also keeping a strong link with the theology of the universal church.

When exactly Africans began to articulate their theological feelings and insights in publications cannot be pinned down to a particular year or a particular book. The process of speaking about and formulating African Theology began in the 1950s and gained momentum in the 1960s. Today, African Theology has become part and parcel of the world-wide Christian heritage. The first specific articulation and use of the term could be the publication of a collection of essays by Roman Catholic priests in 1956. The contributors posed questions and offered reflections on the future of the church in the face of the then political and social process of moving from colonial to independent Africa. They wanted the African voice to be heard on what Christianity and its mission should mean in an Africa freed from colonial and ecclesiastical domination. This urge was also felt in the doctoral thesis of Vincent Mulago of Zaire in 1965. He argued that effective evangelisation is possible only when the (Roman Catholic) Church understands the people. So he wrote: "Having penetrated the mentality, culture, and philosophy of the people to be conquered, we shall have to graft the Christian message onto the proselyte's soul. Only this method will yield a lasting result" (Mulago 1965:23).[1]

9.3 THEOLOGICAL STREAMS

The feeling and urge to relate the Christian Faith to Africa with all its human resources, its history, its cultures and contemporary situation, increased in the 1960s and gave birth to the talk about African Theology. We discern three streams of theological activity which merge, assist or give way to each other.

9.3.1 Oral Theology

This is largely the theology of the whole church of Christ. It comes out in sermons, prayers, catechumen classes, Christian gatherings, discussions of the Faith or of Bible passages. It comes out in stories, in telling peo-

---

1 Before the term "African Theology" was widely used, I referred to and discussed it in my own doctoral thesis written in 1963 at the University of Cambridge, England, later published in 1971 under the title *New Testament Eschatology in an African Background*. Oxford University Press: London. In searching for a name, I spoke of it as: Christian Theology in Africa, African Theology or Theologia Africana. In addition, other terms have also been used, including African Christian Theology, Theology in Africa. The most common term now is simply African Theology.

ple's experiences or dreams, in songs and hymns, as well as in short expressions of how God is seen at work among the people. Oral Theology fits very well into African oral culture which, because of its long historical tradition, is still meaningful and in some places more practical than written culture. It started the very moment when the gospel was proclaimed in Africa, beginning with the apostolic times (in Northern Africa) and has continued to this day. Many of the 340 million Christians in Africa (in 1996) cannot read or write. Even those who can do so, do not usually write down their ideas: they express them more by mouth than by hand.

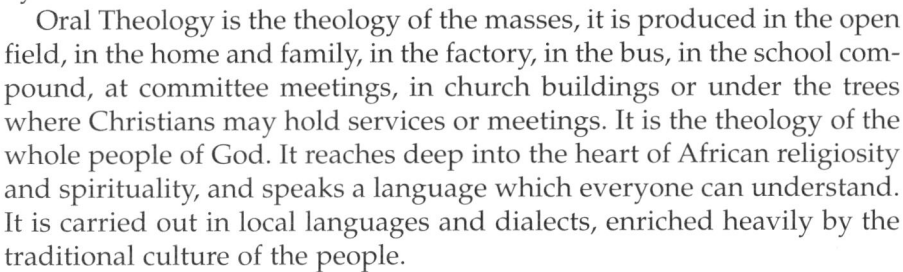

9

African Theology

Oral Theology is the theology of the masses, it is produced in the open field, in the home and family, in the factory, in the bus, in the school compound, at committee meetings, in church buildings or under the trees where Christians may hold services or meetings. It is the theology of the whole people of God. It reaches deep into the heart of African religiosity and spirituality, and speaks a language which everyone can understand. It is carried out in local languages and dialects, enriched heavily by the traditional culture of the people.

Naturally, Oral Theology has its limitations: for example, it is very localised, reaching only a small audience at a given moment. Unless it is written down or taped, it does not reach many people word for word, though its substance can spread widely and form building stones. However, it is generally lost as far as libraries are concerned and it cannot be easily put under academic scrutiny. But in some ways, Oral Theology recaptures the situation of the church in the first two centuries, when accounts of the life, work, teaching and meaning of Jesus Christ were articulated largely through the spoken word. Jesus' own teaching was fundamentally oral, using oral methods, as witnessed in his images, proverbs, short stories (parables) and sayings – all of which were geared to the oral culture of his time.

Similarly, Christian Theology started as Oral Theology and was written down only later – and even then, not all of it. For example, the Evangelist, St. Luke, tells about his use of narrative accounts of the life and work of Jesus in order to compile the third gospel which bears his name:

> Inasmuch as many have undertaken to compile a narrative of the things which have been accomplished among us, just as they were delivered to us by those who from the beginning were eyewitnesses and ministers of the word, it seemed good to me also, having followed all things closely (accurately) for some time past, to write an orderly account for you, most excellent Theophilus, that you may know the truth concerning the things of which you have been informed (Luke 1:1–4).

Luke gathered oral material, plus whatever (little) may have been written down. His friend, Theophilus, had received reports and information about Jesus through oral sources. Luke used those sources to compile his two books, and certainly the other three evangelists did the same.

SECTION A

THEOLOGY

Oral Theology continues to survive everywhere in the world, even among people with written cultures. It anticipates written theology and provides material for it.[2]

9.3.2 Symbolic Theology

This is what Christians express in form of symbols through art, sculpture, dance, drama, rituals, colours, numbers, forms of worship, dress, decorations in churches and people's homes, etc (Thiel & Helf 1984). A lot of Christian symbolism has been brought from the west, but Africa is also cultivating additional symbolism which arises from African creativity, spirituality and articulation. The African Initiated Churches seem to have more freedom here and much of Symbolic Theology is found among them. Christian art, for example, is thriving in all parts of Africa. It is very effective in communicating and explaining the Faith in situations where people may not read or write, but can see and reflect on visual representations. Symbolic Theology relates closely to the context in which the church is growing and living.

9.3.3 Written Theology

African Theology in written form is what began to take shape in the 1950s and has accelerated since the 1980s. Written African Theology is the privilege of a few Christians who have received considerable general and theological education, and who know and have the traditional western tools of reading and writing theology. Theologians who write theology in articles, essays, books, conference papers and formal lectures, are few in proportion to the vast number of Christians in Africa. These are the theologians in the strict academic sense of the term. They normally write in languages other than their mother tongue. The foreign language which they are forced to use sometimes makes it impossible to communicate to the people who only know an African language. But an ex-colonial language makes it possible for them to reach readers and hearers beyond tribal or national boundaries. On the whole, Written Theology is removed from the masses of the African Christians and they have no direct access to it, either because of language barrier or the cost of books and periodicals. It is a luxury to which only a few individuals have access.

Most of the books under the umbrella of African Theology contain

---

2 The importance of Oral Theology was first pointed out in John S Mbiti's "Cattle Are Born With Ears, Their Horns Grow Later: Towards An Appreciation of African Oral Theology" in *Christian Theology and Theological Education in the African Context*. Geneva, 1978, pp. 35–51. In the 1990s the written use of African proverbs and short stories in theological discussions or Christian education has increased and generated interest. These have always been the backbone of oral "theologizing" such as sermons, prayers, catechism, hymns, drama, and other forms of religious education. We are now entering the time when, increasingly, they will be published. See, for example, Joseph G. Healey and Donald F. Sybert, 1996. *Towards an African Narrative Theology*. Nairobi.

select bibliographical lists of other books and articles. Their numbers continue to soar since around 1970.[3]

9.4 SOURCES AND TOOLS FOR DOING THEOLOGY IN AFRICA

At the Conference of African theologians held in December 1977 in Accra, Ghana, a list of sources for doing theology was drawn up. Most theologians agree that these are basic and accept or use them accordingly, with minor modifications or additions. The list is comprehensive and covers the following:

The first and foremost source is the **Bible**. In 1996 there were about 650 translations of the Bible in African languages. The sale and distribution of Bibles increase every year. It is almost the only book that many lay Christians possess and read – and it shapes their lives. It is read and taken seriously by many African theologians. The Accra conference called it "the basic source of African Theology, because it is the primary witness of God's revelation in Jesus Christ. No theology can retain its Christian identity apart from Scripture. The Bible is not simply a historical book about the people of Israel; through a re-reading of this Scripture in the social context of our struggle for our humanity, God speaks to us in the midst of our troublesome situation. This divine Word is not an abstract proposition but an event in our lives, empowering us to continue in the fight for our full humanity" (Appiah-Kubi & Torres 1979:192ff.).

In the second instance there is the **Christian heritage** which has been handed down through the centuries. This heritage originated in Hebrew (Jewish) culture, but soon entered Greek, then Roman and later European and American cultures. In modern times, when it reached Africa, it was wrapped with the dresses of those cultures, but it is rich in spirituality, theological concepts, art, music, liturgies, symbols, etc. The church in Africa has been enriched by this Christian heritage.

The third point we mention is **African culture** in the broad sense, which includes African religion, world-view and values. In particular, it is African religion which has been the most influential force in shaping African world-view. It is still a strong factor today, though often in the background or just beneath the surface. In times of crisis it certainly surfaces. Since African religion is grounded on the conviction of the existence of the one God, Creator of all things, the missionaries who came from Europe and America did not bring God to Africa – rather it is God Himself who brought them there. At many points, African religion resembles the religion of the Jewish Bible (the Christian Old Testament), and some theologians have even spoken of African religion as the Old Testament of Africa – an assertion which is not justifiable. However, the main and new element in the teaching of missionaries was the naming of

---

3 For example, the bibliography on African Theology in the book by H Rücker, *"Afrikanische theologie". Darstellung und Dialog*. Innsbruck and Vienna 1985, contains almost 1000 books and articles.

SECTION A

THEOLOGY

Jesus Christ. A few of us are even saying that some aspects about Jesus Christ can be assembled from or detected in African religion, which means that He was not 100% absent from traditional African religious insights and practices (Bahekuma 1989 and Mbiti 1992). We cannot brush aside African religion. This factor has profound implications for the development and articulation of the theology and life of the church as a whole. The vocabulary used in the churches, the spirituality of the people, the translations of the Bible, pastoral problems, health questions and major life stations (like birth, marriage and death) are all heavily coloured by African religion. The basic materials for the germination and growth of the Christian faith are present in African religion. We could, in this sense, speak of African religion as a preparation for the gospel, even if it stands on its own as a viable religion.

The fourth source is **African history** which goes back, if we so wish, three million years to when the first ancestors of human beings began to roam the savannahs of eastern Africa. More recently however, we take up the pre-colonial, colonial and post-colonial history. Each of these phases has its impact upon the life and thinking of the people. Contemporary history is characterised by rapid social, economic and political change, for better or for worse, and by mass-media, modern technology and contact with other nations. African Theology is taking place in this multi-historical context, which has an impact on theological reflection and output.

9.5 THE MAIN ISSUES OF AFRICAN THEOLOGY TODAY

In reality, African Theology addresses all aspects of the Christian faith. There is a wide diversity of themes and ways in which the theologians handle them. We now mention some items which, currently, seem to be getting more attention than others.

9.5.1 The encounter between African religion and the Christian faith

This began to take place from the very moment the first missionaries preached the gospel. Since African religion permeates all areas of life, the gospel could not be preached outside of this deep religiosity. So questions arise, such as: Is the God of the Bible the same God who is acknowledged and worshipped in African religion? Different answers have been given to this question. Many of the missionaries held the opinion that it could not possibly be the same God. African theologians themselves are more or less unanimous in saying that this is One and the same God. They say that God's revelation is not limited to the biblical revelation. African religion has a revelation of God which lets itself be integrated with the biblical revelation in terms of pointing to one and the same God, Creator and Sustainer of all things, the Father of our Lord Jesus Christ.

When we read a passage such as Hebrews 1:1ff., we feel that this is applicable to us in the situation of African religion: "In many and various ways God spoke of old to our fathers by the prophets; but in these last days He has spoken to us by a Son, whom He appointed the heir of all things, through whom He also created the world." Some theologians say that African religion can be seen as a preparation for the coming of the gospel "in these last days" in which "God has spoken to us by His Son". Theologians hear the words of Jesus applied to our situation with tremendous force, when He says: "I have come not to abolish ... but to fulfil" (Matt 5:17). What does this word mean in the African situation? Theologians are asking themselves in what ways the gospel comes to fulfil our religious longing and yearning.

9

African Theology

Furthermore, the question is raised: What contribution does African religion make to the life of the church in terms of, for example, spirituality, sensitivity to the spiritual realities, respect towards nature and harmony with creation, in the development of relevant forms of liturgy and worship? Liturgy and worship in African tradition utilise, for example, the whole body through singing, dancing, clapping, yelling, shouting and moving rhythmically in giving thanks to God, in calling upon God, in rejoicing in God (Mulago 1986).

Our growing consensus is that African religion has said "yes" to the gospel. The gospel has also said "yes" to African religion. The first conference of African theologians in Ibadan, Nigeria in 1966, took as its theme "Biblical Revelation and African Beliefs". The papers were published in a book of the same title, edited by Kwesi Dickson and Paul Ellingworth, London 1968. In the conference statement we (as I was one of the very young participants) said:

> We believe that the God and Father of our Lord Jesus Christ, Creator of heaven and earth, Lord of history, has been dealing with mankind at all times and in all parts of the world. It is with this conviction that we study the rich heritage of our African peoples, and we have evidence that they know of Him and worship Him. We recognise the radical quality of God's self-revelation in Jesus Christ; and yet it is because of this revelation that we can discern what is truly of God in our pre-Christian heritage: this knowledge of God is not totally discontinuous with our people's previous traditional knowledge of Him.

African Theology takes this interreligious dialogue very seriously. Practically every theological book published since 1980 mentions something of this encounter. Of course, a few theologians maintain that such a discussion or dialogue is nothing but a form of syncretism and should not be undertaken because they do not see any continuity between biblical religion and African religion (Kato 1975 and Adeyemo 1979).

Nevertheless, many theologians are doing or have done research into African religion, basically in order to understand it better on its own merit. This also helps them to see how it relates to the Christian faith. Some of these theologians include the late Harry Sawyerr (Sierra Leone), the late E. Bolaji Idowu (Nigeria), the late Engelbert Mveng (Cameroon), Vincent Mulago gwa Cikala (Zaire), Gabriel Setiloane (South Africa), and

SECTION A

THEOLOGY

A.B.T. Byaruhanga-Akiiki (Uganda). I have also done work in this area and published several volumes on African religion, dealing with matters like concepts of God, prayer and spirituality.

9.5.2 The Theology of Liberation

Since the 1970s, theological discussion in southern Africa has focused mainly on the Theology of Liberation. This was a living issue for Christians there while African peoples suffered the painful experience of oppression by the European settlers, were denied basic human rights, and had little or no say in matters of their own destiny. Further, they were unjustly exploited economically. So for them, the gospel was the good news of liberation "because its message brings a new light to dehumanized and oppressed people", as the Zimbabwe theologian Gwinyai H. Muzorewa writes (Muzorewa 1985).

Among the many theologians of liberation in southern Africa we can mention names like Archbishop Desmond Tutu, Simon Maimela, Takatso Mofokeng, Allan Boesak, Zephania Kameeta (Namibia), Gabriel Setiloane and the late Steve Biko. The first book on Liberation Theology was a collection of essays edited by Basil Moore: *Black Theology, The South African Voice* (1973). The then apartheid government of South Africa banned the book before it was put up for sale. But copies were smuggled out and it was published in America, Britain and Germany. The book says that it is about a theology "in revolt against the spiritual enslavement of African people, and thus against the loss of their sense of human dignity and worth. It is a theology in search of new symbols by which to affirm African humanity. It is a theology of the oppressed, by the oppressed, for the liberation of the oppressed" (Moore 1973:viii). The essays, each in its own way, "call upon African people to throw off the shackles of their own internal enslavement as a necessary precursor to throwing off the external enslavement" (1973:xi). These essays voice the persistent cry of the oppressed. In 1985, the now famous Kairos Document was published in South Africa. It largely took up the issues of Liberation Theology, though it was not necessarily written by liberation theologians as such. It was produced by groups of Christians who met on several occasions to discuss the situation in their country. Among other things, they pointed out that the critical hour, the Kairos, had come in South Africa. The document attacks what is called the Theology of the State in terms of which the then settler government was oppressing people under the guise of keeping law and order. The document also attacked what it calls the Theology of Reconciliation, mainly practiced by the so-called English speaking churches in which the oppressive system of government was not adequately opposed. It discussed the question of violence, pointing out that the apartheid state was the main source and perpetrator of violence against society, especially against Africans. As an alternative to the theologies it rejected, the Kairos Document offered Prophetic Theology and called upon Christians to act. It said that God was on the side of the oppressed people, and Christians should take sides against oppression.

We rejoice that finally, South Africa attained majority rule in 1994. Liberation Theology was a clear voice in the struggle against apartheid, injustice, exploitation and robbery of human dignity and rights. Since 1994, we can look back and see how the yokes of oppression, racism, injustices and exploitation have slid into history, however slowly some of their effects will be healed. Theological development in southern Africa has now to address itself to the new situation; one challenge is overcome, but many others have mushroomed.

9.5.3 Women's Theology

As in all countries of the world, women are the majority in the church. Yet, power is in the hands of the men. Happily, African women are waking up to this form of injustice (see chapter 8), though there are not yet many women theologians. One of them, Mercy Amba Oduyoye of Ghana and Nigeria, published a book in 1986 in which, among other things, she takes as her starting point the Exodus event for the freeing of the whole of humankind, women included (Oduyoye 1986). She gives special attention to the story of the creation of the world and hence of the creation and continuity of human life in the womb of the woman. She says that this should be one of the themes of African Theology. Oduyoye concerns herself with liberation themes affecting the woman who is utilised as a sex object, is exploited in cheap labour, or is put on the periphery of the exercise of church power. Theology should take the experiences of women very seriously.

At a continental consultation on Theology from Third World Women's Perspective, held in Port Harcourt, Nigeria in August 1986, the women affirmed that "Men and women together image God and neither is complete without the other. In Christ we see the fullness of true humanity, therefore Christianity in Africa should be a force for full human development."

Women's theological voice is growing louder and louder and this deserves rightful attention. Women theologians joined forces and published a book of essays in 1992, entitled *The Will to Arise*. They examine the place and role of women in African culture and how this relates to Christianity. They discuss sexual practices in relation to Christian thought and life. Another group examines the place and role of women in the church and the urgency of liberating them to "arise".

9.5.4 Christology

Christology is the theme which deals with the question of who Jesus Christ is. Several answers have been formulated in articles and books (Mofokeng 1983; Mugambi & Magesa 1989; Bediako 1992; Pobee 1992; Mbiti 1977). One area of discussion deals with Jesus Christ in the Theology of Liberation. Here He is regarded as the fighting God, as the Liberator, as being on the side of the poor and oppressed, as the One who frees people from their shackles (Boesak 1976; Kameeta 1983).

A major work on Christology in the direction of the Liberation Theology is the book by Takatso A. Mofokeng (1983), in which he considers Jesus Christ as the Creator of the new humanity. In Him, the Exodus event is taken up again for the whole of humanity. Through his suffering, God the Father suffers also. His resurrection is the eternal event of liberation. Mofokeng explains that the footprints of Jesus in his suffering were being repeated (at that time) in southern Africa in the torture chambers, in the imprisonments, in the beatings, in the cries of the oppressed. Africans were being driven to the cross of Jesus, to the God who hears the cries of the oppressed, and not to the God of the oppressor.

The late Engelbert Mveng of Cameroon (who was murdered in 1995) and Bishop Anselme Titianma Sanon of Burkina Faso see Jesus Christ as the Master of Initiation, because He has gone through the main stages of life according to African tradition. He has survived death, the hardest of them all, and has risen again. Therefore He has the qualifications to be Master, to show us the way of life in its fullness.

In other approaches to African Christianity, Jesus Christ is experienced and proclaimed as the Healer, the One who exorcises the spirits, the One who protects against magic and sorcery, the One who enables childless women to bear. In particular, this is the image of Jesus which is proclaimed and experienced in the African Initiated Churches, many of which carry out healing as one of their main existential functions (see chapter 10).

9.5.5 Church and state

The relationship between church and state is another major concern of African Theology. Wherever it exists, the church finds itself in different political situations, some of which change rapidly or radically within a short time. Just think of the church in socialist countries in Africa like Ethiopia, Angola and Mozambique, in which its freedom was curtailed to a certain degree and where the state was, at least theoretically, committed to an ideology of atheism. However, atheism can hardly find a home in Africa and poses no immediate danger to Christianity. Communism and socialism are on the way out in the 1990s and democracy (at least on paper) is the goal of many countries.

There are Christians living in countries where the state and the church exercise a high degree of co-operation or mutual tolerance, even if at times there may be differences of opinion: for example in Kenya, Zambia, Zimbabwe and most other African states.

There was a time when the church found itself in the situation of apartheid (the "segregation of races") in southern Africa, and was challenged to voice the cries of the oppressed (even though one branch of the church worked hard to justify apartheid!). With the coming of freedom and introduction of democracy, the church's prophetic ministry will not diminish: on the contrary, it will increase. Liberation Theology will have to put weight on new concerns, and may have to give way to new forms of theology.

The church also exists in predominantly Muslim countries like Egypt,

Sudan and elsewhere in northern Africa. Here the church has limited freedom and sometimes the Christians live under pressure, persecution and discrimination. There are Muslim countries outside of Africa such as Libya and Iran, which are reported to encourage, support and propagate military and religious revolutions.

Many African countries are or have been under military regimes. Here, too, some situations of conflict have arisen, and churches have been faced with difficulties, as was the case in Uganda under Idi Amin (1971–1979). The situation in Liberia has not improved much since civil war broke out there in 1990 when the military President Samuel Doe was overthrown and executed. The mass killings of more than half a million people in Rwanda from April to June 1994, even though 80% of Rwanda's population is Christian, shocked the entire world. This means that Christians killed one another, and some were slaughtered in church buildings where they took refuge.

The relationship between church and state in Africa is very fluid and definitive theological studies have yet to be made on this subject.[4] The people cannot survive on the basis of handouts from politicians who come and go like ripples on water. The church has a deeper basis of existence than any regime or individual leader. It can make an enduring contribution to the meaning of life in Africa today and tomorrow, even if it is not without its own shortcomings.

There are other themes in African Theology, such as biblical studies, the nature and mission of the church, questions concerning liturgical life, Christian art and drama, the Ecumenical Movement, and the relationship between human life and nature at large. Unfortunately, there is not enough space in this volume to address each of these issues in detail.

9.6 CONCLUSION

African Theology is in the process of birth and growth. It has to deal with issues that are relevant to the living situation of the church. Much of it is produced orally through art, singing, sermons, daily prayers, in Christian homes and church gatherings, through reading the Bible and telling about Jesus Christ. Written theology is the privilege of a small number of theologians, who are often forced to express their thoughts in foreign languages. At the same time, African Theology is keeping a form of continuity with theologies from other parts of the world. Such a continuity is healthy and ecumenically valuable.

---

4 The former President of Zimbabwe, Canaan Banana, has drawn attention to what he calls "The Theology of Promise", in a book of the same title published in Harare in 1982. See among others, (some essays in) Pobee, J.S., (ed.). *Religion in a Pluralistic Society*, Leiden 1976; Okullu, Henry. *Church and State*, Nairobi 1984, and his *Church and Politics in East Africa*, Nairobi 1974; Gitari, David. *In Season and out of Season*, London 1996; and Enwerem, Iheanyi M. *A Dangerous Awakening. The Politicization of Religion in Nigeria*, Ibadan 1995. With countries becoming more "democratic" and reverting more to '"freedom of speech", we can expect that the relation between church and state will be discussed more openly, with theologians airing their "prophetic voice" as the case may be.

SECTION A
THEOLOGY

Yet African theologians are sometimes apprehensive about being engineered by theologians from other parts who think that their own brand of theology, or method of doing theology, has to be universalised or exported. African Theology does not, and cannot, claim always to have new insights into theology. Often it covers the same ground that has been covered even better by other theologies. It cannot be expected to answer questions which Christians are raising in other parts of the world. It is doing nothing other than, in its own small corner, contributing to the understanding and experience of the gospel. The ultimate test of the viability of any theology is its acceptability before God, since theology is talk about God and before our Lord Jesus Christ, since Christian Theology starts and ends with Jesus Christ.

There is an explosion of Christianity in Africa in the 20th century, according to statistics available. In 1900, out of a total population of 107,9 million, there were 10 million Christians (9,2%), compared to 34,5 million Muslims (32%), 63 million adherents of African religion (58%), and about 1 million (1%) followers of other religions such as Judaism, Hinduism, etc. Projections estimate that by the year 2000, with a total population of 814 million, there will be 394 million Christians (48,4%), 339 million Muslims (41,4%), 72,4 million "pure" adherents of African religion (8,9%), and 8,5 million followers of other religions (1%). Within less than 100 years the southern part of Africa has become predominantly Christian (while the northern third remains predominantly Muslim). African religion, however, continues to be strong, especially in the domain of world-view, often surfacing among Christians (and Muslims) in situations of crisis, or in the search for and assertion of cultural roots.

Increasingly, books and articles are being published which address or contribute to the question of African Theology in its various forms. Interest in African Theology has spread to America, Europe and other Christian theological circles. In addition to African theological creativity, there are some publications by expatriates, but these generally tell or speak about African Theology rather than generating or producing theology which can claim to be African. Some of these expatriate authors raise questions which are pertinent to theological work, but some simply play the role of theological engineers and even manipulate what we ought to say and how we should say it. In any event, all theological writings have to be academically scrutinised since some of them are of poor quality and based on dubious theological grounds.

Oral and Symbolic Theology, together with the rising number of books and articles, are all clear pointers to the fact that African Theology is in a very exciting and creative period in the history of Christianity in our continent. We have to theologise with fear and trembling, lest much of what we cherish as theology may turn out to be worthless rubble before the Lord of all creation.

READING LIST AND BIBLIOGRAPHY

Adeyemo, Tokunboh. 1979. *Salvation in African Tradition*. Nairobi.
Aklé, Y., Kabasélé, F., et al. 1989. *Chemins de la christologie africaine*. Paris. German: Der schwarze Christus. Freiburg, Basel.
Appiah-Kubi, K. and Torres, S. (eds.). 1979. *African Theology en route*. New York: Maryknoll.
Bahekuma, J.M. "African Traditional Religion." In Mugambi, J.N.K. and Magesa, L. (eds.). 1989. *Jesus in African Christianity*. Nairobi.
Bediako, K. 1992. *Jesus in African Culture*. Accra.
Boesak, A.A. 1976. *Black Theology, Black Power*. London: New York.
Boulaga, E. 1984. *Christianity without Fetishes*. New York: Maryknoll.
Bujo, B. 1992. *African Theology in its Social Context*. New York: Maryknoll.
Dickson, K.A. 1984. *Theology in Africa*. London.
Ela, J.-M. 1986. *African Cry*. New York: Maryknoll.
Enwerem, I.M. 1995. *A Dangerous Awakening. The Politicization of Religion in Nigeria*. Ibadan.
Gibellini, R. (ed.). 1994. *Paths of African Theology*. New York: Maryknoll.
Gitari, D. 1996. *In Season and out of Season*. London.
Healey, J.G. and Donald ,F.S. 1996. *Towards an African Narrative Theology*. Nairobi.
Kameeta, Z. 1983. *Gott in schwarzen gettos*. Wuppertal.
Kato, B.H. 1975. *Theological Pitfalls in Africa*. Nairobi
Mbiti, J.S. 1971. *New Testament Eschatology in an African Background*. London: Oxford University Press
Mbiti, J.S. (ed.). 1977. *Confessing Christ in Different Cultures*. Geneva.
– 1978. "Cattle Are Born With Ears, Their Horns Grow Later: Towards An Appreciation of African Oral Theology." In *Christian Theology and Theological Education in the African Context*. Geneva, 1978.
– 1986. *Bible and Theology in African Christianity*. Nairobi: Oxford.
– 1992. "Is Jesus Christ in African Religion?" In Pobee John S. (ed.). *Exploring Afro-Christianity*. New York: Bern.
Mofokeng, T.A. 1983. *The Crucified among the Crossbearers*. Kampen
Moore, B. (ed.). 1973. *Black Theology, the South African Voice*. London.
Mosala, I.J. and Tlhagale, B. (eds.). 1986. *The Unquestionable Right to be Free*. New York: Maryknoll.
Mugambi, J.N.K. and Laurenti, M. 1989. *Jesus in African Christianity*. Nairobi.
– 1990. *The Church in African Christianity*. Nairobi.
Mulago gwa Cikala, M.V. (ed.). 1986. *Afrikanische Spiritualität und Christliche Glaube*. Freiburg: Basel.
Mulago, V. (now gwa Cikala) M. 1965. *Un visage africain du christianisme*. Présence Africaine: Paris.
Muzorewa, G. H. 1985. *The Origins and Development of African Theology*. New York: Maryknoll.
Oduyoye, M.A. 1986. *Hearing and Knowing*. New York: Maryknoll.
Oduyoye, M.A. and Musimbi R.A.K. (eds.). 1992. *The Will to Arise*. New York: Orbis Books.
Okullu, H. 1984. *Church and State*. Nairobi.
– *Church and Politics in East Africa*. Nairobi.
Pobee, J.S. (ed.). 1976. *Religion in a Pluralistic Society*. Leiden.
– 1992. *Exploring Afro-Christology*. Bern.
Rücker H. 1985 *"Afrikanische Theologie". Darstellung und Dialog*. Innsbruck and Vienna.
Serrill, M.S. 1996. "Slaves: On Sale Now". *Time*. 148(1).
Thiel, J.F. and Helf, H. 1984. *Christliche Kunst in Afrika*. Berlin.

African Initiated Church Theology

Stephen Hayes

10.1 WHAT ARE THE "AFRICAN INITIATED CHURCHES"?

It is not really possible to speak of the theology of the African Initiated Churches as a particular tradition. The term "African Initiated Churches" does not refer to a single theological tradition, but rather to a group of denominations characterised by a variety of theological views, teachings, ways of worshipping, and historical background.[1] We can see as much variety in theologies within the groups classified as "African Initiated Churches" as we can see in those outside. Some African Initiated Churches have a Methodist tradition, some have a Congregational tradition, some have an Anglican tradition, some have an Orthodox tradition and some have a Pentecostal tradition. Anything one says about their theology will therefore be an over-generalisation. And many features that people say are characteristic of their theology can often be found equally easily among denominations that are not usually classified as "African Initiated Churches".

It is very difficult, in fact, to say what the "African Initiated Churches" are. Some people have therefore tried to define them by saying what they are not: they are defined in contrast to the "mission" churches, or the "historical" churches, or the "white-led" churches or the "mainline" churches. This does not get us very far in overcoming the problem. Many

---

1 There are several other terms used for the denominations that are usually classified as African Initiated Churches: African Indigenous Churches, African Instituted Churches, and, in older literature, Native Separatist Churches, and several more besides.

SECTION A

THEOLOGY

African Initiated Churches are very active in mission, and so they probably have a better claim to the title of "mission" churches than many of the others. Again, the African Initiated Churches have a history, and so to contrast them with "historical" churches is absurd.

The older term African "Independent" Churches, and the concept of classification that lies behind it, is as problematic. In South Africa in the late 19th and early 20th century, the classification was mainly of interest to white government officials. For them the distinguishing feature was that these were religious bodies that were "not under European control" and in this sense "independent". Now, a hundred years later, thinking that "European control" is an important distinction does not make much sense.

There are still other names like African Indigenous Churches or in some circles even African Separatist Churches, but neither do these get around the problem.

In South Africa alone there are nearly 8000 denominations classified as African Initiated Churches. If we look at other parts of the continent, there are many more.

Instead of trying to define the group of denominations, it might be easier to look at the kind of theology or the approach to theology we are concerned with here. This might make it somewhat easier. The kind of theology that we are concerned with is theology developed or applied in Africa, by Africans, in response to African problems. So we can speak of African Initiated Church Theology.

This immediately raises another question – how does this differ from African Theology and Black Theology? While there might be some overlapping, I suggest that it is possible to make some distinctions. The term African Theology is usually applied to a kind of theology developed by people with academic training in Western Theology, who have tried to incorporate some of the insights of African traditional religions into the framework of their theology. The African Indigenous Theology we are talking about may have some points of contact with such endeavours, but its centre usually lies away from the academic sphere. It is found especially in the so-called African Initiated Churches, but it is also found in other denominations – not so much among the academically trained leaders, but among the ordinary members of the congregations.

Black Theology, too, tends to be more academic, and to draw on theological and philosophical ideas from outside Africa.

10.2 HISTORICAL BACKGROUND

When talking about African Indigenous Theology, it is necessary as well to remind ourselves how much Christian Theology generally owes to Africa and African theologians. According to the earliest traditions of the church in Africa, the Christian faith was first preached by St Mark, who established a church in Alexandria in AD 65.[2]

---

[2] The story of the conversion of the Ethiopian eunuch (Acts 8:26–40) is sometimes cited as evidence of the earliest preaching of the gospel in Africa. It seems, however, that this incident did not lead to the establishment of the church in Ethiopia.

The earliest part of the history of the church is quite obscure. The first Christians may have been of Greek or Jewish background, but by the end of the second century many native Egyptians had become Christian, and vernacular languages were being used in the church. So rapidly did the church grow in the third century that the number of bishops grew to 21, and the bishop of the original centre at Alexandria was given the title "pope" long before the bishop of Rome had begun to use that title.

10.2.1 The contribution of the African Church to Christian Theology in general

In Egypt, during the times of persecution, many Christians fled from the cities into the desert, and even when persecution eased off, some stayed in the deserts to pray. They were the first monks, and by the 4th century the monks were being formed into organised communities. This spiritual movement, which began in Africa, was exported to other parts of the Christian world. Monasticism became the instrument by which much of Europe and northern Asia were evangelized.

A theological dispute that began in Egypt in the 4th century eventually led to the formulation of the statement of faith we know today as the Nicene Creed. It was an African theologian, Athanasius of Alexandria, who wrote the definitive book on the subject. It was the same Athanasius who was visited by a merchant who had been shipwrecked in Ethiopia and lived there for many years, and had gathered a community of Christians there. When this merchant, Frumentius, was finally making his way home, he called on Athanasius to inform him about what had happened and suggested that he send a bishop to the infant church there. Athanasius promptly ordained him and sent him back.

Since the first century, therefore, there has been a Christian Church in north-eastern Africa. This church has had an African Theology, developed by Africans, in African conditions, which has sometimes (as in the 4th century) had a profound influence on Christian Theology throughout the world.

10.2.2 Western missionaries in sub-Saharan Africa

In much of the rest of Africa, however, the Christian faith was first preached by non-African missionaries, mostly from Europe and North America. Their theology had been shaped by the culture and history and conditions in the countries they came from, and was in many ways very different from the original theology of Africa (which, as I have pointed out, still persisted in the north-east of the continent, in Egypt and Ethiopia).

Most of these western missionaries came to Africa in the 19th century, and in the previous centuries their own culture had undergone several transformations that made it very difficult indeed for them to relate to the cultures they found among the peoples of Africa. The cultural changes of the Renaissance and the Enlightenment, and the changes in modes of economic production brought about by the industrial revolution,

SECTION A

THEOLOGY

made their way of thinking vastly different from that of their own ancestors a few generations earlier, to say nothing of the people of another continent.

Where the overseas missionaries preached and their message was accepted by local people, however, a change took place. The local people who accepted the Christian message interpreted it in terms of their own situation, and they in turn preached to others this "contextualized" gospel.[3]

And it was through such African Christians that the Christian message spread. Some of these African Christians were given official titles, such as "evangelist", but there were many more who were evangelists through their actions than had the title. Very few African people became Christians because they had heard overseas missionaries preaching. Most became Christians because the missionaries they heard were their fellow-Africans. The Christian message that was preached soon became African Indigenous Theology, even though it was preached within the so-called "historical" or "mission" churches. It is important to realise this. African Indigenous Theology is not a feature only of a particular group of denominations called "African Initiated Churches". It has developed wherever the Christian message has been preached and passed on by African Christians.

10.2.3 Mission, theology and culture

Why then do we mention African Initiated Churches? What is their significance?

To understand this, it is necessary to go back to the "mission" churches again, the ones that were established by missionaries from overseas. The missionaries were influenced by their culture to have a particular mental picture of what the church "ought" to look like. They had their own ideas of the status and qualifications and salaries of full-time ministers. These ideas varied from denomination to denomination, and they also varied in accordance with the home countries of the missionaries. But most of them had an idea of some kind of academic theological training for their clergy. The academic training was done by the missionaries in various ways, and the theology they taught was based on the image they had of the church as it developed in their own culture in their home countries. This theology was taught in seminaries, Bible schools, theological colleges and eventually in universities. This description is very condensed, and it describes a process that took place in different places, in different ways, over many decades. It is very much simplified, but I

---

3 The word "contextualize" is often used in theology. It is an image derived from weaving cloth (textiles), where two sets of threads are woven together at right angles. The threads going across the width of the cloth are called the weft, while those going down the length of the cloth are called the warp. In contextual theology, the gospel is seen as the warp, and the society in which the gospel is proclaimed is seen as the weft, with the different coloured cloths being woven together so that a unique pattern is seen. The pattern cannot be seen in the individual threads, but only in the whole woven cloth.

have done this to give the historical background.

The result of this was that the African clergy of the "mission" denominations had a theological training based on the theology of the overseas missionaries. They were trained in the methods of interpretation and philosophy of a foreign culture. Their theology therefore tended to be different from that of the untrained and unpaid evangelists who were the real missionaries. The "mission" churches therefore tended to have two theologies – a "clerical" theology and a "peoples'" theology.

10.2.4 The emergence of the "Ethiopian" churches

At the end of the 19th century, when Africans in many parts of the continent were becoming Christians in large numbers, and the number of African clergy was increasing, there was also an important change in Europe and North America. The thirty-five years between 1880 and 1915 constituted the period of the New Imperialism and the Scramble for Africa. The imperialist ideology swept through Europe, and the various countries there were convinced of their national superiority to all other nations, and many of them, France, Britain and Germany in particular, tried to grab territory in Africa. New missionaries came to Africa, but they were less sympathetic to African ideals, aspirations and culture than earlier missionaries. The new missionaries tended to be racist, and considered themselves superior to the African clergy who just then were beginning to be ordained in greater numbers. Some African clergy did not like being treated as inferiors, and broke away to form new denominations independent of white control. Many African Initiated Churches came into being this way. They were led, at least in the beginning, by clergy who had been trained in Western theology, and largely retained the practices of their parent denominations. In South Africa for example, the Ethiopian Church was formed as a break-away from the Methodist Church in the early 1890s. It later split into several groups, and church historians have given these denominations the general term of "Ethiopian" (which needs to be distinguished from the Church of Ethiopia mentioned earlier, which had never been controlled by European or American missionaries).

10.2.5 The emergence of the "Zionist" churches

A few years later, in the early 1900s, some new groups of missionaries arrived in South Africa from America. One group was the Zionists, from the Christian Catholic Apostolic Church in Zion, which had founded a holy city for its members, called Zion City, in the state of Illinois in the USA. They preached a message of divine healing and baptism by immersion. They also taught certain customs, such as not eating pork. The earlier missionaries had a view of sickness and healing that was formed by the Enlightenment culture of Europe and North America. They operated mainly with the "medical model" of sickness and healing, and so their healing ministry was expressed in the establishment of clinics and hospitals. However, the Zionist missionaries healed by prayer alone. The

SECTION A

THEOLOGY

Zionists established several congregations, but a dispute in their home church in America caused the missionaries to withdraw by about 1908, leaving their African congregations to govern themselves. A second group of new missionaries came soon afterwards, from the then new Pentecostal Movement in America. Like the Zionists, they taught baptism by immersion and healing, but they also taught baptism in the Spirit and speaking in tongues. These missionaries were generally known at that time as "Apostolic". Some Zionists accepted the Apostolic message as well, and so became "Zion Apostolic". The churches founded by the Zionist and Apostolic missionaries, unlike the "mission" churches, were not governed by missionaries for a long period. Like the "mission" churches, they spread through the activity of voluntary unpaid evangelists, but unlike the "mission" churches, there was no clerical caste trained in Western Theology to control the process. The gospel, interpreted by African Christians in an African setting, was preached to people who in turn preached it to others.

In Southern Africa, these two distinct historical beginnings – groups that started as schisms from white-dominated denominations because of racism, and the growth of independent Zionist and Pentecostal churches – led writers like Sundkler to distinguish two kinds of African Initiated Churches, which he called "Ethiopian" and "Zionist". This distinction can be useful, provided that one bears in mind that it is not absolute. Any particular group or denomination might fall anywhere on a continuum between the two, with the "Ethiopian" groups tending to retain much of the theology and order of their originating denominations, and the "Zionist" and "Apostolic" groups emphasising healing and (in the latter) the charismatic gifts of the Spirit. For this reason the Zionist and Apostolic groups are sometimes together called "Spirit-type" churches. Sundkler's descriptions were based especially on the KwaZulu/Natal area of South Africa, but in many other parts of the continent the same kinds of distinctions can be found. Though they are not necessarily called "Zionist" and appear to have no direct connection with South African Zionists, there are groups in West Africa that emphasise the building of a holy city, a Zion or Jerusalem. Sundkler also distinguished a third type of movement, which he described as "messianic", in which a living leader, or the founder-leader of a particular group, is seen as a new Messiah, and thus as a replacement for, or completer of, the work of Jesus Christ. This led many people, who wrote after Sundkler's book *Bantu Prophets in South Africa* was first published in 1948, to apply the term "messianic" to almost any African denomination that had a strong founding leader. Sundkler therefore revised and clarified his terminology in a later book, *Zulu Zion* and some *Swazi Zionists* to correct the misleading impression that had been created.

10.3 THE THEOLOGICAL APPROACH OF THE AFRICAN INITIATED CHURCHES

In North East Africa, traditional African Christianity continued in Egypt and Ethiopia, with virtually no influence from outside. In Southern, Central and West Africa, however, the gospel that had come via a long detour through Europe and America, was being interpreted by Africans, in an African setting, to form African indigenous theologies. This happened wherever Africans became Christians, but its development and growth was found in its freest and most unfettered form in the African Initiated Churches, particularly in the Zionist and Apostolic denominations, which were influenced by overseas missionaries for a very short period, usually not more than four to five years. Some African Initiated Churches (AICs), particularly those of the "Ethiopian" type, retained or developed overseas links, often with black American groups, such as the African Methodist Episcopal Church. The rise of the Pan-African movement in the 1920s, under the influence of leaders like Marcus Garvey, had considerable influence on some AICs, resulting in the affiliation of a group from the Ethiopian Church with the African Orthodox Church, the formation of the Afro-Athlican Constructive Gaathly, and the resistance of the Israelite group that led to the Bulhoek massacre. In the 1930s there were estimated to be about 200 American Blacks or West Indians in Cape Town alone (Hill & Pirio 1987:213–217). The Garvey movement also gave rise to the Rastafarian Movement in Jamaica, which regarded the emperor of Ethiopia, Haile Selassie (Ras Tafari) as a new Messiah. This in turn led to the sending of Ethiopian missionaries to the West Indies. Thus there was considerable movement of people and ideas between South Africa, the USA, the West Indies and Ethiopia. At first sight there may seem to be little in common between Rastafarianism and African Initiated Churches – the doctrines of Rastafarianism seem so different from those of Christianity as to make it a new religion altogether. Yet both Rastafarianism and a number of African Initiated Churches were strongly influenced by the Garvey movement. Rastafarianism gave rise to a type of popular music, called Reggae, and one of the best-known Reggae musicians, Bob Marley, joined the Ethiopian Orthodox Church shortly before he died. Rastafarianism provided an opening for missionaries from the Ethiopian Orthodox Church in the West Indies.

10.3.1 Written theology and enacted theology

The Zionist and Apostolic Churches (sometimes described as "Spirit-type" churches) grew very rapidly. Their clergy and leaders required no long academic theological training. New congregations would be started by travelling evangelists and would lead an independent or semi-independent existence, often becoming new denominations. Western church historians described this process as "schism", and referred to these churches as "schismatic" or "separatist" churches. While this may have been true of some denominations like the Ethiopian ones mentioned earlier, it was by no means true of all. In some cases there were schisms when leaders or congregations quarrelled, but in other cases there was consolidation as congregations united under a powerful leader. Similar processes took place all over sub-Saharan Africa. Some of the independent religious groups that developed were not Christian, or were only marginally Christian. Some were syncretist, borrowing some ideas from

SECTION A

THEOLOGY

Christianity, and combining them with other ideas from other sources. Some western church historians thought that all or most of these groups were "syncretist" at best and "heathen" at worst. In part, this was because western-trained theologians had been trained in Written Theology. For them theology was written down in books in carefully-crafted words. The African Indigenous Theology of the African Initiated Churches (and also of their own "mission" churches, if they had only looked closely enough) was not Written Theology, but enacted theology. The theology was expressed not just in words, but in the actions of members of the churches as they preached, prayed, worshipped and healed.

In the last twenty to thirty years some western theologians have studied some of the African Initiated Churches more closely and sympathetically, and have, in effect, become intermediaries in trying to discover their theology and write it down in a way that will communicate it to western theologians. In spite of this, however, the communication remains difficult because questions that western theologians regard as important are not seen as equally important by African indigenous "theologians". I have put "theologians" in quotation marks in the last sentence because that in itself indicates some of the difference. In Western Theology, "theologians" are specialists, with a specialised academic training in abstract theology and philosophy. But in African Indigenous Theology there is little specialization. The enacted theology is a lived theology of many people.

So African Indigenous Theology is less concerned with abstract doctrines than with the manner of doing theology. What is distinctive is not so much the verbal formulation of doctrine as the approach. This chapter therefore does not deal so much with the classical themes of Academic Theology – Christology, trinitology, soteriology and so on. The formulation of such doctrines, even as they are held within African Initiated Churches, is usually left to outsiders. The African Orthodox Church, for example, early on affiliated to the African Orthodox Church in the USA, which was a spin-off from the Garvey movement. It claimed to trace its episcopal succession through the Syrian Jacobite (non-Chalcedonian) Patriarchate of Antioch, but in its constitution it insisted on accepting the teaching of the Seven Ecumenical Councils and the Seven Sacraments, though the Syrian Jacobite Patriarchate of Antioch would only have accepted the first three councils. An East African branch of the AOC affiliated with the Chalcedonian Patriarchate of Alexandria in the 1940s, and the South African branch affiliated with the non-Chalcedonian Patriarchate of Alexandria in 1993, becoming the African Coptic Orthodox Church. It preferred to leave the discussion of the precise Christological formulations to others.[4]

---

[4] The terms "Chalcedonian" and "non-Chalcedonian" refer here to those churches that accepted, and those that rejected, the Council of Chalcedon in AD 451. A majority of Christians in North East Africa (Egypt, Nubia – today Northern Sudan – and Ethiopia) rejected the Council of Chalcedon, and this led a few decades later to a schism that has persisted until today. The non-Chalcedonians are sometimes called Coptic or Ethiopian Orthodox, while the Chalcedonians within Africa are called Byzantine or Greek Orthodox, or Melkites. The western churches, both Roman Catholic and Protestant, also generally accepted the Council of Chalcedon. There is a smaller group of non-Chalcedonians in Syria, who are known as "Syrian Jacobites".

In the Spirit-type churches, one important factor has been the approach to healing and evangelism that is very different from that of the Western missionaries. We have already noted that the culture of the missionaries from Europe and America was strongly influenced by the Enlightenment, whereas African culture was not. The evangelists of the Spirit-type churches therefore applied and taught the Christian gospel in a pre-Enlightenment way. The European and American missionaries spoke of the need to "civilise" Africans before they could preach the gospel to them. Africans had to be taught how to suffer from civilised diseases in order that they could appreciate a civilised cure (Comaroff & Comaroff 1991).

The evangelists and healers of the Spirit-type churches generally avoided this roundabout approach. They shared the African understanding of disease and sickness, and applied the gospel to it directly. In this, they bore a remarkable resemblance to the medieval missionaries of Ethiopia.

10.4 SOME THEOLOGICAL THEMES

So far in this chapter we have looked at some of the different kinds of African Initiated Churches and how they were formed. We have looked at some of the characteristics of their approach to theology, but we have not looked very closely at the theology itself.

In theology, the distinction between the Zionist and Ethiopian-type churches is quite important.

10.4.1 Ethiopian Church Theology[5]

The Ethiopian Church that was founded in Pretoria in 1892 broke away from the Methodist Church over the question of racism in the church. When it broke away, it retained Methodist Church organisation, teaching and theology. It sought affiliation with the African Methodist Episcopal Church in the USA, which, though it had officials called bishops, was nevertheless very much in the Methodist tradition.[6]

Groups in the Congregational and Presbyterian churches in Southern Africa also broke away from their parent bodies. As in the case of the Ethiopian Church, they were primarily concerned with questions of church organisation and leadership, and with the relative power and authority of blacks and whites in the church hierarchy. So they, too, tend-

---

5 In this section, I am not referring to the Church of Ethiopia (Ethiopian Orthodox Church) that was founded in Ethiopia (Abyssinia) in the 4th century, but rather to the "Ethiopian Church" that was formed in Pretoria in the 1890s, and to similar bodies that were formed elsewhere in Africa, usually by secession from bodies that had been started by missionaries from Western Europe and North America.

6 It is worth noting that the Methodist movement as a separate entity was then only 100 years old, as it had broken from the Anglican Church in the 1790s. Today, in the 1990s, the Ethiopian Church is now as old as the Methodist Church when it broke away. The Ethiopian Church is therefore just as much a "historical church" as the Methodist Church was when the Ethiopian Church started. This is why it makes little sense to speak of denominations like the Methodist Church as "historical churches".

SECTION A

THEOLOGY

ed to retain the theology and organisation of the parent bodies. Their secession was not motivated so much by theological differences as by leadership questions. Another group broke away from the Anglican Church, and a significant section of the original Ethiopian Church joined the Anglican Church as the Order of Ethiopia. The African Catholic Church and the Ethiopian Catholic Church in Zion had a fairly strong Anglican background, and some of these churches continued to use the Anglican Book of Common Prayer in their worship. A great many of the Zulu-speaking Ethiopian-type churches used the Congregational Zulu hymnal produced by the American Board Mission.

It is therefore difficult to speak of the "theology" of the Ethiopian-type churches, because their theology is similar to that of the mainly Protestant churches from which they broke away, and ranges from Arminian-Methodist to Calvinist-Presbyterian, and even beyond. A couple of examples may serve to illustrate this.

When, in the 1920s, some members of the Ethiopian Church broke away to join the Garvey-inspired African Orthodox Church, their theology was a mixture of Anglican and Orthodox. The AOC had its origin in America, and its first patriarch was a former Anglican priest, George McGuire, from the West Indies. The first South African leader, Daniel Alexander, was of Xhosa-Mauritian descent. The liturgical texts were peculiar to the AOC, and were midway between Anglican and Orthodox practice. At one point, some congregations in the Pretoria area received an influx of members from the Ethiopian Catholic Church in Zion, and these congregations began using the Anglican Book of Common Prayer. The bishops of the AOC dressed like Anglican bishops. Like many Anglicans, they would also sing choruses accompanied by clapping at big gatherings, such as synods. Many members of the congregations were disaffected Anglicans, and so there was a strong Anglican influence on the theology. The AOC experienced a number of internal splits, so there were also several groups calling themselves the African Orthodox Church. When the largest of these decided, at the beginning of 1993, to join the Coptic Orthodox Church, all the former bishops and some of the senior priests were taken to Egypt for theological training, and they are now introducing Coptic Orthodox Theology and liturgical practices into their congregations. The AOC, therefore, showed a blending of different theological traditions, based on the background of the members (mainly Anglican) and on the self image of their leaders (wanting to identify with Orthodoxy).

Another example is the Oruuano Church and the Church of Africa in Namibia. The Herero-speaking people of Namibia had been evangelised mainly by the Rhenish Mission Society from western Germany, which was an ecumenical mission society, though the first missionaries in Namibia were strongly Lutheran. Eventually, the Rhenish Mission Society in Namibia became the Evangelical Lutheran Church. There were two main political groupings, the Herero and the Mbanderu, and at one point each sought to create a "national" church. The Herero Church was the Oruuano Church (called in English the "Protestant Unity Church") and the Mbanderu Church became the Church of Africa. It could be said that, in terms of Sundkler's classification, these were Ethiopian-type churches. They were primarily Lutheran in theology and ethos. One of the historical principles of German Lutheranism was that of *cuius* regio, eius religio, literally something like: 'Who's region, his religion' meaning (one has to accept) the religion of the ruler. In such a theological ethos, it is hardly surprising that there should be a desire for a national church with close links to the political authority structure of the Herero and Mbanderu groups. But there were also several significant differences from the congregations of the Evangelical Lutheran Church. In many congregations there was a significant Pentecostal or Zionist influence. In the services there was much singing of choruses with clapping accompaniment. South African Initiated Churches of the Zionist or Apostolic-type had established themselves in Botswana, and their influence spread from there to Namibia. The most influential of these groups were the St John Apostolic Faith Church, the St Phillip Apostolic Faith Church, and the Apostolic Spiritual Healing Church. Prophets and other leaders of these churches were often guest preachers at Oruuano services, and at Herero and Mbanderu national occasions. Some traditional Herero customs were also incorporated into church ritual, such as sprinkling with holy water when bad things happened (such as the roof being blown off a church in a storm).

Like the AOC, therefore, the Oruuano Church incorporated different strands of tradition, though the predominating one was Lutheran. Unlike the AOC, however, it was more influenced by the Apostolic churches, and it is to these that we must now turn.

Strictly speaking, therefore, there is no "Ethiopian" Theology. West (1975:17) notes the term "Ethiopian" is used only by people who do not belong to that type of church, except in the case of denominations that have "Ethiopian" specifically in their title. There is no "Ethiopian" Theology, as such, that can be distinguished from that of the denominations that are usually classified as "mainline Protestant". Certainly, particular Ethiopian churches differ from particular "mainline Protestant" churches in their theology, but usually the differences are no greater than those between one mainline Protestant Church and another.

10.4.2 Zionist and Apostolic (Spirit-type) Churches

Unlike the Ethiopian-type churches, however, the Zionist and Apostolic Churches do have a distinctive theology. As the term Spirit-type indicates, their theology tends to be pentecostal-charismatic, with emphasis on the gifts and ministries of the Holy Spirit, especially healing and prophecy.

In South Africa the Zionist Churches, as described above, were started by Zionist missionaries from America, and were followed a few years later by Apostolic missionaries, also from America, from the early Pentecostal Movement. These missionaries generally did not stay very long, and the Zionist missionaries returned to America after only three or four years, because of leadership struggles in Zion City, Illinois.

SECTION A

THEOLOGY

10.4.3 Healing as a sacrament

The Zionist Churches in South Africa continued to preach the message they had received, and some of them added to it the Pentecostal message of the Apostolic missionaries as well. But they also interpreted the message in a specifically African way. The core of this message was divine healing, and this is the main difference between the Zionist-type churches and the Ethiopian type. For the Zionists, salvation was not simply a matter of one's soul being saved after death, but it included healing of soul and body now in this present life. The African Zionists also tended to return to an earlier theological model than their American teachers. American Pentecostals and Zionists, like other Protestants, tended to mistrust sacramental theology, because of their suspicion of anything that could look like Roman Catholicism. African Zionists did not have time to build up this mistrust, and therefore took a far more sacramental approach to healing and worship, making extensive use of such material things as holy water, special clothing and the arrangement of space to express their relationship with the God who has power over disease and sickness.

Zionist Churches believe that people are healed through the power of the Holy Spirit, acting either through a particular person with a healing ministry, or through the congregation as a whole. The healing ministry may be exercised in several ways. The commonest is prayer and laying on of hands. In some cases, the sick kneel in front of the congregation, while in others they kneel in the centre of a circle, and members of the congregation who are not actually laying hands on the sick dance in a circle around them. This is sometimes done in a dedicated holy place – a part of the worship space not used for other purposes. In some Zionist Churches, prayer for the sick is accompanied by rhythmic drumming (West 1975: 92ff.). Holy water is also used in healing, and it is usually blessed and drunk during the service. It is often used for general healing and purification as well as for healing specific ailments. Immersion in holy water – often in a blessed stream or river, is also used for healing in some Zionist Churches.

People with a particular healing ministry are found in many different Christian denominations, and not only among the Zionist and Apostolic Churches. Sometimes such a person becomes well known, and people of other denominations will go to them for healing. They believe that their healing power comes from God. Among the Zionist and Apostolic Churches, however, there are also prophetic healers who predict, heal and divine. Prophets are often those who have themselves been healed. They identify the causes of ailments, and sometimes hold private consultations. The method of healing may vary, but almost always includes prayer with laying on of hands. Blessing with a holy stick, and drinking holy water are also common. The holy water is sometimes mixed with other substances, such as ash. Baths are sometimes prescribed. Enemas and emetics are also sometimes used. Ash is sometimes used on its own, either sprinkled over the patient or around the house as a protective device. It is interesting to note here that in rural areas, members of the Anglican and Roman Catholic Churches (which practise the imposition of ashes on Ash Wednesday at the beginning of Lent) often see the imposition of ashes as very important. In the official teaching of the denominations concerned, the ashes are primarily a sign of penitence and mortality, but many church members see them as a sign of healing as well. Anointing with oil (sometimes in the form of petroleum jelly) is also used. Some of these items, such as ash, are also used in African traditional religion. The hearth or fireplace is particularly associated with ancestral spirits. The Zionists have often reinterpreted traditional symbols in this way.

Among many Zionists, however, there is one exception to this use of material things – the use of medicine is generally eschewed. This includes both western medicine and the African medicine of the herbalist. This was part of the original Zionist teaching, brought from Zion City, Illinois, and it has been retained by most of the offshoots. Though holy water (sometimes mingled with salt or ash) is applied externally and drunk internally, it is seen as sacramental rather than medicinal. For Zionists, the use of medicine is a sign of lack of faith, and their refusal to use it is one of the features that distinguishes them from the "worldly" Christians of other traditions whose faith the Zionists regard as weak. The Apostolic Churches, on the other hand, are more Pentecostal, and like Western Pentecostal Churches, their attitude to the use of medicine varies. Some, especially those of the Zionist-Apostolic type, will tend, like the Zionists, to reject it. Others, which have not been influenced by Zionism, might allow the use of medicine alongside spiritual healing.

Healing is not confined to physical ailments, and many Zionists believe that even physical ailments may have spiritual causes. Many of those who ask for healing are concerned about problems in relationships with members of their families, or with financial problems or worries. In Zionist Theology, troubles and afflictions of all kinds, and not only physical diseases, are seen to be sent by Satan and his demons. They are among the means used by Satan to draw Christians away from God. Healing is therefore closely linked with exorcism, and many of the healing rites are intended, either explicitly or implicitly, to drive out evil spirits and to protect against them. I shall return to this point later when discussing the soteriology of the African Initiated Churches. This theology is not new, however. In medieval Ethiopia, monastic missionaries used healing methods that are very similar to those used by Zionist prophets today. They would heal and exorcise using holy water, holy garments (usually garments of a monk with a reputation for personal holiness), the sign of the cross, etc. They also saw Satan as particularly active in disrupting human relationships by false accusations (the word "Satan" means "accuser"), and politically ambitious people would often use false accusations (and sometimes witchcraft) to discredit their rivals.

10.4.4 Ministry and authority

Another feature of the Zionist-type churches is a dual ministry or authority structure, which West (1975:49) distinguishes as a charismatic author-

SECTION A

THEOLOGY

ity and a legal authority. These two types of ministry are well-known in the history of the Christian Church and indeed they may be found in human society generally. In the first few centuries of the Christian faith, the "legal" ministry took the form of the ministry of bishops, priests and deacons. The charismatic ministries included apostles, prophets, evangelists, healers and, to some extent, pastors and teachers. From the 4th century onwards, the charismatic ministries were found mainly in the monastic movement. In Ethiopia, for example, most of the evangelism and spread of the church was the result of monks whose ministry was in some ways very similar to that of Zionist prophets today – they would heal through prayer and sacramental means, using holy water, garments and the sign of the cross.

In the Zionist-type churches in Southern Africa the two ministries are seen in the ministries of bishops (legal) and prophets (charismatic). The leaders of Ethiopian-type churches, like those of the "mission" churches, are mostly of the "legal" type, and the most common title of the leader is "president". Among the Zionist-type churches, however, particularly in Soweto, the two types of leadership are about equally balanced. There are two further characteristics worth noting: first, that the legal ministry is predominantly male, and the charismatic ministry is mainly female. Secondly, more than half the leaders are self-supporting, and do the same kind of secular work as most of the ordinary members of their churches, and they are also of the same general standard of education as members of their churches. This last point is in marked contrast to the "mission" churches, where the clergy often have a higher standard of education than most members of their congregations, and are usually supported financially by their churches (West 1975:53ff.).

While the structure of the ministry of the church may seem at first sight to be a practical and administrative matter, rather than a theological one, one should bear in mind the point made earlier – that the theology of the African Initiated Churches is an enacted theology rather than an articulated one. Over the last thirty years, since about the mid-1960s, many of the "mission" churches have reflected upon their ecclesiology and their theology of ministry, and it has led them to articulate a theology of ministry that looks remarkably like a theoretical model of the actual practice of many of the Zionist-type churches. After thirty years, however, they still have not been able to achieve what the Zionist-type churches appear to have discovered so effortlessly. What is more, in the 3rd and 4th centuries, churches in North East Africa followed a similar pattern. There would be a bishop, some priests, one or two deacons, and several "widows". The widows were not elderly women who prepared tea, but their ministry was primarily one of intercession, healing and prophecy – exactly as it is at the opposite end of the continent some 1600 years later.

In respect of their patterns of ministry, therefore, the Zionist-type churches seem to have rediscovered an ancient African model, and to have achieved without any special effort what the "mission" churches have been trying, unsuccessfully, to do for years. Statistics have shown that Zionist- or Spirit-type Initiated Churches have been growing much faster than the so-called historical churches. They have generally been more successful in evangelism. In part this is because of their patterns of ministry, which have tended to be more flexible, and to allow more scope for more members of the church to be active in ministry. The "historical" churches, with their emphasis on theological education for their clergy, have gradually lost the active lay ministry of their early days, and have become more "clerical".

10.4.5 Theology and culture

The patterns of ministry and organisational structures are not the only factor, however. Theology is at least as important. I pointed out earlier that the European missionaries who came to Africa in the 19th century were usually imbued with the Enlightenment world-view. The Enlightenment was a movement in Western Europe that emphasised the empirical study of nature and rational reflection on it. There were debates between rationalist and empiricist philosophers about the relative importance of reason and empirical study, but this led to the development of the scientific method used today in all the natural sciences, and, with some modifications, in the human sciences as well. At the beginning of the 19th century, methods of industrial mass production were also being developed, partly as a result of the Enlightenment approach. This enabled goods to be produced more quickly and cheaply than before, and the first countries to experience this "industrial revolution" achieved an enormous trade advantage over others. The first countries to develop such means of production were Britain, Germany, France and the USA. In Africa, cheap goods from those countries swept the market. In Namibia, for example, mass-produced knives and axes from the factories of Sheffield in England were far cheaper (and sharper) than the hand-made products produced by individual local craftsmen. The Sheffield products were brought by traders who exchanged them for ivory, and the local craftsmen were put out of business, and the whole pattern of trade changed.

Many of the early missionaries from Europe were themselves artisans, and had grown up with the capitalist mode of production, which they sought to introduce in Africa. This was part of their "civilising" mission, as they saw it. Western Theology had also become "civilised". The Enlightenment had been built on previous intellectual movements in Western Europe – the Renaissance and Reformation – which led to a profound change in the way of thinking. Western Theology, and especially Protestant Theology, reflected this.

10.4.6 Witchcraft and sorcery

In Europe in the 16th and 17th centuries there was a phenomenon known as the "Great Witch Hunt". Throughout Western Europe, hundreds of thousands of people were accused of witchcraft, often on the most spurious pretexts, and burnt to death. This witch hunt was on an unprecedented scale, and was a complex phenomenon – many books have been written to try to explain it. In part, it was a result of rationalism, and so

SECTION A

THEOLOGY

it was a predecessor of the Enlightenment. At the end of the 17th century, with the rise of empiricism, it suddenly stopped, and in the 18th century there was a remarkable revulsion against witch hunts. Empiricism demanded evidence. It not only demanded evidence that people accused of witchcraft had done what they were accused of doing (casting spells), but it also demanded evidence that the spells worked. In the absence of empirical scientific evidence that spells were actually effective, accusations of witchcraft were simply dismissed. In the 18th century, Western Europeans generally stopped believing in witchcraft. They came to believe that it was unscientific, and that it simply did not work.

The 19th-century missionaries who came to Africa inherited this attitude. But they came to a continent in which most people did believe that there were witches – malevolent people who used spiritual power to cause harm to others. In Africa, most problems, such as illness, misfortune or death, were seen to be caused by malevolent spiritual power, whether by human agency (witches or sorcerers) or not. The western missionaries were ill-equipped to deal with these problems, because their own societies had, in the very recent past, emphatically and decisively rejected the explanation that most Africans accepted. This meant that the gospel the European missionaries preached was irrelevant to pressing African problems. They preached a gospel that had been contextualized to fit post-Enlightenment Europe. In order to evangelise Africans, therefore, Western missionaries came to believe that they must get Africans to abandon African problems, and accept European (Enlightenment) ones. They believed that Africans could not be "evangelized" until they had been "civilised".

The civilising mission included schools. Protestant missionaries translated the Scriptures into local languages. They taught their converts to read the Scriptures. But in the Scriptures these converts found something that was relevant to African problems – Jesus healed the sick, cast out demons, and calmed storms. In Western Europe, theologians were trying to reconcile the culture clash between the Enlightenment and the first-century world of the Scriptures by a process that would lead to the Scriptures being demythologised, while in Africa those same Scriptures were speaking directly to the problems faced by many Africans. While the Enlightenment missionaries sought to solve the problems of witchcraft by building schools to teach people that witchcraft did not exist, the African evangelists they had trained were preaching a Jesus who could cast out demons. This was precisely the same method used by Ethiopian monks five centuries earlier – they did not deny or even question the assumptions or the world-view of African traditional religion. They simply announced that the Christian God could do it better. And even in Western Europe, another five centuries before that, the monastic missionaries who converted the ancestors of the Enlightenment missionaries who came to Africa had used the same methods.

10.4.7 Soteriology

What accounts for the difference is a change that took place in Western

European Theology from the 11th century onwards. In the 11th century a theologian called Anselm, who was Archbishop of Canterbury in England, wrote a book called *Cur Deus homo?* (Why did God become man?). Up to that point, most Christians believed that Christ had come to free us from evil spiritual powers that ruled the world, and prevented us from knowing God. Anselm, believing that sin was primarily an affront to the honour of God for which God had to punish us, thought that salvation meant primarily appeasing God's anger for our sins. Instead of seeing sin primarily as something that God rescues us from, Western European Theology came to see sin primarily as something God punishes us for. This soteriology came to dominate Western Theology. One of the things that it made possible, though it took centuries to develop, was the privatization of religion. It became possible to divorce "religion" from the rest of life, and to see it as something concerned only with one's relationship with God.

Because of this understanding of sin and salvation (soteriology), one of the main objects of the preaching of the Enlightenment missionaries was to induce a sense of guilt for sin in their hearers. One of the constant complaints of the Enlightenment missionaries was the difficulty of doing this. Africans, they complained, had no sense of religion, and no sense of sin. In their frustration at their failure to induce this sense of guilt for sin, they called Africans incorrigible savages, and various other uncomplimentary names. When they came to examine catechumens before they were baptised, they found that this sense of guilt for personal sin was lacking. The catechumens did indeed see that they needed to be saved – but from the power of the devil, from the power of evil. Even in the "historical" churches, this theology took root among the laity. The soteriology of the missionaries, and that of their converts differed. In the "historical" churches, however, this difference was contained, because the clergy were trained in seminaries that taught the official theology, including the soteriology, of the denomination concerned.

In the Initiated Churches, on the other hand, and especially in the Spirit-type Initiated Churches, there were no seminaries to perpetuate this teaching. In addition, the original Zionist and Pentecostal teaching on healing was far more congenial to the kind of soteriology developed by African laity. Among the Pentecostals, too, the idea of casting out evil spirits was not seen as something foreign. The white-led Pentecostal churches tended to keep the soteriology they had inherited from their evangelical Protestant forbears, so there was, to some extent, a dichotomy between their theology and their practice. But for the Initiated Churches there was no such restraint. Thus what most of the Spirit-type Initiated Churches have is a pre-Enlightenment soteriology, where they see salvation primarily as deliverance from the Evil One rather than deliverance from God's anger at their sins. As I pointed out earlier, this is primarily an experiential and enacted theology, not often expressed precisely in words. Salvation is made visible in the here-and-now by healing from sickness, and deliverance from evil spirits and from witchcraft and sorcery.

SECTION A

THEOLOGY

If non-Christians suffering from sickness or other problems that they believe to be caused by witchcraft, go to the "historical" churches with their problems, they are likely to be told that their problems are not real, and that they must exchange them for another set of problems before the church can help them. If they go to a Zionist church, on the other hand, the church will try to help them, by healing, by exorcism, by measures to counter the witchcraft. This led some Western theologians to describe Zionists as syncretist, or as "bridges back to heathenism". But empirical research (that Enlightenment method!) has shown that this is not necessarily so. The Zionists generally have a view very different from that of African traditional religion. Though the starting point is similar in that they share a similar understanding of the problem, the solutions they offer are different. Their soteriology is different from that of most of the Western "historical" churches, but it is nevertheless a thoroughly Christian soteriology, and perhaps a lot closer to that of the Christians of the first five centuries than that of the "historical" churches today. In the pagan Roman empire, many people became Christians because they had been healed by the ministry of Christians after their appeals to pagan deities had failed. The Zionists' success in evangelism and recruiting rests on a similar foundation.

10.5 SUMMARY AND CONCLUSION

The African Initiated Churches are a somewhat arbitrary grouping of Christian denominations, based initially on uneasiness among white government officials about bodies that were "not under European control" – for that reason called African Independent Churches. There are two more-or-less clearly defined types, generally known as Ethiopians and Zionists or Spirit-type churches. The Ethiopian-type groups were usually initially formed by schism from white-controlled denominations, as a form of protest against white-domination of the leadership. Their theology generally follows that of the denominations from which they broke away.

The Zionist or Spirit-type churches, in southern Africa at least, were the offspring of Zionist or Pentecostal missionaries from America who were in South Africa in the first decade of the 20th century. Because of the short time of their exposure to the message of the foreign missionaries, the Zionists took the basic message and applied it to the African situation. While in many respects they retained the basic theology and practice of their parent bodies, the most significant theological development was in their soteriology, where they shifted the emphasis away from guilt for individual sin to deliverance from evil. This soteriology is not necessarily found in all African Initiated Churches, but it is a distinguishing characteristic of a large number of the Spirit-type churches. It is also found in many of the so-called "historical" churches, though it is there more common among the black laity than among the seminary-trained clergy. This theology has made the message preached by the Spirit-type churches more relevant to the pre-Enlightenment cultures of Africa.

READING LIST AND BIBLIOGRAPHY

Barrett, D.B. 1968. *Schism and renewal in Africa*. Nairobi: Oxford University Press.

Chidester, D. 1992. *Religions of South Africa*. London: Routledge.

Comaroff, J. 1991. *Of revelation and revolution: Christianity, Colonialism and Consciousness in South Africa*. Chicago: University of Chicago Press.

Daneel, M.L. 1971. *Old and new in southern Shona Initiated Churches: Volume 1: Background and rise of the major movements*. The Hague: Mouton.

– 1987. *Quest for belonging: introduction to a study of African Initiated Churches*. Gweru, Zimbabwe: Mambo.

Lagerwerf, L. 1987. *Witchcraft, sorcery and spirit possession: pastoral responses in Africa*. Gweru: Mambo.

Makhubu, P. 1988. *Who are the Initiated Churches?* Johannesburg: Skotaville.

Marks, S. & Trapido, S. 1987. *The politics of race, class and nationalism in twentieth-century South Africa*. London: Longman.

Mitchell, R.C. & Turner, H.W. 1966. *A bibliography of modern African religious movements*. Evanston: North-West University Press.

Ndiokwere, Nathaniel I. 1981. *Prophecy and revolution*. London: SPCK.

Oosthuizen, G.C. 1987. *The birth of Christian Zionism in South Africa*. KwaDlangezwa: University of Zululand.

Pauw, B.A. 1960. *Religion in a Tswana chiefdom*. London: Oxford University Press.

– 1975. *Christianity and Xhosa tradition*. Cape Town: Oxford University Press.

Sundkler, B.G.M. 1961. *Bantu prophets in South Africa*. Oxford: Oxford University Press.

– 1976. *Zulu Zion and some Swazi Zionists*. Oxford: Oxford University Press.

Turner, H.W. 1967. *African Independent Church. Vol 2. The life and faith of the Church of the Lord (Aladura)*. Oxford: Clarendon.

– 1979. *Religious innovation in Africa: collected essays on new religious movements*. Boston: Hall.

Turner, Harold W. 1965. *Profile through preaching*. London: Edinburgh House.

Welbourn, F.B. 1961. *East African rebels: a study of some Initiated Churches*. London: SCM.

West, M. 1975. *Bishops and prophets in a black city*. Cape Town: David Philip.

10

African Initiated Church Theology

Pentecostal Theology

Francois Möller

11.1 INTRODUCTION

What is dealt with here is actually "classical" Pentecostal Theology. In the world of Pentecost there are more groups. Burgess, in his book, *Dictionary of Pentecostal and Charismatic Movements,* defines it thus:

> The classical Pentecostal Churches, which had their origins in the US at the beginning of this century, have since grown to be the largest family of Protestant Christians in the world. Known at first simply as "Pentecostal" churches, they were given the added designation "classical" about 1970 to distinguish them from "Neo"-Pentecostals in the mainline churches and the "charismatic" Pentecostals in the Roman Catholic Church (Burgess and McGee 1989:219–220).

However, the distinction between Neo-Pentecostals and Charismatic Pentecostals is rather forced and has been replaced by referring to both groups as Charismatic Pentecostals.

11.2 HISTORICAL BACKGROUND OF THE PENTECOSTAL MOVEMENT

The beginning of the movement can be dated back to 1901 when Agnes Ozman was baptized in the Spirit and spoke in tongues. This happened in the Bethel Bible School in Topeka, Kansas, US, with Charles F. Parham (a Methodist minister) as Principal (1873–1929). Parham's Theology later exercised considerable influence on the Pentecostal Movement. J.R. Goff Jr writes the following of Parham:

> Born amidst a panorama of religious ideas and persuasions, he connected the basic tenets that later defined the movement: evangelic-style conversion, sanctification, divine healing, pre-millennialism,

and the eschatological return of the Holy Spirit power evidenced by glossolalia. (Burgess 1989:660)

Together with a few followers, Parham gave the first impetus to the Pentecostal Movement. However, it was only with the so-called "Azusa Street Mission" in Los Angeles, California, that this movement experienced its first upsurge. The name "Azusa Street Mission" is due to what happened from 1906–1909 in an old building in 312 Azusa Street that previously had been a Methodist Church. For three years William J. Seymor, a black holiness preacher from Texas, held services in which some special manifestations of the Spirit occurred. Many persons were saved and healed, and numbers were baptized in the Spirit and experienced the accompanying tongues, including Seymor himself. Burgess writes of this early period:

> The first persons to receive the experience (of baptism in the Spirit) were poor and disinherited people from the mainline churches, primarily those from the Methodistic and Holiness movements that flourished in the late 19th century. The first avowedly Pentecostal Churches were the Pentecostal Holiness Church led by Joseph King, the Church of God (C.G. Cleveland, Ten) led by A.S. Tomlinson, and the Church of God in Christ led by C.H. Mason. These churches were formed as Holiness denominations before the advent of the Pentecostal Movement. (1989:221)

However, the Pentecostal Movement quickly spread far beyond the Holiness Movement, and soon after 1906 Pentecostal Churches could be found all over in America and in many countries of the world. Many other churches were formed in the US:

> In time, Pentecostal converts without roots in the Holiness Movement formed newer churches. Led by E.N. Bell, the Assemblies of God was formed in 1914 to serve those from a "Baptistic" background. Other churches of this type were the Pentecostal Church of God, founded in 1919 by John Sinclair, the International Church of the Foursquare Gospel founded by Aimee Semple McPherson in 1927, and the Open Bible Standard Churches formed by an amalgamation of two smaller organizations in 1935. (Burgess 1989:221)

11.3 HISTORICAL BACKGROUND OF THE CHARISMATIC MOVEMENT

The Charismatic Movement started in the late 1950s:

> The term Charismatic Movement is here understood in its most common usage to designate what Donald Geen in the late 1950s called the new Pentecost, namely the occurrence of distinctively Pentecostal blessings and phenomena, baptism in the Holy Spirit with the spiritual gifts of 1 Corinthians 12:8–10, outside a denominational and/or confessional Pentecostal framework. (Burgess 1989:130)

A number of ministers and members of non-traditional Pentecostal Churches had the experience of being baptized in the Spirit with the accompanying spiritual gifts. Because of a more open and accommodative attitude than before towards Pentecostal experiences in some mainline churches, many of these people have remained in their churches. They are referred to as charismatics. They initiated various charismatic groups which in most cases operated inter-denominationally. Examples of these are: The Full Gospel Men's Fellowship International founded by the American Demas Shahariah; Mother of God in Gaithersburg, Maryland, founded in 1966 by two newly Spirit-baptized housewives, Edith Difato and Judith Tydings; The Word of God Community in Ann Arbor founded in 1967 by Ralph Martin and Stephen Clark; Emmanuel founded in Paris in 1972 (by far the largest of the European communities); and Maranatha Community in Brussels (Möller 1975:23; Burgess 1989:128–9).

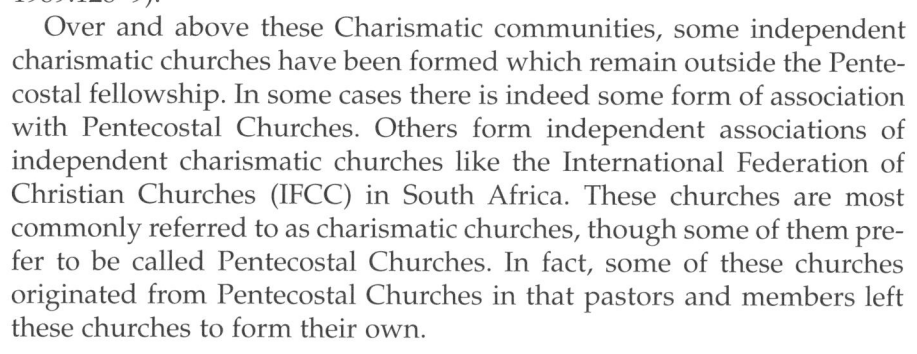

Over and above these Charismatic communities, some independent charismatic churches have been formed which remain outside the Pentecostal fellowship. In some cases there is indeed some form of association with Pentecostal Churches. Others form independent associations of independent charismatic churches like the International Federation of Christian Churches (IFCC) in South Africa. These churches are most commonly referred to as charismatic churches, though some of them prefer to be called Pentecostal Churches. In fact, some of these churches originated from Pentecostal Churches in that pastors and members left these churches to form their own.

11.4 A COMPARISON BETWEEN THE PENTECOSTAL AND CHARISMATIC MOVEMENTS

Because of the lack of a fully-fledged theology in both movements, it is difficult to identify differences between them. This is true even of their doctrines of the Holy Spirit, the one aspect of the faith they emphasize most. Added to this is the fact that there is a great diversity of views in the Charismatic Movement, as the movement itself is so diversified. This is particularly so, concerning the independent churches, for it is difficult to gather the specifics on theological issues.

One possible way out of this dilemma is to look at agreements between the movements and then try to identify differences in emphases. However, most of these differences will not touch fundamental issues, as many Pentecostal and Charismatic Churches are very close to one another in liturgy and spirituality and terms like "pentecostal" and "charismatic" are simply used alternatively.

Jesus Christ is central to both movements and both adhere to the foursquare gospel of Jesus as Saviour, Baptizer in the Spirit, Healer and coming King. The Spirit came to glorify Jesus. In both movements, strong emphasis is placed on a very personal relationship of the believer with Jesus as the revelation of God to humanity.

In both movements concepts like conversion, regeneration and salva-

SECTION A
THEOLOGY

tion are seen as alternatives for the same experience. A specific order of salvation (*ordo salutis*) is foreign to both movements. Whatever this experience of salvation is called, in most cases it is seen as a clearly identifiable crisis experience of a specific "time and date" when the person met Jesus as Saviour.

Because of the emphasis on a personal relationship with Jesus, much is made of the direct and indirect guidance of God in one's life. It is common to hear in these churches the words: "I was led by the Lord to ...", or: "The Lord told me to ...." This guidance is received in a variety of ways, like direct guidance from God being experienced as a firm conviction, urgent desire or strong urge; through the Bible, spiritual gifts; circumstances and people (Möller 1989). Believers are indeed encouraged to exert themselves to hear the voice of the Lord. As matter of control, this guidance is not to clash with the content of the Bible.

Both movements confess that baptism in the Spirit and the accompanying spiritual gifts are intended for the present and have not been terminated and show strong resistance to any theology that denies this:

> The effect of this doctrine was to deny the "cessation of the charismata" teaching that had been the standard teaching of the western churches since the days of Augustine. The cessation view holds that the charismata had been withdrawn from the church at the end of the apostolic age. (Burgess 1989:220; Möller 1975:ch 6)

However, in this instance there are some differences in emphasis. In the Pentecostal Movement, tongues are often referred to as initial evidence that a person is baptized in the Spirit. In fact, it was one of the first essentials of the movement in the beginning of its existence (McGee:1991). From an assignment on the baptism in the Spirit which Parham gave to his students, it can be concluded that "while there were different things that occur when the Pentecostal blessing fell, the indisputable proof on each occasion was that they spoke with other tongues" (Kendrick 1961: 51).

In the Charismatic Movement, tongues are not always seen as essential evidence. It is fairly generally accepted that a person can be baptized in the Spirit without the accompaniment of tongues (Christenson 1968: 54). This is, for instance, true of Latin-America where there is a special upsurge of the Charismatic Movement. This has again and again come to the fore in discussions between classical pentecostalism and the Roman Catholic Church in which I was involved on a regular basis since 1989.

In both movements, there is a strong link between baptism in the Spirit and evangelization. It is emphasized that evangelisation was one of the fruits of the original outpouring of the Spirit (Acts 2). If it is true that, in the Holiness Movement, the emphasis is on the fact that the Spirit sanctifies us and gives us victory over sin and results in holy living (the second blessing), then it is as true that with the Pentecostal and Charismatic Movements the emphasis is on the fact that the Spirit empowers us to witness. With regard to the evangelistic activities of the two movements, P.D. Hocken writes:

11
Pentecostal Theology

It is undeniable that the Charismatic Renewal, at least in the First World, has made most progress in the white, middle-class sectors of society, whereas the Pentecostal movement in its beginning was largely a proletarian phenomenon among poor people of all colours. However, the Charismatic Renewal has from the late 1970s made great progress among the churches of the Third World, most dramatically perhaps in Asia, where it is clearly not the preserve of the middle classes. The probable conclusion is that milieux penetrated by the Charismatic Renewal are those where the historic churches have their strongest membership. (In Burgess 1989:156)

The majority of Pentecostal Churches administer the sacrament of baptism to believers by immersion. In some churches it is done by a threefold immersion, in others by immersing only once. However, in the Charismatic Movement there are some differences. In most cases, the denominational Charismatics accept the forms of baptism in use in their home churches, where the sprinkling of infants is practised. But in the Independent Charismatic Churches, baptism is mostly restricted to believers and is done by a once-only immersion.

Both movements place great emphasis on divine healing. Healing ministries are common, especially where the sick are prayed for. During the founding years of the Pentecostal Movement there was, and in extreme cases there still is, an aversion to the medical profession and medical science, since the use of medicine is seen as a sign of unbelief. However, this view is no longer generally fostered in these movements.

As concerns liturgy, both movements emphasize spontaneous worship. Sometimes worship includes singing in tongues. These forms of spontaneity are increasingly entering other denominations.

The identity of the two movements has influenced their respective mission involvement:

> Charismatic Renewal in the mainline denominations did not immediately release the missionary drive that characterized Azusa Street and the beginnings of Pentecostalism. In the early stages of Charismatic Renewal, the main evangelistic thrust was toward fellow church members to bring them to the baptism in the Holy Spirit, rather than toward the pagan and unchurched. (Burgess 1989:157)

Concerning theological reflection on the experience of Pentecost, Hocken writes:

> The area of theology manifests another obvious contrast between Pentecostals and Charismatics, especially those from Christian traditions with a rich theological inheritance, whether Catholic, Orthodox, Lutheran, Reformed, or Puritan. Charismatics from these traditions, especially priests and ministers, attach more importance to a coherent theological basis for the Pentecostal experience than do Pentecostals and independent charismatics. The spread of Charismatic Renewal to the Roman Catholic Church led to a rapid rise in the theological output on topics of baptism in the Holy Spirit

SECTION A

THEOLOGY

and charismata .... The theological task imposed by Charismatic Renewal has been perhaps most recognised by Lutheran leaders, as shown in the book *Welcome, Holy Spirit*, edited by Larry Christensen (1987), produced by an international team of Lutheran scholars and pastors. (Burgess 1989:158)

Though there is truth in Hocken's words, it should be remembered that theological reflection was a continuous part of the Pentecostal Movement since its origin. This is reflected in the fact that virtually every classical Pentecostal church has a theological training, some of which are related to universities. In southern Africa, the most recent of these is the affiliation of the Theological College of the Apostolic Faith Mission in Johannesburg with the Rand Afrikaans University in 1993.

Added to this are the theological discussions between the classical Pentecostals and the Catholic Church that have appeared since 1972. This dialogue, initiated by David du Plessis (known as "Mr Pentecost"), is conducted annually on international level, mostly in Europe, when representatives from different countries gather for this purpose.

Also in 1975, F.P. Möller, a classic pentecostal, was the first person in both movements to receive a doctor's degree on the baptism in the Spirit and the charismata. It was awarded by the State University of Utrecht.

Rightly, Hocken, remarks that the Charismatic Movement was privileged to be enriched by the age-old theological traditions of the mainline churches. This will, however, not be valued only as an advantage by the classical Pentecostal Churches. They do not see the pentecostal experience as something that can merely be added to the mainline theologies, whether Catholic, Lutheran or Reformed. Baptism in the Spirit and the manifestations of the spiritual gifts influence not only pneumatology, but all of theology. The experience of pentecost has as an essential result that all of theology is to be re-taught and re-formulated. Without this, charismatics will end up in a dualism not only in terms of pneumatology, but of virtually all the other aspects of the faith, as these form a tight and interrelated network.

11.5 A PENTECOSTAL PARADIGM

The word "paradigm" is here understood as the frame out of which and in terms of which the theological reflection of the Pentecostal movement is done. This framework can also be seen as the key to unlocking the Bible, the central truth in light of which the biblical documents are read.

The adjective "Pentecostal" can be misleading, since it could easily be understood that Pentecost is the kernel of this paradigm. This is not true. A Pentecostal paradigm simply means that paradigm which is characteristic of the Pentecostal Movement.

In the formulation of this paradigm, both the diversity of the movement and the limited amount of theological work done, are a problem. So we have to simplify, in the hope that the majority of Pentecostal Churches will recognize themselves in it.

The history of theology reflects a number of attempts to understand the gospel theologically in terms of such a key concept or paradigm. The following examples are obvious: the theology of *hope* (Moltmann), of *salvation history* (Cullmann), of *reason* (Pannenberg), of revolution, of liberation, and existential theology (Bultmann), to name but a few. Reference can also be made to the role of key concepts in theology – such as the church in some trends in Catholic Theology, the *covenant* in the theology of Eichrodt, and the kingdom of God in forms of Reformed Theology (Van der Walt 1973:9).

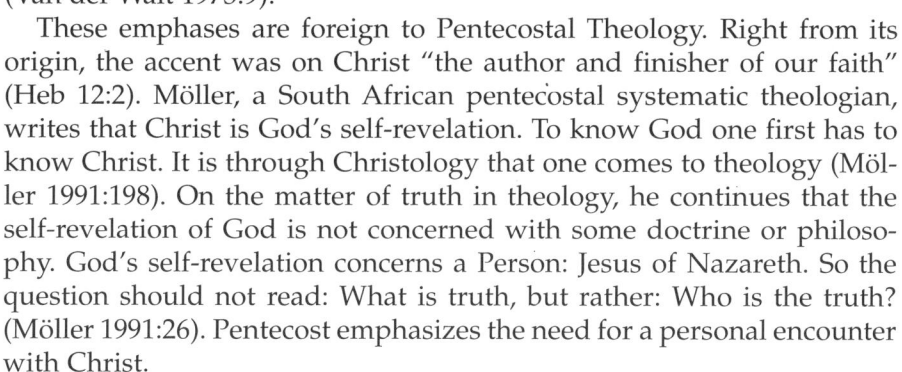

These emphases are foreign to Pentecostal Theology. Right from its origin, the accent was on Christ "the author and finisher of our faith" (Heb 12:2). Möller, a South African pentecostal systematic theologian, writes that Christ is God's self-revelation. To know God one first has to know Christ. It is through Christology that one comes to theology (Möller 1991:198). On the matter of truth in theology, he continues that the self-revelation of God is not concerned with some doctrine or philosophy. God's self-revelation concerns a Person: Jesus of Nazareth. So the question should not read: What is truth, but rather: Who is the truth? (Möller 1991:26). Pentecost emphasizes the need for a personal encounter with Christ.

There are those in the Pentecostal Movement who radicalize this emphasis. Reference can be made to the so-called "Oneness Pentecostalism" which broke away from the Assemblies of God (US) in 1914. At first they were called the "New Issue" or the "Jesus Only" Movement. Since 1930 they call themselves by names like "Jesus Name", "Apostolic", or "Oneness Pentecostalism". Burgess writes that:

> Adherents of the "Jesus Name" Pentecostal movement taught a moralistic view of the Godhead that denied the Trinity while ascribing to Jesus Christ the deity of the Father, the Son, and the Holy Spirit. (1989:221)

However, this emphasis on Jesus Christ at the expense of the Father and the Spirit is not representative of pentecostalism. The doctrine of the Trinity is accepted by the greater majority of pentecostals. Their Christ-centredness is no Christomonism. Rather, they see Jesus Christ as the acme of God's revelation. At the centre of their faith and theology is Jesus Christ: Saviour, Baptizer in the Spirit, Healer, and coming King.

In light of this, it is not far-fetched to call Christ Himself the Pentecostal paradigm. In this sense the name pentecostalism is misleading, as the Spirit is not central to Pentecostal experience or thought. W.G. MacDonald correctly writes that:

> In a movement that highly valued and proclaimed the activities of the Spirit of God, the place of Jesus as God's Christ, i.e. Anointed, and Spirit dispenser, nevertheless, has been central. As with the gifted teachers of the movement, it has never been a simplistic choice based on the either/or fallacy – either pneumatology or Christology. The principle has been reiterated time and time again: The more of the Spirit pervading one's total experience, the more one will have a preoccupation with Jesus as the object of adoration,

11

Pentecostal Theology

SECTION A

THEOLOGY

the focus of doctrine as "the Word of God" (John 1:1; Rev 19:13), the model of spirituality, and the paragon of ethical integrity and fruitfulness. This, of course, presupposes his oneness with God (John 10:30; 17:11,21), and his bearing the unmeasured fullness of the Spirit of God (John 3:34). (Burgess 1989:481)

So, in Pentecost a personal and living relationship between God in Christ through the Spirit on the one hand, and the human being on the other, is simply not negotiable. Any other key concept, like covenant or Kingdom of God or hope or whatever, will be seen as threatening this personal and living relationship between God and the human being. In Pentecostal Theology it is not so much "something" that is at stake, but rather "Someone" – Jesus Christ. Möller further emphasizes this by saying that all revelation comes from and leads back to Christ. So all theological thought should start with Him, the light and the truth (Möller 1991:104). This is more than a mere theoretical truth to pentecostals. The revelation of God in Christ is not only presupposed in, for example, preaching, celebrating the sacraments or in singing, but is constantly expected as a concrete experience in one's life. This existential element in theology is essential to pentecostals.

Pentecostals emphasize that besides the danger of this living relationship being replaced by a paradigm of something, there is also the danger of employing God in the service of such a concept. So it may happen that in a theology of the Kingdom of God, God may be reduced to the main actor in the service of the kingdom, in which case the Creator will become subservient to creation.

W.G. MacDonald amply summarizes the pentecostal view in the following words:

> Because he rose from the dead and by his Spirit was present in the worshipping community, they (pentecostals) did not need to go for a conceptual centre beyond Him, or to place a theological framework over Him. He is alive and interactive among his people. The Christian faith is spelled out from A to Z in Him. He is the First and the Last. ([Rev 1:17] in Burgess 1989:482)

11.6 THE IMPLICATIONS OF THE PENTECOSTAL PARADIGM

It is clear that in the Pentecostal paradigm, truth is related to Christ Himself and not to any theological or even biblical concept. This position has some important implications. Only a few are mentioned here.

As far as the baptism in the Spirit is concerned, what is at stake is not merely a spiritual experience of sorts, but an essential encounter with the glorified Christ as the Baptizer with the Spirit. In encouraging people to seek this baptism, they are in fact encouraged to seek Christ:

> In believer's baptism one must totally yield himself to immersion by another in water; likewise one must totally yield himself to be baptized by Christ in the Holy Spirit ... In any event, what is important is a total surrender to the lordship of Jesus Christ. (Burgess 1989: 47–48)

Möller says that it primarily concerns a revelation of God in one's life, and not merely an experience as such. It is a result, the consequence of the encounter with Jesus Christ as the Baptizer in the Spirit; it is an experience in the God-human relationship (Möller 1975:36).

Even the spiritual gifts are seen in the closest relationship with Jesus Christ. Christ gives the gifts and the gifts witness to Him. Oral Roberts writes: "The ultimate purpose of every gift is to reveal Jesus Christ, to testify of Him and to enable believers to be more complete in Him" (1964: 60). Again, Donald Gee writes:

> Wherever, therefore, the Spirit is working in truth, there comes a revelation of the Lord Jesus Christ. It must inevitably follow that in the manifestation of his gifts there will come supremely a glorification of Christ, and a continuance of his power, both to do and to teach, that will provide nothing less than a re-discovery of those who have conceived of Jesus only as a dim figure of history. (Gee 1937:108)

So the gifts are not given to glorify us, but Christ.

It has already been established that by far the majority of pentecostals accept the doctrine of the Trinity. However, even this they understand in terms of the Christological paradigm. God is called "Father" because Jesus is his "Son" and he is Jesus' Father. For a human to have God as Father, one has to be related to (be "in") Jesus. Without Jesus there is no access to the Father (John 14:6).

This is also true as far as the Spirit is concerned. The Spirit came to glorify Christ (John 16:14) and no one can say that Jesus is Lord except by the Holy Spirit (1 Cor 12:3).

So Father, Son and Holy Spirit, as the triune God, is revealed to us through the God-man Jesus Christ. For the pentecostalist, this means that there is no way for a human being to reach God except through Jesus Christ, the Way.

The sacrament of baptism is also understood in terms of Christ. He instituted baptism and determines how and to whom it should be administered. Möller writes that in Jesus and his gospel we have the fullest and clearest revelation of what God gives us in his grace. Jesus Christ, the light of the world, the One the Spirit opens our eyes to see, is to us the light in whom we understand that which, in the Old Testament, is still unclear and shadowy (Heb 10:1). It is not the other way round. It is not the case that in the light of the shadowy Old Testament we have to understand the bright Light of the New Testament. One always starts with the bright light and in this light researches whatever is dim and uncertain. Applied to baptism, it means that one starts with the teaching of Jesus and the rest of the New Testament on baptism, and only from there does one consider related questions (Möller 1992:412).

The following texts are considered as important: "Are you able ... to be baptized with the baptism with which I am baptized?" "I have a baptism to be baptized with, and how I am constrained until it is accomplished!" (Mark 10:38; Luke 12:50. See also Rom 6:4–5.) The meaning of these texts

SECTION A

THEOLOGY

is that baptism is primarily related to the cross and death of Christ. Other meanings of this sacrament are to be deduced from this primary one.

Concerning election, the point of departure is Jesus Christ as the One elected by God (Möller 1992:94). For pentecostals there is no such thing as being elected before being in Christ. To be elected is to be in the elected One – Christ. So again, election is understood in terms of Christology.

It has become clear that also the Bible is understood and interpreted in the light of Christ. This does not mean that every text is related directly to Him, but rather that Christ, as the revelation of God, is the key to the understanding of the biblical message.

It is an open question how consistent pentecostals are in terms of the other theological loci as far as this paradigm is concerned. Our theological task is never completed and many changes in emphasis and nuance are possible in the years to come. But is seems clear that ever since its conception, Pentecost has not diverted from its emphasis on Jesus Christ.

11.7 CONCLUSION

We have tried to present the main characteristics of pentecostalism, not a complete set of doctrines. The aim was to stimulate readers to further research, but above all to a deeper experience of God's self-revelation: Jesus Christ.

READING LIST

Bennett, D. and R. 1971. *The Holy Spirit and You*. Plainfield: Logos International.
Brewster, P.S. 1976. *Pentecostal Doctrine*. Cheltenham, Gloucestershire, England: Grenehurst Press of the Elim Pentecostal Churches.
Burgess, S.M. and McGee, G.B. 1988. *Dictionary of Pentecostal and Charismatic Movements*. Grand Rapids: Zondervan.
Clark, M.S., Lederle, H.I.L. et al. 1983. *What is distinctive about Charismatic Theology?* Pretoria: University of South Africa.
Duffield, G.P. and Van Cleave, N.M. 1983. *Foundation of Pentecostal Theology*. Los Angeles: L.I.F.E. Bible Centre.
Erwin, H.M. 1968. *These are not drunken, as ye suppose*. Plainfield:Logos International.
– 1984. *Conversion-Initiation and the baptism in the Holy Spirit*. Peabody: Hendrickson.
Gordon, A. 1962. *The Third Force*. Peterborough: College Press.
McGee, G.B. 1991. *Initial Evidence. Historical and Biblical perspectives on the Pentecostal doctrine of Spirit baptism*. Peabody: Hendrickson.
Rodman, W.J. 1988. *Renewal Theology. Systematic Theology from a Charismatic Perspective*. Vol I-III. Grand Rapids: Academic Books.

BIBLIOGRAPHY

Burgess, S.M. and McGee, G.B. (eds.). 1989. *Dictionary of Pentecostal and Charismatic Movements*. Grand Rapids: Zondervan.
Christenson, L. 1968. *Speaking in Tongues and its Significance for the Church*. Minneapolis: Bethany Fellowship.

Gee, D. 1937. *Concerning Spiritual Gifts*. Springfield: Gospel Publishing House.
Kendrick, K. 1961. *The Promise Fulfilled*. Springfield: Publishing House.
McGee, G.B. 1991. *Initial Evidence*. Peabody: Hendrickson.
Möller, F.P. 1975. *Die Diskussie oor die Charismata soos wat dit in die Pinksterbeweging geleer en beoefen word*. Braamfontein: Evangelie Uitgewers.
– 1989. *Goddelike leiding*. Braamfontein: Evangelie Uitgewers.
_ 1991. *Woorde van Lig en Lewe*. Deel I. Westhoven: Evangelie Uitgewers.
– 1992. *Woorde van Lig en Lewe*. Deel II. Westhoven: Evangelie Uitgewers.
– 1994. *Woorde van Lig en Lewe*. Deel III. Westhoven: Evangelie Uitgewers.
Roberts, O. 1964. *The Baptism with the Holy Spirit and the Value of Speaking in Tongues*. Tulsa.
Van der Walt, T. 1973. *Openbaringsgeskiedenis van die Nuwe Testament*. Potchefstroom: Pro Rege.

Charismatic Theology

Jacques Theron

12.1 INTRODUCTION

In order to come to grips with Charismatic Theology, one should first try to understand the early developments of the Charismatic Movement. Specific attention should be given to its Pentecostal roots, to later developments and to its present position. The different churches, groups and scholars that are associated with this kind of theology also need to be identified.

From the onset, it should be noted that Charismatic Theology as such simply does not have a well-developed, identifiable, accepted systematic theology in its own right. Part of the reason for this is that the movement is still very young. Other reasons are that this kind of theology represents a vast number of churches, groups and individuals from totally different theological backgrounds and that the movement, at least in its beginning phases, made use of a kind of oral theology.

We will first look at the historical roots of the movement and then at the characteristics of Charismatic Theology.

12.2 THE ROOTS OF CHARISMATIC THEOLOGY

12.2.1 Historical developments

Pentecostal and Charismatic Theologies are often grouped together since there are very strong historical links between the two streams. Therefore, it is understandable that in the early stages of the development of a "Charismatic Theology", it was dubbed by some scholars as "Neo-Pentecostal Theology". In recent years however, at least in some circles, charismatics have done their best to develop a distinct kind of theology – separated from its Pentecostal connections. To further this trend, other descriptions are being used, for example *Renewal Theology* or even *Third*

SECTION A THEOLOGY

Wave Theology. We will give more attention to these and other theologies at a later stage.

The First Wave in the comprehensive Pentecostal-Charismatic movement began about 1901–1906 – with its earlier roots in religious awakenings among black slaves in the 18th (1741, 1783) and 19th (1886) centuries (cf. Lederle 1990:282). These developments and characteristics are described in the section on Pentecostal Theology.

It is generally accepted (cf. Lederle 1990:283; Spittler 1991:292) that the so-called *Second Wave* of the Spirit or Charismatic Movement broke on to the scene in the early Sixties – beginning among mainline Protestants about 1960, within the (Roman) Catholic Church in 1967 and within the Eastern Orthodox Church in 1971. The movement brought "Pentecost" to the established denominations. This transition was facilitated by initiatives from the remarkable "one-man crusade" of David du Plessis (a South African dubbed "Mr Pentecost" by the American press), the lay Full Gospel Business Men's Fellowship and the healing ministry of Oral Roberts and Oral Roberts University.

Lederle (1990:284) says that the potential for fragmentation and division that the Charismatic Renewal of the Second Wave harboured, came to the fore on the local congregational level. Traditional Christians felt threatened by the renewal movement. Many denominational charismatics exhibited elitist attitudes and spiritual pride. This led to estrangement and tension in many quarters. Sometimes parishes were split, often factions developed and the task of leadership was made more complex. A few smaller denominations were divided into Charismatic and non-Charismatic sections. In most cases, denominations weathered the storm and a Charismatic style of worship was added to the already existing plurality within the church. The three volumes *Presence, Power, Praise* by McDonnell (1980) document the gradual shift in the official pronouncements of churches on the Charismatic Movement from initial alarm or apprehension to cautious acceptance and integration. This was especially true of the attitudes of Catholic and mainline Protestant Church leadership.

The definition of the *Third Wave* poses a problem. Both Spittler (1990: 292) – following the demographer D.B. Barrett – and Wagner (1988: 13–19) say that this phase emerged around 1980, and describe Evangelicals who are not at all inclined to leave their churches nor to call themselves either "Pentecostal" or "Charismatic", but who nevertheless have adopted Pentecostal supernaturalism. They practice the gifts of prophecy, exorcism, prayer for the sick, words of knowledge and speaking in tongues. Thus these authors take the term to refer to a group of denominational (rather than independent) charismatics coming mostly from the more conservative and even the dispensational churches. Their approach would then seem to limit the terms "Charismatic" and "Second Wave" to the *Neo-Pentecostal* grouping of charismatics and prefer "Third Wave" for the *theologically more sophisticated Charismatic* positions.

Lederle's contention (1990:285, 287) on the other hand, is that this term (Third Wave) is more appropriately applied to the rise of *independent*

Charismatic denominations and *networks*. He links this to the fact that, in the Eighties, some denominational charismatics left their denominations because they did not consider them susceptible to radical renewal. They were joined by classical pentecostals who despaired of traditionalism within their churches. These groups formed non-denominational local churches and centres. Others became part of independent Charismatic groupings that were formed, espousing new doctrinal emphases and teachings. He distinguishes at least four streams: the *Faith* movement, the *Restoration* stream, The *Dominion* movement and The *Power Encounter* movement.

12.2.2 The growth of the movement

Hollenweger (1993:152), using the statistics presented by D.B. Barrett, notes that in general, academic theology in the past had no idea of the importance of the continual growth of the Pentecostal Movement. The situation remains the same today. Never in the history of the church did one movement grow from its beginning to more than three hundred million people in eighty years (that is if we include the Pentecostal Churches, the Charismatic Movement and the Independent Churches in the Third World, which historically and phenomenologically belong to the Pentecostal Movement). According to him, the reason for this growth lies firstly in the black and secondly in the oral heritage in the Pentecostal Movement.

Barrett (1989:20–21; cf. 1988:810–830) reports, for mid-1988, about 351 million pentecostals and charismatics and about 318 million Protestants (not including 53 million Anglicans, who officially eschew the term "Protestant"). He further notes the growth of the movement by naming it a "megatrend" in the Eighties. Furthermore, the extraordinary feature of this megatrend is that 80% of all East Asia's Christians are Pentecostal/Charismatic. And their own indigenous mission agencies are spreading throughout the world in countries as distant as Brazil, the United States, Germany, France, Britain, Saudi Arabia, the Gulf states and over fifty other nations.

12.3 FROM ORAL THEOLOGY TO FORMAL SYSTEMATIC THEOLOGY

Spittler (1991:302) says that what distinguishes classical Pentecostalism from all its children in the renewal lies in the character and longevity of the ecclesiastic traditions involved, and especially in the very different valuations of the academic enterprise. Originally, Pentecostalism grew through its oral tradition. It cannot properly be understood and evaluated if this fact is not taken into consideration (cf. Hollenweger 1993:51–153).

The first charismatics more or less started on the same basis with their testimonies, stories, renewed worship, love meals, descriptions of changed lives, but soon education and study gained greater value (cf. Lederle 1988:37).

SECTION A

THEOLOGY

This means, on the one hand, that charismatics could partake in this kind of theological reflection, but on the other hand they also had the privilege of sharing in the ecclesiastical maturity of the major Protestant traditions, with their positive valuation and support of academic inquiry. This ensured that theological outcomes stemming from the charismaticised mainline churches outrank in technicality the modest and pragmatic doctrinal products of the much younger classical Pentecostal tradition (Spittler 1991:303).

12.4 A VARIETY OF THEOLOGIES

In the light of the former emphasis on Oral Theology, and because the Charismatic Movement is just more than about thirty years old, it should once again be noted that there are few well-developed systematic theologies which can be easily identified as specifically "Charismatic". As was indicated above, charismatics in the early Sixties were united in the (Pentecostal) experience of the Spirit. As time went by, many of the charismatics started to pray for whole denominations to be touched by the same Spirit. This led to a process of charismatics becoming more aware of their denominational heritage. In order to reach greater numbers, and allay the fears that the groups of denominational charismatics were en route to Pentecostalism or schism, some serious theological relection and a measure of re-confessionalizing was called for. Thus Catholic charismatics became more conscious of their own traditions. Charismatic dimensions were rediscovered in the thought of the Mystics, and devotion to Mary and loyalty to the pope either increased or just became more visible. In the same vein, Lutherans and Methodists were reappropriating aspects of Luther and Wesley's teachings – or their own sacramental/liturgical traditions as in the case of Anglicans or Episcopalians. Even Calvinists found, to their surprise, that the Reformer advocated the raising of the hands (and hearts!) as a time-honoured posture of prayer (Lederle 1990:283). Spittler (1991:303) says in reference to Protestant Charismatic theologies that they involve considerable diversification: the many varieties of Protestantism, when they are charismaticised, still yield the familiar motifs of each tradition. He adds that Protestant Charismatic Theology, when compared with classical Pentecostal Theology, comes out more academically substantial and capable of much greater variety because of prior centuries of diversification. These theologies reached print far sooner after arrival of the charismatic impulse, and (due to the maturity of the Reformation Churches and the existence of long-standing catechetical resources) are more likely to move beyond edification to critical and societal engagement.

12.5 SPIRIT-BAPTISM SEEN FROM DIFFERENT ANGLES

It is understandable that Charismatic theologians – especially those from the Second Wave – at first did not want, nor ventured, to rewrite the different doctrines of the churches to which they belonged. Instead, they concentrated on the central doctrine of Charismatic experience, namely

Spirit-baptism. This was the main feature which they had to reinterpret in terms of their own theological backgrounds.

Initially, the first generation of Charismatic leaders had generally taken over the categories and framework of Pentecostalism and are therefore termed Neo-pentecostals. Lederle (1990:284) says that although they were less insistent on "the law of tongues" (as Tom Smail dubbed the Pentecostal teaching that everyone should speak in tongues), they preserved the "theology of subsequence" or two-stage pattern to Christian life – referring to the notion that one may receive salvation and only later receive the baptism of the Holy Spirit. He further says that this almost inevitably led to elitist tendencies, dividing Christians into two camps – those who are only saved or born again and those who are also baptised in the Holy Spirit. This teaching was later subjected to exegetical scrutiny and most New Testament scholars found it to be sadly lacking in biblical support. Thus a new process of reinterpretation began.

To understand these developments more adequately, one should take note of the important volume by Lederle (1988). In this indispensable guide to the varieties of Charismatic Theology – originally his doctoral thesis completed at the University of South Africa – he describes and analyses the Charismatic theologies of some forty different writers from the Protestant, Roman Catholic and Eastern Orthodox traditions. He starts with pre-Charismatic interpretations of Spirit-baptism, but then continues to classify the Charismatic authors into three broad groups. As was mentioned above, the first of these categories is called *Neo-Pentecostal interpretations* of Spirit-baptism with a particular emphasis on speaking in tongues as initial evidence. The writers in this category are for example Don Basham (representing the non-denominational Charismatic Movement which, specifically in its early days, was the most authentic form of Neo-Pentecostalism), Dennis Bennett (who is generally considered to be the pioneer of the Charismatic Movement), Terry Fullham (the last two both from an Episcopalian background), Larry Christenson (Lutheran; here evaluated on the basis of his earlier writings), Stephen Clark and Peter Hocken (Catholic), J. Rodman Williams (Presbyterian) and Howard Ervin (Baptist).

The writers in the second category, *sacramental interpretations,* are predictably found among Anglican, Roman Catholic, Reformed, Orthodox and Lutheran thinkers (e.g. Cardinal Suenens, Arnold Bittlinger, J.M. Ford, Donald Gelpi, Kilian McDonnell, Heribert Mühlen, Larry Christenson, Brick Bradford, John Gunstone and Eusebius Stephanou).

In this group "Spirit-baptism" is more or less seen as the "experiential flowering" of baptismal grace. The Spirit, whom the individual received in the sacrament of Christian initiation, is experientially "released" at the time of his or her being baptised in the Spirit. Attempts were also made to replace the questionable terminology of "Spirit-baptism". They were largely unsuccessful (Lederle 1991:284).

The third group of writers include some of the names which have been mentioned already. They are classified under the heading *integrative in-*

terpretations and more strongly reflect denominational allegiance. They vary considerably among themselves: Thomas Smail (Presbyterian/ Anglican), David Watson, Michael Harper and Michael Cassidy (Anglican), Charles Hummel and Morton Kelsey (Episcopal), Culpepper, Hart, Bridge and Phypers (Baptist), Sullivan and (again) Mühlen (Catholic), as well as Donald Griffioen and Barbara Pursey (Reformed/Presbyterian).

Of this group, Lederle (1991:284) says that amongst the more Evangelical charismatics, a broad range of new interpretations were offered to help integrate the Charismatic experience more fully into historic Christian teaching. Thus the validity of the experience of "Spirit-baptism" was acknowledged without accepting its elitist ultimacy or the event- and experience-centredness prevalent in earlier interpretations. It was viewed as the final state of Christian initiation, the infilling with the Spirit, which is repeatable, a mountain-top experience, a new "coming" of the Spirit, a growth or breakthrough experience, or as a part of the long-suppressed experiential dimension of the normal Christian life. According to Lederle, these new interpretative tools enabled Second Wave charismatics to avoid the "unwanted baggage" of Pentecostalism without sacrificing the newly found joy of "life in the Spirit", that is, openness to the spiritual experience of God's presence and the manifestation of the full range of charismatic gifts in the church.

12.6 SYSTEMATIC THEOLOGIES FROM DIFFERENT TRADITIONS

12.6.1 A Charismatic Systematic Theology from a Protestant perspective

In this regard we mainly follow Spittler's thoughts (1991:302–307). It was only in 1988 that the first Systematic Theology, incorporating a throughgoing theological viewpoint, was produced by someone from the Second Wave. In that year, charismatic Presbyterian systematic theologian J. Rodman Williams published *Renewal Theology: God, the world, and redemption*, with the tag line "Systematic theology from a Charismatic perspective". Williams' *Renewal Theology* was conceived as a comprehensive Systematic Theology. In the preface he writes: "my concern is ... to deal with the full range of Christian truth. It will nevertheless be 'renewal theology,' because I write as one positioned within the renewal context". Williams sees his work as not unlike similar works, except in three regards. First, he consciously preserves a style close to conversational, in order to communicate well. Second, he writes unabashedly with the enthusiasm he reports as an outcome of his personal renewal experience in 1965. Third, primarily in Volume II, he readdresses a neglect of charismatic dimensions of the doctrine of the Holy Spirit. It is clear that Williams has moved away from a sacramentalist view and much closer to classical Pentecostal notions (but not quite their language). His thoughts show the benefit of mature reflection and articulated balance. Volume II is a major contribution to the doctrine of the Holy Spirit in a systematic context – a treatment that boldly and extensively develops topics like spiritual gifts and the "coming of the Spirit". Volume III of *Renewal Theology* (1992) deals with the issues of the church, the kingdom and the last things.

Williams does not hesitate to let his personal renewal show through in his writings, not offensively but as a means of engagement with his material. "What I hope the reader will catch," he writes, "is the underlying excitement and enthusiasm about the reality of the matters discussed. The old being renewed is something to be excited about" (1988:12). An illuminating section entitled "The method of doing theology" (1988: 21–28) starts with "seeking the guidance of the Holy Spirit". But theological method, Williams feels, must also show reliance on the Scriptures, familiarity with church history, awareness of the contemporary scene and growth in Christian experience. His style in the use of Scripture more closely parallels the non-technical approach of classical Pentecostalism, and this feature separates his approach from that of the Roman Catholic charismatics. On the other hand, he refuses to endorse the recent emphasis on "scientific creationism" found in the right-wing evangelicalism, which many pentecostals (but far fewer charismatics) would be inclined to accept. Something of Williams' charismatic creativity appears when he considers creation within the categories of "blessing and praise ... marvel and wonder", focusing not "on *how* God created but *that* he did" (1988:98).

The sole available systematic theology by a Protestant charismatic thus shares with pentecostals a high value placed on experience and allows this to show up in the very design of theological topics (joy over creation and for the benefits of atonement). But *Renewal Theology* shows wider knowledge of theological literature and deeper acquaintance with (as well as greater ecumenical openness toward) the broad church. At the same time, it can be observed that Williams uses the Bible pre-critically. In addition, he does, in the main, not engage the broad range of European Theology and exegesis.

Spittler (1991:307) concludes his observation of the writings by Protestant charismatics by saying that as a whole, they reflect a theological style that is more sophisticated than that found in classical pentecostals, but less technical than that of certain Roman Catholic charismatic theologians. These Protestants do not rigidly press the identity-related "distinctive doctrines" of classical Pentecostalism. They openly and positively affirm the total range of the church and work hard at loyalty to their own mainline denominations (rather than vest suspicion in "other" denominations). They more easily affirm the global glory and variety of the church than the restrictive ecclesiology of the Roman Catholic tradition. This cluster of features prompts much hope for the future of theology among Protestant charismatics. As a whole, their style is more sophisticated than that of Pentecostalism, less ecclesiastically exclusive than the Roman tradition, and simply older and hence more mature than the new born "Third Wave".

SECTION A

THEOLOGY

12.6.2 Systematic Theology amongst some Roman Catholic charismatics

In 1967, in the chapel of the Roman Catholic Duquesne University in Pittsburg, the Catholic Charismatic Movement began. And with this new movement has quietly come a large volume of high-quality theology. Roman Catholic charismatics built on the strengths of their own tradition. Thus they paid attention to past writers, wider use of resources in European languages and the support of an ecclesiastic tradition accustomed to the production of Academic Theology.

It is interesting to note that Lederle (1988) finds Catholic representatives in all three of his major categories: Neo-pentecostals, sacramentalist charismatics and the more peculiar group classified as those with an "integrative interpretation of Spirit-baptism". Spittler (1991:308) elucidates his statement that all Catholic theologians show profound allegiance to Roman Catholic presuppositions by saying that the Roman Catholic Church, three times the size of all Protestant churches together, is large enough to embrace charismatic theologians within it, and, for that matter, to absorb the charismatic impulse without conspicuous schism. He further says that two features of certain Roman Catholic charismatic thinkers, so far not apparent in classical Pentecostal or Protestant charismatic writing are (1) the ready use of sophisticated critical methodologies in biblical interpretation and (2) interaction with philosophical schools in order to craft a theological framework.

Spittler (1991:309–310) continues by saying that only two Catholic charismatic works could, in any sense, be taken to reflect a systematic theological intent. Heribert Mühlen, who teaches systematic theology at the University of Paderborn in Germany, published *A Charismatic Theology* in 1978. This volume is a "coursebook" consisting of two seven-week series – one of lectures for understanding, the other of guidance for prayer. The work is intended as a course of study for charismatic parish renewal. The work is not really a systematic theology; it is more a sort of systematic treatment of renewed Christian experience. The other Roman Catholic scholar that Spittler refers to is Donald Gelpi. He says that Gelpi constructs a theology that is decidedly Roman Catholic, North American and charismatic. It is a sort of heavyweight theological "probe" – not a systematic theology as such, nor even one solely biblical in method.

Thus one can say that theological style reaches its most technical, abstract and philosophical level in the Roman Catholic charismatic sector. Their sophisticated critical models of biblical interpretation are blended with very learned philosophic theology – still with a fundamental recognition of individual glossolalic experience.

12.6.3 Charismatic Theology in the "Third Wave"

As was previously mentioned, theologians differ on which groups belong to the "Third Wave". Having relied much on Spittler's descriptions of theologies from the First and Second Waves, we will first pay attention to what he calls the Third Wave, i.e. to the influence of charismatic theology on Evangelicals. Afterwards we will deal with Lederle's view that the Third Wave actually refers to the independent Charismatic Churches.

Charismatic Theology by some Evangelicals

Spittler (1991:310–312) says that Evangelicals – the last major sector of the church at large to be affected by the Charismatic Movement – as a whole keep a careful distance from younger sibling pentecostals. The "Third Wave" terminology, now also adopted by church statistician David B. Barrett, describes evangelicals who see themselves as neither Pentecostal nor Charismatic, but who believe and act like them.

In terms of our question on what theology is for these people, we are confronted with the same problem as with the earlier phases: the Third Wave is too young as a movement to come near to producing anything like a systematic theology. But it has produced a literature that in genre – namely, personal testimony – resembled the first publications of the classical pentecostals, the Protestant Neo-pentecostals, and the Roman Catholic charismatics.

Several personal stories from these charismatised evangelicals have emerged. C. Peter Wagner, who is a sort of anchor to the movement, maps its growth in his book *The Third Wave of the Holy Spirit: Encountering the power of signs and wonders today* (1988).

Committed and supportive expositions of the new evangelical supernaturalism have come from such academic professionals as psychiatrist John White (*When the Spirit comes with power: Signs and wonders among God's people* 1988), anthropologist Charles Kraft (*Christianity with power: Your world-view and your experience of the supernatural* 1989 and *Defeating dark angels: Breaking demonic oppression in the believer's life* 1992), pastor-theologian Don Williams (*Signs, Wonders and the kingdom of God: A biblical guide for the reluctant sceptic* 1988) and former Dallas Seminary professor Jack Deere (*Surprised by the power of the Spirit* 1993). Of these works, Williams proposed a completed theology of the kingdom of God to warrant the realisation of signs and wonders. Kraft speaks from a global worldview, talking of a needed paradigm shift, and of the insufficiency of the Western cultural outlook to deal with these matters.

Spittler sums up his evaluation of this group by stating that as for the theological style of this late-breaking Third Wave, the Bible is taken very seriously and at face value – just as in classical Pentecostalism and among most Protestant charismatics. Buoyant, life-changing, paradigm-shifting individual experience figures prominently. Third Wavers, as a whole, are better trained than classical pentecostals and at least equally as competent as the declared Protestant charismatics. Since for the most part the representatives are professional academics, their testimonies put scholarship to the service of renewal by moving from revitalised personal experience to exploratory essays incorporating the vantage point of their several professional fields.

Charismatic Theology by some of the independent churches

It was mentioned earlier that Lederle prefers the designation *Third Wave* to apply to the rise of independent Charismatic denominations and networks. The *first* of these is the so-called *Faith Movement*. The Rhema churches and many of the independent "Christian Centres" belong to this category. They have a distinctive teaching on the power of the spoken word and on prosperity. There is an emphasis on faith as being at the disposal of the believer. In his book, *Quenching the Spirit*, William DeArteaga describes the development of this kind of faith idealism from its earlier roots in the work of E.W. Kenyon to its present day position. He says (1992:214) that in recent publications the faith idealism theology of Kenyon, which was qualified and bounded by the promises of the Word, was being simplified into a system of absolutes. The new faith-popularisers were presenting a form of Christianity that claimed that suffering and sacrifice were no longer part of the price of the kingdom because proper faith could overcome all adversity. He also describes the reaction to this theology by several people and raises the hope that a more balanced and mature understanding of faith will eventually be produced.

The *second* group of churches belong to the different *Restoration* streams. Andrew Walker (1985) describes their development. Basically, this stream wishes to restore New Testament patterns focusing on relationships (rather than on structures) and the five-fold ministry indicated in Ephesians 4:11ff. Some people feel that these groups tend to have an exclusivist, even elitist attitude towards others, while in their own ranks authoritarianism is not an uncommon phenomenon.

The *third* group or the *Dominion* movement, influenced by Christian reconstructionists, seeks to re-establish the kingdom in all areas, including secular life. An example of this kind of theology can be found in House's *Dominion Theology* (1988).

The *Power Encounter* movement relates in many ways to what was noted earlier on among the charismatised evangelicals. Many of its leaders come from the same background although they find themselves in independent churches. Leaders underscore the equipping of every member for ministry of healing and evangelism through "signs and wonders". John Wimber (1986, 1987, 1991) and Kevin Springer (1988) are good examples of this group. Wimber leads the rapidly growing Vineyard Church Movement.

Once again, it should be noted that the leaders are at this stage only beginning to develop their theological views. Some of them are very influential as leaders of growing churches and this will most probably lead to a further systematisation of their theological positions.

12.7 CONCLUSION

As was shown, it is difficult to portray the content of a systematic Charismatic Theology. Reasons for this include the fact that Charismatic Theology is still in its infant phase of development and has not grown to full maturity. This is a young movement and much theology is done in an oral way. In general, most charismatics come from a more mature theological background than pentecostals. The most developed Charismatic theologies are found amongst Catholics.

Furthermore, the problem is aggravated by the fact that charismatics are found in all the different mainline or historical churches as well as in church structures that are newly formed. People from different theological backgrounds – pentecostal and otherwise – are thus grouped together under one umbrella: Charismatic Churches. A unified systematic theology is unlikely to develop from such diverse backgrounds.

The last comment is that Charismatic Theology will grow regardless. The growth in the number of adherents will continually cause leaders of the movement to diligently reflect on their stance with regard to the different doctrines of their own churches and that of other churches. It can be hoped that this branch of Christendom will eventually have a positive and creative influence on theology in general.

READING LIST

Burgess, S.T. & McGee G.B. (eds.). 1988. *Dictionary of Pentecostal and Charismatic Movements*. Grand Rapids, MI: Zondervan.
Deere, J. 1993. *Surprised by the power of the Spirit*. Grand Rapids, MI: Zondervan.
Kraft, C. 1989. *Christianity with power: Your world-view and your experience of the supernatural*. Ann Arbor: Servant Publications.
Lederle, H.I. 1988. *Treasures old and new. Interpretations of "Spirit Baptism" in the Charismatic Renewal Movement*. Peabody: Hendrickson Publishers.
McDonnell, K. 1980. *Presence Power Praise: Documents on the Charismatic Renewal*. Collegeville, MN: Liturgical Press.
Mühlen, H. 1978. *A Charismatic theology: Initiation in the Spirit*. London: Burns and Oates; New York: Paulist Press.
Wagner, C.P. 1988. *The Third Wave of the Holy Spirit: Encountering the power of signs and wonders today*. Ann Arbor, MI: Servant.
White, J. 1988. *When the Spirit comes with power: Signs and wonders among God's people*. Downers Grove: InterVarsity Press.
Williams, J.R. 1988. *Renewal theology: God, the world and redemption*. Grand Rapids, MI: Zondervan.
– 1990. *Renewal theology: Salvation, the Holy Spirit and Christian living*. Grand Rapids, MI: Zondervan.
– 1992. *Renewal theology: The church, the kingdom and last things*. Grand Rapids, MI: Zondervan.
Wimber, J. & Springer, K. 1991. *Power points*. San Francisco: Harper San Francisco.

BIBLIOGRAPHY

Barrett, D.B. 1988. s.v. "Statistics." In Burgess, S.T. & McGee G.B. (eds.). 1988. *Dictionary of Pentecostal and Charismatic Movements*: 810–830.
– 1989. Annual statistical table on global mission: 1989. *International bulletin of missionary research* 13 (1): 20–21.
DeArteaga, W. 1992. *Quenching the Spirit: examining centuries of opposition to the moving of the Holy Spirit*. Lake Mary FL: Creation House.
Deere, J. 1993. *Surprised by the power of the Spirit*. Grand Rapids, MI: Zondervan.
Hollenweger, J. 1993. "De Pinksterbeweging en academische theologie." *Kerk en theologie* 44(2): 151–158.

House, H.W. 1988. *Dominion Theology: Blessing or curse?* Portland, OR: Multnomah Press.

Kraft, C. 1989. *Christianity with power: Your world-view and your experience of the supernatural.* Ann Arbor: Servant Publications

– 1992. *Defeating dark angels: Breaking demonic oppression in the believer's life.* Ann Arbor: Servant Publications.

Lederle, H.I. 1990. "The Spirit of unity: a discomforting comforter". *Ecumenical Review* 42(3–4): 279–287.

Spittler, R.P. 1991. "Doing Theology in today's world." In Woodbridge, J.D. & Comiskey T.E. (eds.). 1991. *Essays in honor of Kenneth S. Kantzer.* Grand Rapids, MI: Zondervan.

Springer, K. (ed.). 1988. *Power encounters among Christians in the Western World.* San Francisco: Harper & Row.

Wagner, C.P. 1988. *The Third Wave of the Holy Spirit: Encountering the power of signs and wonders today.* Ann Arbor, MI: Servant.

Walker, A. 1985. *Restoring the kingdom: The radical Christianity of the House Church Movement.* London: Hodder & Stoughton.

White, J. 1988. *When the Spirit comes with power: Signs and wonders among God's people.* Downers Grove: InterVarsity Press.

Williams, D. 1988. *Signs, Wonders and the kingdom of God: A biblical guide for the reluctant skeptic.* Ann Arbor: Servant Publications.

Wimber, J. 1986. *Power evangelism.* San Francisco: Harper & Row

– 1987. *Power healing.* San Francisco: Harper & Row.

– 1991. *Power points.* San Francisco: Harper & Row.

Ecological Theology

Martien E. Brinkman

13.1 INTRODUCTION

Ecological Theology, or Ecotheology, has to do with the multi-faced inter-relationship of three fundamental data of theological reflection: God, humankind, and the world of nature. Like God and humanity, nature resists simple definition. We will take nature as a synonym for a more concrete, theological term, rooted in biblical parlance: the earth. We consider the earth as the material-vital aspect of God's creation, including humanity, although humanity has a unique position on earth. This is the reason why we do not to speak of two data, God and nature, but of three, God, humanity and nature (Santmire 1985:9–12).

For many centuries there was a general tendency to consider nature as an entirely static reality, this planet, the earth, being conceived as the stage for the drama of human life. This world-view underwent radical changes during the last centuries. For us, nowadays, the earth is a tiny, fragile planet in one of the many galaxies discovered by terrestrial telescopes. The process of development of this earth began about four billion years ago. It was a process that went on through all kinds of events as matter, then life, and then conscious life, through ever higher and more complex unities characterized by a gradually increasing possibility of freedom until the phenomenon of humanity emerged between 1 and 2 million years ago.

The Christian Church shares in the bewilderment created by this new experience and understanding. For centuries the Bible has been thought of as witness to a static world, governed by a wise and almighty God, whose main interest is to help humankind, the crown of his creation, to their eternal destiny. Christendom, embarrassed by these facts, has often given evasive answers to this new challenge. These answers have either denied the clear facts of science (fundamentalism) or the essentials of the Christian faith (modernism), or else have tried to separate the realms of faith and science by limiting God's work to the inner life and to existential decision, and by denying his relations to the visible realities of nature and history (pietism and theological existentialism).

13.2 GOD IN NATURE AND HISTORY

Against this background, the World Council of Churches' Commission on Faith and Order issued the report *God in Nature and History* (Gassmann 1993) at its meeting at Bristol (England) in 1967. This report also contains many fruitful insights for our times. It stresses the following.

Humanity is part of nature

This is not only the thesis of a materialistic world-view, but also of the Bible (cf. Gen 2:7, 1 Cor 15:47). One should particularly notice the structure of Genesis 1, where creation is recounted as a single history, proceeding from lower to higher realities and crowned by the appearance of humanity. Until recently, Christian anthropology has instead leaned upon idealism with its strong emphasis on the human mind as a priority (spirit) in a way which finds no support in biblical thinking.

Humanity is nurtured by nature

Humanity is totally dependent on its natural environment. Without nature, humanity cannot exist. To this end, Christians should support all those promoting and propagating nature conservation in various countries in their long-standing struggle against the pollution of air and water and in their demands for saving forests and replacing destroyed ones, which counteracts the destruction of forests and resulting erosion of vast regions. Christians should also support their plea for a policy of habitation which takes into consideration the much-endangered biological balance of many areas. What these groups claim for biological reasons, the church has to support for basic theological reasons.

Humanity is threatened and challenged by nature

Nature is ambiguous. She is our mother and our enemy. She brings forth thorns and thistles. Hers are the hurricanes, the floods, the droughts, the earthquakes and the famines. When we not resist nature, she can swallow and suffocate us. Passages like Genesis 3 and Romans 5 give the impression of a "fallen creation". In modern scientific thinking, however, there is no place for the conception that an alteration and deterioration took place in our physical nature and in the physical and biological world around us as a consequence of Adam's and Eve's sin. Modern biology claims that death is inherent in all life. Strife and suffering belong to nature. Floods and earthquakes are part of the same reality to which majestic mountains and fertile valleys belong. In Scripture, an identifiable connection between sin and suffering is sometimes definitely denied (Job, Luke 13:1–5 and John 9:3), but more often it is strongly posited. In the latter case, the biblical writers express something which is as near to our modern mind as it was to them: the unity of humanity and nature, and the decisive role which our guilty deeds play in devastating nature over a period of centuries. In many cases, however, it is nearly impossible to distinguish clearly between the consequences of our sins and the capricious character of nature itself. That brings to our mind what is often called the "tragic" element in God's creation. Much evil and suffering, death included, cannot be explained either as a consequence of our sins or as an expression of God's providence. The reference to God's work in nature and history does not explain everything. For us, nature has also its deep, dark sides. We are not able to find meaning in the evil in the world. Christians are not called upon to explain the tears about this suffering, but to hope for a future in which God will wipe them away (Gassman 1993; Anderson 1984).

13.3 JUSTICE, PEACE AND INTEGRITY OF CREATION

The fifth World Assembly of the World Council of Churches at Nairobi (Kenia) in 1975 initiated the study of a just, participatory and sustainable society. This study provided a new opening for looking at questions about the state of the earth in ecumenical discussions. The evident limits to non-renewable resources presented a radical challenge to the common faith in progress and continuous growth, whether from traditional capitalist models or from socialist hopes for a restructuring of economic relationships. But concern over such "limits" to the earth's resources came into conflict with the demands from rich countries to continue their economic growth and the claims from poor countries for development and economic justice.

In a certain sense, the famous call of the sixth World Assembly of the World Council of Churches at Vancouver (Canada) in 1983 for a "conciliar process of mutual commitment to justice, peace and integrity of creation" can be considered as a continuation of the just mentioned sustainability study. Central to this "conciliar process" was the insistence on the interrelationship between the integrity of creation and issues of justice and peace. The concept of the "integrity of creation" does not presuppose that nature cannot really be changed and threatened, but only damaged, and in that case simply be restored again. It in fact presupposes that humans can utterly destroy nature and therefore that nature should be sustained with the future in view and should be delivered from coercion and corruption (Falcke 1986). It is not looking backwards to a "lost paradise", but is looking forward to a real integration of all the aspects of God's creation. Yet, the concept of the "integrity of creation" did by no means resolve the tension in ecumenical discussions between legitimate claims for social justice and serious environmental concerns.

Another point of difference that remains is the meaning of the uniqueness of the human role within creation. What does being created in the "image of God" mean in terms of humanity's place and value over and against the rest of the created order (Niles 1992)?

With regard to these two issues, the final report of the seventh World Assembly of the World Council of Churches at Canberra (Australia) in 1991 is an important step forward. It stresses that concern for creation

SECTION A

THEOLOGY

and the desire for justice cannot finally be seen as competitive, either theologically or in practice. It underscores the interdependence between them. Social justice cannot happen apart from a healthy environment, and a sustainable and sustaining environment will not come about without greater social justice. Justice is truly indivisible, not only as a matter of theological conviction but in practice. The biblical concept of justice recognizes the need for healthy relationships in creation as a whole. This way of viewing justice helps us understand the link between poverty, powerlessness, social conflict and environmental degradation. Hence, there is no real separation between a theology of liberation and a theology of creation (cf. also Landes 1984).

Moreover, the theme of the Canberra assembly – "Come, Holy Spirit, Renew the Whole Creation" – prompted an important emphasis on the relationship of the Holy Spirit to creation. The Holy Spirit manifests God's energy for life present in all things and reminds us of the total dependence of all things on God. This divine presence of the Spirit in creation binds us as human beings together with all created life and underlines our accountability before God in and to the community of life. This is an accountability which can be imaged in various ways: as servants, stewards and trustees, as tillers and keepers, as priests of creation, as nurturers and even as co-creators (cf. Kinnamon 1991; Castro 1990; Stendahl 1990).

13.4 MAIN ISSUES IN THE ECUMENICAL ECOLOGICAL REFLECTION

In the period from the presentation of the report *God in Nature and History* at Bristol in 1967 up to the fifth World Conference of Faith and Order at Santiago de Compostela (Spain) in 1993, the evolving ecumenical discussion can be characterized by at least five fundamental topical issues on which there is growing convergence.

First, churches in the South as well as in the North are starting to address the threats to creation as part of their mission and witness in their societies. One of the problems that arose early and often in international and ecumenical discussions of environmental questions was a tendency to see this as a luxury problem of wealthy Northern industrialized societies and their churches, as environmental degradation due to decadence. This has changed dramatically in the past decade. While contexts and starting points radically differ, ecumenical discussion on the integrity of creation today generally begins with the presupposition that this is a truly global and ecumenical issue. Dwindling natural resources have been recognized as posing problems to the countries in the South as well. Access to and use of the natural resources and global life support systems is distributed very unevenly over human populations. And this "colonization" of the biosphere is mainly due to high levels of environmental pressure per capita in the North. If the inequality in the level of exploitation of the biosphere persists and if overall levels of environmental pressure remain above the buffering capacities embedded in the biosphere, then the consequences will manifest themselves particularly in the poorest parts of the world, where population growth is also the highest. Environmental resource scarcity, coupled with inequality, will lead to conflicts over natural resources such as oil, water and land (Opschoor 1993).

Second, the integration between ecology and economy, and the interdependence between the protection of creation and the demand for justice is now widely accepted. Of course, in specific contexts it often seems that choices are demanded between ecology and economic justice – like between preserving trees and cooking food. But the ecumenical framework stressed by the justice, peace and integrity of creation process, which insists that in the end the flourishing of creation and the building of justice are one, is now generally accepted ecumenically (Goudzwaard and de Lange 1995).

Third, defending the integrity of creation highlights the critical relationship between cultures and Christian faith. This recognition first became evident when the voices of indigenous peoples began to be heard more clearly. Increasingly, other voices as well have stressed that the threats to creation result from a conflict of cultures. Thus the relationship of cultures and the gospel, which came into sharp focus at the Canberra assembly, and is usually seen as a missiological issue, also becomes a critical part of ongoing ecumenical exploration concerning the theology of creation (Ariarajah 1994).

Fourth, the relationship of the Spirit and creation has become a central theme in this process. Much of the ecumenical discussion in recent years has explored the presence of the Spirit within and upholding all creation. This has enabled interchange, for example, between Orthodox, feminist and indigenous peoples' theological perspectives in attempting to discover a relationship with creation that respects its intrinsic value and reflects biblical understandings.[1]

Fifth, the paradigm of mastery over the earth has been replaced by a search for new models of interrelationship between humans and their earth. There now is an ecumenical consensus that has moved decisively beyond the views which secularized nature as an object for domination and justified a careless and destructive subjugation of the earth. Models that stress the "community of life" and look to the restoration of political, economic and ecological relationships have emerged in new ecumenical developments in both theology and ethics concerning creation.[2] Here we can point to the inspiring efforts within the World Council of Churches

---

1 Cf. the special issue of *The Ecumenical Review* 42 (1990) No.2 with the title of the theme of the World Assembly at Canberra "Come, Holy Spirit – Renew the Whole Creation" and D. G. Hallman (ed.). *Ecotheology: Voices from South and North* (Geneva-Maryknoll: World Council of Churches-Orbis Books, 1994), esp. 175–204 ("Insights from Eco-Feminism") and 207–224 ("Insights from Indigenous Peoples").
2 For listing these five points I am indebted, generally, to W. Granberg Michaelson, "Creation in Ecumenical Theology" in: D.G. Hallman (ed.). *Ecotheology: Voices from South and North*, 96–106.

to articulate a "theology of life".³

13.5 OPEN QUESTIONS

Despite the above-mentioned growing convergence, there are still a lot of open questions (Granberg-Michaelson 1993:103–105). These questions concentrate on issues such as the following.

13.5.1 How do we understand humanity's place within creation?

This issue is far from settled in ecumenical discussions. The Canberra report uses various images to express our responsibility: as servants, stewards and trustees, as tillers and keepers, as priests of creation, as nurturers, as co-creators. All these images stress the view that a hierarchical understanding of *imago dei*, putting human beings infinitely above all creation, must be replaced by a more relational view. But how to express the unique human accountability as moral beings, is still an open question. Response to the environmental crisis is determined partly by what is regarded as an appropriate attitude for humans towards other created things. If the life-giving Spirit of God is related to humans not only in community with each other, but also as they are in mutual interdependence with other created things, then it follows that the value of all created things is to be acknowledged, though this does not necessarily mean that all things are equal in value. The value of all created things is affirmed by speaking, in the weaker sense of the term which does not assume intentionality, of the co-creativity of all created things with God. Co-creativity means here co-operation like the seasons "co-operate" with the Creator to give fertility, etc. The concept of co-creativity in its full sense is only applicable to humans, which makes humans all the more responsible towards nature and implies that there should be urgency in the making of appropriate political and economic decisions and in sponsoring relevant scientific and technological research (Fulljames 1993: 167–173).

If we are convinced that the work of God the Creator is not a work without us, but a work which makes us participants, then living in nature not only means that we are faced with a mystery (the intrinsic value of all created beings), but that we are called to mastery, that is, to take wise decisions and to feel responsible as moral beings. Mystery and mastery are an irreducible pair and need each other: there can be no respectful mastery without mystery and there can be no experience of mystery without the constantly renewed attempt at mastery. Without mastery, humankind abdicates its cultural mandate and its moral responsibility. Without mystery, humankind fails to recognize the enigmatic

---

3 Cf. the report of the meeting of the Central Committee of the World Council of Churches at Johannesburg (South Africa) in 1994, *The Ecumenical Review* 46 (1994) 214–249, especially in the 'Report of the Moderator' (A. Keshishian) 220–230 and in the 'Report of the General Secretary' (K. Raiser), 241–244.

character of the fascinating, but often tremendous character of nature (Brinkman 1988; Gregorius 1978:82–90).

13.5.2 How holy is creation?

The discussion on the relation of Spirit and creation which began at the Canberra Assembly leads not just to affirming creation's "integrity" or its intrinsic value (apart from its utility to humanity), but raises the issue of whether and how creation carries the qualities of the sacred. Christian faith, historically, has always insisted on the distinction between worshipping the Creator (which is required) and worshipping the creation (which is forbidden). We have to remember that the earth is not God, but that the earth is also not without God! That prompts two questions with regard to the exact meaning of our topical stress on the immanence of God's Spirit in his creation. The western Christian tradition projected a transcendent sky-God who becomes immanent only in Jesus of Nazareth. This transcendent God is available to other human beings principally through the work of the Spirit of Christ, that is, by means of the administration of the sacraments and the teaching of the gospel. The rest of creation is more or less neglected in this strong christocentric view of linking transcendence and immanence. Besides this main emphasis, there was, in classical Roman Catholicism as well as in classical Protestantism, always a reference to God's "natural" or "general" revelation in nature, but this was never more than an undercurrent. Nowadays this christocentric tradition is fiercely challenged. Time and again Asian and African theologians discern radical differences between the Semitic and the Asian-African approaches to understanding and relating to nature.

Whatever the differences in detail between Asian and African religions are, one of the significant features of this heritage is that it does not make the universe incidental to human existence. Rather, human life is seen as part of the universe, so that there is a close link between the human predicament and that of the universe. On the practical side, this should lead to love and compassion towards all beings. To violate the earth would be to violate life and also the giver of life, God. This close association and link to the earth and to all in it, expresses itself in many African and Asian traditions as a kinship between the humans and all others. The land thus cannot be owned: it owns us (Ariarajah 1993 *Journal of Black Theology in South Africa* 1991; Eggen 1993; van 't Spijker 1994).

One of the most impressive ways to bridge the cleft between transcendence and immanence might be the growing ecumenical sensibility for the social and ecological meaning of the Christian sacraments. The sacraments of Christian worship use the elements of the created world to manifest the Triune God present among and in us. Therefore, we should not distinguish the "classical" sacraments too sharply from the so-called "sacramentals". The latter comprise the sacramental practice that is most widespread and deeply rooted in the people, and they differ from one circumstance and place to another. Some are linked to the defining moments of life (birth, death, the passage from childhood to youth, from youth to maturity), to places (sanctuaries), to festive times (Christmas, Holy Week), to the agricultural cycle (planting, harvest), to special moments (inauguration of a house, a trip, illness, work). A whole range of symbols are mixed together: images, processions, candles, pilgrimages, blessings, flowers, meals, water rites, etc. They are symbolic expressions of desire, of faith, of piety, of trust in the God of life. We should not fear to include them in the environment of the sacraments, since the early tradition of the church was not too disdainful to identify as sacraments such realities as foot-washing, the blessing of objects, funeral rites, etc. This plea for a sacramental theology of the environment can nowadays be heard especially from Latin-America and Africa, but this sacramental approach to the creation, needed for its re-integration, is already a centuries-old emphasis in Orthodox Theology (Codina 1993:654–676; Daneel 1991:2–26; David 1994; Limouris 1990:1–15).

13.5.3 Is creation's natural, biological order altered by sin?

Much traditional theology assumed that the entry of sin into the world brought predation, decay and physical death to the natural world. Already, the report *God in Nature and History* (1967) denied the existence of such an unambiguous state of original perfection – the so-called *status integritatis* (state of integrity) – and endorses the ambiguous character of nature. In this regard the Canberra report can be considered as a certain relapse into an old pattern of theological thinking. It seems to suggest that there was an "ecological equilibrium in the beginning" which was broken by human sin. Yet anyone who experiences the four seasons knows that, biologically, life has everything to do with the recurring cycles of growth and decay. Should this not be understood as part of the goodness, or rightness, of the creation declared in Genesis (Brinkman 1991:87–98)? The space of life understood as creation is not eternal and therefore not without the cycles of birth and death necessary for life on earth. It is not "the best of all possible worlds". Rather, it is our "good-enough mother" who is not perfect and who can only be perfected by human effort in a limited way, but whom we, nevertheless, gratefully accept as gift of God (Schloz 1987:15–24).

13.5.4 How relevant is God's transcendence?

Most recent theological reflection on ecology and creation has rightly stressed the holistic, interdependent and relational nature of all reality. What has been discovered about ecology becomes a paradigm for theology. Ecumenically, some of the most creative work in this direction reflects on the relational character of the Trinity as a basis for approaching our whole view of life and reality (Moltmann 1985). But in response to this stress on holistic paradigms, some ask how we are to understand God's transcendence anew.

Besides the more "intimate" imagery of the creator-creature relation which the pneumatologically oriented theologians are presently highlighting, there is also the more "distanced" imagery, easily recognized in Scripture. In spite of – or thanks to – the great distance between God and world, this experience of faith does not have to exclude a deep awareness of intimacy. Especially in the Calvinist tradition, but also in many mystical traditions, this dialectic of distance and intimacy has crystallized into a kind of spiritual creation in which our stance towards the Holy and Eternal is primarily characterized by awe and restraint on the one hand, and fidelity and dedication on the other hand. Where this attitude towards the Creator is reflected in the attitude of the faithful towards the created, the positive ecological effects of this form of creation theology cannot be underestimated (Brinkman 1990:150–156).

13.5.5 What about orienting theology around place instead of time?

Traditional Western Theology follows an agenda of time, asking when God's action in history was initiated and when it will be completed. Some non-western cultures, however, move instead around the questions of place. Where is God's reign discovered in relationship to the ground, the mountains, the water and the sky? If justice means the fullest possible flourishing of creation under the conditions of various limits and constraints, then nothing is more basic to justice than adequate space for life's basics. It is the first requirement of community and thus the foundation of koinonia. This leads Sallie McFague to the remark that: "geography ... may well be the subject of the 21st century, since it raises questions like: Where is the best land and who has access to it? What good space is available on this planet and who controls it? Who cares for it? Who will inherit the land? etc." (McFague 1993:101).

13.5.6 Does Ecological Theology, reflecting on creation, provide a new paradigm for doing ecumenical theology?

There are striking parallels between ecological paradigms and ecumenical ones. All things are interdependent and related organically. Diversity characterizes all life and makes unity possible. Connectedness is a given. We are all – the living and the non-living, organic and inorganic – the outcome of the same primal explosion and the same evolutionary history. This reality is the most basic text and context of life and of a theology of life. The universe, however, is anything but harmonious. It is not at all clear from either scientific evidence or common experience that life will triumph over death, at least in forms hospitable to us and numerous other of God's creatures. In fact, it is the threat to life, rather than the celebration of it, that stimulated the ecumenical theology of life in the first place. So amidst deep and deepening gratitude for life, however threatened it is, the turn is to healing and tending and transforming, as co-operators with God, the fragile creation of which we are immensely privileged to be part (Rasmussen in Hallman 1994:112–129). Hence, neither an anthropocentric nor an ecocentric world-view will liberate us from our global crisis, but only a theocentric anthropology which teaches us the real koinonia between God, humanity and nature (Houtepen 1990: 236–252).

SECTION A
THEOLOGY

READING LIST AND BIBLIOGRAPHY

Anderson, B.W. 1984. "Creation and Ecology." In: Anderson, B.W. (ed.), *Creation in the Old Testament*. Philadephia-New York: Fortress Press-SPCK, p. 152–171.

Ariarajah, S.W. 1994. *Gospel and Culture: An Ongoing Discussion within the Ecumenical Movement*. Geneva: World Council of Churches.

– "World Religions and the Wholeness of Creation." In Reuver, M., Solms, Fr. and Huizer, G. (eds.), *The Ecumenical Movement Tomorrow*, 158–171.

Best, Thomas F. and Wesley Granberg-Michaelson, (eds.), 1993. *Costly Unity: Koinonia and Justice, Peace and Creation*. Geneva: World Council of Churches.

Brinkman, M.E. 1988. "The Christian Faith as Environmental Pollution?" *Exchange* 17(51):36–47.

– 1990. "A Creation Theology for Canberra?" *The Ecumenical Review* 42:150–156.

Brinkman, Martien E. 1991. "The Challenge of an Ecumenical Creation Theology." *Exchange* 20:87–98.

Castro, E. (ed.). 1990. *To the Wind of God's Spirit: Reflections on the Canberra Theme*. Geneva: World Council of Churches.

Codina, Victor. 1993. "Sacraments." In Ellacuria, I. and Sobrino, J. (eds.), *Mysterium Liberationis: Fundamental Concepts of Liberation Theology*. Maryknoll: Orbis Books, p. 654–676.

Come Holy Spirit, Renew the Whole Creation: Six Bible Studies. 1989. Geneva: World Council of Churches.

Daneel, M.L. 1991. "Towards a Sacramental Theology of Environment in African Independent Churches." *Theologica Evangelica* 24:2–26.

Daneel, Martinus L. "The Liberation of Creation: African Traditional Religions and Independent Church Perspectives." *Missionalia* 19:99–121.

David, Kenith A. 1994. *Sacrament and Struggle: Signs and Instruments of Grace from the Downtrodden*. Geneva: World Council of Churches.

Eggen, W. "African Roads into the Theology of Earthly Reality"

Falcke, H. 1986. "The 'Integrity of Creation' in the Current Ecumenical Debate." *Church and Society: Report & Background Papers of the Meeting of the Working Group, Potsdam, GDR, July 1986*. Geneva: World Council of Churches, p. 54–61.

Fulljames, P. 1993. *God and Creation in Intercultural Perspective: Dialogue between the Theologies of Barth, Dickson, Pobee, Nyamiti and Pannenberg*. Frankfurt am Main-Berlin-Bern-New York-Paris-Wien: Peter Lang.

Gassmann, G. (ed.) 1993. *Documentary History of Faith and Order 1963–1993*, Faith and Order Paper No.159. Geneva: World Council of Churches, p. 289–311.

Goudzwaard, B. and H. de Lange. 1995. *Beyond Poverty and Affluence: Toward an Economy of Care*. Geneva: World Council of Churches.

Granberg-Michaelson, W. "Creation in Ecumenical Theology."

Gregorius, P. 1978. *The Human Presence: An Orthodox View of Nature*. Geneva: World Council of Churches.

Hallman, David G. 1994. *Ecotheology: Voices from South and North*. Geneva: World Council of Churches: Orbis Books.

Houtepen, A. 1990. "Key Issues in Some JPIC Texts: A Theological Evaluation." *Exchange* 19:236–252.

Journal of Black Theology in South Africa 5 (1991) no.2

Kinnamon, Michael, (ed.). 1991. *Signs of the Spirit: Official Report Seventh Assembly*. Geneva-Grand Rapids: World Council of Churches – Eerdmans, esp. 54–72 (Report of Section I: "Giver of Life – Sustain Your Creation!").

Landis, George M. 1984. "Creation and Liberation." In Anderson, B.W. (ed.), *Creation in the Old Testament*. Philadephia-London: Fortress Press SPCK, p. 135–151.

Limouris, G. (ed.). 1990. Justice, *Peace and the Integrity of Creation: Insights from Orthodoxy*. Geneva: World Council of Churches.

McFague, S. 1993. *The Body of God: An Ecological Theology*. Minneapolis: Fortress Press.

Moltmann, J. 1985. *God in Creation: An Ecological Doctrine of Creation*. London: SCM.
Niles, D. Preman (ed.). 1992. *Between the Flood and the Rainbow: Interpreting the Conciliar Process of Mutual Commitment (Covenant) to Justice, Peace and the Integrity of Creation*. Geneva: World Council of Churches.
Opschoor, J.B. 1993. "Use and Abuse of Creation: Ecumenism and Ecology Tomorrow." In Reuver, M., Solms, Fr. and Huizer, G. (eds.), *The Ecumenical Movement Tomorrow: Suggestions for Approaches and Alternatives*. Kampen-Geneva: Kok-World Council of Churches, p. 135–158.
Rasmussen, L. "Theology of Life and Ecumenical Ethics." In Hallman, D.G. (ed.), *Ecotheology*.
Reuver, Marc, Friedhelm Solms and Gerrit Huizer (eds.). 1993. *The Ecumenical Movement Tomorrow: Suggestions for Approaches and Alternatives*. Kampen-Geneva: Kok-World Council of Churches.
Santmire, H. Paul. 1985. *The Travail of Nature: The Ambiguous Ecological Promise of Christian Theology*. Philadephia: Fortress Press.
Schloz, A. 1987. "The Integrity of Creation." In *Reintegrating God's Creation: A Paper for Discussion*. Church and Society Documents. Geneva: World Council of Churches.
Van 't Spijker, G. 1993. "Man's Kinship with Nature: African Reflection on Creation." *Exchange* 22:89–169.
– 1994. "Man's Kinship with Nature: African Reflection on Creation." *Exchange* 23: 89–148.
Stendahl, K. 1990. *Energy for Life: Reflections on the Theme "Come, Holy Spirit – Renew the Whole Creation"*. Geneva: World Council of Churches.

Postmodern Theology

Marius D. Herholdt

14.1 INTRODUCTION

Postmodernism can take on many specific forms, and is known by names such as revisionary thinking, constructionism, critical realism and deconstructionism. Yet, irrespective of its variety, it is possible to discern a broad postmodern trend that is generally known by its disenchantment with the critical consciousness of modernism, the fragmentary perspective of reality and reductionism. Postmodernism is a serious effort to restore the loss of meaning that is attributed to modernism. In this essay I will outline some of the main features of postmodernism which one has to take into consideration in the construction of a Postmodern Theology. At the same time, I will attempt to write the chapter in a postmodern fashion. This entails an attempt to integrate related ideas by treating each aspect as an expression of a larger whole. Consequently, instead of following a systematic approach, different aspects will deliberately recur repeatedly throughout the chapter from angles of alternative perspectives. This will hopefully allow the reader, after a few readings, to cross reference similar themes as aspects of one coherent whole. (For a treatment of self-organization based on a study of the complex dynamics in literature and science see Haykes 1991.)

14.2 POSTMODERNISM AND MODERNISM

Postmodernism is a global trend that may very well influence the way we think in a very profound way. The term "postmodernism" suggests a distinct period after "modernism", yet postmodernism is more than a time period. It indicates possible progress, a new way of doing science. Probably this movement warrants the term "postmodern" because, in many ways, it follows an opposite approach to that which is distinctly categorised as "modernist". Modernism based the idea of critical con-

SECTION A

THEOLOGY

sciousness largely on the philosophy of René Descartes. The Cartesian legacy includes basic doubt and the idea that truth has to do with that which the scientist can determine objectively. Within this method of science, the values, perspectives and personal faith of the person are regarded as of trivial nature. Consequently, modernism places a high premium on the certainty about reality which is provided by the natural sciences, the mode of living offered by a secular world view and the personal gratification that is guaranteed by autonomous freedom.

Postmodernists hold that the empirical scientific method, with its conviction that truth is bound to objective information, caused an undesirable split between subject and object. The result is an external world distanced from the subject. In theology, this is formulated as the hermeneutical problem. Consequently, the subject has to approach reality (the object) from a critical position of doubt and in doing so, it alienates itself from the world (reality). Modernism lacks an overarching epistemic framework that includes human subjectivity as part of reality; presuppositions and aspirations are not taken to be just as real as external objects. Such an emotionally sterile and rather clinical framework is obviously not suitable for theological reflection that has to cater for religious needs that include the so-called "fuzzy world" of visions, hopes, beliefs, aspirations, and ecstasy. Postmodernism is an effort to restore the value of human feelings as part of experience.

A further outcome of modernism is that of secularity which knows only a reality that is accessible through sensory perception. This resulted in a general loss of meaning because values and transcendent reality that help to constitute meaning do not lend themselves to the scientific criteria of verification. Secularity also involves a strong reliance on human endeavour and competence. The world and the future is seen to be in the hands of human decisions. This often causes a strong conflict in Christians who believe that God is directly in control, that He causes things to happen. The theological formulation of this attitude is evident in certain doctrinal aspects like providence, predestination, the decrees of God and the problem of theodicy. In some theological circles, this tension contributed to the "God is dead" theology.

Another outcrop of secularism is autonomous freedom. If people believe that God is no longer in control, they are inclined to assume control themselves. A secular person does, therefore, not pray for healing, he or she visits the doctor. Secularity does not accommodate transcendence; providence is exchanged for coincidence and the ideal is to assert yourself as the architect of your own destination. This may ensue in a striving for better control and power and an intolerance for failure. The ideal is to be free from all the gods that control human destiny and threaten human decision-making. The strategy is often to increase the skills needed to exert control and to increase information, for knowledge is power. The ultimate experience in this regard is the creation of computer-based reality through which so-called virtual space is created.

Modern Theology has always sounded a warning about the human urge to be formally free. The immanent danger that lurks behind freedom is often that of licentiousness and lawlessness – a total rejection of authority. This tendency becomes quite evident in the political arena, where we often find caricatures of democracy which border on anarchy. As a remedy, Modern Theology has emphasised that freedom is only conditional, that people are free in one sense and that is to obey God. This stance probably does not appeal much to the secularized person who is unwilling to surrender control with the implied risk of suffering hardship. Even Christians are not always sure what it means to obey God, for it is often difficult to discern the will of God.

14.3 SELF-ORGANIZATION

The postmodern approach to the will of God is influenced by the notion of self-organization. This concept points to an intrinsic quality of all entities to generate order, to form patterns by means of the flow of energy through a system. Self-organization, and inter alia feedback, are aspects of the new science of complexity (Mitchell Feigenbaum, David Ruelle, John Casti, Stuart Kaufman, Brian Goodwin, Murray Gell Mann, Ian Stewart, etc.).

It is a bold concept that, as part of a holistic world-view, forms part of a natural theory of the origin of life. It removes the theory of the "God of the gaps" because it promotes belief in spontaneous order ("order for free" or collectively auto-catalytic systems as they are called by Stuart Kauffmann).

Self-organisation has received much prominence as a technical subject due to the work of Ilya Prigogine, winner of the Nobel Prize in 1977, for his work on the thermodynamics of systems far from equilibrium. The philosophical implications (Kellert) of the fact that order and chaos can serve as a source for self-organization and an ensuing new order, has a far-reaching influence. It has boldly challenged the concept of determinism to the extent that randomness and unpredictability have gained a positive meaning as mechanisms necessary to ensure creativity and novelty (Isabelle Stengers, David Bohm and F. David Peat). The philosophical implications of complexity provide new insight into the dynamic and complex nature of reality. People are beginning to believe that we live on the edge of chaos, that the intrinsic dialectic of order and chaos is offering new insights into the meaning of freedom; that this also reflects on the meaning of human freedom and a dynamic understanding of action as a form of self-organization within the evolutionary progress of the world.

The will of God is thus not a predetermined decision that Christians need to discover in a passive mode of obedience. Christians, and for that matter all people, are afforded the right to some human input that co-determines the "plan" for their lives. Many choices are possible, but in the variety of options we are guided by God as creative participant of our lives. Humans need not plug in to a blueprint that renders their own efforts and creative potential sterile, but are co-creators.

These insights are important to theology. Instead of attributing a vertical (earth-heaven) meaning to apparent incidental events, postmodernism may now shift to a lateral approach by trying to trace patterns formed by the network of many apparent incidental events. Attempted self-control, which is individually based, may then be forfeited for the alternative of self-organization which integrates the individual into the network of patterns woven by many seemingly independent events. The interrelatedness of events causes a fuzzy perspective. This "fuzzy" approach to theology results in notions like the following: theology as a process of knowing; the ordering of experience; the growth of coherent meaningful patterns; the approximation of religious reality relevant to experience. Moreover, patterns of self-organization invoke an awakening to community life in exchange for individual control. The dominant model of God in this context is that of the Leader of the community, which means that human life is the greatest opportunity for God's influence (Barbour). The influence of God precipitates in the individual life as the so-called strange attractor where maximum probability is realized. Perhaps one could say in this sense that self-organization is a metaphor for the non-coercive way in which God works.

Postmodernism is, in this sense, a rediscovery of the value of human participation, a quest for wholeness and meaning, a perspective on the continuity between all levels of a multi-levelled reality. Postmodernism aspires to provide an alternative approach to reality in such a way that it could yield a significantly new and improved way of understanding the world. Postmodern Theology, also sometimes referred to as Post-critical or Post-liberal Theology, aims to provide fresh insights, answer existing anomalies, and provide new meaning by moving beyond modernism. This cannot be accomplished by an escape to the inside of the self (existentialism) or even a denial of the valuable results offered by the more critical scientific method. Limited subjective input is combined with limited objective reference to result in a balance between both extremes. The word "limited" refers to the notion that the human mind cannot construct reality completely, nor can the human mind know reality fully.

14.4 THE AGENDA OF POSTMODERN THEOLOGY

Postmodern Theology is thus strongly inclined to philosophy. It is, in a sense, a reaction to modernism and consequently an endeavour to go beyond it. Postmodernism must therefore not be seen as an urge to return to a premodern philosophy. According to postmodernism, the test for theological models is their success in providing meaning in terms of how the world is experienced in relation to the Christian belief in a benevolent God. This can only be accomplished by designing a comprehensive metaphysical scheme in which faith can be fitted into the framework of how we actually experience the world on many different levels. Factors like human experience, the dominant metaphors of faith (especially those derived from the Bible), recent scientific insights into the complexity of material reality and the depiction of reality and constructivist or pragmatically useful epistemologies all blend into a coherent scheme to form the basis for Postmodern Theology.

The agenda for Postmodern Theology will have to be in line with the following or similar trends: Verisimilitude (Karl Popper), where the claim to truth of models is limited to that of an increasing closeness to truth; the theory of the ladenness of theological statements which emphasises the importance of personal presuppositions, participation and the social context of the theologian; contextuality, which means that the real-life situation should also be taken into account; general coherence and complementarity, which means that all things (spiritual and material) are related and constitute an all-encompassing systemic or organic wholeness (Jan Smuts, Von Bertalanffy); complexity, which refers to the openness, organismic nature and self-organization of systems; paradigm theory (Thomas Kuhn) which proposes that knowledge does not grow accumulatively, but by switching from one intellectual framework to another in order to gain increased meaning and answer questions left unanswered by the previous paradigm.

In a sense postmodernism is radically new, in another sense it also includes aspects of modernism. It is radical in terms of the conviction that the whole is more than the sum total of the parts. In terms of a world-view this means that postmodernists do not see the world simply as an unfolding of latent potential. Order is not rearrangement. On the contrary, reality is increasing its sum by creating novelty, by becoming more than the sum of the parts of a system through following a process of evolutionary progress.

Postmodernism has in common with modernism the fact that it refuses to give up the notion of an external world. The difference is that postmodernism does not give autonomous and substantial status to the external world. Consequently, postmodernism deems the participation of the subject as essential to our understanding of the external world. As such, postmodernism hopes to heal the fragmentation of reality, often caused by analysis, systematization and compartmentalization. It builds on the assumption that the human mind is an integral part of the reality it aspires to know. Truth is not something bound to the object alone (naive realism, objectivism, positivism), nor constructed solely by human consciousness (subjectivism, instrumentalism). Truth is relational in the sense that it is both objective and subjective (critical realism). Truth is critical insofar as it is different from reality; it is realist insofar as there is a reference to objective reality. The theological implication of an epistemology where relational truth is emphasised is the conviction that there is no dualism between the external world and subjective life. To give theological expression to this insight is probably one of the greatest challenges of Postmodern Theology.

Postmodernism is technically about a new paradigm (Thomas Kuhn) or intellectual framework. Such a paradigm can only have a universal application if it is comprehensive and influential enough to suggest change on all levels of existence, that is, to the theory of knowledge, the social dimension of language, the value system of society and our under-

14

Postmodern Theology

SECTION A

THEOLOGY

standing of reality, inclusive of our understanding of God. Postmodernism holds promise to be such a new paradigm. Contrary to modernism, it involves the particular rather than the universal, the local rather than the general, the timely rather than the timeless (Toulmin). This means that truth is no longer regarded as something with eternal, unchanging, authoritative and objective, absolute status. Truth is relative to the particular social context and personal presuppositions of the theologian. The importance of contextuality and the social determination of truth are given much thought in postmodern circles. It is instantly clear that such radical changes will, in due course, influence theology profoundly, and ultimately, the Christian understanding of God.

14.5 COMPARING WORLD-VIEWS

There is an increased awareness that a dominating world-view serves as broad filter for the way we perceive and think about things in the world. The modern world-view with its mechanistic understanding, also called the Newtonian (from Isaac Newton) paradigm, provided us with an atomistic understanding of reality, which means that reality was regarded as a substance that was comprised of a mosaic of solid building blocks. The modern world-view "filtered" out non-mechanistic and fuzzy things. Order was supposed to be of a linear nature and was consequently seen as something of a grid-like pattern with exact coordinates of Euclidian nature. The dominant metaphor was that of the cosmic machine that works with deterministic predictable precision. In the new paradigm, nature is regarded as much more organistic and people even talk about the new biology of machines (Kevin Kelly). Along these lines, the science of cybernetics is gaining momentum. It involves a study of patterns and organization which lies on a more functional than substantial level; it is a definite shift from a study of things to that of pattern. This break with substantiality will result in a Postmodern Theology where the old dualism, caused by the division of limited entities, disappears. Heaven is for instance no longer regarded as a place, but rather as something that indicates God's point of departure (or completion); the soul is not seen as an immortal entity, but a process or function of human disposition that transcends mere matter; religion and life are seen as integrated; and postmodern theologians will not attempt to quantify aspects like faith, love and grace. Systems thinking behoves a qualitative study, which means that the postmodern theologian would be more interested in the kind of patterns produced by grace in society than attempting an abstract definition of grace.

According to the old paradigm, even humans were sometimes regarded as intricate machines and human value was consequently measured in terms of production. This trend depersonalized humanity greatly. It obviously also encouraged an analytical and critical methodology of study. Hence, the aim was to dissect, to reduce a system to its constitutive components. The functioning of a system was understood in a deterministic, periodic, linear and static way. This was based on the notion

14

Postmodern Theology

of cause and effect, action and reaction, with the hope of making exact quantitative predictions of the future status of the system. Change was seen as a simple rearrangement and the relationship between spirit and matter as a dualistic pair, that is, two types of entities belonging to mutually exclusive kingdoms. According to this paradigm, scientific knowledge is based on an objective and logical access to reality, known as a positivistic epistemology. The positivistic understanding of truth is that only a mirror image of reality, by means of empirical research, can offer valid information (data).

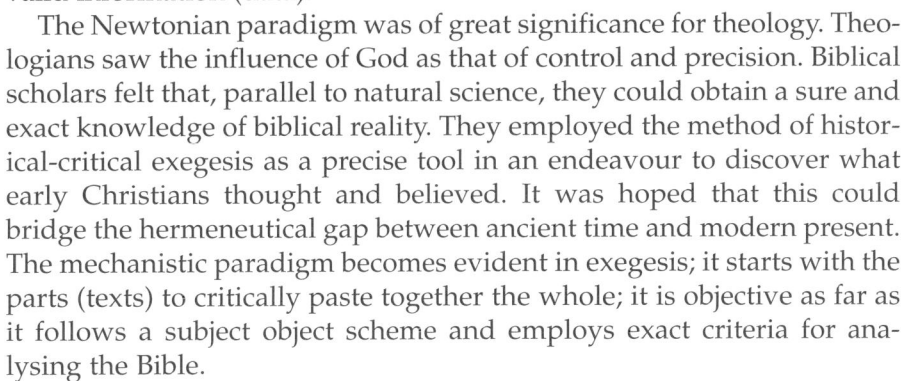

The Newtonian paradigm was of great significance for theology. Theologians saw the influence of God as that of control and precision. Biblical scholars felt that, parallel to natural science, they could obtain a sure and exact knowledge of biblical reality. They employed the method of historical-critical exegesis as a precise tool in an endeavour to discover what early Christians thought and believed. It was hoped that this could bridge the hermeneutical gap between ancient time and modern present. The mechanistic paradigm becomes evident in exegesis; it starts with the parts (texts) to critically paste together the whole; it is objective as far as it follows a subject object scheme and employs exact criteria for analysing the Bible.

Within the scheme of positivism, theologians may be tempted to use the Bible almost as a "textbook" because truth is viewed as a prescribed static set of propositions that lends itself to be discovered. True to the dualistic approach, God is regarded as an other-worldly (transcendent) Ruler or Parent that can only be known through divine revelation. Knowledge about God is consequently endowed with supernatural status which divorces it from any other so-called secular knowledge. Within this scheme, dogmas are believed to be the neatly formulated sum of revealed truth. Due to the elusive nature of God as an object, however, positivists doubted the status of Modern Theology as university discipline due to the fact that it does not fulfil the criteria for objectivity. Consequently, much discussion ensued about the theological validity of the subject-objective scheme for Modern Theology.

On the other hand, postmodern epistemologists (scholars who study the theory of knowledge) claim that knowledge is not neutral or value free. This means that truth in general cannot claim to be eternal and final knowledge. Truth is relative to the questions that we may ask and the needs that we hope to fulfil, it is influenced by the intellectual climate and cultural categories of every period. Theological truth is not exempt from this requirement, for divine revelation necessitates interpretation which opens it up to subjective input. The implication of this is that, in order to serve the church properly, theological thinking cannot take place in a cathedral, that is, outside of a specific religious persuasion and socio-economic climate. In order to be relevant, theologians need to express themselves constantly in the idiom of their day to properly address the religious needs of society. In addition, for the sake of academic integrity, theologians cannot ignore the current philosophical premises of academ-

SECTION A
THEOLOGY

ic subjects or the strong challenges posed by the new (postmodern) discoveries in the natural sciences, like for instance quantum physics and complexity science.

Postmodern science opts for an integrated understanding of reality that is holistic, ecological and systemic. Although analysis still offers a very viable and useful method to explain the way things work, it does not contribute much to the meaning of complex phenomena like life and to the overall coherence of the world. In accordance with the mechanistic paradigm, the tendency is to understand things in terms of their composition. We call this approach reductionism because it reduces the meaning and function of a system to the way its parts work and fit together. According to a holistic approach, the system is more than the sum of its parts because the interrelation brings about interaction in such a way that it adds something to the system (Jan Smuts). The accent is on process, self-organisation and feedback. The essence of all this is non-linear inter-connectedness which means a radical deviation from the cause and effect scheme. This makes the function of complex systems a phenomenon that appears on the edge of chaos. The contribution that the discovery of chaos makes to the emerging world-view is very profound. Chaos should not be associated here with the negative notions of degeneration, anarchy, formlessness and confusion. Chaos serves in a technical sense as an acknowledgement that most systems are unstable, aperiodic, non-linear and dynamic in nature. Consequently, this warrants a qualitative study where probability has a much greater propensity. According to this insight, the world is a much more fuzzy reality where small changes and influences are of great importance (the notion of sensitive dependence on initial conditions). Nothing is negligible. There is even mention of fuzzy thinking, the so-called new science of fuzzy logic (Bart Kosko). Associated with this is the growing realization of the importance of the internal flexibility of a system where the relationship between the parts is not rigidly determined; where, in a manner of speaking, the rules change as the game proceeds.

The holistic paradigm is not a derivative of natural science that is now being artificially applied to theology. Holism or systems thinking is rather a peculiar approach to metaphysics, the philosophical study of reality, that has a bearing on all academical subjects in terms of the dire need to integrate the different aspects of reality into a coherent whole.

14.6 AN ALTERNATIVE EPISTEMOLOGY

An alternative epistemology is also part of the postmodern package. It is the very elusive nature of reality that also leads to an alternative epistemology. I already referred to the analytical method of the mechanistic paradigm. This was in accordance with the positivistic epistemology that included a reliance upon sensory and objective/analytical access to reality, known as the empirical approach. The basic presupposition of this approach is that the universe is a cosmic machine, that matter is, in essence, ordered substance that lends itself to precise mathematical description. With the refinement of research techniques and instruments and the possibility of studying matter on subatomic (quantum) level, this positivistic ideal becomes rather absurd. Scientists are beginning to talk about subatomic entities as processes rather than substance (The dance without the dancers – Gary Zukav); and the role of the researcher as both discovering and constructing reality at the same time. Postmodern epistemologists consequently prefer to talk about truth as modelling reality instead of truth being a mirror image of reality. An applicable slogan that has become very popular is that epistemology models ontology.

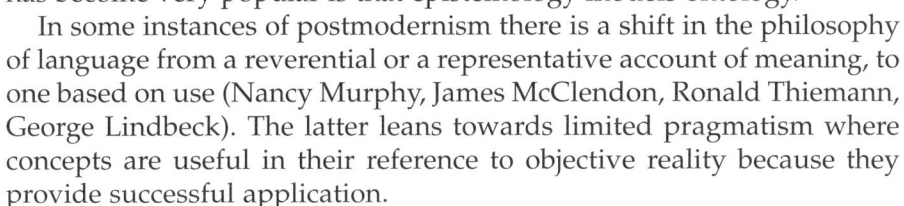

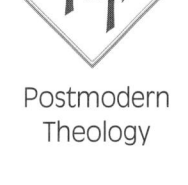

In some instances of postmodernism there is a shift in the philosophy of language from a reverential or a representative account of meaning, to one based on use (Nancy Murphy, James McClendon, Ronald Thiemann, George Lindbeck). The latter leans towards limited pragmatism where concepts are useful in their reference to objective reality because they provide successful application.

14.7 THE CONSEQUENCES FOR THEOLOGY

The shift away from positivism and logical rationalism also has its counterparts in theology. In postmodernism there is a much greater openness for non-conceptual ways of knowing. Due to the increasing awareness that the researcher largely constructs reality (Michael Arbib; Mary Hesse), some postmodernists feel that intuitive and mystical ways of knowing ought to be explicitly included in theological methodology. There is a return to a contemporary literary role for the Bible, motivated by the conviction that the Bible as literature discloses God. This results in an epistemology that takes knowledge as a way of knowing that includes personal experience. The emphasis is then no longer on dogma to explicate the nature and activity of God on rational grounds, but rather on a more poetic literary approach where the sacred can be imaged. The difference is that dogma requires exact understanding, whereas the imaginative dimension of language communicates relative and applied meanings to believers respective to their needs and powers to comprehend (reader response criticism).

In the light of all this, does theology still have a future as a strictly systematic approach to doctrinal issues? Postmodern Theology sees its task in terms of the integration and coherence of all the different loci. This means that postmodernism will view every aspect of theology as an expression of the whole from a specific perspective. To avoid fragmentation, one will have to show how every subdivision of Systematic Theology, that is, ecclesiology, pneumatology, Christology, eschatology, etc. also includes the others. Thus, a study of the church cannot exclude God, Christ, the Holy Spirit, salvation, society, creation, etc. This is of course recognized in Modern Theology, but not included in the modern methodological strategy. Postmodernism asks for more than the recognition of relations; it calls for integration. A suitable metaphor for integration is the recognition that all things interpenetrate one another in a fractal (broken or irregular) way. There are no clear or neat boundaries. This can be

SECTION A

THEOLOGY

very vividly demonstrated on a computer screen with the aid of fractal geometry (Benoit Mandelbrot). The bottom line is that fractals reveal that we find something of everything in everything else.

True to a holistic approach, every theme of the Bible then also needs to show how every single aspect or theme is an expression of all the other themes. According to postmodernism, everything is related to everything else. The so-called order of salvation (*ordo salutis*) serves as an example. Calvinists maintained that regeneration comes before conversion due to election, and Evangelicals saw it in the opposite way. According to systems thinking, salvation is a "package" and there is both conversion in justification and sanctification in conversion. Within this framework, the dichotomy of body and soul also becomes untenable, for humans are holistically viewed as an integrated whole. To talk about the soul is then to refer to the whole human being as a totality from a specific angle. Soul is no longer seen as an entity, but rather as a function of the whole person. The phenomenon of life itself is no longer viewed as a complex process of chemistry or the indwelling of some foreign supernatural entity like the élan vital or soul. In a holistic fashion, life is not foreign to matter itself, yet, due to processes like integration, feedback and self-organisation, soul is that which transcends matter.

The aim of Postmodern Theology is not to provide a rational or exact explanation of God, but to point to coherence between our experience of God and the way we experience the world physically and morally. Postmodernism concerns itself with intelligibility in terms of our being in the world, within the context of ultimate reality. In this sense Postmodern Theology will also lean towards a Natural Theology (Thomas Torrance, John Polkinghorn), without surrendering transcendence, in order to gain an integrated understanding of reality. Consequently, both transcendence and immanence need to be redefined. Traditionally, these concepts serve as metaphors borrowed from the concept of space. In postmodernism they might become more abstract, perhaps changed to metaphors of dimension.

Postmodernism teaches that there is not a fixed body of theological truth available that needs to be communicated from generation to generation. The onus is rather on every generation to discover meaning for themselves by means of metaphoric reference.

14.8 PARTICIPATION

Against this background one can say that the study of theology calls for a commitment to participation. In Postmodern Theology, believers need to include their relationship with God in the process of their theological reflection. In this sense, postmodern theologians are called to both discover and create truth at the same time. The way we model God by means of metaphors bears reference to our spiritual experience and is therefore not groundless. Experience includes cognitive thinking as well as non-conceptual experience that may be of a life transforming nature. In this sense, experiential reality becomes truth; the believer enters a world of meaning where theology serves as an instrument to weave the religious content into one's personal life. The result is that the believer is not called upon to master abstract truth, rather he or she is challenged to make sense of the world by participating in the creation of a new world in terms of which the self can be redefined. Faith is therefore my own experience and theology the story or account of my life. This can of course only be accomplished by making use of language in a creative way – that of imaging or imagining God. This implies that the epistemic construction of God is local and not universal. Every person imagines God personally and differently, although this does not exclude the religious feeling that my God is also your God. After all, we use the same metaphors borrowed largely from Scripture.

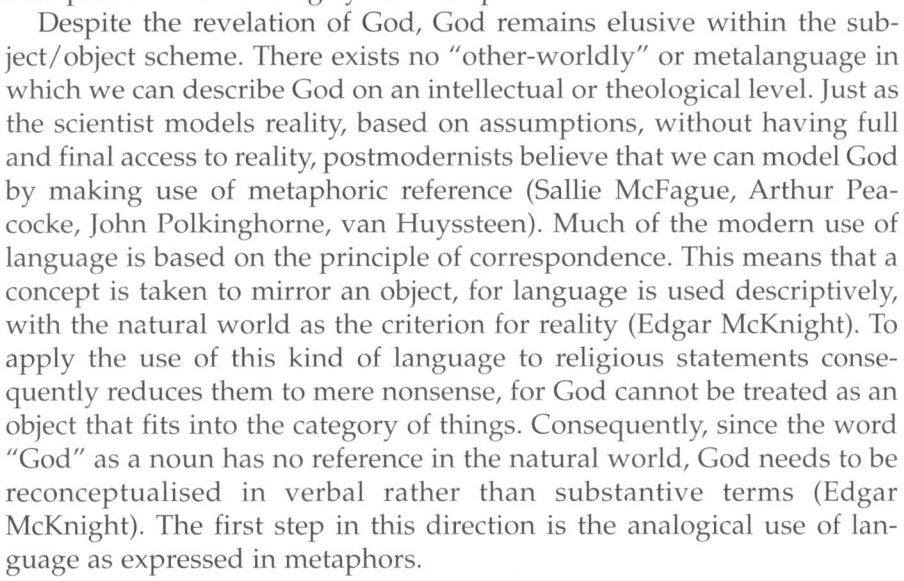

Despite the revelation of God, God remains elusive within the subject/object scheme. There exists no "other-worldly" or metalanguage in which we can describe God on an intellectual or theological level. Just as the scientist models reality, based on assumptions, without having full and final access to reality, postmodernists believe that we can model God by making use of metaphoric reference (Sallie McFague, Arthur Peacocke, John Polkinghorne, van Huyssteen). Much of the modern use of language is based on the principle of correspondence. This means that a concept is taken to mirror an object, for language is used descriptively, with the natural world as the criterion for reality (Edgar McKnight). To apply the use of this kind of language to religious statements consequently reduces them to mere nonsense, for God cannot be treated as an object that fits into the category of things. Consequently, since the word "God" as a noun has no reference in the natural world, God needs to be reconceptualised in verbal rather than substantive terms (Edgar McKnight). The first step in this direction is the analogical use of language as expressed in metaphors.

14.9 METAPHORS

Metaphors are very useful when we have to explain the unknown in terms of the known. They serve as a form of reality depiction. They form a bridge between the direct experience of God by faith, or intuitive knowledge, and the intelligibility of that experience. Understanding at the deepest level forms an integral part of religious experience. It is through revelation that the believer awakens to a new understanding of the relationship between him/herself and God. This means that revelation includes a cognitive element. For instance, the experience of the love, care and authority of God is conceptualised by using the metaphor "Father". Metaphoric reference means that God is likened unto a father but not exhausted by the term, that is to say, He is not other than a father, but at the same time infinitely more than a father. Consequently, the term "Father" is not an absolute reference that excludes God's also being "Mother". This serves to confirm that the particular use of language plays an important part in Postmodern Theology.

A postmodern use of language endeavours to make it possible to con-

SECTION A
THEOLOGY

ceptualise God anew by breaking out of the object/subject scheme. In modern science the concern is with how reality truly is intrinsically. Postmodernism moves beyond the subject/objects scheme and the mere descriptive phase of language. Consequently, in postmodern science the scientist wants to depict or image reality in terms of tentative models. This means that reality is recreated on a mental level with the use of analogical language. We recreate with the intention of obtaining meaning. This should be borne in mind when we do theology, because it is in line with this epistemic trend to go beyond the focus on substance to that of patterns and interrelationships.

There is also an acceptance that truth is relational, which means it is both subjective (creating truth) and objective (discovering truth). Metaphors have reverential value, that is, they refer to objective truth, but are also unlike the object they represent. For this reason, one has to remind oneself that we do not know God, as He is, in Himself, an abstraction. Rather, we know God in his relationships, as He discloses Himself within a specific time frame under peculiar historical conditions.

Against this background it hopefully becomes clear that there is a shift from revelation as timeless truth waiting to be discovered, to the historical importance of revelation. History is thus no longer seen as contingent or incidental, but as an intrinsic part of God's self-manifestation. In addition, the historical dimensions of salvation history, of God becoming incarnated, also serves as an indication of the earthbound direction of God's involvement. Some of the postmodern implications of the "this-worldliness" include a shift towards panenteism or an ecological orientation where the world is seen as God's body (Sallie McFague; Grace Jantzen). In Process Theology (Charles Hartshorne) God is represented as a creative participant. According to this model, God leaves ample room for human freedom and creativity. God is not seen as working in a top-down fashion from a position of absolute authority. In this way, postmodernism is in accordance with the shift away from authoritarianism. God's influence is regarded as internal rather than external, working from the inside out. God and the world are distinguishable, but we can not separate them. An interdependence between God and the world means that the world also to some extend affects God. Of course, this emphasis focuses on God's sympathy and closeness and it is also in line with the contemporary evolutionary and ecological perspectives. This means that the world is an evolutionary entity whose final outcome is not exactly predictable. The world was not created as a cosmos in its final state, but is an emergent process guided by God in his dynamic participation in allowing for an ecological interdependence of all creatures. Consequently, the essence of eschatology is not prediction, but a confirmation of God's involvement, an assurance that in the end all things will be well.

This model also affirms the balance between order and chance in that the universe remains open to change and evolvement. This means that it is not predetermined by God exactly which potentialities will realise.

True novelty may emerge. This view is also in line with the current emphasis on the science of complexity or so-called chaos theory. Chaos theory is a new science which enables scientists to study the irregularities in systems far from equilibrium – the way most real life systems seem to behave. God can thus no longer be conceived as the watchmaker or the puppet master who is obliged to pull all the strings. Brokenness and suffering are part of the way the world is. It is through the interplay of chaos and order that the world attains it's final character – a product which integrates the quality of time into it's essence.

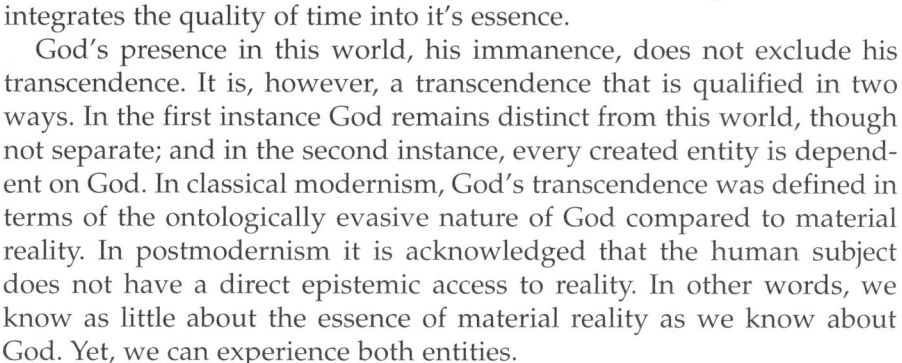

God's presence in this world, his immanence, does not exclude his transcendence. It is, however, a transcendence that is qualified in two ways. In the first instance God remains distinct from this world, though not separate; and in the second instance, every created entity is dependent on God. In classical modernism, God's transcendence was defined in terms of the ontologically evasive nature of God compared to material reality. In postmodernism it is acknowledged that the human subject does not have a direct epistemic access to reality. In other words, we know as little about the essence of material reality as we know about God. Yet, we can experience both entities.

The emphasis on God's immanent actions redefines his power as a persuasive power instead of a controlling power; it is the power of love and inspiration as displayed on the cross – the act of God that evokes a response for surrender and adoration. This picture is one of the sympathetic involvement of a God who guides history towards greater harmony and completeness through the accommodation of human input.

14.10 COSMOLOGY

The relationship between God and the world from a postmodern perspective once again introduces ontology (aspects of physical reality) into the theological debate that, for a long time, was preoccupied solely with moral issues. Theologians are increasingly willing to boldly extend the role of Christ as Saviour to include that of the cosmic Christ, the role that Christ plays in the renewal of the world. There is a rediscovery of the ecological value of this world and the material value of the human body in its eschatological expectation. This tendency gains further momentum with the shift from dualism to reality as a multi-layered process where a continuity between all things exists. This, together with the shift away from positivism, reopens the possibility of a new global awakening to spirituality – a spirituality that does not contrast spirit with matter. Both are aspects of reality.

The effect of sin on the world also needs to be reconsidered. The classical notion is that the Fall is the cause of suffering and death. In postmodernism, suffering and death are natural phenomena – part of the way the world has been since the beginning. The tragedy of sin is not that it caused death per se, but that it qualifies death as a moral dilemma. It is only through the atoning work of Christ that the sting is taken out of death because we participate in his glorious, resurrected life.

SECTION A

THEOLOGY

14.11 INTERDISCIPLINARY DIALOGUE

Another outcome of all this is the reopening of an interdisciplinary dialogue between different subject disciplines. This is based on the conviction that reality is multi-layered and the different objects of study are but complementary aspects of one holistically integrated reality. Apart from this, the new science of complexity serves as a common denominator by reminding us that all disciplines are concerned with patterns and complex systems. This serves as a basis for the different sciences to work closer together under one umbrella, that of the university. A further aspect is that the postmodern epistemology does not exalt empirical research above the methodology of the human sciences. Consequently, theology may regain its status as a university subject.

The realization that theology may not lay claim to a kind of esoteric knowledge holds many consequences. One is the dethronement of theology as the exalted science of the divine. More is gained than lost because the equal footing with other disciplines leads to possible mutual enrichment between theology and natural science. Both enterprises now acknowledge that reality cannot be fully known. This may contribute to better coherence and lend more authenticity to theological statements. The ideal is for the Sunday-world no longer to be foreign to the Monday-world as it used to be within a dualistic framework.

The existential threat that some Christians may experience with Postmodern Theology is a certain loss of traditional certainty. The criterion for truth is no longer a correspondence with reality, but increased meaning, better intelligibility. The new metaphor for certainty is no longer the pillar with its solid foundation (foundationalism), but rather the constant revolving satellite suspended in dynamic equilibrium (explanatory success). In other words, postmodernism relies on an experiential adequacy, determined by the many metaphors which scores of believers have found meaningful throughout the ages (Van Huyssteen) rather than verified or critically justified certainty. The task of Postmodern Theology is to provide an account of faith in order to increase meaning. The method is one of making sense of our religious experience by imaging God in terms of relevant metaphors. And metaphors with staying power eventually become models.

Postmodernism may prove that its models are explanatory more successful than that of previous paradigms, in which case postmodernism may become an established mode of theologising. Postmodern Theology may also be shown to be currently more congruent with contemporary world-views and scientific insights than other traditional approaches. It should, however, be remembered that in terms of the postmodern paradigm itself, postmodernism only serves as a tentative model until a better model can be found. Hence postmodernism is in line with the conviction that we are progressively moving closer to the truth, not by an accumulation of doctrinal knowledge, but by the constant switching of paradigms as determined by the spirit of the time in order to remain relevant.

READING LIST AND BIBLIOGRAPHY

Brueggemann, W. 1993. *The Bible and postmodern imagination. Texts under negotiation.* London: SCM Press.

Capra, F. 1983. *The turning point. Science, society and the rising culture.* London: Fontana.

Capra, F. & Steindl-Rast, D. 1992. *Belonging to the universe. New thinking about God and nature.* London: Penquin Books.

Griffin, D.R. et al. 1989. *Varieties of postmodern theology.* New York: NY Univ. Press.

Hayles, N. Katherine. 1991. *Chaos and Order.* London: Univ. of Chicago.

Peters, T. 1992. *God – the world's future. Systematic theology for a Postmodern age.* Minneapolis: Fortress Press.

The theological challenge of other religious traditions

J.N.J. Kritzinger

15.1 THE CONTEXT OUT OF WHICH THIS THEOLOGY EMERGES

> Jesus ... asked his disciples: "Who do people say that I am?" And they answered Him, "John the Baptist; and others, Elijah; and still others, one of the prophets." He asked them, "But who do you say that I am?" (Mark 8:27–29).

Whatever else these verses mean, it is clear that Jesus did not want his disciples to be in the dark about what people around them believed. Since the very beginning of the church's existence, Christians have confessed their faith in the light of challenges presented to them by surrounding (and often competing) religious communities.

The confession of Jesus Christ as Lord has been the rallying point and "standard" under which Christians have gathered through the centuries, since this was what gave identity and coherence to the greatly diversified Christian movement. In this respect, the Christian church followed in the footsteps of the Jewish religious community from which it emerged. The confession "Hear O Israel: the LORD our God, the LORD is one" or "the LORD is our God, the LORD alone" (Deut 6:4) was the focal point of Jewish identity, wherever Jews were scattered across the world. In the early church, during the time when the New Testament was written, Christians were deeply aware of the multireligious context in which they were living and Christian Theology as such developed out of this "missionary" context where the church was a small (often despised) minority trying to establish itself in the Hellenistic world because it believed itself to be the vanguard of a saved humanity. Bosch has pointed out that mis-

SECTION

A

THEOLOGY

sion was in this sense "the mother of theology". The New Testament authors "wrote in the context of an 'emergency situation', of a church which, because of its missionary encounter with the world, was *forced* to theologize" (Bosch 1991:16).

In other words, because the church from its inception was interacting actively with the communities in which it lived, it has always had a "theology of religions". This is the technical term for the systematic discussion among Christians about the relationship between the Christian faith and other faiths. This is not a separate type of theology or a favourite occupation of a few isolated theologians. Every theologian has a theology of religions, whether it is highly developed and carefully thought out or not. It is not a theological luxury or hobby. It is an essential dimension of every Christian Theology, since it has to do with the church's very identity: what it believes about itself and its calling in society.

A crucial factor in this has always been the position of power the church occupies in relation to other religious communities. When the church is a small and insignificant minority in relation to other faiths, it is constantly confronted with the challenge of other religions and therefore responds to it. But when it is a large and powerful majority community, it often pushes these issues to the background of its theological agenda. In "Christianised" Europe, where for many centuries the church occupied a dominant social and political position, the challenge of other religions was virtually absent from the theological agenda. It was primarily Islam, that perpetual bugbear of the Western mind, which occasionally emerged from the shadows to present a frontal challenge to the existence of "Christian Europe" and which elicited strong responses (mostly negative) from Christian theologians.[1]

And then there was Judaism, which never presented a political threat, and yet occasioned some of the most negative theological statements ever made by followers of the Prince of Peace.[2] Theological anti-Semitism was rife in Europe for many centuries and is often traced back to the New Testament itself (see footnote 3). The triangular relationship be-

---

1 The first time that this happened was in the 8th century, when a Muslim army swept into France, having conquered North Africa and Spain. In 730 AD the Frankish forces under Charles Martel succeeded in stopping their advance at the Battle of Tours and pushing them back into Spain, but the fear of "the Moors" became a permanent feature of European consciousness. The second time that Muslim armies threatened Europe was in the 16th century, when they advanced to the gates of Vienna.

2 One example will suffice here. The accusation against the Jews that they are collectively guilty of "deicide" (the killing of God) was common among European theologians down the centuries. Even in the time of the Reformation we still hear Martin Luther saying:

> Subsequently, after they have scourged, crucified, spat upon, blasphemed, and cursed God in his world ... they pretentiously trot out their circumcision and other vain, blasphemous, invented, and meaningless works ... Therefore, dear Christian, be on your guard against such accursed, incorrigible people, from whom you can learn no more than to give God and his Word the lie, to blaspheme, to pervert, to murder prophets, and haughtily and proudly to despise all people on earth. (quoted in Lochhead 1988:14)

Such theological statements are problematic enough in themselves; the fact that they were part of systematic discrimination against Jews in Europe down the centuries and eventually led to Christian participation (or passivity) in the face of the Holocaust in Nazi Germany is a serious blot on the name of European Christianity.

tween Christians, Jews and Muslims was therefore in the back of the minds of European theologians, but it took centre stage for only limited periods of time (e.g. Aquinas: *Summa contra Gentiles*).

Finally, there was the challenge presented to the church in Europe by the original religions of Europe: the Greek, Roman, Celtic and German religions with their deities and rituals. Contrary to common perceptions, these religions persisted for many centuries in "Christian" Europe and the church dealt with the challenge primarily by "elevating" these "pagan" images, myths and rituals into Christian festivals.[3]

If the other religions of the world featured at all in the Christian theologies of Europe, it was in the circles of missionary activists who, since the 15th century (in the Roman Catholic Church) and the 18th century (in Protestant Churches) were preparing to "go out to the mission field" to evangelise adherents of other faiths. In these missionary circles, dominated for many years by pietist theology and in many cases also by attitudes of colonialist superiority, the theology of religions was generally negative and judgemental. It is one of the delightful twists of history, however, that some European missionaries who crossed seas and mountains to evangelise "pagans", developed a deep interest in the religious traditions they encountered and became recognised scholars of those religions. One example was the German missionary, Bartholomeus Ziegenbalg, who arrived in the South Indian city of Tranquebar on the Malabar coast in 1706. He soon realised the need to study the beliefs of the people of Malabar in order to communicate the gospel to them in a meaningful way and wrote down the results of his investigations in two books, *Genealogie der malabarische Götter* (Genealogy of the Malabar Gods) and *Malabarische Heidentum* (Malabar Paganism). When the leaders at the mission headquarters in Halle (Germany) received these manuscripts they were so upset that they sent a terse message back to Ziegenbalg: You are supposed to eradicate Hinduism from India, not propagate its pagan superstitions in Europe! The manuscripts of the two books lay untouched in the mission archives at Halle and were published only in 1867 and 1926 respectively!

The point of this example is that Christian theologians who live among people of other faiths in situations of religious plurality are far more likely to be drawn into studying those religions and engage in dialogue with their adherents than theologians who live in homogeneous Christian-dominated societies. Christian theologians living as minority

15

The theological challenge of other religious traditions

---

3 Wessels (1994) has traced how the church, in "Christianising" Europe, did not destroy the earlier "pagan" religions, but "elevated" them. The Dutch word "opheffen" (like the German "aufheben") has the double meaning of abolish and elevate. The Christian church in Europe "abolished" the older European religions by "lifting up" into its own life many of the central "pagan" images, myths and rituals.

I put the term "pagan" in inverted commas, because I believe that, like the related term "heathen", it should not be used in a Theology of Religions. Both the Latin word *paganus* and the English word *heathen* refer to people living in the "bundu", thus revealing a feeling of urban superiority over rural people, who are regarded as "backward" or "uncivilised". Such degrading terminology is not fitting in Christian Theology.

SECTION A

THEOLOGY

communities in Asia and Africa, who rub shoulders daily with followers of other faiths and have relatives or friends with different religious commitments, have no option but to take those faiths seriously. But Christian theologians who live in situations of smug Christian superiority and political power usually ignore other religions or look down on them with polite disdain. A theology which faces the challenge of other religions therefore arises primarily out of a context of religious plurality.[4] In such situations the mere existence of other faiths forces itself into the consciousness of Christians as a problem to be explained:

> From now on any serious intellectual statement of the Christian faith must include, if it is to serve its purposes among men, some doctrine of other religions. We explain the fact of the Milky Way by the doctrine of creation, but how do you explain the fact that the Bhagavad Gita is there? (Smith 1972:133)

In contexts of religious plurality, a theological response to the challenge of other faiths is neither a luxury nor the preserve of a few missionary "fanatics"; it becomes a theological necessity. There are theologians living in contexts of religious plurality who withdraw into Christian enclaves, either to ignore the challenges posed by their surroundings or to snipe at other religious communities from the security of their theological fortresses, but both these strategies are theologically irresponsible. We cannot adequately confess Christ in our various contexts if we are unable to tell what other people are saying about Him and about the mysteries of life and death, human greatness and human failure.

A flood of publications is presently appearing on the theology of religions, which signals a very high awareness of the challenge of other religions to the Christian church at the present time. Some regard this as the most important theological question facing the church in the twenty first century. Whereas churches in Asia and many parts of Africa have always lived in situations of religious plurality and therefore had highly conscious and well-developed theologies of religions, it is only in the past few decades that the church in the North has become acutely aware of religious plurality. When Knitter (1985:2) speaks of "the age-old fact of religious pluralism" as "a newly experienced reality for many today", he is speaking primarily for Europe and North America. One can now safely say, therefore, that the challenge which other religions present to Christian Theology is high on the agenda of the church all over the world.

---

4 There is a difference between religious *plurality* and religious *pluralism*. Whereas some theologians use these two terms as synonyms, there are good reasons for distinguishing them. Lubbe (1995:162ff.) has argued convincingly that *religious plurality* refers to "the presence of more than one religious tradition in a particular society, without necessarily implying the existence of any kind of relationship between ... the different components constituting plurality." *Religious pluralism*, on the other hand, is more than mere religious plurality (or diversity), since it implies "the energetic engagement with that diversity" which includes reciprocity, the search for mutual understanding, and a conscious *encounter* of religious commitments (Lubbe 1995:165). In other words, I suggest that pluralism is one theological option in a situation of religious plurality but not the only one, as we shall see below.

15.2 MAJOR TRENDS IN THE CHRISTIAN THEOLOGY OF RELIGIONS

15.2.1 Introduction

In analysing the most influential views held by Christian theologians on other religions, there are two basic ways of proceeding. The first is to make a broad historical survey of twenty centuries of Christian Theology (a "diachronic" approach) and the second is to make a "synchronic" study of different types of theology found in the contemporary context. In this paper, I proceed along the latter lines and find it helpful to construct a set of models or types, since analysis is primarily a "search for patterns" (Spradley 1980:85). Different sets of models have been designed for this purpose, but the most popular has been the triad of Exclusivism, Inclusivism, Pluralism, as developed by Race (1983), D'Costa (1986) and Barnes (1989). In a well-known book entitled *No other name?* Paul Knitter (1985) developed instead a fourfold pattern of models which he labelled Conservative Evangelical, Mainline Protestant, Catholic and Theocentric respectively. Bosch (1976; 1991:478ff.) also opts for a fourfold division (namely exclusivism, fulfilment, relativism and abiding paradox) which is very similar to Knitter's structure, except for the sequence of the categories. Before explaining these models in detail, it may be helpful to show the differences and similarities between these approaches by means of a diagram.

Race and D'Costa	Exclusivism		Inclusivism	Pluralism
Knitter	Conservative Evangelical	Mainline Protestant	Catholic	Theocentric
Bosch	Exclusivism	Abiding Paradox	Fulfilment	Relativism

This comparison reveals just how confusing theological terminology can be, since one cannot assume that theologians mean the same thing when they use a specific term. In explaining this spectrum of Christian attitudes to people of other religions, I will use the threefold division of exclusivism, inclusivism and pluralism before pointing out some weaknesses of this approach and adding other dimensions to it.

The first thing to understand about this approach to the theology of religions is that the underlying focus of this threefold distinction (exclusivism-inclusivism-pluralism) is on *soteriology* (the understanding of salvation) and *Christology* (the understanding of Christ). In other words, the question is whether *salvation in Jesus Christ* is given *exclusively* to those who know Jesus Christ (exclusivism), whether that same grace is available more *inclusively* to people outside the church and the Christian tradition (inclusivism), or whether salvation is not necessarily linked to

SECTION A THEOLOGY

Jesus Christ at all (pluralism). This focus on salvation and Christology often causes the central question of the debate to be phrased as some variation of "Is Christ the only way (to salvation)?" (cf. the titles of Heim 1985 and Nash 1994).[5]

It is important, at the outset, to point out that salvation means different things to different people. To many taking part in this debate, salvation seems to mean little more than the destiny of the individual after death. Put rather crudely, then, for many the issue is: "Can a Buddhist go to heaven?" or more generally: "Who can be saved?" Newbigin (1989: 176ff.) has criticised this "fatally flawed" question for being *presumptuous* (usurping God's sole right to judge), *reductionist* (separating the individual "soul" after death from life here and now), and *individualist* (suggesting that the selfish refrain "for me" exhausts the purpose of God in history). Bosch (1991:488) has likewise rejected this "ahistorical and other-worldly" understanding of salvation in the theology of religions debate and pointed out that salvation has to do rather with the dynamic process of moving humankind and all creation towards the final and all-inclusive peace of God. Be constantly aware then, in what follows, that you do not take for granted that you know what anyone means by the term "salvation".

Furthermore, it is important to understand this approach of constructing models in theology. The advantage of this approach is that it creates some order in an otherwise bewildering variety of theological views. It must be remembered, however, that such models are *constructions* which do not correspond exactly to the state of affairs on the ground. By placing a group of theologians together in a model, one creates a new (theoretical) entity. The exclusivist model is not a church which people have consciously joined and where they are happy to be together. Often people who do not know one another and differ on various points of doctrine are lumped together in the same model because the creator of the model judges that in *terms of a particular issue* (in this case, their view of salvation in other religions) they belong together. A model is therefore like a map; it helps you find your way around, but must not be confused with the territory itself. It only mirrors or approximates the territory and can never do full justice to it. A map also has a specific purpose; there are road maps (for travellers), rainfall maps (for farmers), contour maps (for mountaineers), mineral maps (for people interested in mining), etc. The threefold theology of religions map is a guide for theological travellers who are interested in *the scope of God's salvation* in the world of religions, to help them find their way through this tricky theological terrain.

15.2.2 Exclusivism

This model includes Christian theologies that limit God's salvation to

---

5 The same Christological focus is evident in books like *No other name?* (Knitter 1985) and *No other name* (Sanders 1992), referring to Acts 4:12, in which it is said that there is no other name through which one can be saved but that of Jesus Christ.

those who have heard of Jesus Christ and who have consciously opted to follow him. In other words, this approach believes that it was necessary for Christ to have come into the world for salvation to have become a reality on earth through his death and his resurrection. If Christ had not been incarnated there would have been no salvation on earth. This is what Knitter (1985:116) has called the "ontological necessity of Christ for salvation" because it means that the reality of salvation flows directly from the historical reality of Christ's incarnation and his death on a Roman cross outside Jerusalem around 30 CE.[6] This aspect of the exclusivist model could be expressed as "No incarnation, no salvation."

But the exclusivist model goes one step further. It also believes that salvation is impossible unless a person *accepts* Christ as Lord and *believes* in him. This is what Knitter (1985) calls "the epistemological necessity of Christ for salvation", since it means that salvation does not become a reality merely because Christ died on the cross; individuals need to accept him personally and *come to know* him in order to be saved.[7] This aspect can be summed up by saying: "No conversion, no salvation." So the exclusivist model accepts both the ontological and the epistemological necessity of Christ for salvation.

The practical effect of this theology is the urgent necessity of Christian evangelism to the ends of the earth. If Christ is the one and only way to salvation (both in the ontological and the epistemological sense) then Christians who believe that have the dire responsibility to take the Christian message to everybody on earth. Anything less than that would amount to gross selfishness and lack of compassion. A clear expression of this approach is the statement of the apostle Paul that an obligation is laid on him, since he owes everybody the gospel: "Woe to me if I do not preach the gospel" (1 Cor 9:16).

An important debate within the exclusivist model concerns the question of "general revelation". This could be formulated as a question: Can God be known solely from the Bible, or is it possible for people who have never heard the message of the Bible to know something of God from observing the beauty of nature and the events of history or from obeying

---

15

The theological challenge of other religious traditions

---

6 The word "ontological" is derived from the Greek word *ontos*, which refers to "being" or "reality". At the level of "being" (i.e. what *really happened* in history), the incarnation of Christ was necessary for salvation.

CE is an abbreviation of Christian Era or Common Era. It is used as an alternative to the abbreviation AD, which refers to *Anno Domini*, Latin words which mean "in the year of the Lord" (Jesus Christ). The expression AD therefore contains a specific confession of the Lordship of Jesus Christ, which not everybody shares. It is important to be aware that some other religious communities have their own ways of reckoning the years. For Jews, the year 1997 CE corresponds to their year 5758 (since creation, according to a literal reading of Genesis), whereas for Muslims 1997 overlaps with their year 1417 (*Anno Hijrae*, that is, years since the *hijra* [relocation] of their prophet Muhammad from Mecca to Medina in the year 622 CE). To develop a sensitive Christian Theology of Religions means (among other things) that one should not arrogantly assume one's Christian view to be the only one or the dominant one.

7 The term "epistemological" is derived from the Greek word *episteme*, which refers to the act of *knowing*. Exclusivists believe that Christ is necessary for salvation not only because of his historical death (at the *level of being* – ontological), but also because it is only through knowing him and accepting him (at the level of *knowing* – epistemological) that one can attain salvation.

SECTION A
THEOLOGY

the prompting of their conscience? Or is it even possible that they may attain a saving knowledge of God through God's "general" revelation outside the Bible? Knitter (1985) divides the exclusivist model of Race (1983) and others into two separate models ("conservative evangelical" and "mainline Protestant") precisely to distinguish between these two emphases among theologians who believe that salvation is exclusively tied to the name of Jesus Christ. In the same way, Bosch (1991) distinguishes between "exclusivism" and "abiding paradox", the latter being the view of the Protestant Reformation that salvation is only in the name of Christ, but that God is revealed and known outside of the Bible and the Judaeo-Christian tradition. For Bosch, this abiding paradox gives rise to an attitude of creative tension between *dialogue* (learning about God from listening to "others") and *witness* (testifying to others about the uniqueness of Jesus Christ).

Many radical exclusivists ("conservative evangelicals" in Knitter's terminology) argue that there is no such thing as general revelation and that the world of human religion and culture is the arena of human rebellion against God[8] or (worse still) the fields of demons.[9] In such views, the goodness and love that are evident in the lives of people who are not Christians should be ascribed to the cunning of the devil, who "disguises himself as an angel of light" (2 Cor 11:14), thus creating the (fatally mistaken) impression that a person is actually experiencing the truth.[10] This "conservative evangelical" (Knitter 1985) approach implies a negative and pessimistic view of human nature, suggesting that human beings are totally incapable of doing any good, unless they are reborn "from above" by the Spirit of God.[11]

The practical result of a radically exclusivist theology of religions is a concerted programme of world-wide evangelism, often of the "aggressive" type. In this respect, exclusivist Christians have made a significant contribution to the spreading of the Christian message across the world. Sometimes, however, a radically exclusivist theology gives rise to a praxis which is not at all evangelistic, especially when it teams up with

---

8 Karl Barth's view on "religion as unbelief" is perhaps the best known expression of this approach. He argued in his *Church Dogmatics* I/2 (1978) that religion is the great concern of autonomous and godless human beings, whose minds are (in the words of John Calvin) "idol factories". However, Barth directed this statement not primarily at other religions, but at Christianity itself, as he fought the destructive "German Christian" Theology which supported Hitler and his Nazi ideology.

9 An example of this demonic interpretation of other religions is the approach of Marius Baar, who regards the Allah worshipped by Muslims as an idol, a spiritual power in direct opposition to the God of the Judaeo-Christian tradition: "Mohammed ... who came in his own name and was temporal, knew nothing of eternity and therefore accepted Satan's offer. The Islamic community is now in power because Satan is keeping his promise. We are seeing not just a clash between Christ and Mohammed, but a clash between the Christ and the spirit of antichrist" (in Lochhead 1988:17).

10 Augustine regarded the splendid moral fruits in the lives of people outside the church as nothing more than "splendid vices" (see Gaybba 1994:4).

11 These words are taken almost verbatim from Question 8 of the *Heidelberg Catechism*, an influential instruction manual for young Christians in the Reformed tradition, written in Germany in the year 1563. Defenders of such a view argue that it is not a *pessimistic,* but a *realistic* view of human nature.

"enemy" attitudes to produce ideologies of hostility (see 15.4.2 below) that are intent more on the destruction than the salvation of the "infidel". This was also the destructive logic of the Christian Crusades against Muslims, which did more than anything else to sour the relationship between these two religious communities.

15.2.3 Inclusivism

The second model represents a more open and accommodating view on the reality of God's salvation amidst the religions of the world. It holds to the *ontological necessity* of Christ for salvation, in other words, without the physical coming of Jesus into the world there would have been no salvation. This view they share with the exclusivists. The difference comes in with the question whether someone can be saved without hearing of Christ or personally accepting him as Lord. In other words, the question is whether Christ is *epistemologically* necessary for salvation. In this respect, inclusivists go further than the open-minded exclusivists who accept general revelation by stating that there is a universal revelation of the saving grace of Christ in the life of every human being.[12] By this they do not imply that every human being is automatically saved, but that the possibility is certainly within reach of all religious people and "people of good will".[13] The reason why Bosch (1991:479ff.) categorizes this approach as "fulfilment" is because of the central notion in the inclusivist view that all human wisdom and goodness is a *preparation for the gospel*:

---

12 One of the most influential viewpoints in this regard has been that of the Roman Catholic theologian Karl Rahner. He believed that the grace of Christ "infuses and becomes part of human nature – that is, part of the psychological structures of human consciousness" (Knitter 1985:125). This fact that every human life is "graced" by Christ can be seen in the longing for transcendence and the openness to mystery in the lives of people. In this way people could be "anonymous Christians", living good lives as a result of the grace of Jesus Christ, but without being aware of the fact. Pope John Paul II (1991:15) in his encyclical *Redemptoris Missio* (art.10), says something similar:

> Since salvation is offered to all, it must be made concretely available to all. But it is clear that … many people do not have an opportunity to come to know or accept the Gospel revelation or to enter the Church … For such people salvation in Christ is accessible by virtue of a grace which, while having a mysterious relationship to the Church, does not make them formally part of the Church but enlightens them in a way which is accommodated to their spiritual and material situation. This grace comes from Christ; it is the result of his Sacrifice and is communicated by the Holy Spirit. It enables every person to attain salvation through his or her free cooperation.

Here the epistemological necessity of Christ for salvation has fallen away: people can be saved without knowing Christ or even knowing about Christ, the origin of their salvation.

13 This expression is from art. 22 of the Pastoral Constitution on the Church in the Modern World (*Gaudium et Spes*) issued by the Roman Catholic Church at the Second Vatican Council (1962–1965): "All this holds true not for Christians only, but also for all men of good will in whose hearts grace is active invisibly. For since Christ died for all, and since all men are in fact called to one and the same destiny, which is divine, we must hold that the Holy Spirit offers to all the possibility of being made partners, in a way known to God, in the paschal mystery" (Flannery 1975:924). Article 16 of the Dogmatic Constitution on the Church (*Lumen Gentium*) formulates this as follows: "Those who, through no fault of their own, do not know the Gospel of Christ or his Church, but who nevertheless seek God with a sincere heart, and, moved by grace, try in their actions to do his will as they know it through the dictates of their conscience – those too may achieve eternal salvation" (Flannery 1975:367).

SECTION A

THEOLOGY

Whatever good or truth is found amongst them [moral people who are not Christians – JNJK] is considered by the Church to be a preparation for the Gospel and given by him who enlightens all men that they may at length have life" (*Lumen Gentium* 16, Flannery 1975:368).

In other words, when the church preaches the gospel, it does not move into a vacuum, but into human communities richly endowed with goodness and therefore thoroughly prepared for the Christian message to serve as the perfection and fulfilment of that goodness.

Inclusivists do not, therefore, dispense with the church and its mission in society. They are most certainly not pluralists (see 15.2.4 below), since they stress the fact that all salvation is *due to the grace of Christ* and that this grace is most fully revealed in the church as the body of Christ. They argue that other religions are "lawful" since they contain "supernatural grace-filled elements" (Knitter 1985:127). This makes them the "ordinary" ways of salvation for the majority of humankind, positively included in God's plan of salvation, while the church is the "extraordinary" way of salvation (Küng 1976:111ff.). The role of the church is therefore not to be the exclusive "ark of salvation", but the *sacrament of salvation* for the whole world, in which the fullness of God's purpose with the world is revealed in an exemplary fashion.[14]

Since it is the *grace of Christ* which is operative in all persons and religions, there is *an orientation towards Christ and the church* in all the salvific elements evident in their lives. These experiences of salvation in other religions are therefore incomplete until people embrace Christ, in whom they find their true identity and the fullness of salvation. Here again it becomes clear why Bosch (1991:479ff.) called this approach the *fulfilment* model.

The practical result of this theology does not necessarily spell the end of Christian mission (as some critics of this approach have suggested), but a new understanding of what it should be:

> The Church will not so much regard herself today as the exclusive community of those who have a claim to salvation, but rather as the historically tangible *vanguard* and the historically and socially constituted explicit expression of what the Christian hopes is present as a hidden reality even outside the visible church. (Rahner 1966:133)

15.2.4 Pluralism

The last of the three models in the theology of religions opposes both the ontological and epistemological necessity of Jesus Christ for salvation, since neither Christ not the Christian church plays a key role in this theological approach. Knitter (1985), who follows John Hick quite closely in this regard, calls this the "theocentric" model to indicate that *God*, not Christ, is in the *centre* of this approach. Hick (1973:124ff.) speaks of a "Co-

---

14 This view of the church as sacrament is summarised well by Knitter (1985:130):
> [The church is] no longer an exclusive "sanctuary" of the saved, the church is a "sign raised up among the nations", a "symbol", a *pars pro toto* (part for the whole), a "representative", a "prototype" of the kingdom of God at work throughout all history.

pernican revolution" that is needed in theology, from a church-centred or Christ-centred universe of faiths to a God-centred one.[15] The attempts of inclusivist theologians to overcome the harsh exclusivism of traditional theology ("outside the church there is no salvation") are compared to the "epicycles" proposed by Ptolemaic astronomers, in other words, complex attempts to explain the odd movements of the planets while still retaining an earth centred view of the universe.[16] The implication of this is that Christ is seen as one of many planets (saviour figures) circling the sun (God), rather than being the sun around which everything else revolves:

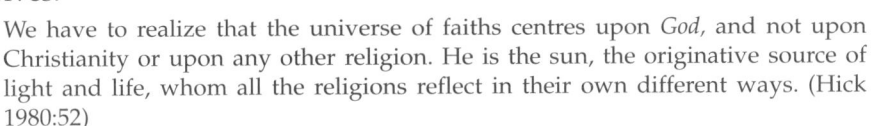

> We have to realize that the universe of faiths centres upon *God,* and not upon Christianity or upon any other religion. He is the sun, the originative source of light and life, whom all the religions reflect in their own different ways. (Hick 1980:52)

Other proponents of this view prefer to call it the "pluralist" approach, because it accepts that there are more ways to God's salvation than Christ and the church, thus accepting religious plurality as something positive (see the distinction drawn between *plurality* and *pluralism* in footnote 4). It is important to note, however, that Christian theologians who support the pluralist position are not necessarily complete relativists, who believe simply that all faiths are equally true. Because, as Race (1983:78) has pointed out, "if all faiths are equally true, then all faiths are equally false." A theologian like Knitter clearly avoids this "debilitating relativism" (Cobb 1975:58) by insisting that he is seeking for an approach "that will be faithful both to contemporary experience and to Christian tradition" (Knitter 1985:xiii) or, put differently, which "allows Christians to be fully committed to Jesus and fully open to other ways" (xiv). In other words, one of the central purposes of Knitter's book is to convince Christians who have given up the doctrine of exclusive salvation in Christ to steer away from a "lazy tolerance that calls upon all religions to recognize each other's validity and then to ignore each other as they go their own self-satisfied ways" (Knitter 1985:9). Such a lazy tolerance, according to which "all cats are grey" is indeed debilitating, since it leads to a position where it literally does not matter to which religion you belong, or whether you belong to a religion at all. In other words, religion

15

The theological challenge of other religious traditions

---

15 The Polish astronomer Copernicus (1473–1543) was responsible for the insight that the sun does not revolve around the earth (as was commonly thought at the time, according to the Ptolemaic view of the universe), but that the earth revolves around the sun. That was a revolutionary insight for the 16th century. Hick and Knitter believe that a similar revolution is necessary in theology from a Christ-centred to a God-centred universe of faiths.

16 "Looking back we can see that it was theoretically possible to stick indefinitely to the conviction that the earth is the centre, adding epicycle upon epicycle as required to reconcile the dogma with the facts. However the whole thing became increasingly artificial and burdensome; and the time came when people's minds were ready for the new Copernican conception that it is the sun and not the earth that is at the centre .... When we find men of other faiths, we add an epicycle of theory to the effect that although they are consciously adherents of a different faith, nevertheless they may unconsciously or implicitly be Christians. In theory, one can carry on such manoeuvres indefinitely. But anyone who is not firmly committed to the original dogma is likely to find the resulting picture artificial, implausible and unconvincing, and to be ready for a Copernican revolution in his Theology of Religions" (Hick 1973:125).

SECTION A

THEOLOGY

becomes strictly irrelevant to life, nothing more than a personal fancy or a private hobby. If all religions are equally true, they could also be equally false.

Since Knitter makes such a strong point of stressing faithfulness to Christ and the avoidance of a lazy relativism, his view differs significantly from classical relativism. The latter is often illustrated by telling the Indian tale which criticises six blindfolded people for claiming to know what an elephant is, after feeling only one part of it (tail, ear, leg, tusk, etc.). Classical relativism says that religions similarly make the false claims of each possessing the whole truth, whereas in reality each is in touch with only one small aspect of it. Knitter's view on a "unitive pluralism" of religions differs from this; it may be idealistic and based on an overly optimistic view of human evolution, but it is a serious *Christian Theology*. This can be seen in the kind of practical effect that Knitter foresees for his theology; he does not understand Christian mission as directed to the conversion of people from other religions to Christianity, but he encourages Christians to be deeply devoted to Christ and to play an active role in the world:

> The primary mission of the church ... is not the "salvation business" (making persons Christian so they can be saved), but the task of serving and promoting the kingdom of justice and love, by being sign and servant, wherever the kingdom may be forming .... The central purpose of mission is being realized as long as, through mutual witnessing, all are converted to a deeper grasp and following of God's truth .... So it can be said that the goal of missionary work is being achieved when announcing the gospel to all peoples makes the Christian a better Christian and the Buddhist a better Buddhist. (Knitter 1985:222)

In conclusion one could say, then, that the pluralist (or theocentric) model accepts the reality of salvation within all religions, while encouraging greater faithfulness of believers to their respective traditions as well as constant interaction between them, resulting in joint service to society.

15.3 CENTRAL BIBLICAL NOTIONS

A superficial way of looking at the use of the Bible in the theology of religions is to list the Bible verses or portions that are most frequently quoted by proponents of the three models discussed in 15.2 above. It is superficial because much more is at stake in this theological debate than merely one's favourite Bible verses. It is, however, a place to begin.

15.3.1 Exclusivism

The most well-known verses used by advocates of the exclusivist model are certainly John 14:6 ("I am the way, the truth and the life") and Acts 4:12 ("No other name"), in which the name of Christ is indicated as the one and only way to God. However, there are many similar verses, such as John 10:9 ("I am the gate") and 1 Timothy 2:5 ("There is one God and one mediator between God and humankind"). Exclusivists interpret them literally, as saying that Christ is both ontologically and epistemologically necessary for salvation. Dualistic notions are the favourites of radical exclusivists, who interpret other religions as demonically inspired. These are drawn from verses like 2 Cor 6:14–18 ("What fellowship is there between light and darkness? What agreement is there between Christ and Beliar?"), 1 Cor 10:20 ("I do not want you to be partners with demons. You cannot partake of the table of the Lord and the table of demons") and 1 John 5:19 ("We know that ... the whole world lies under the power of the evil one").

More open-minded exclusivists tend to emphasise general revelation, which means that they concentrate on portions like Romans 1:18–2:24, in which the apostle Paul speaks of the fact that there are people who did not receive God's special revelation and yet do the law of God, since it is "written on their hearts"[17] (Rom 2:15). Paul's speech on the Areopagus to the people of Athens (Acts 17:22–31) also features prominently, since it stresses the fact that all people "live and move and have our being" in God and are indeed the "offspring" of God (Acts 17:28). Paul's words to the people of Lystra are also quoted in this regard: "He [God] has not left Himself without a witness in doing good – giving you rains from heaven and fruitful seasons ..." (Acts 14:17). All these verses are used to argue for a general revelation of God among the nations of the world, which implies that all people are without excuse before God, since they could have known better than to live in sin and reduce the immortal God to images of mortals or even animals (Rom 1:23). What makes such theologians, who accept general revelation, into exclusivists is that they limit God's *salvation* to conscious faith in Jesus Christ, even though they extend God's *revelation* to all humankind. This seeming anomaly, which Bosch (1976) has called "an abiding paradox", has prompted Knitter (1985:98, 101) to characterise his "mainline Protestant" model as "Revelation – Yes! Salvation – No!"

It is important to point out that the exclusivist model is characterised not only by its selection of Bible verses, but more fundamentally by a distinctive *way of using* the Bible in its theology. Simplifying for the sake of emphasis, one could say that its theological method has two main components, namely *explication* and *application*. This method is derived from the church's preaching practice, since preachers often start by "expounding" a biblical portion as the inspired Word of God, and only afterwards "apply" it to the life of the congregation. For most exclusivist theologians it is sufficient to quote a Bible verse in order to end an argument, since the Bible is the only source of their theology, even though they admit that its message needs to be made relevant to a concrete situation. The study of other religions or dialogue with people of those traditions is therefore not an integral part of theological decision-making; having first estab-

---

15

The theological challenge of other religious traditions

---

17 It should be noted that there is a debate among theologians about whether, in Romans 1–2, Paul is referring to *Gentiles* who have come to know God apart from the Law, or to *Gentile Christians*. Karl Barth, in his rejection of the notion of "general revelation", argued that Paul referred to Gentile Christians in these verses (for all the arguments, see König in *Journal of Theology for Southern Africa*, Vol 15, 1976).

SECTION A

THEOLOGY

lished the truth from studying the Bible alone, exclusivists then proceed to find confirmation for these biblical truths in the religions which they encounter. It is very important to realise that the questions surrounding the use of the Bible in a theology of religions is far more than a quarrel over which verses are most central to its message. The most fundamental questions have to do with the *method* of theology, in which issues like the relationship between text and context, and the relationship between theory and praxis are key factors.

15.3.2 Inclusivism

The inclusivist model operates according to a different theological method. For the protagonists of this model it is not sufficient merely to quote a series of Bible verses in support of a particular position. Karl Rahner, one of the key figures in the inclusivist model, made a detailed analysis of the human condition and emphasised the fact that there is a "supernatural existential" (a longing to be more than who you are) in every human being. He related that to various biblical notions, but it is clear that he regarded it as essential to make a study of human religious experience *while* developing a theology of religions. Roman Catholic Theology after Vatican II proceeded along this path, expressing its appreciation for the beauty and wisdom evident in other religious traditions. In this respect, it draws on a long-standing Catholic tradition (based on the theology of Thomas Aquinas) of seeing God's grace not as destroying human nature, but as fulfilling or perfecting it. In this respect, God is seen as leading and guiding people from their "lower" (but real) knowledge to a "higher" or fuller knowledge of who God is as revealed in Jesus Christ. However, what distinguishes this from the exclusivist notion of general revelation is that the *presence of Christ* among the religions of the world is stressed in an inclusivist approach. Drawing on the view of John's Gospel on the eternal Word *(Logos)* of God as "the true light, which enlightens everyone" (John 1:9), some theologians have developed a theology of the Word, actively present in human lives as the *logos spermatikos*, the Word scattered and working like seed to produce fruits of goodness, love and beauty. Justin, the Christian Apologist from the second century, was the first to articulate this view in a systematic way.[18] He wrote, for example:

> It is our conviction that those ... who are zealous for the good which is delivered to us, and practise it, have some share in God. According to our traditional belief they will, through God's grace, share his dwelling place with us. And it is our conviction that this holds for everyone. Christ is the divine Word in whom all human-

---

18 "Apologist" is a term used for a group of theologians in the early church (second and third centuries) who in many ways laid the foundation for subsequent developments in theology. A number of significant Apologists were Africans, living and working across North Africa from Egypt to (present-day) Algeria. They did not "apologise" for the gospel. The Greek word *apologia* meant a reasoned defence of a position (as in a court of law), and the Apologists presented such a defence of the faith of the church, which was then a small and often persecuted minority, against the criticisms of Greek philosophy, Egyptian wisdom and Roman law. Some of the most important Apologists were Clement, Justin, Irenaeus, Tatian and Tertullian.

ity shares; and such as live in accordance with the light of their knowledge, are Christians, even if they are regarded as godless. (*Apology* I:10,46, quoted in Bosch 1977:32)

It is this notion of *anonymous Christians* which Rahner reaffirmed in the 20th century, which is closely linked to the idea of the *cosmic Christ* who is at work incognito in all communities. In this vein, Panikkar (1964) wrote the book *The Unknown Christ of Hinduism* and the Lebanese Orthodox scholar, Georges Khodr, wrote:

> Christ is hidden everywhere in the mystery of his lowliness. Any reading of religions is a reading of Christ. It is Christ alone who is received as light when grace visits a Brahmin, a Buddhist or a Mohammedan reading his own Scriptures. Every martyr for the truth, every man persecuted for what he believes to be right, dies in communion with Christ. (Khodr 1971:124ff.)

The Pauline image of the Old Testament law as the guardian or educator (Greek: *paidagogos*) which led the people of Israel to the fulfilment in Christ (Gal 4:1–7) is also used in the inclusivist approach. It is interpreted in such a way that the religions of the nations are their "Old Testaments" which prepared them for the coming of Christ. This idea of a preparation for the gospel *(praeparatio evangelica)*, which we have already encountered in the documents of Vatican II (see 15.2.3) is derived from this long-standing Christian view. It was already proposed by Clement of Alexandria, one of the early Christian Apologists, but it found support regularly down the ages. For example, J.N. Farquhar (1913) wrote *The Crown of Hinduism*, in which he argued that "Christianity is the evolutionary crown of Hinduism … for the man who sees in Christ the crown and fulfilment of all religions, the crudest ceremony and the most irrational belief contains germs of truth which have blossomed and reached maturity in him" (in Bosch 1977:95).

15.3.3 Pluralism

As with the inclusivist model, it is insufficient to explain the use of the Bible in the pluralist model by merely enumerating a series of favourite Bible portions. What is critical is to set out the theological method used by the theologians in this approach. Knitter adopts the revisionist method of David Tracy, which he explains as follows:

> Any viable method of theology will have to make use of *two* sources – Christian tradition (Scripture and its living interpretation through history) and human experience (which includes both thought and praxis). Both these sources should be listened to openly and honestly; both must be brought into a mutually clarifying and mutually criticizing correlation. (Knitter 1985:91)

In other words, there is no simple and direct appeal to the Bible. It is possible to *criticise* the Christian tradition (which includes the Bible) if an open and honest listening to human experience today demands it. And this is precisely what Knitter does when he looks at New Testament Christology. He argues that the survival of the human race demands interreligious dialogue, co-operation and peace, but that traditional Christology is a stumbling block in this process and should therefore be reinterpreted. The following statement is a good illustration of this theological method:

> All the traditional Christian claims [exclusivist and inclusivist Christologies – JNJK] are insufficiently sensitive to the way they contradict contemporary awareness of historical relativity and to the way they impede authentic dialogue with believers of other faiths .... One of the principal concerns of this book has been to show that there has been a genuinely new evolution in the "texture" of human experience, very different from the "context" of the New Testament and past dogmatic statements about Jesus .... Not to understand Jesus anew in this new texture, not to open oneself to the possibility of a new Christology, is to run the risk of confining the past to an idolatrous "deposit of faith". (Knitter 1985:171)

Knitter then devotes a whole chapter to a reinterpretation of the New Testament images of Jesus in light of the contemporary "texture" of human experience which he has identified. The result is a Jesus who is unique, but in a non-normative and relational way:

> It affirms that Jesus is unique, but with a uniqueness defined by its ability to relate to – that is, to include and be included by – other unique religious figures. (Knitter 1985:171ff.)

In this way, central theological notions like Incarnation, Resurrection, and the Lordship of Christ get reinterpreted in a fundamental way.

15.4 THE FORMS OF PRAXIS FOR A THEOLOGY OF RELIGION

When discussing the forms of praxis out of which a Christian Theology of Religions emerges and to which it leads, it is helpful first to look at the interlocutors (discussion partners) of Christian theologians who engage in this venture.

15.4.1 Interlocutors

The interlocutors of a Christian Theology of Religions are firstly the adherents of other faiths who, in the process of dialogue (see 15.4.2), challenge Christians to take other truth claims seriously. A theology of religions which does not develop out of dialogue can only be an abstract reflection on vague ideas about other religions. Knitter (1985:206) has formulated it clearly: "To fashion a theology of religions outside the praxis of dialogue would be as inappropriate as it would be for a tailor to make a suit without taking the customer's measurements." The interlocutors are scholars involved in other disciplines, especially Religious Studies, whose views have attained popularity and therefore present theologians with a challenge which demands a response.[19] Knitter (1985: 21–71) has identified three such "popular attitudes" in the west to other religions which demand attention, namely Ernst Troeltsch's historical relativism, Arnold Toynbee's notion of a common essence in all religions, and Carl Jung's idea of a common psychic origin of all religions. In a Christian Theology of Religions there is a constant dialogue with the

---

19 This academic discipline has been variously called Comparative Religion, Science of Religion or Religious Studies. The latter seems to be the dominant trend in the English-speaking world.

Christian tradition, which should be understood as a series of earlier "local theologies", responding to the contexts in which they found themselves (Schreiter 1985). So one's interlocutors are potentially all the Christian theologians who have addressed this question of the relationship between Christianity and other faiths.

There are some Christian theologians who conduct this debate from a safe distance, but the majority of credible theologians in the debate have had intense personal experience of interreligious dialogue and co-operation. Klaus Klostermaier, a Roman Catholic priest who spent many years in India, engaged in dialogue with Hindu scholars "at 104° Fahrenheit", levelled the following criticism at Christians who theologise about other religions from the comfortable distance of air conditioned libraries:[20]

> They have an easy time, the 70° F theologians. They settle down in some library and find enough books there by means of which it can be proved that the non-Christian religions are the normal way to salvation for the non-Christian, that each one finds God even without mission – that one should not disturb the conscience of a non-Christian. In Europe's libraries no goats die of heat-stroke, there are no vultures and no dogs eating the goats .... Many a thing looks different when seen from a European library – more beautiful, more pleasant, and more abstract. (Klostermaier 1969:48)

The point is this: A Christian Theology which faces the challenges posed to it by other religious communities cannot be satisfied to study their beliefs and practices from books. Sustained dialogue with adherents of other religions is the indispensable praxis out of which a meaningful and credible Theology of Religions develops. There are many Christian theologians, however, who are sceptical about interreligious dialogue or opposed to it and therefore limit their interlocutors to fellow Christians. There are others who accept the idea of interreligious dialogue, but only as a means of coming to know people in order to evangelise them more effectively. To them, dialogue is acceptable only if it leads to Christian witness: "Any form of dialogue that compromises the uniqueness of the Christian gospel and the necessity that the adherents of other faiths repent and believe it, should be rejected and supplanted by forms of dialogue that enjoin conversion to Christ" (Hesselgrave 1981:126).

It is clear, then, that one's choice of interlocutors in developing a theology of religions is closely related to the theological model in which one stands. The diagram in 15.4.2 will illustrate the many possible combinations between one's theological model and one's choice of interlocutors (or, more broadly stated, one's attitude to people of another religious tradition).

15.4.2 The praxis of a Theology of Religions

David Lochhead (1988) has written an interesting book, *The Dialogical Imperative*, in which he criticises the approach of theologians like Race,

---

20 Klaus Klostermaier is a Roman Catholic priest who spent years in India in dialogue with Hindus. He has written many books and articles on interreligious dialogue, but one of his first was *Hindu and Christian in Vrindaban* (Klostermaier 1969), in which he tells of his year-long stay in the holy city of Vrindaban, the birth place of Krishna, one of the most popular Hindu deities.

SECTION A

THEOLOGY

Knitter and others for concentrating only on *theological theories* in their Theology of Religions. He argues that it is insufficient merely to explain a person's Christology or understanding of revelation, since there is no direct link between that and the person's praxis in concrete interreligious relationships. According to him, the "missing link" between Christological *theory* and inter religious *praxis* is what he calls the interreligious *ideology* which the person follows. He then discusses four unacceptable ideologies *(hostility, isolation, competition* and *partnership)*, and distinguishes them from *dialogue*, which he regards as the only acceptable ideology for interfaith encounter.[21] Following Lochhead's suggestion, I now want to reflect on the relationship between the three theological models (exclusivism, inclusivism and pluralism) and concrete patterns of interfaith encounter, in order to see what combinations are formed between these. In this way the *forms of praxis* associated with the Theology of Religions can be openly addressed in theology itself and not remain an afterthought or an application of theological theories. By praxis I understand not merely the practical aspect of a theology, *but the process of interaction between theorising and acting*, which always go together. In the diagram below, the categories A, B and C at the top are the Christological/soteriological theories and the categories 1 to 5 on the left are patterns of practical interfaith encounter. The various *combinations* between these two dimensions (i.e. A1, A2, ... C5) represent fifteen forms of *interfaith praxis*. By picturing it in this way, the wide field of interfaith praxis can be mapped out, indicating how a particular soteriological theory combines with a concrete attitude towards people of another faith to produce a distinctive form of interfaith praxis.

Any attempt to distinguish (or construct) these *forms of praxis* in a Theology of Religions can be criticised for being incomplete or one-sided. Even though the process is fraught with danger, I am convinced (with Lochhead) that the discussion of Christological or soteriological theories alone is insufficient. I have constructed five patterns of interfaith encounter, based on the concept of "emotional distance" developed by Overdiep (1985) in a book on Christian approaches to "the enemy". These five types of emotional distance distinguish between people of other faiths as *enemies, opponents, strangers, colleagues or friends*. The first and the last *(enemies and friends)* are closest to a person emotionally, whereas strangers are emotionally the furthest away, since they are the people who leave you cold. The remaining two positions of *opponent* and *colleague* fall between these two extremes.

According to Overdiep, reconciliation does not mean that all enemies have to become friends, since that is an unrealistic expectation. For reconciliation to take place, it is sufficient that enemies become *opponents*, that is, people who play the same game according to the same rules and actively oppose each other, but with respect, thus leaving behind them

---

21 It is not clear in Lochhead's book whether he regards dialogue as a better ideology than the other four or as *the overcoming of ideology* in interfaith relationships. I have interpreted Lochhead as saying that dialogue too is an ideology (like the other four), but the only one that can be justified within Christian Theology (see Lochhead 1988:88).

the bitterness of the battle which was evident when they were still enemies.[22] This distinction is a very useful one in distinguishing forms of interfaith praxis.

Any diagram like this has its weaknesses. The first is that it remains caught in the modernist desire to label and classify, thus enthroning the scholar as a virtually omnipotent subject who makes other people into objects by putting them into boxes. To avoid such abuse of power and the "paralysis of analysis" which it produces, it is important to see the diagram only as a strategy which clears the ground. It does this by establishing a vocabulary and delineating existing theologies (Schreiter 1985), in order to set the scene for new constructive theologising.

A second weakness of the diagram is that it creates the impression that the labels apply only to the blocks on which they are placed. For example, one could get the impression that dialogue only occurs in the approaches of Blocks A4, A5, B4 and B5, or that ethnocentrism is found only in Blocks C1 and C2. This is a false impression, since the label intends to express only *the most characteristic feature* of the particular approach, not every aspect of it.

15
The theological challenge of other religious traditions

	A **Exclusivism** (salvation only through knowing Christ)	**B** **Inclusivism** (salvation through the cosmic work of Christ)	**C** **Pluralism** (salvation possible in any religion)
1. Enemies (= Encounter as threat)	A1 *Hostility* (attacks to destroy falsehood)	B1 *Enlightenment* (witness to overcome ignorance)	C1 *Ethnocentrism* (working against "harmful" religions)
2. Opponents (= Encounter as challenge)	A2 *Competition* (witness to overcome opposition to the truth)	B2 *Fulfilment* (witness to complete what is inadequate)	C2 *Ethnocentrism* (opposing "inferior" religions)
3. Strangers (= No encounter)	A3 *Guilty silence*	B3 *Smug superiority*	C3 *Lazy indifference*
4. Colleagues (= Encounter as opportunity)	A4 *Dialogue for more authentic witness*	B4 *Dialogue for deeper understanding*	C4 *Partnership in serving society together*
5. Friends (= Encounter as joy)	A5 *Dialogue as sharing love with neighbours*	B5 *Partnership in mutual enrichment*	C5 *Partnership in searching for truth*

---

22 Overdiep was not writing specifically about interreligious relationships, but about general human relations of enmity, friendship, etc. I have applied his insights to interreligious relations because I regard it as a very useful way of addressing the problem.

SECTION A
THEOLOGY

Theological theories on salvation patterns of interfaith encounter

A few further comments are in order. The first is that Blocks A3, B3 and C3 represent a watershed across the centre of the diagram. What lies above this are the emotionally negative responses which sees the others as opponents or enemies, whereas below it are the emotionally positive responses which see others as colleagues or friends. The three blocks, A3, B3 and C3, when taken together, express the fact that there are Christians of all theological persuasions who treat people of other religions as strangers and aliens – not to be taken seriously as fellow human beings. For *exclusivist* Christians, who believe that salvation is only available to those who know Jesus Christ, such an avoidance of the "other" can only be interpreted as a guilty silence, amounting to selfish enjoyment of God's grace (Block A3). For *inclusivist* Christians, who believe that Christ is cosmically and anonymously at work in the lives of all people, but that the church is the crown and fulfilment of that universal grace, the treatment of the other as a stranger amounts to an attitude of smug superiority (Block B3): "they may get to our level one day, but that's not our business." For *pluralist* Christians, who believe that salvation is available to all people within their own religious traditions, the avoidance of the other amounts to a lazy and bored indifference (Block C3). From the point of view of the love commandment, all three these responses are a betrayal of the gospel. I almost venture to say that it is better to interact with others as enemies than to ignore them as if they were invisible or irrelevant. The Jewish author Eli Wiesel once said, with reference to the lame response of German Christians to the Holocaust: "The opposite of love is not hatred, but indifference."

The commonest forms of interfaith praxis lie in a band running across the diagram from top left to bottom right, since it is predictable that an exclusivist theology would team up with a more negative type of interfaith interaction (Block A1 – top left), and that a pluralist theology would attract a more positive and open-minded form of praxis (Block C5 – bottom right). The more unusual (and therefore more interesting) forms of interfaith praxis lie at the bottom left and top right corners of the diagram, since it is hardly conceivable that Christian theologians who adopt an exclusivist theology would also develop close friendships with people of other faiths (Block A5).[23] Likewise it seems contradictory to find someone in the top right-hand corner combining a pluralist theory of salvation

---

23 It is primarily among "radical evangelicals" that this kind of interfaith praxis is found, i.e. people with an exclusivist theology of salvation, but who commit themselves to the struggles of suffering and oppressed people. An example is Costas (1981:152):

> The religions may be signs and instruments of God's kingdom if they can accept the scandal of the cross of Jesus amid the human crosses of the world. Since the poor, the powerless, and the oppressed (those whose historical destiny has been marked by the crosses of exploitation, injustice, and oppression) have been given a privileged place in the kingdom, it follows that no religious structure can be an adequate sign of its reality if it is not identified with the dispossessed in their misery and suffering.

A radical praxis of neighbourly love (solidarity with all who suffer, whether they are Christians or not) distinguishes this kind of exclusivist soteriology from other evangelical approaches.

with an "enemy" image of people from another faith (Block C1).[24]

A praxis of inconsistent openness to other religions is another problem with the diagram. As a matter of fact, the whole "Theology of Religions" suffers from the weakness that it assumes a particular theologian will *consistently* relate to *all* religions in the same way. This is often not the case.[25] The most meaningful way to do an in depth Theology of Religions is not to work in vague and general terms, but to examine the interaction between followers of two (or at most three) *specific* religious communities. This is where the specialisation fields of Christian-Jewish,[26] Christian-Buddhist,[27] Christian-Hindu,[28] Christian-Muslim,[29] and Christian-African[30] relations fit in.

15
The theological challenge of other religious traditions

---

[24] I have labelled Blocks C1 and C2 as "ethnocentrism" because the primary reason why someone with a pluralist soteriology would see people of another religion as enemies or opponents (who therefore need to be countered or opposed) is a sense of cultural superiority. The negative attitude of many pluralist Christians to the "barbaric" practices of African religions or of the contemporary Islamic revival is a case in point. Their theological theory affirms that these religions are valid ways of salvation to their followers, but their cultural sensibilities override this "liberal" theological impulse to create a negative or oppositional interfaith praxis.

[25] An interesting example cited by Lochhead (1988:16) are pre-millennialist evangelicals, who belong in Block A1 or A2 with reference to most religions, but in Block B4 or even C4 when it comes to Judaism, since they believe that the rebuilding of the Jewish Temple in Jerusalem is a precursor of the Second Coming and therefore wish to assist Jews in doing that. Lochhead (1988:40ff.) himself proposes a "faithful agnosticism" towards other religions, which means suspending all *a priori* value judgements until one has had enough time to develop understanding by means of dialogue; but when it comes to Judaism he takes a different line: "As a matter of Christian faith, the validity of Judaism is given *a priori*. If Judaism is not of God, then neither is Christianity" (Lochhead 1988:42). It is therefore dangerous to use the models of the Theology of Religions as rigid "boxes" in which to put other theologians.

[26] Christian-Jewish relations have probably been the most painful bilateral relationship for Christian theologians to deal with. The church's track record of anti-Semitism is found on some of the darkest pages of Christian history, and the Nazi Holocaust presents Christian Theology with one of its most serious challenges ever. It is the bilateral relationship with the longest history and also occupies a strategic place in a Christian Theology of Religions. The North American evangelical theologian, Gerald Anderson (1981:119) has developed a "domino theory" in this regard:

> My larger concern is that if the Jewish people – who were the original focus of Jesus' mission – do not need Christ, then a similar theological case can easily be projected ... to apply to other faiths until ultimately it becomes a rejection of Christian mission to people of all other faiths.

[27] In many ways, this is the most developed bilateral Theology of Religions. Regular conferences of Christian and Buddhist scholars and a stream of publications testify to this fact. There is even a journal, *Buddhist-Christian Studies*, which is devoted exclusively to this encounter.

[28] Christian-Hindu dialogue is also a well-developed field of study, with new publications appearing regularly. A good example of this bilateral Theology of Religions is the study of Wesley Ariarajah (1991), entitled *Hindus and Christians*, but this is only one among many important publications.

[29] Apart from the Buddhist-Christian encounter, Muslim-Christian relations is perhaps the most studied and best-developed bilateral interreligious relationship among Christians. It is virtually impossible to oversee or keep up with the publications in this field, partly because it has so many political ramifications in today's world.

[30] The relationship between Christianity and African religion is a neglected area in the dominant Theology of Religions debate. The most quoted scholars like Race, D'Costa, Hick, Knitter, Küng and others concentrate on the interaction between Christians and what are sometimes called the "higher religions". This is a serious underestimation of the power and relevance of African religion (and other "primal" religions world-wide). The critical (and appreciative) dialogue between the Christian tradition and the rich religious traditions of Africa is reflected in books on African Theology that have been written by African Christian theologians, who have been grappling with these issues since the turn of the century, but especially since the 1950s. Two of the earlier "classics" in this regard are the books by Mbiti (1970) and Setiloane (1976).

SECTION A
THEOLOGY

Block A1 also deserves some explanation. The terms *hostility* in Block A1 should not be understood to mean that Christians are intent solely on the destruction or combating of people of other religions. Many proponents of this praxis are involved in evangelistic activities among communities of other religious traditions, although there is a fine line between aggressive evangelism and more destructive forms of interfaith relations that are driven by social forces like racism, nationalism or tribalism.[31] Lochhead (1988:12–17) gives a good discussion of the theological and ideological components of hostility as a form of interfaith praxis.

A final remark on the diagram deals with Block A2. A *competitive* interfaith praxis has two characteristics:

> In the first place, competing communities implicitly acknowledge that they have some similarities. They are, so to speak, in the same business. Secondly, competitive communities place considerable stress on their differences. They stress that the ways in which "we differ from other communities make us superior" (Lochhead 1988:18).

Whereas this is a widespread form of praxis among Christians, it can easily be sucked into a consumerist approach, where "the logic of the marketplace" (Lochhead 1988:22) takes over. Due to its emphasis on the *superiority* of the Christian "product", this praxis is also vulnerable to being co-opted into subtle forms of ethnocentrism and racism.

The diagram is not a perfect instrument, but it helps one to think through the vast variety of ways in which theological theories get hands and feet by becoming aligned to social process on the ground. Or, put the other way around, it helps to show how concrete forms of interfaith praxis find theological justifications to confirm or bolster their actions.

READING LIST

Barnes, M. 1989. *Religions in conversation. Christian identity and religious pluralism.* London: SPCK.
Cracknell, K. 1986. *Towards a new relationship. Christians and people of other faith.* London: Epworth Press.
D'Costa, G. (ed.). 1990. *Christian uniqueness reconsidered. The myth of a pluralistic theology of religions.* Maryknoll: Orbis.
Heim, S. M. 1995. *Salvations.* Maryknoll: Orbis.
Hick, J. & Knitter, P. (eds.). 1987. *The myth of Christian uniqueness. Toward a pluralistic theology of religions.* Maryknoll: Orbis.

---

31 A large section of the world-wide evangelistic and Pentecostal movements fall in Block A1, and many of their preachers are known to have strong judgemental attitudes towards other religions and cultures. But this does not mean that they are destructive people. They are involved in evangelistic work intent on the conversion of others – often understood as an attack on "the fortress of Satan" – but their motivation is that people should be saved from their sins. The term "hostility" in Block A1 should therefore not be interpreted superficially in the sense of being antagonistic to people, although followers of other faiths often do experience it in that way.

Knitter, P. F. 1985. *No other name? A critical survey of Christian attitudes toward the world religions.* Maryknoll: Orbis Books.
Kraemer, H. 1938. *The Christian message in a non-Christian world.* London: Edinburgh House Press.
Lochhead, D. 1988. *The Dialogical Imperative. A Christian reflection on interfaith encounter.* Maryknoll: Orbis.
Race, A. 1983. *Christians and religious pluralism. Patterns in the Christian theology of religions.* London: SCM Press.
Sanders, J. 1992. *No other name. An investigation into the destiny of the unevangelized.* Grand Rapids: Eerdmans.

BIBLIOGRAPHY

Anderson, G.H. 1981. Reponse [to Pietro Rossano's article, "Christ's lordship and religious pluralism in Roman Catholic perspective". In Anderson, G.H. and Stransky, T.F. (eds.), *Christ's Lordship and Religious Pluralism*, Maryknoll: Orbis.
Ariarajah, W. 1991. *Hindus and Christians. A century of Protestant Ecumenical thought.* Grand Rapids: Eerdmans; Amsterdam: Rodopi.
Barnes, M. 1989. *Religions in conversation. Christian identity and religious pluralism.* London: SPCK.
Bosch, D.J. 1977. *Theology of religions.* Study Guide, Missiology and Science of Religion, MSR303. Pretoria: University of South Africa.
– 1991. *Transforming Mission. Paradigm shifts in theology of mission.* Maryknoll: Orbis.
Cobb, J. 1975. *Christ in a pluralistic age.* Philadelphia: Westminster Press.
Costas, O. 1981. A radical evangelical contribution from Latin America. In Anderson, G.H. and Stransky, T.F. (eds.), *Christ's Lordship and Religious Pluralism.* Maryknoll: Orbis.
D'Costa, G. 1986. *Theology and religious pluralism. The challenge of other religions.* Oxford: Basil Blackwell.
Farquhar, J.N. 1913. *The crown of Hinduism.* London.
Flannery, A.P. (ed.). 1975. *Documents of Vatican II.* Grand Rapids: Eerdmans.
Gaybba, B. 1994. "Christology and religious pluralism. The search for a route between inclusivism and pluralism." *Journal of Theology for Southern Africa.* No. 87 (June).
Heim, S. M. 1985. *Is Christ the only way? Christian faith in a pluralistic world.* Valley Forge: Judson Press.
Hesselgrave, D.J. 1981. "Evangelicals and interreligious dialogue". In Anderson, Gerald H. and Stransky, Thomas F. (eds.), *Mission Trends No.5: Faith meets faith.* New York: Paulist; Grand Rapids: Eerdmans.
Hick, J. 1973. *God and the universe of faiths.* London: Collins.
– 1980. *God has many names.* London: Macmillan.
John Paul II. 1991. *Redemptoris Missio* (Encyclical Letter). Vatican: Libreria Editrice Vaticana.
Khodr, G. 1971. Christianity in a pluralistic world – The economy of the Holy Spirit. *Ecumenical Review* 23(2).
Klostermaier, K. 1969. *Hindu and Christian in Vrindaban.* London: SCM Press.
Knitter, P.F. 1985. *No other name? A critical survey of Christian attitudes toward the world religions.* Maryknoll: Orbis Books.
König, A. 1976. In *Journal of Theology for Southern Africa*, Vol 15.
Küng, H. 1976. *On being a Christian.* New York: Doubleday.
Lochhead, D. 1988. *The Dialogical Imperative. A Christian reflection on interfaith encounter.* Maryknoll: Orbis.

Lubbe, G. 1995. *The role of religion in the process of nation-building: from plurality to pluralism.* Religion & Theology 2(2).
Mbiti, J.S. 1970. *Concepts of God in Africa.* London: SPCK.
Nash, R.H. 1994. *Is Jesus the only Savior?* Grand Rapids: Zondervan.
Newbigin, L. 1989. *The gospel in a pluralist society.* Grand Rapids: Eerdmans, WCC: Geneva.
Overdiep, W. 1985. *Het gevecht om de vijand. Bijbels omgaan met een onwelkome onbekende.* Baarn: Ten Have.
Panikkar, R. 1964. *The unknown Christ of Hinduism.* London: Darton, Longman & Todd.
Race, A. 1983. *Christians and religious pluralism. Patterns in the Christian theology of religions.* London: SCM Press.
Rahner, K. 1966. "Christianity and the non-Christian religions". In *Theological Investigations Vol. 5.* Baltimore: Helicon.
Sanders, J. 1992. *No other name. An investigation into the destiny of the unevangelized.* Grand Rapids: Eerdmans.
Schreiter, R.J. 1985. *Constructing local theologies.* Maryknoll: Orbis.
Setiloane, G.M. 1976. *The image of God among the Sotho-Tswana.* Rotterdam: Balkema.
Smith, W.C. 1972. *The faith of other men.* New York: Harper Torchbooks.
Wessels, A. 1994. *Europe – Was it ever really Christian?* London: SCM Press.

SECTION B

Hermeneutics

Contents

16 Biblical Hermeneutics — 261

16.1 Introduction 261
16.2 Formation of the biblical text 261
16.3 The Old Testament in the New Testament 270
16.4 Concluding remarks 272
Reading List 272
Bibliography 273

17 Biblical Hermeneutics: the first 19 centuries — 275

17.1 Introduction 275
17.2 Reading the Bible in the Early Church 276
17.3 Reading the Bible in the Middle Ages 281
17.4 Reading the Bible during the Reformation 286
17.5 Reading the Bible since the Enlightenment 291
Reading List and Bibliography 296

18 Biblical Hermeneutics: the 20th century — 297

18.1 Introduction 297
18.2 On the conflict between explanation and understanding ... 298
18.3 On the conflict over the question who may read the Bible .. 302
18.4 The conflict over reading 307
18.5 The conflict over the responsibility of reading 311
18.6 The conflict over the Bible 313
18.7 Theological Hermeneutics? 314
Reading List 315
Bibliography 316

19 Evangelical Hermeneutics — 319

19.1 Introduction 319
19.2 Definition 319
19.3 Evangelical presuppositions for interpretation 320
19.4 The objective of Evangelical Hermeneutics 325
19.5 The essential method of Evangelical Hermeneutics 327

19.6	From interpretation to application	332
19.7	The outcomes of interpretation	334
	Reading List and Bibliography	335

20 Black Hermeneutics 337

20.1	Introduction	337
20.2	The contexts of oppression and liberative hermeneutics	338
20.3	Biblical notions in African Theological Hermeneutics	345
20.4	The future of Black Theological Hermeneutics	346
	Reading List and Bibliography	347

21 Feminist and Womanist Hermeneutics 349

21.1	Understanding the terms	349
21.2	Women's biblical interpretation in the past	350
21.3	Some approaches to Feminist Hermeneutics	351
21.4	Womanist Hermeneutics	354
21.5	In conclusion	356
	Reading List and Bibliography	357

22 African Women's Hermeneutics 359

22.1	Introduction	359
22.2	The contexts	360
22.3	Women's commitment	362
22.4	Community and motherhood	364
22.5	Hermeneutics of culture	365
22.6	No uniformity	367
22.7	Issues for our continuing study	368
	Reading List and Bibliography	371

23 African Hermeneutics 373

23.1	Introduction	373
23.2	Third-world Hermeneutics as Black, Liberation, and African Hermeneutics	377
23.3	The distinctiveness of African Hermeneutics	380
23.4	The influence of African Traditional Religions (ATRS) and the African Initiated Churches (AICS) in co-determining African Christianity and	

	Theological Hermeneutics	385
23.5	Hermeneutical approaches of some African Theologians: conflicting opinions on the source for African Theology	394
23.6	African Hermeneutics into the future	396
	Reading List	397
	Bibliography	397

24 African Initiated Church Hermeneutics — 399

24.1	Introduction	399
24.2	Terminology	399
24.3	The significance of urban AICS	400
24.4	An African Hermeneutics	401
24.5	Views of the Bible	402
24.6	The preaching of the Bible	403
24.7	Salvation and the African world-view	404
24.8	The role of prophets	407
24.9	Liberation and Zion	409
24.10	Iconic and Messianic Leadership	410
24.11	Concluding remarks	414
	Reading List and Bibliography	416

25 Pentecostal and Charismatic Hermeneutics — 417

25.1	Introduction	417
25.2	Pentecostal Hermeneutics	418
25.3	The dispensation of the spirit	418
25.4	Church life	422
25.5	Christ and the Foursquare Gospel	424
25.6	Further development	426
25.7	A pentecostal reading of the bible	428
	Reading List and Bibliography	430

26 Ecological Hermeneutics — 433

26.1	Introduction	433
26.2	The anthropocentric reading: the dominion model	435
26.3	Actual forms of Anthropocentricity	438
26.4	Physiocentric and biocentric reading: the monistic model	441

| 26.5 | The theocentric reading: the servant model | 447 |

Reading List 450

27 Postmodern Hermeneutics   451

27.1	Background	451
27.2	Hermeneutics and the subject/object scheme	454
27.3	The emergence of a postmodern world-view	457
27.4	The nature and relevance of Postmodern Hermeneutics	459
27.5	The agenda for Postmodern Hermeneutics	467

Reading List 469
Bibliography 469

28 The hermeneutical challenge of other religious traditions   471

28.1	Introduction	471
28.2	What is the Qur'an?	473
28.3	What is Hermeneutics?	474
28.4	The Qur'an and Hermeneutics	475
28.5	The development of doctrine regarding the text	475
28.6	Progressive revelation or gradualism *(Tadrij)*	482
28.7	The contemporary scene	485
28.8	A Quar'anic Hermeneutic of Liberation	488
28.9	Conclusion	492

Bibliography 492

16

Biblical Hermeneutics

W.J. Wessels

16.1 INTRODUCTION

The aim of this chapter is to examine ways in which later writers of the Bible used the older biblical texts in the Bible. The Bible is a set of religious documents in written form. In general, people assume that the Bible was deliberately written for the purpose we use it today, which is as an authoritative and sacred book to be obeyed. However, the fact that the aim of this chapter is to investigate how biblical texts used other texts implies that it is not the obvious conclusion. The use of texts in creating new texts implies an ongoing process in the formation of the documents as we know them today. By studying the biblical documents, it is clear that such a formation process was in existence and that not only did the New Testament make use of the Old Testament, but the Old Testament used even older Old Testament texts already in existence. In fact, in the process of the ongoing use of texts by the people of the Israelite society, new texts were created.

Besides the use of older written texts however, other forms of text should also be considered. In our society today we are so used to books and written documents, that we can hardly think of a time when a predominantly oral tradition was in existence. This seemed to be the case in the early formative years of Israel when oral texts were used and quoted. We will briefly look into this matter.

In this discussion we will explore the formation of the biblical text first, then have a look at the formation and transmission of traditions within the society under discussion. Following this, we will have a brief look into methods applied in the use of texts. Finally, a few conclusions will be drawn with regard to our society.

16.2 FORMATION OF THE BIBLICAL TEXT

The formation of the text of the Bible as we know it today was a process

SECTION B

HERMENEUTICS

which developed over centuries. In actual fact, the process of development went through several stages, of which the first was an oral stage. It was never the intention to write a Bible for the believers, but people who regarded their relationship with their God seriously reflected on this relationship. Contextual reflection means that people, within their specific context and time, reflected on their predecessors' views and experiences of God in relation to their own in an endeavour to make sense of their own experiences. In the long run this unconscious exercise gave birth to the canon of Scripture we know today. The first phase we have to look into is the oral phase or stage.

16.2.1 Oral stage

Today it is widely accepted that such a stage existed in the literary history of Israel (cf. Harrelson 1990:11–12). Thorough research has been done on this oral phase by well-known and respected scholars such as Hermann Gunkel, Martin Noth and Gerhard von Rad, to mention only a few (cf. Rast 1972).

It seemed that a strong tradition of oral transmission of stories existed in early Israelite society. The formation of Israel as a people is closely linked with the history of the biblical traditions of Israel. This formation process is a very complicated matter which need not be discussed in detail here. The important point is that Israel entered into a country which was already occupied by people with their own beliefs of a High God as well as reflections on their relationships with this God. The people of Israel came from different backgrounds and experiences, these they brought with them into their new way of existence as a people of Israel. Some of the people experienced the Exodus and Sinai, while others had different exposures. These experiences were shared with each other orally over long periods of time in the whole process of becoming the people known as "Israel staying in the land of Palestine". These oral texts were conveyed from one generation to another, kept alive and in the process formed a core of traditions, not as fixed in form as was previously believed.

A fair question would be how these so-called traditions were preserved. It is reasonable to assume that the people who had first hand experience of the major events as we know from history, were the first to tell this to their children. Families and tribes were the most important circles for keeping experiences alive and preserving them for posterity in an informal form. Later it seemed, more deliberate efforts were made to preserve traditions. The Old Testament bears evidence of people who performed as storytellers on festive occasions. It seems that there were also other kinds of narrators like court, wisdom, temple, prophetic and apocalyptic narrators (Deist and Vorster 1986:73–74). These people were key figures in the preservation of oral traditions in Israel.

When speaking of the origin of traditions in the broader sense, one should perhaps refer to **regions** with which certain traditions could be associated. The regions in mind are the northern and southern parts of

Palestine. These regions would host northern Israelite traditions on the one hand and Judean (or even Jerusalemite) traditions on the other. The Exodus and Mosaic tradition, for instance, was associated with the first region mentioned and the Zion and Davidic traditions with the Judean region. The two most influential scholars who did research on the tradition history of Israel were Von Rad and Noth. It was Von Rad who argued that the different traditions first had a separate history before they were included in the larger collection of material which later formed the Hexateuch (the first six books of the Old Testament). It was he in particular who referred to the Sinai tradition which was included only at a later stage in a collection with the Exodus and Wilderness traditions. According to Noth, the Pentateuch was formed by five major themes, namely the "Guidance out of Egypt, Guidance into the Arable land, Promise to the Patriarchs, Guidance in the Wilderness and Revelation at Sinai" (cf. Noth 1981:v–vi). These traditions formed the framework of the Pentateuch as we have it today.

Israel's literary history went through a long period of oral transmission before it was fixed in written form. The process is a difficult one to reconstruct, but the transmission was done carefully by traditionalists or circles with an interest in preserving the material for posterity. Israel's history of faith was kept alive. It is not clear when exactly the oral material was written down, although some think of the post-exilic period as the most suitable (cf. Gottwald 1985:93, 102, 107).

It was not an uncommon practise for the people of the ancient Near East to transmit their traditions orally, although in some instances written versions were simultaneously in existence. This being the case, much depended on a well-developed memory. For this purpose poetry was a handy tool. Fixed formulae, parallelisms, metre and the effective use of words (wordplay), typical of poetry, is a feature of ancient Near Eastern literary history as well as that of the Old Testament literature.

During this oral stage, the Old Testament existed in an oral form and was transmitted and applied over some period of time. Research done, especially in the field of folklore, has revealed interesting aspects of the oral stage of traditions which should be taken into account. Without discussing these aspects in full detail, it is important to take note of them.

Many traditions were kept alive due to the fact that they were often performed within new circumstances. The core of the specific tradition was maintained, but the tradition as such was adapted to fit the audience and the circumstances. In this sense, the oration was a new performance, thus keeping the tradition alive.

In some instances, development and adaptations of traditions took place as a natural flow of events. This might have caused a change in characters, location and even the moral of a story (cf. Harrelson 1990: 11–30).

In many instances, the oral stage continued concurrently with a written version of a tradition. This oral expression would then serve as criticism or commentary on the written version of the tradition. This would happen during a more formalised phase of a tradition. Theologising of

SECTION B

HERMENEUTICS

existing traditions, of which Chronicles is an example, forms part of this practise.

The function of all this varied from legitimation of a tradition to renewing and even contradicting it due to changing circumstances. (For an extensive discussion of the nature and dynamics of oral traditions see Vansina 1985.) This brings us to the second phase of discussion, namely the **written documents**.

16.2.2 Written documents

These oral traditions became more fixed in form and content and the need developed to write them down for posterity. This gave rise to the development of the second phase in the process which eventually ended in the formation of the canon of Scripture. As different as the people were who eventually formed the people called **Israel**, so varied were the beliefs and experiences which existed. Exposure to foreign beliefs and the sharing of some convictions gave rise to the forming of knew or adapted beliefs. Some beliefs were adopted from other people, some adapted and still others newly created. As mentioned, most beliefs were expressed in oral literature, but others from different cultures already existed in written form. During this phase of writing, some of these oral beliefs were set in writing, while at the same time new text was formed, using texts already in existence. An example would be the **creation narrative** of which several versions existed, both orally and in written form, in other cultures like the Babylonians and Phoenicians.

Some scholars speak of circles or groups of so-called traditionalists responsible for the collecting, grouping, preserving and transmission of traditions in circulation (cf. Rast 1972:12). There is evidence of scribal activities in the Old Testament. A formal group of scribes existed in post-exilic times, but scribes functioned even earlier in monarchical times. They were functionaries of the kings and were involved in religious activities and with religious texts. They were most probably responsible for overseeing the diversified scribal work done by various interest groups like the priests, tax officials etc., all in service of the royal administration. Scribes played an extremely important part in preserving the texts of tradition throughout the history of Israel (Fishbane 1985:23–25).

When referring to circles of traditionalists, various groups of influence come to mind – of which the priests are the first group to be mentioned because of their location at the sanctuaries. Besides the palace or the location of the royal administration as an assembly point of traditional material, the sanctuaries at Bethel, Shechem, Gilgal and Jerusalem were some of the most important locations which played a meaningful role in the formation of the traditions.

The priests were educated people and ideally situated to hear the different traditions from people coming to worship at these centres. There are definite traces of priestly influence in some of the material in the Pentateuch, which proves the probability of this theory. Some refer to them as the Priestly writers or P as a source. A good example of their activities is the creation narrative in Genesis 1, which shows priestly traces – especially when compared with the other versions of creation in Genesis 2.

Another group which seemed to have played a role in preserving traditions is the Levites. Von Rad (1966:24–25) thought Levitical circles were responsible for preserving the old sacral and legal traditions. Of this, the book of Deuteronomy is an excellent example. There was also a third group of people referred to as wise men, responsible for the creation and collection of the wisdom and didactic material. Finally, there were groups responsible for collecting and transmitting the prophetic material.

Once traditions were written down, it became much easier to detect how later writings made use of earlier texts. First we will take a look at a tradition which has been taken up by later writings. Second, we will discuss quotations within the Old Testament itself and third, the reinterpretation of texts. This will also be done with reference to the New Testament.

16.2.3 Transmission and reinterpretation of a tradition

For the purpose of this discussion, the Exodus and Mosaic tradition is taken as an example. This is one of the major traditions in the history of Israel which has been transmitted, celebrated and reinterpreted. Weber (1989:30–38) took the task of showing how this tradition was treated in the pre-monarchic, the monarchic, the exilic and post-exilic periods.

That which started in pre-monarchic times as an oral tradition and which was regarded as coming from northern Israelite circles (cf. Rast 1972:25), was only tied together with the Sinai tradition at a later stage to form an important core of Israelite belief. This was also the formation period of Israel as a people originating from the various tribes. This tradition served as an opposition to the human king of the monarchic period, therefore an opposition to the royal traditions of the south (cf. 1 Sam 8 and 12; 2 Sam 20:1ff.). The fact that this was a northern tradition was the primary cause of confrontation between traditions.

One of the most important exponents of the Exodus faith was the northern Israelite prophet, Hosea. This prophet reinterpreted the tradition by not only focusing exclusively on God's liberation, but also on his enduring love for his people in spite of their unfaithfulness. His focus was thus on God's liberating love (Hos 11:1, 5). Jeremiah links up with this theme by talking about a new covenant, while second Isaiah refers to a new exodus. This exodus tradition also surfaced during the reformation by Josiah when the "Book of Law" was found in 622. As Weber (1989:31) stated, it served as a critical reminder during the monarchic period.

During the exilic period, the Deuteronomistic history (the books Joshua–2 Kings) was most probably completed and it showed strong tendencies of the Mosaic faith. Israel's misfortune, which led to the exile, was described as the result of the disobedience of the people and their kings. However, hope was expressed that God's covenant love would bring about a new exodus. Using the imagery of the exodus, second

SECTION B

HERMENEUTICS

Isaiah announced a new exodus from the Babylonian exile to Zion (cf. Isa 51:2ff.). This however would not simply be a repetition of the old, but a new act from God's mighty hand (cf. Isa 43:14–21). In the post-exilic times, the feast of the Booths and the Passover celebration were linked with the exodus and the desert journey (cf. Neh 8; Lev 23:39–43).

When reading the New Testament, one can clearly see that knowledge of the Exodus tradition existed. Many thoughts expressed in the New Testament were made against the backdrop of the Exodus and Mosaic traditions of faith. This is true especially when it comes to the liberation work done by Christ Jesus through his life, death and resurrection. There are many parallels drawn between Jesus and Moses. In some instances, Jesus simply replaces Moses (Jude: 5), while in others Jesus is seen as the new Moses (cf. John 6:14; 4:19; 7:40; also Deut 18:15 and Acts 3:22ff., 8:37ff.). In the teachings of Paul which focus on Jesus Christ, what happens in and through Him is the real faith, while Moses and the tradition are only regarded as a foreshadow and a type of this faith. A clear reinterpretation of the Mosaic faith with regard to the Passover is to be found in 1 Corinthians 5:7ff. where Christ is referred to as the paschal lamb (cf. Weber 1989:44–45).

What is clear from the broad overview of the exodus tradition presented here, is the fact that a core of the tradition is transmitted over generations in different periods of history and changing life situations or contexts. In some instances, the application was in a sense conservative, trying to preserve the "original" faith content of this tradition, while in other instances more freedom was taken in the reinterpretation and application within new circumstances. The biggest freedom of interpretation is reflected in the New Testament. This is, in a sense, understandable seen in light of the confrontation with the new phenomenon personified in Jesus Christ. Raised with a knowledge and respect of the Old Testament traditions of faith, but confronted with the newness of Christ resulted in the more free and radical interpretation of traditions.

What we detect in this process of transmission is an identification with the faith of the past expressed in traditions of faith, but also a process of ongoing reinterpretation and application according to the needs of the time or the context.

16.2.4 Quotation of and reference to existing texts

In the formation of the canon which Christians call Bible today, one of the ways in which new texts were created was by using quotations from texts already in existence. When we speak of quotations, we should distinguish between direct quotations of words and sentences and quotations with a slight deviation from the original source which we still regard as quotations. It seems that some direct quotations can be traced back to the original source (Jer 26:18 to Mic 3:12) and are therefore verifiable while others are unverifiable (cf. Savran 1988:7–9).

There are many examples of this phenomenon in the growth of texts which can be mentioned. Proof of this is the extensive study done by

Savran (1988) in his book *Telling and Retelling. Quotations in Biblical Narrative* (cf. also Horwitz 1970). For the purpose of this discussion a few examples will suffice.

The discussion of the chosen examples also serves to show the reasons why texts are quoted or alluded to in the composition of new texts.

16.2.5 Identification and chronology

By this is meant that over a period of time traditions of faith became established in the community of Israel and their teachers, priests, Levites, prophets and wise men identified themselves with these traditions by quoting from them, referring to them, battling against them, interpreting and even using them as a norm for the new times (cf. Reventlow 1990:11–22). Chronologically, these people came later and had knowledge of the existence of such traditions and texts which they applied.

Perhaps it will be wise to make a slight distinction between creating a new text (for instance when a prophet speaks and his words are jotted down in writing) and extensive editing and reinterpretation of existing texts. In the first instance, a prophet might be quoting a predecessor's words or a tradition already in existence and therefore identifying with the past. This identification might be to state the predecessor's words as correct or still applicable in the present situation or as a point of reference (e.g. "... he said that, but I say ...") or even to prove a new point. In this regard, one should perhaps speak of an author of a text.

However, new texts can also be formed by an extensive process of editing and reinterpretation of existing texts. This would, for instance, be the case with those people who took the Torah as a norm for their interpretation and editing. In this regard one would rather speak of redactors or editors.

16.2.6 Torah as a norm

In the process of identification with texts from tradition, it is clear that the Torah was regarded as a norm. Deuteronomy is the first to refer to the codified will of Yahweh by means of the term Torah (Reventlow 1990:15). It is difficult to say when exactly the so-called Torah reached its final form and authority, but there are indications that it was treated by many in the composition of literature as a norm for society. In this regard one thinks of the reformation of king Josiah (639–609) that was ignited, as far as can be gathered from literature, by the discovery of the "Book of Law" in 626 BCE. This most probably consisted of some form of copy of the book Deuteronomy which contained the Torah, i.e. the instruction of Yahweh.

From the research done by many scholars, the conclusion was reached that there was a movement or school of thought in existence which used Deuteronomic theology as a basis for evaluating societies and literature. It is referred to as the Deuteronomists. Some speak of layers of Deuteronomistic work coming from different periods of time before and after the Babylonian exile of 586/7 BCE. Traces of their redactional work were first detected in the historical books which are referred to as the Deuteronomistic history (Jos–2 Kgs). In this literature, for instance, kings were evaluated and categorised according to their obedience to the Deuteronomic Theology.

Besides the historical books, many traces of the work of the so-called Deuteronomists were also found in the prophetic books. This is clear from fixed expressions and thought patterns originating from Deuteronomy. Examples of this are to be found in the books of Hosea and also Jeremiah (cf. the close links between the books of Deuteronomy, Hosea and Jeremiah – both in imagery and expressions). Within the book of Jeremiah for instance, chapter 7:1–15 is a Deuteronomistic version of the narrative also to be found in 26:1–19.

16.2.7 New literary creations from sources in existence

At a stage in Israel's existence, written material came into being and told the history of Israel as a nation. Most probably this was done by the scribes at the palace of the kings. Examples of this are the historical books of Samuel – Kings which overview the monarchical period. We know that these books underwent extensive redactional processes by the hands of what we have referred to as the Deuteronomists.

At a later stage in history, probably the exilic or post-exilic period, a new history was created which also told the story of the kings of Israel and Judah, but from a totally new perspective in time and outlook. This history is referred to as the Chronistic history and its author is called the Chronicler. A clear knowledge of historical notions in circulation is reflected by this work, but presented in a new framework and with different emphases. In this sense, a new text is composed with clear knowledge of material in existing texts. Although a new text is created, it is still a form of interpretation – historical, theological and idealised interpretation (cf. Reventlow 1990:17–20; Fishbane 1985:413).

The Chronicler had a particular theological outlook and this was used as a guideline for selecting, arranging and interpreting knowledge from sources in existence. He particularly idealised the person of king David and emphasised the cultic aspects of Israel. Therefore, the temple in Jerusalem and priests played a key role in this presentation of Israel's history. Judah is also seen as a cultic community. David is regarded as a hero and sections in literature reflecting negatively on him are simply left out. A careful and thorough study of the Chronistic history will illustrate these tendencies clearly.

Chronicles is a creative new interpretation of already existing texts (Deuteronomistic history) without nullifying the existence or importance of the source documents. In our biblical canon they exist side by side, testifying to a process of interpretation which resulted in new text. The Chronistic history is an example of commentary, interpretation and actualization of existing texts (cf. Reventlow 1990:22; also Fishbane 1985:415).

16.2.8 A verifiable quotation

There are quite a number of these types of quotations in the Old Testament. One of the longest quoted sections is Isaiah 36–39 which is excerpted from 2 Kings 18–19. The chosen example I would like to discuss here, however, is the section in Isaiah 2:2–4 which corresponds with Micah 4:1–5.

Both the prophets Micah and Isaiah acted in the southern kingdom of Judah, more or less at the same time. This allows for the possibility that any one of these prophets could be the original expresser of these words. When explaining this obvious quotation, we are faced with different options, which are: Micah quoted from Isaiah, Isaiah quoted from Micah, they both quoted from a third source or this section was interpolated in both texts at a later stage by someone unknown. Arguments for all four options are presented and all seem feasible when explaining this phenomenon. A workable and interesting solution to the problem is the one offered by Van der Woude in his commentary on the book of Micah (1976:127–141). In short, his explanation boils down to the following: The section originated from Isaiah and this is quoted in the book of Micah as part of a dialogue between Micah as the true prophet of Yahweh and so-called pseudo-prophets. This dialogue commences in 2:11c and continues through to 5:14. What we have is a word from these pseudo-prophets followed by a reply from the prophet Micah. Chapter 2:11c–13 expresses the expectation of salvation by the pseudo-prophets followed by Micah's reply in 3:1–12 which is an announcement of renewed judgement. To this, the pseudo-prophets again reply in 4:1–9, followed by Micah's words in 4:10. In 4:11–13 we again have the opponents speaking, with Micah's reply in 4:14–5:3. This pattern follows in 5:4–5, 5:6 and ends in 5:7–14.

According to this theory, the quoted section in 4:1–5 would be part of the reply of the pseudo-prophets. This Van der Woude argues forms part of the pseudo-prophets' false expectation of salvation while they are in actual fact under Yahweh's judgement. These pseudo-prophets quote the prophet Isaiah to substantiate their expectation of salvation, but they are repudiated by Micah who announces doom instead.

In this whole process of quoting, a new text was formed by applying an already existing text within a new and different context. It seems that within the prophetic tradition some form of identification between prophets existed. One can perhaps call it a prophetic lineage or tradition. This is easier to explain when the chronology is clear, which brings us to an example from the book of Jeremiah.

16.2.9 A quotation from within

A very interesting example to illustrate this point comes from the book of Jeremiah. In Jeremiah 23:5–6 and 33:15–16, virtually the same passage appears. At a first glance, it looks like Jeremiah 33:15–16 is a direct quotation Jeremiah 23:5–6. The similarities between the two sections are striking, but a close reading reveals slight differences which are very important. In fact, it seems that 33:15 is not simply a repetition of 23:5–6 within a new context, but a reinterpretation of the section.

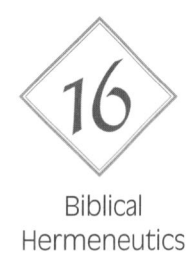

SECTION

B

HERMENEUTICS

Jeremiah 23:5–6 are words from Jeremiah during the reign of king Zedekiah. They reflect the prophet's vision of true kingship. A new king, an offspring of David is expected. He will be chosen by Yahweh and will rule in such a manner as though Yahweh himself were the ruler. In 33: 15–16 this section is reinterpreted within a new context – probably the late exilic or early post-exilic period. This is clear from the formal, contextual as well as theological differences which exist. In the process of reinterpretation, the content is generalised, the emphasis shifted from the king to the city, and the expectation of a priest in the legitimate line of descent is added. All in all, it seems that the reinterpretation is an attempt to explain the non-fulfilment of 23:5–6 for the people of a later period, and addresses the situation of the day (cf. Wessels 1991:231–246).

Besides quotations by authors from other sources, the above-mentioned example shows an interesting process of ongoing interpretation of important issues, in this instance even reflected within the same book. This proves an ongoing process of interpretation within the religious tradition over a period of time. This process which was facilitated by people trying to preserve the Jeremiah tradition is now canonised by tradition. Freedom of interpretation and application existed with the tradition reflecting a dynamic process.

16.3 THE OLD TESTAMENT IN THE NEW TESTAMENT

The question of the relationship between the Old Testament and the New Testament is one which has thoroughly been discussed over the years and is not particularly the issue of this discussion. However, looking at some of the traditions in the Old Testament, it is clear that a continuity between the Testaments exists. If we refer to the chosen example of the Exodus and Moses tradition, there is a definite continuity to be detected.

16.3.1 Quotations from and allusions to the Old Testament in the New Testament

When reading the New Testament, it is clear that a familiarity existed with the Old Testament. Many direct quotations and many almost direct quotations from the Old Testament are made in the New Testament, not to speak of the many allusions and references to the Old Testament. The early Christian church had the Septuagint version of the Old Testament, that is, the Greek translation of the Hebrew text, as their Bible (Hanegraaf 1988:18). Some quotations in the New Testament reflect the Septuagint form, while others are still from the Hebrew text. Typical phrases in the New Testament which refer to the Old Testament are "for it is written", "as it is written", "saying" or "as it is said".

As already mentioned, the writers of the New Testament identified with many of the old traditions, therefore continued to interpret them within the context of their own time. The people of the New Testament regarded the faith of the Old Testament as their spiritual heritage. However, due to changing circumstances and confrontation with new phenomena, interpretation and application of Scripture took different forms. Not only did historical and social circumstances change dramatically over the years – as a general look at the royal history with its religious implication would prove – but a more dramatic event caused a new look at the known and existing. It concerns the person and teaching of Jesus Christ.

16.3.2 Direct quotations from the Old Testament

There are a great many examples of this type of quotation in the New Testament. In some instances the quotation is applied in the New Testament in a straight forward sense, reflecting a natural flow from the Old to the New Testament. In other instances the application in the new time is seen as a fulfilment of the words spoken in previous times. An example of this is the quotation in Luke 4:17ff. of Isaiah 61:1,2, which is claimed in Luke 4:21 as "Today this Scripture is fulfilled in your hearing" (NIV).

Many of the New Testament writers saw Jesus as the fulfilment of prophetic proclamations spoken in Old Testament times. This is clear from several passages in the Gospels. It particularly concerns passages which show expectations of the Messiah to come, claimed by the writers in the New Testament to be Jesus. Passages in mind are Isaiah 9:6ff., 11:1ff., Micah 5:1ff., Jeremiah 23:5–6, Zachariah 9:9–13 to mention a few (cf. Stuhlmueller 1989:91–105).

There are also passages quoted in the New Testament in reference to Jesus Christ which are applied irrespective of the original context of the words. In the speech of Peter in Acts 2:25, a section from Psalm 16:8–11 is quoted, creating a new text which reflects the writer's understanding of Jesus Christ without taking the original meaning into account. This is but one such example.

Not only is Jesus seen as fulfilling the promises of the Old Testament, but the era of the New Testament is also seen as the fullness of time. An example in this regard is the outpouring of the Holy Spirit described in Acts 2, which quotes Joel 2:28–32. This event is seen as the fulfilment of the Old Testament passage.

The main view presented by the New Testament literature is that of the fulfilment of the Old Testament traditions (cf. Fishbane 1985:10).

16.3.3 Allusions to the Old Testament

To illustrate this phenomenon in the process of the composition of new text, reference could be made to the principle of presenting an argument, stating a progression from the lesser to the greater (cf. Russell 1986: 50–52). An example of this would be Mark 2:23–28 with regard to 1 Samuel 21. The disciples picked and ate corn on a Sabbath day and in order to justify their action, reference is made to the Old Testament passage of 1 Samuel 21. This way of argumentation is also followed in the Epistle to the Hebrews by using the words "how much more" to show the progression from the lesser to the better, the fulfilment in Jesus Christ.

Russel also illustrates the phenomenon of allusions of the New to the Old Testament by referring to instances of analogy (Rom 4:2 to Gen 15:6), allegory (4:21–31 – Sarah and Hagar representing the two covenants of Promise and Law) and typology (cf. Nicole 1991:48). Examples of typology would be an Old Testament character like Joseph (Gen 37) interpreted as a "type" of Christ, betrayed by his brothers as Jesus is by Judas Iscariot. Another example would be the reference to the Sabbath in Hebrews 4 as a "type" of eternal Sabbath-to-come. Extensive research on these methods was done by Von Rad, Eichrodt and Zimmerli, to mention but a few prominent scholars (cf. the work edited by Westermann 1963).

16.4 CONCLUDING REMARKS

The people of the New Testament era had at their disposal a tradition of faith in written form. Being children of their time, imbedded within the traditions of the Old Testament, they showed familiarity with the Old Testament, a text much more fixed in nature than was the case with the religious texts at the disposal of the people of the Old Testament.

Their interpretation and application of the Old Testament written text within their time and context shows both acknowledgement and respect, but also a freedom to contextualise. The most formative factor in interpretation, however, is the living experiences of Jesus Christ and the way in which it is said He treated the Old Testament. For many, He fulfilled the promises of the Old Testament prophetic tradition in his person. In some instances, He is regarded as the anti-type of Old Testament figures; in others as a new revelation of God in a new period of time. Some regarded and therefore read the entire Old Testament tradition christologically. Through this whole diverse process of thinking about the Old Testament from a perspective of knowledge of Jesus Christ, new text was formed which resulted in the New Testament as we know it today. Great respect for the old traditions of faith is reflected in the New Testament, but also much freedom in reading and application in the light of their experiences of Jesus.

This identification with and high regard for the traditions of faith reflected in both Testaments should remain within our Christian communities, but so, too, should the freedom to bring in new interpretations due to our living experience of Christ in our own context. The process of interpretation is an ongoing process. Our brief investigation has shown a variety of methods of interpretation and application, and therefore the debate on method of interpretation should not end. There is more than one correct method of interpretation and this is to the benefit of the believing community who should realise that interpretation is a dynamic, open-ended and ongoing process.

READING LIST

Fishbane, M. 1985. *Biblical interpretation in ancient Israel*, Oxford: Claredon.
Harrelson, W. 1990. "Life, faith, and the emergence of tradition". In Knight, D.A. (ed.), *Tradition and theology in the Old Testament*. Reprinted 1977 edition, 11–30, Sheffield: JSOT.
Nicole, R. 1991. "Old Testament quotations in the New Testament". In Ramm, B.L. et

al., *Hermeneutics*, 41–53. Grand Rapids: Baker Book House.
Rast, W.E. 1972. *Tradition history and the Old Testament*. Philadelphia: Fortress Press.
Russell, D.S. 1986. *From early Judaism to early church*. London: SCM.
Savran, G.W. 1988. *Telling and retelling. Quotations in Biblical narrative*. Bloomington. Indiana University Press.
Vansina, J. 1985. *Oral Tradition as history*. London: James Currey.
Weber, H-R. 1989. *Power*. Geneva: WCC publications.
Westermann, C. (ed.). 1963. *Essays on Old Testament hermeneutics*. Tl by Mays, J L. Atlanta: John Knox.

BIBLIOGRAPHY

Fishbane, M. 1985. *Biblical interpretation in ancient Israel*, Oxford: Claredon.
Gottwald, N.K. 1985. *The Hebrew Bible. A socio-literary introduction*. Philadelphia: Fortress.
Hanegraaf, J. 1988. *Ecumenische inleiding in het Oude Testament*. Nijkerk: G F Callenbach.
Harrelson, W. 1990. "Life, faith, and the emergence of tradition". In Knight, D.A. (ed.), *Tradition and theology in the Old Testament*. Reprinted 1977 edition, 11–30, Sheffield: JSOT.
Horwitz, W.J. 1970. "Audience reaction to Jeremiah". *CBQ* 32, 555–564.
Nicole, R. 1991. "Old Testament quotations in the New Testament". In Ramm, B.L. et al., *Hermeneutics*, 41–53. Grand Rapids: Baker Book House.
Noth, M. 1981. *A history of Pentateuchal Traditions*. Tl by Anderson, B.W. California: Scholars.
Rast, W.E. 1972. *Tradition history and the Old Testament*. Philadelphia: Fortress Press.
Reventlow, H.G. 1990. *Epochen der Bibelauslegung*. Band 1. München: Beck.
Russell, D.S. 1986. *From early Judaism to early church*. London: SCM.
Savran, G.W. 1988. *Telling and retelling. Quotations in Biblical narrative*. Bloomington. Indiana University Press.
Stuhlmeuller, C. 1989. *New paths through the Old Testament*. New York: Paulist.
Van der Woude, A.S. 1976. *Micha*. Nijkerk: Callenbach. (POT).
Vansina, J.1985. *Oral Tradition as history*. London: James Currey.
Von Rad, G. 1966. *Deuteronomy*. London: SCM. (OTL).
Weber, H-R.1989. *Power*. Geneva: WCC publications.
Wessels, W.J. 1991. "Jeremiah 33:15–16 as a reinterpretation of Jeremiah 23:5–6". *HTS* 47,1, 231–246.
Westermann, C. (ed.). 1963. *Essays on Old Testament hermeneutics*. Tl by Mays, J L. Atlanta: John Knox.

Biblical Hermeneutics: the first 19 centuries

Dirkie J. Smit

17.1 INTRODUCTION

They asked me to tell you a story. It is the story of "hermeneutics", the story of how Christians used, read, understood and interpreted the Christian Bible through the centuries. It is, as you will understand, a long and complex story. But I shall try.

Let's divide, for the purposes of our story, the history of Christianity into the four well-known periods: the Early Church, the Middle Ages, the Reformation and Modernity. (By now, you will all be familiar with these distinctions. Let's say that the period of the Early Church stretches until roughly the 6th century. The Middle Ages, or medieval times, extend from the 6th to the 15th centuries. The Reformation took place in the 16th century. And the modern period, or the Enlightenment, starts somewhere in the 17th and the 18th centuries and lasts until the present.) As our story unfolds, we can divide these phases of history further, into more specific and accurate periods, if necessary.

Now: *What* did Christians do with the Bible in each of these periods? *Who* were the people who were able to read and interpret it? *Where* did they read it? *Why* did they read it? *For whom* did they read it? And how did they read it? Let's keep these kinds of questions in mind when we try to remember, to reconstruct, the history of Biblical Hermeneutics, the history of the interpretation of the Christian Bible.

By the way: the expression "hermeneutics" was used for the first time only quite recently. Where does the word come from? We do not really know precisely. It refers to Hermes, the messenger of the gods in Greek

SECTION B
HERMENEUTICS

mythology. His task was to explain to humans the plans, the decisions and thoughts of the gods. His explanations, his language, his speech, his interpretations, were meant to bridge the gap between the gods (who spoke) and the human beings (who listened, received, and had to understand). His work, *hermeneuein* (hermeneutics), therefore has something to do with explanation, with speech, with translation, with communicating a message, with interpreting something for people who want to hear and understand. Therefore, the expression "hermeneutics" was coined to refer to this "art of interpretation". And obviously, although the expression is not so old, the activity (of reading and interpretation) has been an essential part of what Christians were doing from the very beginning.

In fact, already the writing of the New Testament documents (and the preaching and witnessing that took place before the writing of the first documents!) was an hermeneutical activity, an activity of interpretation. Writing is already a form of interpretation! The first Christians were interpreting what happened in Jesus Christ. And they were using the documents which we now call the Old Testament to understand what was happening in and through Jesus Christ. In fact, it is very interesting to see what the authors of the New Testament documents did with the documents of the Old Testament, to see how they interpreted them (see chapter 16.3).

17.2 READING THE BIBLE IN THE EARLY CHURCH

What did the first Christians do with the New Testament documents, once they were written and available? Where, and why, and how did they read, or interpret, these documents?

Early Christian worship most probably followed the synagogue pattern (known to them, since they were mainly Jews): it was customary for the Scripture readings, that is, readings from Old Testament documents, to be followed by a sermon. The difference, of course, was that the Christians gave a Christian sermon, or homily, or interpretation, after reading (the same!) Old Testament texts as the synagogue. Probably, however, at some stage of the worship service, they also used the opportunity to read messages to the congregation, and it may be that the Letters and the Gospels were originally used in this way. There are indications in Paul's Letters that he expected them to be read in the assembly. And Justin Martyr (as early as about 155 AD), describing the liturgy of his day, included the reading of "the memoirs of the apostles", which was probably a reference to the Gospels. So the practice of including a Christian lection, that is, a portion of a Christian document (later to become the New Testament) to be read as part of the worship, was established during the first century. When our story continues, remember this: *Christian worship would remain a major social location, that is, a place in society where the Bible is read and interpreted.*

A second major act of interpretation was therefore gradually taking place, namely the combination of (some of the) early Christian documents, together with the Old Testament documents, into a canon, into a

Bible, into an authoritative compilation of religious documents. At least four processes were already at work that would later, at different stages of our story, have enormous hermeneutical implications.

The first process was a simple, very obvious, but still an extremely influential one: the Early Church attached *religious authority* to some documents, which they combined in their canon, and – for a number of reasons – denied the same authority to other documents. The status of the documents that were included in the lists changed. Perhaps apostolic authorship played a role. Perhaps their wider circulation played a role. Their long use in the main churches of ancient foundation and the fact that heretical teaching was absent from them probably played a role. But, whatever the reasons, once authoritatively included (perhaps in a final decision by Athanasius, in 367 AD), and characterised as the "closed" canon of the church, their status changed. They were used in worship. They were preached from. They became known through lectionaries. They were the Word of God. And that changed the way people read, interpreted, and used them.

Ironically, the decisive step towards the formation of the canon came when Marcion, an enthusiastic follower of Paul, drew up a list of Christian documents which he felt were suitable for reading and use in Christian worship. Excluded from the list were the Old Testament documents, as well as some Gospels. To make this long story short, the church declared Marcion an heretic, and gradually compiled and closed their own, authoritative canon of books. The mere fact that books were included in this list, or "library", or "Bible", meant that (future) readers were respecting them, were regarding them as authoritative, as divine, as different from mere human documents, as Word of God, as inspired. This obviously deeply influenced the way they read, used and interpreted these canonical books. They expected something from these books, they trusted them, they believed them.

The second process consisted in the fact that different books, written under different circumstances, by different authors, were now *brought together*, were compiled into one list, one canon, one "book". The most dramatic aspect of this was the combination of Old Testament and New Testament documents into one canon. For centuries to follow, until today, the relationship between the two would be a major challenge to biblical interpretation. Could it be shown that the books of the Old Testament were Christian? How was the Old Testament to be interpreted in the light of the New? The same, however, applies to the individual books as well: bringing them together into a single list or canon influenced, affected, all of them. All the books together became a context in which any particular book was read and interpreted. Each one could now be read through the lenses of the other. Difficult parts in the one could be explained by means of the other. And again, this would become an important rule of biblical interpretation for the centuries to follow. *Sacra scriptura sui interpres:* the Holy Scriptures interpret themselves.

The third process was closely related to the previous one. It is easy to

Biblical Hermeneutics: the first 19 centuries

SECTION B

HERMENEUTICS

understand why the Early Church, faced with this "library" of books, was eager to find a central message, a thrust, a *scopus*, a principle, which kept the documents together; in other words, *a key to the interpretation* of this enormous variety of books.

Without such a key, a major problem arose. Faced with a plurality of meaning, that is, faced with the reality that different readers read these same texts and documents in radically different ways, the readers were obviously faced with the question which readings were more correct, or adequate, and which were less correct, less adequate, or perhaps even wrong and false. They needed some norm, some authority, to help them distinguish between acceptable and unacceptable interpretations. How did they solve this serious problem?

Irenaeus of Lyons (before 202 AD) already argued that the church had an accepted norm, the apostolic tradition, the canon of truth, the *regula veritatis*, the Christian doctrine. And so, reading and using the biblical documents became *subordinated to doctrine*. As our story unfolds, we shall see that this became the major principle of biblical interpretation for centuries to follow.

A fourth process was inevitable. Obviously, the formation of an authoritative canon did not solve this problem of interpretation, but only shifted the problem to a next step. Now they knew which documents were authoritative and were to be used, read, and interpreted, and they somehow agreed on a thrust, a scopus, a material principle, a rule of faith. Soon the next question would arise: If different Christian believers or different Christian groups would disagree about this thrust, this scopus, or this material principle, in short, if they agreed about the authoritative books, but read these books in different ways, *how would they decide such a conflict of interpretation?* Or rather, as they put the question: who would decide the conflict for them? Who would determine what the *regula veritatis* was?

To a large extent they followed a clue already given by Tertullian (160–220 AD). He argued that the proper authority to do this, to distinguish between acceptable and unacceptable interpretations, was vested in the official church. This church had the true doctrine, the so called rule of faith, the *regula fidei*, and it had a hierarchical structure of authority to use and apply this rule of faith, whenever necessary. The solution was, therefore, rather simple: If people disagreed about interpretation, about hermeneutics, the official church would apply its official doctrine and its judicial authority to solve the problem. Vincent of Lérins (–450 AD) would formalise this solution by saying "We hold for true what had been believed everywhere, always, by everyone in the church". And only the official church could determine what that was.

It would not be long before they had to face this question on several fronts. But we shall have to wait a while with that very interesting part of our story.

In the meantime, remember: *In the formation of the Christian canon, several processes were at work that would time and again in Christian history flare up as major conflicts about biblical interpretation. Are these documents some-*

how more authoritative than others? How does the context of the Bible as a single canon or library influence the reading and interpretation of a particular book, part, or text? Is there a single thrust, message, scopus, or material principle at work in this library? And who has the power and authority to determine what this thrust or message is when a conflict of interpretations arises?

But, to continue with our story, after the formation of the canon, the need for interpretation still existed – and in fact grew more urgent! Therefore: where, why, and how did the Christians now read their (new) Bible?

Where? As we have said, they read these documents primarily during worship. They used them liturgically and they explained them, commented on them, applied them, preached from them.

Why? Primarily, one could say, for two reasons. The first, and most common reason, was a practical one. In this (so-called Patristic) age, they used the Bible primarily for moral purposes. These documents provided guidance for the ongoing, everyday life of the church. They were regarded as moral instruction. Appeals made to them were direct and straightforward, and practical. Of course, that was not always so easy with regard to the Old Testament, but they found ways, for example allegorical interpretation (since the Old Testament foreshadows the word of Jesus, they thought it permissible to interpret it through allegories, that is, not literally and historically, but by finding spiritual, Christological meaning hidden in or behind the obvious literal meaning); or typological interpretation (since the work of Jesus was anticipated in the Old Testament, "types", that is, certain Old Testament persons and institutions, could be interpreted as representing New Testament realities); or seeing Old Testament figures as moral and spiritual examples of faith; or retaining parts of Old Testament law that were directly useful; etc.

A second reason gradually developed. From the end of the first century, heretical teachers became a more prominent factor in Christianity. Confusion concerning true and false doctrine was widespread. False teachings had to be rejected and rebutted. The only way to do that was to appeal to the authoritative tradition found in these books. Gradually, particularly the New Testament books were being interpreted with reference to doctrinal controversies and with a view *to develop authoritative theology and doctrine*.

So, the biblical documents were read both as the chief source of moral and spiritual life and as the authoritative source for establishing the truth of doctrine in the age of the great controversies (and in chapter 3 you read something about those great controversies, about the Trinity, and the Person of Christ).

But now for the difficult question: *How* did they read these documents? To a large extent, the early Christians used the skills of interpretation that they knew: from their Jewish heritage and from their Greek (Hellenistic) culture, neighbours and education. From their Jewish tradition, they took over techniques like proof texts, typology, and allegory.

As a general rule one could say that, *time and again, the Christians would read the Bible in much the same way that their cultural contemporaries would*

17

Biblical Hermeneutics: the first 19 centuries

SECTION B
HERMENEUTICS

read other important, authoritative or classical documents. And time and again the result would be that major shifts in culture, and in the ways people read and interpreted documents, would have major impacts on biblical interpretation and would lead to renewed conflicts over biblical reading within Christian and church circles.

During this time, two exegetical schools were founded that would play a major role in the history of biblical interpretation, and in both cases they took over local Jewish interpretive practices. The one was on African soil, in Alexandria in Egypt, the second one was in Antioch, to the north-east. The founding of the Catechetical School of Alexandria some time during the second century was an event of considerable importance for biblical interpretation. Alexandria was a centre of learning. It was the home of the allegorical method of interpretation, practised by the learned Jews, like Philo. Famous leaders of the School included Clement of Alexandria and his successor Origen. Both of them were leading exponents of the method of "spiritual" or "allegorical" interpretation. Taken at their face value, that is, when read "literally", they argued, the biblical documents produced many intellectual and moral difficulties. Every part of Scripture, however, has a spiritual meaning. When read spiritually, the whole Bible shows a wonderful harmony from beginning to end; all difficulties disappear.

In Antioch, a different approach was followed. Well-known representatives of the School of Antioch included Theodore of Mopsuestia (350–428 AD) and John Chrysostom (354–407 AD). They were convinced that the primary level of interpretation was the literal, or the historical level. Not in a hidden spiritual or allegorical key, already available to the readers from outside of the biblical documents themselves, but in the historical and literal meaning of the words themselves, they sought the message of what they read.

Again in Africa, Augustine of Hippo (354–530 AD) would attempt to bring these approaches to a synthesis. He was especially interested in the theory of signs, *semeia*, in what people today call "semiotics". In his very influential book on hermeneutics and preaching, *De Doctrina Christiana*, he argued that biblical interpretation needs an overall perspective, a spiritual key, but according to him that key, or reading perspective, was love, love of God and our fellow human beings. It was, therefore, not a perspective taken from outside the biblical documents, but, as far as he was concerned, the perspective which these documents themselves contained and offered.

However, the contrast between Alexandria and Antioch would remain as a clear indication of one of the major conflicts involved in biblical interpretation for many centuries. Allegorical interpretation looks for the hidden sense of a text with the aid of an interpretive key from outside it, while grammatical interpretation tries to reach the text's sense by studying the linguistic devices and connections within it. This conflict brings us to the heart of the Middle Ages.

17.3 READING THE BIBLE IN THE MIDDLE AGES

Some people say that no significant hermeneutical innovation took place during the Middle Ages, precisely because reading the text was subordinated to doctrine and to ecclesiastic authority. Reading and interpreting the Bible itself lost its power, its excitement. The Bible was simply used by people in authority to prove the doctrine which they already possessed.

But things are a little more complicated. Some developments did indeed take place during these years that would have far-reaching effects on biblical hermeneutics for centuries to follow.

An interesting aspect is that these developments almost all took place in the Latin-speaking world of the western Roman Empire. The writing of the New Testament documents and the formation of the canon (the period which we discussed in the previous section about the Early Church) had mainly taken place in the Greek-speaking world of the eastern Roman Empire. Gradually, however, the political and cultural division between the Greek East and the Latin West led to misunderstanding, lack of co-operation, and finally to estrangement. From now on, all developments concerning the Bible took place in the west. In the East, nothing changed for centuries concerning biblical interpretation.

In the west, however, it was another story. Perhaps the easiest way to reconstruct what happened is to keep in mind that during this time the biblical documents were being read in three different social locations, three different public places that developed one after the other, and most of the time in opposition to one another: first in the *monasteries*, then in the *cathedral schools*, and then in the medieval universities.

"During the Dark Ages", says Barnabas Lindars in his beautiful account of the study and use of the New Testament through the ages, "the torch of learning was kept alight mostly in the monasteries" (Rogerson, J.W., Rowland, C. and Lindars, B. 1988:279). The socio-political developments during these times are important, because whatever happens outside in society and the world often has a major impact on how Christians read and interpret the Bible behind their church doors! In fact, this is a thread running through our story. These were difficult centuries for the Christian Church. Christian hegemony, power, influence and rule, which had once stretched from Britain to Asia Minor, Syria-Palestine and Egypt, was falling apart. Shock after shock followed. Education was becoming very problematic. Life in the cities and towns was dramatically affected. Books and libraries were destroyed. Islamic and Magyar invasions threatened the church, biblical scholarship and interpretation. In fact, only a few people were still able to read. But in the *monasteries*, the Bible was read and studied, as it had been done in the Early Church, to promote the Christian, the moral and particularly the spiritual life. From the 6th until into the 12th century, it was in the monasteries that the biblical learning and reading was kept alive.

In these monasteries, rules of interpretation were necessary so that readers could unlock the spiritual treasures of the Bible. The monastic

SECTION B

HERMENEUTICS

tradition of spiritual reading, called *lectio divina*, was developed and maintained specifically for the edification of the soul in contemplation and discipleship.

To explain it in a very simply way, it normally included three steps, often called *grammar, meditation,* and *prayer.* "Grammar" referred to a reading of the original texts, in their original languages, and to a study of the early commentators. In order to read, they had to know how to write. And they learned how to make books, to copy, to bind and to decorate them. And they read aloud, with the lips and with the ears, not principally with the eyes. "Meditation", or contemplation, referred to the process of thinking about what had been read. "It implied thinking of a thing with the intent to do it; in other words, to prepare oneself for it, to prefigure it in the mind, to desire it, in a way, to do it in advance – briefly, to practice it" (Leclercg 1980:16). "Prayer" was the third step, speaking to God about what they had read and thought. The *lectio divina* was a prayerful reading. The book which was most read and most frequently commented in monastic theology was the Song of Songs.

At this time, the well-known notion of the so-called four senses of Scripture was being employed to its fullest. According to this approach, each part of Scripture has a four-fold meaning: a literal meaning (providing information, e.g. about the history and religion of Israel), an allegorical, doctrinal or Christological meaning (applied to different doctrines of the church and to Christ), a moral meaning (applied to Christian life), and an anagogical meaning (applied to ultimate salvation). Nicholas of Lyra (–1349 AD) would sum this up in a well-known verse, which Grant translates as:

> The letter shows us what God and our fathers did;
> The allegory shows us where our faith is hid;
> The moral meaning gives us rules of daily life;
> The anagogy shows us where we end our strife.

The outstanding interpreters of the biblical documents at the beginning of this period were Gregory the Great (540–604 AD), concerned with education of the clergy, and famous as a celebrated preacher, and the Venerable Bede (673–735 AD), well-known for his extensive writings, particularly of commentaries on Bible books. In these commentaries he made use of earlier commentaries available to them, and then again commented on these. In this way a continuous and authoritative tradition of exposition was growing. The general framework was the rule of faith, i.e. the doctrine of the church, and the precise meaning and application of a particular passage had often been determined in advance in the work of earlier commentators.

This monastic tradition of reading the biblical documents would remain influential in Christianity for centuries. It is not surprising that Jean Leclercq would describe the monastic culture, in a famous study, as "the love of learning and the desire for God". The two elements together depict monastic life: they loved learning, knowledge, grammar, the Bible books, the old commentaries, biographies, in fact, all books, and they desired for God, they were spiritual people, longing for mystical experience of God. And, most important, they believed that these two belong together: that God is known through knowledge, through grammar, meditation, prayer.

But, if learning was so important, what about those people, in fact, by far the majority in medieval society, who could not read? They became aware of the meaning, the teaching of the Bible through *liturgy* and *art*. They could experience the liturgy, hear the familiar Bible stories about the characters from the Bible, listen to the prescribed lections being read and the homilies preached on them, they could partake in the antiphons and the responses that made up parts of the liturgy, and they could see the sculptures, the paintings, the stained glass windows, the carved wooden doors, the altar-pieces. The popular imagination, says Lindars, was nourished by vivid stories and by even more vivid artistic representations of them.

And for those (few!) who could read, books of devotion were produced with pictures of gospel scenes and characters, decorated with verses from psalms and prophets, in order that they could meditate, for the benefit of their spiritual lives.

It is indeed important to remember that some very significant interpretations of the Bible through the centuries *still* do occur in so-called non-verbal ways, for example icons, art, paintings, sculptures, music, illustrations, gestures, liturgical presentations, and so forth.

During this period, the allegorical and mystical interpretation reached a high point. But, while spirituality, theology, learning and reading continued in the monasteries, a new development started that would later have major implications, also for the story of biblical interpretation. A new social location for reading the biblical documents was being established, namely the *cathedral schools.*

Since the time of Charlemagne, about the ninth century, when Christianity once again, after centuries, started to flourish as an official and public religion, it became possible and necessary to "do theology in public", that is, to (learn how to) read the biblical documents in public places outside the monasteries. The education system was improved. More material for study became available. New copies of classic Christian and pagan texts were made and corrected. A new form of handwriting was developed which enabled copyists to produce books (which were still written by hand at that time) in a much quicker way. And, importantly, Cathedrals were required to maintain schools for the education of the clergy. These schools developed a scholastic theology and a scholastic way of reading the Bible which was different, in purpose and in method, from the monastic theology and reading.

So by the dawn of the 12th century there were two types of schools: a school for monks and a school for clerics. The monks were trained individually, under the guidance of an abbot, a spiritual father, through the reading of the Bible and the fathers, within the liturgical framework of the monastic life. In the schools, however, a different form of theology was practised. In this development of scholastic theology, at least four processes with far-reaching results for biblical interpretation were at work.

17

Biblical Hermeneutics: the first 19 centuries

SECTION B

HERMENEUTICS

A first process was the further development of the *gloss*, the exegetical note written either between the lines of a biblical text or in the margins. This method of making notes now became widespread and influential. Both teachers and students moved around from school to school, and found it necessary to record all these comments. Soon they became definitive commentaries, especially as leading commentators compiled glosses as their distillations of their own study of earlier commentators. Lindars comments that it is no accident that this development began at the same time as increasing attention was being given to the study of law – another instance where rules of reading and interpretation at work in society at large impacted on the reading and interpretation of biblical documents! Since the time of Charlemagne, the ancient Roman traditions of law were again taken up. A body of jurisprudence developed, based on the laws of Justinian, but consisting in the form of collections of comments and opinions on the fundamental texts, in the form of glosses of relevant quotations from notable jurists. In biblical interpretation, a similar process was at work. A body of official comments and opinions was growing, comments and opinions of authoritative people, in short, an "official-tradition-of-interpretation" was being established, gradually substituting serious reading of the basic biblical documents themselves.

A second development was at work in the different way of studying and teaching of theology in the schools, namely in the new emphasis on *disputation*, argument, question-and-answer, logic, dialectic and philosophy. The second step in the monastic three-step (grammar – meditation/contemplation – prayer) was replaced by logic, by the practice of critical power and skills, by the practice of logical argument and the construction of philosophical systems. The method of *quaestio* was developed, using dialectic, taught in the liberal arts, to interrogate both the texts, the students, and the teachers. Peter Abelard (–1142 AD) was a famous master of this method. Major commentaries written in the context of the cathedral schools, like the famous *Sentences* by Peter Lombard (1100–1160 AD), were no longer arranged haphazardly (following the biblical documents), but systematically, logically, according to subjects for philosophical discussion. In other words, although the biblical documents remained the official basis for all theological teaching, a change was taking place from Bible study to systematic theology, from studying the biblical documents for the sake of the love of God, to using the biblical documents as divinely inspired source for the study of logic and philosophy. *Lectio divina* (divine reading) or *sacra pagina* (sacred pages) was exchanged for *sacra doctrina*. And the purpose, the third step, also changed. In monastic theology, it was *oratio*, prayer, desire of heaven, wisdom and appreciation. In scholastic theology, it became *disputatio*, argument with others, science, knowledge.

A third development was a more formal one, although also extremely important for the centuries to follow. The Vulgate (Latin) translation of the Bible was provided with numbered chapter divisions for the first time, for easy reference (that is, for easier use in argument in the schools!), and a little later the verses were also numbered, so that concordances and other works of reference could be produced more systematically. And I am sure you can immediately see how the availability of such works would change biblical interpretation simply because the chapters and the verses, that we take for granted, had not been divided and numbered!

A fourth, and extremely important development, was the gradual establishment of yet a new social location, in the form of the first of the *medieval universities*, independent from monasteries and cathedrals. A few centres of learning, like Paris, attracted both teachers, called masters, and students from all over, who set up their own schools alongside the cathedral schools. Soon they created a common organisation, and at the end of the 12th century they had formed a university, known as a *studium generale*, a general study, training students in the liberal arts, preparing them for, amongst other things, theological study afterwards. In practice, the disputations became popular and influential, and the real conflicts were about the question of which classical philosophical traditions, like the teachings of Plato or Aristotle, were to be followed in a particular university setting. Biblical study became less important ... only to re-emerge in a new form!

Early in the 13th century, both the Dominican and the Franciscan orders were founded, both primarily concerned with preaching. Francis was deeply opposed to the scholastic practices of his time, the pride in the possession of books, the rivalry between different teachers, and the neglect of what he regarded as the simple ideals of the gospel. He himself preached simple expositions based on a literal understanding of particularly the Gospels. But, as his Order began to grow, the demand for education for the sake of preaching brought these members, the friars, to the universities, and very soon most of the popular preaching was (again) done by self-appointed and untrained preachers, with the almost inevitable result that various heretical movements grew all over! And so, in order to deal with this problem, Dominic set up his new Order of Preachers to combat this spread of heresies! And, remarkably, they combined their enthusiasm for preaching with solid study and theological education. At least three important processes were at work here.

First, the different orders set up their *own houses of studies* in the vicinity of and even as part of the schools and the universities. They had their own agenda, namely doing the preaching in the church, but they needed theology for that. They read the Bible with a view to preaching, but they did that with the scholarly tools available. In the centuries to follow, that would become a crucially influential trend: communities within the church, and after the schisms of the sixteenth century, even the separate confessional and denominational faith communities would set up their own schools, universities and seminaries where they educated their own students, with their own agendas, but also with due respect for scholarship, the liberal arts, science, and the academy in general. This "dual vision" would have a major effect on the story of biblical interpretation.

Second, a new kind of gloss developed, namely one with the needs of preaching in mind. It was intended to provide further and useful information for preachers. They even started to compile dictionaries and concordances of biblical words. These glosses were usually written in the form of blocks interrupting the continuous biblical text, and were called *postilla*, something like "additions". These informative comments, these additions-for-the-sake-of-preachers, were to become one of the important and influential genres of biblical interpretation.

Third, in spite of their interest in popular preaching, the Dominican Order explicitly refused to make available biblical documents in the vernacular, the *ordinary languages* that the common people could understand. In fact, they were of the opinion that the simple gospel, available without interpretation, would only lead to further heresy. Even the possession of a book of the Bible in the vernacular was regarded as an indication of heresy! The issue at stake was – once again – the question about the authority to read and interpret the biblical documents. And, once again, or rather: still, the answer was that this authority, this power, belonged to the official church and to the orders. Even when they were less interested in scholarly theology and in philosophy and emphasized preaching to the people, the power to do that and to read the biblical documents on behalf of the people still belonged to the official church. Even to suggest something else, was heretical. Gradually this position would be criticised from different corners, and this conflict would be solved in different ways, as we shall see.

These three themes all continue in the next episode of our story: the Reformation of the 16th century.

17.4 READING THE BIBLE DURING THE REFORMATION

The Reformation represents a fundamental change in hermeneutical thinking, in ways of reading and interpreting the Bible. But the Reformation was also prepared by major movements and events which took place in the western world and the western mind. It is necessary to bear this in mind in order to see what happened to biblical interpretation during the Reformation itself.

The Reformation must, of course, be taken together with the Renaissance, the phase of rebirth in western culture, the transition from the medieval to the modern era. The Renaissance was a process of liberation of the western mind from superstition and prejudice, but also from authorities and powers, and the Reformation was very much a product of this development. For the purposes of our story, let us remind ourselves of four processes at work during this time.

The first process was the widespread enthusiasm of these centuries to return to the original sources of their history and culture. *Ad fontes!* they cried. Back to the original sources, ideas, and documents! In general culture and education, this cry referred to the return to the ideas and documents of ancient Hellenistic culture and philosophy, but in religious circles the cry also meant a return to the original *biblical documents*, to the earliest manuscripts, particularly in Hebrew, which they did with the help of Jewish rabbis, but soon also to the documents in Greek. The famous humanist, Desiderius Erasmus (1469–1536 AD), for example, was seriously studying the Greek manuscripts of the New Testament. He published important collections of the works of Greek and Latin Fathers, but was also the first one to publish a printed edition of the Greek text of the New Testament at Basel in 1516.

So people studied these documents anew, they were very interested in philological work on the texts of these documents, they attempted translations in the vernacular, and from time to time they tried to make these original manuscripts and these translations available and accessible to a wider public.

Vernacular translations of the biblical documents, in spite of opposition and official prohibitions, became popular on the European continent. Several movements grew in which people read these documents spiritually, meditatively, with an attention to the literal meaning of the Gospels and with emphasis on psychological and moral aspects. Well known are, for example, the *devotio moderna*, a movement of reform through devotion in the Roman Catholic Church in Holland, which produced for example the famous *Imitation of Christ* by Thomas a Kempis.

Martin Luther would be the first one to produce a vernacular translation from the original Greek when he published his enormously popular and influential German New Testament in 1522. The huge demand immediately made a succession of reprints necessary. French and English translations from the Greek were to follow.

Studying the literal sense of the biblical documents according to the humanist principles at work in the Renaissance included inquiring after the so-called intention of the human author, who used language, including narrative, parables, argument, exhortations, metaphor, etc., to communicate meaning. Reading religious documents like this would start an approach that would bear much fruit, although only much later.

The second process is closely related to the first. Whenever people read, translated and studied the biblical documents for themselves, the old conflict over the authority to interpret these texts, *the conflict arose between Bible and church*, between Scripture and Official Tradition, between literal meaning and doctrine as rule of faith. Several well-known episodes witness to this conflict. Theologians like William of Ockham (1285–1349 AD), John Huss (1372–1415 AD) and Wendelin Steinbach (1454–1519 AD) had all already problematised the possible conflict between a truthful reading of the Scriptures and an authoritarian understanding of the right of ecclesiastic authorities to determine the ultimate meaning of the text.

The criticism which John Wycliffe (1330–1384 AD) expressed against the church of his time was an illustration of this conflict. A desire for church reform, in many places, was born from this tension between how the official church interpreted the biblical documents and what believers thought they heard the gospel itself saying. The claim, held for centuries, that the truth of the biblical documents and the teaching of the church were identical, came under increasing pressure. Wycliffe wanted to restore the church to its primitive purity, which he found in a fairly literal

Biblical Hermeneutics: the first 19 centuries

SECTION B

HERMENEUTICS

and legalistic reading of the New Testament and the commentators of the Early Church. He appealed to the Scriptures to oppose the influence of philosophy and the officialdom in the church. Each person, he claimed, could understand the New Testament's clear and literal teachings; the religious orders had no monopoly on Christian teaching and life. He wanted everyone to have access to the Gospels. There was a growing demand for translations of the biblical documents. The study of Hebrew became more popular. Wycliffe organised an attempt to translate the whole Bible into English for the benefit of the common people, although still from the Latin Vulgate, the only translation available to them. Because of opposition from the scholars, who were still suspicious of translations into the vernacular because they could lead to private readings and interpretations, and therefore to heresies, private initiatives towards translation were forbidden in England in 1407. But it was now only a matter of time.

The third process, which was more of an event than a process, accelerated the other two processes beyond anything they knew before. It was the development of *printing*. The Reformation was a product of the invention of loose-letter printing. It is as simple as that. Without printing, there would have been no Reformation as we know it. It is difficult today for us to imagine a culture, a world, that knew writing but not printing. And yet, that was the way it was. At the end of the Middle Ages every so-called "book", every manuscript, was unique. They were hand-written by authors or copyists, and individually made. The libraries, even the oldest libraries in the cathedrals and abbeys and the largest ones in the universities all had a limited number of manuscripts. The development of printing radically changed that, and thereby changed the world itself. Through industry (paper production) and technology (printing) a new world was created. "Printing conquered Europe. It was to reign supreme over the continent for four centuries and move out to conquer the world" (H-J Martin, in his famous study on *The history and power of writing*, 233ff.). And the Bible played a central role in this new world and in this conquest.

A fourth important process was taking place as a result of the others. Bibles were printed in the vernacular. For the first time, ordinary people had direct access to the Bible. It affected the way they thought and talked. The Bible became part of their *imagination*, of their world-view, of their idioms, of their way of expressing themselves. Luther's German translation, as well as the Authorised Version in England (1611), had an enormously creative effect upon their respective literatures and cultures. Biblical language became part and parcel of everyday speech in all walks of life. The result was that ordinary people were interpreting, applying, using the Bible continuously for everyday purposes. The Bible was, in a sense, now also taken out of worship services and university classrooms and read and interpreted in everyday life. But more than that. People were not interested in the Bible as scholars, in order to study and know the Bible. They were interested in the Bible as believers, in order to study and understand everyday life with the help of the Bible. The Bible became the lenses, the spectacles, through which they looked at life, the means by which they interpreted their world and everyday life. They no longer only interpreted the Bible, but the Bible started to interpret them, their lives, their thoughts, their language. They attempted to live their daily lives in "the strange world of the Bible", looking, seeing through the glasses of the Bible; thinking, talking in the language of the Bible.

We must not underestimate the impact of these developments. For the first time in history, it really became possible to speak of *"The Bible"* in the singular, referring to a single book, that (some of the) ordinary people had access to and which they could also read! It was available in a physical format that made it easier to distribute. The different biblical documents were together in a single volume. They were translated into the ordinary, natural languages that people spoke.

For the first time it became possible to claim that "The Bible" was a single book, with a single message, with a single thrust, a single purpose. It was no longer almost taken for granted that these documents were difficult to understand, that one needed a key to unlock their hidden meaning, that this key was given in the doctrine of the official church, and that the learned and powerful authorities of the official church were the only ones who could unlock these documents. The growing conflict over biblical authority and ecclesiastic tradition came to a head, and the Reformers chose the authority of the Bible itself. *Sola Scriptura!* The Scriptures alone! No longer an official tradition as rule of interpretation! To them the official church was no longer necessary to interpret this Book which they had in their own hands and which they could read and understand. And the fact that the lifestyle of the official church of that time in many ways contradicted what they read in this Book served as further reason to put their trust in the Book and its own message, its own power to speak, through the Holy Spirit, and to convince everyone who could read.

Against this background, it is possible to appreciate what really happened with regard to biblical interpretation. The Reformers read the Bible for themselves and they heard a new message in this Book, *a message of salvation.* This Bible, they would claim, contains all that is necessary for salvation, and it is there for everyone to see, to hear, to read, to understand, it is there in clarity, *claritas,* and in power. The idea of the sufficiency of the Bible was to become a hallmark of the Reformation. They no longer needed the church and its authority to tell them that it was the Word, because the Word itself was powerful, was convincing readers and listeners, was giving its own spiritual testimony, was self-authenticating and was the Word of God itself, powerful unto salvation. And they no longer needed the church and its Tradition to tell them what the content, the message, the scopus, the purpose of the Word was, because the Word itself was clear. Salvation was e*x auditu verbi,* received through listening to the promises of this divine Word and trusting in them.

Surely one can see that biblical interpretation would never be the same again.

The mere fact that the Reformers, like Luther, emphasized the import-

SECTION B

HERMENEUTICS

ance of the Word so strongly meant that there was more interest in the study and reading of the Bible than ever before. Luther insisted that the Bible was the *viva vox*, the living voice of God. The Bible was, primarily, a text for preaching and hearing the gospel of the living God. All philological and historical work, or, as they soon preferred to say: the grammatical-historical study of the Bible, was to serve this end, namely the preaching of the promises, of the life-giving gospel of Christ. The Bible's central theme was Christ, and from this perspective the whole of Scripture was to be interpreted. Biblical Hermeneutics was more than merely applying rules and techniques; something completely different from simply finding the doctrine of the official church back in proof texts; and not an attempt to unlock an obscure and difficult document by using a spiritual key, obtained from somewhere else. No, it became the existential reading of the grammatical historical text itself, because its message, its thrust, its central scopus was clear for everyone to see: the promises of salvation.

There were different emphases amongst Reformation figures and groups about the content of this Word of God and about the nature of this salvation. Lutherans emphasised the material principle of justification by grace alone, Calvinists emphasised the importance of the whole Word as the revealed will of the Triune God, Anabaptists emphasised radical discipleship rather than redemption. The basic claims regarding biblical interpretation and use, however, remained the same. Interpretation was liberated from the rigid control of ecclesiastical authority. The Bible was available (translated from the original Hebrew and Greek!) into the languages that ordinary people spoke and understood, so that they could read the Bible for themselves, since it was God's own Word: the message of salvation, clear, sufficient, self-authenticating.

A heavy responsibility was placed on exegesis, on biblical interpretation itself. The Reformation, therefore, marked the beginning of intense hermeneutical activity that would remain at the heart of theology and church in the post-Reformation era. The church was about preaching this gospel of salvation, this living Word of God. And the study of theology was about the study of this Word.

This had major implications for institutions in society, or, as we have been saying, for the social locations in which the Bible was read. Two examples will perhaps clarify this.

A first example. Very often Protestant Christians, particularly from the Reformed tradition, would attempt to read the Bible "in and for the public sphere", that is, they wanted the princes, the rulers, the cities, the regions, even the countries where they lived, to obey the Word of God and to organise themselves according to the Word of God. Visionary interpretations of the Bible, prophetic interpretations of the Bible and covenantal interpretations of the Bible were all popular. Why? Because they made it possible to claim that societies at large ought to be reformed, organised, according to the authoritative message of God's Word. In the Calvinist tradition, by way of illustration, people like Bullinger (1504–1575 AD) in Zürich and Bucer (1491–1551 AD) in Strasbourg produced covenantal interpretations like this. Bucer dedicated his study on the reign of Christ to King Edward VI of England and advised him how to reform ecclesiastical and civil life, including education, poor relief, luxury, honest gains, marketing, and public inns. It was an attempt to institute a society based upon an Old Testament framework of civil law, and a New Testament concept of the church. (Which poses some questions to us: Would it still be possible to read the Bible like this after a few centuries? And is it still possible today?)

A second example. Activities in the institutions of theological study and training, the universities and the seminaries, would change dramatically. In fact, people have said that Luther only wanted to change the curriculum of study in one of the most insignificant universities of Europe, namely Wittenberg – and the Reformation was the result! Obviously, the study of the Bible was to occupy a central position in the new curricula. But soon it would develop into an autonomous project, soon Old Testament study and New Testament study would evolve as disciplines opposed to and critical of dogmatics, or the study of doctrine, and soon different theological disciplines would become increasingly alienated from one another.

If you listened carefully to our story, you would already have sensed that new developments, new conflicts over biblical interpretation, were just around the corner. They arrived in the form of the Enlightenment, the so-called Modern Period.

17.5 READING THE BIBLE SINCE THE ENLIGHTENMENT

Now our story becomes very complex. A major problem is that, in order to follow our story about the interpretation of the Bible, we must now first listen to a few other stories about the development of interpretation, of hermeneutics in general. You will remember that the early Christians also took over the rules and practices of interpretation available in their heritage and culture. Well, modern Christians are doing exactly the same. We have been reading the Bible in ways that are similar to the ways in which our modern contemporaries read secular documents. And that causes our problem! It is not so easy to summarise all the new developments in interpretation, because the modern world is such a complex world, often called a pluralistic world, with so many trends taking place at the same time!

What was the Enlightenment? Perhaps we can summarise the spirit of the Enlightenment in the two well-known expressions by two of the most famous Enlightenment philosophers, Rene Descartes and Immanuel Kant. Descartes said: "I think, therefore I am" – *cogito ergo sum*. What makes me a human being, is my ability to think for myself; to doubt what people, institutions, traditions, authorities, documents, tell me, and to think and to decide for myself what I shall believe or not. And, much later, answering the question what the Enlightenment was, Kant said: It was the coming of age of human beings; it was the time during which it became possible and necessary for human beings to think for them-

SECTION B

HERMENEUTICS

selves, and not to trust external authorities and traditions any longer.

From this at least three characteristics of the Enlightenment come to the fore which are of crucial importance for our story about biblical interpretation: *a rationalistic mindset, an historical consciousness and a secularization project.*

A first characteristic of the spirit of the Enlightenment was its faith in reason, its *rationalistic mindset*. People believed and trusted in rationality. Rationality (using your intellect) became the opposite of accepting anything on authority. No longer were people willing to believe something because important people, or important institutions, or important documents, or important traditions told them to do so. They wanted to think and decide for themselves. Modernism meant the "flight from authority".

We saw that the Reformation contributed to the critical spirit that rejected the authority of the church. During the Enlightenment, that same critical spirit went further and rejected the authority of the Reformation's Word as well. Once again our principle was at work: the flight from authority taking place in society at large would not leave the religious sphere unaffected. The attitude of trust in the authoritative Word would make place for an attitude of radical doubt and criticism.

As far as social location is concerned, this would become especially clear wherever theology and the Bible were studied within Enlightenment universities. Every discipline would soon and enthusiastically develop a critical methodology. Every discipline, including the so-called human sciences, would try to follow the rational, positivist, scientific natural sciences. Even Old and New Testament studies would soon try to secure their places within the modernist academy by being just as rational and critical as the next discipline. In this environment, the respect for the Bible as the authoritative Word of God would become something of the past. And Biblical Hermeneutics would be changed beyond recognition.

During the time of the Enlightenment, a remarkable development took place in so-called Protestant scolasticism. This was an attempt from conservative Protestant scholars to defend the authority of the Bible. These scholars set out to prove, beyond any doubt, that the Bible was indeed authoritative and true, a final foundation, an inspired, ahistorical, timeless, universal, faultless, inerrant source of knowledge, propositions and fundamental truths. The irony was that, despite their vehement opposition to the Enlightenment, Protestant scolasticism accepted the presuppositions and foundations of science and rationalism, the cornerstones of the Enlightenment!

In some versions of (the more recent) so-called "Evangelicalism" (although the term refer to many different groups and traditions) an attempt was made to bolster and defend the confidence in the truth of the Bible by a theory of verbal inspiration. But the story of evangelical interpretation is told in chapter 19.

Verbal inspiration soon became verbal inerrancy, which soon became biblical Fundamentalism in many circles. In many fundamentalist circles, the need for hermeneutics and interpretation is, in fact, denied, because people claim that the divine Word is so straightforward and clear that no human interpretation is needed. A very instructive discussion of this approach is given by Kathleen C. Boone (1989).

A second characteristic of modernity, of crucial importance for biblical interpretation, was the widespread *historical consciousness*. Because of a number of reasons, people became more aware of history and of their own place in history.

Now historical study regarding the biblical documents led to major advancements. Enormous strides were made with regard to philological studies; the Jewish background of the Old Testament documents was studied intensively; impressive advancements were made regarding the knowledge about and the understanding of the literature and the culture of the ancient world; archaeology made spectacular discoveries; textual criticism of both Testaments advanced dramatically; the history of the phenomenon of religion was investigated; interest grew in the history of the biblical documents themselves, that is when they were written and edited, by whom, together with interest in the real history "behind" the biblical history, in what "really" happened, in who Jesus "really" was, in the growth of the first Christian communities and their beliefs. In short, people became historically conscious, very much aware of the historical and cultural differences between them and biblical times, and very much aware of the historical, human nature of the biblical documents, as mere human products of mere human historical developments. Taken together, all of this contributed to the development of the so-called historical-critical methodology.

This is an umbrella-term which describes a plurality of methods that became extremely popular in Old and New Testament studies. It is impossible to tell the story of the historical-critical study in any detail, but it is an impressive and exciting story, including many famous names like Wolff (1679–1754 AD), Baumgarten (1706–1757 AD), Semler (1725–1791 AD) and many others, and also many methods like form criticism, source criticism, redaction criticism, tradition historical criticism, literary criticism, history of religions, sociological criticism, and so forth.

In general what happened was easy to understand. The Bible was seen as just another human document, just another historical document, although a very interesting, fascinating one. The Old Testament, for example, was not ignored in theological faculties and seminaries. On the contrary, Old Testament studies flourished, but it was studied as "a collection of books from the ancient Near East". Interpretation became the analysis of the literal and historical sense of this ancient text. And in Germany, since the first decade of the 19th century (when De Wette published his famous *Introduction*), critical attempts were increasingly made to present a picture of Israelite religion that differed radically from that implied by the Old Testament itself. The interest was in the reconstructed world of ancient culture and religion behind the Old Testament and obscured by what they regarded as the unreliable accounts found in the Old Testament documents themselves. From South Africa, bishop Colen-

SECTION B

HERMENEUTICS

so contributed 3500 pages of critical work on the Pentateuch! The diversity in and, in fact, behind the Old Testament was emphasised. Almost radical discontinuity between historical phases was presupposed. Any attempt to reconstruct a "theology" of the Old Testament, or for that matter of the New Testament – not to mention the whole Bible! – was soon given up in these critical circles. The same critical spirit dominated historical reconstructions of the historical world behind the so-called historically unreliable New Testament documents as well.

The implications were obvious. The unity of the Bible, often posited in the course of Christian history in a variety of forms to solve the conflict of interpretations, was given up completely in these circles. The authority of the Bible as a reliable, trustworthy and divine book was rejected. The central conviction of the Reformation, that the Bible was God's own Word in a special sense, the message of God's self-revelation to his people, was threatened, and rejected. The idea of a special revelation was no longer acceptable for the modern spirit. In short, a new conflict regarding biblical interpretation had arrived. The issue at stake was the religious value of the Bible itself.

With the idea of the divine authorship of the Bible, the notion of its unity, of its single message, or thrust, or scopus, also came under fire. The most fundamental difference that critical scholarship brought about was in relation to the unity of the Old and the New Testaments. In a typical historical-critical approach, the attention was no longer on the unity, but on the detail.

The so-called Biblical Theology of the late 18th and early 19th centuries still sought to interpret the Old and the New Testaments in their own right, in ways not determined by doctrinal assumptions. In the late 19th and the 20th centuries, however, critical scholars would often reject the possibility of Old or New Testament theologies as such, emphasising the differences, the discrepancies, the pluralities, the discontinuities. Now the division into chapters and verses came in very handy for a radically new purpose! It made it easier to divide the text into small units and to separate them from one another. In fact, a major characteristic of critical scholarship, which it again shares with modernist academic work in general, is the remarkable specialization of people working in the field.

It is necessary, however, to keep the social location of these developments in mind. One can almost say that the historical-critical mentality was more a scholarly way of studying the Bible at universities and seminaries (as just another interesting human document from ancient times and different cultures) than a way of reading, interpreting, and using the Bible. The historical-critical method was, has been, and still is the preserve of scholars. The greater majority of people who constitute the church still know little or nothing about it even today.

This is very important. It means that a major conflict of interpretation was shifted to a conflict between different social locations, *between* universities and the church.

One remarkable aspect of this (institutional) conflict was that many seminaries fell somewhere between these two opposing worlds of academy and church. Many seminaries followed the same fourfold structure of theological disciplines (biblical, dogmatic/systematic, historical, and practical) practised in the universities (where each discipline tried to prove its own scientific character by ignoring the others), while at the same time training students for the ministry. Often that would lead to tension in students' experience of the different disciplines and the conflicting ways in which the Bible was read and interpreted in the different disciplines. Systematic theologians and practical theologians would (still) use the Bible in ways that the Old and New Testament scholars rejected as premodern and pre-critical! Sometimes that would lead to tension between churches and their seminaries, when teaching staff would be accused of not adhering to the authority of the Bible.

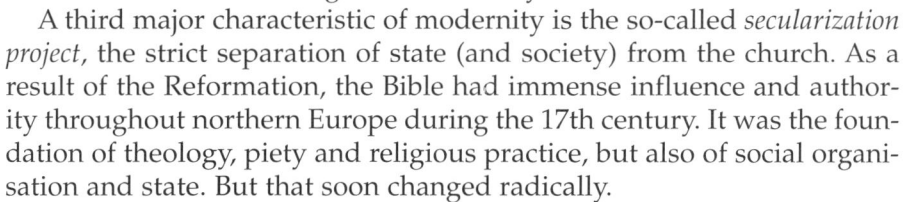

A third major characteristic of modernity is the so-called *secularization project*, the strict separation of state (and society) from the church. As a result of the Reformation, the Bible had immense influence and authority throughout northern Europe during the 17th century. It was the foundation of theology, piety and religious practice, but also of social organisation and state. But that soon changed radically.

It became almost impossible, in Western democratic societies, to interpret the Bible with a view to public life and social organisation. People believed that religious ideas, religious convictions and religious authority all contributed to fanaticism, to irrationality, to lack of tolerance and even war. People were looking for a more rational way to solve their social and political differences, and saw in religion and in appeals to the Bible part of their problem, not part of their solution. Combining rationalism (think for yourself, do not accept ideas on authority) and historical consciousness (we no longer live in the time of the Old Testament covenant and theocracy, or of the small Christian congregations in the Roman Empire), made modern democracy possible: People were equal, and endowed with the same rational capacities, so that they could, collectively, without reading the Bible, decide how to organise their public and civil life together.

The influence of the Bible became limited to the sphere of individual, private life. Pious, personal, spiritual study of the Bible obviously continued. And in churches the Bible was obviously still read in worship, and for preaching and in the liturgy, but it was no longer interpreted with a view to society itself.

The picture must be clear. In scholarly circles, biblical interpretation took place in a scientific, analytical, rational, historical way – without much impact on or relevance for the church and Christian living, or for public life at large. In the churches and in their personal lives, Christians were reading the Bible, but without paying much attention to what scholars did or to what happened in society.

Small wonder that a fourth, almost counter-development of major importance for biblical interpretation took place, namely the development of biblical *hermeneutics* in a technical sense, now for the first time deliberately using the term "hermeneutics" to explain what was at stake. And

17

Biblical Hermeneutics: the first 19 centuries

SECTION B

HERMENEUTICS

what was at stake? The claim that biblical interpretation involved more than mere rational, historical or private study of the Bible.

Perhaps one can summarise the basic thrust of this developing biblical hermeneutics by saying that the convictions gradually grew that historical study alone is not enough, that completely objective, neutral, scientific, prejudiceless study of the Bible is impossible, that "understanding" is still something different from "explanation". Historical enquiry can only find answers to historical questions. Literary enquiry can only find answers to literary questions. Historical enquiry can explain a lot about the historical nature of these texts and documents, and has produced a wealth of valuable historical knowledge. Literary enquiry can explain a lot about the literary nature of these texts and documents, and has produced a wealth of valuable literary knowledge. But reading and understanding these documents as religious documents, as sacred, or inspired, or divine, or authoritative writings, requires something more, something different. But what?

That is another story, which is told in chapter 18.

READING LIST AND BIBLIOGRAPHY

Ackroyd, P.R. et al. *The Cambridge History of the Bible.* 1963–1970 three volumes, Cambridge University Press.

Boone, K.C. 1989. *The Bible tells them so. The discourse of protestant fundamentalism.* London: SCM.

Coggins, R.J. & Houlden, J.L. (ed.). 1990. *A dictionary of biblical interpretation.* London: SCM Press.

Grant, R. & Tracy, D. 1984. *A short history of the interpretation of the Bible.* Philadelphia: Fortress Press.

Jeanrond, W.G. 1991. *Theological hermeneutics. Development and significance.* New York.: Crossroad.

Leclerg, J. 1980. *The love of Learning and the Desire for God – A study of monastic culture.* New York: Fordham.

Martin, H-J. 1994. *The history and power of writing.* Chicago: Chicago University Press.

Rogers, J.B. & McKim, D.K. 1979. *The authority and interpretation of the Bible. An historical approach.* San Francisco, CA: Harper & Row Publishers.

Rogerson, J.W., Rowland, C. & Lindars, B. 1988. *The study and use of the Bible.* Grand Rapids MI: Wm B Eerdmans.

Romer, J. 1989. *Testament. The Bible and history.* London: Michael O'Mara Books.

Thiselton, A. 1992. *New horizons in hermeneutics.* Grand Rapids, Michigan: Zondervan Publishing House.

Biblical Hermeneutics: the 20th century

Dirkie J. Smit

18.1 INTRODUCTION

What is the story of Biblical Hermeneutics, of reading the Bible, in Western Theology during the 20th century? Where does the discussion stand at the moment? I have already briefly told you the story of hermeneutics, of reading and interpreting and using the Christian Bible through the first nineteen centuries (chapter 17). But what is the state of the present discussion?

Once again, this is a very difficult question! This much is obvious from the many articles and books that are available, with thousands of pages, trying to tell us this story – and often in contradicting ways! In reminding ourselves of the story of the way Christians read and used the Bible during the first nineteen centuries, we often remembered the specific conflict about biblical interpretation that dominated a certain period of Christian history. In order to understand the contribution made during a particular phase of history, it was often useful to ask: *What* did they disagree about? *Who* disagreed *with whom*? And *how* was the issue resolved at that time? Who won the argument? How was that conflict over Biblical interpretation solved at the time?

Now, the interesting thing is that the 20th century can also be described in terms of the specific *conflicts of interpretation* that we experience. In fact, many people say that we live in a time that is characterised like never before by a conflict of interpretations, a time characterised by the fact that different Christians read, use and interpret the Bible in different ways.

What are these conflicts that characterise 20th century Biblical Herme-

SECTION B

HERMENEUTICS

neutics in the west? In a way, they are the old conflicts of ages past in new forms, but also in their old forms. Different people would describe them in diverse ways, but I would like to tell you about five of the major ones – and you will recognise all of them!: The conflict between *explanation and understanding;* the conflict over the question who may read the Bible; the conflict over the question *what we do when we read;* the conflict over the *responsibility* of reading the Bible; and the conflict over the question *what the Bible is.*

18.2 ON THE CONFLICT BETWEEN EXPLANATION AND UNDERSTANDING

The first issue is almost obvious. So many *exegetical methods*, or approaches, have developed in the past that it is almost impossible to know how to respond to them. What must we say about this multiplicity of exegetical methods? How do you read the Bible once you have heard about all these methods? Before one started studying theology, it was often easier to read and understand the Bible than during and after your studies! Then you did not know about historical criticism, and literary criticism, and psychological exegesis, and social-scientific approaches, and structuralist exegesis and rhetorical criticism and what-have-you. It was rather easy to read the Bible. And even to preach.

But once we know about all these exegetical methods, how are we to respond? Are some of them better, more adequate, than others? Should we choose between them? Should we select one or more, and use only them and defend them?

Some people believe that this is indeed the answer. We must select. They may, for example, be convinced that a historical approach is the only legitimate one. If you do not use historical-critical methods, they would argue, you cannot properly analyze a text. Or others would say that a literary approach is the only legitimate one. They would often claim that we do not have enough historical knowledge in any case, so that we must concentrate on the literary structures within the text, on the genre, or on the narrative, or on the document as an ancient letter, or whatever.

Other people, however, believe that there may be an element of truth, of value, of usefulness, in all these methods, or in most of them. Usually they will therefore simply be eclective, which means that they pick and choose, they decide, from time to time, from text to text, from occasion to occasion, what they want to use and what not. In reality, what they use often depends on what they have available. A preacher, for example, may not have a solid or an interesting literary analysis of a specific pericope available. Therefore she or he may just use the historical analysis that they do have on their shelf! Or vice versa. Many theological students and many theologians read the Bible like that. This means that they are in principle willing to use almost any exegetical method, as long as it provides interesting or useful results. They do not really care. They do not really think that there is a serious conflict of interpretation at stake between the different methodologies.

And still *other people* may try to combine all these methods into one. These are, therefore, also people who believe that all or most of the exegetical methods are based on a valid suppositions and provide some valid information about the text. They may attempt to include all these methods, focused on different aspects of the text, in an all-inclusive, comprehensive, exegetical approach or theory. They may, for example, be convinced that it is indeed important to take account of the historical, the structural and the pragmatic aspects of a text. Then they attempt to develop an exegetical approach that will include the results of all three these ways of looking at texts. Many people have made attempts like this. One of the best-known representatives is, in fact, a South African New Testament scholar, Bernard C. Lategan. He has published many contributions over the years in which he has argued that proper explanation of a text must take all the different dimensions into account.

So in summary one can say that many people, when they hear about the "conflict of interpretations" that is so typical of 20th-century Western Biblical Hermeneutics, would immediately think of all these methods, and of the so-called "conflicts" they may cause. They think that the conflict of interpretation is caused by the different exegetical methods, and one must either choose, or use whatever you have, or combine them into a single approach.

However, there is a *much more fundamental problem here*. The real conflict of interpretation lies deeper that this. All these methods are attempts to "explain", to analyze, to dissect, to study, the biblical text; but is that enough?

Many people would say "no" and argue that it is not enough. Why not? They would argue that "understanding" is something different from "explaining". And, they would argue, what we normally do when we read the Bible is not to "explain" it in a scholarly, scientific, academic way, but to "understand" it, to hear what it has to say to us.

In fact, during the 20th century, more and more people have started to realise this and to emphasise that "understanding" and "explanation" are two different ways of looking at a text. And more and more people are of the opinion that *this conflict between understanding and explanation may be far more fundamental* than the differences between different exegetical, scholarly methods. In other words, they would argue that the basic conflict is not between the different scholarly, exegetical methods, but between all these methods on the one hand ("explanation"), and totally different ways of reading the Bible on the other hand ("understanding").

> In order to understand this story of Biblical Hermeneutics a little better, it may be helpful to make a small detour, and to remember briefly the story of the development of so-called *philosophical hermeneutics*. This is a rather complicated detour. Therefore it is done in smaller print. Readers not interested may leave this and subsequent small print sections out. As we have seen so often, biblical interpretation is always closely linked to the general ideas about reading and interpretation at work in the broader culture of the specific time. Over the last two centuries, the story was exactly the same. In the western cultural history at large, a movement countering the influence of "scientism" and "historicism" grew. These expressions mean taking the importance of a scientific approach and an historical metho-

Biblical Hermeneutics: the 20th century

SECTION B

HERMENEUTICS

dology too seriously, making these approaches absolute and expecting all knowledge and all truth from them. One such counter-movement, claiming that there is more to knowledge and truth that scientism and historicism can offer, was called the development of philosophical hermeneutics. The easiest way to summarise this story is to link the development to a few important individuals, each with a crucial contribution: Schleiermacher (1768–1834), Dilthey (1844–1911), Heidegger (1889–1976), Gadamer (1900–) and Ricoeur (1913–).

Schleiermacher was the first one to develop a fully-fledged general philosophical hermeneutics for the interpretation of texts. He started with the reality of misunderstanding written texts and oral communication. The danger is that we misunderstand those texts and oral expressions that we think we do understand! It is, therefore, necessary to start with the more fundamental question: What is understanding? When do we really understand a written or oral communication? In technical, philosophical jargon: What are the preconditions which make understanding possible? The language that speakers (or authors) and listeners (or readers) share make understanding possible, but true understanding needs something more: We must understand the intention of the author. And it is precisely the individuality of the author (as well as our own individuality) that makes understanding difficult and misunderstanding possible. The language we share cannot adequately express the unique experience of the individual author or speaker. The receiver (reader or listener) must therefore reconstruct, *reproduce*, the intention or meaning of the speaker, writer or sender in his or her own consciousness. Is this possible? Yes, because we are "congenial", that means, we, both listeners and speakers, as human beings, share the same human spirit. We can, in principle, understand someone else. So this is where hermeneutics becomes necessary. Interpretation involves two steps: A first, grammatical interpretation, and a second, technical, or in his terms: psychological, interpretation. The former step only prepares the way for the second, which is understanding in the full sense of the word: Through "feeling", divination, it is possible to experience what the speaker or writer wants to communicate.

Dilthey broadens the idea of a general hermeneutics by applying it to the phenomenon of *history*. He is not interested in the interpretation and understanding of human communication, but in the more general question: How do we understand history? How do we interpret, reconstruct, history? Like Schleiermacher, he still concentrates on the power of human consciousness to reconstruct and to interpret and understand. Both the possibilities and the problems of historical understanding are rooted in human historical consciousness. On the one hand, our historical consciousness provides a link with the past. We feel ourselves part of it. We feel we can reconstruct and understand it. On the other hand, our historical consciousness also causes an experience of alienation from history, an experience of "then" and "now", an experience of distance. Interpretation and understanding require the conscious effort to overcome this historical distance which we experience. The one who wants to understand must transpose him- or herself out of the present to the past, must re-construct, must re-experience the original experience. Is that possible at all? Well, the re-experience will never be exactly the same, never identical with the original experience, but will inevitably be co-determined by the interpreter's historical horizon. Nevertheless, some access is possible, some form of understanding the past, as expressed in the tradition and the cultural manifestations of the past. It is possible, because we share, through our historical consciousness, with the past and the tradition. So the "text" to be read and to be interpreted is, for Dilthey, not the real, physical texts of human communication, but the text of the whole cultural heritage of humanity. This is the task of human sciences, as distinct from natural sciences. Accordingly, human sciences follow a distinct methodology as well, the method of understanding *(Verstehen)* in contrast to explanation *(Erklären)*.

Heidegger broadens this idea. The hermeneutical problem, according to him, is even more fundamental and all-inclusive: It is ontological, i.e. it has to do with reality, with meaning, with *life itself*. We do not merely want to understand texts (Schleiermacher), or history, tradition, and culture (Dilthey), but life itself, reality, being. To be human is to be interpreting. To be human is to be involved in hermeneutics. To be human is to attempt to understand. Interpretation is the modus, the way, in which reality appears to us. The text to be interpreted is reality itself. Our own existence is at stake in this process of interpretation. How does this take place? Well, says Heidegger, we never start with a clean slate. We experience reality in history, as historical beings. We confront reality, daily, as the people we already are. We come with our own ideas, beliefs, convictions, questions. We come conditioned by our own horizons. In experiencing reality, in the process of interpretation, we are changed. Our horizon of understanding is continuously challenged by new possibilities of being, of life, of reality. In responding to them, we are affected, changed, transformed. On our way through life, we do not remain the same. Next time, we experience in new ways, and are again challenged, and changed, etc. He calls this the hermeneutical circle: the interpreter (the human being) brings pre-understandings to the process of interpretation. The pre-understanding is challenged, modified, affirmed, revised, or whatever. The modified understanding becomes the new horizon, the new pre-understanding in the next phase of the process. When, or where does all of this take place? Heidegger makes much of the importance of language. Language, he says, is the house of being. It is in language that reality reveals something of itself, and where we find new challenges and new possibilities for being human. It is in language that we encounter and interpret reality itself.

Gadamer draws some very important implications from all of this in his philosophical hermeneutics. The insight that the truth we are looking for as human beings is the truth of disclosure, of something being disclosed, shown, revealed to us, is important to him. This means that hermeneutics cannot be only a question of method, of objective and scientific inquiry. His famous study is in fact called Truth and method. Truth is only found in a conversation with reality, in a dialogical process, through which possibilities for our existence are acknowledged and accepted. A conversation, a dialogue, unfolds between text and interpreter, each with its own horizon. True understanding takes place when the two horizons meet, or fuse. That is the goal of interpretation, and the medium through which it takes place is language.

Ricoeur argues that a religious text is only properly understood when it leads to action. He says that the real power of a text, and especially a religious text, is its transformative power. Put simply, this means that these texts "refer" to something, to a new way of living and being, to "a world in front of the text". These texts have the power to suggest, to propose, to open up, to make possible, to produce "a world in front of the text" and invite the readers or hearers to adopt or inhabit this world. They propose a new way of living, they invite readers to an alternative world, they suggest a new way of looking at life, of thinking, of being, of acting. They appeal to readers to be transformed, to be changed, to act in a new way; in short, to inhabit this world of the text. It is immediately clear why imagination plays an important role in this kind of hermeneutics. "Imagination" is the ability to see this new world, to see the possibilities for action offered to us by the religious text. And it is easy to understand why systematic theologians, particularly church theologians, have often been attracted to this kind of hermeneutics. This makes it possible to claim that the Bible is God's Word, that God is speaking through this Word, is inviting readers, challenging them, confronting them, calling them. This makes it possible to claim that the Bible has a message, a thrust, a scope, a purpose, and that the only proper way to hear this message and to understand the Bible is to pay heed to this message, to answer the call, to believe the divine Word behind and in the human words; in short, to act, to be transformed, to follow. These ideas are today very popular in liberation-hermeneutical circles. (See chapters 6,7,8,20,21 and 22.)

Biblical Hermeneutics: the 20th century

SECTION

B

HERMENEUTICS

Does this short account of Philosophical Hermeneutics make any sense? To many people who read and interpret the Bible it has made a lot of sense, especially during the 20th century. Biblical Hermeneutics has taken over many of the basic ideas and insights of Philosophical Hermeneutics and popularised them in theological and church circles.

To understand the Bible is something different from merely explaining it, i.e. using scientific and critical methods to analyze and study it; to understand the Bible involves taking it seriously as some form of disclosure, as a classic, or a sacred text, as Word of God, as revelation and canon; to understand the Bible is not an objective process, but the readers or listeners are fully involved, with their own horizons of understanding, their prejudices, expectations and questions; to understand the Bible is to be transformed, to be called to action; understanding the Bible takes place when the horizon of the reader and the horizon of the biblical text fuse, combine, become united, when the reader enters the world to which the Bible is inviting us.

But I am sure some of you will already feel that there is a problem somewhere, that this kind of language causes other conflicts of interpretation to come to the fore.

18.3 ON THE CONFLICT OVER THE QUESTION WHO MAY READ THE BIBLE

One obvious conflict of interpretation, embedded in what we have said so far, is the conflict over the question *who* may then read the Bible. *To whom does the Bible belong?* Who has a right to read and interpret the Bible? Who may claim that they know how to approach and how to read and how to use and how to understand the Bible?

Can you see the problem? If it is true that the presuppositions of the readers (or listeners) are important, then the question *who we are* will also be important! Then, obviously, different people will read, interpret, understand, appropriate the same texts in different ways, because they are different people! If our horizons fuse with the horizon-of-meaning in the biblical texts, then people with different horizons will obviously hear the same things in the Bible differently! Can we then all be correct in what we think we hear in the Bible, or is there a serious conflict of interpretations here? If our imaginations co-determine what we see in the Bible, then different people will see different worlds there, and will feel themselves called to different forms of action. Can that be correct and acceptable? Or will some be right and others wrong?

The problem is therefore that *who we are will make a difference to how we read*. Where we come from, how we think, what we believe, what we want to know, what we want to do with the Bible – all of this will cause major differences, sometimes even conflicts, between our respective interpretations, sometimes even of the same biblical text.

During the 20th century, people interested in hermeneutics, and therefore also in Biblical Hermeneutics, have used different concepts, different notions or ideas to emphasize different aspects of this fundamental insight: who we are makes a difference to how we read.

They have, for example, often used the expression *"context"* to underline the importance of the life-situation, the economic, social, political, historical, cultural, gender, psychological "context" we come from. Many people have therefore pleaded for (or against!) a *contextual* hermeneutics, i.e. a form of reading and interpretation that takes these "contexts" seriously.

Others prefer the expression *social location* to refer to the same kind of reality. They often want (Bible-)readers to be conscious of who they are and where they come from, to take their particular socio-political cultural location into account, and to acknowledge that they read the way they read because they are socially "located", "constructed", "made" and "pre-fabricated" like that.

Still others talk about *"reading from this place"*. You can immediately hear that it points to the same issue. We never read the Bible abstractly, ahistorically, universally and without limitations of time and space. We are who we are. We read the Bible as very specific people, in and from a very specific place, and with very specific questions, reasons, purposes and interests.

Yet others want to emphasize precisely these diverse purposes or reasons that Bible-readers may have, and accordingly they speak of *interpretive interests*. And obviously these reasons or interpretive interests may often be in conflict with one another, with the result that people have conflicting interpretations! You get in the Bible what you want, the argument goes.

Still other people point to the fact that we do not read primarily as individuals, but in groups, in traditions and in communities. We read the Bible the way we are accustomed to read the Bible. In a particular social location we read with particular interpretive interests and according to particular methods, because we have seen other people in that location, in that community and in that tradition, do it in that way. People emphasizing this aspect use the expression *community of interpretation*, and argue that, within particular reading communities, we accept the rules, the practices and conventions that have developed there over the years, and we also read like that (at least, while we are there!).

And finally (because we must stop somewhere!) some people use the expressions *official interpretive culture* and *unofficial interpretive culture* to describe this aspect. It means that we learn how to read the Bible within a certain "culture": the culture of our specific church, or the culture of the university classroom, or whatever. Sometimes this culture is "official". There is an official canon of interpretation. Everybody knows that and must adhere to that. Authorities protect these rules for correct interpretation. This means that if we do not read the Bible in this way, people say it is wrong, and they censure us. (They do not like our sermons, they do not allow us into the ministry, they accuse us of heresy and falsehood, or they fail us in the exams.) Sometimes, however, this culture is "unofficial". Then people are not consciously aware that they follow rules and prescriptions. They think that is simply the only proper way to read!

SECTION B

HERMENEUTICS

They are not aware that they have been told and taught to read like that in their particular social location, community or tradition. Instead, they believe their way of reading the Bible comes naturally. They take it for granted. And they think that all other people who use and read the Bible in different ways, and come to different interpretations, are wrong, uninformed and stubborn.

So, who we are always makes a difference to how we read the Bible, and this leads to conflicts of interpretation.

Is it possible to describe some of these social locations, these places where people with diverse interpretive interests read the same Bible according to the conventions of diverse "communities of interpretation" and according to the taken-for-granted rules of diverse "interpretive cultures"?

The most common way of doing that is to use the very popular distinction between the three so-called "publics" of theology, namely the church, the academy and society. One could argue that some people read the Bible primarily as a religious document, as *the revelatory book of the church*; others interpret the Bible primarily as *a classic scholarly document*, to be studied as any other historical and literary text; and still others use the Bible primarily as *a valuable possession of society* at large, of culture, of art, of morality and politics. Obviously, one can further distinguish a large number of variations within each of these broad categories.

> For those who are interested, let me tell this story in a little more detail. Just more than a decade ago, Scholars Press published some of the papers read during a major conference at the University of Chicago, under the title *The Bible as a document of the university*. Edited by Hans Dieter Betz, the papers published were "The Bible as a document of believing communities" by James Barr, "The Bible as a document of the university" by Gerhard Ebeling, and "The Bible and the imagination" by Paul Ricoeur. This division suggests a useful typology. This leaves us with a broad outline for *a threefold typology of reading communities with different interpretive interests*, with different reasons why they read, interpret and use the texts we call the Bible, with different views of these documents: *The Bible as document of believing communities, the Bible as document of society, and the Bible as document of the university*. This also reflects the historical order in which these communities with their diverse interpretive interests developed. At first, Christian believing communities used these documents in a variety of ways for religious purposes. When and where Christianity became a dominant or official religion, more and more groups used these documents, in a variety of ways, for public, social and political purposes. Since the founding of universities, and through the successive radical philosophical and institutional changes that universities experienced, groups within these universities have read these documents in a variety of ways for scholarly purposes. Within each of the three categories of reading communities a wide variety of more particular interpretive interests can obviously be distinguished.
>
> *Amongst believing communities who read the Bible with religious interpretive interests* there obviously exist a wide variety of viewpoints. There are many Christian communities that confess the Bible to be the Scriptures (but they may have widely divergent ways of reading these Scriptures, see e.g. *The Bible in the churches. How different Christians interpret the Scriptures*, edited by Hagen). There are people who claim that the Bible is the Word of God (and they themselves represent a wide spectrum of viewpoints, from, on the one extreme, Protestant fundamentalism, with claims about an inspired, inerrant, literal and authoritative text, as described

by Kathleen Boone in *The Bible tells them so. The discourse of Protestant Fundamentalism*, to far less fundamentalist claims and notions). There are people who regard the Bible as a sacred and revelatory text (see the extremely clear and useful *The revelatory text. Interpreting the New Testament as Sacred Scripture*, by Sandra Schneiders). There are people who appeal to the Protestant *sola scriptura* principle (see the useful collection of studies in *Sola Scriptura. Das reformatorische Schriftprinzip in der säkularen Welt*, edited by Schmid & Mehlhausen). There are people who call the Bible the book of God (see e.g. the contributions and discussion of a recent Arnoldshainer conference, published as *Das Buch Gottes: elf Zugänge zur Bibel*). There are people who approach the Bible as the book of the church (see Phyllis Bird's popular, but instructive, *The Bible as the Church's Book*). There are people who regard the Bible as canon (see e.g Childs and his supporters). There are many people who appeal to the authority of the biblical texts in all kinds of contexts, particularly ethical and doctrinal discussions, saying "The Bible says ..." (see Kelsey's well-known and still very helpful analysis in *The uses of the Bible in Christian ethics*). There are people who appropriate the Bible in the first place as a resource book for worship (in lectionaries, hymns, litanies, prayers) and specifically as a book to preach from; or as a resource book for spiritual reading, mostly private and meditative (see Muto, *A practical guide to spiritual reading*). A very strong and instructive defense of this kind of interpretive interest is to be found in Fowl & Jones, *Reading in communion*. They argue that, in order to be able to read and understand the Scriptures, "Christians need to develop the moral and theological judgement which enables faithful discernment of Scripture's claims on contemporary life," and to develop such judgement, "requires the formation and transformation of the character appropriate to the disciples of Jesus." They even say very clearly: "This requires the acquisition of a very different set of skills, habits and dispositions from those required of the professional biblical scholar ... Christians develop such character in and through the friendships and practices of Christian communities." The important point for our present purposes is that, in spite of all the obvious differences between these approaches, which often causes fundamental differences in the ways in which these respective groups read the same biblical documents, they share the same basic set of interpretive interests, namely that some kind of faith, belief or commitment is necessary in order to read and understand these documents properly.

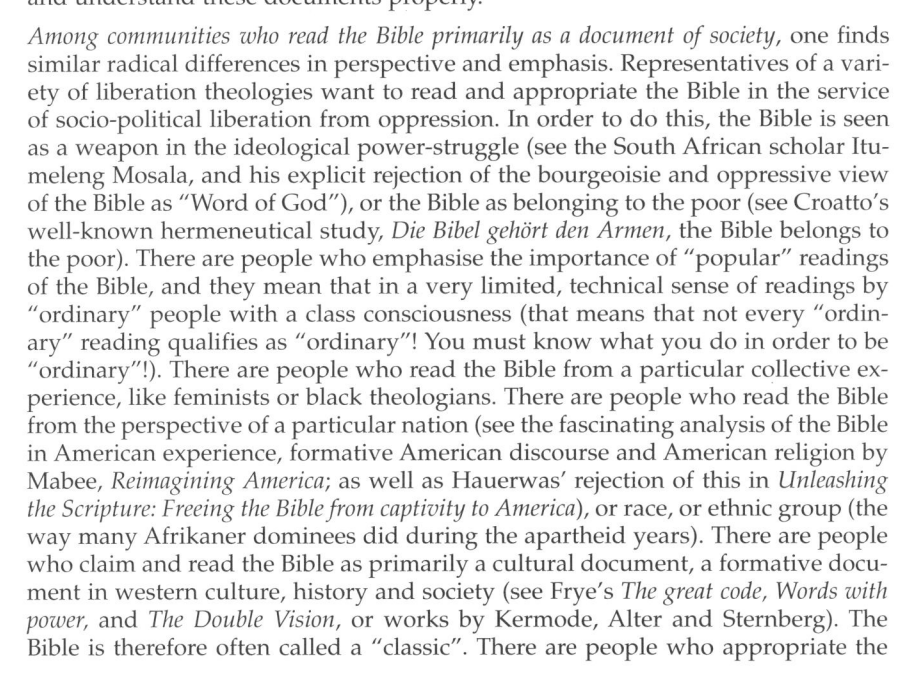

Among communities who read the Bible primarily as a document of society, one finds similar radical differences in perspective and emphasis. Representatives of a variety of liberation theologies want to read and appropriate the Bible in the service of socio-political liberation from oppression. In order to do this, the Bible is seen as a weapon in the ideological power-struggle (see the South African scholar Itumeleng Mosala, and his explicit rejection of the bourgeoisie and oppressive view of the Bible as "Word of God"), or the Bible as belonging to the poor (see Croatto's well-known hermeneutical study, *Die Bibel gehört den Armen*, the Bible belongs to the poor). There are people who emphasise the importance of "popular" readings of the Bible, and they mean that in a very limited, technical sense of readings by "ordinary" people with a class consciousness (that means that not every "ordinary" reading qualifies as "ordinary"! You must know what you do in order to be "ordinary"!). There are people who read the Bible from a particular collective experience, like feminists or black theologians. There are people who read the Bible from the perspective of a particular nation (see the fascinating analysis of the Bible in American experience, formative American discourse and American religion by Mabee, *Reimagining America*; as well as Hauerwas' rejection of this in *Unleashing the Scripture: Freeing the Bible from captivity to America*), or race, or ethnic group (the way many Afrikaner dominees did during the apartheid years). There are people who claim and read the Bible as primarily a cultural document, a formative document in western culture, history and society (see Frye's *The great code*, *Words with power*, and *The Double Vision*, or works by Kermode, Alter and Sternberg). The Bible is therefore often called a "classic". There are people who appropriate the

SECTION B
HERMENEUTICS

Bible as source of inspiration for literature, theatre, art, poetry and cultural expression. There are people who emphasise the role of (both receptive and creative) imagination in reading the Bible. A powerful example of this approach is Josipovici's *The Book of God. A response to the Bible*, with the premise "we have to trust the book itself and see where it will take us." Again in spite of all these crucial differences, there remains a common interpretive interest. In terms of these approaches, people read the Bible in the first place neither for religious nor for scholarly purposes. They all have some other interest, whether personal or social, whether political or aesthetic, in reading the Bible. Neither faith nor academic tools are necessary for their reading of the Bible. In fact, they may often be a hindrance.

Finally, *between communities that read the Bible as a document of the university*, there are equally fundamental differences. Both the institutional setting (seminary; department/school/faculty of religion or theology or divinity; faculty of arts or social sciences; departments of languages, history or culture) and the methods or approaches towards the text lead to important differences. Still, the interpretive interest shared be these communities is a scholarly one, the conviction that neither religious convictions nor social interests should determine objective, scientific interpretation.

Do you agree that this causes a problem? Many 20th century readers of the Bible have become only too aware of the unlimited number of conflicts that are caused by the tensions between these three types of reading communities. Some of us experience some of these conflicts in very personal ways, for example as theological students, as ministers of religion, as teachers of theology, as people involved in social and political struggles, or as scholars. In the apartheid years, people opposing apartheid sometimes said that the Bible had also become "a site of struggle".

But again there are stronger and weaker versions of the conclusions people draw from this fundamental insight into the contextuality of our readings.

In the first place, it is again possible to argue that *some contexts, some social locations are more suited* for reading the Bible or even that there is *only one suitable or legitimate* context in which to read the Bible. In our overview of the history of the use of the Bible we have encountered this same conflict and this same "solution" again and again. Quite often some official church or group acted as if it had the true, proper and only authority to interpret the biblical documents.

In the 20th century this claim is for example very popular amongst liberation theologians. They often speak about the so-called *"epistemological privilege of the poor"*, which simply means that the poor, the marginalized, the suffering people of the world are either in a much better position, or are in fact the only people, able to hear the gospel and to understand the Bible. Their social location of suffering gives them an hermeneutical advantage, the argument goes. Representatives of a number of different liberation theologies have therefore popularized the notion of "contextual hermeneutics", not in a general and descriptive way, simply stating that all readings are inevitably contextual, but in a purposeful, prescriptive way, arguing that a context of poverty, or marginalization, or oppression, or suffering provides the only legitimate context for reading the Bible as the Book of "God's good news to the poor". But this story is told elsewhere in this volume, by different liberation and contextual theologians themselves. There are the voices of Black Theology, Feminist Theology, Womanist Theology, African Theology, and others.

In the second instance it is again possible not to choose between different contexts, but simply to follow the rules, the procedures and the conventions of the particular context in which one finds oneself at a specific point in time. On Sunday when you preach in your congregation, you do it according to the culture that the people there know and respect. (And you hope that your university lecturer in Biblical Studies will never attend the worship service!) During the week, however, or in the university examination, you quote Bultmann and Barth and you talk about socio-historical exegesis in the most difficult jargon you can find, knowing that you will never again use this in real life. That is possible. *Many people* who studied theology are doing it precisely like this. They use completely different interpretations of the Bible in different social locations, with different interpretive interests, according to different interpretive cultures, but somehow they often do not experience that as a conflict of interpretation, because these social locations never meet. The minister or student of theology simply shuttles between these worlds that are so far apart. On Sunday they do this. During the week they do that.

Still other people, however, – and that is a third option – are not satisfied with these worlds being apart. They believe that the worlds should meet, because they can all learn from one another and benefit from the interaction. They believe, for example, that preachers and ordinary Christians can benefit from the use of scholarly methods, but also that scholars can benefit from listening to the way ordinary people read the Bible.

So once again we face the same issue as earlier. Many people, when they hear about the "conflict of interpretations" that is so typical of 20th-century Western Biblical Hermeneutics, would immediately think of all these contexts, and of the so-called "conflicts" they may cause. They think that the conflict of interpretation is caused by the different social locations, and you must either choose, or use whatever you have where you are, or combine them into a single approach and learn from one another.

This is simply a reality of our story, as many of you will know from experience. Most of us regularly face this choice in some form or another. And hidden underneath these questions is an even more fundamental issue for hermeneutics, namely the question: *When is someone a competent reader of the Bible?*

18.4 THE CONFLICT OVER READING

The realisation that our context, that the question who we are, plays an important role in biblical hermeneutics, has gradually shifted our attention to a next question, namely the question: *what we are doing when we read the Bible?* What does "reading" mean? *Why* does our context or location or place or horizon influence our readings? *What do we do with and to the text that we read?*

SECTION B

HERMENEUTICS

You will remember that this question was also one of the major causes of conflict in the history of the use of the Bible. Because of many, often very practical, very material reasons and developments, the way people read the Bible often changed dramatically during the centuries, and each time it caused major conflicts. In our century, once again, this is the case.

This shift in emphasis has also taken place outside the circles of church and theology. So, once again it is the same old story. We also learn from what people are doing in culture and society at large. And during the 20th century people have increasingly been making similar claims in other disciplines, in other circles, as well: in philosophy, in literary studies, in historical studies, and in many others. Perhaps it is fair to say that the most important development during the 20th century regarding Biblical Hermeneutics has been the emergence of so-called literary criticism. This has impacted on Biblical Hermeneutics like the rise of historical consciousness did during the Enlightenment! "Literary criticism" – like "historical criticism" – is an umbrella term, covering many diverse things. Basically, however, it underlines that people have become more aware than ever of the crucial importance of the fact that the biblical documents are precisely that: documents, texts, literary products, like all other literary products. They have, accordingly, focused on aspects of these documents like genre, structure, plot, characterization, development and narrative. The results have been impressive and far reaching in their implications.

Again, one finds a number of theories and approaches, and this is not the place to go into any detail. One specific trend is, however, important. This emphasis has again led to many new expressions. You will hear about *reader-response* theories, about *reception hermeneutics*, about *communicative hermeneutics*, about *audience criticism*, about famous names like Wolfgang Iser and Werner Jauss, and many others. The basic point remains the same: these scholars have made us aware that readers are more actively involved in the reading process than we often think. Reading is not simply reading "what the author intended", or reading "what the document says". Reading is not such a passive process. It is not simply listening, acknowledging, receiving. It is not simply taking notice of the "meaning" or the "content" of the document. No, not at all, these people argue. The reader is making an enormous input. Readers associate, remember, conclude, imagine, expect and "fill gaps" in the texts, providing their own additional information, drawing their own conclusions. That is how reading takes place, which simply means that different readers read the same document in different ways, with diverse experiences and sometimes opposing views of what the document says. To a large extent, (good) authors indeed expect their (competent) readers to do that. But often readers can read against the grain, in ways totally different from what the author intended or what the text "says".

From the circles of Liberation Theology, Severiano Croatto has made this point very strongly. He argues – like so many others – that reading is in fact *the production of meaning*. Reading does not simply mean "finding" meaning that is already there, fixed, eternally, objectively (hidden, embedded, buried) in the text. No, readers also produce meaning, they make meaning, they give meaning to the text, they add meaning to the text.

Obviously when this is true, exciting new possibilities for reading the Bible become possible, and become necessary. For example, it becomes important to ask how people actually read, understood and used a particular document, like a specific biblical pericope. If the text only offers a *potential* reading, which real readers then have to actualize, it becomes a very interesting question how real readers actually did that and are still doing it. It is no longer possible to ignore what other, real-life readers of flesh and blood did with the Bible and are doing with the Bible. If they have been legitimately "producing" new meaning and if they are still legitimately producing new meaning, it becomes interesting to take notice of what they are doing! The study of "actual reception", of the "responses" of "real readers", of "empirical readers", becomes necessary. But obviously, a study of actual reception is only possible where a *record* of such readings exists. Now we can have records of all kinds, both from the past and the present. This has led to a further distinction between historical and contemporary empirical research. Empirical research presupposes real readers, or rather: evidence of their reading in some form or another. Think for example of the *first readers* of biblical texts. How did the people in Rome actually respond to Paul's letter? Unfortunately, the problem is that very little evidence of these first readings exists. We know too little. But we have some evidence of later readings of the texts. These successive readings together constitute the so-called *reception history* of the text. And more and more fascinating 20th century studies are made of specific episodes in this history. Obviously, by far the most accessible source of empirical readings is to be found with *contemporary readers* of the Bible, all around us.

Small wonder that this new interest has been called *"the democratization of biblical interpretation"*! Reading, interpreting and appropriating the Bible is no longer simply the exclusive domain of a privileged few, whether authoritative church bodies or respected scholarly guilds. Particularly in South Africa, this new interest is widespread and popular.

So the conclusion is clear. If all readings are productions of meaning, all readings are equally valid and worth taking note of ... Or not? Or is this a false conclusion?

Again, we hear both very radical and less radical conclusions being drawn from this fundamental insight into the nature of the reading process. A typically radical conclusion comes, for example, from the ranks of so-called *postmodern* and, more specifically, *deconstructionist* thinkers. (I say "so-called" because there is no one fixed meaning for postmodern, and people can call a number of extremely different things "postmodern". See chapters 14 and 27.)

Deconstructionist thinkers deconstruct. They reject and oppose constructions, also constructions of meaning. Whenever someone says that a

Biblical Hermeneutics: the 20th century

SECTION B

HERMENEUTICS

text means this or it means that, a typical deconstructionist would argue that there is no meaning inherent in the text at all, that the only meaning is the meaning we, as readers, give to the text, because in the process of producing our own meaning, we combine it with other texts we have read before and other ideas we bring from somewhere else, and in fact even produce the text as well.

Now, deconstructionists have a point, as you can see. Every word we read (they say), we only understand 1) because we are reminded of other times, other places, and other contexts when and where we also heard those words; and 2) because this word does not mean the same as other words, because it is different from other words. Can you see the point? Words do not have meaning in themselves. They get some meaning *for us* and only *for some time* because they remind us of other texts and of other words. But in principle this process will never stop! When we want to understand the other texts and the other words, we shall again need yet other texts and other words! Meaning is always personal, for me, and temporary, fleeting, just for a moment. When "a text" says something about "love", for example, three people reading the same text and the same word will have different associations attached to the word "love", because they will be reminded of different experiences of love and of different words that do not mean love ... So, they would argue, the text (and the word) does not really mean anything. No-one can "construct" the meaning of a word or text. The reader gives (temporary) meaning to the text (and to the word) because she or he remembers and differentiates. But the next moment, when reading the same text or hearing the same word, the same person can be reminded of other experiences and other differences, so that she or he will give new meanings to the text (and to the word). So, it is clear that deconstructionists have a point. And yet, one must ask if that is really the full story. Doesn't a text mean anything? Doesn't a word mean anything? Can we, arbitrarily, in whichever way we want, give any meaning at all to any word and any text? Is any reading really possible and all readings really equally valid and legitimate? Is there nothing determinate, nothing definite, about a text? Is a text really subject to an infinite number of incompatible, yet all equally valid, readings? Can "meaning" be deferred, be postponed, forever, because a text can presumably always mean something else as well?

A second popular approach is to agree that all readings are legitimate, but to conclude that different readers and readings must therefore listen to one another and converse with one another. The truth, the real meaning, the best reading, will then supposedly be found somewhere in between, where diverse readers try to convince one another of what they heard in the biblical documents. In church circles, this is a typically ecumenical approach. People accept that others read the Bible in their own ways, for good reasons, and they want these different Christian groups to listen to one another and to learn from one another.

A third approach, and often a dominant one, is to be rather sceptical about all of this. For diverse reasons many people are convinced that the reading process must somehow be controlled. They believe that you cannot just do whatever you want to with the Bible and you cannot make the Bible say anything and everything. They believe that there are some constraints in the text, some meaning, some indications of which readings are possible and which are not. They believe that some readings are better than others. They believe that some readings may even be wrong. They believe that the issue of competent readers of the Bible is a legitimate question. They believe that we should indeed look for and meaningfully argue for *more adequate readings*, for *more responsible readings*. And with this notion of "responsibility" in interpretation, we come to yet another stage in the major conflicts over biblical interpretation in the west during this century.

18.5 THE CONFLICT OVER THE RESPONSIBILITY OF READING

During the 20th century, it has become increasingly clear that *reading* the Bible is a *social activity*. Most of the time it has important social consequences. People believe what they hear and read there. They are influenced, formed, moved, inspired, motivated by what they read and hear there. Accordingly, the people with the power, the influence, the positions and the authority to speak on behalf of the Bible are influential indeed. The people who are able to read, to interpret, to explain the Bible, to tell others what to read and when to read and where to read and how to read have considerable power, at least in certain circles within society.

Interpretation of the Bible, even scholarly activity, is therefore also a *social activity* with considerable social effects. People are influenced by these authoritative claims about what the Bible says or does not say.

Writing about the Bible, writing theology, writing books and articles and sermons and expositions is also an extremely powerful *social activity.*

Preaching is a social activity with considerable social implications. Every Sunday, millions of people listen to preachers speaking on behalf of the Bible, on behalf of God. Christians believe that the preachers proclaim the Word of God. They accept that. They (often) try to live according to that.

It is obvious why a well-known North American scholar (David Tracy), discussing hermeneutics, said: *Sometimes, interpretations matter!* Sometimes, biblical interpretation deeply influences our lives.

It is therefore not without reason that a so-called "hermeneutics of suspicion" developed in western thought during the 20th century. Precisely because reading the Bible, interpreting the Bible, using the Bible, preaching from the Bible and writing about the Bible are all social activities, precisely because they are all so powerful, precisely because they all influence our lives, precisely because they all matter, some people have become suspicious.

The three so-called *"masters of suspicion"* taught us to be suspicious of three different processes. *Marx* taught us to be suspicious of *interests*. We must – for example – ask: Why do these people prefer these texts (and not others)? Why do they read these texts like this (and not in different ways)? Why do they want us to behave in this way? Whose interests will be served if we were to believe them? *Nietzsche* taught us to be suspicious of *power*. We must – for example – ask: Are these people not using their readings of the Bible to influence, to force, to coerce us? Do they not use religious language, God-talk, appeals to the Bible, simply to legitimate, to give more authority and power to their own ideas and viewpoints? And *Freud* taught us to be suspicious of *unconscious* elements, needs, longings and desires that influence and drive us and may determine our

SECTION B
HERMENEUTICS

readings of the Bible, even without us being aware of the fact! In hermeneutical thought in the 20th century these ideas have been developed further by many others. You will often hear of people like Habermas who developed the notion of interests, and Foucault who developed the notion of power, and Lacan, or Derrida, who developed the notion of the unconscious. For biblical interpretation, the general implication of what they have taught us is easy to understand: We must be careful of readings, we must be suspicious, we must not take every interpretation for granted, we must not believe everyone who appeals to the Bible.

It is obvious why many South Africans have strongly agreed with these contributions. We have seen and experienced how the Bible and how interpretations of the Bible have been used to serve interests, to legitimate power-relations, and to mask unconscious desires and motives. It is also obvious why particularly women are using the insights of a hermeneutics of suspicion to defend themselves against the oppressive male usage of the Bible so widespread in our culture and society.

It is for reasons like this that talk about *the politics of interpretation*, or *the ethics of reading*, or *the ethics of interpretation*, or *the ethics of writing* has become commonplace in 20th century hermeneutics, and especially popular in South Africa. South Africans have often said that the interpretation of the Bible has itself become *a site of struggle*. We have been warned against *ideological* readings of the Bible. Ideology originally referred to the use of ideas in order to fight a social struggle, the use of ideas in a public, social and political conflict, the use of ideas to serve the public interest of your own group. Readings of the Bible can indeed be ideological in this sense. They can become weapons in a social struggle, serving the interests of groups.

These expressions all refer to the fact that not every reading is acceptable. They suggest that there is power at work in biblical interpretation, and that questions of *responsibility* therefore become crucial.

It is also clear why rhetorical criticism has become a popular trend in feminist, but also in South African theological and hermeneutical circles. "Rhetoric" reminds us that the important question is not only what is said, but also *by whom* it is said, *why*, and to *whom*. This applies to the biblical documents themselves, but particularly also to our interpretations of these biblical documents! Who is reading the Bible? And why? And for whom? On whose behalf? These are important questions.

But what is the answer, the solution? Some people become so suspicious, so critical, so sceptical, that they reject every possible usage of the Bible as irresponsible and illegitimate.

Some, however, prefer to say that it is indeed possible to interpret the Bible responsibly, that it is not necessary to reject every usage of the Bible. But then the questions remain: *When* is a reader of the Bible competent? And *when* is an act of interpretation of the Bible responsible, adequate, legitimate, acceptable? When do we read *this book* responsibly? This brings us to a fifth and final conflict of interpretations, namely the debate about the nature of this book, this document, which we call "The Bible".

18.6 THE CONFLICT OVER THE BIBLE

Somehow this may be the most fundamental cause of all the other conflicts about biblical interpretation. Ultimately we often disagree about the nature of this text, the nature of this book. Bernard Lategan recently said: "There is an urgent need to change the order of our questions. Instead of asking: What is the best method to use?, the first question ought to be: What is the 'object' to be interpreted?" (Mouton et al, 1988:68)

We already touched on some of the conflicting answers people give to this question when we thought about the different social locations in which we read the Bible. In our communities of faith, we regard the Bible as *a religious document*, in society we often regard it as *a cultural classic*, in the academy we often regard it as *an ancient literary collection*. And, as we have seen, each of these can be further divided into a large number of views. For example, not all people who regard the Christian Bible as a religious document read it in the same way. Not at all! In fact, some of the most bitter conflicts within Christian and church circles arise from the fact that some believers reject the way other believers view the Bible! This is one of the most fertile grounds for accusations of false teaching and heresy! In a recent study, called *Models for Scripture* (1994), John Goldingay distinguishes between a number of ways according to which Christians see the Bible: Scripture as witnessing tradition, Scripture as authoritative canon, Scripture as inspired Word, and Scripture as experienced revelation. One can add even more, or prefer other expressions. Christians, believers, who all attach religious value to the Bible, disagree (sometimes strongly) about the way to express this value. And obviously their different views of Scripture will also lead to different approaches to the reading, the use, and the interpretation of Scripture. That is clear for anyone to see. Yet they will share some respect for the authority and/or power of the Bible.

The differences in approach and the differences in interpretation become even larger when people do not see the Bible as a religious book in the first place, as is often the case in society and the academy. It is because of these basic options – *with* their many subdivisions – that major conflicts of interpretation are experienced.

In fact, we have seen that this basic option was often also the main reason for conflicts during the history of biblical interpretation: during the formation of the canon, during the time of the Reformation, during the Enlightenment.

Somehow all the other conflicts come together in this one: The question whether people expect something from the text or not influences the conflict between explanation and understanding; the question what the text is definitely determines the conflict over the question who may read this text, to whom it properly belongs; the question whether we can do with the Bible what we like while reading, or whether there is a message, something in the text that readers must respect, has a bearing on the conflict over the question what reading is; and, obviously, the view of the text will impact on the notion of the responsibility of interpretation.

Small wonder that someone like Jeanrond argues that we must first talk about the nature of the text before we can talk about the nature of interpretation.

8.7 THEOLOGICAL HERMENEUTICS?

Is this the full story of Bible reading and -interpretation in the 20th century in the west? Does it in the end result in conflict upon conflict, with no agreement, no consensus, no vision? Not at all. Many theologians and most Christians (still) read the Bible with trust, with confidence, with expectation. They practice a hermeneutics of consent, of engagement, of trust, of transformation; in short, a theological hermeneutics.

Perhaps one can summarise much of what we have learnt by saying that we now know that we must remember to *respect the other*.

As people who live since the Enlightenment and the historical awareness it brought about, we must respect *the otherness of these ancient literary texts*, the fact that they speak to us over centuries, and from cultural worlds far different to our own. As people who live in the late 20th century, after the so-called "linguistic turn" and the growing importance of literary theory, and therefore read these documents as strange literary documents, with strange genres (prophecy, law, gospels, parables, apocalyptic), we acknowledge that we must respect this literary *otherness* of these documents, their structure, their sign systems, their pragmatic intent, their communicative function.

As people who read these documents in a tradition, a living tradition, of mothers and fathers who read these same documents through the centuries and taught us to read them also, we must respect *the otherness of this tradition*, its diverse voices, its witnesses, its summaries, whether in doctrine, song or morality of what these readers before us read and heard.

As people who read these documents in community with others, with sisters and brothers, close and far, we must respect their readings and their interpretations, *the otherness of other readers*. Therefore we must read together with others. As people who read these documents from our own social locations, from the places where we are, we can not ignore our own experiences and questions and the experiences and questions of people around us with regard to these documents. We must respect *the otherness of new contexts* and the light they can throw on these documents. As people who know that interpretations matter, that reading is power, that the Bible has been used as well as abused, that the Bible has been used for terrible purposes, as a weapon against humanity and against creation itself, we must respect *others when they are critical* of what we do with our interpretations.

And finally, as people who hope to hear God's Word speaking to us from these documents, we must respect this Other, the transformative power of these documents that we call the Bible. Somehow, in theological hermeneutics, Christians believe that this Bible touches us, changes us, inspires us, moves us, saves us. After all, that is why we continue to read these documents.

READING LIST

There are many excellent *studies available on 20th century hermeneutics*. Perhaps the single most impressive one is A. Thiselton's recent study *New horizons in hermeneutics*, Zondervan Publishing House, Grand Rapids Michigan, 1992. It is intended as "an advanced textbook on hermeneutics" and discusses everything and everyone in great detail! He is also known for his earlier work, *The two horizons*, Eerdmans, Grand Rapids Michigan, 1980.

Another extremely useful study is W.G. Jeanrond's *Theological hermeneutics. Development and significance*, Crossroad, New York, 1991 (with a very helpful bibliography, on pages 207–212). It is also a textbook, but much easier than Thiselton's. Jeanrond is known for his earlier study, *Text and interpretation as categories of theological thinking*, Crossroad, New York, 1988. You can read anything that he writes on hermeneutics.

If you are looking for something shorter or something specific, try the very good *A dictionary of biblical interpretation*, London, SCM Press, (eds.), R.J. Coggins & J.L. Houlden, 1990. It is a wonderful source, with very good contributions.

You can also read anything you find by Bernard C. Lategan. Two of his influential essays in South African circles are, 1984 "Current issues in the hermeneutical debate", *Reading a text. Source, Reception, Setting. Neotestamentica* 18, 1–17, and 1992 "Hermeneutics", *Anchor Bible Dictionary III*, New York, Doubleday, 149–154.

Finally, you will find many books (often edited) by Donald K. McKim in the libraries that you can use. A particularly helpful one is *A guide to contemporary hermeneutics. Major trends in biblical interpretation*, Wm B. Eerdmans, Grand Rapids MI, 1986.

On the conflict between explanation and understanding, one could read the more philosophical introductions again (Jeanrond, Thiselton). On the different scholarly methods available, we have a number of very interesting collections available that explain and often even demonstrate the diverse and sometimes conflicting results of these methods. See e.g. *Fishing for Jonah*, E. Conradie, D. Lawrie et al., University of the Western Cape, Bellville, 1995; and *To each its own meaning. An introduction to biblical criticisms and their application*, (eds.), S.L. McKenzie & S.R. Haynes, Westminster/John Knox Press, Louisville, KY, 1993. Some of the best scholars in the world in this field have contributed, including Yehoshua Gitay from Cape Town.

On the issue of the (proper) readers of the Bible, see the introductory essays in Betz, H.D. (ed.). 1981. *The Bible as a document of the university*, Chico, CA, Scholars Press.

On the Bible as a book of believers, see e.g. Bird, P.A. 1982. *The Bible as the Church's book*, Philadelphia, Westminster Press; Fowl, S.E. & Jones, L.G. 1991. *Reading in communion. Scripture and ethics in Christian life*, London, SPCK; or Jodock, D. 1989. *The church's Bible. Its contemporary authority*. Minneapolis, Fortress Press.

On the importance of ordinary readers, the South African theologian Gerald West has done important work. See e.g. his thesis, 1991. *Biblical hermeneutics of liberation. Modes of reading the Bible in the South African context*, Pietermaritzburg, Cluster Publications, or essays like 1991. "The relationship between different modes of reading (the Bible) and the ordinary reader", *Scriptura* S9, 87–110; or 1993. "The interface between trained readers and ordinary readers in liberation hermeneutics", *Neotestamentica* 27/1, 165–180.

Kathleen C Boone, *The Bible tells them so. The discourse of Protestant fundamentalism*, London, SCM Press, 1989, offers a fascinating study of fundamentalist Bible reading; Mark A. Noll, *Between faith and criticism. Evangelical scholarship and the Bible in America*, Grand Rapids, MI, Baker Book House, 1986, provides very instructive information on the debates between evangelicals and scholarship (in America); and Donald K. McKim also edited a beautiful volume called *The Bible in theology & preaching. How preachers use Scripture*, Abingdon Press, Nashville TE, 1994.

On cultural readings of the Bible, see the impressive *The postmodern Bible. The Bible and culture collective*, Yale University Press, 1995.

On the reading-process, you will find some of the most influential essays in a volume edited by Jane P. Tompkins, *Reader-response criticism: From formalism to post-structuralism*, John Hopkins University Press, Baltimore, 1980. (But be warned: these es-

18

Biblical Hermeneutics: the 20th century

SECTION B
HERMENEUTICS

says are difficult. It seems that people, when they write about the importance of reading, make reading very complicated ...)

South African biblical scholars have done some very good work in this regard as well. Two helpful essays are Combrink, H.J.B. 1988. "Readings, readers and authors: an orientation", *Neotestamentica* 22, 189–204, and Lategan, B.C. 1992. "Reader response theory/audience criticism", *Anchor Bible Dictionary V*, New York, Doubleday, 625–628.

Two volumes of well-known journals are also very instructive, namely *The Bible and its readers, Concilium 1991/1*, Beuken, W., Freyne, S. & Weiler, A. (eds.), and *Semeia* 48, 1989. *Reader perspectives on the New Testament.*

And, since literary theory has made such a major contribution towards the appreciation for the reading-process, someone may want to read about the Bible and literary theory. An interesting volume is *The book and the text. The Bible and literary theory*, (ed.). R. Schwartz, Cambridge, MA, Basil Blackwell, 1990.

On the responsibility of reading, one could read some of the essays in the interesting volumes by Lundin, R. Thiselton, A.C. & Walhout, C. 1985. *The responsibility of hermeneutics*, Grand Rapids: Wm Eerdmans, or by Jobling D. et al. 1991. *The Bible and the politics of exegesis*, Cleveland, OH, The Pilgrim Press.

Two major studies in this regard that have recently been published, are D. Patte, *Ethics of biblical interpretation. A reevaluation*, Westminster John Knox Press, Louisville, KY, 1995; and *Reading from this place. Volume I. Social location and biblical interpretation in the United States*, F. Segovia & M.A. Tolbert (eds.). Augsburg Fortress Press, Minneapolis, 1995.

A South African, Jan Botha, has written a very good doctoral thesis on the ethics of reading, *Reading Romans 13: Aspects of the ethics of interpretation in a controversial text*, D.Th dissertation, University of Stellenbosch (1991). It will be published in the USA in 1995, in a scholarly series.

On the conflict over the nature of the Bible itself, one could read Goldingay, J. 1994 *Models for Scripture*, Wm B. Eerdmans, Grand Rapids MI, or an excellent study by Sandra Schneiders, *The revelatory text: Interpreting the New Testament as sacred Scripture*, San Francisco, Harper, 1991.

An interesting volume is *The Bible in the churches. How different Christians interpret the Scriptures*, Hagen, K. et al. (eds.). New York, Paulist Press, 1985.

On theological hermeneutics, three excellent contributions are Kelsey, D.H. 1975. *The uses of Scripture in recent theology*. Philadelphia, Fortress Press; Tracy, D. 1990. "On reading the Scriptures theologically", in *Theology and dialogue*, Marshall, B.D. (ed.). Notre Dame, Notre Dame University Press, 35–68; and Wood, C.M. 1981. *The formation of Christian understanding An essay in theological hermeneutics*, Westminster Press, Philadelphia.

Several churches or church consultations have also published useful studies. Three examples that you may find interesting are *The Journal of Ecumenical Studies*, Vol XXVIII, Summer 1991/3 (on the Consultation "Scripture, Tradition, and the Church," with contributions by i.a. Rusch, Marty, Meyer, Gassmann, Gros, Reumann, Froehlich, Fackre); the Catholic document by the Pontifical Biblical Commission, *The interpretation of the Bible in the Church*, Vatican City 1993; or the document by the Reformed Ecumenical Council, *Hermeneutics and ethics*.

In the volume edited by Watson, F., 1993. *The open text. New directions for biblical studies?* London, SCM Press, one finds a variety of very interesting contributions on contemporary possibilities for Bible study.

I have not included references to all the other forms of hermeneutics that will also be discussed in this book. Remember, however, that some of the most exciting hermeneutical work is done in those circles.

BIBLIOGRAPHY

Betz, H.D. (ed.). 1981. *The Bible as a document of the university.* Chico, CA: Scholars Press.

Bird, P.A. 1982. *The Bible as the Church's book*. Philadelphia: Westminster Press.
Boone, K.C. 1989. *The Bible tells them so: The discourse of Protestant fundamentalism*. London: SCM Press.
Fowl, S.E. & Jones, L.G. 1991. *Reading in communion. Scripture and ethics in Christian life*. London: SPCK.
Godingay, J. 1994. *Models for Scripture*. Grand Rapids, MI: Wm B. Eerdmans.
Jeanrond, W.G. 1991. *Theological hermeneutics: Development and significance*. New York: Crossroad.
– 1988. *Text and interpretation as categories of theological thinking*. New York: Crossroad.
Kelsey, D.H. 1975. *The uses of Scripture in recent theology*. Philadelphia: Fortress Press.
Lategan, B.C. 1984. "Reading a text: Source, Reception, Setting." *Neotestamentica* 18, 1–17.
– 1992. "Reader response theory/audience criticism." *Anchor Bible Dictionary V*. New York: Doubleday.
– 1992. "Hermeneutics." *Anchor Bible Dictionary III*. New York: Doubleday.
Schneiders, S. 1991. *The revelatory text: Interpreting the New Testament as sacred Scripture*. San Francisco: Harper.
The postmodern Bible. The Bible and culture collective. 1995. Yale University Press.

Evangelical Hermeneutics

William Klein

19.1 INTRODUCTION

After reading this essay students should understand:
- the *definition* of hermeneutics;
- the essential *presuppositions* evangelical interpreters bring to the task of biblical interpretation;
- the *objective* of interpretation – what is the goal of the interpretation of the Bible according to Evangelicals;
- the essential *method* by which a student can come as close as possible to the true meaning of a passage of Scripture;
- how to move from the meaning of a text to *valid application* of that meaning;
- the *outcomes* of interpretation: the uses to which we put the Scriptures rightly interpreted.

19.2 DEFINITION

A definition is required right at the outset. The term *hermeneutics* comes from words in the Greek language that mean "to explain, interpret or translate" or the results of that process: "interpretation or translation". Using this verb, Luke writes that Jesus *explained* to the two disciples on the road to Emmaus what the Scriptures said about him (Luke 24:27). However, this task of explaining the text is today rather called exegesis, while hermeneutics is used for the theory behind this task of exegesis – the principles we use to understand what a section of the Bible means.

Unconsciously, we all apply *hermeneutics* – that is, principles of interpretation – whenever we engage in any communication process. When we converse with a friend, read a newspaper or watch a television programme, we employ hermeneutics, even though in our own culture and

SECTION B

HERMENEUTICS

in familiar surroundings we are usually completely unaware of the process. We decode what we hear and settle on its meaning.

But when we get out of our own culture or language, or into some unfamiliar domain, we become aware of our inability to understand. If you should stumble into a lecture on astrophysics, you might hear terms like "antiquarks", the "weak anthropic principle", or "neutrinos". Help! you exclaim. You need help in making sense of what you heard.

So it is when we come to understand the Bible. Though we may have it translated into a language we can read, when we open its pages we enter a world that is very different from our own. The greatest challenges to understanding the meaning of the Bible grow out of distances. First, we encounter the *distance* of *time*. We are far removed – over nineteen centuries – from the time the last words in the Bible were written. *Cultural* distances separate us from the worlds of the biblical writers. We do not easily understand the meaning of all of the cultural practices reflected on the Bible's pages. Most of us are unfamiliar with the *geography* of the biblical worlds. We cannot picture what life was like for people in very different parts of the world. In addition to all of the above, we are separated from the biblical writers by *language*. We do not speak Hebrew, Aramaic, nor the Hellenistic Greek of the first century CE. We may also be unfamiliar with the literary conventions of the ancient authors.

Our point should be clear: in order to understand the meaning of the Bible, we need principles and methods which will help us bridge these distances – be they linguistic, historical, social or cultural – between the ancient and modern worlds. To avoid interpretation that is arbitrary, erroneous, or that simply suits our own (or someone else's) personal preferences or prejudices, the biblical reader needs rules or principles for guidance. A deliberate attempt to interpret on the basis of sensible and agreed-upon principles provides the best guarantee that an interpretation will be accurate. We assume that people communicate in order to be understood, and this includes the authors of the Scriptures. Hermeneutics provides a strategy that will enable us to understand what an author or speaker intended to communicate.

19.3 EVANGELICAL PRESUPPOSITIONS FOR INTERPRETATION

One matter is very important to assert at the outset: methods and approaches have proliferated through the centuries (see chapters 17 and 18). From interpreting texts very literally to wild and expansive allegorizing; from interpretation as the handmaiden of church tradition to the "no-holds-barred" interpretation of rationalistic scientism; and from a view that the Bible represents God's revelation to one that sees the Bible merely as a human document – the Bible has been subjected to a seemingly unending array of investigative methods. Who is to say what we ought to do, or how the Bible should be handled? Readers of this essay will feel more attracted to some of the methods or perspectives than to others. But the question is really not one of our preference nor which one(s) might attract us more. The question is one of "rightness". What is the best way of interpreting the Bible? Which method (assuming we could limit it to one at the moment) is most in keeping with the character of the Bible and does the Bible the most justice?

It is at this point that Evangelicals resort to a discussion of *presuppositions*. Much depends on our starting point and the answer to this question: what is the *nature* of the document we are interpreting? Another issue is also crucial: *who* is doing the interpreting? Our answers to these questions matter greatly. We need to consider carefully both of these in turn. In fact, they make all the difference in the methods and outcomes of interpretation. All interpreters operate with their own presuppositions. A distinct set of presuppositions sets one interpreter off from another. What are those that characterize the evangelical?

19.3.1 Presuppositions about the nature of the Bible

Evangelicals believe they stand in the long line of Hebrew and Christian believers who affirmed that God is a God who reveals Himself, and that the Bible is the collection of God's written revelation to his people. In other words, the Bible is *inspired*. It is not merely inspiring; it owes its origin to divine inspiration. The texts they appeal to include 2 Timothy 3:16 and 2 Peter 1:20–21. Hence, the Bible is a supernatural document; it is God's self-disclosure. This in no way denies that the Bible is also a very human book. God's people composed the books of the Bible out of their own experiences and from the vantage point of their own cultures and circumstances. But in the midst of all that, God used their writings to convey his message.

But what is the relationship between the written texts the authors produced and that divine message? Can we assume that the Bible is to be equated with the "Word of God"? Or does God's Word come to us *through* the reading or proclamation of the Bible? Does the Bible merely *contain* the word of God or does it somehow *become* the Word of God? These are important questions that anyone who seeks to interpret the Bible must address.

For Evangelicals, the Bible is the Word of God. They often use the terms "plenary" inspiration and "verbal" inspiration to convey their belief that the entire Bible is inspired down to the very words. This suggests a crucial implication: the Bible is *authoritative and true*. What God says is true; He does not deceive. Hence, to reject the teaching of the Bible is to reject what God has inspired his people to write. Since God is true and Truth, what He has revealed is faithful and reliable.[1] But what does it mean for a document like the Bible to be true or reliable? True in what sense? Are only the underlying realities to which it points true? Does it only teach what is true morally or ethically? Normally, Evangelicals would not want to limit the Bible's truth merely to the Bible's essential

19

Evangelical Hermeneutics

---

1 Obviously we can't defend this view here, nor consider all its implications or ramifications. In my estimation, however, this is the view assumed in the New Testamet itself. See John 10:35; 17:17; Titus 1:2; and Matthew 5:18. Likewise, the Psalmist declares that all God's commands are utterly perfect (119:96).

SECTION

B

HERMENEUTICS

message or its structure or view of reality.

Yet to posit that the Bible is "true" is not a simple matter for Evangelicals. Evangelicalism does not represent a monolithic whole on these issues. The terms infallibility and inerrancy – terms fraught with controversy – often figure into the debate. (See chapter 5 on Evangelical Theology.)[2] Some insist on using these terms in the belief that what they convey represents the Bible's own view (e.g. Matt 5:17–20; John 10:34–35) as well as the view of the believing church throughout its history.[3] We need to observe a bit of the range of positions among Evangelicals.

There are other Evangelicals who are clearly unhappy with the concept of the Bible as an errorless or infallible document. They emphasize that the Bible, being the Word of God, is still a human book, and thus they distinguish between its spiritual and incidental teaching. Though it is true in its major tenets – in matters of faith and the plan of salvation – they allege the Bible does contain factual errors and inconsistencies. These occur especially in matters of science or history, or in numbers or dates. Simply put, the Bible does not measure up to what we today consider as scientific precision. They eschew major attempts at harmonizing various texts or authors, believing that they may indeed conflict with one another. They remain convinced that such a view best does justice to the data of the biblical documents themselves. Dewey Beegle says the Bible contains not only revelation from God, but also religious and theological judgements of many fallible humans, representing merely human traditions. The Bible is "inspired from cover to cover, human mistakes and all."[4] For these Evangelicals, inerrancy is a dogma as unacceptable as papal infallibility.

Other Evangelicals prefer to speak in terms of a more limited inerrancy: the Bible is true in the main, but that essential truthfulness does not extend to every detail.[5] An example of this type of approach is evident in R. Gundry's work, *Matthew. A Commentary on His Literary and Theological*

---

2 The issue of inerrancy has caused much controversy and division in the Southern Baptist Convention in recent years. Reports on the issues may be found in P.D. Wise, "Biblical Inerrancy: Pro or Con?" *Theological Educator* 37 (1988): 15–44; R. James, (ed.). *The Unfettered Word: Southern Baptists Confront the Authority-Inerrancy Questions* (Waco: Word, 1987); and C. Sullivan, *Toward a Mature Faith: Does Biblical Inerrancy Make Sense?* (Decatur, GA: SBC Today, 1990).
3 Some of those who make this assertion include J.N.D. Kelly, *Early Christian Doctrines*, rev. ed. (San Francisco: Harper & Row, 1978); T. George, *Theology of the Reformers* (Nashville: Broadman, 1988) and B.B. Warfield, *The Inspiration and Authority of the Bible* (Philadelphia: Presbyterian and Reformed, 1948). An opposing interpretation occurs in J.B. Rogers and D.K. McKim, *The Authority and Interpretation of the Bible: An Historical Approach* (San Francisco: Harper & Row, 1979).
4 D.M. Beegle, *Scripture, Tradition and Infallibility*, rev. ed. (Grand Rapids: Eerdmans, 1973), p. 208. Beegle is an evangelical who denies inerrancy. See also his *The Inspiration of Scripture* (Grand Rapids: Eerdmans, 1963).
5 This is the contention of, *inter alia*, J.B. Rogers and D.K. McKim, *The Authority and Interpretation of the Bible: An Historical Approach*. Advocates of limited inerrancy include S.T. Davis, *The Debate About the Bible: Inerrancy versus Infallibility* (Philadelphia: Westminster, 1977) and C. Pinnock, *The Scripture Principle* (San Francisco: Harper & Row, 1984). An adamant critic of inerrancy (clearly not an evangelical) is J. Barr. See his *Beyond Fundamentalism* (Philadelphia: Westminster, 1983) as well as several earlier books.

Art.⁶ Essentially, Gundry (an avowed Evangelical), believes that the Jewish literary tradition was more concerned with purpose than with historicity. Writing from this standpoint, Matthew felt free to take artistic liberties with historical facts in order to convey his theological message in the best possible way. We must judge Matthew's accuracy not on the basis of whether the "facts" presented in his Gospel actually occurred (many of which, Gundry asserts, did not), but on the basis of how well he succeeded in getting his message about Jesus across to his readers. It is this message that is conveyed inerrantly and which we are to trust.

Full or complete inerrantists, on the other hand, insist on the truthfulness of the Bible in all its details, including history. Such a view leads these evangelicals to seek to harmonize conflicts, for they see them as only *apparent* contradictions or errors.⁷ At the same time, most would insist that their assertion of the Bible's truthfulness must be properly nuanced.⁸ Inerrancy, properly speaking, applies only to the original autographs, not the copies or versions we possess today. What God inspired the original authors to write is inerrant; errors may indeed have crept into the manuscripts during centuries of transcription and translation. At the same time, inerrancy does not imply a dictation theory of inspiration. That is, verbal, plenary inspiration does not mean that God dictated the words of the Bible so that the authors functioned as mere typists or stenographers. In fact, God worked in and with the authors in the process of their writing so that, employing their own abilities, cultures, and backgrounds, God moved them to write what He wanted to say. Nor do inerrantists of this type believe that the actual words of Scripture have special power. They wish to insist upon the critical study of Scripture and not deny its humanness: we must engage in historico-grammatical exegesis to get at its meaning. In other words, inerrancy does not settle issues of hermeneutics and application. Inerrancy does not imply a crass literalism. It agrees that the Bible often does not use exact language (that is, what we would expect today given our scientific precision). All inerrancy says is that what the Bible says is *true*.⁹

So these Evangelicals affirm the Bible is true in the sense that all it

---

6 (Grand Rapids: Eerdmans, 1982). The second edition, revised in view of criticisms, has a new subtitle: *A Commentary on His Handbook for a Mixed Church under Persecution* (Grand Rapids: Eerdmans, 1994).

7 The success of this approach can be seen in C.L. Blomberg, *Historical Reliability of the Gospels* (Leicester, UK and Downers Grove, IL: InterVarsity, 1987).

8 For a sensibly nuanced view of inerrancy see P. Feinberg, "The Meaning of Inerrancy," in *Inerrancy*, N. Geisler (ed.) (Grand Rapids: Zondervan, 1979), pp. 267–304. At the same time, many inerrantists don't particularly like the term itself. What it affirms about the Bible's truthfulness is laudable and important. But the term "inerrancy" does not occur in the Bible, and it implies a kind of mathematical precision to readers today that is not always appropriate for the texts themselves.

9 Inerrantists insist that the following are *not* errors: non-agreement in parallel accounts, since authors employed their own styles and purposes; differences in how complete or final statements are, for Scripture evidences a progress of revelation; inexact quotations, given that we cannot apply modern standards to quotations in an ancient culture; scientifically imprecise statements of natural phenomena, since the biblical descriptions are popular, not technical; and difficulties or problem references, since our knowledge is still limited and, admittedly, some problems are not resolved as yet (but this does not mean they cannot).

SECTION B

HERMENEUTICS

intends to teach is true. What the Bible's authors intended to communicate by their writings will not lead their readers astray in any way. Truthfulness is determined by the human authors' intentions, intentions superintended (or inspired, to use the Bible's term) by the Holy Spirit. This is why, as we will see below, the discussion of the Bible's genres is so crucial. We judge a work's truthfulness in terms of what the author sought to say via the kind of literature employed. When Isaiah 55:12 asserts that "... all the trees of the field shall clap their hands," we do not accuse the writer of writing nonsense or error. The genre of poetry governs the line's truthfulness.

The fact that the Bible is divinely inspired also implies that it is a *spiritual document*. That is, more than being merely an inspiring book, the Bible, through the illumination of the Holy Spirit, has the capacity to change lives spiritually. The Bible embodies God's living word, a word that has inherent power (Isa 55; Heb 4:12–13). In it we find life-giving and life-changing truths because they derive from the all powerful God Himself. It gives spiritual direction to our thoughts and guidance to our lives. To treat the Bible as a merely human book – even a very good one – robs it of its central purpose as God's revelation to his people.

The Bible is a book characterized by both *unity* and *diversity*. Its origin as God's revelation achieves its unity. This produces the Bible's overall coherence and keeps it from being contradictory. In it God presents his message to his creatures. Yet it comes through many authors over many centuries, through various cultures in a diverse collection of kinds of literature. These realities make the Bible a diverse book. We do the Bible an injustice when we neglect or ignore either of these realities.

Evangelicals assume that ordinary people can understand the Bible. It is not the domain only of the clergy, scholars or experts. Nor is the Bible a puzzle or cryptogram whose key only some enlightened ones possess. Those willing and qualified to handle the Bible on its terms can understand its meaning.

Finally, Evangelicals assume that the Bible has been given to the church as a collection of sixty-six books that constitute a Canon – the authoritative and complete record of God's revelation to his people.

19.3.2 Presuppositions about the nature of the interpreter

People come to the Bible with different concerns or agendas, with different presuppositions and world-views, and from different backgrounds and cultures. As a book, the Bible can serve many purposes for students or readers. Evangelicals believe, however, that correct interpretation must take the Bible on its own terms, and, therefore, those readers who understand and adopt those terms are in the best position to understand its message accurately. For example, a reader who is convinced on other grounds that miracles cannot happen will not understand the gospel accounts of Jesus' miracles in the same way as another reader who is open to the occurrence of such supernatural events. Interpreting the Bible is not only a matter of techniques and tactics; it is also a question of the stance of the interpreter. What do you see when you read a text? What do you think when you encounter its claims or read its descriptions?

As interpreters, Evangelicals seek to work within the Bible's own framework, and they accept the existence of an all-powerful, all-knowing God and the reality of the supernatural. They accept the Bible as divine revelation, and, as such, are predisposed to bow to its message (even if they don't like what it teaches). This stance makes all the difference. This position is not merely one of blind dogmatism or of pious preference. Evangelicals believe they have sufficient grounds for such an approach – that there are rational, historically defensible arguments to accept for instance, the reality of the miraculous.

19.3.3 Presuppositions about methods

Evangelicals are committed to get at the true meaning of the biblical text. Hence they are open to all methods that open up that meaning. Since the Bible is a collection of historical and literary documents which embody God's revelation to his people, any historical or literary techniques that help us understand and unpack the meaning of those documents are to be embraced. Certain methods in the hands of some interpreters clearly violate Evangelical presuppositions that were mentioned above. For example, some form critics may assume that miracles cannot happen and so explain the presence of a miracle in a gospel account as an embellishment of the later church. So a method may subscribe to, or grow out of, an anti-supernaturalistic presupposition. Evangelicals feel it improper to employ any method that, by its very nature, denies or weakens the Bible's claims about its own origin in God's divine revelation.

In the end the issue is one of authority. Who possesses the final authority, God or his creatures? Given the Evangelical presupposition of the divine character of the Bible – it is God's Word – they allow the Bible to have the final say. They study and interpret it with what they deem to be the best and most appropriate methods to gain an understanding of its message. But they eschew any approaches whose very nature denies the Bible its rightful authority – and that is a matter of presupposition.

19.4 THE OBJECTIVE OF EVANGELICAL HERMENEUTICS

Given what we have observed in the preceding sections, the goal of interpretation for Evangelical interpreters is the *meaning of the text*. That is, the objective of hermeneutics is to enable interpreters to arrive at *the meaning of the text that the biblical writers or editors intended their readers to understand*. Certainly this is not the only approach interpreters may take. Personal experience, plus a review of the survey of the history of interpretation, indicates that people have various objectives when they read the Bible. Some may hope that the Bible "speaks to them", whatever that might mean. Some expect "meaning" to be created in their encounter with a biblical text. On a more subtle level, church communities or denominations want texts to affirm their established understanding of theology. They want the texts to support what they already believe.

Evangelicals affirm that the proper goal of the task of interpretation is

SECTION

B

HERMENEUTICS

to extract the *meaning of the texts themselves*. That is, they seek the meaning the people at the time of the texts' composition would have been most likely to accept. That is the goal of interpretation. Once they possess that textual meaning (what the author intended to say, recovered from the text itself), Christians can then apply that meaning to their lives, communities, and world. But application must follow from and grow out of the correct meaning of the text itself. Both these steps require elaboration. First we address the question of meaning. Then we must ask how we move to application.

We cannot always perceive a text's meaning accurately or easily. Our modern preunderstandings and prejudices may cloud our ability to see the meaning clearly. But these difficulties do not obscure the goal: the text's meaning. It is God's word that we seek to unpack; only the inspired text possesses authority as God's word. Any other meaning besides the text's meaning is a meaning imposed onto the text. For the Evangelical, this would violate the divine character and purpose of the Scriptures: to reveal God's meaning.

Further elucidation is in order. To repeat: "The meaning of a text is: *that which the words and grammatical structures of that text disclose about the probable intention of its author/editor and the probable understanding of that text by its intended readers.*"[10] This statement clarifies how interpreters can pursue that meaning: it entails both a text's language and its history. So the valid approach must be a historical and literary one that enables readers to understand the language of the text.[11] A correct interpretation of a text will be the one that is consistent with language in the ways that people typically write and understand in a given genre of literature. In other words, "We seek to understand a text in the normal and clear sense in which humans ordinarily communicate by that type of literature."[12] Any approach that imposes arbitrary or rare meanings on words, grammar, or historical features has no claim to accuracy. Novelty is not a goal in interpretation. Nor is relevancy – *at the level of interpretation*. What a text means is fixed by its historical meaning.[13] The *significance* a text has *today* is another matter. An historical meaning can have multiple significances. That is the distinction between meaning and application.

Application is not optional, according to Evangelicals. Both Testaments affirm that the design of God's revelation is to evoke appropriate responses from God's people. When people put God's principles into

---

10 William W. Klein, Craig L. Blomberg, and Robert L. Hubbard, Jr. *Introduction to Biblical Interpretation* (Dallas: Word, 1993), 133.
11 Space forbids raising the question of whether a text has only one fixed meaning or may have several levels of meaning – as some in the history of the Bible's interpretation surmised. For a fuller discussion of the issues, see W.W. Klein et al., pp. 119–132 and the further literature to which that discussion refers.
12 W.W. Klein et al., p. 146.
13 Of course evangelicals insist that Scripture is relevant to people today. This grows out of their convictions about the revelatory nature of the Bible. But they also insist that a valid application must grow out of a valid interpretation. It is no virtue to find a relevant application for a meaning that the biblical text does not teach. That is a gross misuse of the Bible. To bind people to practice what the Bible teaches means we must interpret it accurately.

practice they are blessed, and when they disobey, they incur his discipline, if not punishment (see Deut 30:11–20). Jesus emphasizes that his words must be put into practice; only the foolish disregard what He says (Matt 7:13–27). James writes in no uncertain terms about the requirement of response to God's word (Jas 1:22). The biblical writers envisioned that the words of Scripture would serve the people of God for generations to come (e.g. Deut 31:9–13; Neh 8:1–18; Matt 28:19; 1 Cor 10:6; Rom 15:4). The statement of 2 Timothy 3:16–17 rings true for Evangelicals: "All Scripture is inspired by God and is useful for teaching, for reproof, for correction, and for training in righteousness, so that everyone who belongs to God may be proficient, equipped for every good work" (NRSV). But before we explain the approach to move from meaning to application, we must describe the Evangelicals' method for understanding the meaning of the texts.

19.5 THE ESSENTIAL METHOD OF EVANGELICAL HERMENEUTICS

If the goal is to get at the meaning of the ancient texts, then the method involves those tactics and techniques that enable interpreters to arrive at that meaning. It concerns issues of lexical analysis (what words mean), historical and cultural background, literary criticism, literary genre, Hebrew and Greek grammar, and the like. Why can a native speaker and citizen of Pretoria read and understand a column in a daily newspaper published in that city? The answer lies in the competencies that he or she possesses. They include linguistic, cultural, historical, and political competencies, among others. The Evangelical method of biblical interpretation seeks to provide a modern reader with as full a measure as possible of those same kinds of competencies so he or she can understand an ancient biblical text.

Evangelicals posit, therefore, that the correct method of interpretation concerns itself with five essential arenas: (1) literary context, (2) historical-cultural background, (3) word meanings, (4) grammatical relationships, (5) and literary genre. That is, an accurate understanding of any text must fit the obvious sense of the literary context, the facts of the historical and cultural background of the world at the time, the normal meaning of the words of the language in that context, the proper ways the language uses grammar, and the genre of the text that is being studied.[14] We must explain each of these in turn.

---

14 For a full discussion of these elements, see W.W. Klein, et al., pp. 155–374. In these pages, the authors discuss not merely the general rules of interpretation for both prose (155–214) and poetry (215–255), but also pay special attention to understanding the specific genres to be found in both the Old (259–322) and New (323–374) Testaments. Another superb treatment of the genres of the Bible is G. D. Fee and D. Stuart, *How to Read the Bible For All Its Worth* (2d. ed.; Grand Rapids: Zondervan, 1993).

SECTION B

HERMENEUTICS

19.5.1 Literary context

An accurate meaning of any text is the meaning that best fits with the sense of the context in which the text occurs. Language functions in context; to construe a meaning out of context is to misconstrue it. Several reasons account for the importance of context. First, context provides the flow of thought of a text. Second, context helps a reader to understand the meanings of the words of a text. Since most words have multiple meanings, only the context gives an accurate guide to the appropriate meaning. Finally, context unpacks the correct relationships between the units (sentences and paragraphs) of a passage. It helps the reader to understand the flow of the argument or the narrative.

A simple and famous example illustrates the principle of literary context well. Consider the sentence, "Flying planes can be dangerous." Without a literary context, the sentence is ambiguous due to the various functions that participles can play in English. Yet a reader can readily determine the correct meaning if the preceding sentence reads, "The instructor always began his first lecture with the new class of would be pilots with the words, ..." Another meaning results if the preceding sentence is: "As he clung to the Empire State Building, King Kong was heard to exclaim, ..." For biblical interpreters it matters greatly, for example, that we understand the literary context for Romans 8:28 and its promise that "all things" will work together for good. The "all things" are defined in the context as those things God has determined with respect to the salvation of his people. Nothing can separate God's people from his love for them. The "all things" do not include their economic or social circumstances.

The Bible may be said to have multiple contexts. A specific text can be located in an immediate context, the book context, the author's context (if he has written more than one book), the context of the Old Testament or New Testament, and the context of the entire Bible. We understand "the Day of the Lord" in Joel 2:31 by noting the author's uses of this crucial phrase in 1:15; 2:1, 11; 3:14. This implies that we are open to see that Paul's use of the concept of faith is different from James' uses. We understand their characteristic uses by a study of their work or works. An interpretation that disregards the context(s) in which a text occurs, or that violates the context, can have no claim to validity.

19.5.2 Historical-cultural background

Given the distances between the ancient world(s) and the modern world(s), interpreters must discover as much as they can about the ancient world in which a text occurs if they are to understand that text correctly. If we are to comprehend an ancient text accurately, we must come to appreciate, as much as possible, the perspective of the ancient writer and readers. Since the ancients were in a world of their own, we must "walk in their sandals" to understand their writings as they would have. Also, we must appreciate the mindset of the ancients – how they thought about things and the world "back then". Instead of remaking the message into our own image in light of our cultures, we need to feel and think as they did.

Fortunately, archaeology, historical research, sociology and other cultural studies have unearthed much data about the ancient world. We may never completely close the gap between their world and ours, but we cannot stop trying. To interpret in ignorance of what we can know about the biblical worlds is to risk misunderstanding and error.[15] The task involves exploring the general background of the biblical book one is studying and then researching any specific features of a text whose meaning is obscure due to distance from the modern world in time and culture. This may include such items as: world-view, societal structures, physical features, economic structures, political climate, behavioral patterns and religious practices.

Many Bible students completely misconstrue the meanings of "hot", "cold", and "lukewarm" in the letter to the church at Laodicea (Rev 3: 14–22). By disregarding the historical situation of the city of Laodicea and through employing alien spiritual meanings for the terms for temperature, we might jump to erroneous and misleading conclusions. One might wrongly conclude that Jesus prefers people to be spiritually *cold* (or be actively opposed to Jesus) rather than to be merely a lukewarm Christian. This is absurd, and, fortunately, a conclusion dispelled by correctly understanding the situation of the city. Laodicea was located near both hot springs and a cold stream. Both are useful, desirable, and have their place. It was the water that eventually flowed into the city through an aqueduct that was tepid and lukewarm; it was putrid.[16] Christians need to be useful to Jesus – hot or cold.

To understand why Jesus called Herod Antipas a "fox" requires an understanding of the connotation foxes held in *his* day, not ours. To understand Matthew's reference to "phylacteries" (Matt 23:5) requires historical study; no amount of personal pondering on the meaning of the text will help the reader understand what the Pharisees were wearing. Many specialized works, not to mention introductions, Bible dictionaries, encyclopedias and commentaries, provide useful insights into historical and cultural features.[17]

19.5.3 Word meanings

Here the principle is simple: "The correct interpretation of Scripture is the meaning required by the normal meanings of the words in the context in which they occur."[18] We cannot imagine communication without

19

Evangelical Hermeneutics

---

15 One of the features of W.W. Klein et al., *Introduction to Biblical Interpretation*, is the extensive annotated bibliography at the end. In the section on historical and cultural backgrounds, many fine volumes are listed (pp. 471–480).
16 For helpful analyses of this section see C.J. Hemer, *The Letters to the Seven Churches of Asia in Their Local Setting*, JSNTSup 11 (Sheffield, UK: JSOT, 1986), pp. 186–191 and M.M.S. Rudwick and E.M.B. Green, "The Laodicean Lukewarmness," *ExpT* 69 (1957–58): 176–178.
17 A fine volume is C.S. Keener, *The IVP Bible Background Commentary. New Testament* (Downers Grove, IL: InterVarsity, 1993). It provides background helps for every section in the New Testament.
18 W.W. Klein et al., p. 183.

SECTION

B

HERMENEUTICS

words; they are foundational. Yet a glance at any dictionary of any language will demonstrate the range of meanings specific words may have. What is more, the meanings of words change over time. This explains why the translators of the AV (KJV) used "prevent" when they translated 1 Thessalonians 4:15: " ... we which are alive and remain unto the coming of the Lord shall not prevent them which are asleep." In 1611, the word "prevent" had a more etymological sense of "go before". Now its meaning has changed to something like "to keep from happening, avert." More recent translations employ "precede" or "come first".

The fact that words cover a range of meanings suggests that interpreters must be sure that they identify the precise sense a word has in a specific context. A quick look in a lexicon at the Greek word *kosmos* (world) will show how wide a range of meanings a single word might have.[19] To understand John's assertion that "God loved the *world*" (3:16) one must know the possible meanings "world" might have, and which of those best fits the context of John 3. Honest interpreters may not merely choose the meaning they prefer, or the one that fits a personal prejudice. Again, the touchstone is intention: what meaning of the word did the author most likely intend, and what meaning did the readers most likely understand?

Biblical interpreters must assure themselves that they have a good grasp of the meanings of the words of the passage they are studying.[20] They must be prepared to investigate any words in a passage whose meanings they do not understand adequately. These include difficult terms, rare words, theologically loaded words, or simply those words the student is unsure about. Many resources are now available, at least in English, to aid students in establishing the proper sense of the words they encounter.[21]

Once the interpreter has selected the words that require further study, the steps for study are only two: determine the range of meaning a word had in the ancient world and select the meaning that fits best in the context of the passage. Though the word *kosmos* (world) could mean a number of things at the end of the first century CE, in the context of John 3 the author most certainly meant "people". God loved the people on this planet so much that he sent his son to die.

In recent times it has become clear that meaning is more often than not conveyed in phrases rather than in single words. In Amos 1:3, older translations read something like *"For three transgressions* of Damascus, and for four, I will not turn away its punishment." It sounds rather odd because the meaning is in the phrase and modern translations correctly read something like: *"Because of the repeated transgressions of ..."* So a word

---

19 In their *Greek-English Lexicon of the New Testament Based on Semantic Domains*, 2 vols. (New York: United Bible Societies, 1988), Louw and Nida note nine different senses for *kosmos*: universe, earth, world system, people, adorning, adornment, tremendous amount, unit, and supernatural power (vol. 1, p. 146). In English, one could consider words like "hand" or "trunk" to illustrate the wide range of meanings words may have.

20 The best help for doing word studies is found in M. Silva, *Biblical Words and Their Meaning* (Grand Rapids: Zondervan, 1984).

21 For such word study resources see the annotations in W.W. Klein et al., pp. 464–472.

by word translation, a so-called literal translation, is often a bad one. Look at another example: "For in it (that is in the gospel) the righteousness of God is revealed *from faith to faith*" (a "literal" translation, Rom 1:17) does not make good sense. The meaning is not in the separate words, but in the Greek phrase, and should be translated as something like "through faith and faith alone."

19.5.4 Grammatical-structural relationships

Languages communicate by combining words together according to grammatical rules. Languages have their own systems for putting words together coherently. To understand the Bible, students should ideally understand something of how the Hebrew and Greek grammatical systems work. Of course, not all students have either the opportunity or the time to master the biblical languages. Fortunately, many scholarly works – especially commentaries – provide reliable insights into how the grammar of Hebrew or Greek functions.[22] Interpreters must avail themselves of such resources if they are available. When they are not available, the student should collect as many possible translations in his or her own language as are available. Then they can study the grammar and structures of a passage on the basis of a comparison of the versions. The translations will sharpen the student's understanding of many important grammatical and structural matters.

What should the student look for? First, seek to identify the natural divisions of the section to be studied. Seek to study in larger thought units, not in fragments (as verse divisions sometimes encourage). Of course, divisions will depend on the type of literature studied. In Proverbs, the natural divisions may consist of one proverb. In other genres, a section might consist of a single psalm, a paragraph, a speech (e.g. Job 23:1–24:25), or a subsection – like Jesus' Sermon on the Mount (Matt 5–7).

Observe the flow as the writer's logic or train of thought develops. One might wish to produce some type of diagram or grammatical analysis to see the development of the author's argument.[23] It is important to observe when an argument turns, for example, on time, location, purpose, result, a condition, contrasts, manner, or means. So we must determine what kind of condition 2 Peter 1:10 expresses: "For if you do these things, you will never fall."

In addition, note the impact of the key verbs. Languages use verbs to designate the mood, aspect, time, kind and voice of the action or state being expressed.[24] Is an action viewed as continuous, as an undifferentiated whole, or as a completed state? Does the author make a statement, ask a question, give a command, express a possibility, make a wish, or seek to prohibit some course of action?

---

22 See the lists and descriptions of the major commentaries in W.W. Klein et al., pp. 488–491 and at the end of the book by Fee and Stuart, *How to Read the Bible For All Its Worth*, pp. 252–254.
23 See an example in W.W. Klein et al., p. 207. The authors cite other books that present various methods of structural analysis in note 143 on p. 206.
24 Many of these issues go far beyond the scope of so limited an essay. Students should see the standard Hebrew and Greek grammars for detailed analyses and insight into the more technical matters of grammar.

19.5.5 Genres

Literature comes in various types, and the competent interpreter understands the formation and function of each literary type, for each type has its own cues that tell us how it must be understood and, therefore, interpreted. For example, poetry is not like narrative. Poetry conveys its message through tightly structured, rhythmical patterns and metaphorical language. On the other hand, narratives normally function more "straightforwardly". "The trees clap their hands for joy" makes good sense in poetry, but we would be extremely puzzled to encounter such a sentence in an historical narrative. Knowing the genre is crucial for interpretation.

The careful interpreter takes the time to learn and understand the various genres in the Bible. The tools for understanding one genre might not serve as well in another. A narrative might teach a lesson by telling a story. Read the saga of Joseph and learn the lessons of God's sovereignty and a man's faithfulness. An epistle makes a point more didactively. Paul urges very pointedly: "Be angry and sin not" (Eph 4:26). A parable makes its case through a captivating, down-to-earth story. Its details provide local colour to enhance the main point(s) and ought not be taken in the same way as the details in a description in a narrative. A prophet sometimes acts out a message (see Jeremiah), while an apocalyptist writes in other-worldly pictures. The point is to take each type of literature *on its own terms.* We must not expect the Bible to be all of one kind of writing. The Bible is a book of diversity, as noted above.

What are the genres of the Bible? In the Old Testament we find narratives of various kinds – proverbs, riddles, parables, songs, lists, legal materials, poetry, prophecy, apocalyptic prophecy and wisdom literature. In the New Testament, the interpreter encounters gospels (kinds of "theological biographies") and forms within them (parables, miracle stories, pronouncement stories), Acts ("theological history"), epistles and Revelation (apocalyptic).

While the general principles of interpreting literature (context, historical-cultural background, words and grammar) apply to all writing, each genre or form has unique features that interpreters must note if they are to understand accurately.

19.6 FROM INTERPRETATION TO APPLICATION

A unique dimension of Evangelical Hermeneutics grows out of its central presupposition that the Bible constitutes God's written revelation to his people. The Bible is no mere object of scholarly study or only a source book for discovering the religious yearnings of ancient peoples. The Bible, Evangelicals affirm, has a legitimate and vital role to play in the modern world. In fact, it can speak in a relevant way to the issues of life in today's diverse world with its manifold cultures. Despite its origins among ancient peoples centuries ago, it retains its unique value and remains consistently applicable (since it is God's message), when that application grows out of principles of sound and accurate biblical interpretation. Assuming we know what a text means, how do we move from the correct meaning of a passage to appropriate application?

Before we go any further, however, we must acknowledge that the terrain of application is strewn with obstacles. People make the Bible say all sorts of things. One will frequently hear sincere Christians say words to this effect: "What this verse says to me is ...", and one has difficulty in understanding how what follows in any way grows out of the verse in question. It is possible to speak about legitimate versus illegitimate applications. At the same time we can speak about application that is more authoritative and application that is less authoritative. What do we mean?

The biblical writers spoke to people in their age seeking to elicit appropriate responses in God's people. For example, those responses included actions to perform or to avoid, concepts or beliefs to adopt or to shun; the authors sought to engage God's people in worship of the Creator; or they provided examples of either godly or ungodly behavior. The modern reader might well understand what the ancient author sought to evoke from the original readers, but that does not mean Christians today ought to respond with precisely the *same* response. The objective of application is to seek to apply the *principle* found in the original teaching and to apply that principle in appropriate ways today. Though the Bible was written to address specific situations, its character as God's Word guarantees its continuous applicability. Its principles apply to God's people throughout history. What happened to God's people in the past happened as examples for God's people today.[25] How, then, do we move from original meaning to application today?

Though different approaches may be found, Evangelicals suggest something like the following four-step strategy:

1. Determine the original application(s) intended by the passage.
2. Evaluate the level of specificity of those applications. Are they transferable across time and space to other audiences?
3. If not, identify one or more broader cross-cultural principles that the specific elements of the text reflects.
4. Find appropriate applications for today that embody those principles.[26]

Klein et al. use the following diagram to illustrate the approach:

THEN   **NOW**

Application   Application
↑   ↑
Principles   → → → → → Principles[27]

Evangelical Hermeneutics

---

25 See how Paul uses this very same logic when he applies the Israelites' wilderness experiences to his readers in Corinth (1 Cor 10:1–13; especially vv. 6 and 11). In his *Taking the Guesswork Out of Applying the Bible* (Downers Grove, IL: InterVarsity, 1990), Jack Kuhatschek devotes an entire book to helping Christians apply the Bible correctly. On "principilizing" the meaning of Scripture, see H.A. Virkler, *Hermeneutics. Principles and Processes of Biblical Interpretation* (Grand Rapids: Baker, 1981), pp. 212–232.
26 W.W. Klein et al. *Introduction to Biblical Interpretation*, p. 407.
27 W.W. Klein et al. *Introduction to Biblical Interpretation*, p. 424.

SECTION B

HERMENEUTICS

The starting point is the discovery of the meaning of the text. That leads the interpreter to an understanding of what the original biblical author was seeking to accomplish "back then". With that original application in view, the interpreter seeks to move across the centuries to the current time and culture in which he or she lives. The interpreter's goal is to find appropriate and corresponding applications for those principles that have continuing relevance for people today. This process shows how crucial the previous steps of interpretation really are. Unless the student understands the original meaning of the text, he or she is not in the right position to move to correct application.

For example, a favourite and familiar incident from the Gospels is the one in which Jesus calmed the storm on the Sea of Galilee (Matt 8:23–27 and parallels). A student may be tempted to move too quickly to an application like, "If Jesus could calm the physical storms on the sea for his disciples, surely he can calm the storms of my life." This may be a true sentiment, but it is not a sound application from *this passage*. Surely prudent principles of interpretation lead us to conclude that the author intended to call attention to Jesus and to elicit faith in him as the Lord over all – even the physical creation.[28] The point is Christological – who is this Christ? – and the need for his disciples to have faith in Him. This is the principle which Christians today can apply: Christ is the one we must follow, for He is Lord over all.

Apart from growing out of the original intention of the text, an application has little authority; it may be applying Christian principles, but it is not applying the Bible. This also implies that the farther an application moves from the original author's intention, the less confidence we may have that an application has the full authority as God's Word for today. How, then, may God's Word be used today?

19.7 THE OUTCOMES OF INTERPRETATION

Once we have an approach to discovering the meaning of a passage from the Bible, and to understanding how to connect meaning and application, how do God's people respond to his message? The Bible is no magic talisman or Ouija board; it is a message of divine communication from God to people. It is understandable and useful. To what uses can people put its message? Several obvious answers suggest themselves.

Certainly, one can read the Bible to gain the information it contains. That is, it has value as an educational medium, reporting history and insights. Of course, the Bible has always served to lead God's people into worship as they respond to God's revelation of Himself in Jesus Christ. Scripture also informs the ways the church worships and the ways it understands theology. It is the source book for the faith of the faithful. Hence the Bible serves as the basis for the preaching and teaching ministries of the church. To learn the Christian faith requires learning what

---

28 See C.L. Blomberg, *Matthew*, NAC (Nashville: Broadman, 1992), pp. 149–150.

the Bible teaches. This is more than cognitive information or propositional truths. As God's message to fallen creatures, the Bible provides comfort and guidance: instruction in godly living as well as care in times of need.

We need a crucial reminder at this point:

> We can confidently promise people from the Bible only those things that God has in fact *intended* to say. A responsible system of hermeneutics will restrain well-intentioned, but misguided, help.[29]

And again:

> The Bible communicates in various ways and serves many purposes. ... But if the Bible is to retain its integrity and potency as God's communication to his people, we must understand the intention of its message. To impose our own meaning is not a valid option. ... We must know the meaning of the Bible's message before we can expect that meaning to perform what God intended.[30]

The evangelical contribution to the contemporary hermeneutical debate is a clarion call to take the Bible as seriously as it deserves to be. Evangelicals reject the charge of bibliolatry; they do not worship the Bible simply because they hold it in high regard. Rather, they insist, they worship the God of the Bible – the one who has taken such effort to reveal his message in it. To misconstrue its message for whatever reason or to read one's own agenda into the Bible – rather than to let the Bible speak its own message – subverts its intention.

READING LIST AND BIBLIOGRAPHY

Barr, J. 1983. *Beyond Fundamentalism*. Philadelphia: Westminster.
Beegle, D.M. 1963. *The Inspiration of Scripture*. Grand Rapids: Eerdmans.
Blomberg, C.L. 1987. *Historical Reliability of the Gospels*. Leicester, UK and Downers Grove, IL: InterVarsity.
Cotterell, P. and Turner, M. 1989. *Linguistics and Biblical Interpretation*. Downers Grove, IL: InterVarsity
Davis, S.T. 1977. *The Debate About the Bible: Inerrancy versus Infallibility*. Philadelphia: Westminster.
Dockery, D.S., Mathews, K.A., and Sloan, R.B. (eds.). 1994. *Foundations for Biblical Interpretation. A Complete Library of Tools and Resources*. Nashville, TN: Broadman & Holman.
Erickson, M.J. 1993. *Evangelical Interpretation. Perspectives on Hermeneutical Issues*. Grand Rapids: Baker.
Fee, G.D. and Stuart, D. 1993. *How To Read the Bible for All Its Worth*. 2d. ed. Grand Rapids: Zondervan.
Feinberg, P. 1979. "The Meaning of Inerrancy." In cd. Geisler, N. (ed.), *Inerrancy*, . Grand Rapids: Zondervan.
George, T. 1988. *Theology of the Reformers*. Nashville: Broadman.
Gundry, R.H. 1982, 1994(2). *Matthew. A Commentary on His Literary and Theological Art*. Grand Rapids: Eerdmans.

---

29 W.W. Klein et al, p. 395, emphasis retained.
30 W.W. Klein et al, pp. 398–399.

SECTION B

HERMENEUTICS

Hemer, C.J. 1986. *The Letters to the Seven Churches of Asia in Their Local Setting.* JSNT Sup 11. Sheffield, UK: JSOT.

James, R. (ed.). 1987. *The Unfettered Word: Southern Baptists Confront the Authority-Inerrancy Questions.* Waco: Word.

Kaiser, W. and Silva, M. 1994. *An Introduction to Biblical Hermeneutics.* Grand Rapids: Zondervan.

Keener, C.S. 1993. *The IVP Bible Background Commentary. New Testament.* Downers Grove, IL: InterVarsity.

Kelly, J.N.D. 1978. *Early Christian Doctrines*, rev. ed. San Francisco: Harper & Row.

Klein, W.W., Blomberg, C.L., and Hubbard, R.L., Jr. 1993. *Introduction to Biblical Interpretation.* Dallas, London, Vancouver, Melbourne: Word Publishing.

Kuhatschek, J. 1990. *Taking the Guesswork Out of Applying the Bible.* Downers Grove, IL: InterVarsity.

Larkin, W.J. 1988. *Culture and Biblical Hermeneutics.* Grand Rapids: Baker, Repr. Washington, D.C.: University Press of America, 1994.

Louw, J.P. and Nida, E.A. 1988. *Greek-English Lexicon of the New Testament Based on Semantic Domains*, 2 vols. New York: United Bible Societies.

Mickelsen, A.B. 1963. *Interpreting the Bible.* Grand Rapids: Eerdmans.

Osborne, G.R. 1991. *The Hermeneutical Spiral.* Downers Grove, IL: InterVarsity.

Pinnock, C. 1984. *The Scripture Principle.* San Francisco: Harper & Row.

Ramm, B. 1970. *Protestant Biblical Interpretation.* 3d. ed. Grand Rapids: Baker.

Rogers, J.B. and McKim, D.K. 1979. *The Authority and Interpretation of the Bible*: *An Historical Approach.* San Francisco: Harper & Row.

Ryken, L. 1984. *How to Read the Bible as Literature.* Grand Rapids: Zondervan.

Ryken, L. and Longman, T. 1993. *A Complete Literary Guide to the Bible*, 3d ed. Grand Rapids: Zondervan.

Silva, M. 1983. *Biblical Words and Their Meaning.* Grand Rapids: Zondervan.

Stein, R.H. 1994. *Playing by the Rules. A Basic Guide to Interpreting the Bible.* Grand Rapids: Baker.

Sullivan, C. 1990. *Toward a Mature Faith: Does Biblical Inerrancy Make Sense?* Decateur, GA: SBC Today.

Tate, W.R. 1991. *Biblical Interpretation. An Integrated Approach.* Peabody, MA: Hendrickson.

Thiselton, A.C. 1980. *The Two Horizons.* Grand Rapids: Eerdmans.

– 1992. *New Horizons in Hermeneutics.* Grand Rapids: Zondervan.

Virkler, H.A. 1981. *Hermeneutics. Principles and Processes of Biblical Interpretation.* Grand Rapids: Baker.

Warfield, B.B. 1984. *The Inspiration and Authority of the Bible.* Philadelphia: Presbyterian and Reformed.

Wise, P.D. 1988. "Biblical Inerrancy: Pro or Con?" *Theological Educator* 37.

Black Hermeneutics

Timothy G. Kiogora

20.1 INTRODUCTION

The term "hermeneutics" is used to refer to methods of interpreting a text, originally a biblical text. "Hermeneutics" was regarded by biblical scholars as a "science" confined to comparative textual studies with the object of locating the original composition, genre and period of the writing of the text, authorship and such related technical matters. This in itself was a noble task. The only problem, however, was that the Bible was reduced to an object of endless rational investigations by scholars who viewed it in terms of its various parts and not in terms of the *meaning* of events reported in the texts for the present historical situation.

It is important to remember from the outset that the interpreter of any text, biblical or otherwise, is located in a concrete historical context. For the biblical interpreter, it is this concrete historical context and the revealed meaning of the text which forms the essence of the message to be deduced from the text. In other words, a text's meaning is fully revealed as it is opened to the reading of the "signs of the times" (J.S. Croato 1983: 160). The contribution of Liberation Theology over the last several years has been precisely in raising the question of the relevance of the reading of biblical texts in the light of social, political, and economic situations of Third World peoples. This awareness that there needs to be a clear correlation between text and context (past and present) presents us with an alternative hermeneutics.

In this essay we shall see, in outline form, the precise contributions of the hermeneutics of Black Theology within the larger framework of other theologies of liberation. In all cases, the point of departure for theologies of liberation is an inquiry into the context in which we are to hear God's word and discern God's involvement in the transformation of societies, as opposed to mere inquiry into the meaning of a biblical text for philosophical interests of curious investigators.

SECTION B

HERMENEUTICS

First, we shall look at the varieties of contexts out of which an alternative theological hermeneutics arises, showing how Black Theology was shaped by contextual readings. Second, we shall look at some biblical notions involved in the formulation of different forms of Black Hermeneutics of Liberation, some of which may be useful in the present global, cultural, political and socio-economic process.

20.2 THE CONTEXTS OF OPPRESSION AND LIBERATIVE HERMENEUTICS

For purposes of brevity, we shall comment here only on Latin American, North American and African contexts which gave rise to forms of liberative theological hermeneutics. However, elsewhere in this volume (e.g. chapters 7, 8, 21, 22) it will become clear that oppressive contexts are characterized by not only socio-political and cultural, but also by gender domination. Moreover, liberative theological hermeneutics have also been propounded in Asia, but we shall not have space here to outline the Asian perspectives.

Black North American theologians and Latin American theologians began to use the term "liberation" at the same time, but independent of each other. In 1969 James Cone, the foremost black North American theologian, wrote *Black Theology And Black Power,* followed by *A Black Theology of Liberation* in 1970. In 1971, Gustavo Guitierrez, a pioneer Latin American liberation theologian, published his *A Theology of Liberation* in Spanish. Both of these theologians use the term "liberation". Why did theology have to be "liberating"? Let us look at each of their contexts.

20.2.1 The Latin American context and approach

The main issues in Latin America leading to a different theological hermeneutics involve the nature of a colonial Christianity (Christendom) and the consequent socio-political and economic domination of the masses of people by a few in spite of this Christianity. Enrique Dussel, an historian of Liberation Theology, has shown that Latin America was colonized by a people confident in their allegedly "Christian civilization" which had been developed since the time of Constantine's "church-state" marriage in the 4th century. Thus Latin and Hispanic Christendom was imposed on Latin America. Specific historical events are outlined by Dussel to show how this Hispanic Christendom impacted the peoples of Latin America (1974:3).

So the conquest of Latin America brought with it Christianity. According to Dussel, it was as if by divine right that "non-believers" had to be forcibly converted to Christianity. By both ecclesiastical and political authorities, the conquest of the peoples of Latin America was effected in a period of over three hundred years. In this period (1492–1808) most of the land was taken by "conquerors" and the native populations were reduced to servants of the big landlords (Dussel 1974:401–39).

The Catholic Church in Latin America remained foreign to indigenous Indians of Latin America because of its alliance with the ruling classes

20
Black Hermeneutics

(5%) who owned 80% of the land, and its ignorance of the culture of the Indian peoples. Although a lot of the Indians were christianized, this did not in itself seem to change their historical condition of powerlessness and poverty in their own land. Over the years not even inter-marriage between the Indians and Spanish peoples seemed to improve the situation of the poor. Indeed, Latin America, as historians insist, was characterized by two classes: the rich and the abject poor. In all this, the church in Latin America seemed to cling to a theology of two realms: the earthly realm and the heavenly realm, with the gospel only related to the latter. Hence, there needed not to be cause for alarm about the poverty of the people. This kind of church, however, was not a true church of the people since their cries could not be heard by it. It was an alien church, "imported" from Spain.

In the 19th century the features of Latin American colonialism were irreversibly altered with the rise of independent states and a growing secularism. However, although there was also a growing sense of nationalism and new political thought, the reality of much of Latin America remained that of dependence on Anglo-American programs of "development aid". For example, after the Second World War, western donor countries believed Latin American countries would soon reach high levels of economic growth only if more money was invested in these countries. Altogether some $9.6 billion was invested in Latin America between 1950 and 1961, *but* at the same time $14.4 billion was taken out of Latin American economies (Dussel 1981:4).

The rise of "developmentalism" in the 1960s did not produce the expected economic growth. Instead, poverty increased, illiteracy was high and foreign-owned businesses were everywhere. "Development" was not really what it was meant to be, but rather proved to be a further erosion of the people's resources and energies.

What is important to note here is the unique perspective of Latin American theologians in their analysis of their political and socio-economic context, particularly their ability to open up theological discourse for interaction with the so-called "secular" academic discourse. For example, economists Fernando H. Cardoso and Enzo Falletto of the Latin American Study Centre disputed the relevance of the theory of development in Latin America, showing why this theory does not eventually lead to economic emancipation, but rather to more poverty and dependence on external aid. Of this situation, Latin American theologians like Gustavo Gutierrez, Louis Juan Segundo and Miguez Bonino were fully aware. They exposed the reality of "underdevelopment" and the need to break the cycle of dependence as one aspect of liberation. For them the process of the liberation of Latin America was a matter of theological significance and not just academic, university or "secular" involvement. History was one, and God was in charge of all history, and what takes place in it.

Latin American Liberation Theology came to its own with the publication of Gustavo Gutierrez's book *A Theology of Liberation* in 1971. In the book Gutierrez states his object: "To think through (our) faith, to streng-

SECTION B

HERMENEUTICS

then (our) love and to give reason for (our) hope from within a commitment which seeks to be more radical, total and efficacious" (Gutierrez 1971:ix). The theme of the *unity* of the task of liberating human beings from all forms of captivity within *this* history underlies his writing. Concerning Liberation Theology, he clearly states: theology is critical reflection on praxis (or practice). A critical reading of history must lead to a new hermeneutical approach to the Bible. Thus reading the Bible from the position of the observer will be different to reading the Bible from the point of view of one committed to historical change, Gutierrez and others were to insist. This also means, in effect, that the powerful read the Bible from a position of power and domination, while the poor and powerless read from a position of suffering, looking for clues in the biblical texts for liberation from their oppression.

Latin American Liberation Theology depended on a critical reading of history and the conviction that poverty arose from unjust social structures and was not God's will. The phrase "preferential option for the poor" was coined to indicate one of the most important hermeneutical keys in the Theology of Liberation. God, the theologians insisted, being by nature just and merciful, is more inclined to hear the cry of the poor. Moreover, by virtue of their poverty, the poor are the weak in society, and God prefers to operate in the world from the perspective of the weak, the poor, or those at the periphery of human made "centres". Anything that dehumanizes persons – and poverty does that – distorts God's very image in human beings. To challenge this dehumanization is a missiological task.

Reflection on the plight of the poor, powerless and peripheral peoples in Latin America (and beyond) became for liberation theologians a necessary prerequisite for doing any theology. The gospel, they insisted, is "good news" to the poor (Luke 4:18–21) and is consistent with God's total involvement in salvation history. We shall see how this theological assertion was enjoined by black theologians in the latter part of this essay.

Liberation theologians in Latin America made another distinct contribution in their use of social analysis as part of theological hermeneutics. From this perspective, social reality is interpreted in such a way that hidden ideologies are unearthed. Religion and theology may be termed "ideological" when they hide, through dubious justifications, vested interests (Segundo 1976:39). The reading of Scriptures and the teaching of history, they held, may be used to domesticate a people to accept an evil social order uncritically. Thus the reading of both Scripture and history must be done in the context of the struggles for emancipation. Only in this way does Jesus truly become the liberator.

The discovery of "hidden interests" through the hermeneutics of suspicion led many liberation theologians to an appreciation – but not total embrace – of Marxist analysis of social conflict (Bonino 1975:96). They saw the Christian faith as capable of shaking itself off from previous ideological interests to become a vehicle for the liberation of the people of God. (Marxists would not accept any religious claims to liberation.)

20.2.2 The North American context and approach

Perhaps as a sign of the times, the rise of Black Theology in the United States and South Africa in the 1970s lent more credibility to a totally new theological movement whose real beginnings are difficult to pinpoint. Possibly this is due to the fact that there were simultaneous developments in Latin America, North America and Africa, partly because of the collapse of the colonial orders around the world after the Second World War, and partly because of a growing critical interchange of ideas in the years that followed. How then did Black Theology as a theological movement in North America develop, and what shape did it take in Africa? We now turn to these two aspects.

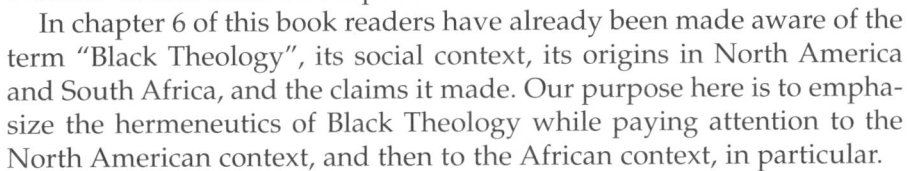

In chapter 6 of this book readers have already been made aware of the term "Black Theology", its social context, its origins in North America and South Africa, and the claims it made. Our purpose here is to emphasize the hermeneutics of Black Theology while paying attention to the North American context, and then to the African context, in particular.

Historically, Black Theology was a reaction to the split which appeared in the Civil Rights Movement in North America in 1966 which produced the Black Power Movement. The latter, historians now agree, was a call by younger people within the Student Nonviolent Coordinating Committee and Congress of Racial Equality for all Black North Americans to be more assertive in their dealings with racism (Witvliet 1987: 05). White church leaders put pressure on black church leaders to condemn these young people and the slogan "Black Power". However, the National Committee of Negro Churchmen (NCNC) declared open support for the sentiments behind the Black Power call, putting Dr. Martin Luther King's Freedom Now movement (a non-violent civil rights campaign) in a dilemma. Before this crisis, the black race had never been explicitly challenged to examine their "blackness" in theological terms, apart from worshipping in distinct styles from those of white communities.

Recalling the "subversive praxis" of the "invisible church" during the long years of slavery, black churchmen in North America recognized that indeed there existed a "black theology", a theology of self determination and affirmation. Like the children of Israel against Egyptian slavery, black Americans had to revamp their faith in a God capable of ending their oppression (Witvliet 1987:161).

Three issues may be identified as constituting the early concerns of Black Theology in North America: criticism of the black church which simply internalized a docile Jesus (an American white Jesus) alienated from their culture, suffering and aspirations; reviving the true vigour of the black church and rejecting the view that the church is an irrelevant obstacle to true liberation; finally, challenging the "closed discourse of white theology" and exposing its traditional alliance with a dominant social order without challenging and changing it. James Cone took up the latter task in his writings from within the academy, particularly his *God Of The Oppressed* (1975).

SECTION B

HERMENEUTICS

Black Hermeneutics is the hermeneutics of the experience of black Americans in North America in the light of the biblical witness. Just like Latin American Liberation Theology, Black Theology takes the primacy of context seriously. The experience of black Americans since the days of slavery has been characterized by the negative association of "black" with something inferior, evil, and therefore less than that which is "white".

Black Theology is a positive reading of the Bible so that the oppressed, in this case the black person, is situated at the centre of God's historic plan of salvation. Here "blackness" is extended to include *all* the oppressed, not just black people. Thus, Black Theology is not just a simplistic hermeneutical dead-end. It makes connections with all other forms of Liberation Theology, although its starting point is the particular historic suffering of black people in North America as the underclass. This point needs to be stressed, because it is the only connection Black Theology has with other theologies of self-determination.

Two sources of Black Theological Hermeneutics may be identified. First, the "spirituality" of the black church, the backbone of most black people and their survival while weathering the storm of racial discrimination and abuse. Their spirituality refers to how, in their own ways, simple folk, not sophisticated theologians, gave an account of God's presence among them, and what hope this awareness gave the people (James Cone 1972).

The second source of Black Theological Hermeneutics is the ongoing assessment of the condition of black people in North America in past and contemporary struggles for their true identity and dignity. In this process, all reality has to be reassessed, including the nature of the desirable church and society. Also important in this respect has been the critical examination of black history (Harding 1981; Blassingame 1979; Levine 1977).

The first source is disputed by black historians of religion who argue that the church was not the only connection black people had with God, and that indeed black people, even as they left Africa, had a God-centred religion which was a critical source of their philosophy of life (Cone 1975). In this regard, a more inclusive and expanded hermeneutics is called for. Other critics would go as far as saying that black religion and Black Theology are so burdened with other traditions that it is difficult for them to be useful vehicles of understanding the true meaning of "blackness". Charles Long represents this radical school of thought which questions the very basis of Black Theology (Witvliet 1987:188).

The importance of Black Theological Hermeneutics, all things considered, has been its attempt to break away from a theological tradition dominated by members of a race that did not incorporate the experience of oppression as a necessary starting point in its theology. The historic injustices of oppression caused by racist attitudes was exposed to be contrary to God's will, and ancient biblical motifs concerning God's intervention on behalf of the oppressed revived. We shall sketch these momentarily, after a brief examination of the influence of North American Black Theology in Africa.

20.2.3 The African context and approach

Theological Hermeneutics in Africa focuses on the historical dehumanization of Africans on two levels: the political and socio-economic level and the anthropological religio-cultural level. Consequently, liberation from political and socio-economic domination and Africanization have been two important approaches (Martey 1993). In South Africa, Black Theology has been associated more with the struggle for political and socio-economic liberation in South Africa than religio-cultural (Africanization) issues which have tended to dominate the agenda of theologians in the other parts of Africa. Regrettably, Black Theology in Africa has been mistakenly seen as separate from what has been called African Theology. This separation is regarded by some as superfluous and a misperception of the total reality affecting Africans. (See chapters 9 and 23 in this regard.) In this paragraph we will concentrate on Black Theology in *South Africa*.

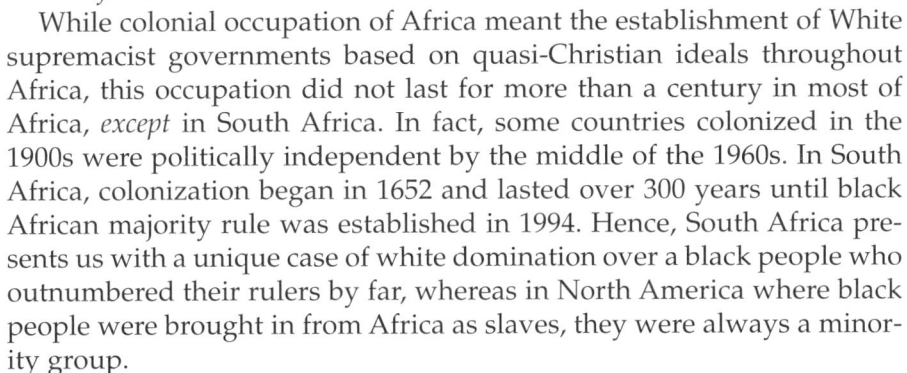

While colonial occupation of Africa meant the establishment of White supremacist governments based on quasi-Christian ideals throughout Africa, this occupation did not last for more than a century in most of Africa, *except* in South Africa. In fact, some countries colonized in the 1900s were politically independent by the middle of the 1960s. In South Africa, colonization began in 1652 and lasted over 300 years until black African majority rule was established in 1994. Hence, South Africa presents us with a unique case of white domination over a black people who outnumbered their rulers by far, whereas in North America where black people were brought in from Africa as slaves, they were always a minority group.

The origins of Black Theology in Africa are to be located in the struggles of black South Africans against white supremacy established by a minority Afrikaner government and its peculiar doctrine of apartheid (separation of races). The Afrikaners, mainly descendants of the original Dutch colonizers of South Africa in the 17th century, had also successfully co-opted the Dutch Reformed Church in their claim to the special providence of God. They saw themselves as a people whose nationhood was blessed by God (Martey 1987:19). They remembered their escape (the "Great Trek") from British domination in the 18th century during the British occupation of the Cape Province as proof that God had a clear destiny for them. In their scheme of things, black peoples were to serve them, and indeed, African populations were reduced to farm workers and tenants in their own lands. But Africans, although initially conquered through superior fire power, remained in a state of restlessness.

By 1910 the Whites (mostly Afrikaners) had firmly consolidated their power as the Union of South Africa government. Two years later, the South African Native National Congress (later the African National Congress) was formed as a black African response to Afrikaner rule. But there were other responses from Africans too, particularly the more militant Pan Africanist Congress, all focused on the political liberation of black Africans from Dutch Afrikaner rule.

SECTION B

HERMENEUTICS

The banning of both the African National Congress and the Pan Africanist Congress following the Sharpeville massacre of black Africans in 1960 gave Africans an opportunity for a higher solidarity based on a philosophy of black consciousness, which fully blossomed into the South African Student's Organization (SASO), led by Steve Biko in the 1970s. The Black Consciousness Movement addressed itself to the meaning and resources of black African resistance to white rule and its psychological and physiological hold on Africans.

Black history, culture and religion were seen as crucial resources in this encounter with institutional racism in South Africa, and the goal was first and foremost to free the African's mind (Martey 1987:24). The Black Consciousness Movement was backed by theological expressions from various Christians who were now being challenged to develop a critical hermeneutics of their Christian existence in a religious, but racist, country.

The Black Consciousness Movement was banned in 1977. By that time, however, Black Theology had come to its own, with *Essays On Black Theology* (1972) already on the record. The Black Theology Task Force of the Institute for Contextual Theology carried on the work of organizing and transmitting ideas in biblical perspective from a wide spectrum of South African theologians relating to the struggle of South Africans against apartheid. The various trends in South African Black Theology have already been outlined in chapter 6. Here we shall only comment on the hermeneutics of Black Theology in South Africa in general.

Black Theology in South Africa, as we have noted above, grew from the Black Consciousness Movement. It sought to interpret reality from the perspective of the underdog – the majority black African population.

In the broader South African Christian community, three kinds of theology have grown side by side: *the theology of the state* (Afrikaans churches), *the theology of reconciliation* (liberal white churches), and *prophetic theology* (with black-dominated theologians) based on a radical understanding of the God of justice of especially the Old Testament prophets. It is important to note this "mixed up" religious atmosphere of South Africa within which a black theological hermeneutic was to operate.

The distinctive hermeneutic of Black Theology started from the suspicion that the theology of the state (civil religion) and that of the liberal churches helped to legitimize the conditions in which black Africans found themselves. Seeking to discover afresh the relationship between Christian faith and the struggle for liberation from oppression, Black theologians adopted a hermeneutics of correlation between the biblical witness and the political, socio-economic and racist context of South Africa. Thus the South African context and the Bible were seen as two "texts" deserving careful reading in order to bring about radical social change. This they regarded as "prophetic" theology.

Black Theology viewed the South African situation as one of conflict due to issues of power and the distribution of resources (Mosala 1989). Thus much of the energy was spent on analyzing the critical elements of this conflict, such as race, class, ideology and ethnicity, as they helped to keep the political, social and economic arrangements intact. Accordingly,

God was seen as one who took sides with the oppressed (Maimela 1986: 102). The situation of Israel in Egyptian bondage was likened to that of black Africans in South Africa, and the same God who helped free Israel from Egypt was invoked.

In Black Theology, Jesus is seen as God entering the very experience of the poor and oppressed, and a further claim is made that the suffering of the poor and oppressed is the suffering of God. Salvation in Black Theology is seen as a cry for a God-affirming social order, and not just a simplistic, emotional personal affair. However, liberation from human structures which dehumanize persons is not seen as the final coming of the reign (kingdom) of God, but rather only points to God's final act of liberation, the effect of which has already began. It is through the divine-human Jesus that human beings have been authorized to participate in changing social structures for the better. In Black Theology, liberation is viewed as *the* core of the Gospel of Jesus Christ, and not just an aspect of it.

20.3 BIBLICAL NOTIONS IN AFRICAN THEOLOGICAL HERMENEUTICS

The struggle of oppressed and poor blacks led Black Theology into a critical analysis of the South African situation and its peculiarities of racist ideology. Now, in post-apartheid South Africa, Black Theology has to revisit its earlier commitment that was focused on the political struggle of the majority, and re-examine the broader South African situation of poverty and underdevelopment that is still present under a majority government. The question is: Is there indeed a broader biblical tradition to which African theologians may refer? While not attempting to answer this question entirely, it is necessary, by way of conclusion, to evaluate some biblical notions which were at the core of Black Theology.

It is important to note that in Black Theological Hermeneutics the underlying presupposition was that *divine revelation happens within a specific social context*. Therefore the knowledge of God leads to a certain ethical life because of the very nature of God. The following biblical themes obtain in Black Theology.

20.3.1 God is a liberating God, revealed in situations of oppression

Black Theology recognizes God as the God of history. As such, the Old Testament account of God's revelation to an oppressed people (Israel) in the book of Exodus is taken very seriously. Some relevant passages are: Exodus 2:24–25; 15:1–2; 19:4–5; 20:3. Here, the distinctiveness of God's name is that it is associated with liberation from Egypt (particularly Exod 20:2–3, where Israel is warned against "idols" or gods who are not associated with the history of liberation from Egypt). Knowledge of Yahweh in the Old Testament is through his historical activity on behalf of the oppressed. In return, Yahweh concludes a covenant with Israel so that they may become responsible stewards of God's historic intervention. Through Israel, and despite of her lapses, God's liberating Lordship over all the earth will be realized (Isa 49:6; 42:4; 53:1ff.). Hence, God's liberating activity is not to be confined to Israel's history.

20.3.2 God defends the poor and defenceless

The crushing power of oppressors, Black theologians argue, is censored in the Bible. This is shown in passages like Isaiah 3:13–15 (God will indict oppressors); Proverbs 17:5; 19:17 (to insult the poor is to insult God, to be generous to them is to honour God); Proverbs 23:10–11 (God is a powerful guardian of orphans). Theology, as James Cone was to insist, is partisan: on the side of the poor and defenceless (1975:71).

20.3.3 The God revealed in Jesus Christ is a liberating God open to all humanity

Black Theology sees an obvious connection between God in the Old Testament and the coming of Jesus Christ who begins his mission in the world by referring to Isaiah 61:1–2 (Luke 4:18–19). Divine revelation is not separable from concern for the poor which Jesus takes up as the point of departure in his ministry. The divine plan of salvation is viewed as a continuous activity from the Old Testament to the New Testament, and to the present.

Jesus overcomes Satan and the demons (Luke 11:20), and this action is consistent with the theme of liberating the poor from all obstacles (Cone 1975:77). Such obstacles are found among the blind, lame, lepers, the deaf and the lifeless (Luke 7:22ff.). The reign of God is inaugurated through acts of liberation of the dispossessed (Luke 6:20, Matt 15:30). In Black Theology, Jesus' focus on the poor and the powerless forms an hermeneutical point of departure to the assertion that divine freedom as made possible by Jesus' crucifixion and resurrection, and is even *more* than the freedom made possible in history (Cone 1975:80). Here the Old Testament's view of God as one who wins battles, and the New Testament's view of a Saviour who is vulnerable before his enemies (and gives up his life for the sake of many), need to be carefully distinguished. In the New Testament's perspective, socio-political limitations do not necessarily negate the kind of freedom Jesus brings to human beings. Yet, in much of Black Theology, this recognition that socio-political liberation is not central in the New Testament has not been attended to adequately. However, the very notion that Black Theology is prophetic theology implies that it does not transcend the historical limitation of Old Testament concerns, and the timeless task of ongoing witness remains in a world where socio-political problems may only form part of the situation to be addressed. That is as it should be, for prophetic theology always points into the future, beyond itself.

20.4 THE FUTURE OF BLACK THEOLOGICAL HERMENEUTICS

Black theologians who hold onto the view that Blacks have suffered various forms of oppression and that they need more than political and socio-economic liberation (the main emphasis of Black Theology) seem to agree that the bigger issue for Africans is the dislocation of Africa's cultural-spiritual self. That is to say, Africans need to have a picture of the fullness of life which is consistent with a communitarian hermeneutic.

The South African situation has changed, at least in terms of a power-shift: from minority rule to a majority rule based on an open democratic dispensation. This change has meant political liberation for both the oppressed and former oppressors, raising the hopes of all South African peoples and indeed of all Africans. In which way, then, will theology in South Africa reflect broader community interests beyond merely political ones? How will Black Theology view socio-economic deprivation of the masses under a government they have themselves elected? Clearly, these will be some of the issues facing Black Theology in South Africa.

The term "black", as applied to theology in Africa, will probably in future be found redundant in view of the collapse of minority white rule in South Africa. Instead, reflection on the realities of present-day Africa in the light of the *Missio Dei* (God's historic mission) will no doubt be a multi-faceted task no longer concentrating on the blackness of people. Poverty, ethnic and gender conflicts, class and cultural ruthlessness, authority and right governance will constitute the core of this task.

Perhaps the greatest hope of a credible theological hermeneutic in Africa lies in the formation of truly visionary communities of faith committed to an inclusive society that reflects justice and mercy. The fragmentation of African communities and the absence of compassionate, shared leadership in much of Africa remains a most vexing problem. In the struggles ahead, the Bible still presents Africans with the living word of God for their peculiar circumstances.

READING LIST AND BIBLIOGRAPHY

Boff, Leonardo and Clodovis. 1987. *Introducing Liberation Theology*. Maryknoll: Orbis Books.
Croato, J.S. 1983. "Biblical Hermeneutics". In Fabella, Virginia and Torres, Sergio (eds.), "The Theologies of Liberation." In *Irruption of The Third World*, Maryknoll: Orbis Books.
Cone, C. 1975. *The Identity Crisis in Black Theology*. Nashville Abingdon Press.
Cone, J. 1986. *A Black Theology of Liberation*. Mary Knoll: Orbis Books.
– 1969. *Black Theology and Black Power*. Minneapolis: Seabury Press.
– 1975. *God of The Oppressed*: Minneapolis: Seabury Press.
Guitierrez, G. 1974. *A Theology of Liberation*. Maryknoll: Orbis Books.
Maimela, S.S. 1986. "Current Themes and Emphasis in Black Theology." In Mosala, I.J. and Tlhagale, B. (eds.), *The Questionable Right To Be*. Maryknoll, Orbis Books.
Maimela, S.S. 1990. *Modern Trends In Theology*. Johannesburg: Skotaville Publishers.
Martey, E. 1993. *African Theology: Inculturation and Liberation*. Maryknoll: Orbis Books.
Moore, B. (ed.). 1974. *The Challenge of Black Theology In South Africa*. Atlanta: John Knox Press.
Mosala, J.I. 1989. *Biblical Hermeneutics And Black Theory In South Africa*. Eerdmans Press.
Wilmore, Gayraud and James Cone (eds.). 1979. *Black Theology: A Documentary History, 1966–1979*. Maryknoll: Orbis Books.
Witvliet, T. 1987. *The Way Of The Black Messiah*. London: S.C.M. Press.

Feminist and Womanist Hermeneutics

Denise M. Ackermann

What do the ancient writings we call "The Bible" really mean? How are we to understand them, coming as they do from contexts and languages so different from our own? Do women and men understand the Scriptures in the same way? Do the writers from those ancient communities have the power to speak to the lives of women today? What happens when women read the Bible? How do women deal with the fact that the Scriptures are often discriminatory towards them? How should the Bible be normative for the faith and the daily lives of women? These and many other questions lie at the heart of the task of Feminist and Womanist Hermeneutics.

21.1 UNDERSTANDING THE TERMS

The meaning of hermeneutics is explained, *inter alia*, in chapter 17. Any attempt to define the word "feminist" is not easy and is often confusing because any definition requires taking a specific political stance and depends on how the person doing the defining views the past, present and future relationships between women and men in their particular contexts (Fiorenza 1993:20ff.). Women are not simply a mass of similar or like-minded people. Women live in very different circumstances and cultures. Their histories and material circumstances vary greatly. Some women in the Third World understand the term "feminist" as referring exclusively to white North American and European women seeking their liberation. Other Third World women are comfortable describing them-

SECTION B

HERMENEUTICS

selves as feminists, allowing their own interests and analysis of their particular contexts to shape their views. Unfortunately, certain early feminists fell into the trap of making universal assumptions about women and were blind to their own race and class prejudices. Today, however, feminists stress issues of difference and context in recognition of the fact that women come from diverse historical and social locations.

Against this background, it is not surprising that African-American women in their particular struggle for racial and gender justice have, in order to distinguish their approach from that of feminists, preferred to call themselves womanists.[1] As their experiences differ from those of white North American women, African-American women read the Scriptures through their own particular lenses. So also do African women whose approach again differs from both those of European feminists and womanists. (See section on African Women's Hermeneutics, chapter 22.)

All understandings of feminism have, however, certain elements in common. Existing relationships between the sexes and the way in which society is structured are found to be discriminatory and unjust. Feminists seek the transformation of society in which women's rightful place is affirmed and ensured. Broadly speaking, feminism can be described as "a lived experience, a political struggle for liberation, but ... also an intellectual activity" which women share (Ramazanoglu 1989:45).

People have always interpreted what they read from their particular contexts. Because women's experiences are diverse, the term "Feminist Hermeneutics" covers a number of different approaches to interpreting the Scriptures. Elisabeth Schüssler Fiorenza suggests that the goal of feminist biblical interpretation and the historical reconstruction of the Scriptures is "the critical praxis of emancipatory struggles for liberation" (Fiorenza 1993:20). Before examining how feminist scholars move towards this goal, it is necessary to say something about the history of women's biblical interpretation.

21.2 WOMEN'S BIBLICAL INTERPRETATION IN THE PAST

The Bible, as the source document of the Christian faith, has been read by women for centuries. However, reading the Scriptures selfconsciously *as* women, directing questions to it from women's experiences of the family and their place in societal and religious structures, is a more recent phenomenon. One hundred years ago, in 1895, part 1 of *The Woman's Bible* was published in the United States (Reprinted, Stanton 1986). Elizabeth Cady Stanton, its chief architect, stated in its preface that the aim was to revise those texts and chapters of the Scriptures which refer directly to women and exclude them. According to Fiorenza, this project contained two insights which are critical for Feminist Hermeneutics today: first, that "the bible is not a 'neutral' book, but a political weapon against women's struggles for liberation," and second, that "this is so be-

---

1 This term derives from Alice Walker's use of "womanist" in *In Search of Our Mothers' Gardens: Womanist Prose*. (San Diego: Harcourt Brace Jovanovich, 1983), pp. xi–xii.

cause the bible bears the imprint of men who never saw or talked with God" (Fiorenza 1994:7). *The Woman's Bible* was highly controversial, not only for its political implications, but for its radical interpretation of portions of the Scriptures. Cady Stanton's understanding of the male-centred nature of biblical texts and its implications for women remained largely unheeded by the majority of women for the next sixty years and more.

The women's movement of the 1960s and 1970s gave rise to a renewed interest in reading the Scriptures from women's perspectives in North America. Letty Russell edited *The Liberating Word: A Guide to Nonsexist Interpretation of the Bible* (1976) and Phyllis Trible's *God and the Rhetoric of Sexuality* (1978) appeared. These, and subsequent works, opened up a new feminist understanding of the Bible. Since then, feminist biblical scholarship has become an ever-expanding and exciting field of study and has contributed greatly to contemporary biblical research. Its richness lies in its diversity and an article of this nature cannot do justice to the many different approaches employed by feminist theological scholars. Accordingly, only certain trends in Feminist and Womanist Hermeneutics will now be examined.[2]

21.3 SOME APPROACHES TO FEMINIST HERMENEUTICS

Today, the question of scriptural authority is central to all discussions on Feminist Hermeneutics. To begin with, certain feminist theologians have found the Scriptures to be irredeemably male-centred. For them, its language and origins in the patriarchal culture of antiquity and the way it has been used down the centuries to discriminate against women, rob it of authoritative status for women.[3] Women who share this view have moved away from Christianity and sought other sources for their theology (Daly 1973; Downing 1987; Christ 1980; *Journal of Feminist Studies in Religion* 1989). They have rejected the authority of the Bible in their lives.

However, feminist scholars who work within the Christian tradition find themselves in an ambivalent situation. On the one hand, the Bible is undoubtedly a male-inspired document which holds patriarchal views, and on the other hand, it also serves as an inspiring and authoritative text for women trying to liberate themselves from patriarchal views and structures. Where does its authority lie for women in this situation? In wrestling with this question, different approaches to Feminist Hermeneutics emerge. I shall deal briefly with four of these approaches found in the work of Rosemary Radford Ruether, Letty Russell, Phyllis Trible and Elisabeth Schüssler Fiorenza.

---

2 Asian, Hispanic, Latin American, European and African women are all involved in finding their own particular hermeneutic approaches. See, *inter alia*, the following works: Fabella and Oduyoye 1988; Kwok 1989; Isasi-Díaz 1993; Tamez 1989; Oduyoye and Kanyoro 1992 and Hopkins 1995.
3 Patriarchy is understood as "a legal, social, and economic system of society that validates and enforces the domination of male heads of families over dependent persons in the household" (Ruether 1988:148).

SECTION B

HERMENEUTICS

Feminist liberation theologian, Rosemary Radford Ruether, starts with women's experience of oppression. She rightly points out that what have been called the objective sources of theology, namely Scripture and tradition, are themselves codified human experience: "Human experience is the starting point and the ending point of the hermeneutical circle" (Ruether 1983:12). She continues: "The uniqueness of Feminist Theology lies not in its use of the criterion of experience, but rather in its use of *women's* experience, which has been almost entirely shut out of the theological reflection of the past. The use of women's experience in Feminist Theology, therefore, explodes as a critical force, exposing classical theology, including its codified traditions, as based on *male* experience rather than on universal human experience" (Reuther 1983:13). At the same time as she insists on the criterion of experience, Ruether is at pains to point out that women's experiences differ greatly. According to her the critical principle of Feminist Theology is "the affirmation of and promotion of the full humanity of women. Whatever denies, diminishes, or distorts the full humanity of women is, therefore, to be appraised as not redemptive." Conversely, whatever promotes the full humanity of women "is of the Holy, does reflect true relation to the divine, is the true nature of things, is the authentic message of redemption and the mission of the redemptive community" (Reuther 1985:115).

Reuther comments that this principle is hardly new and rests on the theological concept that *all* of humanity is made in the image of God. It is, however, a central theme in Feminist Theology. With this approach she discerns a liberating-prophetic critique running through Scripture which places God on the side of those who are oppressed and marginalized by the ruling elites. Thus Ruether can say: "The word of God comes as a critique of these elites, calling them to reform their ways in order to be faithful to divine justice" (Reuther 1989:172).

Letty Russell, also a feminist liberation theologian, is, like Ruether, unequivocal about the biblical basis of her theology, the patriarchal nature of biblical texts notwithstanding. The Bible, she writes: "... continues to be a liberating word as I hear it together with others and struggle to live out its story. For me the Bible is 'Scripture', or sacred writing, because it functions as 'script', or prompting for life" (Russell 1985:138). Russell's interpretative key, arrived at through her own life story and in particular from many years of pastoral experience among the poor in East Harlem, New York, is the witness of Scripture to God's promise of bringing about the restoration of the creation in the Christ event: "That which denies this intention of God for the liberation of the groaning creation in all its parts does not compel or evoke my assent (i.e., it is not authoritative)" (1985:139). Russell acknowledges the similarity between her interpretative key and that of Ruether. For her, the Bible opens up possibilities of new life as we perceive glimpses of God's partnership at work in both the biblical story and in our own lives.

Russell further explains that in God's act of renewing creation, women and men are set free to develop new ways of relating to one another, to the world, and to God:

> This freedom of living in the "already, but not yet" of the New Creation is key to those who are struggling with structures of oppression and with biblical texts that are used to justify and even to bless these structures ... (1985:139).

Ultimately for Russell the authority of the Bible rests not in *authority understood as domination*, in which reality is seen in the form of a hierarchy or a pyramid. This understanding reinforces ideas of authority in a chain of command in which women are subordinate to men and in which authority is exercised over community. Russell proposes that *authority as partnership* expresses a feminist understanding of reality as a circle of interdependence. Rather than a chain of command, authority is exercised *in* community, thereby enforcing co-operation and respect for difference among people.

Phyllis Trible, a biblical scholar who in her work focuses on the Hebrew Scriptures, employs a literary critical approach informed by a feminist perspective (Trible 1978 and 1984). She reads the biblical stories in order to find God's intention in the texts. This requires listening to the text and interpreting it as accurately as possible. This process or journey through the Scriptures brings the reader face to face with the fact that the Bible is a mirror of both the horror and the holiness of life. In her book, *Texts of Terror*, for example, she turns to the dreadful tales of women such as Tamar, Hagar and the daughter of Jephtha, allowing them to speak "... on behalf of their female victims in order to recover a neglected history, to remember a past that the present embodies, and to pray that these terrors shall not come to pass again" (Trible 1984:3). With her hermeneutical approach, Trible hopes to find fresh insights in her reading of the text which may inspire repentance for the sins of patriarchy and hopefully lead to new beginnings and a biblical theology of womanhood (Trible 1985:149).

No feminist theologian has devoted more time, skill and painstaking scholarship to the hermeneutical question than Elisabeth Schüssler Fiorenza.[4] She recognizes that "... the Bible is source for women's religious power as well as for their religious oppression throughout the history of Christianity to the present" (Fiorenza 1994a:35). Unlike Ruether, Fiorenza does not see the goal of Feminist Hermeneutics as "women's full humanity", since humanity as we know it is male defined. She finds her hermeneutical centre of feminist biblical interpretation in the concept of "women-church", a term used to describe "the movement of self-identified women and women identified men in biblical religion" (1994a:126).[5] In her writings, Fiorenza sets out her critical feminist interpretive model in great detail, insisting that such a model must be both feminist-critical and historical-critical. This model, instead of accepting biblical authority unquestioningly, begins with a *hermeneutics of suspicion*. Readers are

---

4 For Fiorenza's critique of Ruether, Russell and Trible's hermeneutical methods, see *In Memory of Her*, pp. 14–21.
5 It is necessary to note that both Russell and Ruether work with the concept of women-church as well. See, for instance, Ruether's *Women Church: Theology and Practice* (San Francisco, Harper and Row, 1985).

SECTION B

HERMENEUTICS

invited "to investigate biblical texts and traditions as one would 'search' the place and location where a crime has been committed" (Fiorenza 1994:11). This is followed by a *hermeneutics of re-vision* which "'searches' texts for values and visions that can nurture those who live in subjection and authorize their struggles for liberation and transformation."[6] The goal of this two-part strategy is a critical assessment of the ancient texts in such a way that cultural stereotypes are challenged and "a different cultural and religious imagination" produced (Fiorenza 1994:11).

Fiorenza's hermeneutic, like Russell's and Ruether's, is firmly developed within a liberation framework. In such a framework illusions of objectivity are abandoned in favour of the realization that all interpretation takes place through the filter of the lens of the interpreter. Feminist Theological Hermeneutics is therefore critical hermeneutics. Fiorenza does not regard the Bible as a mythical archetype, but as "the historical prototype, or as a formative root model of biblical faith and life" (Fiorenza 1994a:34). Biblical texts are therefore placed under the authority of feminist experience. This insistence on the authority of women over the Bible makes Fiorenza's work different from Ruether's and Russell's.

21.4 WOMANIST HERMENEUTICS[7]

The particular history and context of African-American women and the lack of awareness among early feminists as to their own class and race biases, compelled African-American women to forge their own hermeneutical approach. A history of slavery, racism, dislocation and struggle for liberation shapes this approach. Womanist Hermeneutics is, like Feminist Hermeneutics, not a monolithic exercise, but is characterized by certain features which are singular. Among these is first the reliance on the work of African-American women writers,[8] and second African-American women's experience of community in the black church.[9]

Why is the literary tradition of African-American writers so important for womanist biblical scholars and theologians? According to womanist ethicist, Katie Cannon, these writers are recorders of the black experience who "convey the black community's consciousness of values which enable them to find meaning, in spite of social degradation, economic exploitation and political oppression" (Cannon 1988:78). These writings are

---

6 *Ibid*. For a more detailed discussion of Fiorenza's hermeneutic, see *Bread not Stone: The Challenge of Feminist Biblical Interpretation* (Boston, Beacon Press, 1984). For further elaboration see also *But She Said: Feminist Practices of Biblical Interpretation* (Boston, Beacon Press, 1992) and *Discipleship of Equals: A Critical Feminist Ekklesialogy of Liberation* (New York, Crossroad, 1993).
7 I acknowledge insights gained from conversations with womanist ethicist Joan Martin who with patience and kindness helped me to understand something of the character of Womanist Hermeneutics.
8 *Inter alia*, see the work of Zora Neale Hurston, Audre Lorde, Toni Morrison, Paule Murray, Mildred Taylor and Alice Walker. See also feminist theorist Bell Hooks (who prefers her name to be written without capital letters, thus bell hooks), and the work of Patricia Hill Collins.
9 Joan Martin also alerted me to further characteristics of Womanist Hermeneutics. They require *audacity* to analyse white-dominated structures in such a way that black women are made wiser; *responsibility* to interpret in and with the black community; an aesthetic which celebrates life and, lastly, an *awareness* of who black women are in relation to white women.

embraced "for their fidelity in communicating the baffling complexities and the irreducible contradictions of the black experience in America" (*Journal of Feminist Studies in Religion* 1993:30). In order to find a deep innate understanding of the social, cultural and political environment in which black people live, womanist theologians turn to this literary tradition.

In particular African-Americans have had to grapple with their history of slavery and its consequences for their lives right up to the present time. This history of slavery is a recurring theme in the work of the women writers who play such an important role in Womanist Hermeneutics (cf., *inter alia*, Morrison 1987). What does it mean for the faith experience of black people to have had slavery practiced and condoned by Whites who called themselves Christians? In reflecting on this question, Cannon identifies three distorted perceptions which made it possible for white Christians to condone slavery:

> As property, slaves were not seen as fully human; as Africans they were classified as heathen savages to be saved through enslavement; and as Christians, white and black, they were expected to believe that slavery was divinely willed in the Bible. (In Fiorenza 1994:6)

Sojourner Truth, a freed slave, summed up her hermeneutic by referring to the white minister's use of texts from Paul's writings in which slaves are enjoined to be obedient to their masters and saying: "I promised my Maker that if I ever learned to read and if freedom ever came, I would not read that part of the Bible" (in Thurman 1949:32). Within this harrowing history, African-Americans seek liberating themes in the Bible and find encouragement to resist racist discrimination and to celebrate their worth and dignity.

Affirming the God who has a special interest in and care for the oppressed and marginalized characterizes all liberation theologies. Working in this tradition, womanist theologian Dolores Williams recounts making a startling discovery. She finds two traditions for interpreting the Bible in the black community. The first is a Black Liberation Hermeneutic which claims God as the liberator of the poor and oppressed. This she calls "the *liberation tradition of African American biblical appropriation*" (Williams 1993:2). The second tradition, which Williams herself embraces, is the one that lays emphasis on female rather than male activity. This female-centred hermeneutic she calls "*survival/quality-of-life tradition of African American biblical appropriation*" (1993:6). She finds a biblical prototype for African-American women's experience in the figure of Hagar, the slave woman who was cast into the desert by Abraham and Sarah. Williams writes:

> In black consciousness, God's response of survival and quality of life to Hagar is God's response of survival and quality of life to African-American women and mothers of slave descent struggling to sustain their families with God's help. (1993:6)

What exactly is the "black church" which plays such an important role in the faith and actions of African-American women? To begin with, the "black church" was for a long time the sole place where black people were in control. As such, it was "the heart, centre, and basic organization of Black life" (Russel 1985:34). Today, according to Williams, "The black church does not exist as an institution." In fact, it escapes precise definition. It is not confined to one place. For some it is invisible, rooted in "the soul of the community memory of black folk." For others, it is the core symbol of four hundred years of struggle by African-American people against white oppression in which God is involved on their side. And, for yet others, it is the place where black people come to worship "without white people being present." Despite these differences, Williams writes "but we know it when we see oppressed people rising up in freedom." It is "the heart of hope in the black community's experience of oppression, survival struggle and its historic efforts toward complete liberation" (Williams 1993:204–206). Williams distinguishes between this invisible black church rooted in the soul of the black people and the visible African-American denominational churches which she finds guilty of sexism and poor leadership (1993:206–209).

According to Cannon, the role of the black church in biblical interpretation during the time of slavery served as a two-pronged weapon. On the one hand, confidence that the omnipotent power of God is with them, comforted the slaves and helped them to survive this oppressive system. On the other hand, it also made them discontented with their chattel condition. Black women, despite particularly noxious exploitation by their white masters, shaped their specific resistance and survival through their religious consciousness nurtured in this dual reality. After the abolition of slavery, black women continued to struggle against racist socio-political and economic structures. In Cannon's words: "The Black woman began her life of freedom with no vote, no protection, and no equity of any sort" (Russel 1985:35). Throughout their history, the black church has played a vital role in developing biblical teachings which resonate with the socio-economic and political experience of black women and men. In this endeavour, the experience of black women and their understanding of who Jesus is for them forms a powerful impetus for liberation. Cannon explains that the "Black womanist identifies with those biblical characters who hold on to life in the face of formidable oppression ...[they] search the Scriptures to learn how to dispel the threat of death in order to seize the present life" (Russel 1985:40). In summary, the prophetic and liberating tradition in the Bible remains the central authority for womanist theologians as it does for most liberation theologies. This tradition is interpreted in the light of the black contextual experience in all its diversity, as articulated by African-American literary tradition and the life of community in the black churches (*Journal of Feminist Studies in Religion* 1992:136).

21.5 IN CONCLUSION

When women interpret the Bible, they do so from specific historical and social contexts. There can accordingly be no single hermeneutic which is valid for all women. This article deals briefly with only two particular methods. But within both Feminist and Womanist Hermeneutics there are many different approaches, as neither feminists nor womanists are homogenous groups of people. Both share the search for a shift from a paradigm of domination to one of radical equality. This requires a continuous re-articulation of our interpretations as our different social and historical contexts change.

Despite the fact that the Bible reflects the patriarchal ways of the societies in which the biblical writers lived, despite the notable absence of women's voices in the Scriptures, despite serious critiques advanced by feminist biblical scholars on traditional interpretations of the Bible and their challenges to the uncritical use of biblical texts and despite the androcentrism of these texts, both feminist and womanist theologians still claim the Bible as the source book for their theologies which has the power to speak to the lives of women today.

READING LIST AND BIBLIOGRAPHY

Cannon, Katie G. 1988. *Black Womanist Ethics*. Atlanta: Scholars Press.
– 1993. "Womanist Perspective Discourse and Canon Formation." *Journal of Feminist Studies in Religion*. 9(1–2).
Christ, Carol P. 1980. *Diving Deep and Surfacing: Women Writers on Spiritual Quest*. Boston: Beacon Press.
Daly, Mary. 1973. *Beyond God the Father: Toward a Philosophy of Women's Liberation*. Boston: Beacon Press.
Douglas, Kelly Brown. 1992. "Teaching Womanist Theology: a Case Study." *Journal of Feminist Studies in Religion*, 8(2): Fall.
Downing, Christine. 1987. *The Goddess: Mythological Images of the Feminine*. New York: Crossroad.
Fabella, V. and Mercy A. Oduyoye (eds.). 1988. *With Passion and Compassion: Third World Women Doing Theology*. Maryknoll: Orbis.
Fiorenza, E.S. 1984. *Bread not Stone: The Challenge of Feminist Biblical Interpretation*. Boston: Beacon Press.
– 1994. *Searching the Scriptures: Volume 2, A Feminist Commmentary*. New York: Crossroad.
– 1994a. *In Memory of Her: A Feminist Theological Reconstruction of Christian Origins*. New York: Crossroad, Tenth Anniversary Edition.
Fiorenza, E.S. (ed.). 1993. *Searching the Scriptures: Volume 1, A Feminist Introduction*. New York: Crossroad.
Grant, J. 1989. *White Women's Christ and Black Women's Jesus: Feminist Christology and Womanist Response*. Atlanta: Scholars Press.
Hopkins, J. 1995. *Towards a Feminist Christology: Jesus of Nazareth, European Women, and the Christological Crisis*. London: SPCK.
Isasi-Díaz, A.M. 1993. *En La Lucha: In the Struggle, A Hispanic Women's Liberation Theology*. Minneapolis: Fortress Press.
Journal of Feminist Studies in Religion, 5/1, 1989.
Morrison, T. 1987. *Beloved*. London: Chatto and Windus.
Newsom, C.A. and Ringe, S.H. (eds.). 1992. *The Women's Bible Commentary*. London: SPCK.
Oduyoye, M.A. and Kanyoro,M. (eds.). 1992. *The Will to Arise: Women, Tradition, and the Church in Africa*. Maryknoll: Orbis.
Pui-lan, K. 1989. "Discovering the Bible in the Non-Biblical World." *Semeia* 47.

SECTION B
HERMENEUTICS

Ramazanoglu, C. 1989. *Feminism and the Contradictions of Oppression*. London: Routledge.

Reuther, R.R. 1983. *Sexism and God-Talk: Toward a Feminist Theology*. Boston: Beacon Press.

– 1985. "Feminist Interpretation: A Method of Correlation." In Russell, Letty M. (ed.), *Feminist Interpretation of the Bible*. Philadelphia: Westminster Press.

– 1988. "Sexism as Ideology and Social System: Can Christianity be liberated from Patriarchy?" In Johnson, P.A. and Kalven, J. (eds.), *With Both Eyes Open: Seeing Beyond Gender*. New York: Pilgrim Press.

– 1989. "Religion and Society: Sacred Canopy vs. Prophetic Critique." In Ellis, M. and Maduro, O. (eds.), *The Future of Liberation Theology: Essays in honor of Gustavo Gutiérrez*. Maryknoll: Orbis Books.

Russel, L.M. (ed.). 1976. *The Literary Word*. Philadelphia: Westminster Press.

– 1985. *Feminist Interpretation of the Bible*. Philadelphia: Westminster Press.

Stanton, E.C. et al. 1986. *The Woman's Bible*. Salem, NH: Ayer.

Tamez, E. 1989. *Through her Eyes: Women's Theology from Latin America*. Maryknoll: Orbis.

Thurman, H. 1949. *Jesus and the Disinherited*. Nashville: Abingdon.

Trible, P. 1978. *God and the Rhetoric of Sexuality*. Philadelphia: Fortress Press.

– 1984. *Texts of Terror: Literary-Feminist Readings of Biblical Narratives*. Philadelphia: Fortress Press.

– 1985. "Postscript: Jottings on the Journey." In Russell (ed.), *Feminist Interpretation of the Bible*. Philadelphia: Westminster Press.

– 1985a. "Black Feminist Consciousness." In Russell.

Townes, E.M. (ed.). 1993. *A Troubling in My Soul: Womanist Perspectives on Evil and Suffering*. Maryknoll: Orbis Books.

Walker, A. 1983. *In Search of Our Mothers' Gardens: Womanist Prose*. San Diego: Harcourt Brace Jovanovich.

Williams, D. 1993. *Sisters in the Wilderness: The Challenge of Womanist God-Talk*. Maryknoll: Orbis Books.

African Women's Hermeneutics

Mercy Amba Oduyoye

22.1 INTRODUCTION

The women's revolution is one of the main challenges of our time. Part of this is the Feminist Movement. The theological aspect of the revolution which we are concerned with is Women's Theology, which is referred to by a number of names. In the United States of America with its multi-cultural experience, we have Theologia Mujerista of the Spanish-speaking women, Womanist Theology of the African-American women, and the Feminist Theology of the white American women. These theologies are distinctive by reason of the different life experiences of these women – all of whom are American, but for whom being American means different things. Basically however, they are all concerned with an approach that African women will name "a motherhood" agenda, but the particular names highlight aspects of domination that are more keenly experienced in their community. Economically disadvantaged as the descendants of migrants, forced or voluntary, socially marginal as people of minority cultures, and blatantly discriminated against as people of colour, these women's theologies bear the marks of a people whose humanity is trampled over.

In this chapter we deal with *African* Women's Theology. It falls into the mould of those women who are doubly and triply burdened – women whose humanity needs to be proclaimed.

Surveys of the theological reflections of women bound together in The Circle of Concerned African Women Theologians (hereafter referred to as The Circle) are already being undertaken by women in Africa and be-

SECTION B

HERMENEUTICS

yond. The fact that we are meeting on our own initiative has often come as a surprise to many. Since theology is defined as the activity of academics in seminaries, colleges and universities, The Circle's definition of who does theology becomes itself an affirmation that "every Christian is a theologian". We want to develop tools for reflecting on our faith. The hermeneutics of contemporary Christian Theology in Africa assumes all too easily that women and men experience the world in the same manner. Yet the illustrations of life's realities are those of men. Up to very recently, women faced with oppressive religio-cultural structures found nothing but the call to acquiescence in the theology of African male theologians and preachers. Even when economic and racial issues are theologized, the outcome often does not empower women to struggle for full humanity, but only to the extent that traditional culture allows. It has been left to women to craft tools adequate to the real questions we face as African women, be they Christian, Muslim or of any other faith. We are searching and testing the available tools and asking fresh questions on the religions and cultures that we participate in.

The survey I offer here is structured into five sections. The first four sections are the hermeneutical principles that I have found:

1. Bible, Church and African tradition are interpreted contextually.
2. Community and motherhood agendas are the basis for interpretation.
3. Interpretation includes translation into African cultures.
4. There is no expectation of unanimity in interpretation.

Finally, I will conclude with a look at the agendas of African women as they struggle to develop their own hermeneutical interpretation.

22.2 THE CONTEXTS

Any effort related to theology anywhere, and especially in Africa, has to state clearly the religious and other contexts. In contemporary times one cannot, for example, assume that theology means Christian Theology. The religious context in which Christians do theology in Africa is not a homogenous one. Muslims and the adherents of traditional African religion can also tell us about God and God's activity in the world. In this contribution, however, the reference to theology is restricted to Christian Theology. It is Christian Theology done in a context of a living and dynamic culture that is imbued through and through with traditional religious symbols, beliefs, rites and rituals, a whole world-view that we drink with mother's milk and breathe till death. Christian theologians in Africa can never forget this.

The second is the context of the church itself. The church in Africa is also multi-faceted. Each Christian community or denomination has a peculiar ethos by which it is distinguished, but all are one in Christ. Every church has got a rather monolithic theology because usually one is told from the pulpit and through catechises what is to be believed. However, often the socio-economic and political realities say the contrary. Sometimes the church's own silence in the face of oppression and the perplexities of contemporary life, and especially in the face of the marginalization of women, belies its preaching of a caring God. Church theology leaves no room for debate and often counsels what amounts to fatalism as a response to dehumanisation. Churches teach doctrines concerning what is to be believed and nurture members to develop what sometimes amount to domesticated ethical and moral attitudes by which their lives are guided. This theology, mostly done from pulpits, is simply to be received as no dialogue is possible in that format. There are indeed other church structures for this dialogue, but unfortunately not all who "go to church" avail themselves of these. However, even ordinary Christians cannot afford to stand aloof. They should themselves participate in the task of articulating the Christian faith and making it operative.

Women in The Circle are trying to promote this "theology by the people". The people, Christians in the pews, do reflect theologically on their lives and even on the sermons they hear. Only, nobody invites them to share their reflections. Women theologians of The Circle are training themselves to affect this situation. By their participation in forums of church women, they suggest fresh approaches to old theological statements. They join a wider circle of Christian women in reviewing the church's history and the manner in which Christianity and African culture have interacted. The publication of *Women Hold Up Half The Sky* (Ackermann 1991) in South Africa, and *Life, Women and Culture. Theological Reflections* (Edet 1990) in Nigeria are examples of this approach to reflecting theologically on the participation of women in church and society.

We begin with stating that the concept "men" does not include women and that most of the time we delude ourselves in thinking we are included. We face realistically the experience that even when we are present, our concerns and views are not required for decision-making that affects the whole community. Acknowledging the truth and telling it as it is, is an important hermeneutical principle.

Until churches and universities began to Africanize their leadership, church theology was basically "mission theology". It was theology crafted to make Euro-American Christians out of African "pagans". It was a theology supposedly devoid of politics, economics, and ethnocentrism, but which in fact simply denied the existence of the primal religion and culture of Africans. Much of it assumed the superiority of Euro-American structures of meaning, life-styles and world-view. Much of the mission theology persists today in a variety of modes. Its proponents include African men and women. What these people need to realize is that all theology is contextual.

The first noticeable change was in the curriculum of Religious Studies Departments of the state universities. Full attention was given to developing them as places in which Traditional African Religion, Christianity and Islam met, interacted and dialogued. This more faithfully reflected the reality people lived in. A more sensitive reading of and research into Africa's primal religion was undertaken and the content of its beliefs and

SECTION B

HERMENEUTICS

practices were reflected upon for their theological content. In this regard, J.S. Mbiti's *The Prayers of African Religion* (1975) may be regarded as seminal in that he moved beyond the phenomenology of African religion to its theology. African theologians educated in the western systems now feel empowered to do their own thinking and thus to craft Liberative Theology, reflecting on their faith in terms of the situations in which they live. Associations of theological institutions and of theologians have developed, as have several journals of theology. All these have been structures and sources of inspiration and of intellectual stimulation and sharing. Women seek to contribute to these, and especially to seek to impact the articulating of the theology of African religion and to analyze the implications of African culture for Christian theology.

Africans do theology from the actual experience of living in Africa with its poverty and wars that cause famine and the displacement of people, and the so-called international debt that has turned Africans into slaves on their own continent. African theologians who follow biblical paradigms know that human knowledge about God comes with experiencing God in history. It is therefore not helpful to idolize the received pattern of theologising from the experience of the European Reformation of the 16th century or from the pietistic movement, as these are not related to how Africans experience God. It also means that there is a need for relating biblical situations of agony – cries and prayers like those of Hagar, Moses and the burning bush, and Amos – to the exploitation of the market economy and the blatant cheating that accompanies trade. African theologians seek a word from God that will liberate the minds of Africans and set their feet on the path of recovering the dignity of humanity in Africa. This is the prophetic theology that strengthened the hands of the anti-apartheid struggle in South Africa. It is this prophetic theology that African women theologians have taken up. They hermeneuticaly employ the biblical poor.

22.3 WOMEN'S COMMITMENT

The struggle against hunger and sheer destitution stretches the energy and imagination of the majority of African women. The contemporary women's challenging of traditional attitudes has unleashed energy that is now being utilised in the search for physical, material and spiritual provisions for a quality of life worthy of the label "human". The traditionally vulnerable status of women is being transformed as women work towards human rights, legal rights and human dignity. Women struggle for the right of self-defense in the face of the violations of their persons and their rights. African women continue to offer themselves as living sacrifices, but they expect and challenge men to do the same for the integrity of the whole community. While women continue to give their life and time to others, they actively look for fairness and for reciprocity. The response of women theologians is to join other women's movements in seeking transformation that will permeate all aspects of life, involve domestic and social issues, change the lifestyle of men and communities, and usher in an era of dignity and respect for all. Women theologians work to undergird the women's struggle to stimulate transformation of society. This is a struggle for life that is the outcome of a spiritual force, a strong affirmation that the Holy Spirit empowers those who work for justice and compassion to prevail. Women doing theology have committed themselves to act justly and to see justice done, conscious that that is the road to true peace. They seek a holistic approach to life, having realised that therein lies our survival and our wholeness.

The many roadblocks placed in the path of women are being identified. When women ask: "Who will roll the stone away?", they recall the resurrection experience and move out in faith. In Africa, women have begun to write up the stories of women who have been a part of the church's mission. We owe it to ourselves and to posterity to unveil women's presence in history. In doing this, they are also asking other theologians to pay attention to the vulnerable elements of society. An "unjustified" page has attention paid only to the left hand margin. "Justifying" a page means also attending to the right hand margin. Likewise, no human community can be described as just and complete as long as either margin is ignored. Hence the great store placed on inclusiveness as essential for an empowering and Liberative Theology. We often speak of women, young people and other disadvantaged persons as "being marginalized". Being marginalized is a state which leads persons to develop a low self-esteem, accept their status as non-participants and even prepare arguments for their own exclusion. Against this, the practice of Jesus of Nazareth and his involvement with the "marginalized" of his day has become a guiding principle in African Women's Theology.

African women theologians take the Pauline teaching about incorporation seriously. For this reason we seek in the theological task a way of participating in the transformation of the human community. Several members of The Circle have written reflections on what Jesus means to them and to Africans as a people. Some have contributed to anthologies on Christology. The common thread in all this is that Jesus is the friend who stands in solidarity with the marginalized and works to transform not only individual lives, but also the oppressive situations and structures that hold all, but especially women, in bondage. African women constantly refer to Jesus as the one who respects their humanity and is always ready to restore that which is perishing. Through Bible studies, the gospel events in which Jesus interacts with women or stands by them to affirm them have inspired a lot of reflection.

Another strong thread in African Women's Theology is the call to women to dispense with the coping devises evolved over centuries to cushion the effects of powerlessness as they are seen to contribute to the persistence of oppression. They have turned attention to the need for a prophetic word as belonging to a global movement aimed at enhancing life. They concern themselves with struggling against the violence perpetrated against the vulnerable members of society. If a word before is worth two after, and women's voices are stronger than the brawn of men,

SECTION B

HERMENEUTICS

then speaking up is indispensable in the task of whittling down the spiral of oppression. The theological effort is a resistance against the temptation to contribute to one's own marginalization for the sake of maintaining peace without justice. African Women's Theology is theology in the prophetic vein that declares it is not right that the perpetrators of injustice should be left to enjoy ill-gotten peace of mind.

African women theologians see themselves as part of a global movement aimed at enhancing life. They concern themselves with understanding so that they may resist the political and economic liaisons that impoverish their people and buttress unjust structures. They work for people's participation. With determination they struggle against the culture of silence which is the cloak of injustice underneath which the vulnerable are violated.

22.4 COMMUNITY AND MOTHERHOOD

This motherhood agenda of making space for life, caring for it and ensuring that others also respect, honour and care for life, has meant that in doing theology, The Circle has a principle of mutual-mothering as well as seeking the interests of the communities to which one belongs: church, academy or sociological group. All these affect one's theological reflection. Doing theology involves knowing what others have written on the subject, doing your own research, listening and studying the contemporary scene and context and finally having something to say on the subject. The women's process does not end here, for the divorce of theology from ethics does not make for commitment and responsible living. The life-centred approach has meant that theological reflection begins with life-stories, community experience and diagnosing of the challenges of community. Doing theology becomes a process that needs field research and participation in action programmes geared to reflecting on and responding to situations. This should be done from our theological perspective and spirituality that portrays the integrity of persons and communities which seek justice, shalom and mutual respect. These become principles for the critique, criticism or affirmation of religions, doctrines and cultural demands.

While individual theological reflection is the usual style of the academia, The Circle is also promoting a community approach as a practical demonstration of the mutual mothering which we believe will enable us to craft theologies that respond to the realities we live. Women jointly research, or else bring their individual research findings to a forum of the sisters, where they are heard, discussed, sharpened and refined in accordance with the cardinal ideas of the researcher. This process also enables mutual learning and discovery of fresh approaches to the questions we seek to answer. In this we are backed by the principle that it is not only formally trained theologians who think theologically. Prayers, songs, biblical insights, questions on culture, explorations of culturally based beliefs offered by women in the pews of churches and elsewhere are in themselves theological and therefore resources for theology.

This community-oriented perspective has also directed us towards an inter-disciplinary approach. We take into consideration the variety of theological disciplines, the study of other religions, the findings of sociology, economics and politics. Oral tradition, folk tales, proverbs and ritual are resources for doing theology and their presence in the discourse makes theology attractive to persons who ordinarily would put themselves beyond the theological quest. Fiction written by Africans has become for us a source from which to discover the theology and spirituality of Africans, be they Christian or Moslem, but especially that of the traditional religio-culture. Herein lies the hermeneutic of continuity and interaction that we find critical if we are to be relevant contributors to the development of theology in Africa. Rosemary Edet, Teresia Hinga, Elizabeth Amoah and Mercy Amba Oduyoye have all developed theological courses from these sources. In meetings of The Circle, we consciously used African languages in plenary sessions and interpretation in committee work, thus making possible inter-cultural dialogue and wider participation of women who are outside the academic communities. In this way we contribute to making African Theology whole, hence more relevant and powerful.

Based on the affirmation that theologians exist outside the academies and ecclesiastical structures, we have availed ourselves of the creative theological expressions of church women's groups, Christian women's prayers and the songs they weave from events and sayings of the Bible, and their commentaries on them. Church women of Africa are enthusiastic students of the Bible. This gives the foundation for developing among them a conscious theological statement of the faith by which they live. In their organisations they create plays to retell stories and to dramatise their relevance in daily life. In this way of appropriating the Bible we are confronted with a hermeneutic of affirmation that comes from the similarity between the religio-culture of much of the Hebrew Scripture and that of Africa's traditional religio-culture. This love for the Bible as a source of theology is what demands of women theologians in Africa that they do their own reading, study and interpretation of the Bible.

We have opened a way for women to express their theology in prayer, poetry and song, and we have been offered dramatic presentations by church women, the eloquence of whose theology we have been thankful for.

22.5 HERMENEUTICS OF CULTURE

The question which Philip put to the Ethiopian: "Do you understand what you read?" is one that all theologians face, whether the reading is of Scripture, culture, or the actualities of the day. In the attempt to do our own theology, we have had to pay keen attention to the traditional religio-culture and its influence in our daily lives and in the pronouncements that emanate from churches. To create a holistic and balanced view of biblical events, stories and teachings, women are affirming the presence and action of women in the Bible. Where, up to now, these have

SECTION B

HERMENEUTICS

been glossed over, they are highlighted, as in the case of Puah and Shipporah, Tamar the daughter of David, Tamar the daughter-in-law of Judah, Dinah the daughter of Jacob, Jephtah's daughter, "the concubine" of the Levite and many more. Women re-read and re-interpret the lives and actions of the women which men's theology either ignores or demonizes, by researching into the cultures that were contemporary to the biblical writings or into the myths of other peoples. The violent men of the Bible, whose actions are glossed over when their violence is against women, are called up for re-examination, and the courageous and compassionate women whose lives are glossed over are recalled to be role models. Women do all this firm in the belief that no bird can fly with one wing only. Through all this is the affirmation that we as women are simply human beings seeking to do the will of God and to live before God, sometimes failing, sometimes succeeding, but always conscious that this world belongs to God and not to the male human being. Through this theological effort, women demonstrate that they have taken up the responsibility to live fully their vocation to be human. Being in the image and likeness of God brings with it direct responsibility to God for what happens to one's community and to one's person.

We see here theology born out of the need to live as active participants in history. We have an affirmation that it is contrary to human dignity, and a denial of the affirmation that we are created in the image and likeness of God, if we do not live out the implications of this assertion. In this theology, women seek to keep afloat the vision of life described as life in all its fullness.

African Women's Theology is firmly grounded in the conviction that theology does not culminate in words. Theological statements must take on flesh and become alive among people. To realise this, we attempt to unveil the theology that comes through the practice of religions in Africa. We are suggesting that theological messages are coded into myths and ritual practices that are the common heritage of all Africans, whatever their religious affiliation. The theological community in Africa is therefore seen by women theologians as one that is multi-faith and multi-cultural.

In many parts of Africa one finds extended families in which the three dominant religions of Africa are practised. In the same family there will be rites that pertain to traditional religio-culture, there will be celebrations of Muslim feasts and fasts, just as they will do with Christian rites and festivals. What is important is the cohesion of the community. So the family celebrates the significant events in the religions in solidarity with those of its members who are adherents of the particular religion. Simply comparing beliefs and practices is insufficient for touching the spirituality, ethics and morals associated with the religions, and certainly is insufficient for the crafting of a theology adequate for multi-religious living. We see doing theology as living conscious of the energy that makes us human and binds us together to inhabit the earth, holding firm to and affirming its integrity.

One of the fundamental questions is how we discern the hand of God.

Who speaks for God? A second question is how we reach an agreement on what it means to be truly human. For us these are very critical questions as the norms of society seem determined and dictated from men's perspectives. We attempt to theologise from a principle which states that human beings are to live conscious of the reality of God as the source and energy that makes us human and binds us together to inhabit the earth and to respect our mutual dependence. Underlying our theological reflection on humanity and community is an affirmation that it is better to seek to please God than to please the human male. It becomes clear that women are no longer ready to swallow men's interpretation of culture.

22.6 NO UNIFORMITY

Many African theologians have taken the position that it is not helpful to theologise from the experience of the European Reformation of the 16th century or from the Pietistic Movement because these are not related to how Africans experience God in action. It also means that there is need for paying more attention to the use of a liberative methodology in the teaching and development of African Christian Theology. The Theology of Liberation in Africa includes the liberation of African culture and the liberation of Africans from cultures that are debilitating. Africa struggles against the socio-economic weight of western powers. Africa works to rehabilitate the humanity of the African that has been eroded by the ravages of white racism. African Liberation Theology comes from these concerns (cf. chapters 6 and 20) and it is within this context that African women theologians also work.

Women theologians who constitute The Circle tend to concentrate on asking basic questions related to African religion and culture. They seek the reasons behind the beliefs and the practices. Teresa Okure summarizes well the basic principle by which African women theologians interpret and understand religion and culture when she writes as follows on human development:

> All serious efforts, aimed at promoting true human development, will demand that we identify and strive after eliminating from our cultures those elements, factors and practices which are inhuman and dehumanising, whether these are found in social culture, political culture, scientific and technological culture, economic culture of even religious and church culture. (Okure 1989)

Hence for African women theologians, breaking with the culture of silence is an important principle. We are seeking the truth about these cultures. Whom or what do they serve? For we believe that it is only the truth that shall free us from the negative aspects of culture.

A study of the methods and interpretive structures of African Women's Theology reveals a variety marked by the context and the community in which the discourse takes place. Teresa Okure's biblical studies are offered in the context of New Testament scholarship and yet her highly scholarly work is firmly located in the concerns of African Christianity and of women's experience. Rosemary Edet with her doctorate in Religious Education pointed us to religion in African creative writings in

SECTION B
HERMENEUTICS

her book *The Resilience of Religious Traditions in the Dramas of Wole Soyinka and James Ene Henshaw* (1984). In both of them one finds a hermeneutic of affirmation as well as continuity between the biblical and the African tradition.

Nyambura Njoroge, Isabel Phiri and Christina Landman offer us an historical study of Christianity in their countries from the stance of women, which arises out of a hermeneutic of suspicion that the men and missionary versions were not conscious of the presence of women in the churches and have therefore ignored their contribution to its development. Those studying African Traditional Religion and Christian ethics, like Elizabeth Amoah, have opened the way for serious study of Africa's religio-culture from the women's perspectives. Here the need to balance the hitherto androcentric interpretation of culture comes to the foreground. The younger women such as Vibila Vuadi and Joyce Tsabede are already reflecting on the primary materials cited above. Some theologise from their study of Islam although they are themselves Christian, while others like Rabiatu Ammah, a Moslem, share their theological reflections of the same African experience.

Many more of the women of The Circle are pastors and do their theology in sermons and have to wrestle with cultural realities, including how women are portrayed in creation myths, the power of life-cycle rituals and the taboos associated with them. They not only have to theologize in words, but also in deeds, having to provide pastoral care for women struggling with these realities. The challenge of these cultural practices to how the Christian faith is stated and lived, is one which women have undertaken to wrestle with more than men. As Musimbi Kanyoro (whose doctorate is in linguistics and who has been a Bible translator) has indicated, there is need for an intentional study of hermeneutics, especially with regard to the use of cultural realities as a biblical hermeneutic.

Where physical life is threatened, women have begun to break away from traditional responses of acquiescence to challenge the roots of their hurts, that is, the patriarchal mode of thinking and its paternalism towards women. Since, in African culture, women have been battered for centuries, the women theologians have become bold in speaking out, and have generated energy to move against all forms of sexual harassment. No longer do women feel it disloyal to admit to male violence in their lives. The Christian vision of humanity under the rule of God demands that we do justice and resist evil. When this call to resistance conflicts with the cohesion of community, the choice is the resistance. This choice is based on the principle that, in the final analysis, if it dehumanizes women, it dehumanises the whole community and the whole of humanity. We understand the well-being of women as integral to the well-being of the whole community.

22.7 ISSUES FOR OUR CONTINUING STUDY

This chapter is an attempt to indicate in a preliminary fashion the hermeneutics of African Women's Theology. We have a lot of work still to do and the development of hermeneutics is one such area. We do need to discuss whether the perspectives named here, or others, are the basis on which we do our interpretation of biblical and church traditions. We do have a choice, of course, to keep raising issues that are important for African women and this we shall continue to do as we work on the question of hermeneutics. In Africa, we pride ourselves on being community oriented. In the church we have a vision of a community of women and men equally yoked before God and equally in the image of God. This puts on all theologians the duty to break the silence around various manifestations of oppression. Theology is to serve the need to transform power, and to become itself a transforming power. The theological task is incomplete until its effects are seen in lives that glorify God because persons side with God who is just and compassionate. We have placed an emphasis on publication as a method of publicising the dehumanization that goes on in society. If we are to help redefine what brings shame to persons, families and communities, we cannot continue merely to talk among ourselves.

Aware of the domesticating use of the passion of Jesus, women are redefining what is salvific sacrifice. They have insisted that the crucifixion of Jesus is qualitatively different from the lives of the many crucified women of our societies. Jesus was a living sacrifice. He knew what He was doing. He knew that the liberation of human life depended on his acceptance of the cross. He willingly took it up so that He might become the way to reconciliation and the beginning of a new humanity under God. The crucifixion of women by religion and culture is aimed at boosting the male ego and at fuelling male determination to reduce the humanity of women to something other than the image of God. It is to break this spell that women have undertaken to break the silence around their real situations, to refuse the image of the vulnerable ones, and to become rather a community of resistance. Doing theology has become a way of setting the records straight by telling our own stories. It is an affirmation of the right and duty of women to be actors and thinkers in their communities.

Life, as women see it, demands co-operation and partnership. As Mary, mother of Jesus co-operated with God in the Christian history of salvation, all women in theology seek to co-operate with God. The vision of a people under God relating to one another in love and compassion, has guided our daily lives and attitudes. Women's vision of life as consisting of healing and caring, excludes marginalization. It is a motherhood agenda that constantly focuses loving attention on the least and spares no effort to retrieve the lost coin. They see life as Mary sees it, as a "magnificat" of the God who transforms and liberates. With Mary as model, women theologians proclaim that without women's participation the transformation of human society towards justice, peace and compassion will not happen, because it takes women to insist that hierarchical and periphery/centre paradigms should give way to caring communities. It takes women to resist the biases against women, to reconstruct tra-

African Women's Hermeneutics

SECTION B

HERMENEUTICS

ditional theological themes or provide fresh visions and perspectives on Christian Theology.

The concerns of African women in theology for Africa's religio-cultural history and realities have meant that while we share the feminist and womanist critique of the non-inclusiveness of the language of traditional theology, it has not taken up much space in our work. This should not be read as a dismissal of the issue, as African women often highlight the feminine imagery with regard to God and the Christ, and the inclusiveness of the perspectives of Jesus of Nazareth. Patriarchy and power that feature prominently in feminist theology are also part of the African women's concerns. The hermeneutics of suspicion that accompanied the exegesis of Scripture and the re-reading of Christian history by feminists and womanists form part of African women's theological methods. In Bible study we have shown sensitivity to marginalized cultures, and exclusivist passages used against women who may have been black attract attention. We even find black women marginalized from the Bible, as in translations where the black woman of the Song of Songs (1:5), is depicted not as black, but as "sunburnt".

African women theologians join both womanists and feminists in the concern for justice and liberation. All dominating systems are named, analyzed and deconstructed. With the womanist, the African women lift up the factor of slavery, which we continue to experience as the economic injustice embodied in world trade, and in the class system of masters and servants, maids and mistresses. We experience, as do African-American women, the triple burden of being black, female and poor, and our own special fourth of being African.

When, as African women, we resist male domination, we are accused of seeking to emasculate the African male. It is expected that the horror of this accusation will bring us guilt feelings and make us give up our bid for the recognition of our full humanity. However, we analyze these burdens with the tools available to us and seek to reflect theologically on them in order to develop a spirituality that overturns them and replaces them with what is life-giving.

With all women liberation theologians we have acknowledged that numerical strength does not necessarily promote women – though we represent at least half of humanity. But with patriarchy's marginalization of women's perspectives, women's numbers do not count that much. Further we know that as women theologians we are a minority. But if we search for truth and side with justice, our numerical weakness will not be a handicap. The combination of these two factors move us to refuse the role of a silent majority as women and to associate ourselves with the prophetic seeking to pronounce God's "No" to injustices and to proclaim God's "Yes" as we find apt expressions for the announcement of the good news of the gospel of Jesus Christ.

READING LIST AND BIBLIOGRAPHY

Ackermann, D. et al.1991. *Women Hold up half the Sky: Women in the Church in Southern Africa*. Pietermaritzburg: Cluster Publications.

Edet, R. 1984. *The Resilience of Religious Traditions in the Dramas of Wole Soyinka and James E. Henshaw*. Rome.

Edet, R. and Umeagudosu, M. (eds.). 1990. *Life, Women and Culture: Theological Reflections. Proceedings of National conference of a Circle of African Women Theologians*. Lagos: African Heritage Research and Publications.

Fabella, V. and Oduyoye, M.A. (eds.). 1988. *Passion and Compassion: Third World Women Doing Theology*. Maryknoll, New York: Orbis Books.

Mbiti, J.S. 1975. *The Prayers of African Religion*. London: SPCK.

Njoroge, N. *African Christian Social Ethics*. (Ph.D. thesis Princeton Theological Seminary).

Oduyoye, M.A. 1986. *Hearing and Knowing: Theological Reflections on Christianity in Africa*. Maryknoll, New York: Orbis Books.

– 1992. *The Will to Arise: Women, Tradition and the Church in Africa*. Maryknoll, New York: Orbis Books.

Oduyoye M.A. and Kanyoro, M. (eds.). 1990. *Talitha 'Qumi: Proceedings of the Convocation of African Women Theologians*. Ibadan: Daystar Press.

Okure, T. 1988. *The Johannine Approach to Mission*. Tübingen: JCB Mohr.

– 1989. "A Theological View of Women's Role in Promoting Cultural/Human Development." *Ecclesiastical Review* 31.

Okure, T. et al. (eds.). 1990. 32 *Articles Evaluating Inculturation of Christianity in Africa*. Eldoret: AMECEA Gaba Publications: Spearhead.

Phiri, A.I. 1992. *Women in African Church and Culture: A Critique of Patriarchy*. (Ph.D. Thesis University of Cape Town).

African Hermeneutics
Cornel du Toit

23.1 INTRODUCTION

Questions abound when one takes up the topic of African Hermeneutics. What is African Hermeneutics? (What is Africa?) Is it possible to speak of hermeneutics if one lacks an established theology as with the African Initiated Churches (AICs) or African Traditional Religions (ATRs)? If hermeneutics is the science of interpretation and understanding, can there be different legitimate ways of practising it? If not, then Western Biblical Hermeneutics remains the only source of reference and interaction. This cannot be accepted and we must enlarge our understanding of hermeneutics to include a holistic look at religion, religious understanding, interpretation, and communication. This does not exclude hermeneutical rules, established to guide our interpretation. Nevertheless, hermeneutics is more than the science of reading and interpreting texts. The world of texts exceeds biblical and sacred texts or any specific literary work. It is impossible for the African to separate interpretation and understanding from all other aspects of life – and this is the concern of this article.

The three important religions in Africa are Islam, Christianity, and the African Traditional Religions. These religions could again be subdivided into a multiplicity of subdivision, traditions, and so on. One could also consider the theologies of Afro-Americans and liberation theologies from the Third-World, since their hermeneutics have exerted an important influence on African Hermeneutics. One could also try to give a formal description of the history and theologies of different African religions, which would not necessarily answer the question of hermeneutics. One might also try to find common hermeneutical denominators like colonialism, oppression, and poverty, with which to describe these religions. These may all be very important hermeneutical keys as the question of poverty, for example, shows. Perceptions of God, religious experience, self-esteem, world-view and the like are all vitally determined by one's

SECTION B

HERMENEUTICS

basic living conditions. It would seem sacrilege to expect a western hermeneutic consciousness from people lacking the basic means of existence.

Looking at the Christian tradition, one has to reckon with different cultures, the histories of the so-called mission churches and the establishment of black "main-line" churches, or one could concentrate on those churches that have inculturated Christianity and given it a specific African identity (like the African Initiated Churches (chapters 10, 24). One has to bear in mind the influence the African Traditional Religions have exerted on AICs, and their importance for African theologians writing from a post-colonial perspective.

When one reads present-day African theologies it soon becomes clear that African Hermeneutics is of a very specific kind[1] and includes the African world-view and culture, its histories and religions. African Hermeneutics considers the Bible and African Traditional Religions as sources of equal importance.

Hermeneutics, as we have seen, is the science of interpretation and gets its name from the Greek myth of Hermes, the winged messenger of Mount Olympus, whose job it was to interpret (Greek: *hermeneuein*) the sayings of the Oracle at Delphi. But how are African oracles interpreted and by whom? How are African messages conveyed and received by the African people? The voices of the ancestors, mediating the will of the gods, have been muffled for many years, overwhelmed by many voices of missionaries proclaiming the one and only way to the one and only truth. Until recently this truth was accepted in Africa, with all the delights and burdens it brought. After many years of servitude and struggle, however, these yokes have been lifted and Africa is taking stock of its gods. The single truth proclaimed in Africa divides into many different church denominations and traditions, each claiming to have the correct interpretation, the best hermeneutics, the best messengers of God. One can imagine Africa's scepticism about the claims of Western Hermeneutics.

From the very beginning, the Christian hermeneutical tradition was inclined to find the single spiritual truth within a particular biblical passage. We do know, however, that most texts allow for numerous interpretations, and that to accept one single truth is almost invariably a sad reduction of reality. Western Biblical Hermeneutics cannot be understood apart from its preoccupation with the book of the Bible, seen as the final revealed truth of God. Anyone claiming to represent the one and only interpretation of this truth could also, on this higher biblical authority, expect acceptance of his or her interpretation. But this has changed with current developments in hermeneutics and our new insights into the nature of understanding.

---

1 In the past little serious attention was given by African theologians to the problem of Biblical Hermeneutics. Fasholé-Luke (quoted in Parratt 1983:91) indicated that, historically, the missionary penetration of Africa was done by male Europeans with a fundamentalist view of the Bible, and until fairly recently this factor has tended to circumscribe biblical studies on this continent.

African Hermeneutics

Even in the western world hermeneutics has shown truth to be open, dynamic and subject to reinterpretation and recontextualisation. The so-called hermeneutical circle shows the interpretative process as an involvement in examining a certain text or event through a systematic investigation of the general and the particular, the results of which, in turn, are related to what is already known by the interpreter. This process continues in a circle, moving from one subprocess to another, until the interpreter is convinced of a satisfactory interpretation. But the process is never-ending. Understanding, the interpretation of texts, and the search for truth are continuing and open-ended processes. This implies that any final meaning keeps evading us. Our existence remains a mystery. We keep on trying to explain this mystery to which the multiplicity of texts and interpretations bear proof. No final hermeneutical method is possible. The dream of developing an ontology hermeneutics is not only impossible but contradicts the open endedness of human nature (Ricoeur 1974:23).

But what is the case in Africa? What is the relationship between African and Western Hermeneutics, if one can speak of it at all? Does Africa and the west meet in the same way as the premodern and postmodern meet?[2] Parratt (1983:92) urges African theologians to take the problem of a genuine biblical Hermeneutics seriously, as a preparatory stage of African Theology, and argues that a good deal that passes under the name of African Theology is inadequate because it lacks a solid foundation in biblical exegesis. This does not mean that they should simply quote European scholars as authorities. He enthusiastically quotes D.N. Wambudta, who stresses the need for African theologians to return to the original biblical languages, and who warns against interpreting the Bible too easily in the light of African religions, rather than according to its own canons (Parratt 1983:92). This insistence has led to a reaction by many African theologians who concentrate exclusively on African Religions as their source, and discard the Bible altogether. African theologians have today become more confident about what Maluleke (1996:4) calls African Christianity. This means following a hermeneutics demanded by the African text, which is much broader than a certain phase in Western Biblical Hermeneutics. Parratt displays an insensitivity to the nature of African culture and the hermeneutics he proposes is still solidly embedded in the western world-view, culture and literary theory, epistemology, view on the nature of truth, and so on, which have all changed since the time Parratt wrote his article.

The time has passed, however, in which Western Hermeneutics/Theology is normative. In many instances, western theologians are looking at African religiosity with renewed interest. Not only has the religious

---

2 Thornton (1996:144–145) mentions that the South African condition is more postmodern than it is post-colonial. In contemporary South Africa there are literally no names, no vocabulary, to discuss major aspects and parts of its political situation. There is no agreement on what are the boundaries of "black" or "white". No one knows whether to refer to "tribes", "ethnic groups", "language groups", "peoples" or "races".

SECTION B

HERMENEUTICS

point of growth shifted from north to south; the southern growth point also has interesting features. It is not a duplication of western Christianity, it has a deep spiritual strength, it operates within an oral culture, it is free from western metaphysical constraints, it renders important critique on western culture, science and technology and it offers an alternative to western forms of doing theology, succeeding in relating in interesting ways traditional religious ideas with those brought to Africa. Faith in the west has lost its innocence and is seen as an ever-interpreting faith seeking a second naiveté (Thiselton 1992:348). Although Africa is critical of western interests, it can offer them this religious innocence which is still intact in African communities. The individualism, typical of modernism, is foreign to African people who hold a hermeneutics of potential or initial trust because of shared beliefs, practices, conventions and traditions.

Hermeneutics is not a western or scholarly prerogative. All people practise hermeneutics since they communicate every day and are challenged to understand correctly, to relate conflicting ideas and to express their ideas again when misunderstood. People practise hermeneutics when listening to the radio, when reading a paper, when talking politics, or when participating in gossip! This hermeneutical activity can be cultivated to become an art, enabling us to understand and speak more carefully. Although hermeneutics may be studied by a minister of religion or a theologian, it actually belongs to the community. In African context, hermeneutics is the *indaba* of the community. It means listening to the sage and asking him or her critical questions. It means challenging the system that we may have become accustomed to – especially if we find it oppressive or outdated. It means listening to the stories of our fathers to explain difficult present-day problems, and telling our own stories. We relate to stories since they embody our understanding of ourselves, our fears and hopes. Through stories, as in the case of texts, we reinterpret and renew our existence. Existential issues have always been very much part of African self-understanding and hermeneutics.

Although people see and interpret things differently, there are always good reasons why they understand what they do. Hermeneutics helps us to understand why people differ. It shows the power strategies people use to get their point accepted. It also helps us to come to agreement. The task of hermeneutics is not to undermine creative and individual approaches to understanding (and so create an one-dimensional way of seeing things), but to make us aware of our specific *culture of understanding*, of possible logical mistakes in the process of interpreting, and of possible power strategies underlying our style of interpretation. It also helps us to understand ourselves and others and to recognise the influence of culture, religion, pre-understanding and many other factors which co-determine the understanding process. Hermeneutics concerns our **world-view** – that is, the way we try to find meaning in our lives and world; it concerns our understanding of God and humans, our relationship with the past and the ancestors, and how it affects us today; it concerns our present difficulties in our families and communities, our suffering and hardships, it also concerns our understanding of the future and how we act to influence it. Hermeneutics concerns the language we speak, how we express ourselves and understand the expression of others (communication); it concerns our customs and belief systems and how they influence our views, and other aspects of our lives. African Hermeneutics comes naturally in the sense that most aspects of life are integrated into a harmonious unity.

23.2 THIRD-WORLD HERMENEUTICS AS BLACK, LIBERATION, AND AFRICAN HERMENEUTICS

To place African Hermeneutics one must remember the wider context of so-called *Third-World Hermeneutics* in which it developed. The term *Third-World Hermeneutics* stresses the contextual nature of hermeneutics in the Third-World countries. Theological developments in Third-World countries could not ignore the poverty, exploitation, illiteracy and suffering of the people of these countries. For them hermeneutics meant first and foremost to understand and interpret the situation in which they found themselves. To read a text is to read life through the lens of the text. The hermeneutical process moves from life to text and from text to life. In this two-way movement texts question our lives, and our existential experiences are also brought to the text. We not only understand and interpret ourselves and our world in a certain manner, we are also affected and changed by the texts we allow into our lives. This is especially the case in Third-World Hermeneutics.

Third-World Hermeneutics implies that there is also a First and perhaps a Second-World Hermeneutics, from which it differs. Third-World countries have often found the gods and the guns, the texts and the truths of the oppressors to be quite intimidating and difficult to disagree with. Third-World Hermeneutics alleges that to understand a text, text and reader must meet on the same level.[3] When text and reader meet each other as free entities, without the purpose of simply overpowering the other, then free discourse, critical questioning and creative inter-action become possible. Third-World Hermeneutics refuses to meet any text like a victim approaching its oppressor. It challenges and reinterprets the text. The text is to serve life. Third-World Hermeneutics recognises that texts are brought to us by text bearers and that these often structure the text – receiver relationship through the way they read, interpret, explain and preach these texts. Hermeneutics and the art of politics are often not to be distinguished.

Third-World Hermeneutics refers to the way countries with a background of colonialism, exploitation and a missionary history try to un-

---

3 This does not exclude the fact that texts want to convince, inspire, teach, change and influence the reader. In communicating with another I also want to convince, influence and the like. I can, however, not meet a text like another person. Texts tend to have the last say – as they are written and therefore fixed. My dialogue with the text becomes but another text. The world of texts is therefore not fixed and autonomous, but open. This comes to the fore in the inter-text (the influence of other texts in a specific text) in which texts are always in communication with each other.

SECTION B
HERMENEUTICS

derstand what has happened to them.[4] It develops from the perspective of colonialism, poverty, underdevelopment, economic exploitation, and cultural victimization. The Third-World is, however, such a large and complex concept that one has to distinguish different contexts and histories. To narrow Third-World Hermeneutics down to Africa does not simplify the task. Hermeneutics in Africa cannot be separated from Black Theology in America or in Africa, because of the reciprocal influence between the two continents.

Although African Hermeneutics overlaps with Latin American Hermeneutics, and Black Hermeneutics, there are also specific distinctions to be made. It is, however, inevitable that this chapter will refer to and deal with the whole concept of hermeneutics in the liberation context. I will try not to overlap too much with what has already been said.

Black Hermeneutics refers, according to Thiselton (1992:419–420), to three distinct contexts. Black Theology in South Africa focuses on issues pertaining to colonial history and apartheid; North American Black Theology finds expression in the historical memory of slavery and its aftermath; African Hermeneutics in African states mainly concerns *contextualization* and the relation between the Bible and African cultures. Although the Black Theology of the North American, James Cone, has influenced Black Theology in South Africa, his context and approach are different. All these movements stress experience and struggle as contexts of hermeneutics. Thiselton (1992:423) has correctly indicated that it is tempting, but one-sided, to suggest that African Hermeneutics stresses contextualization, where Latin Americans speak of praxis, and North American Black Theology speaks of black experience.

Black Theology in South Africa, although it took its example from Afro-American forerunners, has predominantly been a South African phenomenon, promoted by people like Basil Moore, Manas Buthelezi, Steve Biko, Allen Boesak, Frank Chikane, Desmond Tutu, Mokgeti Mothlabi and many others. Many African theologians have felt that Black Theology has put too much emphasis on political and economic liberation at the expense of the spiritual component. Black theologians have been equally critical of African Theology, feeling that they encouraged a cheap alliance between African culture and Christ. In the apartheid era it was felt that promoting the uniqueness of African Theology might promote the idea of apartheid. It was also feared that some indigenous church groups may concentrate on Africanisation to the detriment of the liberation struggle. Reconciliation between Black Theology and African Theology came about in 1977 in Accra, Ghana, with the Pan-African Conference of Third-World theologians, when James Cone indicated that they were not as different as had previously been suggested (Schoffeleers 1988:109–110).

Developments in **Afro-American** and **Liberation Hermeneutics** influence African Hermeneutics, and vice versa. Africa remains, however, the

---

4 One example is the book by R.S. Sugirtharajahl, *Voices from the margin. Interpreting the Bible in the Third World*, which looks at Africa, Latin America, India and Indonesia, amongst others.

one focal point for Afro-American Hermeneutics, the other focal point being the Afro-Americans' own history and experience of enslavement. It is, however, not limited to these issues. Afro-American Hermeneutics is also concerned about its place in a post Christian, postmodern, pluralistic and global context (Coleman 1993:69). According to Coleman (1993: 71–71), Black Theology in America developed as a conscious discipline in the mid-1960s, underwent a second phase between 1970 and 1975, when African-American theologians took their case to Euro-American colleges and seminaries, a third phase when it focussed on global issues affecting them, and they have now embarked upon the fourth phase, namely the utilisation of indigenous resources along with interdisciplinary strategies in their theological discourse. This specifically includes researching the religious past of African people for expressions of faith that may be translated into the present. While they concentrated in the 1970s and 1980s on Marxist social analysis, they are now concentrating on developing interdisciplinary skills to examine and appropriate multi-layered discourses within the cultural history of American people, by examining what Coleman (1993:75–76) calls "tribal talk". This is mediated through African Hermeneutics, exposing African folklore, traditions and practices.

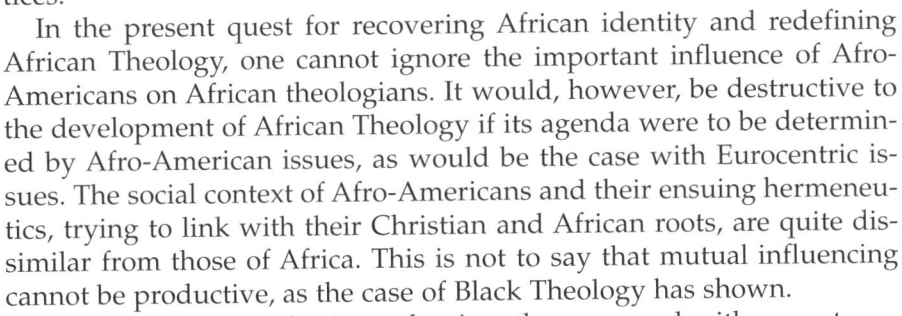

In the present quest for recovering African identity and redefining African Theology, one cannot ignore the important influence of Afro-Americans on African theologians. It would, however, be destructive to the development of African Theology if its agenda were to be determined by Afro-American issues, as would be the case with Eurocentric issues. The social context of Afro-Americans and their ensuing hermeneutics, trying to link with their Christian and African roots, are quite dissimilar from those of Africa. This is not to say that mutual influencing cannot be productive, as the case of Black Theology has shown.

African Hermeneutics is predominantly concerned with ways to reconstruct African Theology independent from western theological influences. It is the effort to understand and interpret the religious significance of African culture and to determine the theological character of African Traditional Religions. Present-day African theologians are aware of the pressure imposed on African Hermeneutics during the liberation period, but do not focus exclusively on it. They concentrate on the anticolonial struggle and on post-colonial reconstruction, trying to find what is typical of Africa and searching for an African intellectual self-definition. The quest for an African Hermeneutics testifies to the need for thinking autonomously and creatively in a context of political threat, economic need and the presence of western influences. This essay tries to come to grips with developments during the last two decades, during which African theologians have started to make a decisive effort to recover what is typical of African Theology. There are several ways in which this is done. Our concern is to deal not with those thinkers who wanted to recover African religions without taking notice of the influence of Christianity, but those who took African religious reality as their point of departure. Thinkers like J.B. Sanquah and Okot p'Bitek prepared

SECTION

B

HERMENEUTICS

the way by concentrating on what African Traditional Religions are all about (see Awolalu 1991:129–131).

African Hermeneutics obviously cannot refer to a single approach in interpreting and understanding African religions. There are also different degrees to which theologians concede the world-view, ideas and practices of African Traditional Religions. African Theology can be practised neither in isolation, nor by ignoring the very formidable presence of Christianity in Africa. It is easier to agree on commonalities like the influence of colonialism, the impact missionary work had on Africa, the common struggle against poverty, illiteracy, underdevelopment and so on, than to agree precisely on how to integrate African Traditional Religions into an African Theology.

Many African theologians are very critical of those who endeavour to synthesise African Traditional Religions with any other religious tradition. Onunwa (1991:120–121) for example, refers to the debates, conferences and polemics of the mid-1950s and early 1960s on "indigenization", "Africanization", "Theologia Africana" or "Black Theology", which were concerned with practical methods of making Christianity an authentic "African Religion", using some elements of the traditional religions, in order to make Christianity relevant to the traditional situation. Christianity had to be interpreted in the context of their traditional religious experience, language and culture. For Onunwa this means that they subscribed to the idea of Christianity being superior to the traditional religions, despite their efforts to show the Traditional Religions as a people's search for ultimate meaning. When Christians or any other interest group use African Traditional Religions as a means to an end, this is, for theologians like Onunwa, simply not acceptable.

23.3 THE DISTINCTIVENESS OF AFRICAN HERMENEUTICS

It is unwise to restrict African Hermeneutics to any specific characteristic. A more precise delineation may become possible as this hermeneutics develops and is studied. It includes the reactionary and socio-critical. For the purpose of this contribution I shall define African Hermeneutics as the effort to rid Africa of the unacceptable legacy of colonialism, to recover African traditional ideas and to indicate how this is as important a source as the Bible in providing Africans with their specific spirituality.

23.3.1 Hermeneutics without a book but not without a text: The African way of reading life

The text that African Hermeneutics tries to understand is much wider than the biblical text, or western-oriented theology, since it includes the African world as text. As Awolalu (1991:131) puts it: "African Traditional Religion has no written scriptures or records, yet we can say that it is written everywhere for those who have eyes to see." Religion permeates every aspect of peoples' lives and can be found in their riddles and proverbs, songs and dancing, rites and ceremonies, myths and folk-tales, shrines and sacred places, and in their artistic designs.

African Hermeneutics

African Hermeneutics is a contextual hermeneutics, aware of the legacy of colonialism, the history of African oppression and exploitation, but determined to recover African identity and formulate a theology which takes cognisance of African culture and African Traditional Religions. African Hermeneutics is an understanding of Africa by Africans, for Africans. John Pobee (1996:54) quoted Éla in this regard, saying that one of the primary tasks of Christian reflection in Black Africa is to reformulate our basic faith through the mediation of African culture. African symbolism must replace the cultural presuppositions of western Christianity, namely *logos* and *ratio*.

In the post-colonial era, African Hermeneutics seems to be more concerned with Africanisation than with liberation, although the latter is not excluded. For Pobee (1996:57), African Theology must restore the identity and ethos of *homo africanus*. There is resistance to this approach, which is seen by Muthukya (quoted by Pobee 1996:56) as the heathenisation of the church.[5]

African Hermeneutics is a hermeneutics without a book, but not without a text – the text of African suffering and dependence. The Bible (book) is read with this text in mind. As Éla (1991:259) puts it: "The colonised peoples never had a complete view of Christianity exactly because they were restricted to the 'book' without the 'text'. Bereft of a historical, critical sensitivity that would relate the salvation message to a particular context of colonial domination, the missionary church kept Africans in line with taboos and sanctions instead of launching them into the historical adventure of liberation – where, precisely, the living God is revealed."

African Hermeneutics **differs from hermeneutics in the west**, but not because rules determining understanding in one context are not valid in another. It is, however, a question of different emphases, a different language and culture, a different self-understanding and world-view. Hermeneutics depends on the specific concept of truth one has, the emphasis placed on the written or the spoken word, the way people integrate theory and practice, one's critical aptitude, and so on.

Onwu (1985:146–150) has already stressed the problems of language and world-view as specific problems of African Hermeneutics. Many biblical concepts simply do not exist in African culture, or have a totally different meaning. This especially concerns the personality of Christ, who can be labelled Black Christ, African Chief, Elder Brother, Great Ancestor. While we know that the African world-view easily assimilates the Old Testament world-view, the Bible was brought to Africa framed in a Western world-view. Onwu (1985:150–153) mentions the fact that, by the time Christianity was introduced into Sub-Saharan Africa in the mid 19th century, the world-view of the Christian theologians was reminis-

---

5 The full quote reads as follows: "This is what they mean by African Christianity. No mention of the one and only saving Gospel of Our Lord Jesus Christ. No mention of sin. No place for the authority of an inspired Bible. Instead their arguments are based on the traditional background of the African people, their culture, customs and belief. If natural culture and religious customs are acceptable to God, why did Christ send his disciples to preach the Gospel to every creature in the uttermost parts of the earth?"

SECTION B

HERMENEUTICS

cent of only the biblical one. Under the influence of the Enlightenment they had already outgrown the biblical (as well as African) world-view. They could hardly still make sense of the biblical references to demon possession, and to angels and spiritual forces operating in the affairs of human beings. These, however, fitted perfectly well within African cosmology, which believed that spiritual forces, both evil and good, operated in the world – a world of charms and amulets, sacrifices, ancestral worship, witches and wizards.

23.3.2 Protesting hermeneutics

Theological Hermeneutics would be sterile if it ignored the physical constraints influencing peoples' experience. African Hermeneutics can be typified as a hermeneutics of protest, against factors crippling its people. African Hermeneutics is a reactionary hermeneutics, trying to come to grips with post-colonial Africa.

Part of this process concerns the effort to understand and deal with the impact of a post-missionary era. For Éla (1991:257), the God of missionary preaching was a distant God, foreign to the history of the colonised peoples. Exploited and oppressed, they found it difficult to identify this God with the God of Exodus. The primary role of the Bible, and especially the Old Testament, in African religious movements is to express the reaction and revolt of African Christians.

23.3.3 Hermeneutics of sociocritical theory

According to Thiselton (1992:379), Socio-critical Hermeneutics can be defined as an approach to texts, traditions and institutions which seek to penetrate beneath their apparent function to expose their role as instruments of power, domination and social manipulation. The idea behind this kind of hermeneutics is to achieve the liberation of those over whom power or social manipulation is exercised. Socio-critical theory provides the theoretical hermeneutical framework for Liberation Hermeneutics, which includes on a meta-critical level African and Black Hermeneutics.

Socio-critical Hermeneutics becomes imperative in a context of oppression where texts, and especially religious texts, are subservient to the existing ideologies. Radical critique of knowledge, for Habermas, is only possible as social theory (Thiselton 1992:282–283). Hermeneutical understanding as social critique must test traditions in relation to their embodiment of social force and epistemological distortion.

The real challenge for Africa is the ongoing development of an African Hermeneutics and an African religion in which the reinterpretation and critical accommodation of African Christianity, African Traditional Religions, and other factors of importance, will be determinative of a future theological profile. This may prove to be much more important to African identity than Liberation Theology was. This process cannot, however, be artificially constructed by any group of theologians with specific blueprints in mind. One can expect this process to develop spontaneously, being unflanked by developments within the African Initiated

Churches. These developments may be similar to religious developments all over the world where one finds the accommodation of a multiplicity of religious styles existing in juxtaposition.

For Itumeleng Mosala only a materialist reading of biblical texts, which takes up the conflicting social and political forces and interests, can constitute a genuinely Socio-critical Hermeneutic (see Thiselton 1992:425). In Mosala's own words (1989:5–6): "The notion that the Bible is simply the revealed 'Word of God' is an example of an exegetical framework that is rooted in an idealist epistemology. I criticize that position in this study because it leads to a false notion of the Bible as non-ideological, which can cause political paralysis in the oppressed people who read it."

Thiselton (1992:429) rightly warned against the danger that any selective use of texts to encourage the oppressed in the end mirrors the strategy of the hermeneutical method of the oppressors, who use texts to re-enforce and re-affirm their corporate identity and interests.

23.3.4 Can the Bible be the neutral Word of God?

There is a close relationship between the biblical world and that of traditional Africa. Parratt (1983:90) has remarked that the world of traditional Africa, like that of the Gospels, is one in which supernatural powers impinge on the human world in every respect, since every aspect of life is subject to spiritual powers. The biblical references to demon possession, the healings and miracles performed by Jesus and the apostles, fit perfectly well into the African world view.

However, this is true not only of the apocalyptic background of the New Testament. It is the AICs, in particular, who have shown a considerable preference for the Old Testament. This can be ascribed to many factors, especially the similarities in world-view, the Exodus tradition, the emphasis on the poor, and the fact that the Old Testament deals with so many aspects of life, like the social, agricultural, family and ritual aspects, all important to African religion (Parratt 1983:91).

Special thought should be given to the question whether the Bible can be the neutral word of God. Uka (1991:153ff.) challenges the idea that African Theology has to be rooted in the Bible as well as the idea that there cannot be a valid theology of African Traditional Religions. African Theology is not theology if it is Christian Theology or imported theology. He is also critical of the way in which African theologians in the past simply interpreted Christianity in African terms. This sentiment is underscored by Maluleke (1996:6) when he refers to Bediako, who said that the Christianization of the pre-Christian tradition of Africa could be seen as one of the most important achievements of African Theology. Africanization, however, should not be confused with indigenization, which has already been achieved by the African Initiated Churches. What is at stake is the intellectual question of how African Christianity, employing Christian tools, can set about mending the torn fabric of African identity and hopefully point the way to a fuller and unfettered African humanity

SECTION **B**

HERMENEUTICS

and personality. For Uka (1991:154), African Theology is the theology of African Traditional or Indigenous Religions – not the African Theology that tries to solve the problems of indigenization of a new and foreign religion. African Traditional Religions must be freed from those western concepts which have for a long time restricted and imprisoned them. It remains, however, to be seen how Uka will employ "Christian tools" to mend African identity.

In this connection a debate is raging concerning the equation of the Bible with the Word of God. For Maluleke (1996:12), the equation of the Bible with the "Word of God" is not only naive, but a dangerous form of naivete. He sees this equation as being debilitating for Black and African Theologies and as much more harmful than the equation of colonialism with Christianity, or of the African past with Christianity. The reason is that this equation has been used to legitimate the demonisation of African traditional culture and religions. The point is that the equation of the Bible with the Word of God implies that it is possible to appropriate the Bible unideologically. For Maluleke (1996:11), the equation of the Bible with the Word of God has been the most consistent tool in questioning the validity of both African Christianity and African Theology. It is African Theology's reference to African Traditional Religions and Black Theology's reference to liberation that has caused both to be dismissed on the basis of lack of biblical grounding. This argument is fundamental in determining the nature of African Hermeneutics. From an African point of view, this exclusive stance has caused divided loyalties, since Africans have had to deny the importance and appeal their very own traditions and customs had and still have on them. From a western point of view it has offered the opportunity to impose western ethics, world-view and theology on Africa. Although there is a case to be made that the Bible is often intolerant, Western Hermeneutics itself had to relativise this to accommodate the multiplicity of diverging truth claims from its own traditions.

There is, however, more to the issue. What then is the status of the Bible in Africa if it is not to be seen as the Word of God? This is once again the peculiar character of African thought. It does consider the Bible the Word of God, but not so as to exclude many ideas, customs and rites from African culture and traditional religion. Africa knows the secret of accommodating (not indigenising) divergent ideas. In a holistic manner, all things are integrated. African thought does not operate on the level of western metaphysics, where a substantial ontology determines the detached nature of things as they exist in and for themselves. One has to differ from the oft-quoted remark by Leopold Senghor that reason is Hellenist and emotion is Negroid[6] (See Serequeberhan 1994:6). Africa does

---

6 Elsewhere Serequeberhan (1994:45) quotes Senghor as follows: "White reason is analytic through utilisation: Negro reason is intuitive through participation. European is empiric, the African mystic. The European takes pleasure in recognising the world through the reproduction of the object ... the African from knowing it vitally through image and rhythm. The African does not realise that he thinks: he feels that he feels, he feels his *existence*, he feels himself; and because he feels the Other, to be reborn in knowledge of the world."

not separate in a Cartesian manner the mind from the body, or reason from emotion – as is often done in the west. African thought is rational and emotional. African Hermeneutics favours a relational ontology where life-giving interactions determine what are considered important and true. On this level the Bible has become important to them, but in a way that it does not exclude the simultaneous influences of past traditions.

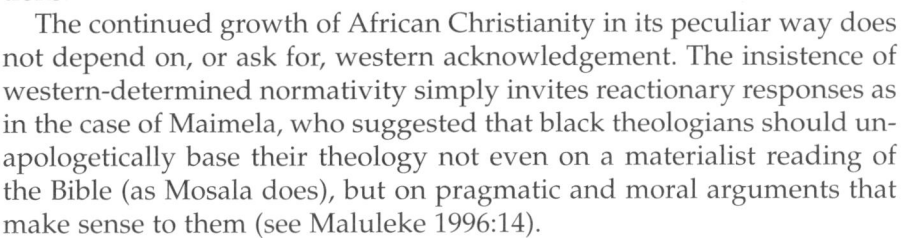

The continued growth of African Christianity in its peculiar way does not depend on, or ask for, western acknowledgement. The insistence of western-determined normativity simply invites reactionary responses as in the case of Maimela, who suggested that black theologians should unapologetically base their theology not even on a materialist reading of the Bible (as Mosala does), but on pragmatic and moral arguments that make sense to them (see Maluleke 1996:14).

For Maluleke, the way out of this trap is to confront not only the Bible, but all other sources and interlocutors of theological discourse precisely at a hermeneutical level *(ibid)*. Canaan Banana has proposed that what he calls "oppressive" texts, must be removed from the Bible and that the religious experiences of other peoples ought to be added to the Bible (see Reed 1996:282–288). It must be stated that the Bible does not belong to the west. It belongs to those who read it and live from it. The danger is real that in reacting against the abuse of any text, the text may be identified with those misusing it.

23.4 THE INFLUENCE OF AFRICAN TRADITIONAL RELIGIONS (ATRS) AND THE AFRICAN INITIATED CHURCHES (AICS) IN CO-DETERMINING AFRICAN CHRISTIANITY AND THEOLOGICAL HERMENEUTICS

To understand African Hermeneutics and the reason why it focuses increasingly on the ATRs, attention must be given to these religions. To determine their importance, statistical information is given below (23.4.1). The numbers of their adherents, however, do not seem to explain their influence sufficiently; the answer can rather be found in the quest for African identity (23.4.2). A watershed point concerning the importance of the ATRs was reached when theologians began to reckon them as a religion and not as pagan (23.4.3). African Traditional Religions are the mainspring for African customs, narratives, symbols and rites, indispensable for developing an African Theology and Hermeneutics (23.4.4). The African Initiated Churches represent the group in which Christianity and African Traditional Religions came to be integrated in a fascinating way. This will be dealt with shortly (23.4.5). Our hermeneutical concern is the way African theologians understand themselves, African religion, its place in the world of religions, and how they visualise (idealise) its future. The idea is not to idealise or romanticise the ATRs, but to recognise the important influence they have. Sarpong (1991:289) sounds a warning note in this regard when he says that, like all other cultures, African traditional cultures contain several objectionable elements. This is not to say that they do or did not fulfil a social function now or in the past. A careful examination of many an African custom, no matter how repulsive it may be to modern people, will reveal that it once played – or even now plays – a meaningful role in the social life of the people.

23.4.1 Geographical distribution of adherents of African Traditional Religions in some African countries (percentage relative to the population of each country)[7]

There has been a dramatic drop in numbers of followers of the ATRs since 1900, as the selected list of statistics below shows. This is because most Africans were converted to Christianity or Islam. Trends displayed are representative of the whole of Africa. If these trends continue one would expect that the ATRs, would eventually become totally insignificant. How is this to be understood in the light of the renewed interest in the ATRs and the fact that most prominent African theologians try to accommodate the ATRs' ideas in their work? One would perhaps be wrong in expecting a revival of the ATRs, or in thinking that they will eventually replace African Christianity. It would perhaps also be a mistake to assume that they will eventually die out as an active religious group, as the statistical trend seems to indicate. Renewed interest and appreciation for the ATRs may even stimulate the ATRs' growth. Although statistics reflect a drop in numbers of adherents to the ATRs, they do not display their influence in African life and on African theologians. One can expect that the cause of the ATRs in a democratic and post-apartheid South Africa will be promoted by a renewed spirit of nationalism. One can also expect ATR ideas to become more of an academic concern as the process of urbanisation speeds up. Theologians favouring ATR ideas are mostly not religiously observant in the ATR context. It is in groups like the AICs that these ideas come to fruition (see Schoffeleers 1988:114–119).

ATR ideas will be influential in the reformulation of African Christianity. They give access to African culture, and provide African theologians with material to develop an African Christian Theology. Schoffeleers (1988:103) stated that African religions are essentially monotheistic and in that fundamental respect fully in accordance with biblical revelation. He believes that Christianity can borrow suitable ideas from the ATRs and *vice versa*.

---

7 Data arranged by Chidi Denis Isizoh from the entries made in D.B. Barret, *World Christian Encyclopaedia*, Nairobi, 1982.

Geographical distribution of adherents to ATRs

Country	1900	Mid-1970	Mid-1975	Mid-1980	Projection for 2000
Botswana % of population	102 900 85,7	347 200 56,3	362 560 52,5	3 909 104 9,2	4 915 003 4,4
Congo % of population	526 500 97,5	79 580 6,7	76 240 5,7	73 240 4,8	75 800 2,8
Ghana % of population	1 987 000 90,3	2 864 000 33,2	2 690 600 27,3	2 451 400 21,4	1 177 500 5,6
Lesotho % of population	271 200 88,9	137 210 13,2	100 310 8,7	80 200 6,2	61 000 3,0
Madagascar % of population	1 556 000 60,.3	3 408 050 49,2	3 859 780 48,1	4 390 180 47	7 591 000 42,7
Malawi % of population	714 000 95,2	1 075 200 24,7	1 059 800 21,6	1 057 400 19	1 049 000 11
Mozambique % of population	2 504 900 96,4	4 757 300 57,8	4 832 300 52,3	4 963 700 47,8	6 197 000 35,1
Namibia % of population	129 600 91,3	33 100 5,2	28 300 4,0	27 800 3,5	26 400 2,0
South Africa % of population	2 793 000 57	3 889 210 18,1	4 189 700 17	4 534 400 15,9	6 519 000 13,1
Swaziland % of population	79 200 99	115 700 28,3	112 360 24	113 490 20,9	127 260 13,5
Zimbabwe % of population	479 800 96	2 469 000 46,5	2 729 500 43,5	3 034 300 40,5	4 440 000 29,3

African Hermeneutics

23.4.2 The quest for African identity

Many African theologians today have taken up the task of formulating a truly African religion, based on African traditions and influenced by the history of Christianity in Africa. This is a holistic hermeneutics which

SECTION B
HERMENEUTICS

wants to read the African text in its interrelated plurality in the African world. Holism does not negate differences, but accommodates them. African Hermeneutics is an endeavour to understand and interpret the many paradoxes – the competing, and even opposing, elements determining African life. Although some African thinkers want to rid Africa of all foreign influences, foreign gods and practices, this is not possible. Not only is it difficult to determine what these influences are and "extract" them from African life – the interdependence of all countries on economic and technological levels simply makes this impossible.

There remains, however, much to be done in regaining African identity. In pre-colonial times, non-Africans wondered and wrote about African religion. Africans were seen mostly as spiritually lost, wicked, and wilful sinners. African religion was negatively portrayed as ancestor-worship, animism, idolatry, fetishism, paganism, polytheism and the like. During colonial and post-colonial times, Africans writing about their religion were over-dependant on western Christian ideas. A post-colonial African Hermeneutics wants to rectify this situation by writing a theology of the people, by the people and for the people (see Uka 1991:161).

But is it possible to know what African identity exactly was, before colonialism, and do the majority of people want to restore this former identity?[8] These are difficult questions and one realises that the quest for African identity is a focal point of the very complex process of cultural reinterpretation. It seems that the strongest rationale behind the wish to recover African identity is the urge to rid Africa of its negative self-image, mindset of dependency, its poverty and underdevelopment. Poverty has become a very macabre part of African identity (Pobee 1993: 397).

The quest for identity can often be linked to a context in which people's identity is threatened and disfigured. In the case of Africa, colonialism and continued economic and other forms of dependence on the west can be named as such threats. Anger has always been a result of the denial of identity. Africa has reason, in this regard, to be angry. Violence is seen by some as a way to freedom, as part of the struggle for a changed self-image, which takes place both among the subjugated and against the dominator (Taylor 1994:65). The history of liberation struggles testifies to this.

From a western perspective, the search for African identity may be experienced as inconvenient as it inhibits the process of development. This is because the promotion of African culture is wrongly perceived as preventing the development of a technological society. The lack of technological advancement must be ascribed, rather, to the general underprivileged background of black communities and the absence of proper

---

8 Root-searching and root-thinking do not impress everyone. Kristeva (1993:2–3) sees the cult of origins as a hate reaction. Hatred of those others who do not share my origins and who affront me personally, economically, and culturally: I then move back among "my own", I stick to an archaic, primitive, "common denominator".

education from the pre-school level onwards. There is a strong recognition that Africa needs development and this seems to be impossible in isolation from western aid, ideas and involvement. Apart from this, the question must be answered whether development – which is inconceivable without science, technology and industry – can be purely African. If a so-called Afrocentrism (there are many African identities) is to be promoted, this cannot be done by isolating Africa.

The recovering of African identity is often described with the metaphor of finding one's roots. Finding one's roots is determined by what one is looking for, and how one appropriates what one finds. The quest for identity is in many cases (such as in South Africa) highly politicised and cannot be completed without dealing with the past. Although the past can never be restored, it remains important for understanding oneself in the present. "Root thinking" can give direction to the present. There may be recognition, insight and identification when encountering one's past. Root thinking can be stimulated, but should not artificially be enforced upon communities. To a large extent Africans need not excavate too deeply to find their roots. They can simply affirm and appropriate these roots. The African world-view is oriented more towards the glorious, perfect, primordial state of the past and less to an unknown, uncertain future. The world of the ancestors is always the best, closer to the perfect origin and it therefore has more potency than the present or the future. The best in life lies in the past, the world of the ancestors and the origin. Anything passed down from the ancestors – such as culture, religion, and technology – must be maintained and protected and passed on to the next generation. The moral obligation to retain and continue traditions and conventions overrides the desire for change (Turaki 1991: 134–135).

Western identity is an open identity. This excludes the idea of a fixed and stable identity and replaces it with the notion of a continuous and dynamic process of re-identification. The western notion of identity must be linked to mentality or attitude, which indicates the volatile nature of western identity. This does not mean that the west has no identity or that it is not interested in identity. The very process of continuous re-identification and relating to a multiplicity of identities emphasises its importance.

To Pobee this does not mean that Africa's identity is to be found solely in Africa. The search for African identity is not wholesale acceptance of either an African or a European oriented culture; it is an acceptance of what is good, presumably for the dignity and well-being of *homo africanus* (1993:394). There is not one African identity.[9] There is no going back to some supposedly pristine African (Pobee 1993:390). Pobee finds Africa's identity in present characteristics. African identities are tied to the

---

9 This complicates the quest for African identity, especially in the light of its ethnic and cultural nature. African identity is local and contextual, bound to issues occupying a community's mind and influencing its world-view. African identity differs not only from community to community, but is quite different north and south of the Sahara (Bloch-Hoell 1992:101).

question of who people are, and these questions are directly linked to their relationship with God (1993:392). This relationship has been inhibited by colonial attitudes. For the growth of a genuine African identity, Africa must be exorcised not only of the spirit of colonialism but also of a missionary paternalism. Africa must develop authentic African theologies (1993:393, 395). Africa must find its identity in the religion typical of Africa. The development of authentic African theologies is a necessary undergirding of African identities (1993:395). Pobee identifies some characteristics typical of *homo africanus* (1993:396–398): the view of the sacred and secular as one; a communitarian epistemology and ontology; a distinguished sense of finitude, bound up with Africa's vulnerability and high mortality rate; the experience of reality through song, dance and ritual; and the culture of poverty (see Pasteur & Toldson 1982:93).

Africa must reject all factors that render African spiritual resources impotent. This means that, to a large extent, western rationalistic theologies and ecclesiastic initiatives must be rejected, for the difference between the spiritualities of the African Initiated Churches and black mainline churches is conspicuous.

23.4.3 The ATRs as source of present African Theology: reading the African text

As we have seen, the effort to develop and reformulate African Theology depends heavily upon African Traditional Religions which give access to African lifestyles, myths and narratives, practices and rites, and the broad oral tradition. The ATRs' world-view, their view on God, nature, the ancestors, community life, medicine and healing, the past and future, and so forth, all provide the lens through which traditional Christian doctrines about God and human beings, Christ and sin, protology and eschatology and the like are being reinterpreted. Apart from the Bible as source for African Theology, the ATRs provide the complementary source, without which present African Theology, is unthinkable. ATR ideas are, however, not used in a syncretistic or eclectic manner, nor does the concept of indigenisation[10] simply fit the hermeneutical processes active in African Theology. The practice of using culture as a determinative factor in formulating theology is foreign to the history of Christian Theology, which alleges to use the Bible as the only source of God's revelation.

To understand the development of African Theology, it is imperative to know African world-view and culture, especially as represented by the ATRs. A few remarks will be made in this regard.

An interesting question is whether an implicit theology exists for the ATRs. Uka (1991:156–160) applied six determinative theological criteria

---

10 Bediako (1995:82) confirms in this regard that the struggle for the indigenization of the church by the Christianisation of the pre-Christian heritage has passed. The debate will now rage over the abiding relevance of the old religions in the transition to the new Christianity in Africa.

(which Macquarie identified[11]) to African Traditional Religion, to indicate its theological nature. Although African Traditional Religion fits these criteria, it does so in a peculiar way, which requires a specific hermeneutics to accompany this theology. These criteria are experience, revelation, Scripture, tradition, culture and reason:

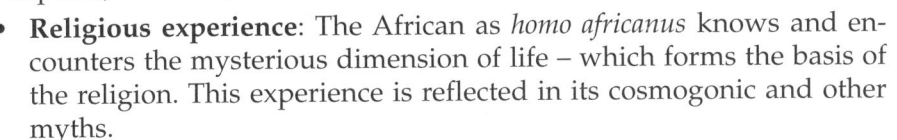

- **Religious experience**: The African as *homo africanus* knows and encounters the mysterious dimension of life – which forms the basis of the religion. This experience is reflected in its cosmogonic and other myths.
- **Revelation**: African religion is no book-religion and lacks this primary theological source. Africa is not, however, without its experience of revelation. The holy is revealed in nature, at special places, through symbols, idols and myths.
- **Scripture**: The text of African Traditional Religion is not written. Its sources include songs, arts and symbols, wisdom sayings, myths, legends, beliefs and customs, prayers, riddles, names of people and places, et cetera (Uka 1991:157; Parratt 1983:90).
- Like Scripture, the **traditions** of the ATRs are mainly transmitted orally from generation to generation. African Hermeneutics cannot be understood apart from the storytelling typical of its oral tradition. Oral Theology has been described as theology in the open air, unrecorded theology, generally lost to libraries (Uka1991:163).
- African **reason** is integrated with all other faculties of the human being. The Africans believe in God and spirits, but they are not interested in rationally defining these realities, and most of the theological terms, displaying a rational preference, mean nothing to them (see Uka 1991:160).

Although these factors may be present in the ATRs, they do not as yet constitute a theology. This only comes to the fore to the extent that African theologians, coming from a Christian background, use these ideas to formulate an African Theology. Bediako (1994:94; 1995:262) underscores the idea that it is in African Christianity that the primal heritage in Africa is likely to acquire a more enduring place. In this sense the ATR has become the *praeparatio theologia* in the African context. What remains fascinating is the much-overlooked fact that ATR explains why Christianity has found fertile ground in Africa. The ATR has been an important pre-

---

11 One could be critical of the approach to once again use western criteria against which to measure African religion. The norm remains western even if African religion fulfils it in a peculiar way. African Traditional Religions simply do not have a theology as it is known in Christianity. What they do have is a very rich religious experience and tradition, myths, symbols, rites and so on. These have been interpreted in the past by westerners in an anthropological and not theological manner. It remains to be seen how African theologians will develop an African Christian Theology which uses the ATRs as one source among others. It remains, however, almost impossible not to compare or equate religions with one other. It is just as impossible not to use identical or analogous terms, metaphors, symbols and so on to describe a specific religion. This should not be done with a feeling of inferiority or subservience to religious traditions other than one's own.

paration for the gospel in Africa and forms the major religious substrate for the idiom and existential experience of Christianity in African life (Bediako 1995:82–83). This implies that, on the one hand, African Traditional Religions can no longer be regarded as "pagan" or idolatrous, and on the other this propensity of the ATRs for the gospel implies that Christianity can no longer be dismissed as a foreign religion and could be regarded as a natural complement of indigenous religious traditions (Schoffeleers 1988:103).

The fear that Christianity will disappear from the African continent, or be replaced by the ATRs, is unfounded. One can expect, however, to find in future a very unique form of Christianity in Africa. In this regard Mbiti (see Bediako 1995:82) even speaks of a new era in African Theology, in which African theologians themselves realise that the Christian way of life is in Africa to stay. The Ecumenical Association of Third-World Theologians (EATWOT) and the Fellowship of Mission Theologians from the Two-Thirds World are examples of this.

23.4.4 ATR ideas influencing the hermeneutics of African Theology

To understand the impact of ATR on African Theology, reference is made to the nature of the primal world-view as explicated by H.W. Turner (quoted in Bediako 1995:93–96). The following features are mentioned with reference to and critique of analogical notions in the west (and in Western Theology):

> A sense of kinship with nature in which animals and plants, like human beings, have their own spiritual existence and place in the universe as interdependent parts of a whole. African ontology considers God, spirits, human, animals, plants, and inanimate creation to be one. To break up this unity is to destroy one or more of these modes of existence, and to destroy one is in effect to destroy all of them (see Bediako 1995:102). The idea of the interdependence and interrelatedness of all of creation is increasing"ly acknowledged in western world-view and cosmology. This "ecological aspect' of primal religions explains the religious approach to the placing of human beings in the world. This attitude explains the appeal of natural theology, which is receiving renewed interest in the west.
>
> Human beings are finite, weak and impure or sinful, and stand in need of a power beyond their own. This conviction can be linked to the Christian idea of the sinful nature of human beings, but without the associated notion of guilt.
>
> Human beings are not alone in the universe and must respect the spiritual world of powers or beings more powerful and ultimate than themselves. Humans can enter into a relationship with the benevolent spirit-world and share in its powers and blessings and receive protection against evil forces. This belief can be related to Christian pneumatology, and sharply criticises western autonomy and self-centeredness. This aspect is sadly lacking in western science and technology and is a prerequisite for the revival of spirituality.
>
> There is an acute sense of the reality of the afterlife, which explains the important place of ancestors. This openness towards life after death has become foreign to a western closed and rationalistic world-view. The belief in the ancestors has interesting links with Christology.
>
> Humans live in a sacramental universe where there is no sharp division between the physical and the spiritual. One set of powers, principles and patterns runs through all things on earth and in the heavens and welds them into a unified

cosmic system. There is also a new appreciation for these ideas in the western world. A new biology, and a renewed interest in human consciousness and its relatedness to ideas from quantum physics, have brought this to our attention. The work of Pauli, Bohm and others testifies to this.

The primal religious world-view is decidedly *this-worldly*. This *this-worldliness* encompasses God and humans in an abiding relationship which is the divine destiny of humankind, and the purpose of the universe (Bediako 1995:101). This holistic approach proposes an answer to western dualism and the unhealthy and often artificial separation between the holy and the profane.

23.4.5 An example from the Ifa-tradition

Ifa (Eze 1993:266) is a process of seeking knowledge through divination. *Ifa* (also called the Eha process) is closely connected with the Nigerian Yoruba and has occupied an important place among African people for many centuries. The core of *Ifa* is a literary text comprising thousands of aphorisms, poems and riddles called *Odu*. *Odu* also contains elaborate exegesis on the text. Esu is the ashé principle, or the creative Word, as revealed yet hidden in the *Ifa* text (Eze 1993:273–274). When interpreting the text the *babalawo* (Ifa-follower) adopts a "hermeneutic" posture depicting the way of rational reflexivity, under the inspiration of *Esu*. As a way of inquiry *Ifa* values interpretation as a dialogical event, views knowledge as existential and not dis-interested, does not see truth as a set of general principles universally applicable to particular situations, sees truth as a process, and regards rationality as non-hierarchical (Eze 1993:280).

Although the verses of the text are fixed, their interpretation is open. Textual objectivity is seen as submission of one's intuitions to the inter-subjective process of inquiry, through which a possible (re)birth of understanding may occur. The meaning of a text is not imposed upon the inquirer who brings his/her pre-conceptions to determine what is objectively valid. Truth is the dialogue between the text, the *babalawo* and the interpreter. *Ifa*-hermeneutics accept that our capacity for understanding is limited. It sees the nature of truth as limited, acknowledging its simultaneous accommodation of truth and untruth, concealment and unconcealment, presence and absence (Eze 1993:281–183).

These principles are sound and in line with some of the latest ideas found in Western Hermeneutics. The advantage of *Ifa*-tradition, however, seems to be the existence of a rich textual tradition absent in many parts of Africa. The history of African Biblical Hermeneutics seems to lag behind the insights produced by *Ifa*-hermeneutics.

23.4.6 Bridging the ATRs and mainline Christianity: The role of the African Initiated Churches (AICs)

Sarpong (1991:288–289) says that the church has not become "African" enough. He refers to the fascinating *Vatican Propagation of the Faith* issued in 1659 to missionaries in China and Indo-China, giving the following directives:

SECTION B

HERMENEUTICS

Put no obstacles in their way; and for no reason whatever should you persuade these people to change their rites, customs and ways of life unless these are obviously opposed to religion and good morals. For what is more absurd than to bring France and Spain or Italy or any other part of Europe into China? It is not these that you should bring but the faith that does not spurn or reject any peoples' rights and customs, unless they are depraved, but, on the contrary, tries to keep them. Admire and praise what deserves to be respected.

The AICs in South Africa comprise about 7 000 groups of churches, of which the Zion Christian Church is the largest. According to the 1991 statistics, the AICs in South Africa represented 31% of the Black population, the mainline Christian churches (excluding the AICs) 34 %, and the ATRs and those with no religion 33%. The respective percentages for the 1980 census were 17,7% (AICs), 53% (mainline Christian), and 28,4% (ATRs and no religion). This indicates a dramatic growth for the AICs, and a limited growth for the ATRs and those with no religion. The trend is clearly that of more and more black people leaving the mainline Christian churches for the AICs.

The AICs play a very important role on the African religious scene. They resemble at this stage, for many African theologians, the best example of the direction in which African religion should develop, since they incorporate traditional and Christian (predominantly Pentecostal) ideas. They include predominantly disadvantaged people from the black working class.

The important place the Bible takes among them is well known. The booklet *Speaking for Ourselves*, states: "We [the AICs] read the Bible as a book that comes from God and we take every word in the Bible seriously. Some people will say that we are therefore 'fundamentalists'. We do not know whether that word applies to us or not but we are not interested in any interpretation of the Bible that softens or waters down its message. We do not have the same problems about the Bible as White people have with their scientific mentality" (quoted by West 1991:158).

Their knowledge of the Bible is of an oral nature. The Bible as text makes no sense to them. Mosala, quoted by West (1991:159–160), argues that they do not appropriate the Bible in terms of what it says, but in terms of what it stands for – a canonical authority. Their hermeneutical weapons are drawn from the sense of mystery generated by the authority of a basically unknown Bible. They appropriate the mysteries of the Bible and of traditional society in order to cope with their perception/sense of being as a subordinate class. The "mystery" of the symbols of the Bible is important in this hermeneutics of mystification. Mosala (West 1991:160) further indicates that race, gender and class are absent as hermeneutical factors in the AICs appropriation of the Bible, while African symbols and discourses are very much part thereof.

23.5 HERMENEUTICAL APPROACHES OF SOME AFRICAN THEOLOGIANS: CONFLICTING OPINIONS ON THE SOURCE FOR AFRICAN THEOLOGY

The African hermeneutical identity depends to a large extent on the theologians practising this hermeneutics in doing their theology. Instead of concentrating on only one or two names, we will try to give a picture of how some of the players approach the task. African theologians, as can be expected, differ in their hermeneutical approaches to African religion. Although it is a generalisation, one can distinguish two groups, referred to as the "old guard" (including well known theologians such as E.W. Fashole-Luke, Bolaji Idowu, John Mbiti, Itumeleng Mosala and Harry Sawyer) and the "new guard" (including such theologians as Eboussi Boulaga, Jean-Marc Ela, Ambrose Moyo, Kwame Bediako and Mercy Oduyoye) (Rogers 1994:245–246). Most African theologians involve themselves, to a greater or lesser extent, in liberation issues and the post-colonial urge to find what is typical of African religion. As can be expected, their theologies are dynamic and this especially comes to the fore in the work of younger theologians more exposed to post-colonial conditions. Their work should not, however, be pinned down to specific theological topics. As articulated by Sarpong (1991:288), the African can pursue a particular cause or act in a definite pattern for twenty years or so, and when the westerner concludes that he will continue to do so for the rest of his life, the African suddenly breaks this pattern.

Old-guard theologians have taken Western Christian Theology, developed it in African terms, and called it "indigenization". African traditional values and experiences have become a passive partner, subordinate to presumably superior Western Theology. They practise a western form of hermeneutics which does not suit or serve the African context. They stress the centrality of the Bible and see it as the basic source for the development of African Christian Theology. They see the Old Testament, in particular, as a source for developing a *Theologia Africana*. Fashole-Luke, while favouring African traditional religion as a source of nourishment for African people, warns against the notion that African traditional religion is a preparation for the gospel (see Rogers 1994:247). Mbiti's approach is to take biblical themes, compare them to the African world-view and culture, and discuss the question whether biblical themes can be apprehended by Africans. African concepts like time and history, for example, cannot express the biblical understanding of eschatology. The African world-view is cyclical and the rhythm of nature ensures that the world will never come to an end. Idowu sees African traditional religion as a *praeparatio evangelica* in the sense that he believes that God has not left Himself without witness in any nation, and that it is therefore necessary to find out what God has done, in what way he has been known and approached in Nigerian history and upon what, traditionally, Nigerians base their faith now and their hope for the afterlife (quoted in Rogers 1994:249).

New-guard theologians of the 1980s reject the indigenisation process, affirming African traditional values, avoiding what was called western bourgeois values. Their primary work was produced in the 1980s, in response to the call for liberation in South African religious circles. Ogku Kalu and Manas Buthelezi (one of the leading figures in promoting Black

SECTION B

HERMENEUTICS

Theology in South Africa, along with Basil Moore) were calling for scholars to use the hermeneutical perspective of liberation when interpreting the Bible. The content of the biblical message must be transposed from the first-century situation to that of the hearer in such a way that the biblical situational and indigenous elements are replaced by those of the 20th-century hearer in South Africa (Rogers 1994:252–253).

In 1984 the Congress of African and European Theologians convened in the Cameroon to consider the appropriate forms of theology for African people. They stressed the need for a new hermeneutic biblical tradition reflecting the political realities (Rogers 1994:253–258). Theologians like Marc Ela, Mercy Oduyoye, Eboussi Boulage and Ambrose Moyo supported this approach. Boulage distrusted even the name "African Christianity" because it symbolised African acceptance of the domination of Africa by the west on social, political, economic and scientific levels. He still accepts the Bible as part of Christianity from within an African perspective, and he favours an "aesthetic Christianity" that responds to biblical themes of a universal nature. He sees the contribution of African Christians to African civilisation as still to come. Elá concentrates on an African reading of Exodus and voices his suspicion against enculturation/indigenization. Africa has to develop its own models of faith. Mercy Oduyoye stresses that Christian Theology in Africa must be constructed from the vantage point of the "underside of history". For her, the Old Testament provides the key to an authentic African Theology. Moyo calls for dialogue between Christianity and African traditional religion. ATR should not take precedence over biblical revelation. He wants to liberate the church in Africa from the white missionary establishment. The AICs are already free from this domination. Rogers (1994:258–260) concludes that while the "Old Guard" theologians were reluctant to enter the political realm, the "New Guard" is strongly committed to a hermeneutic that is a response to the current "oppressive regime" where and whenever it occurs. The "Old Guard" was open to indigenization whereas the "New Guard" follows a style of confrontation. The "Old Guard" saw African Traditional Religion as *praeparatio evangelica*, whereas the "New Guard" considers the ATRs in their own right. However, both "Old" and "New Guard" theologians agree that an African perspective on the Bible is essential to buttress a "living theology" appropriate to African Christian experience. African Traditional Religion is considered a worthy source for understanding African religiosity.

23.6 AFRICAN HERMENEUTICS INTO THE FUTURE

An exciting future, presenting many challenges, awaits African Hermeneutics. One could expect the liberation theme to remain important, but shift its emphasis to economic upliftment and African politics. The task of developing an African Religion, integrating Christian and African traditional ideas, is far from complete.

No single hermeneutical or methodological approach seems to fit the African context. A poly-methodological and multi-hermeneutical approach seems the best way to go. In the past, the search for an appropriate approach was influenced by the idea that African religion is so different a type of study that it can be studied only anthropologically because of its ethnic and preliterate context. Evans Pritchard (quoted by Metuh 1991:147–148) has warned against the danger of reductionism in using any categorical approach to study African religion. African religious concepts and categories need not fit into the well-known western ideas of monotheism, polytheism, pantheism and animism.

The vibrancy of African Theology and Hermeneutics will be determined not by the theologians, but by the spiritual reality of everyday life. This was the secret of African religion in the past and will be its force in future.

READING LIST

Bediako, K. 1995. *Christianity in Africa. The renewal of a non Western religion.* Edinburgh: Orbis.
Eze, E.C. 1993. *Rationality and the debates about African philosophy.* Published dissertation, Michigan: UMI dissertation services.
Maluleke, T.S. 1996. "Black and African theologies in the New World order: A time to drink from our own wells." *Journal of Theology for Southern Africa,* 96.
Mosala, I.J. 1989. *Biblical hermeneutics and black theology in South Africa.* Michigan: Eerdmans.
Pasteur, A.B. & Toldson, I.L. 1982. *Roots of soul. The psychology of black expressiveness.* New York: Anchor.
Ricoeur, P. 1974. *The Conflict of Interpretations.* Evanston, Northwestern University Press.
Serequeberhan, T. 1994. *The hermeneutics of African philosophy.* London: Routledge.
Thiselton, A.C. 1992. *New horizons in hermeneutics.* London: Harper Collins.
Uka, E.M. (ed.). 1991. *Readings in African Traditional Religion. Structure, meaning, relevance, future.* New York: Peter Lang.
West, G. 1991. *Biblical hermeneutics of liberation. Models of reading the Bible in the South African context.* Pietermaritzburg: Cluster.

BIBLIOGRAPHY

Appiah, K.A. 1994. "Identity, authenticity, survival: Multicultural societies and social reproduction." In Gutman, A. (ed.), *Multiculturalism. Examining the politics of recognition.*
Awolalu, J.O. 1991. "African Traditional Religion as an academic discipline." In Uka, E.M. (ed.), *Readings in African Traditional Religion. Structure, meaning, relevance, future.* New York: Peter Lang.
Bediako, K. 1994. "Jesus in African culture." In Dyrness, W.A. (ed.), *Emerging voices in global Christian theology.* Grand Rapids: Zondervan.
— 1995. *Christianity in Africa. The renewal of a non Western religion.* Edinburgh: Orbis.
Bloch-Hoell, N.E. 1992. "African identity. European invention or genuine African character?" *Mission studies,* ix(1).
Coleman, W. 1993. "Tribal talk: Black theology in postmodern configuration." *Theology Today,* vol L/1.
Elá, J.M. 1991. "A black African perspective: An African reading of Exodus." In Sugirtharajah, R.S. (ed.), *Voices from the margin. Interpreting the Bible in the Third World.*

SECTION B

HERMENEUTICS

Eze, E.C. 1993. *Rationality and the debates about African philosophy*. Published dissertation, Michigan: UMI dissertation services.

Kristeva, J. 1993. *Nations without nationalism*. New York: Columbia University Press.

Maluleke, T.S. 1996. "Black and African theologies in the New World order: A time to drink from our own wells." *Journal of Theology for Southern Africa*.

Metuh, E.I. 1991. "Methodology for the study of African religion." In Uka, E.M. (ed.), *Readings in African Traditional Religion. Structure, meaning, relevance, future*. New York: Peter Lang.

Mosala, I.J. 1989. *Biblical hermeneutics and black theology in South Africa*. Michigan: Eerdmans.

Onwu, N. 1985. "The hermeneutical model: The dilemma of the African theologian." *African Theological Journal*, 14(2).

Onunwa, U.R. 1991. "African traditional religion in African scholarship: A historical analysis." In Uka, E.M. (ed.), *Readings in African Traditional Religion. Structure, meaning, relevance, future*. New York: Peter Lang.

Parratt, J. 1983. "African theology and biblical hermeneutics." *African Theological Journal*, 12(2).

Pasteur, A.B. & Toldson, I.L. 1982. *Roots of soul. The psychology of black expressiveness*. New York: Anchor.

Pobee, J.S. 1996. "A Passover of language. An African perspective." In Saayman W. and Kritzinger, K. (eds.), *Mission in bold humility*. New York: Maryknoll.

– 1993. Africa in search of identity." In Reuver, M., Solms, F. and Huizer, G. (eds.), *The ecumenical movement tomorrow*. Kampem: Kok.

Reed, S.A. 1996. "Critique of Canaan Banana's call to rewrite the Bible." *Religion and Theology*, (3)3.

Reuver, M. 1993. "Emerging theologies: faith through resistance." In Reuver, M., Solms, F. and Huizer, G. (eds.), *The ecumenical movement tomorrow*. Kampen: Kok.

Ricoeur, P. 1974. *The Conflict of Interpretations*. Evanston: Northwestern University Press.

Rogers, R.G. 1994. "Biblical hermeneutics and contemporary African theology." In Hopfe, L.M. *Uncovering ancient stones*. Indiana: Eisenbrauns.

Sarpong, P.K. 1991. "Christianity meets traditional African cultures." In Uka, E.M. (ed.), *Readings in African traditional religion. Structure, meaning, relevance, future*. New York: Peter Lang.

Serequeberhan, T. 1994. *The hermeneutics of African philosophy*. London: Routledge.

Schoffeleers, M. 1988. "Black and African theology in Southern African: A controversy re-examined." *Journal of Religion in Africa*, (xviii)1.

Sugirtharajah, R.S. (ed.). 1991. *Voices from the margin. Interpreting the Bible in the Third World*. New York: Orbis.

Taylor, C. 1994. "The politics of recognition." In Gutman, A. (ed.), *Multiculturalism. Examining the politics of recognition*. Princeton: Princeton University Press.

Thiselton, A.C. 1992. *New horizons in hermeneutics*. London: Harper Collins.

Thornton, R. 1996. "The potentials of boundaries in South Africa: Steps towards a theory of the social edge." In Werbner, R. and Ranger T. (eds.), *Postcolonial identities in Africa*. London: Zed.

Turaki, Y. 1991. "Culture and modernization in Africa. A methodological approach." *Cultural diversity in Africa: Embarrassment or opportunity?* Potchefstroom: PU vir CHO.

Uka, E.M. (ed.). 1991. *Readings in African Traditional Religion. Structure, meaning, relevance, future*. New York: Peter Lang.

West, G. 1991. *Biblical hermeneutics of liberation. Models of reading the Bible in the South African context*. Pietermaritzburg: Cluster.

African Initiated Church Hermeneutics

Allan H. Anderson

24.1 INTRODUCTION

This chapter deals with the hermeneutical approaches in Pentecostal-type African Initiated Churches (hereafter AICs). What follows is the result of research conducted in Soshanguve, in the north of Gauteng, between 1991 and 1993, and published in two books, *Bazalwane* (Anderson 1992) and *Tumelo* (Anderson 1993). Many of the insights and remarks referred to in this paper were made by members of these churches during numerous interviews conducted.

24.2 TERMINOLOGY

In a study on AICs an initial explanation of terms used is essential. In my previous studies (Anderson 1992:2–6, 64–72; 1993:5–6), the category "African Pentecostal" was a general term referring to three different groups of churches: first, "Pentecostal mission churches", those churches originating from predominantly white Pentecostal missions (the majority of whose members are now Blacks); second, younger African initiated Pentecostal or Charismatic Churches, not very different from Pentecostal Mission Churches, but founded and governed by Blacks and independent of white control; and third, the vast majority of AICs quite different in some respects from the first two groups, called "Pentecostal-type churches". This term includes these latter churches because of their historical and theological continuity with the Pentecostal movement (Anderson 1992:20–22, 28–31). They are sometimes as old as Pentecostal

SECTION B

HERMENEUTICS

Churches, and are founded, governed and propagated exclusively by Blacks. Most of these churches (but by no means all of them) use the words "Zion" and/or "Apostolic" in their church name. These are the churches that will form the subject of this chapter.

The common historical, liturgical and theological roots that these different church groups have in the American Holiness movement and in the Pentecostal and Christian Zionist movements (Anderson 1991:26–29; 1992:20–32) means that they still have much in common, despite significant and sometimes striking differences. The similarities are also evident in their hermeneutical approaches. All these churches have a literal approach to the Bible, which is used to justify their emphasis on the working of the Holy Spirit in the church with supernatural "gifts of the Spirit", especially healing, exorcism, speaking in tongues and prophesying – although there are sometimes pronounced differences in the practice of these gifts. The emphasis on the Spirit, which earlier researchers alleged was evidence of a weak Christology (Anderson 1991:4–5), is a common characteristic, where the Holy Spirit is the agent of healing and deliverance for people who submit to the ones chosen by God to bestow his power. These churches also all claim biblical precedent for their common practice of adult baptism by immersion. These factors distinguish them from most other Christian groups.

The semantics of the terms used should not unnecessarily detain us. It is true that the churches referred to have developed their own distinctive African expression of Christianity. But so have African churches whose origins are in Europe or North America, whether Pentecostal or not. There is much about all types of Christianity in Africa that is contextualized. This terminology is not an attempt to claim Pentecostal ownership of Zionist Churches, but simply to describe the fact of affinity between Pentecostals and Zionists. These commonalities have their roots in history and are so significant that they may not be ignored. It is really not so important whether one calls them "Pentecostal-type", "Zion-type" (Sundkler) or "Spirit-type" (Daneel) – all this terminology suggests links with the Pentecostal movement. My use of "Pentecostal-type" to describe the majority of AICs in South Africa is an attempt to avoid generalizations and an overlooking of the obvious differences that exist between these churches and Pentecostals, acknowledged by members themselves. The term should not detract from their distinct character in liturgy, healing practices, their different approaches to African folk religion, and their unique contribution to Christianity in a broader African context. The churches discussed here are mainly "Pentecostal-type" churches, including the largest AIC in Southern Africa, the Zion Christian Church.

24.3 THE SIGNIFICANCE OF URBAN AICS

According to official census figures, AICs made up a massive 46% of the total black population of South Africa in 1991, compared to 33% for the older "mission churches" (CSS 1992:121–123). Significantly more black

South Africans today belong to those churches originating with African initiative than to those originating from foreign missions. This has important ramifications.

In Soshanguve, the largest single church is the Zion Christian Church (with a star emblem, hereafter ZCC), accounting for over 10% of the total population. All the Pentecostal-type churches together in this township (mostly "Zionist" or "Apostolic") accounted for 32% of the total. Adding other Pentecostal Churches to this figure would mean that 41% of all the people in Soshanguve belonged to African Pentecostal Churches. The growth of African Pentecostalism in particular, and the AIC movement in general, has appeared to have been at the expense of older mission churches, which have declined drastically in relative membership, from 70% in 1960 (West 1975:2) to 60% by 1970 and 33% in 1991 (CCS 1992: 121–123). Various factors could contribute to what amounts to a decline in mission church relevance in South Africa. The rapid increase in urbanization among black South Africans since 1960 and the insecurities inherent in the urbanization process provide strong incentives for people to seek new, culturally and socially meaningful religious expression. The rejection of "white" values and religious expressions such as found in mission churches, and the high birth rate during these years also could be contributing factors. Whether the momentous political events of 1994 will do anything to reverse this trend is debatable, but if the decline continues, the mission churches could be only 20% of the population by the turn of this century, compared to 50% for the AICs.

24.4 AN AFRICAN HERMENEUTICS

The hermeneutical approaches of members of Pentecostal-type churches are considered from the perspective of how members read and interpret the Bible in their everyday situation. The attraction of the Pentecostal-type AIC hermeneutics for African people is that, probably above all other considerations, these churches are believed to provide biblical answers for "this worldly" needs like sickness, poverty, hunger, unemployment, loneliness, evil spirits and sorcery. Church respondents in Soshanguve told of their healings, deliverances from evil powers, the restoration of broken marriages, success in work or in business ventures and other needs which were met in these churches. All of these experiences were usually backed up, either implicitly or explicitly, by scriptural support. The Bible is understood as a source book of supernatural answers to human need.

The Bible, however, is also used in some AICs as a rationale for practices which can hardly be termed biblical. Even though those with a western orientation may have difficulty with the way the Bible is sometimes used to support what are essentially African traditional religious practices, the fact that African people are able to contextualize the Bible for themselves is extremely significant in any evaluation of this uniquely African Hermeneutics. An appreciation for the "Africanness" of their understanding of the Bible, and the fact that the churches are founded

SECTION B

HERMENEUTICS

and led by Africans, who have read and interpreted the Bible for themselves, is very meaningful. One Zionist said that she appreciated the fact that the church encouraged her to stick to her African traditions. ZCC respondents said that they preferred this church to other churches because it was an "African" church. AICs are specifically geared to fulfil African aspirations and meet African needs.

The Bible is also seen in these churches as an ethical rule book. Some members had very definite opinions of biblical ethics. ZCC members, for example, said that the ethical rules observed by members were the most important teachings in the church, and that they were based on the Bible. One ZCC member said that his church was a place where people were at peace with each other, and where love, respect and honesty prevailed. These sentiments express the dignity and sense of self-worth that an African hermeneutic gives to South Africans who have long been the victims of exploitation and personal affronts to their humanity. There are rigorous ethical rules in the ZCC, whose members, like those of most other Pentecostal-type AICs, are almost unanimously opposed to alcohol, tobacco and pork. As far as food taboos are concerned, a ZCC minister said that because Jesus Christ had cast out demons from a man and had put them into pigs, pork was therefore unclean and forbidden for church members. Pigs had seven evil spirits in them, he explained.

24.5 VIEWS OF THE BIBLE

AICs have a unique contribution to make to the reading and understanding of the Bible in an African situation. Without doubt, the Bible plays a very important, although not an exclusive role. It is usually understood in a literal, "fundamentalistic" fashion – that is, Pentecostal-type AIC members believe that the Bible, both Old and New Testaments, is the inspired and inerrant Word of God, the absolute authority for faith and ethics. It was very important to most respondents that their churches were established solidly on the teachings of the Bible – even if their various interpretations of the Bible's teachings differed. Members spoke of the importance of the Bible as God's message revealing both God and ourselves to us, a guide for life and a solution for human weal and woe. Harold Turner (1965:11) considers that the acceptance of the authority of the Bible was "undoubtedly the best single visible mark of a genuine Church among the African independent movements".

The evidence of continuity with African traditional ideas that is sometimes evident in AICs becomes meaningful for African people searching to find their cultural roots in an impersonal urban society. Therefore, in some AICs, the source of revelation is not confined to the biblical record. Also for some members, the Bible is not the only ultimate authority. In this regard there is a departure from a "fundamentalistic" hermeneutics. This, too, is a reflection of the influence of traditional African holism. There is no perceived contradiction between the authority of the Bible on the one hand and that of the ancestors or a church leader (whether living or deceased) on the other. Some respondents said that they were in a particular church, not because they heard a message from the Bible, but because it was the church revealed to them by an ancestor. The pattern for this response was usually that either the respondents or one of their family members were ill. The ancestor appeared in a dream saying that if they would go to a certain church, bishop or prophet, they would be healed. They followed this instruction, and remained in that church thereafter, often believing that the continuation of their healing was contingent upon their continued membership of the church. The conviction that a particular church was pleasing to the ancestors was sometimes very strong. Often this was accompanied by a tolerance and accommodation of traditional African beliefs and rituals in that church. In these cases, traditional spirituality has superseded Biblical Hermeneutics. It would therefore appear that some AIC members take traditional beliefs as the standards by which the Bible is interpreted.

24.6 THE PREACHING OF THE BIBLE

It was nonetheless important to members that the teaching of their churches and the preaching of their ministers were based on the Bible. Preaching usually begins with a reading from the Bible. The preaching is often interspersed by phrases like "the Bible says" to reinforce the message. Although preachers sometimes do not make a conscious effort to explain the Bible or to contextualize its message, the Bible is given pride of place on most occasions. For example, ZCC preachers (and there are several at each service) begin their sermons by reading a passage from the Bible. The lack of biblical training by many AIC preachers (who are often laypersons) may explain why the Bible is sometimes not expounded, but it does not detract from the emphasis on its authority.

Preaching often centres on salvation in the here and now, on material security which (at least in the ZCC) "embraced health, wealth, and influence in community affairs and occupations" (Lukhaimane 1980:58). Van Wyk (in Lukhaimane 1980:49) rightly observed that the ZCC is "touching some real needs of their people" with an "openness to scriptural teaching". Members base their life and faith on the Bible, the Word of God, as the final authority for all that is taught, practised and preached. For this reason, preachers give pre-eminence to the Bible, and use it to justify and reinforce their messages. Through the Bible, people learn about God and his ways, and it is believed to be the means by which God is able to speak to his people today. The Bible forms the basis and provides the conditions for holy living, and those who follow its instructions will be enabled to overcome all kinds of difficulties.

In a few churches it is not the Bible per se, but the leader who interprets it correctly and declares its message to his followers, who has the ultimate authority. Nevertheless, the authority of the Bible itself is unquestioned, even in these churches. Preaching must always be founded on what the Bible says, either directly or implicitly. Preachers use the Bible to exhort people to love one another and be faithful to the church, to be obedient to the rules of the church, and (in some cases) to confront

SECTION B

HERMENEUTICS

some traditional religious rites, teaching or practices in other churches.

With a few Pentecostal-type church members, the belief in the centrality of the Bible was not as clear. The International Pentecost Church (hereafter IPC) is one of the fastest growing AICs in the Transvaal. To some IPC members it seemed that the final authority was the word that their leader Ntate (Father) Modise heard from God and pronounced to his people. One member said that Modise's teachings were not necessarily straight from the Bible, but that they were the words from God. But another said that Modise was the interpreter of the Bible for his people. When he explained the Word of God, it helped his followers to live in the right way. Other members even expressed views about the Bible that were fairly "evangelical". One member, for example, said that the Bible was God's word which taught people the laws of God and enabled God to speak to people. In the IPC services we attended, the Bible was read as frequently as in any other church; and Modise himself makes extensive use of it during his protracted preaching. It appeared that the Bible's authority was upheld in the IPC by Modise and by his preachers, and that no significant difference existed in this respect between the IPC and other churches.

24.7 SALVATION AND THE AFRICAN WORLD-VIEW

In Pentecostal-type AICs, the Bible is interpreted holistically. "Salvation" is an all-embracing term which is usually seen as a sense of well-being evidenced in freedom from sickness, poverty and misfortune, as well as in deliverance from sin and evil. Healing from physical sickness is a major theme in these churches and in the lives of their members, and becomes a very important part of their hermeneutics. Because the Bible is interpreted literally, healing is seen as part of the biblical revelation, and reference is made to Old Testament prophets, Christ Himself and New Testament apostles who practised healing.

Inus Daneel (1974:186) wrote that, in the Spirit-type churches of Zimbabwe in the 1960s and 1970s, the healing treatment by the prophets was the most frequently mentioned reason for people joining these churches. In our research healing was probably the main reason for people joining various Zionist and Apostolic Churches. Because of the significant number of second generation Christians in these churches, the ongoing healing offered to members in fact makes healing one of the most important factors in the continued expansion of these churches.

This healing offered to people usually relies heavily upon various symbolic healing methods, especially the sprinkling by holy water, which has become a sacrament in many AICs providing ritual purification and protection. These healing methods are not used in other Pentecostal Churches, where the emphasis is on the laying on of hands with prayer. This is in fact one of the main differences between Pentecostal-type churches and other Pentecostal Churches. The symbolic healing practices are often justified by referring to the Bible, where Jesus used mud and spittle to heal a blind man, Peter used cloths to heal the sick, and Old Testament prophets used staffs, water, and various other symbols to perform healings and miracles.

Healing is not usually separated from evangelism. A person joins the church because felt needs are met – and this includes healing from physical sickness and discomfort. The majority of people in South Africa are still largely underprivileged, which means, *inter alia*, that efficient medical facilities are scarce and expensive. As Bengt Sundkler (1961:223) put it, many people "receive the Zionist Healing Message as a gospel for the poor". Pentecostal-type AICs take the Bible literally on the issue of divine healing: it was practised by Old Testament prophets, by Jesus and by the apostles, and the Bible says that healing will accompany one who believes in it.

The fact that people believe themselves to be healed means that this unique message of the Bible is more powerful to them than anything else they have ever experienced. This is in fact evangelism, or "a gospel for the poor". So too, Sundkler (1961:233) said that "The Message of Healing is in fact the strongest asset of Zionist evangelization". Healing is certainly one of the main activities in Pentecostal-type churches. Sundkler (1961:228) wrote: "I have stressed repeatedly that prayer for the sick is not just a detail of Zionist Church services, but it is their most important feature." A ZCC member related to us that he had been ill for a long time and had tried diviners, medical doctors, and other prophets – to no avail. Then his father appeared to him in a vision and said that he should go to the ZCC. "I went there", he recalled, "they healed me, and that is why I still go there. There is no other church like the ZCC. The others failed to heal me." Lukhaimane (1980:63) said that healing was the reason for 80% of Engenas Lekganyane's followers joining the church. It was "a faith healing and a miracle performing church (*ke kereke ya Mehlolo*)" (1980:46). Daneel (1988:90) wrote of the most significant Zionist leader in Zimbabwe that it was "Mutendi's ability to heal the sick, exorcise the most powerful of evil spirits and even raise the dead which caused the people to flock to his Church."

The International Pentecost Church (IPC) that has already been referred to, is a sabbatarian church largely based on the personality of its leader and former ZCC minister Frederick Modise, and particularly on his healing powers. This is the main reason for people flocking to this church and indeed, it appears that a person who receives healing from Modise has extreme pressure to thereafter join the IPC. The ability of Modise to heal the sick, coupled with a proclamation of the total inadequacy of all other healing methods offered by churches, prophets or diviners, form the core of the IPC's highly pressurised recruitment drive, particularly at Silo, the church headquarters at Zuurbekom. In the outlying branches of the church, visitors are urged to make the monthly pilgrimage to Modise at Silo. Once they do this, they are virtually assured of a place among the "chosen". Modise does not use symbolic healing such as that practised in the Zionist and Apostolic Churches, but there is a strong symbolism associated with the accompaniments to the healing rituals at Silo.

SECTION B

HERMENEUTICS

Daneel (1974:187–191) showed the major role that healing played in the initial phase of church expansion in Spirit-type churches in Zimbabwe. This was also the case in South Africa, demonstrated in the histories of Zionist pioneers Elias Mahlangu, Edward Motaung and Engenas Lekganyane, amongst many others (Anderson 1992:40–44).

There are several other important questions in a discussion of AIC views on salvation, such as the question of the accommodation of African religious practices in Christian faith. The ancestor cult, for example, is still practised in its totality by many AIC members. In some of these churches the ancestor cult is absorbed into Christian beliefs. The ancestors are not seen to be at variance with Christian truth, as they often appear to people to reinforce Christian faith. To illustrate, a member of the ZCC in Soshanguve related how she came to join the church, during which process several factors were simultaneously at work. She had suffered from severe headaches for some time. One night she dreamt that she saw her grandfather in ZCC uniform coming to her. He said that if she wanted help she should go to Moria (the ZCC headquarters), where she would find a prophet who would pray for her healing. She obeyed, and the prophet came to her and said "I saw you in a dream; you are suffering from headaches". He prayed for her, and she was healed. The prophet told her that to stay healed she had to remain a ZCC member for the rest of her life. She considered, however, that the main reason that she was in the ZCC was because it was the church shown to her by her grandfather. At the same time, the prophet was exploiting his healing power as an effective method of recruiting a new member for the church.

Salvation is related to more than a truncated concept of the "salvation of the soul" in the life hereafter. It is oriented to the whole of life's problems as experienced by people. Salvation is deliverance and protection from evil in all its forms, including evil spirits and sorcery, misfortune, natural disasters and disease. Whether God uses direct power through African prophets or the protection of ancestors to achieve his purposes is not always an issue. The Pentecostal-type churches proclaim a message of deliverance from sickness and from the oppression of evil spirits, and a message of receiving the power of the Holy Spirit, which enables people to survive in a predominantly hostile spirit world. The Spirit enables members to find that their Christianity is relevant to all of life in all its facets, and not just to a western dualistic "spiritual" part of it. Members see salvation in more inclusive terms than do more western influenced churches. Salvation has also to do with the whole of church life, as it is experienced in the sacraments, prophetic practices, healing, deliverance from evil, and also in obeying the rules of the church. The AICs reckon more adequately with Africa's holistic world in their concept of salvation.

Church members relate the Bible directly to their troubles. Our respondents said that affliction and trouble came from various sources: from Satan, from failure to keep the instructions of the Bible or of the church leaders, from hatred and fear of other people, from witchcraft and sorcery, from the ancestors, and even (said some) from God. The solution was to trust in a power that was greater than the power that was against you. Most said that faith in God and his ability to bring deliverance was the prerequisite for salvation. To many, this meant times of special or prolonged prayer, sometimes with fasting, and the reading of God's Word, the Bible. As in the healing practices, methods of deliverance differed. Some said that deliverance was effected through the use of symbols like holy water, ashes, ropes, staffs and whips to drive away evil spirits. Instructions given by church leaders were also to be carried out carefully before deliverance was obtained. Although the possibility of the attribution of magical power to the healing symbols themselves exists, the symbolic objects used were almost invariably believed to be powerless without faith in God and were not usually seen as having any intrinsic power in themselves.

The African traditional world is filled with fearsome and unpredictable occurrences demanding a Christian answer. Hermeneutics in Africa must be relevant to the whole of Africa's existence, and proclaim biblical deliverance from sin, from sickness, and from the very real fear of evil that haunts many people. Whether the source is Satan, sorcery or the omission or commission of a person – evil, trouble, misfortune, disaster and affliction are the lot of people everywhere. The Pentecostal-type churches in Africa are endeavouring to provide a solution to this compelling need.

The understanding of biblical salvation proclaimed in these AICs has to do with deliverance from the totality of evil forces ranged against a person's existence. The methods used to receive this salvation and the perceptions concerning the means of grace sometimes differed. Nevertheless, members believe that the Bible reveals an omnipotent and compassionate God who concerns Himself with the troubles of humankind. Bishops, prophets, ministers, evangelists and ordinary church members exercise the authority that they believe has been given them by God to announce the good news that there is deliverance from sin, from sickness, and from every conceivable form of evil and "darkness".

24.8 THE ROLE OF PROPHETS

A discussion on hermeneutics in AICs must reckon with the very important fact of the African prophets, who are seen as continuing in the biblical prophetic tradition, particularly that of the Old Testament prophets. Their pronouncements are accepted as revelations from God, but they are never accorded infallibility on the level of holy Scripture. When a ZCC prophet once proceeded to prophesy over me, he was chided by his superior church officials for prophesying to a visitor without permission.

The prophets are the ones to whom God reveals his will and through whom He manifests his power. For most members, the source of the revelation of the prophets is the Holy Spirit. He is the one who gives the prophets the power to heal sickness and overcome evil generated by the deep-seated fears and insecurities inherent in the traditional world-view. African prophetic practices must not only deal with the *results* of evil;

SECTION B
HERMENEUTICS

they must also reveal and remove its *cause*. Sometimes the revelation of the cause is by itself sufficient to guarantee the solution to the problem, and the supplicant is satisfied. Diagnostic prophecy, therefore, is the most common form of prophecy found in Pentecostal-type churches. These revelations by the Holy Spirit become one of the major causes of attraction for outsiders seeking answers to their particularly African problems – an efficient recruitment method. Prophecy in Africa also often becomes an extremely effective form of pastoral therapy and counsel, mostly practised in private, a moral corrective and an indispensable facet of Christian ministry. It can become an expression of care and concern for the needy; and in countless cases, it actually brings relief.

Prophetic healing therapy in AICs must not be simplistically dismissed as a repetition of traditional divination. The fact that there are so many parallels between the *forms* of the old traditional practices and those of the new prophetic ones does not mean that the *content* of prophecy is the same as that of traditional divination. The parallels are often the very features that make prophetic healing rituals so significant to so many people. That most of the people do not see it as the same as divination was illustrated in our research. One woman observed that, unlike traditional diviners, the prophets do not seek to draw attention to themselves, but to point the sufferers to God who alone can bring healing. This was the reason why she had received healing through the prophets. The similarities sometimes are the greatest strengths for people seeking meaningful African solutions to their problems. For many members, therefore, prophetic healing practices represent at the same time a truly Christian and a truly African approach to the problem of pain and suffering.

There was, however, obvious confusion in the minds of some members in their understanding of prophecy; and this was especially true of some ZCC members. In these cases, it was indeed difficult to distinguish between prophecy and divination, or between the source of revelation as being the Holy Spirit or the ancestors. To some members, the prophet played an identical role to the traditional diviner in declaring the will of the ancestors. The possibility of syncretism still exists in the minds of some still steeped in traditional thought forms and oriented to the African spirit world. And yet, in these apparent syncretistic tendencies there remains the possibility that "The chief motive of the prophet is to respect the existential reality of the patient's thought world and confront it with the Christian message" (Daneel 1988:117–118).

The role of prophets and prophecy in most Pentecostal-type churches is of utmost importance in understanding this African Hermeneutics. As revealers of God's will from the Scriptures and dispensers of God's power to meet human needs, the African prophets become the agents of salvation. The Holy Spirit gives them revelations and the ability to overcome many African problems, including sickness and all kinds of evil. This becomes salvation from pain, fear and suffering for many people. Of course, human error is inevitable in healing practices. In many Pentecostal healing services observed over the past 25 years, sick people have apparently gone away unhealed, and so-called "miracles" are claimed which eventually prove to be no miracles at all. This human failure does not mean that God's power and ability to heal is thereby negated.

24.9 LIBERATION AND ZION

A fundamental theme of AIC hermeneutics is that of liberation. African people themselves, without the help of white missionaries (representing former oppressive colonial powers), have discovered in the Bible their own freedom from bondage. They have discovered that, contrary to previous assumptions, the Bible is not a "white person's book", providing answers to questions which African people are not asking. Particularly since the translation of the Bible into the vernacular, Africans have discovered that the Bible is relevant to Africa, that it does fulfil African aspirations and meet African needs, and that the Bible has much to say about issues that were largely left unaddressed in mission churches.

The principal leaders of Zionist and Apostolic Churches are seen as Moses figures, bringing their people out of slavery into the promised land, the new "City of Zion". This reading of the Bible sees the Exodus event as a deliverance from the old life of trouble, sickness, oppression, evil spirits, sorcery and poverty. The new Israel incarnate in Africa is moving out of Egypt towards the new Jerusalem, the Zion of God, where all these troubles will be in the past. The people of God are the members of this new African Church who have been able to discover their promised land for themselves.

The concept of Zion, the new Jerusalem, the holy place which is not in some far off Asian land at some distant time in the past, but is right here and now in Africa, is a prominent theme in the hermeneutics of the Pentecostal-type AICs. Most Zionist and Apostolic Churches in South Africa have a church headquarters where the founder or bishop lives, a sort of healing colony to which members must make regular pilgrimages on holy days for church conferences. This African Zion is seen as a place of blessing, of deliverance, of healing – in short, the place where the closeness of God is keenly felt. It is also the place where the means of grace and the manifestation of God's presence in the sacraments are administered by the bishop. The conferences of the church at "Zion" are therefore of the utmost importance.

ZCC members are expected to visit Moria, the church headquarters near Pietersburg, at least once a year, either at the Easter conference or at the conference in September. The importance of this pilgrimage is that members thereby meet the bishop and obtain his blessing on their lives, especially through the sacrament of communion. The Easter Festival at Moria is obviously the highlight of the ZCC year. More than a million people, all dressed in ZCC khaki, gold and green, congregate there annually. To experience this vast throng, as I did at Easter 1992, is awe-inspiring. There are probably few Christian conferences in Africa that draw as many people as this one does. The highlight of the weekend's activities is when Bishop Lekganyane, resplendent in the green and gold bishop's

SECTION B

HERMENEUTICS

attire, at the head of the brass band, takes the podium to address the assembled and expectant multitude.

The IPC annual conferences also take place at the church headquarters at Easter and in September, the month when Modise received his "anointing" by the Holy Spirit. The IPC Zion is called Silo (Shiloh) – like the ZCC Moria, this is a reference to the Old Testament holy place and priesthood. Before Silo was constructed, the church pilgrimage was made to Jerusalem, at Oskraal near Pretoria. For IPC members, the monthly weekend at Silo is also a type of church conference to which they are expected to go.

24.10 ICONIC AND MESSIANIC LEADERSHIP

One of the problems in the study of AICs is whether the followers of a charismatic leader have "messianized" or even "deified" their leader. Most AIC leaders of the Pentecostal-type are credited with extraordinary and supernatural powers, given them by God. It is important that any western interpretation of what I would term the more "radical" AICs (those furthest away from western church norms) consider the African context in which the adulation of the church leader is couched. But at the same time, one cannot ignore the fact that sometimes Christ is overshadowed, and sometimes even replaced, by the founder or leader of the church. When this happens, we may refer to such churches as "messianic", but they are very few in South Africa. I will illustrate this aspect of Pentecostal-type hermeneutics by referring to two prominent and quite different AICs, the ZCC and the IPC.

The ZCC was termed a "messianic" church by early researchers, and it is true that the bishops (both living and deceased) are extremely important figures there. Bishop Lekganyane is the personality around which many of the church activities centre. Lukhaimane (1980:37) said that Engenas Lekganyane was "to his underprivileged followers ... a messiah who had come to deliver them from bondage, especially from the horror of superstition and the power wielded by the medicine man." Both Sundkler (1961:323) and Martin (1964:161) referred to Lekganyane as a "messiah", although they had no empirical evidence to support this contention. The Lekganyanes themselves, and official ZCC literature, have expressly denied any messianic titles or divine status to the Lekganyanes. In the church magazine, The *ZCC Messenger*, for example, Rafapa (ZCC 1992:6) states that the three Lekganyanes, "the apparently worldly spiritual leaders of the Church only vicariously preside for God." It is believed by ZCC members that Engenas Lekganyane passed on his prophetic powers to his successors, first Edward and then Barnabas (Ramurumo). Lukhaimane (1980:43) states that the bishop "fulfilled the same functions between God and man that the *badimo* [ancestors] had done in traditional religion. He was a messiah, a prophet for his followers."

It is true that for some members the deceased Lekganyanes sometimes appear to fulfil the protective functions of the ancestors. In an article entitled "The Lord is my Shepherd", Dr J.L. Maaga (ZCC Messenger 1992: 12–13), a medical practitioner and a ZCC leader in Mamelodi, Pretoria, described a trip he made to accompany Bishop Barnabas Lekganyane to the Transkei, during which white extremists tried to force his car off the road. He reported that a large white Mercedes Benz, driven by "the late Bishop Edward", came to his rescue. Nevertheless, Maaga's intention in relating the incident was to show the protective power of God, of which Bishop Edward was a mere agent. His purpose was to show how "the Lord would look after me during the trip". Although Lekganyane did what any ancestor might have done, the result of this encounter was that this ZCC member praised God for his protection: "I blinked a few times, and with a joyful heart began to sing '*Ke na le modisa*' [I have a shepherd]".

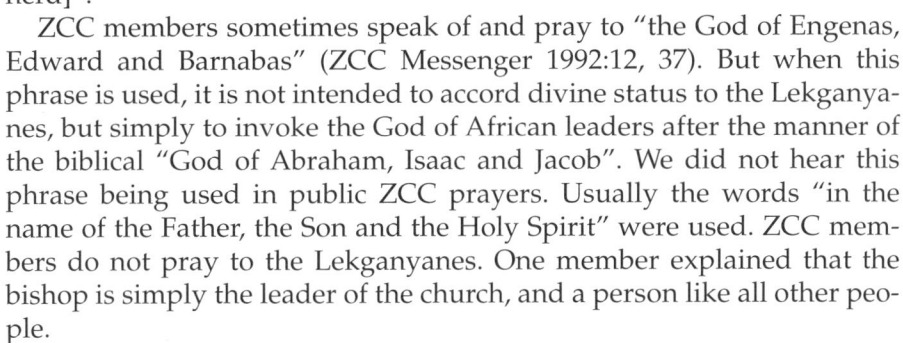

ZCC members sometimes speak of and pray to "the God of Engenas, Edward and Barnabas" (ZCC Messenger 1992:12, 37). But when this phrase is used, it is not intended to accord divine status to the Lekganyanes, but simply to invoke the God of African leaders after the manner of the biblical "God of Abraham, Isaac and Jacob". We did not hear this phrase being used in public ZCC prayers. Usually the words "in the name of the Father, the Son and the Holy Spirit" were used. ZCC members do not pray to the Lekganyanes. One member explained that the bishop is simply the leader of the church, and a person like all other people.

The appearance of the bishop at the annual Conferences is to many ZCC members the climax of the weekend's festivities, and all the faithful long to be as close to him as is humanly possible, to receive some of his power. The impressive sight of Bishop Barnabas Lekganyane marching at the head of his brass band, swinging his bishop's mitre, is obviously the high point of proceedings, and an emotional occasion at church conferences. Not even the presence of the three leading political leaders in South Africa (Mandela, De Klerk and Buthelezi) at the 1992 Easter Festival detracted from the bishop's glory.

In the activities of ZCC prophets, the bishop is often mentioned as being present to help and to guide; but the meaning of these expressions is unclear. ZCC members did not emphasize the role of the bishop; in fact the great majority did not mention him at all. The ZCC cannot really be named a "messianic" movement, because in the perceptions of ZCC members Lekganyane does not in any sense replace or supersede Jesus Christ, even though he is given the honour and respect that would have been given to a traditional paramount leader.

On the other hand, in the IPC members constantly refer to their leader, Frederick Modise, as the *Moemedi* ["Representative"], the ever-present one who is able to exercise supernatural powers and mediate between his followers and God. The question to be asked is to what extent he is regarded by his followers as a sort of living messiah, a mediator between humankind and God. Members of this church do not agree in their views of Modise – although it would appear that all believe that he is some sort of mediator. To some he undoubtedly has divine status, and a personality cult centres around him. Modise's picture appears above the "altar" in the centre of the auditorium at Silo, on shirts worn by the faithful, on

SECTION

B

HERMENEUTICS

all official church literature and throughout the offices at the headquarters. The faithful buy photographs of him and hang them on the walls of their homes. One IPC member told us that she believed that these photographs brought Modise into her home; he looked after the home and guarded the property. Another member told us that Modise was a mediator who prayed to God on people's behalf, and that through him people could know the will of God. He was the only one who knew how to "pray spiritually". Whenever the faithful encountered difficulties, they would pray according to Modise's instructions. One member said that she also prayed to Modise himself: "I pray to him to heal me even when he is not present. He is able to heal you even though he is (physically) absent."

In IPC church services, Modise is called *Moemedi* [Representative], also a Tswana translation for "counsellor" or "advocate" in the English Bible – a title describing the mediatorial work of both Christ and the Holy Spirit. In English, he is referred to as the "Comforter" (with a capital "C") in printed literature of the IPC, which in the old Authorized (King James) Version of the Bible is a title of the Holy Spirit. He is praised in singing by this name, which sometimes takes the place of the name of Christ or of God in hymns and songs. People are exhorted in every IPC service to go to Silo to meet Modise himself, who will heal them of all their sicknesses, solve all their problems, and bring them success and prosperity.

Modise is addressed as "our Father" by his followers, and they are "his children". These various appellations appear to go beyond traditional respect. One of the most illuminating interviews in Soshanguve revealed that Modise is, at least in the minds of some of the members, divine. A member for eight years, with Modise's photographs all over her house, believed him to be both omniscient and omnipresent:

> Our teachings are above the teachings of the prophets. Modise is not a prophet. He knows all of us who are his children. He protects us when we are sick. When I am sick I simply remember him and he heals me ....

She went on to say that Modise was the Holy Spirit:

> The world will never have true freedom apart from Modise. The world is waiting for *Moemedi* .... Even the Whites are waiting for him; but they don't know that he has already come. Jesus said "If I do not go the *Moemedi* will not come". Fortunately, he has come, on 14 September 1962 [the date on which Modise was healed, marking the birth of the IPC].

When she was pressed to explain the relationship between Modise and the Holy Spirit, she was even more explicit:

> The Holy Spirit came during Pentecost, and lastly when he entered Father Modise. No-one in this world has the Holy Spirit except him; in fact, he is the Holy Spirit himself. Jesus was rejected and denied. Modise is also being rejected and denied, because people say he is a mere person – they said that Christ also was a mere person. He (Modise) is the *Moemedi,* or the Holy Spirit.

She went on to say that the proof of Modise's divinity was that he healed people "without touching them". He heals people "when he forgives their sin". "Father Modise is my God", she concluded. "I trust him in everything I do. God is one with him. He is a member of the Trinity – God the Holy Spirit – because he has been chosen by God."

Not every member of the IPC has the same degree of reverence for Modise that this respondent had; although several expressed similar sentiments. Our field assistant, Samuel Otwang, attended the weekend activities at Silo in March 1992. During the lengthy proceedings, several speakers made reference to Modise in terms that accorded him divinity. One minister (in Modise's presence) said that the people who spoke about accepting Jesus into their lives were deceivers. Jesus had gone away from this world and had sent *Moemedi*. People now should accept *Moemedi*. Another minister told the two thousand or so visitors who had come that weekend that there was no-one else like *Moemedi*. He was God, because he had power to forgive sins. The visitors should simply humble themselves and accept his words. Modise's power to reveal and forgive sins, and the coercive nature of the confession to him before healing, appear in fact to accord to him divine status.

Frederick Modise himself told us in August 1991 that he was a man and not God. Another IPC member, who had no pictures of Modise in her house, said that Modise is definitely not God nor the Holy Spirit, and that Modise himself had told his followers that he was not divine. He was God's Messenger, the one who stood before God on behalf of people's sicknesses, weaknesses and problems. This was the meaning of his title *Moemedi*, she said. When IPC members prayed, they prayed to God and not to Modise. Modise was a sinner as much as anyone else, she said; but God healed him in hospital and spoke to him. He is "special" because he just speaks the Word, and thousands are healed simultaneously. Another IPC member gave a similar view when she said:

> Modise is not God – he is simply the overseer of the church. I also call him God's messenger, *Moemedi*, because he is the one who stands on your behalf for whatever sickness or problem you have. He is not the Holy Spirit, but is a person like us. We do not pray to him; we pray to God. Some of the things people say [about Modise] are not true.

There are at least some grounds for characterising the IPC as a "messianic" church. The teaching in the church seems to indicate that although Modise is not Christ, he has taken the place of Christ, at least in the opinion of some ministers and members. There is actually no real place for the Holy Spirit in IPC theology. The references to the Holy Spirit in John 16 are consistently applied to Modise. The greeting repeated by the IPC faithful at every service: "We thank God for Jesus; we thank Jesus for *Moemedi*" appears to accord Modise a place in the Trinity itself, whether consciously or not.

But this is a subject for which there are no certain answers at present. There are many secrets in the church which outsiders are not permitted to know. Modise alone knows the name of God. Together with the "Lord's Prayer" and the secret formula to be used by members, these things can only be revealed to members. For these reasons, and perhaps intentionally, there remains much mystery associated with this church and its leader. Nevertheless, the widespread belief by both church lead-

SECTION B

HERMENEUTICS

ers and members that Modise has divine status and is in some way part of the Trinity has apparently not been effectively or actively repudiated in the IPC's preaching and practice. For these reasons the IPC is a church where the term "messianic" might be appropriate.

The so-called emphasis on the Holy Spirit has not resulted in a weak Christology or an impoverished hermeneutics for most Pentecostal-type churches. Christ is not relegated to the periphery, and there is certainly no conscious attempt to dethrone him. The Bible is the measuring rod by which most teaching, preaching and practice is conceived and continuously modified; for this reason church members bear witness to the lordship of Jesus Christ. Faith in Jesus Christ was expressed by many members of these churches in clear terms which did not indicate any Christological weakness. The honour that is given to the heads of the churches must be understood in the African context only to mean respect for leaders; and it cannot usually be assumed that this has gone beyond traditional esteem. The reverence for the principal leader of an AIC to the extent that he may have appeared on the surface to have overshadowed Christ may in fact be an attempt on the part of his followers to achieve "the closest possible identification with biblical figures and the re-enactment of biblical events", observed Daneel (1988:300). For these reasons, most of the arguments for "messianism" are unconvincing, and it is only in the IPC where they might be pertinent.

Martin (1975:171) modified her earlier harsh judgement on the ZCC and other "messianic movements" with the following comments:

> In the light of what we have observed among the Kimbanguists, the tendencies of the various "messianic movements" in Southern Africa would have to be studied afresh every few years. What still appeared yesterday to be a messianic movement may today already be becoming a church of Jesus Christ on the basis of the ever-renewing Spirit of God.

This reminds us of Schreiter's (1985:158) observation:

> The conversion process ... is much slower than we had first thought .... What appears to be syncretism ... may be but reflective of the stages in the conversion process .... The firm foundations we experience today were not easily achieved. No doubt they may have looked like a dangerous syncretism to an earlier generation.

What today may appear to be an aberration of Christianity or "syncretism" from a "foreign" perspective, may in fact be stages on the way to total conversion, a goal which western Christianity itself has probably not yet attained. Anyone who tries to evaluate African phenomena from outside the cultural matrix in which those phenomena are found, may be making "foreign" evaluations which do not accurately account for the realities. To assume that the rapidly moving, fluid phenomenon of the AIC movement is static and in its final form is to start with a false premise.

24.11 CONCLUDING REMARKS

In view of these comments, it is doubtful that the ZCC, or most AICs in

Southern Africa, can today be termed "messianic", nor "syncretistic" movements. We would be foolish to assume that the Holy Spirit is not working there, renewing these churches as churches of Jesus Christ. To be sure, the bishop is a most important figure in the ZCC; but he can hardly be said to have taken the place of Christ. Even when a deceased bishop appears to help or protect a ZCC member, or when the prophets mention these functions, it is understood to signify the guidance of God and not that of the bishop; God is praised as a result. ZCC members do not pray to their bishops, living or dead, and this church cannot assuredly be said to have departed from "orthodox" Christology.

The IPC, on the other hand, seems to be at least a movement on the way to *becoming* messianic. Modise's status in the church is clearly rising among his followers. To many IPC members, he has become a divine figure who stands as the "Representative" of God. He has indeed taken the place of Christ in this church, at least in the perceptions of some of its members. He alone wields divine power to reveal and forgive sins; he alone has the power to heal sicknesses with his words; he alone knows the secrets of God and the mysterious divine name; to many he is in fact the Holy Spirit personified. Modise alludes frequently to the Bible – in fact, there is a strong tendency in this church for the members (and Modise himself) to consider their leader as the sole interpreter of the Bible, the only one who has the secret knowledge needed to apply its wisdom to the lives of IPC members. Modise preaches material prosperity and physical health to his followers using Scriptural support. He declares that people are not supposed to be poor or sick; God's will revealed in the Bible is that they have plenty and be healthy, provided they follow Modise's recipe for success. Visitors at Silo are exhorted to leave "Egypt" (their old churches) and join the promised land of Modise and the IPC. These churches were, declared one preacher, tombs of death and deception.

In many Pentecostal-type churches, confession of sins precedes baptism, and therefore is a prerequisite for the cleansing and admittance to the company of the "saved". In the IPC, however, confession of sins must be made to Modise himself, the "Representative" of God, before healing can be received. Only a person who has been "healed" in this way (Modise calls it "spiritual healing") can be admitted to the chosen flock. There is believed to be no salvation outside the IPC and Modise. The fact that Modise has the power not only to forgive sins, but to identify *what* the sins are and to force a confession, is of extreme theological importance in an assessment of the IPC. He thereby becomes the only one in whom salvation is deposited, alone holding the keys of the gate to the kingdom of heaven.

In any case, one cannot judge an essentially religious phenomenon as if it is in its final, static form. Even that which appears strange to our particular sensitivities, coloured as they are by our theological and cultural presuppositions, may be a dynamic and fluid movement on the way to becoming a truly African expression of the Lordship of Jesus Christ. As

SECTION B
HERMENEUTICS

Turner (1979:166) has reminded us, "Any evaluation of the independent churches must begin by recognizing certain ways in which many of them have made a radical departure from pagan worship." This, he says, amounts to a "radical breakthrough to worship of the one true, living, loving, and all-powerful God of the Christian Scriptures." One of the central features of many Pentecostal-type AICs is the rejection of key elements in traditional religion, particularly traditional divination and the ancestor cult. Daneel (1987:26) has reminded us that the AICs teach us "how the gospel is adapted to or presented in confrontation with existing indigenous customs and values". He considers the approach of the AICs to traditional religion and culture to be one of the main contributions of these movements to African Theology (1990:56). To Daneel, contextualization is not "a simplistic adaptation to traditional thought", nor is it "accommodation in the Roman Catholic sense of the word", but is rather "an adaptation that, while displaying parallels with traditional religion, essentially implies a continuing confrontation with and creative transformation of traditional religion and values" (1990:56).

Any hermeneutical reflection that is done here has been made with circumspection and hesitancy. It can never be definitive when the phenomena under discussion are dynamic and under a constant process of change.

READING LIST AND BIBLIOGRAPHY

Anderson, A.H. 1991. *MOYA: the Holy Spirit in African context.* Pretoria: UNISA.
– 1992. *BAZALWANE: African Pentecostals in South Africa.* Pretoria: UNISA.
– 1993. *TUMELO: the faith of African Pentecostals in South Africa.* Pretoria: UNISA.
CSS. 1992. *Population census 1991.* "Summarised results before adjustment for undercount". Pretoria: Central Statistical Service
Daneel, M.L. 1974. *Old and new in Southern Shona independent churches. Vol II.* The Hague: Mouton.
– 1987. *Quest for belonging.* Gweru: Mambo Press.
– 1988. *Old and new in Southern Shona independent churches. Vol III.* Gweru: Mambo Press.
– 1990. "Exorcism as a means of combating wizardry: liberation or enslavement?" *Missionalia* 18(1).
Lukhaimane, E.K. 1980. "The Zion Christian Church of Ignatius (Engenas) Lekganyane, 1924 to 1948: an African experiment with Christianity". M.A. thesis, University of the North, Pietersburg.
Martin, M-L. 1964. *The Biblical concept of messianism and messianism in Southern Africa.* Morija: Morija Sesuto Book Depot.
– 1975. *Kimbangu: an African prophet and his church.* Oxford: Basil Blackwell.
Schreiter, R.J. 1985. *Constructing local theologies.* London: SCM.
Sundkler, B.G.M. 1961. *Bantu prophets in South Africa.* Oxford: Oxford Press.
Turner, H.W. 1965. *Profile through preaching.* London: Edinburgh House.
– 1979. *Religious innovation in Africa.* Boston: G K Hall.
West, M. 1975. *Bishops and prophets in a Black city.* Cape Town: David Philip
ZCC. 1992. *The ZCC Messenger* Vol 22.

Pentecostal and Charismatic Hermeneutics

Marius D. Herholdt

25.1 INTRODUCTION

Biblical Hermeneutics, as an academic discipline, has to do with the methods of interpreting the ancient biblical texts for a modern audience. It is therefore basic to a proper understanding of Scripture and provides insight into the peculiar way a specific church group approaches the Bible. In this chapter, I will concentrate on the presuppositions held by members of the Spirit-movement – presuppositions which exert an influence on their hermeneutics. This should enable the student to come to grips with the key issues of Pentecostal and Charismatic Hermeneutics.

By the Spirit-movement, I refer to that stream of evangelical and baptist Christians who place a high premium on the use of the charismatic gifts in their church services. Popularly they are known as the Pentecostals and Charismatics and they are part of one of the fastest-growing streams in the Christian world.

Although Pentecostal and Charismatic Hermeneutics are still in the initial stages of development, the role that they play is of vital importance. In fact, no group can function effectively without some basic hermeneutical method. This is inescapable because hermeneutical principles form a pattern for understanding and interpreting. In other words, hermeneutics provide a framework and guideline which assist humans in the quest of finding meaning and making sense out of life.

An essential presupposition of modern hermeneutics is that the art (or science) of understanding requires a recipient that is not passive. It is integral to human nature to derive some form of understanding, to un-

SECTION B
HERMENEUTICS

ravel the meaning of experience and circumstances that befall us. We always ask questions such as how, why, what? Understanding requires an act of participation, a process of making knowledge our own. This process does not take place in a naive way. Certain definite guidelines based on intuition, conditioning, or more formally, on critical principles, constantly regulate our interpretation. An important epistemological insight is that no knowledge is value free. The social and religious contexts always play a major role. The point of departure, the presuppositions we work with, is so deeply ingrained in our thought processes that we are normally not consciously or objectively aware of it. This underlines the necessity to give a thorough and honest account of one's religious background to enable one to trace the rudiments of a specific hermeneutic. Let us therefore proceed to consider how Pentecostals and Charismatics may answer the how and why questions.

25.2 PENTECOSTAL HERMENEUTICS

Against this brief background, the student will realise why it becomes necessary to study the broader Pentecostal context. Although no clearly defined Pentecostal Hermeneutic exists, my assumption is that Pentecostals are precisely Pentecostal because they subscribe to a "common Pentecostal point of departure." The difference between pentecostalism and other denominational traditions is fairly significant and profound. It probably warrants a search for a distinct Pentecostal approach that may be developed into a coherent hermeneutical scheme. Such a scheme could be helpful in making the biblical message relevant for Pentecostals today.

There are mainly three areas that make up a common Pentecostal point of departure, irrespective of minor differences between separate Pentecostal and Charismatic groups:

- The very peculiar function of the charismatic gifts and, consequently, the emphasis on the pivotal role of the Holy Spirit;
- The peculiar understanding of the church and the physical role of the body in worship;
- The fourfold role of Christ in the idiom of the so-called Foursquare Gospel.

25.3 THE DISPENSATION OF THE SPIRIT

As the word "Pentecostal" suggests, one would expect the role of the Holy Spirit to be pivotal to Pentecostal experience and consequently also to Pentecostal Hermeneutics. This also applies to Charismatics. I do not suggest that the Holy Spirit is unimportant to other traditions, but I hope to show that the role of the Holy Spirit is of peculiar hermeneutical significance. In mainline Christian traditions, God is the father figure, but in Pentecostal and Charismatic traditions God is the Holy Spirit present in the service. The tendency is to view the post-New Testament era as the era of the Holy Spirit. The outpouring of the Holy Spirit is thus interpreted as an event of profound historical significance in contrast to the dispensation of the Father (Old Testament) and the dispensation of Christ (New Testament events leading up to the ascension of Christ).

Pentecostals need to understand the role of the Holy Spirit against the background of religious experience, especially as it becomes expressed in Pentecostal liturgy. Praise and worship, as it is known, is the religious space where the Holy Spirit is felt and where the gifts normally find expression. This activity of the Holy Spirit is the active, ever-present God occupying Himself with the affairs of believers. To put it in more theological words, this manifestation of the Holy Spirit is the current mode of God in contrast to the specific way God operated in previous historical dispensations.

Pentecostals have a very peculiar approach to the Trinitarian doctrine. They lean towards a process understanding of God, in which He is consecutively operational in history as follows:

- Old Testament: Authority (the Father),
- New Testament: Redemption (the Son), and
- Today: Mission (the Holy Spirit).

The current mode, initiated by the outpouring of the Spirit on the day of Pentecost, does not leave the previous modes behind, but integrates them as applied in prayer: We pray to the Father in the name if Jesus Christ and in the power of the Holy Spirit.

To return to the emphasis on the Holy Spirit within Pentecostal and Charismatic denominations: obviously one needs to look closely at the ramifications of the idea of mission as set out above. "Mission" in Pentecostal and Charismatic circles includes ideas such as outreach, revival, supernatural phenomena like healing and speaking in tongues, revelation, praise and worship, and inspired preaching. This range of religious phenomena is typical of Pentecostal practice. It is a mission in the power and presence of God, who is working dynamically and immanently in the midst of believers. The aim of the Holy Spirit is, in the words of a biblical idiom frequently used in Pentecostal circles, to "gather the harvest". This motivates the urgency for believers to be equipped with power and charismatic gifts (1 Cor 12) to successfully participate in evangelization. Divine healing of the physical body and the direct message of God, expressed as prophecy, are all part of the gifts employed to persuade sinners "to accept Jesus Christ as their personal Saviour".

Through baptism by immersion, the new converts are then accepted into the Christian Church. They are, in turn, discipled and taught to worship God in praise and worship which takes on a peculiar form of spontaneous, often loud and active participation in Pentecostal and Charismatic Churches. The more excessive the worship, the greater the revival that borders on feelings of ecstasy and a yearning for the supernatural. Insights about spiritual matters that prove to be helpful in practical life are normally taken by Pentecostals as revelations granted by God. In Charismatic circles, this is the so-called *Rhema* word, in contrast to the *Logos* word (the written word), that Charismatics frequently refer to. A

25

Pentecostal and Charismatic Hermeneutics

SECTION B

HERMENEUTICS

Rhema word speaks into the situation, it is a relevant word – the word that is received as a direct word from God. Rhema can be expressed in counselling or conversation, but most frequently Rhema is expressed as preaching. Preaching is accepted as inspired when it is persuasive and motivational, when it becomes a word for today. The circle is complete when the new converts reach the stage when they, in turn, can bring in new converts to help fulfil the mission of the Holy Spirit.

To think about God as the present power of the Holy Spirit provides definite theological clarity about the Pentecostal tradition. It does not explain the claim that God is real in our midst, but does describe *how* God is real. He is real in the sense that believers experience his power and working in a way that is open to sensory perception. He is not above us, but in front of us and next to us; God is not far from us, but working within us.

We can state certain accents of Pentecostalism against this background: religion is experience, not dogma; God is an overwhelming presence operating in a communal setting, not the abstract God of theological thought or the private God of the individual ascetic; God is not merely a transcendent Being that works in an authoritarian, top-down way, but the immanent this-worldly Spirit whose divine nature is revealed in the supernatural working of the charismatic gifts. He is the God of all ages, but is now working in a universally different and unprecedented way, a way that is only possible because of the peculiar nature and constitution of the church. The church is the ecclesiastical space where the manifestation of the Holy Spirit is most evident. Consequently, the paired concept Spirit/church is a key concept in Pentecostal Theology. This I will work out in more detail in the next paragraph.

The mode of the Spirit as the presence of God means to the Pentecostal believer that God is willing to make his power available. This power finds expression in different ways, such as the gifts, the courage to witness, supernatural phenomena such as healing and, to a lesser degree, especially in Charismatic circles, even dramatic joyful expressions like so-called "laughing in the Spirit" or "dancing in the Spirit". Irrespective of the particular kind of phenomenon encountered, the underlying principle is always that the power of the Holy Spirit elevates one above the normal. In a more personal way, it also means that God is willing to bless his children. The power of the Holy Spirit is not a blind force; He is the God that loves us, saves us, cares for us and abides with us. As Father, He comforts us and employs us in his service; as Son, He saves us, heals us and sets us free to celebrate redemption; as Spirit, He qualifies us for his service and instructs us.

Of particular significance is the fact that Charismatic and Pentecostal Churches make liturgical provision for the manifestations of the Holy Spirit. Peter Hocken is correct in his assessment that:

> What is new in Pentecostalism is not the occurrence of particular pneumatic phenomena nor the initial opening-up of the pneumatic dimension in individual Christians; rather it is the organisation, embodiment and expectation of all these gifts within the life of Christian communities, i.e. the articulation and organisation

in corporate church life of what has over the centuries been known only spasmodically in isolated instances. (Hocken 1977:35)

The value of glossolalia (speaking in tongues) in re-enacting the presence of God is of particular interest in this regard. Tongues is a verbal expression of the supernatural working of the Spirit. The interpretation of tongues follows the message in tongues so that the unintelligible message is made known to the other believers. Therefore, this gift has cognitive value in becoming the direct communication of God. This divine communication establishes an intimate and personal bond between God and the believers. The verbal gifts are expressions of God's thoughts and will, and although this does not take the place of the Bible, it adds a dimension of directness in the way God is perceived to reveal Himself. Yet, this revelation also requires human participation, for it is when believers speak under the anointing of the Spirit that they hear the voice of God. They speak, yet not out of themselves, for they speak as the Spirit leads them to.

The Bible is the background to the space where Pentecostal believers find themselves living out their faith. Yet, occasionally Pentecostals may switch to a "biblical mode" in correspondence with the tradition that the Bible is the rule of faith. In many such instances, Pentecostals employ particular texts to confirm or critically survey certain dogmatic convictions or institutionalized practices. Apart from the Bible, the charismatic gifts serve also as a way for God to guide and inspire his people. In this regard, Gilpen aptly remarks that: "Pentecostal meetings are characterized by the ecstasy, exuberance and exercise of the gifts of the Spirit, both for worship and the guidance and direction of God's people" (Gilpen 1976:117). To summarise, Pentecostals and Charismatics use the Bible to offer more formal instruction, whereas the gifts serve as a mode of personal communication in our walk with God. The former requires diligent study and the latter require a direct openness to the Holy Spirit. The significance of this is that it provides an interpretative (hermeneutical) framework by which Pentecostals and Charismatics understand God to be present in a direct and actual way to operate or communicate in the circle of believers.

Believers actually participate in this working of God as they experience his presence and respond to his unction. Furthermore, the Spirit employs the human faculties so explicitly that the content of what God is doing inspires, reveals, guides and urges surrender of the self. In commenting on charismatic experience, Heribert Mühlen confirms this truth:

> When we see and hear how other people surrender themselves to God in praise, giving thanks and faith, then we see and hear something of the Spirit of Jesus himself (Acts 2:33). This experience cuts us to the heart (Acts 2:37), lays hold not just of our understanding, not just of our will, but of all our being and resources. (1978: 348)

Pentecostals are often misunderstood as individualising the Spirit. The presence of the Spirit, however, goes far beyond the sphere of private experience. In fact, it first and foremost involves church life.

Pentecostal and Charismatic Hermeneutics

25.4 CHURCH LIFE

I already mentioned the fact that the paired concept of Spirit/church is central to Pentecostalism. Let me expound on this. The Holy Spirit as the mode of God's presence in this age was shown to be of major hermeneutical significance. The church, on the other hand, is the result of the work of the Holy Spirit and also the liturgical space where the Spirit manifests its power. It can be said that the Spirit not only helps believers, but also enables believers to help, serve and testify to others. What Allen Anderson says of the Spirit-type churches may equally apply to Pentecostalism: "The Spirit-type churches went a long way towards meeting the physical, emotional and spiritual needs of Africa, offering a solution to *all* of life's problems and a way to cope in a threatening and hostile world" (Anderson 1991:103). The potential is there to develop this broad approach into a fully-fledged holistic idea – for it is for this very reason that Pentecostals encourage participation. Phrases such as "let us join hands", "let us pray together", or "we belong to one another" are frequently heard in Pentecostal circles.

This unity is the result of the Holy Spirit who joins believers together and fills all hearts as a common denominator. The Spirit is not only there for the individual believer, He is there for "us". More precisely understood, the Spirit is only there for the individual because the individual is part of the community. The Spirit was poured out, not on the individual, but on the community of believers. This could explain why the charismatic gifts are mostly in operation during services where the group worships. This bonding factor leads to the idea that the body of Christ is the dominant metaphor for the church. Consequently, the church is no longer merely the people of God like in Old Testament times. The idea of the body of Christ (or *corpus Christi*) has a much more organic and intimate connotation. A body is formed by an interaction between the parts, a symbiotic harmony between the members.

Whereas Reformed Churches base their sense of belonging on the covenant relationship, Pentecostals base the group bond on the more organic metaphor of the body. Pentecostals may distinguish in this way between Israel and the church. This distinction is so crucial that it becomes an hermeneutical principle. The newness of the church implies a significant break with the past, a new dispensation or era in God's dealing with humankind. Accordingly, Pentecostals will underline the uniqueness of the New Testament in its application to the church, and especially the ongoing working of the Holy Spirit. The body of Christ is an entity that is only possible because of the completed work of Christ. Jesus and the cross really made an historical difference, inaugurated a new epoch.

The church is the place where the Bible becomes manifested, where all the Bible truths are lived out and that which is latent becomes actual. Consequently, the sermon is meant not only to be an exegesis, but a power to save and to heal and to set the captives free. Pentecostals expect the authority of the Word of God to make a difference by the transformation that takes place when people believe the Word. The quest here lies on a different level – a level of understanding and experience rather than of interpretation. The scope of understanding is application, experience and growth, whereas interpretation is a scholarly approach to the Bible, but with a critical edge. Pentecostals have engaged in scholarly exercises, but the emphasis is largely on the Word that is alive and that gives light and affects transformation. The very Spirit who inspired the Word causes a "melt down" of the written Word so that it becomes alive. Pentecostals not only see a text within the context of a passage or chapter, but also within the church as the wider context. In this way, they understand the Word also by the way it inspires, edifies and strengthens believers.

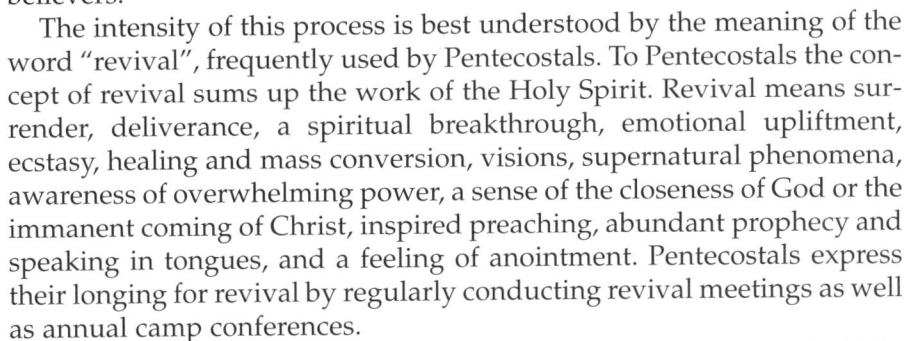

The intensity of this process is best understood by the meaning of the word "revival", frequently used by Pentecostals. To Pentecostals the concept of revival sums up the work of the Holy Spirit. Revival means surrender, deliverance, a spiritual breakthrough, emotional upliftment, ecstasy, healing and mass conversion, visions, supernatural phenomena, awareness of overwhelming power, a sense of the closeness of God or the immanent coming of Christ, inspired preaching, abundant prophecy and speaking in tongues, and a feeling of anointment. Pentecostals express their longing for revival by regularly conducting revival meetings as well as annual camp conferences.

The Pentecostal Church, then, is about revival, about the way the Holy Spirit affects believers and the way people react to Him. The Holy Spirit is at home in the church. He is concrete in his manifestations because it involves people as physical human beings. The human faculty of speech is in the service of the Holy Spirit; He works in the church when people lay hands on the sick; He speaks when people speak under the unction of the Spirit. The church is the place where the Holy Spirit includes people bodily in the flow of power. Liturgical conduct is normally emotionally expressive and actively participatory. At the basis of this is the idea that the physical world is a vehicle of the spiritual because God accepts the homage of the body in worship. Indeed, the Holy Spirit works in nature and touches the material world, but it is through the human body that He becomes intelligible. It is through the material body responding to the flow of the Spirit that God reaches out in his infinite mercy and tender love. It is here, in the church service, that believers may witness the truth of his Word and understand the depth of his revelation. In the revival atmosphere, the full scope of the Bible becomes displayed and the heart of God's message to save and help, becomes evident. It is through preaching that the Bible becomes alive, and it is through the miracles of faith that the Bible shows itself to be true.

The Holy Spirit works within the parameters of the Bible. By believing what God says in the Word, and by putting it into practice, the Spirit becomes manifest in the church. Pentecostals experience the Holy Spirit as a relationship rather than as an entity, for it is in the community that the Spirit becomes manifest. Believers feel the Spirit when they act on the metaphors of the Bible. These metaphors provide access to the Spirit and

SECTION B
HERMENEUTICS

to experience. Believers use the body to uplift the human spirit to God, daring to reach out to Him because we have examples in the Word of people who dared to reach out. To understand the texts does not mean to take an objective stand. We therefore do not interpret the text so much as follow the text, to be interpreted by the text. We understand the texts as much as we touch the reality of God on the invitation and demand of the text. It is not understanding alone that is important, but also orientation; it is not interpretation that is sought, but the challenge to respond to the Word at face value. Interpretation only follows obedience; truth results from experience and dedication. The counterbalance to the subjective experience of the Word is the bodily participation in worship, which acts as visible sign that people are responding to the Word. Peter Hocken puts it very well:

> The Pentecostal acceptance of the body in prayer and worship has important consequences for the sign element in Christian life ... Pentecostals do not simply exalt subjective experience over objective doctrine. What is distinctive in Pentecostalism is that the objective counterbalance to subjective experience is not primarily doctrine but visible signs. (1977:35)

The Bible then ultimately speaks to the body, to the whole human being. The Bible itself is like a body to the Spirit, for the body is a medium through which things can be moved and the world can be touched. Yet, the Spirit should be "released"; the body should become active. This is accomplished when the Word is carried out as believers change from being hearers to becoming doers of the Word. The body becomes a metaphor for the way the process of understanding proceeds within the framework of communication. This is why the Bible "speaks" as if it has a mouth, the Bible can comfort and uplift as if it has "hands", it can guide and comfort us as if it walks alongside us.

A text, like the limb of the body, does not stand on its own. It is part of an organic whole. Every text is, in its organic connectedness, an expression of all other texts; every text is related to the whole body of Scripture. Every text then points away and beyond itself to a whole that sustains and supports it. Exegesis is no longer a painstaking analysis, but a meaningful encounter; it does not tolerate mere interest, but invokes respect. It is precisely through the human response to the Word that the church is formed and that the church as the body becomes an extension of the Word, a living expression of the Word. Thus the Spirit can leave the pages of the Word and enter the church to fulfil those blessings promised in the Word. This is how the Word becomes clear.

25.5 CHRIST AND THE FOURSQUARE GOSPEL

The church was properly formed after the atonement of Christ had been completed. This opened the way for the Holy Spirit to work in an unprecedented way because a multitude of believers was now at his disposal. The Spirit need no longer be a stranger on earth, because converts form the channel for his operation. The Spirit is the dove that looks for an abiding place. This is why He fills people. In Pentecostal and Charismatic circles, this is called the baptism of the Holy Spirit. Although not a "Pentecostal", Hendrikus Berkhof puts the meaning of this fulfilment in good theological perspective when he writes:

> The power to partake of that which the Spirit has granted us, in the wider contexts of his work in humanity, is the sign of spiritual maturity. Such maturity has to do with the mystery of our individuality. The Spirit in justification occupies the centre of ourselves; in sanctification, the whole circle of our human nature; in filling us, he occupies our individuality, the special mark which I and I alone bear, the special contribution which I have to make to the whole of life. (1977:90)

By putting it this way, Berkhof shows the filling as a third category of the Spirit's work next to salvation and sanctification. To Pentecostals and Charismatics, these individual contributions have to do with the charismatic gifts. Yet, that which occurs in the worship service remains anchored in Jesus Christ in a most profound way: The pastor preaches because Jesus is the Saviour; the believers pray for the sick because Jesus is the Healer; the people testify and are used in the charismatic gifts because Jesus baptizes them in the Spirit; and all of this is done in anticipation of the second coming because Jesus is the coming King. Donald Gee confirms that Pentecostals popularly refer to this fourfold approach as the Foursquare Gospel (1949:122). The Foursquare Gospel describes the hermeneutical value of the Pentecostal Christology. In the words of Henry Lederle:

> I would venture to suggest that the essence of Pentecostal faith lies in the doctrine of Jesus Christ and that it can be found in the specific concentration on Jesus as Saviour, Spirit baptizer, Healer and soon coming King. In these traditional four elements (cf. the Foursquare Gospel) I believe we have the epitome of Pentecostal faith. (1988:37)

The central question here is what the implications of this understanding of Christ are for Pentecostal Hermeneutics. In the first instance, it reminds us that the Bible has to do with the good news (gospel) that Jesus saves, and here I mean salvation in a comprehensive sense of making all things new and whole. Consequently, interpretation of the Bible serves understanding, and understanding is part of the process of becoming whole. We are renewed in the sense that we become integrated into the grand scheme of the universe; a quest to find our place in the multitude of seemingly disconnected things. We need to see the interconnectedness of all things, the intelligibility of the cosmic order. We discover meaning to the degree that we see things fit together in a way that is wholesome and conducive to our well-being. Thus the interpretation of the Bible is part of a process that answers to the criteria of becoming whole and all that it entails.

Against this background, we may take the Foursquare Gospel to describe a process that answers to the need of wholeness. This means that Christ not only provides salvation or healing superfluously. On the contrary, without the things offered within the package of the Foursquare Gospel, reality will remain marred, fragmented, unintelligible and incomplete. Without Christ, humans are lost in the most terrible sense. This not only has moral consequences, but also touches the reality of existence. Without wholeness, people live a shadow existence. Brokenness, incompleteness, sickness and degeneration threaten all people in the deepest sense. Against the background of this threat, Christ is proclaimed as the only solution. The Spirit of God rests upon Him to heal the broken hearts and set the captives free. In this fragmented life, He becomes the integration point, the fulcrum of all existence. In Him we find rest, coherence and peace.

The four facets used to describe the work of Christ I understand as a reference to the whole of life, that is, moral life, church life, physical and political. Let me explain. Christ as Saviour saves people from sin and liberates them from moral degradation; as Baptizer, Christ brings people into the new community known as the church and endows them with gifts to be of service to one another; as Healer, He touches our bodies (the physical) and brings wholeness; and as coming King, He promises to return to reign with peace and righteousness. His authority as King is experienced in the way the Bible often addresses us with power and coercion.

All the modalities of life can be included under these four aspects. Christ is therefore presented as sufficient to fulfil all needs and solve all problems. This hermeneutical presupposition is very important because it stresses the central role that Christ plays, as well as the necessity of his atonement. In the context of the fourfold office, He is the living Word that conveys truth about life. In the all-sufficient answer to human misery, we discover the real magnitude of the problem of existence. In Christ, God gives the decision to remedy all things. All Bible stories converge on this truth and all detail falls into one of the following categories – categories that are broad enough to fit any instance of need:

- **Salvation**: Liberation, restoration, return, freedom, righteousness, forgiveness, feeling of bliss, future expectation, status.
- **Healing**: Wholeness, sanctification, relief, integration, meaningfulness, quality of existence.
- **Baptizing**: Service, power, social togetherness, a sense of belonging, spirituality, usefulness, individuality.
- **Reign**: Peace, righteousness, fairness, authority, guidance, thankfulness, abundance, global purification, sound ecology.

The intertwined threads of these four strands run through the Bible as fairly clear indications of the message of God's good news. They serve as broad hermeneutical categories within which Pentecostals will interpret everything that they read in Scripture. They create the expectation that whatever God does, He is doing to help us. In the words of the songwriter:

> Christ is God's answer to all our longing,
> Christ is the answer to all our needs,
> Saviour, Baptizer, the Great physician;
> O Hallelujah, He's all I need.

25.6 FURTHER DEVELOPMENT

As Pentecostalism and the Charismatic Movement – both as fairly young

25 Pentecostal and Charismatic Hermeneutics

streams in the history of Christianity – advance and become progressively institutionalised, they may pave the way for deeper academic reflection. In a western world that places a high premium on academic prestige and scientific method, Pentecostals and Charismatics are under exceeding pressure to participate in serious theological research. I am uncertain that the current approach to research is very helpful in explaining the Spirit-movements. Modernity, where analysis, causality (every effect has a direct cause), and reductionism (everything can be reduced to its parts) play a major role, forms too rigid a mental framework to be helpful in describing the Pentecostal sentiments characterised by spontaneity and freedom. Perhaps a postmodern paradigm (mental framework) (cf. chapter 14, 27), with its emphasis on an integrated (holistic) approach and organic (the world is not a machine) reality may provide a basis for a more promising method. In such a setting, the understanding of the texts may form part of the very effect it produces. Interpretation is not the discovery of an already existing objective truth, but the outcome of participation as believers attempt to apply the living Word to real life situations. In this sense, the goal of the interpretation of the text is not only to understand, but also to apply. Logically, this implies a zone of pre-understanding that impels us to make use of a text in the first place. In the application, however, deeper meanings of the text become unlocked. We simultaneously discover and construct the truth of the text. Consequently, a plurality of meanings become possible.

Consistent with the emphasis placed on the active role of the Spirit and on the charismatic provision for believers to minister unto one another, Pentecostalism cannot afford to be a book-based religion. The painstaking reference to a book, irrespective of it being traditionally the Holy Bible, is too much of an academic enterprise to satisfy Pentecostal and Charismatic expectations. Prophecy, messages in tongues and inspired preaching as a comprehensive divine message best suit Spirit movements. This does not mean that the Bible is not important at all. It rather means that the church is the actual place for spiritual growth, and not the Bible itself. The Bible functions as the source for new growth, but does not specify the growth. It is rather like the food that we eat; it provides the necessary nutrients that cause cell growth, but does not decide the colour of the eyes or how tall a person will grow.

In practice, then, the Bible is not taken as a rule book or as a fixed or absolute truth. The rich images and metaphors, the many examples of God's intervention in human existence and the many Bible promises stimulate the religious imagination and challenge one to discover the Bible truth as living truth for oneself. Prophecies and preaching are inspired by the comprehensive images and stories derived from the Bible, rather than by the text itself as a single verbal unit. Such an approach makes it easier for the Bible texts to become integrated into the mind in order to enrich and stimulate what is already present in the form of images and stories. After all, the mind is an already occupied zone teeming with many rich images and expectations. The major images present in the Pentecostal mind are

SECTION B

HERMENEUTICS

the Spirit giving gifts to believers, the church as the actual place where growth takes place, and the fourfold work of Christ directed at fulfilling certain needs.

There is, unfortunately, a lack of uniformity among Pentecostal and Charismatic groups. This makes it difficult to find a common hermeneutical approach. Nevertheless, the broad categories discussed here may be a fruitful starting point in deciding that which is basic to Pentecostal and Charismatic Hermeneutics.

25.7 A PENTECOSTAL READING OF THE BIBLE

Traditionally, the Pentecostal reading of the Bible has been a loose type of reading, rather like looking for gems on the surface – all texts are seen to be level (of equal importance). Some texts are, nevertheless, of more relevance to Pentecostals than others due to the support that they render to distinct Pentecostal doctrine like the charismatic gifts. Consequently, Luke (Acts) is more often quoted than Paul. Pentecostals, like many Christians from other traditions, often succumb to a fundamentalist understanding of Scripture and the text is taken at face value. On the other hand, the amazing thing is that Pentecostal scholars are often inclined to follow contemporary academic hermeneutical streams without considering whether they are in line with Pentecostal tradition and presuppositions. This needs to be remedied if Pentecostals want their hermeneutics (and consequently exegesis) to be true to their roots.

Factors that influence a Pentecostal Hermeneutic, in terms of the typical characteristics that I have identified, are the following: [1] The consensus of the church; [2] the charismatic guidance of the Holy Spirit; [3] the Foursquare Gospel; [4] the newness of the current dispensation; and [5] the importance of mission and revival. In order to develop the hermeneutical consequences of these factors, I need first to translate them into theological categories, namely: [1] the ecclesiastical space of religious life; [2] the supernatural communication of God; [3] the Christocentric moment and the fourfold office of Christ; [4] the notion of novelty; [5] and the divine imperative. By engaging in a more exact formulation of key factors, a further uncovering of theoretical issues becomes more plausible. Let us consider each theoretical aspect briefly.

25.7.1 The ecclesiastical space of religious life

To both Pentecostals and Charismatics, inspired preaching is very important. Preaching is the moment when the Word comes alive, when God speaks forcefully into individual lives. The ideal for preaching is not exposition or teaching, but the touching of lives. The mood is therefore experiential rather than cognitive. One could conclude that the experiential mode serves as an hermeneutical level where truth and reality converge to become a power of persuasion and ultimately transformation.

The consensus of the church also serves as an atmosphere where the intensity of this "Word-becomes-alive" reality becomes intensified. This consensus is often in the form of some kind of response like "amen"

(Pentecostals) or spontaneous laughter (Charismatics) or non-verbal signs like nodding or bodily gestures. Of course, Pentecostals also read and study the Bible at home, but by far the most understanding takes place under that which is termed "anointed preaching". This is only possible when the ecclesiastical space is properly constituted, and hence this is a crucial factor in Pentecostal and Charismatic Hermeneutics.

25.7.2 The supernatural communication of God

The essence of prophecy and glossolalia is that God speaks to his people. The message is normally one of comfort and encouragement; and although the content is in line with the Word, it is a word that extends the pages of the Bible. Indeed, to Pentecostals and Charismatics, the Bible is not a limited book, for Acts still continues. Pentecostalism is a Spirit religion, for the charismatic gifts serve as a medium for God to address his people in a very relevant way.

The hermeneutical bearing of this is that the concentration of hermeneutical effort is on God's side, and not on human endeavour. Believers actively engage in the charismatic gifts, but it is God who speaks and makes his message known. The kerygma is not a static set of truths that waits to be discovered, for God speaks when believers speak as the Spirit gives them utterance. The input of the believer therefore contributes to a reader-response type of communicative understanding of the Word.

25.7.3 The Christocentric moment and the fourfold office of Christ

Christ is the picture that serves to brings the pieces of the puzzle together into a coherent whole. He is the integration point that evokes meaning. Deeply embedded in the roots of the Pentecostal perspective, lies the fourfold office of Christ, that is, Saviour, Healer, Baptizer and coming King. In the final analysis, this is what God has set out to do and around which the Bible content revolves. Especially the functions of Healer and Baptizer are peculiar to Pentecostals and Charismatics.

The fourfold office serves as a broad hermeneutical category according to which much of Scripture will be interpreted. Hence, this Christocentric moment, as we may call it, is normative in the sense that nothing in the Bible may contradict it or directly, or indirectly, fail to contribute to it as central message.

25.7.4 The notion of novelty

How new are the things that God works? Newness can be the result of a rearrangement of old components; it can be the unfolding of latent potential; or it can be new in a novel sense of a first appearing without any direct bearing to any prior entities. It seems to me that the latter possibility is basic to a Pentecostal and Charismatic understanding of the things that God does. In this regard, the radical newness of the new dispensation of the Spirit, or the newness of a new creation, or the novelty of glossolalia may serve as examples.

SECTION B

HERMENEUTICS

Newness is therefore more radical than freshness, rearrangement or emergence. It is sheer novelty. As a conceptual scheme, novelty only becomes possible when one bravely dares to break with the old philosophical notion of cause and effect. This break can now be substantiated from a scientific (quantum mechanics) as well as philosophical (non-Cartesian order) point of view. In a sense, novelty has to do with the abundance of possibilities, or the infinite spectrum, of meaning. It is akin to the impossibility to provide the exact temperature due to the infinite number of decimals that it may entail. To make it easy, we work with intervals of tenths and ones. Likewise, words are perhaps merely rough intervals for an infinite amount of meanings. The closest we can get to true meanings are nuances.

If we apply this rather sophisticated construct to hermeneutics, it implies, amongst others, the following: Exact meanings (or interpretations) can never be attained with certainty – we only approximate truth; God speaks newly into new circumstances and needs in such a way that the Word is constantly extended; a cognitive understanding of the Word must of necessity be supplemented by non-conceptual aspects of understanding in order to "fine-tune" nuances missed by the broad verbal intervals employed by the intellect; the Word is not static, for novelty is only possible in a very dynamic interplay of complex forces; the reality of the Word is probably a multi-levelled reality where many different levels of authentic meaning co-exist.

25.7.5 The divine imperative

By this I mean the goal of God is mission and revival. Both mission and revival serve as counterparts of the final outcome to indicate the direction that God is heading. Mission points outwards to sinners and revival inwards to believers. Mission is a description of the big evangelical embrace of God to include sinners in his kingdom; and revival is a description of the total blessing, ecstasy, and bliss that God wants believers to enjoy. Revival is nothing less than a foretaste of heaven.

Irresistibly, one reads the Bible with the end result in mind. Consequently, Pentecostals will fit texts into certain categories by which both mission and revival can be advanced. Concepts like kingdom, witnessing, baptism, salvation, victory, blessing, miracles, charismatic gifts and worship, which all have a bearing on mission and revival, will consequently serve as key concepts in a Pentecostal and Charismatic understanding of the Bible.

READING LIST AND BIBLIOGRAPHY

Anderson, A. 1991. *Moya. The Holy Spirit in an African context*. Pretoria: University of South Africa.
Berkhof, H. 1977. *The doctrine of the Holy Spirit*. Atlanta: Knox.
Clark, M.S. & Lederle, H.I. 1989. *What is distinctive about Pentecostal Theology?* Pretoria: University of South Africa.
Fee, D.G. 1991. *Gospel and Spirit: Issues in New Testament hermeneutics*. Massachussets:

Hendrickson.
Fourie, S. 1990. *Prophecy, God's gift of communication to the church.* Pretoria: University of South Africa.
Gee, D. 1949. *The Pentecostal movement.* London: Elim.
Gilpen, G.W. 1976. "The place of the Pentecostal movements today." In Brewster, P.S. *Pentecostal doctrine.* London: Brewster.
Herholdt, M.D. 1990. *Christus die Saligmaker, Geneser, Doper en komende Koning: Vertrekpunte vir 'n Pinksterteologie.* Pretoria: University of South Africa.
Hocken, P. 1977. "The significance of Pentecostalism." In Tugwell, S., et al. (eds.), *New heaven? New earth? An encounter with Pentecostalism.* Springfield, MO: Templegate.
Hollenweger, W.J. 1977. *The Pentecostals.* London: SCM.
Lederle, H.I. 1988. "The proprium or distinctive element of Pentecostal Theology." *Theologia Evangelica.* 21.
Möller, F.P. 1975. *Die diskussie oor die charismata soos wat dit in die pinksterbeweging geleer en beoefen word.* Braamfontein, Johannesburg: Evangelie Uitgewers.
Mühlen, H. 1978. *A charismatic theology.* London: Burns & Oates.
New Heaven? New Earth? 1976. London: Darton, Longman & Todd.
Nichol, J.T. 1966. *The Pentecostals.* Plainfield, NJ: Logos.
Spittler, R. (ed.). 1976. *Perspectives on the New Pentecostalism.* Grand Rapids: Baker
Williams, J.R. 1972. *The Pentecostal reality.* Plainfield, NJ: Logos.

Ecological Hermeneutics

Luco van den Brom

26.1 INTRODUCTION

"There can be no peace among human beings if there is not peace with nature." These words were spoken by the nuclear physicist C.F. von Weiszäcker in a sermon on Good Friday 1986. The danger he has in mind consists in "unintelligent forms of economic growth" which destroy nature (von Weiszäcker 1986:312ff.). It is evident for many people that crimes against the environment, like pollution or felling the rain forests, can endanger the development and well-being of the human species. We recognize in this example a consciousness about a delicate balance between the human existence and the so-called natural world. Pollution of the environment, deforestation, several modern western forms of technological industrialization, etc. are like the fouling of one's own nest. And we may raise the question whether a damaged world is the one the Creator has in mind. Such a simple question is an example of an ecological way of reading the Bible and understanding the religious tradition. Ecological interpretation stresses the relevance of the insight that human beings belong to a wider community than human relationships such as family, tribe, nation or race. This community also includes the various organisms of the environment which can be called the *oikos* (house) for human beings. Trees, herbs, flowers, insects, beasts etc. belong to this community.

The awareness of such a wider community may be part of a worldview, as it is the case in the next example: "A thing is right when it tends to preserve the integrity, stability, and beauty of the biotic community. It

SECTION B

HERMENEUTICS

is wrong when it tends otherwise." These words of Aldo Leopold (1949: 225) spell out a fundamental ecological world-view including a specific notion of the good. His words give expression to a consciousness of belonging to larger biological structures than merely human ones. People are not only part of social and political networks, but they are also organisms because of their being embodied. This ecological consciousness is also morally significant.

The word "ecological" is used here for the interdependence of the various organisms to one another and to their environment in a biological community. The interactions among the organisms and all aspects of the environment in a specific region must be considered as a kind of a functional unit or system. The different elements of such a system are interrelated by means of food chains, through which nutrients are cycled and energy is transported. This interrelatedness of the organisms tends towards delicate stability which contains, however, the possibility of destabilization. Fluctuations or changes at some places in the environment can have serious repercussions elsewhere in the system.

Within this ecological framework, Leopold defines his moral and aesthetic criteria. Actions are measured by their consequences for "the integrity, stability, and beauty" of the ecological system. This means that right and wrong do not refer to the condition of the individual organisms, but to the well-being of the system as a whole. This also has implications for the meaning and value of the individual organisms. The meaning or significance of any individual consists in its relation and contribution to the ecological system as a whole.

Within the dominant framework of western culture, Leopold's stance has its contrast in the view of science of Francis Bacon (1561–1626). He claims that science is significant as far as it contributes to human control over the natural forces to the benefit of humankind. Bacon is a controversial figure in the history of science because of his "original" method of scientific research. His approach consisted in a kind of elimination of hypotheses whose predictive consequences were not in agreement with the observed facts. This method of falsification was not original, but he presented it so effectively that he inspired many scientists in their search for the basic principles of nature.

The understanding of the basic principles, however, is not the main purpose of scientific research, according to Bacon. Humanity lost the dominion over nature since the Fall, but science is quite a good instrument to recover human supremacy over the non-human world. This recovery of the lost control over nature is commissioned by God. Therefore, progress in knowledge of nature should not be the purpose of science, but its practical application in a technology which leads to the improvement of the quality of *human* life. Bacon's point of view implies a distinction between the human species and the rest of its environment, between humanity and its ecosystem. And, by consequence, human beings are the lords and masters of all other living creatures.

My aim in this chapter is to contribute to the clarification of an Ecological Hermeneutics. Traditionally, people meant by hermeneutics the science and art of interpreting classical or fundamental texts. It was important to discover the basic principles for the understanding and interpretation of the religious texts. With the introduction of the critical methods of reading the Scripture, biblical scholars began to relate these texts to their historical background in order to understand the original meaning of these texts (the so-called historical-critical method, see chapter 17). In the 19th century, the interpretation of biblical texts was not a matter of asking about the meaning and relevance of those words for us as modern readers. This question of the meaning for us was left to doctrinal, i.e. confessional, theology because the subjective meaning was not part of the objectively knowable truth about the text.

However, this critical approach is also applicable to itself. The idea that the historical background is all-determining for the exact understanding of biblical texts reveals much of the world-view and interests of the 19th century scholar. In their view, classical texts like the Scripture are historical *objects* which belong to a specific era in the past. The idea that classical texts could also be *instruments* that are helpful to give meaning and sense to our present context was not part of their so-called objective or positivistic framework. At best, the 19th century biblical scholar could understand classical texts as instruments of communication with a past period. But even then, the texts remain objects. In an instrumental view of reading texts, however, we recognize the usefulness of the biblical text as instrument also in a new context of a new reader. In order to figure this possibility out, we have to realise the interaction or interrelation between a world-view and the way we understand religious texts as relevant for a context of the modern reader. Our world-view will certainly influence the way we read texts and vice versa. A good example is given by Bacon's way of reading texts. In his classical western point of view, humanity is apart from the rest of nature. And he justifies his anthropocentric world-view by a traditional anthropocentric reading of the first chapters of the Bible.

26.2 THE ANTHROPOCENTRIC READING: THE DOMINION MODEL

According to the anthropocentric understanding of the universe, the world is designed for the benefit of the human species. The value of stones, plants and animals is dependent upon their contribution to the human well-being. Everything exists solely to do people good. This anthropocentric prejudice determines the reading and interpretation of the biblical texts and their meaning for a religious understanding of the created universe.

Many theologians in the western Christian tradition will not even raise the question of our responsibility to non-human organisms. Traditional moral theology, for example, denies that human beings have direct responsibility to animals as they do have to other human beings. The argument for this denial is often based upon a hierarchical interpretation of the order of things in the created world. Because of this hierarchy, all

SECTION B

HERMENEUTICS

nature has a purpose, and flora and fauna have no other purpose save that of serving the human being. In this way Genesis 1:29 is understood: "Fill the earth and subdue it, rule over the fish in the sea, the birds of heaven and every living and moving thing." Which means that humanity has the dominion over the other creatures. In theology, Thomas Aquinas is a well-known defender of this dominion model for which he uses a logic of perfect being.

Influenced by Aristotle's philosophy, Aquinas claims that "the order of things is such that the imperfect are for the perfect, even as in the process of generation nature proceeds from imperfection to perfection" (*Summa Theologiae* II/II.64). This order is ordained by God in such a way that all things in the world occupy their appropriate place in order to serve all those things which are ranged above them. The anthropological consequence of this view is that the world is made exclusively for the benefit of humanity. God Himself transcends this order of the created things in order to maintain it by his providence. In this order, God governs the highest creatures, which are the intellectual ones. The lower creatures are ruled by the higher ones. Because humanity (together with the angels) belongs to the category of the intellectual creatures, the animals are subordinate to humanity in accord to the divine providence. Wild animals, however, have some knowledge, and "so they are set above plants and other things that lack knowledge". In this anthropocentric understanding of the world, all non-rational creatures have merely an *instrumental* value for the human agent. Therefore, human agents can use plants for the benefit of their animals and both plants and animals for the benefit of humanity. Hence both their life and death are subject to the human interest.[1] They are under the human dominion.

When the value of flora and fauna is instrumental, it is difficult to raise the question of human responsibility to the flourishing of non-human creatures. Aquinas claims that:

> one who holds dominion over his own acts is free in his activities, "for the free man is he who acts for his own sake". But one who is acted upon by another is necessarily subject to slavery. So, every other creature is naturally subject to slavery; only the intellectual creature is by nature free.

The human agent is a rational creature and, therefore, free to act for his own sake; but the plants and the beasts belong to the category of creatures "acted upon by another". Accordingly, they are at the disposal of the human free agent. They are to be understood as human property and, therefore, human beings can act with them at their own discretion. And so animals and plants have no moral status in themselves. The argument for this moral claim is based upon the criterion of possessing reason or mind. Only an intellectual being can attain to God in Himself by knowing and loving. "Therefore, the rational being is the only one that is required in the universe, for its own sake" (Aquinas, *Summa contra Gentiles*

---

1 Aquinas, *Summa contra Gentiles* III.78.1; III.81.1&2; III.112.1&2. This is in line with Aristotle's ideas in *Politics* 1256^b; 1254^b; *Metaphysics* 982^b. See Robin Attfield, *The Ethics of Environmental Concern*, Oxford 1983, Ch.2.

III.112.3). Other beings cannot love God because of their lack of rational life, and they cannot be object of the love of charity because of their inherent lack of value. God can love the non-human creature in so far as it is useful to the human one.

This anthropocentric understanding of the world, influenced by Aristotle's philosophy, determines the way of reading biblical texts. This point of view selects certain interpretations of the texts, while biassed by an anthropological perspective on every element of creation. It chooses among the notions given by the theological scheme to specify the reading of the text. This can be illuminated by Aquinas' understanding of Genesis. According to his anthropocentric understanding, Aquinas understands the text of Genesis 1:26 merely in an intellectual way: being created in the divine image and likeness is interpreted as being an intellectual or rational creature with some understanding. In the human way of life, the body is subject to the mind, and the material or non-rational parts are under the control and command of the intellectual. Aquinas has projected this anthropological order on the order as it is found in the universe. Accordingly, the relationships between humans and the rest of creation are understood in terms of intellectual subordination, and not, for example, in terms of interrelationships that consist in a mutual dependency. Rationality separates human beings from the rest of creation. This justifies the use of non-human creatures indiscriminately, like killing animals for food or fun, or (mis-)using plants or inanimate objects in whatever way.

Aquinas utilizes Genesis 9:3 ("all living and moving creatures shall be food for you; I give you them, as I gave you all green plants"[2]) to argue that it is not a sin to kill animals. He is referring to an idea that was a Manichaean doctrine, at least according to Augustine. The Manichees appear to have taught that it is morally wrong to kill animals and to eat them (Augustine, *De moribus Manichaeorum* ch. 15–17). This doctrine is based on a dualistic understanding of the universe whereby everything contains at least a part of the godhead. Aquinas recognizes a contradiction between this Manichaean doctrine and Genesis 9:3. It is almost incredible that he concludes from the biblical prohibition of cruelty against animals (e.g. Deut 22:6) that this is not said because of the animals, but because of human good. An act of cruelty against animals is forbidden for two reasons. The first one is that such an act might remind people of the possibility of such an act against *human* beings. The second reason is that the interests of other people could be damaged by it (Aquinas, *Summa contra Gentiles* III.112.9–13). This means that animals as valuable creatures are completely out of the picture, and that, therefore, human beings have no moral responsibility to them at all. This extreme hermeneutical prejudice will understand the biblical texts anthropocentrically, i.e. to the exclusive benefit of humans. This has as moral result the conviction that people have to care for other people only. One step further: in an anthropocentric hermeneutics, the biblical texts are not read from the perspect-

Ecological Hermeneutics

---

2 See Genesis 1:29 with its vegetarian ideal.

SECTION B

HERMENEUTICS

ive of responsibility to the whole of creation, because plants are for the good of animals, and inanimate objects, plants and animals are for the good of humanity.

By making human beings the centre of creation, this type of theology creates its own difficulties. First, it is not easy to understand how the rich variety of all biological species could be designed for the good of human beings only. This is not *a priori* evidence, but more like a hermeneutical bias. Second, another difficulty concerns the problem of evil or at least apparent design faults like diseases, storms, natural disasters. In what sense might be a hurricane or a volcanic eruption for the benefit of humanity? Third, with its stress on human salvation and anthropocentricity, it casts out the rest of creation from liberation and redemption. This is the result of not considering at least the possibility that anything else has meaning unless it is subservient to human beings. Actually, this means that there is no theological future for the rest of the creation: plants and animals appear to be excluded from the liberational and recreational work of the triune God, because they cannot be objects of the love of charity. Lacking rationality, they cannot be treated as analogous to human neighbours.

26.3 ACTUAL FORMS OF ANTHROPOCENTRICITY

The anthropocentric reading and the related dominion model have dominated the western culture and religious traditions. These ideas were introduced into other continents, partly through Christian missionary activities. However, it is simply not true that these anthropocentric ideas belong to the past, notwithstanding the ecological consciousness in the ecumenical Conciliar Process since 1983 (the sixth World Assembly of the World Council of Churches in Vancouver). This Conciliar Process emphasized the interrelationship between both justice and peace on the one hand and integrity of creation on the other hand. Justice and peace are concepts and aspects in social life, whereas integrity of creation concerns the whole biological balance of the ecosystem of the earth. In the following debate, the issue of the priority within the three topics is raised: "integrity of creation" is a typical modern western concern, while "justice and peace" are the concerns of South American and African Liberation Theology. At the seventh World Assembly of the WCC in Canberra in 1991, the consonance of both the social and the ecological topics was highlighted by emphasizing the activity of the Spirit in all creation, especially as the energy for all life. Because of this Spiritual energy, humanity shares life with all organic forms and has its accountability for the good of the whole of creation. This good is part of the broader concept of justice and includes more than the social, mental, and physical well-being of people.

So far so good. From an eco-hermeneutical point of view, however, we might feel suspicious of this stress on consonance of integrity of creation and social justice. All depends on the way the concepts are used relative to each other. Justice is often construed as primarily an anthropological concept that can be merely used in an anthropocentric way. It is not *prima facie* clear how the concept of justice could apply to the relation between people and animals. We could raise some questions in this context. How far does justice concern the treatment of animals? In what sense does justice affect the natural environment? How far is the natural environment more than simply a background or stage for humanity's agency and development? It is evident that a healthy environment is a fundamental condition for the possibility of a desirable situation of social justice. Therefore, we could say that the principle of equality demands a healthy environment not merely for privileged people, but for humanity as a whole. It is simply unacceptable that some people should live in towns far away from the polluting industries because they belong to the favoured classes while others are condemned to live on the rubbish dump because of their lower economic or social status. But again, does this principle of equality also pertain to the natural environment of flora and fauna, or should its application be limited to merely human relationships?

Liberation theologians tend to emphasize that environmental issues are a fancy problem of the industrialized countries that are rich enough to allow themselves the luxury of puzzling their brains about such matters. Environmentalist theologians, on the other hand, blame liberation theologians for being anthropocentric because of their exclusive stress on social justice for all human people. Andrew Linzey, for example, criticizes Gustavo Gutiérrez for reducing the universal cosmic understanding of Christ's work to an anthropocentric form of salvation (Linzey 1994:62ff.). Indeed, Gutiérrez claims on the one hand that "the work of Christ is a new creation". This is in line with Paul's theology as expressed in 2 Corinthians 5:17 and Galatians 6:15. This new creation results in "a new chosen people, which this time includes all humanity" saved from sin and liberated from all individual and social consequences of sin. This salvation which thus includes all people, is extended by Gutiérrez to the whole of creation: in Christ *the whole universe* is reconciled with God (Col 1:15–20). This all encompassing cosmic salvation, on the other hand, is related by Gutiérrez to a hierarchical understanding of creation with humanity as its crown. He interprets the prescription of Genesis 1:28 (to dominate the earth) in a rather anthropocentric way for all labour "is worth nothing if it is not done for the good of humanity" (Gutiérrez 1988 rev: 90). Particularly these last words are criticized by Linzey: they reveal the anthropocentric hermeneutic of Liberation Theology.

"The good of humanity" is the final moral standard in Liberation Theology which appears to regard ecological issues as secondary or even irrelevant. It seems that any other project that does not enlarge the good of humanity, is "worth nothing". It is for that reason that Liberation Theology is considered to be anthropocentric. However, to be fair, it is important to qualify this so-called anthropocentrism of Liberation Theology. This theology is not talking about humanity as such, but focuses on the challenge posed by a political, cultural and economical splitting up of the human species into "persons" and "non persons". These "non-persons"

26

Ecological Hermeneutics

SECTION B

HERMENEUTICS

are the people who are not recognized as human by the dominant social order: they are the poor and the exploited, the dehumanized and the oppressed. The question is how to proclaim to the marginalized people that they are children of God's kingdom, which means that they are really human, participants of the new history of liberation. The analogy is the making of a nation out of liberated ex-slaves in the Exodus story. That story tells us of a radical change: the oppressed non-persons became a completely human community with its own Mosaic standards. By using this picture of Exodus, Liberation Theology argues for the *unity* of humanity by denying the splitting up of the human species, and restoring the human identity of the "non-persons". In this sense, liberationalist theologians are not to be blamed, as they use the same notion of unity or wholeness as the environmentalists, but only apply it to humanity. They claim that people who are dehumanized because of the exploitation by others, should be treated as full human beings. By so doing, the moral category of human being is enlarged: all humans are to be treated in a humane way because of what they are. Therefore we cannot simply charge Liberation Theology for being anthropocentric.[3]

In order to cope with environmental problems, churches of the west encourage the use of the *stewardship* model instead of the dominion model. This hermeneutical model stresses the human responsibility for the rest of creation. According to this model, we should not interpret Genesis 1:28 as an invitation to exploitation of the rest of creation, but as an exclusive commission to humanity, as special creature, to show concern for the sustainability of the created world as the basis for all life forms. It is relevant, however, to ask for the intended object of this stewardship. We might be stewards for the good or well-being of a family or clan or a larger community. It is not evidently clear that stewardship concerns the well-being of the rest of creation! Sustainability means the maintaining of the quality of the biosphere for the future of ourselves and new generations. From an ethical point of view, sustainability implies an extension of the meaning of the principle of equality. Future generations equally have rights to the natural resources of the earth, just as the present generation does. This means that people yet unborn also have a moral status: we are urged to manage our earth for them too.[4] We are at risk of leaving a polluted biosphere without adequate natural resources for them. This moral feeling, however, that can be described as "Think of your grandchildren" remains anthropocentric for it concerns only the

---

3 Leonardo Boff in his book *Ecology and Liberation: A New Paradigm* (Maryknoll 1995) argues for an "ecologico-social democracy" that is aware of both the relations among people and their relations to their environment (84). His argument starts from the notion that we all proceed from the same act of love of the Creator. That means that there is a universal interrelatedness among all beings (77) and we can interpret this sacramentally: "God makes of all reality a temple" (51, panentheism!). Therefore he uses the concept of ecology for the mental, social and environmental aspects of life (78).

4 Hans Opschoor uses the term *intergenerational equity* for this concern for future generations: leaving them enough possibilities for wealth and welfare. See his "Use and abuse of creation: ecumenism and ecology tomorrow." In Marc Reuver e.a. (eds.), *The Ecumenical Movement Tomorrow*, Kampen 1993, p. 52ff.

human species. This stewardship model conceals from our eyes that we ourselves are just part of creation. Therefore it does not change our anthropocentric perspective, but maintains the human being as trustee over the non-human creatures.

26.4 PHYSIOCENTRIC AND BIOCENTRIC READING: THE MONISTIC MODEL

We will get a completely different hermeneutical perspective when we turn the anthropocentric model upside-down: we are for the good of nature or Nature. This means that Nature exists for its own sake and has its own intrinsic value. It also means that human beings exist for Nature's sake and purposes. We are not the top of all creatures or the best of Nature, but merely part of it. The meaning of the existence of humanity consists in its relatedness to Nature and its contribution to the continuation of Nature as it ought to be. Humanity is thus subordinated to Nature, and it loses its meaning if it does not contribute to the pro-existence of Nature. This way of understanding our place in the world is monistic in the sense that it underscores the unity and overall balance of our world and our participation with it. In other words, the existence of humanity has an instrumental value that consists in the contribution to the ecosystem of our whole planet. It is well-known that the environment has an important influence upon the development of organisms, but the opposite thesis is also defended. That is to say that on a large scale, complete systems of organisms can influence their inorganic environment in such a way that it maintains a balance of processes which makes the continuance of life possible. For example, we can imagine that in a certain area there is a balance between the numbers of mammalians, reptiles, birds, insects, bacteria, trees, plants, minerals, water, oxygen, etc. A change in the numbers of one species can influence the others in such a way that some of them might even become extinct, and by doing so, threaten the continuation of the balance. Sometimes a new balance between the remaining species can come into existence. So we can imagine the existence of a new ecosystem of the earth without the human species after its self annihilation. That means that, *inter alia*, the existence of Nature is not bound up to the existence of humanity.

The large system which makes the continuance of life possible on earth, is sometimes dubbed the goddess name "Gaia".[5]

It is a small step from a geophysiological concept to the question about the human role in or contribution to this system that seeks to maintain

---

[5] New Age writers might be attracted by such ideas. At a more scientific level, James Lovelock adopted the same position in his writings. He proposes that we could describe our earth in a "geophysiological" way, i.e. as a complex system of the biosphere, atmosphere, oceans, and soil that constitutes a cybernetic system which seeks to provide an optimal physiological environment for life on earth. It is important to be aware of the fact that this is self regulating. See his *Gaia: A New Look at Life on Earth*, Oxford 1979, 11; cf. his *The Ages of Gaia: A Biography of Our Living Earth*, Oxford 1988, xiv. By calling this system "Gaia", Lovelock has caught the imagination about green issues, especially because of connotations of the pagan earth goddess Gaia.

SECTION B
HERMENEUTICS

the balance for the sake of life. It depends upon how we understand human agency in this system. Is it moral activity or merely biological activity like a symptom of life? When we agree that human agency and behaviour can be judged from a moral point of view, we presuppose some form of freedom of choice as necessary for human action. In which case the kind of action will matter. However, when human activity is merely a symptom of life, it will not matter what kind of action human beings perform because their actions are part of a large self-maintaining system. This is to say that, in the long run, this ecosystem will seek to create a new balance that will integrate the effects of any human action, morally good or bad. The consequence might be that in maintaining the balance this ecosystem of the earth may change into a less comfortable environment for various life forms, including human beings. From the perspective of this system as a whole, the loss of the human and other species may not even be problematic because these species are merely instrumental in maintaining a specific balance of the system that might change after their extinction. For example, a nuclear war could destroy the whole human species while this would *not* be an ultimate disaster for the ecosystem as a whole. Maybe we are merely a temporary element in the large chain of terrestrial life forms, and once we have done the job of maintaining a part of the chain of life, we may perish like other species before us or contribute to other future life forms. This view of life minimizes the uniqueness and privileged status of the human species and emphasizes the dispensability of specific forms of life, including humanity. We could characterize this understanding as monistic or holistic because of its accent on the subordination of the individuals to the system as a whole, although we should not stress this qualification too much in a philosophical sense that everything is an expression of one and the same substance.

This way of understanding the world can determine the hermeneutical perspective. As we have seen, an anthropocentric hermeneutic tends to underscore those aspects of the Scripture that refer to the special privileged status of humanity against the rest of creation, and pays attention to the human dominion or, at least, stewardship over the non-human part of creation. In the light of an anthropocentric perspective, we recognize here an anthropology that accentuates the supremacy and independent moral status of humanity and that, therefore, gives priority to a "hard" interpretation of Genesis 1:26–28; 2:19–20. In such an anthropology, Psalm 8:6 ("Thou makest him master over all Thy creatures; Thou hast put everything under his feet") will take priority over e.g. Psalm 8:5 ("What is the human that Thou shouldst remember him?"). A physiocentric hermeneutic pursues the opposite course and stresses the human fragility and the dependence of the human species upon the rest of creation. It points out the similarities between the human and non-human creatures by referring to Ecclesiastes 3:18–22. Its author tells us that the human beings and the beasts are both "creatures of chance ... death comes to both alike". And above all: "Human beings have no advantage over beasts" (3:19) because their origin and destiny are the same: "all came from the dust, and to the dust all return." Ecclesiastes is a voice within the Wisdom tradition of the Old Testament period that contradicts the conventional opinion that humanity belongs to a category apart from the beasts, and underscores their equivalent value. This insight of Ecclesiastes can be extended to all nature. All creatures have value from a theological viewpoint.

The physiocentric perspective could also be developed in another mood that does not primarily minimize the status of human beings, but emphasizes that environmental problems are also spiritual problems because of the sacredness of our earth. The United Nations Conference on Environment and Development, held in Rio de Janeiro June 1992, was meant to address a whole range of serious problems concerning the health of our planet. Some of the participants of the conference were deeply convinced that a human civilization cannot flourish on a dying planet. Other delegations have attempted to rob the climate treaty that aims at the reduction of polluting production processes of any real force. Whereas the so-called developed countries were concerned about the rain forests in the so-called developing countries, the latter stressed their awful problems to meet the simple basic human needs. It illustrated the inequality in access to the natural sources that are necessary for human life: the Northern countries can consume far more energy than the Southern countries.[6] Apart from these controversies, it is remarkable that the conference was surrounded by a religious atmosphere that was evident in statements of non-governmental organizations like "the universe is sacred because all is one" and in symbols like a "tree of life". Apart from this very vague religious monism, however, it is significant that people have recognized that environmental problems cannot be met by merely technological solutions, but primarily by a complete change of mind, religiously or spiritually.[7]

The ambience of Rio has shown that a monistic physiocentric perspective is a life option for many people. However, a physiocentric outlook does not provide us with a criterion for right action. Leopold's proposal ("something is right when it helps to preserve the integrity of the ecosystem") is inadequate. It neglects evolution because there all species are temporary and many of them are extinguished during the process, partly because of changes in the ecosystem of the day, partly because of the evolution of other species, etc. The biosphere is always changing and if such is the case, it is not clear what is meant by integrity of an ecosystem. In a biological outlook, this criterion cannot even claim that pollution by

Ecological Hermeneutics

---

[6] Barbour informs us that "one-fifth of the world's population now accounts for 70 percent of the world's energy use, which is more than nine times as much per person as in the remaining four-fifths of the world" (*Ethics in an Age of Technology*, London 1992, 116).

[7] The final report of the WCC Assembly in Canberra (1991) recommends "*a universal declaration on human obligations towards nature*" to this UN conference and emphasizes the responsibilities of both producers and consumers of goods. Cf Michael Kinnamon (ed.), *Signs of the Spirit: Official Report Seventh Assembly*, Geneva 1991, 243 (cf. also p.69). For a helpful comment on this UN conference, see Loren Wilkinson, "Christianity and the Environment: Reflections on Rio and Au Sable", *Science and Christian Belief* 5 (1993), 139–145.

human beings is really wrong, because such an action will be absorbed in the ecosystem towards a new temporary balance. Many other species have polluted their habitat as well and could leave it or otherwise die. In which of these cases is integrity and stability preserved? Therefore, the criterion does not discriminate between right and wrong and, consequently, we cannot claim that a physiocentric outlook is sufficient for an Ecological Hermeneutic. Although this is the case, this approach, with its concern for the status of life and ecosystems, is also important in two trends in theology: in the ethics of the "reverence for life" and in eco-feminism, while both interpret nature and female as victim of the male or human exploitation.

The idea that the *"reverence for life"* is significant for Christian ethics because of a certain kind of unity of life forms, is defended with the argument that all life forms are created by God and, therefore, being *his* creatures, they need to be respected. Albert Schweitzer is well-known as the theological thinker who developed the concept of "reverence for life" as basic for ethics. He blamed the western cultural tradition for its interests in more sophisticated and academic problems rather than in elemental questions such as those regarding life in all its magnificent forms. The philosophical tradition of the Cartesian ego that gives priority to "I think and therefore I am" is too biased by abstract reflection and neglects the richness and abundance of all life forms. The Cartesian device needs replacing by another self referring description "I am life which wills to live, in the midst of life which wills to live." Therefore, we need to develop a life-affirming ethic that is concerned with our relationship to the world of life forms. This relationship is understood by Schweitzer as *spiritual*, that is, "understanding self-devotion to the world to be self-devotion of human life to every form of living being with which it can come into relation" (Schweitzer 1967:212). Schweitzer's description of the context of human life as linked up with a web of life forms makes it a good example of a physiocentric or rather biocentric perspective.

The devotion to every life form expresses itself in an ethic that shows the same reverence to all forms of a will-to-live as it does to our own life. This is the basic principle for all moral life and a biocentric version of the golden rule: *Good* is to maintain and further life whereas *bad* is to destroy life or to obstruct it. This principle is universally applicable to all life forms, human and non-human, including plant life. That means that life as such is worthy of reverence without exception. In consequence, the moral agent is responsible to all that lives, and will, for example, neither tear a leaf from a tree nor pluck a flower nor crush an insect without necessity. These examples show that this moral prescription is absolute in such a way that we are guilty most of the time because it is impossible to avoid the injury of other life forms in our daily life. Schweitzer's philosophy starts from the immediate consciousness that the individual life form is involved in a web of life, and through life united to the Source of life. Which means that all life forms have value being given by God, that is, life is sacred. This religious dimension illustrates that, in Schweitzer's view of life, it is impossible to avoid wrongdoing because to live means to destroy other forms of life and such actions are wrong, although unavoidable. Therefore, having good conscience is impossible (Schweitzer 1967:209). This philosophical viewpoint understands the human life form as a continuous tragedy, that is, human beings cannot alter their destiny of being destroyers of life, whether they want to or not. This inbuilt destination looks like a secularized form of the doctrine of original sin and is morally ineffective because an inbuilt destination is not open to a decision. And morality without the possibility of decisions is a contradiction in terms.

Such a biocentric point of view itself is also open to serious critique for not using its terms in a clear way. In the description of the human moral consciousness that "I am life which wills to live, in the midst of life which wills to live", Schweitzer seems to suggest that the human will-to-live is equivalent to the will-to-live in non-human life forms. There might be an instinct or an impulse to survive in plants and simple organisms that could be called "a will-to-live". However, such an impulse differs completely from the will-to-live of human beings. We have to acknowledge that the human life form does have traits which we can consider as forms of an animal instinct to survive, for example in a situation of serious threat. But apart from that, human beings can also act intentionally which means that they can freely decide *how* to live. Which means a kind of lifestyle that can even contradict their animal instinct. For example, people can act in a generous and unselfishness way. Such an option is not open to plants and many animals. Therefore, "the will-to-live" is an ambiguous term. That is also the case with the term "life". All organisms share these typical characteristics that we dub the name "life", but that does not mean that they participate in an abstract idea of life that exists independent of the various life forms and could be called "life-in-itself".

Besides the equivocal use of the terms, there is a biological problem for an ethic of reverence for life. The different plant and animal species vary in their way of living whereby some species are predatory, or parasitic, or herbivorous, or competitive with other species for the same resource, or co-operative with other species, etc. This means that the interactions which occur between members of different species are not always beneficial, but sometimes create negative effects too. Plants are eaten by herbivorous animals, which in turn serve as food for carnivorous ones, which in turn are attacked by parasites or bacteria. In the complexity of these interactions between species in a biotic community, it is difficult to apply the principle of reverence for life in a straightforward way. How can we determine which of the species or their individual members should be protected against their "natural enemies"? Some bacteria cause diseases in plants, animals, or other bacteria, which diseases are sometimes lethal for the hosts. From an intra-species perspective, the principle of reverence has to respect that bacteria reproduce, and by doing so they sometimes cause diseases. From an inter-species perspective, the same principle cannot cope with the problem of how to justify the host's production of antibodies or the use of medicine as defence against those foreign substances, as bacteria are.

SECTION B
HERMENEUTICS

We can conclude that Schweitzer's biocentric perspective is not applicable to our natural environment and cannot make sense for an ecological ethic because of its semantic weakness and its factual inadequacies. However, it reminds us that we as human beings are part of an enormous web of life forms that fulfils the vital role of a biotic community.

Ecofeminism is a branch of feminism that combines attention to women studies with concern for environmental issues. It rejects the distinction of anthropocentrism versus biocentrism or physiocentrism as lacking subtlety. It defends instead that all forms of oppression like sexism or racism or environmental abuse arise from a common root, that is, a hierarchical structure of domination. This cosmological hierarchy places females and other species beneath men and provides the model for a "logic of domination" that is shared by all forms of social oppression. Therefore, one cannot get rid of one system of oppression without stopping the others.[8] The recognition of this hierarchy provides the distinction of androcentrism versus biocentrism. Ecofeminism is very diverse and varies from forms of animism ("white magic") to reinterpretations of Christian Theology.[9] Remaining within the Christian tradition, the Irish theologian Anne Primavesi proposes that theology has to deconstruct the language of the Scriptures by recognizing the sexist and otherwise oppressive speech in order to replace it by feminist vocabulary. This can be done by replacing the traditional notion of hierarchical transcendence which regarded Jesus "as the normative divine male" by an egalitarian conception that "all beings live in a relationship with God". God's love is not exclusively for human beings, but is concerned about all creatures in the same way (Primavesi 1991:152ff.). She proposes that we should use the term "resouling" of nature to dub this relationship of all creatures to God. In spite of that, she challenges the *absolute* goodness of God, because otherwise the source of sin is either Eve or nature. Therefore, God is the source of both good and evil. However, her argument implies a kind of ontological dualism of good and evil that denies the goodness of God's creation.

Rosemary Ruether confirms this fundamental dualism with her defence of a duality of the feminine and the masculine in the divine. She criticizes the goddess myth of a palaeolithic period of peaceful matriarchy, but also rejects the traditional Christian concepts of God's kingship and life-after-death. To overcome the competitive character of the modern culture, she introduces the notion of the covenant as basic for a new ecological way of thinking: being conscious of "the living interdependency of all things". She uses the process concept of divine creativity in order to understand this covenantal notion as so fundamental that the

---

[8] See Rosemary Radford-Ruether, *Sexism and God-talk: Toward a Feminist Theology*, Boston 1983, 73; Karen J. Warren, 'Feminism and Ecology: Making Connections', *Environmental Ethichs* 9 (1987), 3–20; Susan Power Bratton, 'Ecofeminism and the Problem of Divine Immanence/Transcendence in Christian Environmental Ethichs', *Science and Christian Belief* 6 (1994), 21–40.

[9] Some goddess-ecofeminists reject the Christian tradition and replace it by a spiritualist form of the Gaia hypothesis; e.g. Starhawk.

individual gives its "small self back to the Great Self" (Ruether 1992: 200ff., 242ff., 251ff.). By so doing, Ruether replaces a teleological temporal eschatological perspective by a universal periodical return into the Divine; this looks like creation as a form of divine emanation. This is a one-sided way of understanding Christian Scripture and its reception, and abandons both the Divine transcendence and the personhood of the individual human being in favour of a universal consciousness of a cosmic ecological monism which bears some similarities to a pantheistic mysticism.

26.5 THE THEOCENTRIC READING: THE SERVANT MODEL

A theocentric perspective starts with the claim that "the earth is the Lord's and everything in it". It relativizes anthropocentric and biocentric perspectives by referring to God the Creator as the real owner of the creation (Clark 1993:140–144, 160ff.).[10] The created world is given to all the creatures that make up the biosphere. This outlook considers all creatures as beings under God and, therefore, it denies the absoluteness of the two other perspectives by claiming that these are too one-sided and restricted. The anthropocentric perspective neglects a fundamental aspect of human responsibility for the rest of creation: humanity received it from God. A theocentric viewpoint excludes a final human autonomy by relating it to the ultimate Divine authority and sovereignty. Whereas it stresses the duality of Creator-creature as basic, it understands the relationship of Creator and creature in terms of both transcendence and immanence. This means that God does not coincide with (the process of) the created world and, simultaneously, that his agency also occurs in that world. This insight denies the possibility of overcoming the conceptual dichotomy of divine transcendence and immanence by the use of the distinction of spirit and body. For example, it denies Sallie McFague's proposal that we talk about the world as God's body, empowered by the Divine spirit. Her way of speaking stresses the organic interrelatedness of the human and non-human creatures. However, by so doing, it also subverts the notion of human responsibility, because human beings as parts of the Divine body cannot have freedom of action. It is difficult to see how this metaphor can avoid pantheistic language because McFague seems to deify nature (McFague 1993).[11] By underscoring the Divine transcendence and immanence, the theocentric outlook rejects the pantheistic tendencies of a biocentric or physiocentric approach as well.

The theocentric perspective combines elements of the two other perspectives and tries to avoid their disadvantages. Thus, from the anthro-

---

10 Clark uses the term "sacramental theism" for his outlook, which means that we could recognize an eternal "beauty" and "justice" incarnated in the world we live in.
11 This is an exciting book which challenges various classical doctrinal issues with new interpretations, but at the end of the day it looks like a christianized version of the biocentric outlook.

SECTION B
HERMENEUTICS

pocentric viewpoint, it adopts the notion of the human agent as a responsible being and, therefore, with the most special place in all creation, because the human being is the only creature that can act deliberately and intentionally. On the other hand, the human being is not the whole of creation, but a part of the larger system of creation. A biocentric viewpoint will describe such a system as the total interdependence of all life forms.

Whereas in an anthropocentric perspective the human being is ranked between God and the rest of creation, humanity, in a theocentric perspective, is ranked at the same level as the other creatures. This does not deny the uniqueness of the human species, but underscores both its relativity and its special role for all creation. The biocentric approach may underline the human relativity, but the theocentric approach accentuates the contribution of humanity to the well-being of creation as a whole. The human skill and technology are meant to strengthen the quality and welfare of creation. Concepts like "stewardship" or "trustee" might suggest that the rest of creation is there for human agents to deal with as they like. Therefore, from the Christian viewpoint, our role as agent could be better described as that of a *servant*, refraining from using our power over creation merely for our own good, but using it to enhance creation's well-being. Human beings are God's servants in order to bring release for all creation. The Spirit of God works through them to the benefit of other creatures. For this role the standard example is Jesus Christ as the Good Shepherd. The image of a shepherd (John 10:1–21) reminds us that just like a shepherd, servants may abandon (a part of) their longings and needs in order that the rest of creation could be saved from serious decay. This means that human creatures are responsible for the way the power they were given is used for the sake of all creation, whereas they themselves are part of the larger ecosystem.

The role of the servant, however, can also be understood in another way: human creatures are called to give expression to the blessing of the Creator on behalf of the whole of creation. Being language users, they can express the gratitude of other creatures because of their existence. Above all, they can pray and intercede for all living creatures, being their representative before God. This way of considering the special position of human creatures also implies that they should serve the interest and value of other species as being their own. This means that the moral community of the human species is not restricted to its own members, but includes other creatures as well. Therefore, technological developments which contribute to the social welfare of people are to be tested to see whether they fit into the development of the ecosystem. This is important, since technological developments are subject to decisions of agents, whereas ecological developments are subject to non-intentional biological factors. Which means that both processes are not *a priori* parallel and, thus, we might expect the ecological evolution to run more slowly than the technological revolution. So, when human beings have to serve the interests of the moral community as their own, it will be relevant for them to pay special attention to the interrelationship of these two processes.¹²

Jürgen Moltmann argues for this double function of the human agent. He claims that we can develop an anthropology from two perspectives. On the one hand, the human being is *imago mundi*, that is, a microcosm which represents the macrocosm before God. A human being is, in this sense, a "priestly creation" that "lives, speaks and acts" on behalf "of all other creatures". This *imago mundi* character implies that the creation stories of the Bible are interpreted as accounts of the status of the human being as "one creature among others". This hermeneutical perspective underscores Genesis 2:7 that "the LORD God formed Adam from the dust of the earth" and acknowledges that humanity remains bound up with the earth. On the other hand, the human being is *imago Dei*, that is, God's representative in the community of creation on earth. Human beings reflect the glory of God before the rest of creation. Moltmann interprets this image of God aspect as a commission to contribute to the history of the completion of the creation in the feast of an eschatological sabbath. Human beings are simultaneously both *imago mundi* and *imago Dei*, which means that they are part of an ecosystem without being merged into it (Moltmann 1985:186–190; 215–243).¹³

This double aspect of anthropology underlines the point that "creation exists *for* God" (Linzey 1994:24ff.). This means that we cannot claim that plants and animals are simply instrumental to human needs. Although humanity is viewed as representative of the rest of creation, we cannot conclude that therefore humanity is the sole aim of creation. Richard Griffiths, for example, argues that "the value that God places on *all* nature is a biblical principle which means that the Christian does not have to draw the line anywhere in valuing the world" (1982:6ff.). His argument is that the differentiated creation has intrinsic value to God. This is expressed by the creation story that tells us that He made the animals *before* humanity and was the first one to enjoy them as He pronounced them good, before and apart from the creation of humanity. That is to say, the non-human creatures are made by God and for God. Griffiths' idea of the God-given worth of the rest of creation apart from the human creatures helps us to see humanity in its proper context: that

---

12 In this regard, I would like to note that the moral community is larger than the community of possible moral agents and includes all entities whose well-being is of mutual interest. This means that, in this description, the moral community includes the ecosystem which the community of agents belongs to. This ecosystem and its parts, however, can encompass, but are not all, moral agents. The moral agents belong to a social system as a family, tribe, nation, or a religious community etc., and within such systems alone the development of morality is possible. Therefore we have to distinguish between a social system and an ecosystem. A member of a social system always belongs to an ecosystem, but not the other way round, whereas the moral community includes both social systems and an ecosystem and its members.

13 The late Ecumenical Patriarch, Dimitrios, defended an analogous view in his *Orthodoxy and the Ecological Crisis* (1990), but he understands the role of the human agent in a sacramental way as "the priest at the Eucharist" offering "the fullness of creation and receiving it back as the blessing ... to share with others" (7ff.). Cf, for similar ideas, Metropolitan John D. Zizioulas, "Preserving God's Creation." In Elizabeth Breuilly and Martin Palmer (eds.), *Christianity and Ecology*, London 1992, 47–63.

is, as *imago mundi*. The ultimate value of *flora and fauna* is not related to the judgement of human beings, but to God's, because creation is intended by God in order to work in it his purposes (cf. Ps 19). Being the Creator God who is worthy of worship, He cannot be indifferent to his own creation. A creator who is indifferent to his creation, is not worthy of worship. Just because He is *God the Creator*, He intends this creation and, therefore, it is good (by definition). Analogously, we can understand that the mythological Leviathan is referred to as "Thy plaything that Thou hast made" (Ps 104:26). The same Psalm reports that the various parts of creation are so arranged that they as a whole work together to accomplish the divine purposes and express God's faithfulness. In a wonderful poem, God's supremacy and immanent agency are illustrated by reference to all the creatures in heaven and on earth, whereas the human being is given a small place amongst the other creatures (vs 23). This makes it clear that such a theocentric hermeneutical perspective can relativize anthropocentric prejudices. If the differentiated creation has intrinsic value to God, it is impossible for human beings to be indifferent to the rest of creation.

The theocentric outlook as a hermeneutical tool is to be preferred to the anthropocentric and the physiocentric alternatives. On the one hand, it recognizes the special status of humanity by emphasizing its responsibility, but it rejects the anthropocentric notion of humanity as the final end of creation as if human beings were God's favourites. On the other hand, a theocentric perspective makes it possible to consider the non-human creatures as beings with intrinsic value to God, which is not instrumental to the existence of human beings. It makes sense of the interrelatedness between the human existence and the rest of nature without denying the special function or role of human beings. The double role of representative of both God and all creation underlines the two aspects of human life: spiritual and biological. The theocentric perspective helps human beings, aware of their fundamental double-sidedness, to recognize the limits of the ecosystem.

READING LIST

Attfield, R. 1983. *The Ethics of Environmental Concern*. Oxford: Blackwell.
Clark, Stephen R.L. 1993. *How to think about the Earth: Philosophical and theological models for ecology*. New York: Montray.
Griffiths, R. 1982. *The Human Use of Animals*. Brancote: Grove Books.
Gutiérrez, G. 1988rev. *A Theology of Liberation*. London: SCM.
Linzey, A. 1994. *Animal Theology*. London: SCM.
Leopold, A. 1949. *A Sand County Almanac*. New York.
Moltmann, J. 1985. *God in Creation: An Ecological Doctrine of Creation*. London: SCM.
McFague, S. 1993. *The Body of God: An Ecological Theology*.Minneapolis: Fortress.
Primavesi, A. 1991. *From Apocalypse to Genesis*. Kent: Burns and Oates.
Ruether, R.R. 1992. *Gaia and God, An Ecofeminist Theology of Earth Healing*. San Francisco: Harpers.
Schweitzer, A. 1967. *Civilization and Ethics*. London: E.T.
Von Weiszäcker, C.F. 1986. "A Council for Peace: A Sermon on Good Friday." *The Ecumenical Review* 38

Postmodern Hermeneutics

Marius D. Herholdt

27.1 BACKGROUND

Hermeneutics, traditionally known as the art or science of understanding, has received much prominence since the eminent theologian Friedrich Schleiermacher (1768–1834) presented lectures on the subject to his students. The word hermeneutics derives from the Greek noun *hermeneuein*, which is synonymous with the Latin verb for interpreting, namely *interpretare*. As a science, hermeneutics is the theory behind interpretation, especially in relation to literature. Theological Hermeneutics, which concerns us here, relates to the interpretation of the Bible.

Wilhelm Dilthey (1833–1911) followed in the footsteps of Shleiermacher, but focused on literature and brought the deeper sense of understanding to light. The distinction was made that we *explain* nature, but we *understand* the life of the soul. With this, hermeneutics was opened to epistemology, the theory of knowledge. This brings me to the subject/object division that is a helpful scheme to briefly trace the development of hermeneutics to the present time. Differences in epistemological trends are the results of different ways of relating the knowing subject (truth?) with the knowable object (reality).

Dilthey himself was more of an empiricist, which explained his quest for objectivity. This is popularly known as the copy theory because truth is taken to be a copy of reality. The greater the correspondence, the more true the statement about reality. He considered historical objectivations as "givens" that could be understood with the help of hermeneutical techniques.

SECTION B
HERMENEUTICS

The subject/object epistemological distinction was given a definite direction by Karl Barth's *Römerbrief* (1919) which exploded into the theological world. The gist of this book was the fresh proclamation of Paul's thought in the language of the day based on the supposition that the wisdom of Paul's time is also the wisdom of today. This is seeing a parallel between Paul's questions and answers and those of any other period in history in terms of the eternal Spirit of God that gives continuity between yesterday and today.

Since Barth, the subject may no longer reflect in an interrogatory way on the text as object, but in a reversed sense, the object puts the subject in question. This means that the object demands that the right questions be asked because the object is the ultimate. This contribution of Barth is summed up by James Robinson (1964:23) as "the view of the relation of subject to object basic to the historical method, to the effect that the subjective element is to be eliminated so as to attain the highest possible objectivity," has been relativized by the basic recognition of the hermeneutical relevance of the subject. This means that in the role of the subject as a heuristic medium of understanding, the text is taken into consideration by the subject.

The clear shift that this represents can only be appreciated when, with the help of Heidegger (a German philosopher 1889–1976), we are reminded that the Cartesian[1] principle of sufficient cause[2] implies that everything must give account of itself. Therefore, every object must give account to the investigative subject. In a theological sense, this was unacceptable to Barth who did not see God as an object that is accountable to the subject. In Barth's stance, he differed harshly from Adolf von Harnack who saw theology as a science by which intellectual mastery over the object can be achieved.

Martin Heidegger also had a concern for understanding that superseded hermeneutics. This means that prior to interpretation there is already a quest for meaning that is bound to language. This is because the human being is a linguistic creature. It is very difficult to understand Heidegger, but it boils down to this: in his hermeneutical perspective, he does not think that it is the author of a text that speaks, but language itself speaks in that it expresses something (being) that shows itself, that shines forth in the text. Existence objectifies itself in the language and therefore the language need not be objectified. This connection between language and being is expressed in Diogenes Allen (1985:274) when he points out that Heidegger succeeded in opening hermeneutics to transcendent dimensions:

> His analysis of human existence or *Dasein*[3] can be viewed as part of his attack on the split between subject and object. His analysis is an attempt to present the world given *with Dasein*, prior to the split into subject and object, and prior to conceptualization.

---

1 Formulated in the Cartesian (referring to the philosopher René Descartes) period.
2 Nothing is without a cause.
3 The German word Heidegger uses for human existence, for the fact that a person exists.

This means that a human being, on the deepest level, experiences reality as existence. In the ensuing process of interpretation, the focus is not on understanding, but rather on language (Robinson 1964:44). At this level, subject and object are not distinguished because the subject matter addresses itself to human thought to which the human being answers. This is a response to being.

An important contribution to the fact that hermeneutics concerns all human enquiry was made by Hans Georg Gadamer (b.1900), once a student of Heidegger. Gadamer calls this the universality of the hermeneutical problem.[4] According to Gadamer, the natural sciences are not based on exact observational data, for these facts answer to some questions based on presuppositions. The questions that determine answers are then hermeneutical questions. This brings Gadamer to the conclusion that understanding is bound to language. Therefore, "for Gadamer himself, the boundless intersubjectivity that characterizes all human language and communication constitutes the 'universal aspect of hermeneutics' (Thiselton 1992:323).

The question was whether textual meaning is only intertextually derived, or whether intersubjectivity, like social conditioning aspects, is also interacting in the process of understanding. For instance, to Ludwig Wittgenstein (1889–1951) and Habermas, language is essentially social.

Another important development en route to postmodernism was the switch from a hermeneutical paradigm of understanding to the literary paradigm of reading. This turn towards literary theory, Thiselton (1992: 471) points out, is one of the most significant developments for biblical hermeneutics. This is a convergence of the text and the reader where the ideal is not to discover the eternal truth implicit in the text. The reader is thus seen as actively and participatively constructing the meaning of the text from the perspective of the social context of readers. Meaning ought to be qualified here as not one particular meaning, but rather a variety of meanings as the text discloses itself and transforms the audience.

This movement coincides with the renewed interest in literary theory that stresses reader involvement, interaction and response. This is sometimes referred to as narratology, which means that the text is read as a narrative that involves the reader through identification with characters of the narrative. Closely linked with this, is Ricoeur's use of metaphor that involves the creative imagination of the reader constantly making new connections and discovering new possibilities of human action.

Another important aspect of literary theory is the aspect of semiotics,[5] in which codes become important. Semiotics is a study of the function, meaning and structure of signs. With this, the context of the reader is largely extended to that of the whole world that may be used as semiotic apparatus. Roland Barthes and Jacques Derrida developed from semiotics a hermeneutics of deconstruction.

---

4 This was the title of an essay written in 1966.
5 For example Ferdinand de Saussure.

SECTION B
HERMENEUTICS

Deconstruction is regarded as the strongest philosophical context of Postmodern Hermeneutics. Deconstruction differs from structuralism in the sense that it does not view the text as an independent unit that influences the subject, but views both the subject and text as part of an intertextual world. Intertextuality is a network that constitutes a new "text" with a transformed meaning.

Thiselton (1992:117) explains that the deconstructionism of Roland Barthes and Derrida holds that we know reality only in language, but it is an "unreal reality" like a game that is played, not against the background of a fixed, stable reality, but rather a field of freeplay and infinite substitutions.

This brief overview of the development of hermeneutics and the accompanying shifts discloses how immensely complex this subject is. Seeing that postmodernism involves epistemological issues that highlight the intricacies involved in the subject/object scheme, I want to devote some special attention to this.

27.2 HERMENEUTICS AND THE SUBJECT/OBJECT SCHEME

Hermeneutics, as a theoretical reflection on the processes of understanding in general, is thus very clearly influenced by the frame of reference that is used. Furthermore, hermeneutics is intrinsically linked to epistemology, or the theory of knowledge. Epistemology deals with the nature, foundations and criteria of knowledge, whereas hermeneutics deals with the way we interpret knowledge (?) in the cognitive process of understanding.

The constants at play in the total hermeneutical process are that of transcendence and immanence, subject and object. Philosophically speaking, these constants are opposite poles on the ontological (pertaining to existence) and epistemological lines. It can be graphically presented as two intersecting planes:

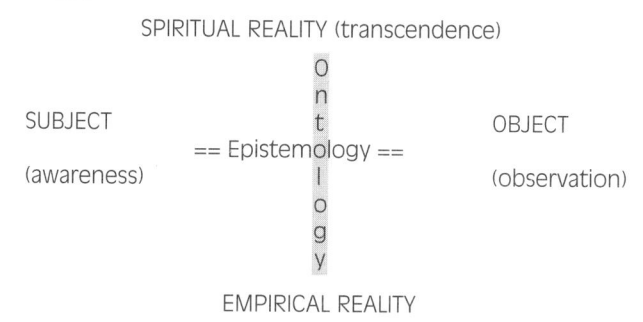

```
            SPIRITUAL REALITY (transcendence)
                       O
                       n
                       t
   SUBJECT             i                OBJECT
              == Epistemology ==
  (awareness)          l              (observation)
                       o
                       g
                       y
              EMPIRICAL REALITY
```

The diagram explains how different theologies are methodologically the result of different points of hermeneutical departure. Revelation Theology proceeds from the pole of spiritual reality in terms of God disclosing Himself "supernaturally" to humans. Contextual theologies on the other hand, depart from the empirical pole in terms of, for instance, the sociopolitical circumstances. Existential Theology places a lot of emphasis on existential awareness, whereas a theology of history will start with objective "facts". Many positions in between are of course also theoretically possible.

A critical perspective brings to light that there appears to be a constant tension between opposite poles. Revelational theologies do not seem to be sufficiently contextual due to a methodological point of departure *from above*. Here, the truth is an eternal, timeless truth, belonging to a world of truth contained in the Bible or the doctrines of the church (Herholdt 1992:7,9). Contextual theologies on the other hand, seem to lack the full dimension of spiritual awareness and moral salvation because of its departure *from below*. Here, truth is more pragmatic and less authoritative (Herholdt 1992:16). Hermeneutics is "not simply the understanding of ancient texts, it also means comprehending all manifestations of life and knowing how to relate them to the evangelical message" (Boff 1978:41).

In theologies departing from the subjective pole, religious feeling and subjective experience will be dominant. Inversely, more objective theology will place a strong emphasis on aspects like historical critical exegesis, the text itself, history, creeds and dogma.

A brief overview of hermeneutics illustrates the constant switch between the subjective and objective poles in the quest for understanding the Bible. The church father, Origen, from the Alexandrian school, proposed an allegorical explanation meant to reveal hidden truths. The school of Antioch on the other hand, preferred a more objective stance with the literal-historical approach. Spiritual understanding was relegated to second place for the sake of historical interest. Objective interpretation was continued in the Reformation and after the Enlightenment historical exegesis was brought to the point where, with the loss of canonical authority, the Bible was reduced to a document with the status of ordinary literature. Concurrent to this, Reimarus defended the thesis that Jesus merely preached a message of virtue and Ernst Troeltsch propagated the idea that God does not interfere in history. It seems then that an objective epistemology tends more towards the empirical pole due to the fact that spiritual reality is not readily objectively accessible.

The failure of historicism to construct an historical Christ lead to a more subjective approach known as "the Christ of faith", with emphasis on the more "spiritual" aspects and the message of Christ. This was especially expounded by D.F. Strauss who based his theology on the philosophy of Hegel, who stressed *Christ as idea* rather than as an historical figure. The culmination of this school of thought is probably the "implicit Christ" in the existential theology of Bultmann. According to Bultmann, the message or *kerygma* of Christ was based on the *Dass* – the fact that Jesus lived – and not on the *Was*, or historical facts of his life.

Against this background, it becomes clear how it occurred that the text was then no longer regarded as an historical document, but instead as an account of the existential relationship between God and humans in which the *Selbstverständnis* (self-understanding) of the reader comes into focus. As an existential category, this self-understanding is not a self-opinion, but at a deeper level, a way of reacting to reality. Out of this ap-

SECTION B
HERMENEUTICS

proach developed the so-called New Hermeneutic of Ernst Fuchs and Gerhard Ebeling. They believed that, contrary to literalistic repetition (objective), the text can only speak in a different situation by being said differently (Thiselton 1986:80).

The history of hermeneutical development can thus be explained as a competition between subjective and objective approaches to reality. The content of the subjective and objective varies from time to time. As pointed out above, the subjective emphasis was translated by the existential movement as the self-understanding of human beings. At later stages, like that known as deconstruction or poststructuralism, the shift is more to communicative processes with emphasis on the subjective (reader). Language as metaphor without a final meaning, the so-called open-endedness, is the content of the subjective pole within the framework of reader-response. It allows for redescription (Ricoeur) which has to do with the world that is opened in front of the text (Vorster 1985:59).

Reader-response[6] means that once the Bible was written, it is no longer the intention of the author or the reaction of the original audience that counts, but the text alone which bears the meaning. This is referred to as the "speech-event" of discourse that must be distinguished from the "language-system" which is the atemporal, non personal, non-communicative category of language (Tracy 1975:74). This concern with the "event" and "meaning" in discourse, together with the reformulation of the "dialectic of explanation and understanding",[7] is seen by Tracy (1975:75) as the two most important developments in contemporary hermeneutic theory. Simply put, this means that there is no longer a dichotomy between explanation and understanding,[8] but the two aspects belong together in interaction (dialectic). The text does not refer the reader to a meaning "behind" the text that needs to be understood (such as the original intention of the author), but rather to an explanation of the author's way of being in this world.

The objectivity of the text is therefore no longer its "historicity", but rather its "logicity". This means that the content of the objective pole shifted from the emphasis on textual production and origin (historical critical method) to textual interpretation. The text as object is the scope of **structuralism**, which endeavors to eliminate subject as well as history from the text. Instead, the emphasis is on language as a fundamental category leading to text-immanent exegesis. The objective element is therefore no longer history, but the text itself. Yet structuralism remains an objective approach. The main trend has been a shift from the author to the text as an auto-semantic unit and currently to the reader as the one who attributes meaning to the text.

Judging from these shifts, it becomes clear that a unilateral point of departure always results in a tension between the opposite poles. Invariably, one has to ponder the possibility of providing equal weight to differ-

---

6 Reader-response theoretists: Stanley Fish, David Bleich, Wayne Booth. A related movement in Reception Theory: Wolfgang Iser and Hans Jauss.
7 As it is labelled by Ricoeur.
8 As was proposed by Dilthey.

ent poles in order to ensure greater hermeneutical coherence. Postmodern Hermeneutics differs then from modernism exactly in the sense that a radically different relation between the subject/object poles is established in terms of relational truth. The degree to which this leads to greater coherence and less tension between the knowing subject and knowable object will determine the successfulness of Postmodern Hermeneutics.

Another criterium is based on the way Postmodern Hermeneutics fits in with a postmodern world-view. In other words: the question is whether Postmodern Hermeneutics can add meaningfulness to the way people today are trying to make sense of this world.

27.3 THE EMERGENCE OF A POSTMODERN WORLD-VIEW

There is a postmodern[9] world emerging. In this area of understanding, the conceptions of reason and knowledge initiated by the era of the Enlightenment (c. 1600–1780) no longer provide adequate answers. Postmodern thought raises the question whether the 20th century situation in the areas of philosophy, natural science, art, culture and society has changed so much that it deserves to be seen as a new period beyond modernity (Ford 1989:291).

In a very enlightening article on Postliberal Hermeneutics, Albert Outler (1985:284) points out that there is a growing consensus to the effect that neither neo-orthodoxy nor neo-liberalism is adequate for the oncoming age. Outler (1985:290) continues:

> In the ghostly world of artificial intelligence, new questions about human selfhood and individuation have begun to emerge. At the very least, the embargo on "God-talk" as the Encompassing Mystery, self disclosed in Scripture, has been lifted, at least by a little.

But if this is so, then the agenda for hermeneutics has been changed significantly.

But what will come in the place of neo-orthodoxy and neo liberalism? What is the content of postmodernism? Perhaps Ihab Hassan was the first to use the term *postmodernism* formally in 1971 in relation to literature (Oden 1990:71), although the process theologian John Cobb used the term *postmodern* already in a 1964 essay to refer to a certain type of Philosophical Theology (Griffin 1989:7). In the 1980s, postmodernism[10] was gradually applied to hermeneutics. Although the term has not found general acceptance, it is rapidly gaining popularity in different disciplines with a more or less fixed connotation that may be characterized as pluralist, pro-metaphor, relational, holistic, relativistic, indeterminate, evolutionary, post critical, and participatory. The implications that this has for a post critical hermeneutic will be spelled out later.

To understand this distinction, it is necessary to contrast the eras of premodernism, modernism and postmodernism briefly.

During the 11th and 12th centuries there was, mainly due to scholas-

---

9 Postmodernism is a nascent phenomenon and its ramifications are therefore not yet clear.
10 The terms postliberal or postcritical are also used.

SECTION B

HERMENEUTICS

tic theologians like Thomas Aquinas, a synthesis forged between Aristotelian (Greek) philosophy and Christian ideas. James Miller (1989:2) lists the main elements of the premodern world as a vertical metaphysical dualism, separating the heavenly from the earthly spheres; the use of organic metaphors to describe things; a reliance upon tradition as a source of knowledge; and a view of humanity being at the centre of the cosmos (geocentric world-view).

The first break with premodernism came with Galileo Galilei (1564–1642), a brilliant Italian mathematician, astronomer and physicist. His telescopic observations cast doubt on the Ptolemaic geocentric theory of the universe which was, according to Roman Catholic interpretation, confirmed by Scripture. Another aggravation to the church was his *Letter on Sunspots* which suggested that the sun decayed. It conflicted with Aristotelian cosmology which held that the celestial bodies were eternal and perfect. In 1633, he was forced to recant and was placed under house arrest. His ideas, however, prevailed.

Two influential thinkers, the French philosopher René Descartes (1596–1650) and the German philosopher Immanuel Kant (1724–1804), were especially significant in the formation of the modern world-view. Descartes, who is often hailed as the father of the modern era, founded a kind of "horizontal dualism" (Miller 1989:3) by dividing the world into the domains of matter and mind (or spirit). In this sense, he deviated from the Aristotelian idea that people are rational animals by positing an incorporeal mind housed in a mechanical body – the so-called ghost in a machine.

The critical idealism of Kant, on the other hand, opened the way for a critical rationality. Kant was mainly interested in the theory of knowledge, or epistemology as it is also called. Epistemology concerns itself with the question: How do we know what we know? Kant's critical philosophy finds its full expression in the critical epistemological attitude that empirical observation and the reason were the only sources of absolute knowledge. This laid a foundation for the enterprise of the natural sciences.

The Cartesian dualism which sustained the world as a vast machine opened the way for Newton to formulate his laws which apply for the falling apple as well as for the trajectories of the planet. According to modernism, the celestial and terrestrial worlds no longer operated differently. Universal causality, the view of action and reaction, made scientific predictions possible. Certainty of knowledge became important to the positivist. This positivistic trend also becomes evident in neo-orthodox theologies of the modern world. The revelation of God, like in the theology of Karl Barth, was looked upon to provide absolute knowledge of God and his purpose for the world. It also becomes clear that the doctrine of Predestination (Calvin) fitted nicely into the Newtonian world-view.

The most significant thing about modernism is the comprehensive dualism. The distinction that Descartes made between two substantial domains in terms of mind and matter, Kant made between the reality of the external world called *phenomena*, and the categories of the mind or product of the interaction of mind and world, called the *noumena* (thing-in-itself). Because logical positivists accepted this dualism, but then denied the reality of the non-empirical aspect, modern science became an impersonal, objective search for facts. The existential philosophers and theologians, on the other hand, neglected the objective side of the dualism. They focused on mind and personhood rather than on the natural world. Existential spirituality is thus transcendental.

Now, at the turn of the century, we encounter a radical world-wide intellectual revolution that "is perhaps as great as that which marked off the modern world from the Middle Ages" (Allen 1989:2–5). This is primarily spurned by some amazing discoveries in physics like quantum theory, chaos theory and non-reductionism. To the meaning of these I will shortly return.

Diogenes Allen thinks that the breakdown of the modern mentality is evident in at least four areas. First, whereas modernism has, in the intellectual world, seen the idea of God as superfluous, it can no longer be scientifically or philosophically maintained that we live in a self-contained world. Second, modernism has failed to provide a basis for morality and society. Third, the optimism of scientific progress to save us from vulnerability to nature and social bondage has become tarnished. In the fourth place, the assumption that scientific knowledge is inherently good and always beneficially applied has become suspect. The time is ripe to look to a new mentality popularly known as postmodernism.

27.4 THE NATURE AND RELEVANCE OF POSTMODERN HERMENEUTICS

Postmodern Theology also struggles with the subject/object dilemma, but from a different angle. Positivism, the epistemological approach of modernism with its ideal of objective knowledge, is making way for an approach with greater coherence between the objective and the subjective poles. Of course, there are different varieties of Postmodern Theology, as outlined by David Griffen (1989:3) like **Constructive** or Revisionary (David Griffen, William Beardslee, Joe Holland); **Deconstructive** or Eliminative (Jacques Derida, Jean Francois Lyotard, Richard Rorty, Mark Taylor); **Restorationist** or Conservative (William Rutler), and **Liberationist** Theology (Cornel West, Harvey Cox). Yet, those approaches which hold to both the objective and subjective poles seem to be more successful. For instance, the objective approach of deconstruction to the facts of experience proves, paradoxically, that an objective approach is not possible (Griffen 1989:4).

The postmodern trend of constructionism is the conviction that truth is neither objective nor subjective, but relational. In the words of Wentzel van Huyssteen and Ben du Toit (1982:10):

> Relational truth wants to say that truth – also that of the Bible – does not solely exists objectivistically apart from humans for humans, it is also not subjectivistically created by humans, but becomes disclosed rather within a relation of the believer's involvement on something else. (translation MDH)

SECTION B

HERMENEUTICS

The epistemological insight of relational truth, known in some circles as **critical realism**, thus conditions the hermeneutics of the exegete. Whereas modern exegesis in the vein of positivism approached the biblical texts as an object, Postmodern Hermeneutics favours reader-response hermeneutics. The locus of revelation is no longer the historical events behind the texts, but the text as language that involves the reader. Reader-response Hermeneutics is therefore a relational approach because it is both subjective and objective in the sense of what the text produces in the reader. In the words of Sandra M. Schneiders (1989:62):

> Thus, the positivistic objectification of the text which resulted inexorably in the dilemma of the subject-object paradigm of understanding by analysis has begun to give way to a hermeneutical paradigm of understanding by participative dialogue.

Participative dialogue is in line with a critical realist epistemology with its basic presupposition that truth is constructed, but that it truly refers to some objective reality. Theories in a critical realist sense are taken to be representations of the world as reality, but not as mirror images of reality.

The roles of metaphors in constructing are very serious epistemic devices. The nature of metaphors is that they refer in an ontological way to reality as an epistemic way of expressing the *unknown* by way of the *known*. A metaphor is the way in which we understand, as well as enlarge, our world and change it. It is the only way we have of dealing with the unfamiliar (McFague 1982:18).

Calling God "Father" may serve as an example. We experience the caring love of God religiously, but we need to express it more cognitively. Fatherhood is not taken here in a literal sense, for God never fathered children in the normal sense of the word. Yet, in terms of his love, care and authority, God may be called Father for it conveys in a very real sense something about the nature and actions of God. It ought, however, to be clear that we cannot take this designation in a literal or absolute sense. God is not exhausted by the term Father, nor does this mean that God cannot also be justifiably referred to as Mother. This approach suits Feminist Hermeneutics well, which is part of the postmodern trend. Its aim is to move away from sexists trends and to take seriously the fact that God is on the side of the oppressed, which includes women (Fiorenza 1986:376).

The term "Father" is, according to metaphoric theory, not a pure objective designation, because the reader already approaches the Bible with presuppositions of the concept and therefore the text forms part of a much broader frame of reference. In a sense, the Bible is then constructed by the theologian who uses the Bible in the context of a more comprehensive argument (Van Huyssteen 1987:35). This means that there is no fixed meaning in the Bible, no eternal truths that can be uncovered, because truth is historically contextual.

Against the objection that this appears to lead to relativism, critical realists will point out that, unlike instrumentalism, critical realism is not reluctant to make ontological claims. Critical realists claim that the text truly refers to some reality. The text can therefore not replace the events or person of whom it is merely a testimony. Instrumentalism on the other hand, emphasizes that theories are the product of creative imagination, with the result that the biblical text is seen as functional (and not ontological) in the sense of evoking religious experiences.

Critical realism is an effort to establish the coherence of truth, to keep the subjective and objective together as integral parts of reality. This is relational truth which is explained as follows:

> Truth is not merely something outside of humans, nor a human endeavour nor even the product of both. It does not concern truth (objectively) that needs to be appropiated (subjectively), but both in one. (*God met ons* 1980:12–13, translation MDH)

27

Postmodern Hermeneutics

The fragmentation of knowledge and the so-called certainty of objective knowledge is no longer tenable. Empirical sciences can no longer claim to enjoy better academic status, for in postmodern terms, natural science is not solely objective, for "hermeneutic considerations apply in the natural sciences, particularly in connection with the theoretical interpretation and 'world models' (Arbib & Hesse 1986:171). This means that scientists approach experiments with preconceived notions which determine the experimental approach and therefore also the results. In the words of Fritjof Capra (1992:123), this is referred to as new paradigm thinking:

> In the old paradigm scientific descriptions were believed to be objective, that is, independent of the human observer and the process of knowledge. In the new paradigm it is believed that epistemology, the understanding of the process of knowledge, has to be included explicitly in the description of natural phenomena.

Whereas hermeneutics originated in the work of biblical scholars explicating the meaning of the canonical text, it can be said that in the postmodern era, science has become more aware of human input in its methodology because the experience of nature and culture cannot be disjoined (Rolston 1987:219). In this sense, Postmodern Hermeneutics has gained a much broader definition than being merely a science that concerns the understanding of texts. It cannot be divorced from epistemological issues that undergird our understanding in terms of the poles of subjectivity and objectivity. Nor can interpretive symbol systems be ignored that are cultural, historical and religious at their cores (Rolston 1989:219). This is why a postmodernism approach that is more integrated in its approach will give birth to Postmodern Hermeneutics that will opt for greater coherence.

Since Thomas Kuhn's famous book, *The structure of scientific revolutions* (Chicago: University of Chicago Press, 1970), it has become fashionable to talk about paradigm shifts. Technically, a paradigm is defined as a disciplinary matrix "... disciplinary because it refers to the common possession of the practitioners of a particular discipline; matrix because it is composed of ordered elements of various sorts" (Kuhn 1970:182). Simply put, a paradigm refers then to a framework of understanding, formed by a matrix, in which problem solving takes place. When anomalies increase, they can only be solved by switching to a new paradigm, a revolution in that particular science, that is accompanied by a change in

SECTION B
HERMENEUTICS

world-view. Old problems are then seen in a new perspective because the epistemic contours have changed.

As has been shown already, historical criticism as an objective study of the biblical text dominated the hermeneutical scene for a long time. In terms of Kuhnian theory, we can now refer to historical criticism as a dominant paradigm and identify its domain assumptions and basic presuppositions. These refer to the reality and subject matter which is studied. How did scholars perceive the text? Probably as something that could be analyzed, because knowledge of the canon was obtained by taking the Bible apart and studying each part as if it were an entity on its own. This is technically known as the method of reduction. Vorster (1988:34) observed that three criteria apply to this method:

> This approach is critical in as far as arguments are given for conclusions that are reached. It is objective in as much as the scientific community accepts the methods and results intersubjectively. It is mechanistic in as far as the parts dominate the whole while the parts fit together like a machine.

This means that the historical-critical approach regards the texts as fragments that are pieced together. In such an approach, the continuity between texts, and consequently the coherence of meaning, is diminished. With the epistemological changes from objective knowledge (the emphasis on the author or text) to a more subjective approach (the focus on the reader, not to discover meaning, but to attribute meaning), the need for a more integrated whole is experienced. Postmodern Hermeneutics is thus a paradigm shift in this sense.

Elizabeth Schüssler Fiorenza (1986:366) sees the paradigm of historical-critical hermeneutics as an effort to see exegesis and history as objective, value-free, rationalist and scientific. In post-critical hermeneutics, the notion of holism or a systems view, the insight that a Bible narrative is the remaking of reality (creating a narrative world) (Vorster 1985:60) and that value free knowledge is not possible, are important factors constituting the postmodern paradigm.

It is realized that a system cannot simply be explained as the sum total of its parts because parts interact by way of information. For instance, none of the parts of an airplane can fly. This is to say that the system has properties that only relate to the system as an integrated whole.

If we apply this to the text, it means that the Bible should be seen as a network of intertextuality. Each part is an expression of the whole and cannot be isolated from the rest without reducing its meaning. The mechanistic way of piecing texts together is now exchanged for a more organic understanding of how the parts interrelate. The texts can therefore no longer be regarded as objects, but are transformed into elements of communication. Within this communication, the interpreter can now attribute meaning by referring to the text.

The role of metaphors is once again important here. Where the Bible is regarded in a objective way, it corresponds with the notion of timeless absolute truth to be discovered hidden in the text. In such a sense, the Bible is an archetype with an ideal form that serves as a fixed blueprint for religiosity. In a communication paradigm where there is no fixed meaning or margin between texts, the Bible is more of a prototype that is always open to transformation.

The idea of metaphoric understanding fits this notion of the Bible as prototype well because in a metaphor there is always openness toward new clarity, it lends itself to flexibility and new insights (Syverson 1978: 28,32). A metaphor describes a more unfamiliar object or action in a non-literal way by comparing it with something that is explicitly clear, for instance: *he is as strong as a lion*. The metaphor supposes a correspondence between the two things that are compared, but also a difference which does not make them equal. This means that the metaphor itself may not be taken for reality, although the metaphoric reference constitutes a reality which could not, at least initially, be known in the same way.

Metaphors are thus a way to access the unknown by way of the known. This insight fits religious language well because believers have no meta-language with which to describe God. The Bible never portrays God as a being that can be empirically known by human beings (Exod 33:20; John 1:18; 1 John 4:12). Religion claims an experiential knowledge of God, whether it be mediated by faith or intuition. Yet humans do not posess a meta-language by which to express this knowledge. Critical realism, for instance, claims that on an epistemic level, God can only be known by way of metaphoric reference. This means that the experiential knowledge of God is made cognitively known by way of indirect reference.

This can be explained with reference to the way Christians address God. Except for the name *Yahweh*, which has no earthly equivalent, there are no novel references employed for God. The common word "God" (Hebrew: *El*) used for God in the Bible, has cognate forms in other Semitic languages which mean "god" or "divine being" in the wider sense of the word. Furthermore, God is known in terms of earthly categories like a rock, a father, a creator, a shepherd. All these metaphors presuppose a kind of similarity between God and the concept used. Adjectives befitting these concepts immediately come to mind. A rock speaks of permanence, is unmovable and strong; fatherhood of care and authority; creator of competence, innovation, creativity; and shepherding of provision, guidance, nursing, care and collectiveness. In terms of critical realism, the metaphors then truly refer to God in the sense that He is also experienced as caring, loving, strong, authoritative. Yet God is not reduced to or limited by metaphors, because they is not literally meant. He remains much more than the metaphor can express.

If one accepts metaphorical understanding as a viable hermeneutical option, certain theological implications come with the package. In the first instance, it emphasizes the human role in comprehending the revelation of God. Certain judgements are called for in terms of relating the way God is experienced to something known, like for instance shepherding. In other words, God does not tell us that He is a shepherd. He rather nurses us, cares for us and guides us to the extent that we come to think of Him as a shepherd. Here again we have the subjective (referring to Him a Shepherd) in the "objective" (experiencing Him as caring and loving).

Postmodern Hermeneutics

SECTION B
HERMENEUTICS

Second, reality is no longer equated with the truth parallel to the relation between an object and its mirror image. In this case, God as Ultimate Truth is only approximately known so that, in a sense God, remains a mystery. God is both like and unlike our metaphors of Him. No metaphor can exhaust Him. Yet, this is not negative religion[11] because God is not totally different and mysterious. Some things can be said about God, albeit tentatively.

Against this background, it also becomes possible to ask about the relevance of certain metaphors in the day and age that we are living in. If, for instance, God told us that He is a Father, then it might not be permissible to change it, but if we have called Him Father because of what we have experienced Him to be, then we would be wrong to take it as an absolute term.[12] For instance, Sallie McFague (1982:164ff.) challenges the relevance of the metaphor "Father" in the light of a feminist approach and the fact that we no longer live in a patriarchal society. She then proposes the use of "Friend" as a model that has a lot to offer.

In the fourth instance, this is more of a functional approach than an ontological[13] approach. It is functional because we understand God not in Himself (ontologically), but in his relationships, the way He acts and deals with human beings and his creation. Such a trend clearly favors religious experience above speculation. Yet postmodern hermeneutics is an intellectual enterprise without ruling out the validity of faith. The acknowledgment that presuppositions play an important role in our theories opens up the possibility that beliefs, whether religious or not, may play a major role in the construction of models.

From these theological implications it becomes clear that postmodern hermeneutics has a profound influence on theology as a whole. Whether postmodernism constitutes progress can only become clear when we contrast Postmodern Hermeneutics with that of Premodern and Modern Hermeneutics.

How well does Postmodern Hermeneutics serve us? Does the tentativeness of models enhance our understanding in a postmodern era or threaten our security? How well does it fit in with concepts that are part and parcel of postmodernism, like holism, feminism, the underachievement of theories, models in science, theory-ladenness, intelligibility and coherence, contextuality and praxis, and plurality?

Anthony Thiselton (1992:143ff.) finds that premodernism has much in common with postmodernism, in contrast to modernism. He cites three examples: Modernism is more profoundly individualistic than pre- and postmodernism; pre- and postmodernism both allow more room for the notion of the texts as processes and variables (see further on); and modernism is more critical than pre- and postmodernism.

It is necessary to expound Thiselton's distinctions further in order to

---

11 A technical term used to describe religions where God is so totally different and mysterious that nothing can be said about Him.
12 Texts in which God calls Himself Father can not be used as a proof of the fact that He reveals Himself that way. It could simply be that God acknowledges the use of our metaphors.
13 Ontological, pertaining to existence.

understand them better. The French philosopher, Descartes, plays a major role in the transition from premodernism to modernism. His rationalism subjects all else to methodological doubt, while the individual becomes the epistemological point of departure as the only thing that is not doubted.[14] Inversely, the postmodern individual is part of a larger whole, a network of beliefs, traditions and customs that influence and form the individual's understanding.

The awareness of a social dimension of science forces one to take the social context into consideration and to realize that science is always a time-conditioned product of the social context. Hans-Georg Gadamer strongly advances this. Although Gadamer is strongly influenced by Heidegger, he does not start with the self or *Dasein* like Heidegger. Gadamer sees the self as part of a community and tradition. We not only grasp the truth, but are also grasped by the truth. In Gadamer's major work, *Truth and Method* (1960), he advances the idea that we are always changed by that in which we participate and which we experience. The true essence of a work of art is that it changes the person who experiences it and therefore it cannot be reduced to an aesthetic experience: "This alienation into aesthetic judgement always takes place when we have withdrawn ourselves and are no longer open to the immediate claim of that which grasps us" (Gadamer 1980:128).

Whereas premodernism reveres the corporately shared beliefs, Postmodern Hermeneutics is radically suspicious and does not hesitate to "deconstruct" it. Another element enters the social context here, namely that of transformation and action. Whereas the aim of Gadamer's philosophical hermeneutics was that of understanding, the social hermeneutic of Jürgen Habermas was more praxis orientated. Action is required and not just understanding.

In postmodernism, there is a sense of pluralism which means that a text does not have only one fixed meaning. Already in premodernism, allegorical ("spiritual") interpretation allowed for different levels of meaning. Premodernists distinguished between the historical, moral and allegorical levels of the text. The postmodern acceptance of the fact that theologians work with tentative models also leads to a positive outlook on pluralism. Pluralism allows different theologians to learn "incomparably more about reality by disclosing really different ways of viewing both our common humanity and Christianity" (Tracy 1975:3).

Premodern theories of interpretation are classified by Anthony Thiselton (1992:145) as representing a hermeneutic of innocence. This means that the testimony of the church to the apostolic faith, as revealed in Christ, is never questioned. In modernism, critical thinking is more rampant. It started from Descartes as a methodological doubting of tradition, runs through Kant's critique of reason and Wittgenstein's critique of language. Postmodern Hermeneutics is a postcritical hermeneutic, for although it is suspicious of recurring patterns of tradition, it accepts that

---

14 *Cogito, ergo Sum* meaning: 'I reason, therefore I am', expressed the conviction that the thinking person cannot doubt his/her own existence.

SECTION B
HERMENEUTICS

aspects like tradition and culture constitute an important conditioning of the process of understanding. An important part of the extra-individual influence on interpretation is the postmodern world-view that is strongly informed by the new science and its philosophical ramifications. The new science came about during the 1980s where strange new concepts like systems thinking, chaos theory, evolution, non-determinism, quantum mechanics, the uncertainty principle, relativity theory, self-organization, complexity and synergetics, play a major role.

These concepts present a radical breakthrough to a new way of thinking. The magnitude of this revolution only becomes clear when one is able to see it against the rudiments of the modern world-view. The modern world-view can be traced back to Isaac Newton (1642–1727), who developed a comprehensive system of mechanics in his *Philosphiae naturalis principia mathematica* (1687) with reference to the solar system. It had wide philosophical repercussions, as is illustrated by the work of the French philosopher and mathematician, Pierre Simon La Place (1749–1827), who developed Newtonian science into a system of mechanical determinism. The ensuing theological implication is that the hand of God was removed from history because creation was perceived to be a self-contained entity. This world-view is popularly known as the clockwork paradigm, which is the theological counterpart of deism.

Against determinism, the philosophical meaning of the new physics boils down to non-determinism, where aspects like the interplay of randomness, non-linear dynamics and the uncertainty principle[15] indicate a nascent postmodern world-view. It is not easy to define a world-view. Better to indicate its general features and function. Michael Macnamara (Pretoria: J.L. van Schaik, 1980:21ff.), in his philosophical reflection on world-views, indicates that every world-view has a set of key propositions which are the result of all the cognitive, affective and conative aspects of the human being. The world-view is influenced by culture and itself also influences culture. Popularly expressed, a world-view is the comprehensive way a person sees the world or reality. It serves basically to orientate the human person and to provide meaning by integrating the disparate pieces into a coherent whole.

Quantum physics focuses attention once again on relationships, because at a quantum level all things including space and time, seem to be integrally linked. The resulting world-view is no longer mechanistic, but relational; reality is no longer substance, but function. This is what Paul Davies refers to as the matter myth.[16] Danah Zohar talks[17] about a quantum world-view. Of course, this type of world-view goes beyond common sense. Notwithstanding, its influence is already widely felt, because the westerner today is much more academically informed.

---

15 The student who is interested in these aspects, is referred to a popular treatment in *Does God play dice, the new mathematicas of chaos*, by Ian Steward, 1989. Penguin and *Chaos, making a new science*, by James Gleick, 1988. Sphere Books.
16 Paul Davies & John Gribbin in a book by that name, 1991, Penguin.
17 See *The quantum self*, 1991, Flamingo.

Joanne Wieland-Burston (New York: Routledge, 1989:70–71) thinks that in culture, science is today fulfilling the same role as folk custom and beliefs in earlier ages, namely to accept and integrate chaos as a fact of life.

27.5 THE AGENDA FOR POSTMODERN HERMENEUTICS

Because world-views, as constituted by new insights, influence knowledge in all areas, it is imperative to evaluate the impact of their philosophical implications for hermeneutics.[18] In this way, the postmodern view of texts as an interrelated network and contextuality[19] are traced back to systems thinking, holism and a relational perspective on reality; Reader-response Hermeneutics traced back to subject participation in scientific experiments; pluralism and types of disciplinary matrices based on Kuhn's theory of paradigm shifts. Historical progress is in line with evolution and process thought; tentativeness on variable interpretation is congruent with the uncertainty principle; metaphoric reference is in line with the invisible subatomic particle in quantum mechanics; and multi-levelled interpretation and inter-penetration of texts correspond with the qualitative study of complex dynamics.[20] These shifts are probably the future agenda for Postmodern Hermeneutics.

This brings one to the important question of how a person inclined towards postmodernism would read and interpret the Bible. Many options are open within the framework of postmodern trends. I shall endeavour to sketch a general scenario.

A postmodern person will not approach the Bible as if it contains some body of truth that needs to be discovered. Truth lies rather within the relationship of the reader with the text. Truth is therefore not prefabricated, but dynamic and co-determined by the needs, presuppositions, religious background and cultural heritage that the person brings to the Bible. The enlightened student may immediately remark that this smells of relativism. Within the postmodern understanding this is not the case. Postmodernism emphasizes the role of models as problem solving constructs. The truth is therefore an applied truth that must function in the following sense: Providing meaning, intelligibility, and answering anomalies. This can only be authentic if there is an objective reference to the world of the text as the reality that pertains to the divine. Some models will of course be more successful than others, and consequently not all models are equally acceptable.

The postmodern person will probably not approach the Bible with the critical and methodological stance that is typical of the historical-critical

---

18 An excellent treatment of this subject is to be found in *Science and Hermeneutics* by Vern S. Poytress, 1988, Grand Rapids, Mi:Academie.
19 For a good insight of how contextuality influences interpretation of the Bible, see *Voices from the margin, interpreting the Bible in the third world*, by R.S. Sugirtharajah, 1991. Chicago: The University of Chicago Press.
20 An excellent treatment of this theme is discussed in *Chaos and order, complex dynamics in literature and science*, 1991. Chicago: The University of Chicago Press.

SECTION B
HERMENEUTICS

method. The postmodernist is also a post-critical person who trusts in non-conceptual ways of knowing. This means that spiritual experience will intuitively be relied upon to guide the reader into relevant meaning. Postmodernism points away from a book religion. The Bible does not serve as a fixed record of God's communication, but as an example of the way in which people experienced and understood God in the past. This history of revelation does not preclude believers from experiencing God currently in different ways. The metaphors of the Bible, like Jesus as the resurrection and the truth, God as Father and friend, the good shepherd, and the light of the world all serve an explanatory purpose. This leaves room for the possibility of new metaphors that are congruent with that of the Bible because the concept "God" is not exhausted by certain metaphors.

The postmodern reader lives in an integrated world where spiritual reality and worldly reality are part of the same multi-levelled reality. Consequently, spiritual matters are not approached as an esoteric realm. The biblical statements must correspond with the way the world really is. Brokenness and death are part of the natural world; sin is the outflow of the imperfect human disposition; coincidence happens because different unrelated events randomly cross; and evolutionary thought and spontaneous order are in line with recent scientific insights. These presuppositions will contribute to a different reading of the texts than was the case previously.

Biblical truth in a postmodern sense is contextual and ecological, i.e. has a bearing on everyday life and worldly issues. The Bible is not concerned only with ethical and moral issues, but also touches upon the status of created entities. Salvation, liberation and preservation are equally important. It tells a story, not of God in heaven or people on their way to heaven, but of God coming to this world to dwell amongst his people. God is expected to guide this world, not by an external coercive force, but through his immanent participation and persuasive love.

Postmodernism can be typified as a soft approach to the Bible. This means that it is not so much analytical as poetic; not so much technical as creative; more pre-occupied with narrative than trying to delve into the original meaning of the text. By "poetic", I mean that language is not used descriptively in terms of the principle of correspondence. Language is used in an analogical way to create meaning, to talk about God in verbal rather than substantive terms. It is also creative in the sense of the participation of the reader and that which comes about is not a re-arrangement of information, but a novel insight applicable to a unique situation. In other words, the Bible writer is not called upon to translate ancient Scripture for today, but to enter into the reality of the Bible and to experience it as his/her own story.

The postmodern reader approaches the Bible in a holistic fashion. This means that every text is an expression of the rest of the Bible, that every theme also includes all other themes in some sense. No theme is "quantisized", for the content of the text is not seen as an exact and final explanation of any theological theme. Texts are rather seen as overlapping fields where the probability of truth approximation in a qualitative sense becomes more feasible. There are no clear boundaries or final statements, and consequently the God who speaks in the Bible, speaks again when we speak into our own situation on the basis of what we read in the Bible.

This agenda for Postmodern Hermeneutics may in the end also result in particular exegetical techniques and specific tools. Postmodernism is a fairly recent development. If it should lead to a deepened sense of wellbeing and an improvement of meaning, if it could lead to a more comprehensive understanding of the world, the postmodern agenda would have accomplished its goal.

READING LIST

Allen, D. 1989. *Christian belief in a postmodern world: The full wealth of conviction.* Louisville, Kentucky: Westminster/John Knox Press.
Brueggemann, W. 1993. *The Bible and postmodern imagination.* London: SCM Press.
– 1980. *God met ons, over de aard van het Schriftgezag.* Utrecht: Tijl-Libertas.
Fiorenza, E.S. 1986. Towards a feminist biblical hermeneutics: Biblical interpretation and liberation theology. In McKim, D. (ed.), *A guide to contemporary hermeneutics: Major trends in biblical interpretation..* Grand Rapids; Mi: Eerdmans.
Griffin, D.R. 1989. Introduction: *Varieties of postmodern theology in Varieties of postmodern theology.* Griffin, D.R., Beardslee, W.A. & Holland, J.A. 1989. New York: City State University of New York Press.
McFague, S. 1982. *Metaphorical theology, models of God in religious language.* London: SCM Press.
McKnight, E. 1988. *Postmodern use of the Bible: The emergence of reader oriented criticism.* Nashville: Abingdon Press.
Miller, J.B. 1989. The emerging postmodern world. (p. 1–19) In Burnham, F.B. (ed.), *Postmodern theology: Christian faith in a pluralist world.* San Francisco: Harper & Row.
Oden, T.C. 1990. *After modernity ... What? Agenda for theology.* Grand Rapids, Mi: Zondervan.
Outler, A.C. 1985. "Towards a postliberal hermeneutics." *Theology today,* vol XLII, October 1985, p. 281–291.
Schneiders, S.M. 1989. Does the Bible have a postmodern message? in *Postmodern theology: Christian faith in a pluralist world.* Burnham, F.B. (ed.). San Francisco: Harper & Row, (p 56–73).

BIBLIOGRAPHY

Allen, D. 1985. *Philosophy for understanding Theology.* Atlanta: John Knox Press.
Capra, F. et al. 1992. *Belonging to the universe. New thinking about God and nature.* London: Penguin Books.
God met ons: Over de aard van het Schriftgezag 1980. Die Gereformeerde Kerke in Nederland se rapport oor die aard van Skrifgesag. Utrecht: Tijl-Libertas.
Griffin, D.R. et al. 1989. *Varieties of postmodern theology.* New York: N.Y. University Press.
Fiorenza, E.S. 1986. *In memory of Her: a Feminist theological reconstruction of Christian origins.* New York: Crossroads.
Herholdt, M.D. 1992. *The dialectic of order and chaos. A model for understanding the rela-*

tionship between God and reality. Doctoral dissertation, University of Port Elizabeth, S.A.

Kuhn, T.S. 1970. *The structure of scientific revolutions.* 2nd. ed. Chicago: University of Chicago Press.

McFague, S. 1982. *Metaphorical theology, models of God in religious language.* London: SCM Press.

Miller, J.B. 1989. The emerging postmodern world, in *Postmodern theology: Christian faith in a pluralist world,* (ed.) F.B. Burnham. San Francisco: Harper & Row, p. 1–19.

Oden, T.C. 1990. *After modernity ... What? Agenda for theology.* Grand Rapids: Mi: Zondervan.

Outler, A.C. 1985. Towards a postliberal hermeneutics. *Theology Today,* vol. XLII, October 1985, p. 281–291.

Robinson, I.M. 1964. *A new quest to the historical Jesus.* London: SCM.

Rolston, H. 1987. *Science and religion: A critical survey.* Philadelphia: Temple University Press.

Schneiders, S.M. 1989. Does the Bible have a mostmodern message? In Burnham, F.B. (ed.), *Postmodern Theology: Christian faith in a pluralist world..* San Francisco: Harper & Row, p. 56–73.

Thiselton, A.C. 1986. *The new hermeneutic,* p. 78–107 in McKim 1986.

Tracy, D. 1997. *Blessed rage for order: The new pluralism in Theology.* New York: Seaburg.

Van Huyssteen, J.W.V. 1987. *The realism of the text: A perspective on biblical reality.* Pretoria: University of South Africa.

Van Huyssteen, J.W.V. & Du Toit B.J. et al. 1982. *Geloof en skrifgesag.* Pretoria: N.G. Kerk Boekhandel.

Vorster, W.S. 1988. Towards a post-critical paradigm: Progress in New Testament scholarship. In Mouton, I., van Aarde, A.G.C.P., Vorster W.S. (eds.), *Paradigm and progress in theology.* Pretoria: HSRC, p. 31–38.

Wieland-Burston, I. 1989. *Chaos and order in the world of the Psyche.* London & New York: Routledge.

The hermeneutical challenge of other religious traditions

Farid Esack

The eternal cannot enter time without a time when it enters. Revelation to history cannot occur outside it. A Prophet cannot arise except in a generation and a native land, directives from heaven cannot impinge upon an earthly vacuum (Cragg 1971:112).

28.1 INTRODUCTION

The discussion on the relationship between revelation and history is not a common one in Muslim circles today, despite the fact that virtually all Muslims believe that the Qur'an speaks to them and their problems as much as it spoke to the first Muslims. Where does this silence come from? Are there any voices "out there" attempting to break the silence? How are Muslims struggling to relate their stable and unchanging texts to ever-changing social and political contexts? These are but some of the questions which a number of us, Muslim theologians and scholars of the Qur'an, are beginning to ask as we try to understand our own community and the way it relates to the word of God.

In this chapter 1 want to look at the relationship between the Qur'an and history in three areas: First is the period of revelation itself; here I shall deal with the idea of progressive revelation, i.e. God's word being revealed bit by bit in terms of the needs of a specific community. Second is the area where theology and dogma became formalized; here I shall explain the theological bases for the orthodoxy's attitude to the Qur'an.

SECTION B
HERMENEUTICS

This also explains why hermeneutics, in its present sense, is not really a serious discipline in qur'anic studies. Third is the area of contemporary challenges to traditional notions of text and context; here I shall look at the ideas of two of the more important scholars who write in English and deal with Qur'anic Hermeneutics and who also have an appreciation of contemporary developments in historical and literary criticism. I conclude with a brief survey of the challenge of Liberation Theology to the more objective approaches towards Qur'anic Hermeneutics offered by the scholars referred to above and some of my own ideas from the perspective of Liberation Theology.

In the Christian world, theology usually refers to the study of faith from the perspective of religious belief. It is usually studied and taught by people who actually believe in a particular faith tradition. Religious studies, on the other hand, is usually studied as a more "objective" subject and is often taught by people who do not necessarily believe in that or any other particular religion. Many others, including much of the Muslim world, do not make any such distinction and see the study of religion and theology as a purely "internal matter". They argue that faith is needed to truly understand religion.[1]

While the interpretation of religious texts is usually connected to theology, hermeneutics relates far easier to religious studies. This is because interpretation is the act of understanding the text, while hermeneutics looks at the interpreter, the text being interpreted and the conditions under which interpretation takes place. In other words, while the believer may say: "In looking at a text, I simply want to understand what the word of God is saying to me", the hermeneuticist will stand aside and try to look at the problems involved as the believer or anyone else, reads and tries to understand Scripture. This does not mean that the one cannot be the other, because many deeply religious people are also critical thinkers in the same way that some people can question their own behaviour and ideas and ask: "Why did I do such a thing?" or "Why do I really believe in God?"

For Muslims the difference which is made between "confessional" theology – theology based on personal beliefs – and interpretation of Scripture on the one hand, and the "objective" study of religion and hermeneutics on the other, can also be extended to revelation and history. Muslims do not believe in a God who at some stage became incarnate, and so, for them, God always exists outside the area wherein people operate and where the ordinary laws of nature and society apply. In other words, while God is everywhere and acts all the time, he really exists outside and above history. The Qur'an, being the direct and unaltered revelation of God, which Muslims believe to be relevant for all ages, is also seen to exist outside history.

---

1 This explains why non-Muslims interested in studying Islam are always met with suspicion by Muslims. Because Muslims connect the study of their religion to the desire to live it out more fully, they do not see the point in any "outsider" wanting to understand it. "Outside" interest in the study of Islam, they believe, can be for one of two reasons only: a desire to know more in order to embrace Islam as a religion, or a keenness to learn about the "Muslim enemy" in order to deal with them from a more knowledgeable perspective.

What do Muslims believe about their Scripture and how do these beliefs affect the way they view hermeneutics? Can one speak about Qur'anic Hermeneutics in the same way that it has become common to speak of, for example, New Testament Hermeneutics? In order to understand these questions we need to take a closer look at what the Qur'an is and what is meant by hermeneutics.

28.2 WHAT IS THE QUR'AN?

From the Arabic root *qara'a*, (to read) or *qarana*, (to gather or collect) the word is used in the Qur'an in the sense of "reading" (Q. 17:93), "recital" (Q. 75:18) and "a collection" (Q. 75:17). From this literal meaning, especially the idea of a "collection", it is clear that the word is not always used by the Qur'an in the concrete sense of a Scripture as it is commonly understood. It rather refers to a revealed oral discourse which unfolded as a part of God's response to the requirements of society over a period of twenty three years (Q. 17:82 & 106). From its contents, it is clear that the Qur'an engages those who believe in it, who doubted it and who rejected it.[2]

It is only towards the end of this process that the Qur'an is presented as "Scripture" rather than a recitation or discourse. In this sense, it resembles the Bible which also started off as essentially oral discourse. Because the Qur'an already became a written text during the time of Muhammed and a uniform canon was available throughout the Muslim world some twenty one years after the death of Muhammed in 632 AD, it has avoided many of the problems of authenticity and canonization which biblical scholars and early church councils have had to deal with.

For Muslims, the Qur'an as the compilation of the "speech of God" does not refer to a book inspired or influenced by Him or written under the guidance of God's Spirit; rather it is viewed as his direct speech. It is thus defined as "the unique revelation, the Speech of God revealed to the Prophet Muhammed through the Angel Gabriel literally and orally in the exact wording of the purest Arabic" (Ibn Manzur n.d., 3:42). This view of the Qur'an can be compared to some of the premodern positions in biblical studies which regarded the Bible as divine dictation. Unlike the early Church Fathers, however, who recognized the human side of the biblical text to some degree, this was never the case with the Qur'an. The intersection between the human and the divine is seen in another and secondary form of authoritative Scripture which Muslims have, the *hadith qudsi*, or the divinely dictated sayings of Muhammed.

A clear and definitive distinction is made between the Qur'an and the Hadith, the sayings of Muhammed. The Hadith, including those sayings regarded as divinely inspired (*hadith qudsi*) wherein Muhammed would commence a statement by saying "God said", was collected over a long period of time after his death. Scholars differ on the authenticity of some

---

2 These three categories are normally described as the "believers" (*mu'minun*), "hypicrites" (*manafiqun*) and "rejectors" (*kafirun*). For a detailed examination of the contemporary application of these terms, see chapter five of Esack (1996).

SECTION B

HERMENEUTICS

of these and some Hadith collections have greater canonical authority than others.

The Muslim equivalent of the Bible is thus not the Qur'an, but the Hadith. We see, for example, that the Qur'an is valued for what it is more than for what it does, unlike the Bible, which for the Church is authoritative "because of what it does and not because of an inherent quality" (Gnuse 1985: 3). For Muslims, the Qur'an occupies the space which Jesus Christ occupies in the life of Christians. It is thus not surprising that, unlike Christianity which has a person at its centre, for Muslims the Qur'an, and not Muhammed, stands at the heart of Islam as a world-view, and is the only valid contemporary revelation. (This also explains why Muslims do not like being described as "Muhammedans".) For Muslims, to invoke the Qur'àn is to invoke God. The Qur'an is God speaking, not merely to Muhammed in 7th century Arabia, but from all eternity to all eternity to all humankind. It represents, as Cantwell-Smith says, "the eternal breaking through time; the knowable disclosed; the transcendent entering history and remaining here, available to mortals to handle and to appropriate; the divine become apparent" (1980:490).

28.3 WHAT IS HERMENEUTICS?

The difference between the act of interpretation on the one hand, and the rules for this as well as the problems surrounding it on the other, has been known from the earliest days of both biblical and qur'anic studies. Such a distinction is basic to hermeneutics. Thus, "while the term hermeneutics itself dates back only from the 17th century, the operations of textual exegesis and theories of interpretation – religious, literary, legal – date back to antiquity" (Palmer 1969:35). According to Palmer (1969:35) hermeneutics deals with two broad areas: the rules and methodological principles of interpretation as well as the study of the ideas and required conditions for all understanding (e.g. "What is understanding? What is a text? When does one actually understand a text and is there a single "true" understanding of a text?"). Carl Braaten covers both approaches when he defines hermeneutics as "the science of reflecting on how a word or an event in a past time and culture may be understood and become existentially meaningful in our present situation" (Braaten 1966: 131). "It involves," says he, "both the methodological rules to be applied in exegesis as well as the epistemological assumptions of understanding meaningful in our present situation" (1966:131).

How do we make sense of a word written two thousand years ago, or for that matter even only yesterday? How is a word written or spoken in desert understood in a jungle? Take the Arabic language, for example, the word *jamal* (camel) has the same root as *jamil* (beauty). Non-Arabs would require a sizeable leap of imagination to connect the camel to beauty unless they understand and appreciate the camel through Arab eyes.

Looking at the meaning of hermeneutics, one may think that it only deals with understanding a text and not really with the nature of the text, e.g. is a particular text the word of God or that of an ordinary person? This is not really the case, because depending on who you think or believe wrote a text, your attitude towards it will be very different. This attitude will also influence the way you understand the text and how seriously you take it, in other words, what authority it has for you.

28.4 THE QUR'AN AND HERMENEUTICS

Having briefly outlined some of the issues which hermeneutics as a contemporary discipline deals with, I now go on to look at how a number of key hermeneutical issues relate to the understanding of the Qur'an as outlined above.

28.4.1 All language and speech are widely believed to be the result of social interaction. We cannot, for example, imagine a word in our own individual minds for a specific thing which does not exist and make that word meaningful. The word "meaningful" itself means "understood by someone else". We are thus limited by language. If God uses human language, then does this mean that God is also "limited" or confined to the limitations of language? If so, then what does this mean for the all-powerful nature of God?

28.4.2 If the Qur'an is the word of God, then how does one actually understand it as the Author wanted it to be understood. Can one actually get into the "mind of God" to grasp what God really meant? Some may suggest that while this is not possible, a person can let God take over his or her mind and inspire him or her. In this way, they may say, "the true meaning" of a text is revealed to that person. The implications of both these paths ("getting into the mind of God" and "God revealing the true meaning" are the same; i.e. an individual ends up claiming to own a "true understanding" which others cannot question. While this may be useful for some people at a very personal level, there are problems in trying to persuade others to accept something they do not share.

28.4.3 Given that the Qur'an was revealed over a specific period of time in a specific context or contexts, the question arises as to whether it is possible to really understand it outside that context, or even the various contexts, in that period. If the meaning depends on the context, then what does this mean for the authority of the text as Scripture which is believed to be valid for all times and all places?

28.5 THE DEVELOPMENT OF DOCTRINE REGARDING THE TEXT

I shall now look at the two most important doctrines which Muslims uphold with regard to the Qur'an and look at how some of the hermeneutical ideas raised above were implicit in them. Both of these doctrines have profoundly affected the nature of qur'anic scholarship and explain why critical studies of the Qur'an as a text, with some very rare exceptions, are absent from Muslim scholarship. In looking at the way these two doctrines developed, I shall also try to show: a) a pattern in the early

SECTION B

HERMENEUTICS

period when Islamic theology was being shaped from a broader interpretation of dogma to a narrower one, and b) that there is actually a clear relationship between doctrine and socio-political reality or history.

28.5.1 The doctrine of inimitability

From the beginning of announcing his prophethood, Muhammed encountered intense and bitter opposition to his mission from the Quraysh, the tribe to which he belonged. One of the forms that this opposition took was to denounce the source of his claims and thereby his truthfulness. He was accused of being bewitched, possessed by an evil spirit and being a mad man. By these accusations, his opponents wanted to suggest that he was unworthy of being followed. Furthermore, the new literary style of the Qur'an did not fit in with the Arabic poetry which was common at that time. The Qur'an was thus dismissed as something false which Muhammed produced with the help of others. In response to these accusations, The Qur'an challenged Muhammed's opponents "produce a discourse like it" (Q. 52.33–4), "ten similar chapters" (Q.11.13) or even "just one chapter" (Q.10.38). The Qur'an then confidently declared that "they would not be able to produce the like thereof, even if they diligently assist one another" (Q.7.88). Muslims regarded the apparent failure of Muhammed's opponents to take up the challenge as proof that the Qur'an came from God.

The need to prove the truthfulness of Muhammed's mission occurred within a concrete religio-social situation of proclamation and rejection. This, in turn, led to the qur'anic texts dealing with this challenge. After the death of Muhammed, this need combined with another one, that of providing the Muslim community with a waterproof authority for doctrine. Given that Islam has never had a formal church which could define tradition as a source of authority, these two requirements produced a **systematic** concept of *i'jaz*, i.e. the unique and miraculous nature of the Qur'an which led to the Qur'an being the only source of doctrinal authority.

Muslims maintain that Muhammed was illiterate and thus incapable of producing any literary work, least of all one of such quality as the Qur'an. They have always believed that the miraculous and unique nature of the Qur'an is proof of Muhammed's prophethood. The belief that the qur'anic revelations cannot be equalled or improved by any human power in the beauty of its language and its contents was given a more precise form in the teaching that every prophet was given a verifying miracle and that Muhammed's miracle was the Qur'an. (In the same way, they argue, Jesus Christ was given the miracle of raising the dead to life and Moses that of having the sea parted, as proof of their truthfulness and the supporting presence of God.)

The supernatural nature of the qur'anic revelation was from the beginning the most important argument which Muslims used to support the case for Muhammed's prophethood. The term *i'jaz*, however, acquired its technical meaning only at the time of Ahmad Ibn Hanbal (d.855), a key Muslim theologian. Most scholars agree that it was first elaborated fully by the Mutazilites, a group regarded as the pioneers of scholastic theology in Islam. What is clear, is that while today there appears to be complete agreement among Muslims about the doctrine of the uniqueness of the Qur'an (*i'jaz*), this "agreement" is not always well-founded in early qur'anic scholarship or in contemporary discussion on the Qur'an.

Some of the Mutazilite scholars argued that the Qur'an is not unique by itself, but that God will prevent anyone from successfully imitating it. (It's like saying that a particular song can be copied by someone other than the original singer. However, as soon as someone actually tries to do so, then his or her voice becomes hoarse.) Most Muslims rejected this concept of deflection, *sarfa* (lit. "turning away"). Instead, they insisted that the Qur'an's language, style, and meaning are so beautiful by itself that these simply cannot be imitated. (To return to my singer example: it's like saying that the original musician's voice is so beautiful and unique that it is impossible to imitate it.)³

There are three pillars upon which Muslims base the doctrine of inimitability: the superior nature of the guidance which the Qur'an offers, its eloquence or the sweetness of its language, and its literary style. All three of these pillars show how the Qur'an is intimately related to Arab society. In other words, that revelation and history are really closely connected. In showing this relationship, I shall also elaborate somewhat on the contents of the Qur'an itself.

28.5.1.1 The superior nature of the Qur'an's guidance

The ongoing relationship between revelation and history is seen from both the contents of the Qur'an and the way it was revealed in small parts over a period of twenty three years. Muhammed received his first revelation in the city of Mecca where he was born. After about ten years, during which both he and his followers faced intense persecution, he went into exile in Medina, where he lived for thirteen years until his death in 632. Islamic scholarship has therefore divided Qur'anic revelation into two distinct periods, the Meccan and Medinan. Although this distinction is not made in the Qur'an as presently arranged, all scholars of the Qur'an believe that if one wants to understand the Qur'an, then it is important to know where each revelation occurred.

The Meccan texts focus on the three essential elements of Islamic doctrine: The absolute oneness of God, the prophethood of Muhammed and the final accountability of people in the presence of God. In support of these basic doctrines, the Qur'an supplies stories of earlier prophets and

---

3 There were also differences on ohter issues: Abu Muhammed ibn Hazm (d. 1064), for example, refused to acknowledge the aesthetic qualities of the Qur'an as proof of its uniqueness, while al-Juwaini (d. 1085), a prayer leader of the sacred mosques in both Mecca and Medina, refused to recognize its linguistic superiority at all. There has, however, been a significant minority of scholars who have attempted to re-open debate as new horizons in text criticism and linguistics unfold. The two most notable contemporary scholars among these are Fazlur Rahman and Mohammed Arkoun whose views we will look at shortly. However, they have remained confined to the margins of Quar'anic scholarship, and in Rahman's case, were also persecuted for their views.

SECTION B

HERMENEUTICS

their struggles to establish the law of God. It also contains responses to the philosophical, religious or a-religious arguments of Muhammed's opponents. The way these beliefs are meant to influence one's life are spelt out in clear ethico-moral instructions which are also characteristic of this phase of revelation.

It has often been said that Muhammed's life was a commentary of the Qur'an. It is equally true that the Qur'an is a commentary of his life. The Meccan revelations, especially, are noted for their intense poignancy when they console him in the face of utter confusion during the first revelation and rejection, even persecution, by the Quraysh, his tribal kinsfolk.

While Muhammed was a bit of a lone voice supported by only a handful of followers in Mecca, in Medina, the city to which he fled after thirteen years, he became the head of a city-state. The Medinan revelations, therefore, deal with the issues of community building and the problems arising from them. Laws regarding socio-political relations based on the ethico-moral instructions revealed in the Meccan phase were now supplied in some detail. The intellectual and political challenges presented by the new neighbours of a governing Islam, the Jews and the Christians, were also dealt with.

The Qur'anic exhortations, guidance and warnings in both phases of revelation have as their backdrop accounts of the remote past as well as prophecies of the worldly and unseen future. This backdrop, the breadth of Qur'anic guidance and the all-embracing nature of its contents are seen by many Muslims as further manifestations of its uniqueness. Although its contents show the various phases of the prophetic period, yet the fact that it could come up with such deep meaning and profound guidance is regarded as impossible for Muhammed, who, the Qur'an emphasises, was an ordinary and illiterate human being.

Despite Muslim belief that the Qur'an comes from beyond the material world, the Qur'an clearly needs a moment in history in order to become meaningful. Belief in the divine nature of the Qur'an does not mean that it is not contextual Scripture. It is still a Scripture speaking to people in terms of their contexts, where they are now. This notion is also confirmed in the other elements comprising its uniqueness.

28.5.1.2 Eloquence

The most widely accepted basis for the uniqueness of the Qur'an is its linguistic and aesthetic character, in the words of a contemporary scholar of the Qur'an, "its eloquence and rhetorical beauty, and the precision, economy and subtlety of its style" (Ayoub 1984:2). Two points made earlier are also seen in the way ideas about the Qur'an's linguistic and aesthetic character were formalised as theological dogma: a) the way revelation is connected to history and b) a trend in Qur'anic scholarship to move from flexibility to rigidity.

On a number of occasions the Qur'an says that it is a unique and inimitable "Arabic Qur'an" (Q. 12: 2, 13:37, 16:103) because it wanted to speak in a perfect manner to a people who took great pride in the expressive quality of their language. In fact, it may be said that the roots of the doctrine of uniqueness are located in this pride of the pre-Islamic Arabs. Arab poets competed with each other by composing eloquent poetry. Their linguistic skills and eloquence were sources of immense pride and the subject of ongoing inter-tribal rivalry and boasting. The word *arab* itself means "eloquent expression" or "effective oral communication" and non-Arabs were called *al-'ajam*, that is, "those who cannot express themselves eloquently".

Much of the early discussion about the linguistic components of the Qur'an centred on the question of non-Arabic words in it: "Does the Qur'an contain any non-Arabic words or not?"; "If it does, then does this mean that it is worth less than a purely Arabic Qur'an?; "Can any language be said to be 'pure'?" These were some of the questions debated and the verses referring to "clear Arabic" were used to support the arguments of those who held that the Qur'an did not contain any non-Arabic terms.

The earliest commentators of the Qur'an, particularly those associated with Abd Allah ibn 'Abbas (d. circa 689), a nephew of Muhammed, recognized and freely discussed a large number of non-Arabic words in the Qur'an. Early Islamic literature suggests that Ibn 'Abbas and "his school" had a special interest in seeking the origins and meanings of these words. Yet, later scholars insisted that the Qur'an does not contain any non-Arabic words and put forward various theories so that the contradictions between Ibn 'Abbas and the purists did not appear as such.

Jalal al-Din al-Suyuti (1973:135) says that some prominent scholars who regarded the qur'anic expression "clear Arabic" to mean "pure" argued that the inclusion of non-Arabic expressions or words in the Qur'an would have cheapened the miracle of the Qur'an testifying to Muhammed's prophethood. This opinion, based on theological doctrine rather than sound linguistic principles, has now become the predominant view of the orthodoxy. This opinion, today still seriously defended, thus rejected the idea that non-Arabic words were borrowed from other languages at the time of the qur'anic revelation or were naturalised Arabic words borrowed in the centuries before the Qur'an's appearance.

The idea of the qur'anic Arabic being completely pure is really connected to the doctrine of the Qur'an being unique and a miracle, and has little to do with the natural development of any language because all human speech is interrelated. However, there are two reasons why this was rejected by the orthodoxy: a) The Qur'an was not really regarded as human speech, but as God's, which does not have to follow any linguistic principles and b) for the orthodoxy, God's own eternity and self-subsistence became the same as those of his revelation. The Qur'an and its language thus came to be viewed as equally timeless and independent of any non-divine elements, non-Arabic included.

28.5.1.3 Literary arrangement (Nazm) and rhetorical style (Uslub)

Not only does the Qur'an repeatedly assert its arabicity in a linguistic sense, but it also conveys its message in terms familiar to the Arabs.

SECTION B

HERMENEUTICS

Similarly, many of its stories merely allude to some events without going into any detail; it assumes that the hearers have some prior knowledge of the story or allegory. The significance of the Qur'an's literary arrangement and rhetorical style can only meaningfully be appreciated by those fully conversant with Arabic culture and language and it would be of little use to dwell at length on the issue here.

However, an important question arises here: would "literary arrangement and rhetorical style" have developed as pillars of the miraculousness of the Qur'an if it were revealed in a non-Arab society where language and linguistic skills did not occupy the elevated place which it does in Arab society? For Muslims, it was as if Arab society was challenged by God on their terms. The achievement of the Qur'an is that it does this so successfully and still engages numerous adherents from countless other cultures in an entrancing manner.

28.5.2 The doctrine of uncreatedness and eternity

Is one's voice and the sounds which one makes part of one's being, or are they something that one actually produces? Is Jesus Christ begotten as a part of God or was He created? In some ways, these questions resemble the ones which tore the early Muslim world apart on the subject of the Qur'an. The doctrine of the Qur'an's uncreatedness arose from discussions around the question of the Qur'an as the speech of God in the sense of it being a divine attribute or not. Another dimension of that question gradually acquired greater significance: "Is it created or not?" Finally, in the first half of the 9th century, the somewhat mild non-assertive "not created" was substituted for a more definite "uncreated". The question now at stake was: "Does the Qur'an co-exist with God in all eternity, or did God create it in time?"

This controversy had a major influence on Islamic scholarship in general and, more specifically, on qur'anic scholarship. This debate, however, is the outcome of a scholastic theological discipline which emerged about two centuries after the death of Muhammed. The forerunners of this theology, who were also essentially responsible for the debate on the nature of the Qur'an, were the Mutazilites. In order to understand some of the underlying issues in this debate, it is necessary for us to have some idea of Mutazilite Theology.

The key point of Mutazilite Theology was their emphasis on the absolute unity of God and on his justice. In fact, they described themselves as "the people of justice and unity". In dealing with the issue of God's attributes, therefore, and in particular with the attribute of speech, their main concern was to uphold his absolute unity and uniqueness. To suggest that anything, even divine revelation, shared in any of these characteristics, they argued, would lessen or cheapen God's beyondness. It was like saying that if Jesus Christ shares in God's divinity, then somehow that divinity is lessened. The Mutazilites, in fact, accused their opponents of being influenced by Christianity which, they said, had equated the Word of God, Jesus Christ, with God. This debate can also be compared to the one in the early Church whereby biblical authority was contrasted with that of God and Jesus Christ and some argued that to accord the biblical inerrancy and infallibility would be to detract from the authority of God and Jesus Christ.

Their second principle, that of divine justice, led to a rejection of notions of God's arbitrary rule and predestination. If the Qur'an were eternal, they reasoned, it followed that all the events narrated therein were pre-ordained. The players in all of these events, the believers, rejectors and hypocrites would thus all have had their fate sealed, even before birth. Both their basic doctrines, therefore, meant that they rejected the eternity of the Qur'an and a belief in its createdness.

We do not know for sure when exactly serious theological discussion commenced on the nature of God's speech. The earliest references indicate that al-Jad ibn Dirham (d. 743) and al-Jahm ibn Safwan (d. 745) argued for its created nature and that this discussion was confined to a few scholars until the time of the *Mihnah* (lit. "test" or "trial", a type of inquisition) in 833. An increase in state interest in scholastic theology is, however, detected from the time that the Abbasides, the second dynasty of the Islamic Empire, came to power in 749 in Baghdad, and the period of Harun al-Rashid (d. 809) especially saw debate on this issue becoming quite extensive. This reached new heights – intellectually, politically and emotionally – during the reign of Abu-'l Abbas al-Mamun (813–833). The compelling nature of the controversy is evident from the establishment of the *Mihnah*, towards the end of al-Mamun's reign in 833. Most leading officials and other prominent personalities were forced to publicly profess that the Qur'an was created. Failure to do so led to persecution and even to death. With a few exceptions, most theologians submitted publicly. A large number of jurists, however, continued in secret to uphold the doctrine of an uncreated Qur'an.

The *Mihnah* continued intermittently under the next two rulers until it was abandoned in 848. The repression and persecution during the *Mihnah* enlarged the theological and doctrinal positions in a manner which was unknown until then. The new orthodoxy, who came to power after the *Mihnah* and who believed that the Qur'an was uncreated, now enforced their ideas with a rigidity that was unknown in the period before the *Mihnah* and denounced all their theological opponents, the Mutazilites. The middle of the road position that the Qur'an is uncreated, but an event originated in time was rejected as heresy. Even those who doubted the heresy of those who supported the moderate position were denounced as "rejectors of the faith".

The *Mihnah* brought about two significant changes in theological attitudes, particularly regarding the Qur'an:

1. Before the *Mihnah*, the traditional scholars preferred to keep quiet on the question of whether the Qur'an was created or not; some even regarded it as necessary and virtuous to do so. During and after the *Mihnah*, this attitude of suspension of opinion was changed into an insistence on a declaration in favour of its uncreatedness and even a bitter denunciation of those who maintained silence.

2. The *Mihnah* resulted in ideas about the Qur'an becoming rigid and transformed into dogma; a mere insistence that the Qur'an is truly the word of God and a simple denial that it is created was changed into a positive doctrine affirming its uncreatedness, eternity and pre-existence.

28.5.3 The influence of doctrine on Qur'anic Hermeneutics

As we have seen, unlike early biblical scholarship which was at least unanimous about the Bible being a "work", God's and/or that of humans, in Islam the nature of the Qur'an as a work is itself disputed, as was the question of its historical eventness. Traditional qur'anic scholarship makes a neat and seemingly unbridgeable distinction between the production of Scripture on the one hand and its interpretation on the other. In other words, it insists that questions of the way Scripture came into the world and its nature are settled matters which cannot be discussed or re-opened. The interpretation of Scripture, however, can continue. This means that, other than biblical scholarship, qur'anic scholarship either refuses to or is unable to work with that part of hermeneutics which deals critically with the nature of the text. It can however, deal with questions of interpretation and how a text is received by the Muslims in different areas and different periods. In this respect, qur'anic scholarship may follow the path walked by early biblical scholarship, whereby classic Christian exegesis and polemics at the time of the Reformation was characterised by accusations of exegesis being a product of human systems going wrong without questioning the birth of Scripture. (Koch 1969 & Reventlow 1986).

28.6 PROGRESSIVE REVELATION OR GRADUALISM *(Tadrij)*

I now turn to the question of how, from a qur'anic perspective, God who exists beyond history, speaks to people who live within it.

In discussing the uniqueness of the Qur'an, I have looked at the relationship between revelation, language and the contents of the Qur'an on the one hand, and the community which it first addressed on the other. We saw that the Qur'an is clearly a Scripture within history. Wherever it may have originated according to Muslim belief, the Qur'an's claims to be a guide to people who are located within history means that revelation remains related to history. Muslims, like others, have connected with a reality which may transcend history but also acts within it.

The Qur'an presents God as actively engaged in the affairs of this world and of humankind. One of the ways in which this constant concern for all of creation is manifested is in the sending of prophets as instruments of progressive revelation. Thus, qur'anic scholarship has always been interested in the history of events surrounding the revelation of the Qur'an. The idea of progressive revelation, step by step with regard to the needs of the community, is reflected in two key notions connected to revelation, occasions of revelation (*asbab al nuzul*, sing. *sabab*) and abrogation (*naskh*).

28.6.1 Occasions of revelation (Asbab al-nuzul)

Asbab al-nuzul is a discipline within qur'anic studies which deals with the transmission of the occasion or "cause" (*sabab*) of the revelation of a chapter or verse and the time, place and so forth of its revelation. These occasions, incidents or events which led to revelation have been transmitted by the Companions of Muhammed and are subjected to the same critical scrutiny for reliability as the sayings of Muhammed, the Hadith. Given the general impression in the Qur'an of a God who is constantly involved in the affairs of humankind, this is certainly a credible reason for the presence of a *sabab*. The *sabab* as Rippin says, "is a constant reminder of God and is the rope – that being one of the meanings of *sabab* in the Qur'an – by which human contemplation ascends to the highest levels even while dealing with the mundane aspects of the text" (1988:1).

28.6.2 Abrogation (Naskh)

Literally, *naskh* means "the removal of something by something else" and "annulment". In qur'anic studies, it means the elaboration of different modes of abrogation or cancellation. These modes may be classified as follows: a) The qur'anic abrogation of divine Scriptures which preceded it; b) The abrogation of some qur'anic texts which are said to have been blotted out of existence; c) The abrogation of some earlier commandment of the Qur'an by the latter revelations; d) The abrogation of a *sunnah* (practice or injunction of Muhammed) by a qur'anic injunction.

There is a lot of disagreement among scholars of the Qur'an around these various categories, both in principle as well as in the detail. In issues of principle, some will ask the question whether any text of the Qur'an really abrogates another, or whether a saying or an act of Muhammed can be allowed to abrogate a law in the Qur'an. In questions of detail, some will say that verse A is abrogated by verse B, while others will say that it was abrogated by verse C or that it was never really abrogated.

Whatever the various opinions surrounding abrogation, there is unanimity about the "situational character of the Qur'an" (Rahman 1965: 10). Both the entire, as well as specific, revelation generally came down in the context of specific social conditions. As the early Muslim society was developing, the qur'anic revelation also kept changing along with the changing conditions and environment.

28.6.3 Progressive revelation in today's task of interpretation

I now turn to the question of how Muslims use the concept of progressive revelation in order to understand the will of God for society today.

For Muslims committed to discovering the will of God for society today, the message of the Qur'an "despite its being clothed in the flesh and blood of a particular situation – outflows through and beyond that given context of history" (Rahman 1965:11) This word of God thus remains alive because its universality is recognised in the middle of an ongoing struggle to rediscover contemporary meaning in it. The challenge to the

SECTION B

HERMENEUTICS

believers is to discover their own "moment of revelation", their own frustrations with God and joy with his consoling grace and their own being led by the principle of progressive revelation. Furthermore, for the numerous Muslims who experience existence as marginalized and oppressed communities or individuals, this discovery clearly has to take place amidst their own Meccan crucibles of the engagement between oppressor and oppressed, Abyssinian sojourn amidst the gracious and warm hospitality of Christians and attempts at nation-building in Medina.[4]

Contemporary Muslim attempts to contextualize the message of the Qur'an draw significantly on the principle of progressive revelation despite varying attitudes to abrogation. Using abrogation as the cornerstone of their reformist methodology were Taha Mahmud (d. 1985), the executed Sudanese scholar, and the Republican Brothers. The use of abrogation as the most significant element in the methodology to reinterpret Islam has been detailed in the works of the group's most prominent legal scholar, Abdullahi al-Na'im, in his works on civil liberties, human rights and international law (al-Na'im 1990, 1991). (Although their premises would differ widely, their ideas have the same effect as those of biblical scholars who say that only portions of Scripture is inspired, "and thus those parts which might disagree with modern understandings would offer no offense, since they were part of the biblical writer's limited world-view" – Gnuse 1985:9).

Other latter-day reformists such as Sir Sayed Ahmad Khan (d. 1898) and contemporary scholars such as Isma'il al-Faruqi (d. 1988), have rejected abrogation and have argued that the revelations which came earlier in certain circumstances and which were modified or improved later were not actually abrogated. Instead of viewing previous rulings as abrogated by subsequent ones, it is more appropriate to continue regarding them as valid – to be implemented in conditions similar to those in which they were revealed.

All reformist scholars, however, argue that all exegesis must study the time and place, what the Germans call *Sitz im Leben*, in order to understand how directives respond to the specific situations. "From these specific directives or 'divine answers', further significance must be drawn by translating them faithfully into the idiom of the time situations which we now confront" (Cragg 1988:95). Furthermore, they also share a commitment to the inner unity of the Qur'an. Particularly the events occasioning revelation, Rahman emphasizes, must be studied as a part of an integrated and self-consistent qur'anic hermeneutic (1986). The objective is not to search for chunks of isolated historical incidents which occurred in the prophetic era and then attempt to construct a "politically correct"

---

4 This is a reference to the three periods in the life of the Muslim community during the time of Muhammed. The first thirteen years were spent in Mecca as a persecuted minority and the next ten in Medina as a nation with its own government. For Muslims living as religious minorities amidst just and peace-loving Christians, the Abyssinian paradigm also become important. Two groups of Muslims were sent to Abyssinia by Muhammed to escape the persecution of the Meccans. In Abyssinia they were warmly received by the ruling Christians who afforded them protection and hospitality.

view on the basis of these. The Qur'an is not merely the collection of a number of individual and disjointed injunctions, but "an exposition of an ethical doctrine where every verse and sentence has an intimate bearing on other verses and sentences – all of them clarifying and amplifying one another" (Asad 1980:iiv).

To summarize, revelation was closely related to the day-to-day spiritual, social, legal and ideological requirements of Muhammed and the early Muslim community. An understanding of that interaction and context is a condition for re-applying it. To understand the Qur'an in its historical context does not mean that one wants to confine its message to that period; rather one has to understand it in order to make it relevant for contemporary society. An incident during the Battle of Siffin (657) between the forces loyal to Muhammed's nephew, 'Ali, and Mu'awiyah, the governor of Syria, neatly illustrates this point. Mu'awiyah held up a copy of the Qur'an and insisted that it should arbitrate between the two sides in order to end the war. 'Ali responded by saying "here is the Qur'an; it is a book between two covers. It does not speak, but needs interpreters, and interpreters are people." In the last part of Ali's statement lies the crux of hermeneutics and the point of departure with many people who look at their Scriptures only from the perspective of faith. The most important thing 'Ali seems to be saying is not to confine the argument about what the Word says, but to look at who is reading the Word.

28.7 THE CONTEMPORARY SCENE

Given some of the problems which the traditional understanding of the Qur'an poses for hermeneutics and the limited number of scholars engaged in critical qur'anic scholarship, it is difficult to speak of trends in contemporary Qur'anic Hermeneutics. This is not to say that nothing new has occurred in qur'anic scholarship since the end of the *Mihnah*. Indeed, the rise of intellectual modernity in the west in general and the development of historico-critical studies around language in particular have impacted on Qur'anic scholarship, even if only marginally. Here one may also note that it is very rare that Muslim scholars would examine trends in biblical studies in order to examine whether they have any relevance for approaches to the Qur'an. While trends in Biblical Hermeneutics will not have any impact of qur'anic studies, the other factors mentioned earlier will increasingly force Muslims who feel compelled to go beyond defensive apologetics to confront the unthinkable in qur'anic scholarship and to ask the same questions about the text which others have asked about texts, sacred or otherwise.

To date though, little has been written about the relationship between the Word of God and history in an historical or literary critical manner or about the explicit or implicit ideological assumptions underlying its theological orientations; a key concern of contemporary hermeneutics. The most notable exceptions in the west are Fazlur Rahman, a Pakistani scholar who died in 1986 and Mohammed Arkoun, an Algerian scholar who lives in France. I shall reflect on some of their views in order to get

SECTION B

HERMENEUTICS

an idea of the way things are being approached by some Muslims who are also committed to live alongside modernity and all its implications for belief in a text of divine origin. Rahman is arguably the foremost reformist scholar in contemporary Islam who remains rooted to traditionalism, while Arkoun represents a radical break from all traditional ways of thinking and is the clearest example of Islamic scholarship embracing contemporary hermeneutical and literary criticism.

28.7.1 Fazlur Rahman

Among contemporary Muslim scholars, the concern for the contextuality and "programmatic character" (Cragg 1988:92) of the Qur'an is best represented by Rahman. His views on the Qur'an and revelation are covered in a chapter in his book *Islam* (1966), while his ideas on hermeneutics and interpretation are dealt with extensively in *Islam and Modernity – Transformation of an Intellectual Tradition* (1982). Rahman believes that the Qur'an is the divine response, "through the Prophet's mind, to the moral and social situation of the Prophet's Arabia" (1982:5). He clearly affirms the ontological otherness of the Qur'an as "*verbally revealed* (italics in original) and not merely in its meaning and ideas" (1966:30–31). This "divine message broke through the consciousness of the Prophet from an agency whose source was God" (1988:24). Rahman insists that while the Qur'an "itself certainly maintained its otherness, objectivity and the verbal character of the revelation", it had "equally certainly rejected its externality vis-à-vis the Prophet" (1966:31). In other words, at some point the word of God was also the word of Muhammed.

Rahman is arguably the first modern reformist Muslim scholar who links the question of the origin of the Qur'an to both its context and interpretation. He, however, displays very little insight into hermeneutics as a contemporary discipline and does not deal with the crucial question of the relationship between the genesis of a text and interpretation. Instead, he concentrates on ways of interpreting the Qur'an.

Rahman regrets the "general failure to understand the underlying unity of the Qur'an" which has lead to "a piecemeal ad hoc and extrinsic treatment of it". It is his criticism of the "extrinsic treatment" of the Qur'an which reveals the inadequacy of his hermeneutical methodology and his insistence on an "objective" appreciation of the Qur'an's meaning. Rahman strongly argues there are intellectual constructs which can "objectively" be arrived at and "objectively" defined as "Islamic". Rahman argues that an interpreter can break free from the shackles of his/her "effective history" (Gadamer's term); he says that it is possible to understand something without being influenced by the many things which have gone into that person's life (1982:8–11). In *Islam & Modernity*, Rahman argues the case for an "adequate hermeneutical method" which is "exclusively concerned with the cognitive aspects of revelation" (1982:4). Such a method, he argues, is concerned about an understanding of the Qur'an's message which will enable those who have faith in it and want to live by its guidance, in both individual and collective lives, to do so "coherently and meaningfully" (1982:4). The hermeneutical key for the "purely cognitive effort" is thus faith and the willingness to be guided. "While faith may be borne from this effort," he says, "more patently, faith may and ought to lead to such cognitive effort" (1982:4).

28.7.2 Mohammed Arkoun

The discussion on revelation and historicity led by Mohammed Arkoun is more radical than any other Muslim scholar. Arkoun argues that today's crisis of legitimacy for religion, and Islam in particular, forces scholars to "only speak of heuristic ways of thinking", that is, we have to work our way through by trial and error (1987b:10). In his article "Rethinking Islam Today" (1987b:8–13), he argues that everything which a person can think of is tied to his or her history. If the Qur'an is to have any social or cultural use then it must be linked to history. According to him, there is no access to the absolute outside the concrete world in which we live. He thus insists on "historicity as a dimension of the truth" (1988: 70).

Arkoun's ideas are best understood in his description of revelation and the way it moved on to become a written text, that is, Scripture. He distinguishes between three levels of revelation:

1. Revelation as the word of God which is limitless and unknown to us as a whole because only fragments of it were revealed through the Prophets.
2. The way the word of God was manifested in history through, for example, the Israelite Prophets (in Hebrew), Jesus of Nazareth (in Aramaic) and Muhammed (in Arabic). Originally this level was oral; it was memorised and transmitted orally during a long period before it was written down.
3. The Word of God becoming a text which people can handle and pass on to others. It becomes a Scripture and is available to believers only through the written version of the book which is preserved in the officially closed canons. This "word of God becoming text", according to Arkoun, was influenced by many historical facts depending on social and political agents, not on God (1989:5).

28.7.3 Rethinking Rahman and Arkoun

Both Rahman and Arkoun have made an enormous contribution to the methodology of interpretation and the Qur'anic Hermeneutics respectively, despite the lack of depth in Rahman's work and the repetitive nature of that of Arkoun over the last few years.

Rahman, however, seems to ignore his own insistence on a unified approach to the Qur'an and Islamic studies and, in this absence of grey areas, a sense of open-endness and questioning is the most serious inadequacy in his approach. Faith leads to understanding, he insists, without seeing that they can be intrinsically linked to each other. Similarly, he deplores what he calls "Islam's pitiable subjugation of religion to politics, rather than genuine Islamic values controlling politics" (1982:139–40) without acknowledging the dialectical relationship between the two. His

SECTION B

HERMENEUTICS

criteria of knowledge are based on understanding and he entirely ignores action as a basis for it, nor does he indicate an awareness of the way action leads to and shapes understanding.

Arkoun ignores the fact that his epistemological critique and intellectualist solution themselves function within history. One cannot view revelation and tradition historically and ideologically and then take an ahistorical or "ideology-less" view of one's own critique. His call for "knowledge as a sphere of authority to be accepted and respected unanimously: a knowledge independent of ideologies, able to explain their formation and master their impact" (1988:69) effectively advances the ideological interest within which this knowledge functions. Invaluable as his critique of tradition and interpretation may be, a fundamental question remains: "For whom, and in whose interests?" This is undoubtedly a political question and may suggest wanting to use the text as pretext. I do not believe that this can be otherwise, nor that it is intrinsically objectionable to do so.

28.8 A QUR'ANIC HERMENEUTIC OF LIBERATION

Most of the contemporary Muslim qur'anic scholarship may broadly be described as falling into two categories: the traditionalists and the modernists. Traditionalists often appear to be merely restating dogma which is rigid and seemingly unconnected to socio-economic reality or history. Most traditional scholars work on the assumption that they, too, are living in some historical vacuum. Jane McAuliffe notes that it is "frequently difficult to determine from internal evidence alone whether a [Qur'an] commentator had ever seen a Mongol or a Crusader or had ever conversed with a Christian or conducted business with one" (1991:35). While this rigidity and insulation may have helped to protect dogma from the encroachments of modernity, it has left Muslims ill-equipped to deal with the various challenges which invariably accompany the encounter with modernity and the crucial problems of racism, sexism, structural poverty and the environmental crisis.

On the other hand, modernist scholarship, as we have seen from the examples of Arkoun and Rahman, pay a lot of attention to objectivity. Scholarship, however, does not take place in a vacuum and all scholars, as hermeneutics reminds us, approach any text with their own biases or pre-understandings.

In the context of the South African struggle for liberation, the context in which I place my own thinking, it was not a sacred Scripture such as the Qur'an which was stimulus for the interest in hermeneutics; rather, it was the social and political context in which we tried to understand it and the way it functions so that it means different things to different people. The South African experience presented many of us with the problem of making sense of the Qur'an in a particular context, that is, the problem of contextuality. "How does the Qur'an make sense to us when we are imprisoned for our commitment to justice?" was a key question.

When one lives in a world of injustice, of women suffering many forms of oppression by men, of racism and economic exploitation, then one must also ask where the scholar fits into all of this and whom does his or her studies and research really serve? In the absence of an answer to the question "For whom, and in whose interest?", intellectual pluralism simply becomes "a passive response to more and more possibilities, none of which shall ever be practised" (Tracy 1988:90). As David Tracy reminds us, such pluralism results in "a general confusion in which one tries to enjoy the pleasures of difference without ever committing oneself to any particular vision of resistance, liberation and hope" (1988:90)

For those who eke out an existence on the margins of society, living under the yoke of oppression and struggling alongside others in the hope of liberation, a pluralism of splendid and joyous epistemological neutrality is not an option. On this basis a number of scholars, including the present author, have argued that we must re-interpret the meaning and use of Scripture in a racially and sexually divided and economically exploitative society and develop ways of reading the Qur'an which will advance the liberation of all people. Amina Wadud Muhsin, based in the United States, is one of the foremost scholars of the Qur'an who have interpreted the Qur'an in order to support the struggle for gender equality. Ali Asghar Engineer, a pioneer Muslim liberation theologian who is based in India, has argued for the re-interpretation of the Qur'an through the eyes of the oppressed. My own thinking on the Qur'an and hermeneutics is also placed within the context of the struggle of the oppressed for freedom and dignity.

28.8.1 Through the eyes of the oppressed

I believe that there is something which can correctly be described as a South African qur'anic hermeneutic, which is a way of reading the Qur'an from our own perspective as people who first experienced the crucible of oppression and now the challenges of liberation. This way of reading the Qur'an flows from, and relates to, direct involvement in the struggle for liberation, reconstruction and reconciliation. It is a synthesis of action for justice and the theological reflection on that action. This "action – theological reflection – action" paradigm bears a close resemblance to that of Christian Liberation Theology, and is a resemblance which I freely acknowledge.

The Qur'an is addressed to *al-nas* (the people) and the social reality of "the people" is the most important factor in our hermeneutic. If that social reality is essentially one of hunger, humiliation and deprivation on the one hand, and activism to remove these yokes on the other, then that forms the basis of our hermeneutic. I want to briefly summarize the way I, and others in the stream of progressive Islam to which we belong, have employed certain hermeneutical notions. The extent to which these notions contribute significantly to developments in South African Islamic Theology in the long-term remains to be seen.

The methodology employed by us is one which Arkoun describes as "regressive-progressive" (1987:17). This means a continuous going to the past – not only to project on fundamental texts and the demands and

SECTION B

HERMENEUTICS

needs of the present, but (also) to discover the historical mechanisms and factors which produced these texts, and assign them such functions. The process of revelation of the Qur'an within a social context has to be examined, and its meaning within that particular (past) context understood. This process of understanding, however, takes place within the present personal and social context which is one of suffering, hunger and a struggle for justice.

Because these texts are an inseparable part of our identity and active in our ideological system, we have to rework them in order to give a contemporary and contextual meaning to them (progression). This two-way process of going back to the Qur'an and then to the present context is necessary for a contemporary meaning to come forth. Out of this regression-progression process we have extracted six hermeneutical principles for understanding. Before getting to these, two issues need to be addressed.

First, how does one "know" that certain methodological principles of interpretation are more "correct" than others? We never know. There are no guarantees that one "knows". We may, however, succeed in reducing the possibilities of "erroneous" interpretation and enhancing the possibilities of an interpretation which supports the basic ethos of the Qur'an. What we are assured of is that this "tentativeness" will deprive us of a revolutionary or religious arrogance and place us firmly at the mercy of God's Grace.

Second, how does one acquire the right to determine and define hermeneutical keys or methodological principles for interpretation? The progressive Muslim in the midst of a struggle for survival in the hell of apartheid has had to make sense of diverse interpretations of the Qur'an. The six methodological principles which will now be discussed have opened avenues of understanding for us in our struggle for integrity as human beings and coherence as Muslims. They are valid for us and for whoever finds themselves in similar situations may appropriate them.

1 *Taqwa* (Consciousness)

Taqwa, literally meaning "to ward off", "to heed" or "to preserve". It is usually employed to mean the "fear of God". Rahman refers to it as "an inner torch" (1986: 50); in other words, it is the inner light which guides a person. *Taqwa* is emphasized in the Qur'an as a condition for "correct understanding". *Taqwa* is the protective measure against the random use of qur'anic texts for legitimating ideology which may be inconsistent with the qur'anic world-view. A qur'anic hermeneutic of liberation is one which is not only liberated from theological ideas which seek to keep people happy in their suffering and political reaction. It is also one which is free from the purely personal whims and fancies of individuals, even if those individuals come from the ranks of the oppressed and marginalized.

2 *Tawhid* (Divine unity)

Tawhid refers to the unity of God and is often used to contrast the Islamic understanding of God with the Trinity of Christianity. In social terms, *tawhid* implies a rejection of the dualistic conception of human existence.

In other words, no distinction is made between the sacred and the profane; humankind and human concerns are thus regarded as sacred. Socio-politically, *tawhid* operates as the opposite of a society which absolutizes race and racial divisions, as well as the elevation of some classes above others. In terms of hermeneutics, it implies a search for an holistic understanding of the Qur'an. Such understanding will guard against the selective and arbitrary choosing of some texts above others.

3 Al-nas (The people)

Described as "the family of God" by Muhammed, the people are vital in the divine scheme. The interpreters and the addressees of the Qur'an are "the people". Given the stewardship of humankind on the earth, the Qur'an has to be approached in a manner which gives particular support to the interest of the people and to the fact that this approach must be given preference over those which support the interests of a small privileged minority or class. Furthermore, understanding has to be shaped by the experience and aspirations of humankind.

4 The mustad'afun fi 'l-ard (The oppressed and the marginalized)

It is within a socio-political context of suffering and injustice that the Qur'an is understood with the object of transforming society. This reality of oppression must shape understanding. Throughout the history of God's engagement with people, one sees what Christian liberation theologians have described as "the preferential option for the poor and the marginalized". In the Qur'an this is clear from the many specific instructions to Muhammed to remain close to the marginalized, from the way Prophets are always seen to arise from among the poor, and in the express desire of God to side with the poor. The eyes of the oppressed and the poor, in other words their experiences and hopes, are thus vital elements through which to read and understand the Qur'an.

5 'Adl wa qist (Justice and equity)

In a context of injustice the Qur'an, by its own admission, is compelled to be a tool for a comprehensive revolt against injustice in all its manifestations. This means that the Qur'an must be read through the eyes of the desperate need for justice in an unjust world. This perception of the Qur'an excludes any "objective", "scholarly" or entirely didactic reading of it. Any attempt at such an approach in conditions of poverty and injustice is cowardice or, at best, escapist. To attempt neutrality or objective exegesis amidst oppression and injustice is, I believe, to compromise one's integrity as a believer, and it goes against its basic spirit.

6 Jihad wa amal (Struggle and praxis)

"Those who struggle in our way," says the Qur'an, "to them we shall show our ways" (Q. 29:69). This verse implies a dialectical process whereby struggle informs guidance as much as guidance informs struggle. In other words, the meaning of the Qur'an is disclosed to the seeker whilst he or she is engaged in a struggle to establish its meaning. As a person reflects upon the relevance of the Qur'an's message and acts upon whatever insights one gets, one will find that greater insights are opened in the middle of that struggle. This also means that as your commitment to work for a more humane and just society increases, so will your understanding of the word of God deepen.

All of the hermeneutical keys above operate within a circle of qur'anic reflections and praxis which means a permanent relationship with the Qur'an as a book of inspiration, guidance and broad understanding.

28.9 CONCLUSION

I acknowledge that a number of my ideas have been developed both in concert with a specific struggle for justice as well as having been enriched by thinkers who are not Muslim, but deeply committed to the liberation of all people from the many forms of injustice in the world. I have no doubt that Islam also has much to teach people of other religions in a number of ways as humankind confronts the challenges of creating a world in which it is safe for children to be children.

However, in the context of this current volume, there is another question which needs to be addressed: "What are the challenges which qur'anic hermeneutics pose for biblical studies?" I feel compelled to say that there is nothing which we have to offer biblical studies or Biblical Hermeneutics. For the reasons which I have outlined above, Muslims have not even begun to ask the questions which Biblical Hermeneutics has long been confronted with and has also dealt with. I have no doubt that as Muslims increasingly engage modernity they will be compelled to deal with all of those issues, because all of our lives are so intertwined and whatever we do impacts on others. It is, perhaps mercifully, too late for any religious group to return to their shelters. The cake cannot be unbaked, nor can the sugar be separated from the flour or the water.

BIBLIOGRAPHY

Al-Na'im, A. 1990. *Toward an Islamic Reformation – Civil Liberties, Human Rights and International Law*. New York: Syracuse University Press.
Ahmad, R. 1968. "Quranic Exegesis and Classical Tafsir." *Islamic Quarterly Review*. Vol. XII. No 1,2.
Arkoun, M. 1987a. *The Concept of Revelation: From the People of the Book to the Societies of the Book*. Claremont, California: Claremont Graduate School.
Arkoun, M. 1987b. *Rethinking Islam Today*. Washington: Centre for Contemporary Arab Studies.
Ayoub, M. 1984. *The Qur'an and its Interpreters*. Vol.1, Albany: State University of New York Press.
Bell, R. 1970. *Introduction to the Qur'an*. (ed. & rev.) Montgomery Watt in Islamic Surveys. Edinburgh: Edinburgh University Press.
Braaten, C. 1966. *History of Hermeneutics*. Philadelphia: Fortress.
Cantwell Smith, W. 1980. "The True Meaning of Scripture: An Empirical Historian's non-Reductionist interpretation of the Qur'an." *International Journal of Middle Eastern Studies* 11.

Esack, F. 1991. "Contemporary Religious Thought in South Africa and the Emergence of Qur'anic Hermeneutical Notions." *Islam and Muslim Christian Relations*, 2:2 (December 1991)

Macintyre, A. 1988. *Whose Justice? Which Rationality?* London: Duckworth.

Martin, R.C. 1982. "Understanding the Qur'an, Text and Context." *History of Religions*. 21,4.

Le Roux, C du P. 1989, 1990 & 1991. "Hermeneutics – Islam and the South African Context." *Journal for Islamic Studies*, nos. 9 & 10.

Muslim-Christian Research Group. 1989. *The Challenge of Scriptures: the Bible and the Qur'an*. Maryknoll, New York: Orbis Books.

Palmer, R.E. 1969. *Hermeneutics – Interpretation Theory in Schleiermacher, Dilthey, Heidegger, and Gadamer*. Evanston: Northwestern.

Patton, W.M. 1897. *Ahmad b. Hanbal and the Mihnah*. Leiden: E.J. Brill.

Rahman, F. 1966. *Islam*. London: Weidenfield & Nicholson.

– 1982. *Islam and Modernity – Transformation of an Intellectual Tradition*. Chicago: University Press.

– 1986. "Interpreting the Qur'an." *Inquiry*. May, 1986.

Suyuti, Jalal al-Din al-. 1973. *Al-Itqan fi Ulum al-Qur'an*, 2 vols. Beirut: *Maktab al-Thaqafiyyah*.

Watt, M. 1950. "Early Discussions About the Qur'an." *Muslim World*. XL 50:27.